Democratizing Luxury

DEMOCRATIZING LUXURY

Name Brands, Advertising, and Consumption in Modern Japan

Annika A. Culver

University of Hawai'i Press
Honolulu

The College of Arts and Sciences
at Florida State University provided funding
through the Humanities Book Publication Fund.

© 2024 University of Hawai'i Press
All rights reserved
Paperback edition 2024

Printed in the United States of America

First printed, 2024

Library of Congress Cataloging-in-Publication Data

Names: Culver, Annika A., author.
Title: Democratizing luxury : name brands, advertising, and consumption
in modern Japan / Annika A. Culver.
Description: Honolulu : University of Hawai'i Press, [2024] | Includes
bibliographical references and index.
Identifiers: LCCN 2023030766 (print) | LCCN 2023030767 (ebook) |
ISBN 9780824895167 (hardback) | ISBN 9780824896713 (epub) |
ISBN 9780824896720 (kindle edition) | ISBN 9780824896706 (pdf)
Subjects: LCSH: Branding (Marketing)—Japan—History—Case studies. |
Marketing—Japan—History—Case studies. | Advertising—Japan—
History—Case studies. | Consumers' preferences—Japan—History—
Case studies. | Women consumers—Japan—History—Case studies.
Classification: LCC HF5415.12.J3 C85 2024 (print) | LCC HF5415.12.J3
(ebook) | DDC 658.800952—dc23/eng/20230828
LC record available at https://lccn.loc.gov/2023030766
LC ebook record available at https://lccn.loc.gov/2023030767

ISBN 9780824899141 (paperback)

Cover illustration: Poster of Mitsukoshi by Sugiura Hisui

University of Hawai'i Press books are printed on acid-free
paper and meet the guidelines for permanence and
durability of the Council on Library Resources.

For my father
Lowell W. Culver (1932–2022)

Contents

Preface	ix
Acknowledgments	xiii

Introduction: Defining Luxury and Accessibility to Quality in Japan   1

Chapter One
Craftsmanship and Proto-branding in the Tokugawa Era   29

Chapter Two
Commodifying Western Modernity, New Japanese Corporations,
and the Department Store   60

Chapter Three
Modern Girls and Salarymen Consuming the West   92

Chapter Four
Frugality, Patriotic Consumption, and the Military   124

Chapter Five
Consuming the Bright Life   162

Chapter Six
Consuming Japaneseness and Global Brand-Name Recognition   195

Chapter Seven
The Rise of "Cool Japan" and Japanese Luxury-Consuming
Communities in the Virtual World   236

Conclusion: *Nihon-shiki* Commodity Fetishism   276

Notes	285
Bibliography	357
Index	379

Preface

Japanese name-brand luxury evolved alongside a consumer society emerging in the late nineteenth century with several iconic Japanese companies associated with certain luxurious qualities and style for accessible consumer products like soap, toiletries, timepieces, and liquors. *Democratizing Luxury* begins by examining craftsmanship developing from long-standing artisanal traditions coupled with nascence of brand names spreading throughout Japan during the Tokugawa era (1603–1868). The book covers Japanese consumer-based businesses developing in parallel with Japan's late nineteenth-century imperial expansion and progresses into the interwar period, wartime, and postwar eras. Individual chapters focus on luxury consumer items with relatively affordable prices often featuring advertising toward women, including beverages, beauty products, fashion, and timepieces. Western ideas of modernity merged with earlier artisanal ideals to create Japanese connotations of luxury for these readily accessible products.

Composing an advertising model, this luxury is portrayed as available to all, which I term "democratizing." For modern Japan, growth of a democracy began alongside a modern consumer society's development, with modes of consumption and advertising driven by newspaper readership and models of citizenship. Thus, I examine an "imagined community"[1] of consumption,[2] with political choice ensured by limited voting, but still idealistically viewed as potentially universally attainable. I also pose several important questions directly addressing these themes. How are consumer choices related to political landscapes seemingly promising greater choices for different social worldviews? How is affordable luxury tied to concepts of the good life, viewed in different time periods as the 1920s "culture life" (*bunka seikatsu*), 1950s "bright life" (*akarui seikatsu*), and 1980s "delicious life" (*oishii seikatsu*)?

Between the late nineteenth century and the postwar period, control over family disposable income made Japanese middle-class women an important market. This growth of purchasing power among women consumers corresponded with diffusion of Japanese consumer items throughout the empire and globally in the postwar period. In the following chapters, I present case studies of companies producing high-quality yet affordable commodities for particular markets, like Shiseidō, Suntory, Seiko, Casio, and Sanrio, and avant-garde fashion houses including Issey Miyake and Comme des Garçons, along with street fashion company Bathing Ape. *Democratizing Luxury* thus features comprehensive histories of the origins of iconic Japanese name brands and their unique connotations of luxury and accessibility in modern Japan and elsewhere.

Interestingly, Japanese companies (or their prototypes) have capitalized on affordable luxuries ever since a flourishing domestic mercantile economy began in the late Tokugawa period, complete with name-brand shops, rock-star artisans, and mass-produced woodblock prints by famous artists. Beginning in the late nineteenth century, personalized service became de rigeur in department stores like Mitsukoshi, at Shiseidō cosmetic counters, and in designer boutiques. Shiseidō now markets its services globally as communicating invented traditions of *omotenashi* (whole-hearted hospitality), a set of "Japanese values" of hospitality found in purchasing and consuming its products.[3] However, a long history of affordable luxury exists for many Japanese name brands, where it masqueraded as available to all consumers, and especially women, with wide product ranges at all price points. In the postwar period, with growth of a new middle class of cautious, yet hopeful, consumers, Japanese companies sought to rebuild a mass consumer base while democratizing luxury in making it widely available at reasonable prices and maintaining earlier business patterns of accessibility, high quality, and exemplary service.

What insights can a historical glimpse into a nearly 150-year history reveal about branding, consumption, gender, and how these companies now market products globally while still capitalizing on their Japanese origins? In prewar times, as companies spread their products throughout the Japanese empire, they focused on nationalizing name brands. In the postwar world, with Japan's renewed expansion as an economic and cultural powerhouse, Japanese products spread globally, beyond the former empire, whose regions and countries now became centers of manufacturing for Japanese firms, such as China and Southeast Asia.

What exactly is enticing about particularly "Japanese" luxury goods? And, how are they emblematic of "luxury" in craftsmanship, detail, and design? How do we define luxury, and its particular expression in a Japanese context? A Japanese luxury product's uniqueness partially stems from the consumer's ability to partake in the commodity in small portions or taste a microcosmic whole in sampling the brand. Japanese companies also succeeded in validating consumption as acceptable versus profligate during wartime and peace, while assuaging consumer fears of hedonism and wastefulness by creating quality and value amid continuing postwar trends toward savings and frugality. This book seeks to elucidate such cultural contexts, along with the roles of consumption, gender, and class in Japanese advertising of certain products often geared toward women.

SCHOLARLY CONTRIBUTIONS

Democratizing Luxury illustrates how Japanese name brands evolved and developed connotations of luxury over exclusivity in a mass consumer society originating in the late nineteenth century. It uses case studies of companies producing Westernized nonessential consumer products with artificially created markets, like beauty products, Western alcoholic beverages, and fashion. Advertising made products seem accessible to ordinary consumers, especially women. Such products capitalized on Western and Japanese modernities from their early history until the present global moment. My approach as a cultural historian covers aspects of modern Japanese business history utilizing multidisciplinary sources and analyses.

Academic books featuring consumption, advertising, and products in modern Japan were usually written by business scholars or art historians and typically focus on one Japanese company. Instead, as a multidisciplinary and interdisciplinary historian, I provide a broad historical overview while focusing on women's impact on consumption and branding in transwar Japan (1920s–1950s) and investigate accessible luxury as an advertising model in imperial, postwar, and contemporary Japanese contexts.

Few scholarly texts or analyses exist that comprehensively explore the history of iconic Japanese consumer products and how brand names expanded among consumers domestically and then globally.[4] Inspired by Japan's remarkable 1970s and 1980s successes, earlier

English-language studies resembled business histories lauding instrumental figures, like Sony's founder. From sociopolitical perspectives, scholars like the late Ezra Vogel hailed "Japan as number one" (1979) while other studies captured "secrets" of Japanese business successes or unique business models informed by traditional cultural norms. In the millennium, historians and anthropologists began examining consumption with investigations of certain products, like electrical appliances[5] or toys.[6] Recent case studies exist for individual companies or products becoming pop-cultural phenomena like Hello Kitty,[7] while art historians[8] and cultural historians[9] have analyzed prewar commodities' cultural and social values in Japanese advertising.

Democratizing Luxury incorporates these ideas into interdisciplinary and multidisciplinary perspectives by assigning political value to consumption and showing how mass-produced products afford symbolic capital or "luxury" to consumers. To inform customers of standardized and industrially created products' alleged superiority, advertising spread knowledge of companies and their products. Political connections between propaganda and advertising were porous in prewar years and beyond. The Japanese word *senden* meant either propaganda or advertising, but it also infers instructional components. Thus, I examine Japanese advertising's political aspects, where in certain eras, consumption was portrayed as modern, patriotic, democratic, or even specifically expressing Japanese values. In Japan, connections persist between consumption and perceived national benefits, with consumption either deemed insufficient or excessive; hence, the Japanese government often attempts interventions to spur or curb consumer demand, as revealed in Sheldon Garon's 2000 study on savings and thrift in wartime Japan and his 2011 analysis of Japan's frugality campaigns throughout the transwar period.[10] Oscillation between these two extremes represents a pendulum where an ideal center-point surfaces in steady demand satisfying both corporations and Japan's government. Subsequent chapters investigate this compelling relationship's origins, along with multifaceted resources mobilized to capture consumer desires.

Acknowledgments

Democratizing Luxury developed during a decade of research and writing. This book was written amid constellations of support from academic, governmental, corporate, archival, and personal sources. For early research in 2010 and 2012, I utilized archives at Duke University's Bostock and Perkins Library, where the formidable, now-retired Kristina Troost helped me ferret out articles and advertisements in prewar Japanese-language periodicals like *Chūō kōron* (Central Review) and other sources. Along with assistance by numerous individuals at archives, academic institutions, corporations, and online communities in the United States and Japan, I thank my home institution, Florida State University (FSU), for a fully funded fall 2019 sabbatical allowing a semester's teaching hiatus. This valuable time dedicated to research permitted me to develop a book proposal and earn an advance book contract with the University of Hawai'i Press. A spring 2021 research semester at FSU once again supported my full attention to writing. I also appreciate the insight of FSU colleagues in the history and modern languages departments.

Company archives reveal how Japanese companies officially present their histories and "frame" name brands to ordinary consumers, fans, and scholars, while boutiques portray contemporaneous brand marketing. Corporate museums dedicated to products and company history democratize access, and also cultivate manufactured artisanality and craft narrative histories. From 2012 to 2018, personal interviews with museum curators, store managers, scholars, and librarians supported my research to develop deeper understandings of accessible luxury in Japanese contexts and how advertisers and retailers portrayed products of iconic Japanese name brands over time.

In June–July 2012, a US Department of Education HOPES grant funded three weeks of research in Tokyo, Japan. That June, I met with

xiv   *Acknowledgments*

Shiseidō corporate representatives, including Ogura Mihō, of Shiseidō's Corporate Culture Department. In July I visited and toured the archives and museum at Kaō Corporation's Tokyo corporate headquarters, where I was hosted by Machida Saori, the firm's public relations officer, with further assistance from Corporate Culture and Literature Department representatives. Additionally, I toured exhibits at the Tobacco and Salt Museum in Shibuya and at the Advertising and Design Museum Tokyo (ADMT) to understand early Japanese capitalism's underpinnings and advertising practices.

In May 2013, a China and Inner Asia Council research grant from the Association for Asian Studies funded my month-long stay as a visitor at the Princeton-based Institute for Advanced Study (IAS), where I utilized resources at Princeton University's Firestone Library, and Martin Heijdra provided invaluable assistance. IAS members, along with Professors Sheldon Garon, Janet Chen, and Susan Naquin, kindly provided suggestions for resources and methodological approaches.

In 2014, a First Year Assistant Professor (FYAP) grant from FSU supported June travel to the Shiseidō company archives and Shiseidō corporate museum in Kakegawa, Shizuoka prefecture. Marumo Toshiyuki, the museum's curator and director, generously offered a private archival tour and showed advertising posters from wartime Japan. Additionally, Nakano Seishi, a volunteer now retired from Shiseidō's Corporate Planning Division, provided excellent advice and gave me copies of *Hanatsubaki* (Camellia Magazine) covers and other materials. In July, ADMT librarian Kuriya Hisako kindly assisted me in finding secondary materials, while I conducted research on Tokugawa-era prehistories for advertising (including *kanban* signage and logos) and examined advertisement transformations from the 1970s to the present. At the Edo-Tokyo Museum, I investigated material cultures of artisans in displays of merchant life, while librarians at the Ochanomizu-area *Shufu no tomo* (Housewife's Companion) archives assisted my search for soap, cosmetic, and liquor advertisements geared toward women.

At Waseda University in 2012 and 2014, I utilized the Central Library's Nishigaki Collection of materials on prewar advertising, department stores, and corporate cultures. In 2016 and 2018, urban historian Satō Yoichi provided helpful advice on framing postwar Japanese society and consumption practices during his research at FSU's archives and my research at Waseda. In summer 2014, when I visited Kyoto University, historian Kishi Toshihiko offered useful comments on propaganda and advertising. Professors Satō and Kishi continue to post

Acknowledgments xv

informative Facebook updates on visual media and Japan's transwar urban culture.

In summer 2018, while a Next Generation Fellow of the American Friends of the International House (AFIH), I lodged in the I-House's congenial surroundings in Roppongi, Tokyo. Lectures by W. David Marx and Nancy Snow at Temple University Tokyo proved inspirational. At the National Shōwa Museum, Audio-Visual Division Library Manager Sakajiri Asako and Audio-Visual Division Head Research Librarian Orihara Rie helped me research postwar consumption and material cultures through vintage Japanese photographs and songs. Fieldwork included participant observation at boutiques and department stores like Mitsukoshi. To investigate watch collecting, I "shopped" as a consumer browsing merchandise at Shinjuku pawnshops and Ginza-area watch stores.

The 2020–2022 global pandemic prevented further research trips to Tokyo, so I scoured online communities for Casio and Seiko watch *otaku* (enthusiasts) and visited online sites for the Toshio Kashio Museum of Invention and Seiko Museum, which feature vintage timepieces and company archival materials. Brand consultant Philip Santiago also kindly answered my questions about Japanese street fashion during phone interviews.

To understand luxury retailing in the United States, Europe, and East Asia, and for broader perspectives, I gained practical field experience. Since spring 2019, I have belonged to the Harvard Alumni for Fashion, Luxury and Retail, a special interest group for alumni. I thank the group's founder, fashion blogger Timothy Parent, for correspondence on logos and brand names in East Asia. The group enabled attendance at virtual talks and networking events to investigate global fashion and luxury retailing. From March 2020 into summer 2021, I engaged in online opportunities to learn how contemporary American marketing industry practices compared to Japan. Beginning in March 2020, I became a "Fashion Advisor" and completed marketing and advertising surveys for Nordstrom, a high-end US department store. In August 2020, I served on a US focus group for New York City–based corporate marketing specialists from Creed Perfumes, a luxury French perfume retailer, to develop strategies to access broader US market shares by attracting more diverse customers with lower-range purchases to consume products more frequently. Consequently, for winter 2020–2021, Creed created a $165 coffret of fifteen samples with an informational booklet for perfume fans to compare favorites.

Curated coffrets like this one now include incentives for future purchases like a $50 credit toward a full-sized bottle. I also engaged in Shiseidō's personalized online beauty consultations and attended webinars on the Vital Perfection and Future Solutions skin-care lines to learn about the company's newest products and marketing innovations. Such opportunities composed my real-life fieldwork experiences as a consumer and short-term national and international marketing consultant.

I am also grateful for the expert shepherding of the manuscript by Masako Ikeda, acquisitions editor at University of Hawai'i Press, and John Donohue, production editor at Westchester Publishing Services. In addition, Sandy Sadow created an excellent index.

Last, I thank my family and children for sharing my enthusiasm. RH read through numerous drafts and suggested useful theoretical materials. Family members accompanied me to Japan, went on shopping trips, and enjoyed Japanese name brand goods while becoming fierce devotees of commercial Japanese food and snacks and other pop-culture "goods." My father unexpectedly passed away during this book's completion, which I dedicate to him.

DEMOCRATIZING LUXURY

INTRODUCTION
Defining Luxury and Accessibility to Quality in Japan

Democratizing *Luxury* investigates how certain iconic Japanese companies developed and created advertising to stimulate purchasing of originally Western-style consumer products whose connotations of affordable luxury transformed in the late nineteenth century to the present from cheaper substitutes to higher-quality Japanese essentials: soaps, cosmetics, liquors, watches, fashion, and even gift trinkets. Currently, Japanese company logos continue to advertise particular quality standards to domestic and global consumers—crucial to brand names communicating aspirational luxury and even cultural attributes.

This study describes characteristics of these targeted customers amid analyses of how mass consumption formed in modern Japan, often through what I call "consuming communities" created by mass media advertisements generating narratives promoting consumption in the Meiji period (1868–1912). I explore consuming communities' early ties to news media, along with Japanese bourgeois women's important roles as arbiters of household consumption, and the products they purchased as frugal, discerning consumers. This chapter also covers product commodification; in Japanese capitalism, advertising processes have long amplified commodity fetishism linked to particularly Japanese forms of luxury for particular consumer goods, marketed in multifaceted ways to attract middle-class consumers, which I term "democratizing luxury": accessible high-quality, "manufactured artisanality," and seasonal or limited editions. This approach has enabled steady profits amid a state and society valuing frugality where consumers expect high quality at

2 *Introduction*

affordable prices, along with a fictive artisanal tradition that helps distance industrial products from capitalism's occlusion of labor.

CONSUMING COMMUNITIES: IMAGINED COMMUNITIES OF CONSUMPTION

During the time period featured in this book, subsequent chapters examine what I call "consuming communities," with Japanese women holding disproportionate sway over family purse strings from the early Meiji period into the present. Concurrently, married men with white-collar positions, known as *sarariman* (salaryman/salarymen), purchased small personal luxuries, like liquor and watches. These consuming communities were composed of individuals united by certain imagined consumption practices displayed in print advertisements and other media, where consumers and advertisers initiated complex interplays determining which products became popular—a concept subsequent chapters discuss in depth. Such consuming communities began in the late nineteenth century among middle-class housewives, which by the 1910s included markets of single working women, and into the early to mid-twentieth century, when children and young men began to participate in consumption purchases. Newspaper and magazine advertisements displayed images appealing to these groups, with easily recognizable markers of status, domestic environments, clothing, and other clues resonating with each target group to showcase various products.

Benedict Anderson's now-classic 1983 study *Imagined Communities* examines expansion of the vernacular, enabling mass readerships to feel connected through printed media like newspapers, and posits that print capitalism helped disseminate socially constructed ideas of nationhood, which included images, from which communities chose to feel national belonging.[1] Generally, his study relates to construction of European political communities, but he also asserts that readers consumed ideas in editorials, articles, and even political ads appearing in newspapers and other media. Here, Anderson presumes fairly widespread literacy enabled by vernacularization distanced from Latin and classical languages, a phenomenon occurring in Japan after compulsory education's initiation in 1872, and inscription of nearly 90 percent of children into elementary schools before the 1890 Imperial Rescript on Education, along with centralized government control over education. Many newspapers also included *rubi* (phonetic *hiragana*, or syllabic Japanese, script in smaller text alongside *kanji*, or Japanese characters) to allow less-literate readers to comprehend articles and stories. Alongside newspaper and magazine articles, product advertisements often appeared juxtaposed amid discussions of contemporary political trends, so even if individuals were poor readers, they could still consume product depictions and settings, and certainly might remember brand names expressed in visually prominent product logos.

Therefore, examining Japan's newspaper development is helpful in understanding how and why consuming communities began forming around certain concurrently initiated companies and products— notably in the 1870s, when Imperial Japan advanced universal education after abolishing status distinctions. Though many companies boasted Tokugawa-era precedents dating back two and a half centuries, conglomerates like Mitsui and Company (established in 1876) began operations as modern corporations in the late nineteenth century. Smaller companies dealing in personal consumer products and comestibles also started then, including Shiseidō (1872), Kaō (1887), Seikō (1881), and Kotobukiya (later, Suntory) (1899). It is unsurprising that large-circulation newspapers were created roughly contemporaneous to the establishment of these iconic Japanese companies now producing consumer goods known worldwide. This development supports the book's premise: that Japanese name-brand luxury evolved alongside a consumer society emerging in the late nineteenth century with emblematic Japanese companies whose names became associated with certain luxurious qualities and style. Print media first served as a message delivery mechanism by product advertisers for growing companies during urbanization and industrialization, driving modern Japanese capitalism.

Whereas the earliest Anglo-American newspapers began organized circulation in the late eighteenth century, large-scale publication and dissemination failed to exist in Japan until the mid- to late nineteenth century. The *New York Times,* now the largest and most popular US newspaper, published its first issue in 1851, and antecedents of today's large-scale British newspapers developed between 1860 and 1910. Japanese newspapers followed similar trajectories in the 1870s and 1880s. For example, *Asahi Shimbun* (Morning News), Japan's current second-largest circulation newspaper, began in Osaka in 1879 with a 3,000-copy run for the first to fourth issues, and then grew to a 21,461 average daily circulation with Japan's largest readership by the 1880s.[2]

For Japanese, these time periods also corresponded with democratic growth and the expansion of domestic voting rights, with political freedoms discussed in columns placed alongside product advertisements. In 1890, the new Parliamentary Election Law granted votes to propertied Japanese males paying direct national taxes of 15 yen, which included 450,365 men, a number that historian Maurius Jansen posits as consisting of the former samurai class.[3] By the 1928 election, these numbers included landless men, though women could not vote until 1946 with the American-crafted postwar constitution's universal suffrage stipulation. Since the Enlightenment project's beginnings, democracy and capitalism were linked, as representative politics were believed to temper radicalism and thereby ensure capital's smooth workings, which also served industrialization purposes under assumptions of political choice. The marketplace seemingly mirrored growing political options as illusions of consumer choice, while advertisers clamored to position products as "unique" in competitive marketplaces filled with mass-produced commodities.

Japan's oldest general-circulation newspaper, *Mainichi Shimbun* (Daily News), began in 1872 as *Tokyo Nichi-Nichi Shimbun* (Tokyo Day-by-Day News), and the country's most popular news daily, *Yomiuri Shimbun* ("Selling by Reading" News), started in 1874. Its rival, the aforementioned *Asahi Shimbun,* began publication in Osaka and, with government and corporate support from Mitsui and Company, opened an office in Tokyo in 1888; in 1908, the Osaka and Tokyo branches merged into one news corporation. In the early twentieth century, it hired as writers and journalists literary luminaries like Natsume Sōseki (1867–1916), who joined the paper in 1907 and solidified fame with his iconic work *Kokoro* (Sincerity, 1917), running in *Tokyo Asahi Shimbun* from April to August 1914.[4] Osaka *Asahi Shimbun* also featured serialized novels like Tanizaki Jun'ichirō's (1886–1965) satirical *Chijin no ai* (A Fool's Love, 1924–1925),[5] a cautionary tale of a young man besotted by a café waitress, appearing in March to June 1924 before its censorship and resumption in the lesser circulation, but more compartmentalized, women's magazine *Josei* (Woman).

Newspapers targeting specialized business and commerce-oriented readerships also began in the critical 1870s, with Mitsui and Company initiating its in-house journal, *Nikkei* (also the Tokyo Stock Exchange's abbreviation) in 1876, which soon thereafter expanded into general readership. In 1946 it received its contemporary name, *Nihon Keizai Shimbun* (Japan Economics News), now recognized as the American *Wall Street Journal*'s Japanese equivalent. Additionally, in 1882, liberal education reformer Fukuzawa Yukichi (1835–1901) founded *Jiji shimpō* (Current Events News), now known as *Sankei Shimbun* (Industrial and Economic News), a competing publication with a conservative angle.

In contrast to commercial newspapers, larger general-circulation newspapers enjoyed wide readership by all ages and genders. They also experienced extensive archiving from their beginnings, thus accruing value to scholars determining impacts of mass consumption through serialized fiction or political commentaries, and especially, highlighting advertising's role throughout Japan's modern history. However, other media were also important in expanding commercialization and product knowledge in the late nineteenth to mid-twentieth centuries.

In 1867, Japan's first modern magazine, *Seiyō zasshi* (Western Magazine), started circulating just before the Meiji revolution precipitated the country toward industrial nation-state status. However, magazines specifically for women only developed in the early twentieth century, with *Katei no tomo* (Home Companion) established in 1903, preceding its later *Fujin no tomo* (Women's Companion) incarnation; *Fujin Gahō* (Women's Pictorial) was founded in 1905 by journalist and novelist Kunikida Doppo (1871–1908), and *Shufu no tomo* (Housewife's Companion) was initiated in 1917.[6] Literary historian Maeshima Shiho posits that women's magazines enjoyed broader audiences beyond their targeted "feminization" and asserts that women's magazines led to interwar Japan's democratization of print and reading cultures.[7] So-called women's magazines, rich in images and "popular" reading materials, presumably circulated among readers of all genders and ages. Maeshima additionally highlights that women's magazines pioneered "inclusion of various article genres written in highly colloquial styles, extensive use of visuals, stress on entertainment and people's private lives, and increasing collaboration with other industries," which later characterize postwar Japanese periodicals.[8] Since Japanese women held inordinate control over household consumption, examining print media like women's magazines and large-circulation newspapers is crucial to determining the impacts of these consuming communities.

WOMEN, COMMODIFICATION, AND JAPAN'S "BIRTH" OF CONSUMERISM

Japanese advertising, and the consumption it generated, certainly connects to broader global histories of consumerism. Yet, because Japanese women basically controlled household finances during the late nineteenth century and beyond,[9] most notable is middle-class housewives' negotiated acquisition power for their homes and families coinciding with Meiji-era modernizations. These included state-sponsored paradigms like *Ryōsai kenbo* ("Good Wife, Wise Mother"), assimilated via the new universal education system, and initiation of the 1898 Meiji Civil Code, which subjected Imperial Japan to compulsory heterosexuality and patriarchal family structures mimicking Western patterns modeled after Anglo-Saxon Victorian-era norms. Essentially, to appear modern, the Japanese state encouraged imposition of a quasi-dictatorship of the bourgeoisie, with the family's corresponding bourgeoisification and acquisition of all the concomitant bibelots it demanded.

Along with the growth of middle-class women's economic power through the family's decision-making ability in running households came realizations that acquisition could obtain promises for an aspirational life. Aspirational allure to maintain a certain lifestyle and acquire certain commodities was both manufactured by advertisers and supported by the state as important means of social control. Middle-class consumption drove individuals to pattern themselves after certain ideals, attainable by purchasing, which also led them to function as good employees and as educated, knowledgeable consumers. An economy driven by continuous consumption thus accrued national benefits, but its constituents needed guidance to prevent excessive spending. Hence, this book also argues that democratization of luxury for small consumer items resulted in symbiotic relationships between consumers, corporations, and the state.

In the late Meiji period, amid growing prosperity, leisure, and disposable income associated with a rising middle class, early corporations realized they needed to target middle-to-upper-class married women. Though women in Japan could not vote and held few political rights or social protections, many housewives chose how to decorate their living spaces and ran families according to new social models deemed modern and Western, applying scientific methods of household management. These new developments gave middle-class Japanese women feelings of agency in ordering their world, although their roles remained circumscribed by the state's gendered needs. Historian Jordan Sand asserts that contemporaneous Japanese experts on domestic management, influenced by Anglo-American ideas about interior decorating's impact upon inhabitants' moral values, viewed the "home as a moral sphere under female dominion."[10] In the Tokugawa era and earlier, home decorating had been men's purview, and in the late Meiji

Introduction   7

period some male commentators began lamenting elite women's domination of home decoration.[11] These complaints not surprisingly coincided with ambitions toward adopting certain standards of living depicted and described by various media in articles and advertisements.

Women's magazines were thus crucial in constructing hypothetical bourgeois lifestyles, and the iconic companies that I examine first advertised products to housewives there and in newspapers. Juliann Sivulka's investigation of late nineteenth- and early twentieth-century American consumer culture argues that advertisers viewed "consumption as a feminine activity." Sivulka states that in the United States, "among the middle- and upper-class households, men, in theory, earned wages outside the home, while women transformed these earnings into well-decorated homes, fashionable bodies, and well-developed children."[12] Similar processes occurred in Japan, where, along with newspapers containing political columns, general-interest segments, and serialized novels punctuated by advertisements, readers of women's magazines like *Shufu no tomo* and *Fujin kōron* (Women's Review) acquired relatively synchronous contemporaneous ideas of bourgeois lifestyles. In investigating *Kingu* (King) and *Ie no hikari* (Light of the Home), two early twentieth-century "central originators of a Japanese mass culture"[13] and termed "family magazines" (which could include women's magazines with broader readerships transcending gender and age), Amy Bliss Marshall notes, "In creating a mass audience that desired magazines to read, these media also created a conduit for communicating other aspirations to that audience. . . . There was complete harmony between, on the one hand, the lessons readers learned about how to be dutiful participants in society and the empire they saw in the articles, and on the other, the instructions that advertisements delivered in how they could assume *things*, in addition to ideas in order to make themselves happy and productive."[14]

Even today, in Japan and the United States, this assertion holds for how mass media shapes consumer wants and desires. Communications scholar Erin Duffy employs the term "manufacturing authenticity"[15] to refer to aspirational consumption, appearing recently in popular US women's magazines like *Glamour* and *Cosmopolitan*. She examines how advertisements for "real" products, teamed with promises of external and internal beauty, use "manufactured" authenticity to promote consumption. Ads for Dove soap, for example, show allegedly "real" women of various ethnicities and body sizes enjoying the product's intended effects, thereby better representing the general

8   *Introduction*

American population. Supposedly "real" women use these inexpensive yet allegedly high-quality beauty products in settings appearing inclusive to consumers (or where inclusion is viewed positively in aspiring toward better lifestyles).

In modern Japan (and elsewhere), the brand is not necessarily what is consumed but rather the aspirational promises it offers consumers. However, in a Japanese model of consumption, instead of yearning for a commodity unaffordable to ordinary consumers, it is better to *have* the product than to want it—the essence of democratizing luxury in Japan, where corporations with clever advertisers ensure that, once lured, every consumer among all spending levels can buy a name-brand product from favored companies. In the past, most notably in literature like Murasaki Shikibu's iconic Heian-period (794–1185) novel *The Tale of Genji,* pure longings for love, political ideals, or aesthetic perfection were viewed as pinnacles of traditional elegance,[16] while in modern times, emotional consumption processes seemingly compelled by commodities themselves have instead led to quick consummation of such socially approved longings now directed toward material objects. In a discovery exploding during Japan's mid-twentieth-century prosperity, advertisers who successfully tapped into such emotional consumption processes surrounding products could create winners and, amid late capitalism's media saturation, determined that name brands themselves activated this media-generated longing.

Clearly, the young college student narrator of Tanaka Yasuo's 1980 Bungei Prize–winning novel *Nantonaku, kurisutaru* (Somehow Crystal), a 1981 prestigious Akutagawa Prize finalist, snarkily celebrates such unabashedly materialist culture. He revels amid consumption in contemporary Tokyo, with the book featuring overwhelming numbers of footnoted side commentaries on places and objects composing a litany of superfluous brand names.[17] This novel of obvious social parody marked an allegedly hedonistic time of tremendous prosperity. In the 1980s, during the Japanese Bubble Economy's heyday, corporate profits reached their peak, and in late 1980 during the book's publication, Japan's net worth (national wealth) stood at 1,363 trillion yen, or 5.6 times the GDP.[18] Western countries began studying the "Japanese model" of economic success, and political sociologist Ezra Vogel published his influential 1979 text *Japan as Number One: Lessons for America.*[19] Yet, aspirational themes surrounding products initiated in Japanese advertising also point to similar forms of worldwide commodity fetishism—a theory useful for understanding how consumerism functions after activation by shrewd advertising and marketing practices.

COMMODITY FETISHISM IN A JAPANESE CONTEXT

As a concept initially developed by Karl Marx (1818–1883) in 1867, commodity fetishism argues that commodities mediate social relations, with corresponding occulting of labor, and reveals how abstract and subjective value become perceived as concrete and objective.[20] For an item to become a commodity, three elements must be present: use value, exchange value, and requirement of labor to produce it. Commodity fetishism, in particular, pertains to (potential) use value. However, in this book's later chapters, when I refer to specific brand-name items produced by iconic companies, I use the term "product" instead of "commodity," since "product" implies specificity in grouping mass-produced items of one type, whereas for purposes of theoretical analysis, "commodity" references a more general term applying to broader categories of items. Hence, a study on consumption and advertising of certain iconic products with connotations of accessible luxury merits discussion of "commodity fetishism," and how it functions in Japanese contexts.

In *Capital,* and more specifically in "The Fetishism of Commodities and the Secret Thereof," Marx identifies "the mist-enveloped regions of the religious world" as an analogy for understanding commodity fetishism. He indicates that commodities are a "mysterious thing," and that they take on "the fantastic form of a relation between things" as "independent beings endowed with life."[21] Thus, Marx appears to ascribe a certain spiritually infused animism (which he attributes to religion) to mass-produced objects resulting from their imputed use value, and he therein views "the Fetishism which attaches itself to the products of labor, so soon as they are produced as commodities, and which is therefore inseparable from the production of commodities."[22]

In his key investigation of fetishism's source as a term, intellectual historian William Pietz asserts "the fetish, as an idea and a problem, and as a novel object not proper to any prior discrete society, originated in the cross-cultural spaces of the coast of West Africa during the sixteenth and seventeenth centuries."[23] He believes the word developed from *Fetisso,* an African pidginized usage of the Portuguese

10 *Introduction*

word *feitiço,* describing common people's magical practices in the Late Middle Ages, which derived from the earlier Latin *facticius,* or "manufactured."[24] Thus, its origins contained notions of manmade enchantment or magic. In areas surrounding the Guinea (Mina) Coast, Pietz argues that new social formations arose from "intercultural spaces" where objects were translated and transvalued when "triangulated among Christian feudal, African lineage, and merchant capitalist social systems."[25] Essentially, European understandings of what was perceived, and later described as "fetishism," developed from structures of mercantilist exchange value in a colonial setting.

According to Pietz, Protestant Dutch merchants of the Dutch West Indies Company, arriving in the seventeenth century after the Portuguese (driven out by 1642), attempted to explain West African customs and social relations based on supposed worship of Fetissos and their bewildering personifications of material objects.[26] In the late seventeenth century, Dutch merchant Willem Bosman observed West African society through a commercial lens, and in 1703 he described these objects in an influential Guinea Coast study, positing that moral topsy-turvyness or "ideologization of the fetish discourse"[27] served as advertisements favoring Enlightenment principles. Here, "the exploiting priests, the irrational women, the superstitious polity, and the despotic king constitute the basic character system of Bosman's Guinea as a world that will remain morally upside down until knowledge and power are reunited."[28] Bosman's resultant travelogue, *A New and Accurate Account of the Coast of Guinea,* addressed to Dutch West Indies Company directors as a ruthless boss' second-in-command, achieved wild popularity; key eighteenth-century intellectuals read numerous translated editions, including Enlightenment political philosopher John Locke (1632–1704) and Scottish economist Adam Smith (1723–1790), a proponent of free-market capitalism.[29] Bosman's text cast wide influences over his society and Europe's amid great intellectual ferment. In 1757, historian and literary philosopher Charles de Brosses, author of *Du Culte des dieux fétiches, ou parallele de l'ancienne religion de l'Egypte avec la religion actuelle de Nigritie* (The Cult of Fetish Gods, or Parallels between the Ancient Religion of Egypt with Contemporary Religion in Niger) (1760), first employed the word *fétichism* (fetishism).[30] Marx also apparently read this book outlining quasi-materialist theories of religious origins, from whence he applied the translated French term to a section in *Capital.*[31]

Introduction 11

In investigating fetishism's genealogy, Pietz outlines several themes arising in what he calls "the history of fetish discourse": "Irreducible materiality; a fixed power to repeat an original event of singular synthesis or ordering; the institutional construction of consciousness of the social value of things; and the material fetish as an object established in an intense relation to and with power over the desires, actions, health, and self-identity of individuals whose personhood is conceived as inseparable from their bodies."[32] The "social value of things" and objects' power in constituting personal identity also appear in modern, and global, forms of commodity fetishism.

In the early twentieth century, Sigmund Freud (1856–1939) developed his own psychosexual theory of the fetish; his 1927 essay "Fetishism" posited that during a young boy's maturation, while regarding his mother's foot or shoe, he might imagine a (nonexistent) phallus beneath her undergarments, and his substituting a reassuringly familiar object (like a shoe) for this fanciful body part represented personal fears of castration.[33] Feminist psychoanalyst Louise J. Kaplan views such concepts of castration and lack as psychologically destructive, arising from Freud's aggressive misogyny (and homophobia).[34] Nevertheless, within Freud's understanding of fetishism, desire's "magical thinking" creates substitutes for the original, along with pleasurable new attachment forms,[35] which also appear in advertising's manufactured yearning for commodities. Literary scholar Elaine Apter more positively views fetishism as "compromise" of a "hexed state of mind," where "fetishism emerges as an ever-shifting form of specular mimesis, an ambiguous state that demystifies and falsifies at the same time, or that reveals its own techniques of masquerade while putting into doubt any fixed referent."[36] This "specular mimesis," or chimeric attachment, applies to fantasies of commodities, replicated in myriad forms in newspaper and magazine advertisements, and film, television, and online images during the roughly 150 years covered in this study.

Pietz's historicized understanding of fetishism, coupled with Freud's idea of the fetish as "substitute for desire," form a bridge between the discourse's origins and Marx and Freud's understandings of fetishism that helps unveil the power of commodities and, particularly, Japanese relationships to objects infused with residual premodern Shintō notions. In a specifically Japanese context, people's relationships to things could even evince commodity fetishism's naturalization (or "domestication").

12 *Introduction*

In contemporary times, decluttering guru and former Shintō priestess Marie Kondo's (b. 1984) global "cult" reveals popular appeal for enduring remnants of a uniquely Japanese relationship to things in her attitude toward objects of daily use, where she thanks them before tossing or donating them. Her mid-2010s popularity reached a point where pundits coined the English word "Kondoization" to describe decluttering a garage or apartment to gain clarity and determine which objects "spark joy," and thus, merit keeping.[37]

Nowadays, most items causing clutter in dwellings are mass-produced in industrial settings and are thus alienated from hand-manufacturing's artisanality, lacking the (hypothetical) craftsperson's aura. Yet, Kondo asserts that "a dramatic reorganization of the home causes correspondingly dramatic changes in lifestyle and perspective. It is life transforming."[38] Of course, moral influences of living environments, including ordering of furnishings in homes, is not a new concept, and in the late nineteenth century these moral influences distinctly preoccupied Anglo-American reformers, whose ideas were also adopted in Japan. In addition, houses and apartments in Japan occupy less space than in other countries—thus increasing propensities toward clutter or appearances of stockpiled or hoarded possessions, and therefore, more likely to cause owners' distress over the mess. More importantly, according to Kondo, "When you put your house in order, you put your affairs and your past in order, too."[39] She characterizes success for individuals in maintaining clutter-free lives as stemming from how "they are surrounded only by the things they love."[40] This concept that objects maintain emotional resonance and influence life outcomes appears to echo culturally Japanese values gleaned from Kondo's former profession as clergy.

In popular literature and contemporary trends, late capitalist societies with social formations based upon accumulation of things seemingly have not mastered emotional relinquishment of objects no longer deemed useful. As objects habitually substitute for actual relationships, and often, alienate their owners from having them due to lack of "space" in homes (and psyches), object fetishism even reaches radical limits. The popularity of US reality TV shows like *Hoarders,* with its 2009 premiere attracting 2.5 million viewers, speaks to widespread American interest in pathologically extreme consumption endpoints reaching levels of even accumulating waste.[41] In the 2011 *New York Times* best seller *Stuff: Compulsive Hoarding and the Meaning of Things,* psychologist Randy Frost and sociologist Gail Steketee unpack

Introduction 13

hoarding's psychological ramifications as a disorder afflicting over six million people, which causes nearly unbreakable attachments to objects owned while prompting desires to acquire more.[42] Their book details narratives of treated patients who recognized their problem with accumulating things but greatly feared psychological distress caused by giving up future options of acquiring more objects. With material objects' unremittent encroachment upon personal living space, clutter in homes thus became proxies for unresolved psychological issues and traumas, while further acquisitions postponed their resolution.

Interestingly, Kondo's periodic decluttering practice is the very antithesis to mass consumption, or an action possibly countering socially conditioned continuous consumption marked by permanent accumulation of mass-produced commodities. Ironically, removing accumulated objects that no longer inspire positive emotions, and replacing them with newer ones allegedly generating greater happiness, could also stoke endless consumption engines. Certainly, falling into such cycles was not Kondo's intention, who instead advocates keeping only objects one needs and enjoys using. Unsurprisingly, in her critique of capitalism, political philosopher Cynthia Kaufman notes how "consumerism is one of the central memes of capitalist reproduction."[43] Naturally, capitalism's fuel now and in the past is consumption, while modern consumption is driven by creation of a robust, self-replicating commodity fetishism spurred by advertising meant to ensure healthy, ever-replicating consumerism. However, Kondo's tidying and organizing practices likely represent Japanese attitudes toward things based on Shintō ideas about human relationships with objects, combined with Buddhist conceptions of impermanence, that can engender unique forms of religiously infused commodity fetishism in Japan.

Some clues intimating this are found in Marx's writings. In *Capital*'s first part, commodity fetishism is described as the commodity possessing a mystical quality. The so-called product becomes imbued with a quasi-religious character in the commodification process, through projection of certain commonly held values upon it, where the real world reflects spiritual dimensions of commonly held belief systems, or what Marx calls religion. Commodity fetishism, in fact, melded well with preexisting Japanese religious ideas. Understanding aspects of Japan's indigenous religion, Shintō, with its set of premodern animist beliefs and practices based on living and inanimate things' diffuse divinity,[44] adds interesting dimensions to commodity fetishism. In premodern times, Japanese relationships to things were informed

14 *Introduction*

by Shinto-influenced animism, where useful objects or unusual natural features were popularly believed as inhabited by *kami* (spirits, gods) or possessing *kami* nature.[45]

Religious scholar Angelika Kretschmer notes how "mortuary rites for inanimate objects" are still practiced in Japan for "retiring" once-useful objects no longer employed, like broken needles in a *hari kuyō* (needle offering) ritual.[46] In the past, and even today, Japanese can take advantage of ritual tool kits emerging from Shintō practices to separate themselves emotionally from objects no longer needed. These "rites of separation" or *kuyō* can be performed for "needles, chopsticks, combs, dolls, clocks, personal seals (*hanko*), knives, shoes, scissors, and semiconductors,"[47] including useful objects or tools used by tradespeople or artists like tea ceremony whisks or calligraphy pens.[48] During the 1970s and 1980s amid Japan's arguably most saturated point of industrialization and capitalization, a "*kuyō* boom" mushroomed from a burgeoning occult boom (intersecting with cash-strapped religious institutions' fund-raising motives).[49] Though historical antecedents exist, this popular recourse to religious beliefs imbuing objects with spiritual or "living" qualities—like fetishizing mass-produced commodities in advertisements to make them unique—notably developed during commodification's apex exactly when social relations between people began experiencing alienation.

According to Marx, in Asian contexts, products became commodities once "primitive societies" began breaking down with industrialization, while rural individuals increasingly became workers involved in large-scale production.[50] Of course, feudal societies, whether in Europe or Asia, did not intentionally produce commodities serving as entities of projected social value. However, "a society based on the production of commodities," or basically, an industrial society, is characterized by conditions where "the producers in general enter into social relations with one another by treating their products as commodities and values, whereby they reduce their individual private labor to the standard of homogeneous human labor."[51] This pertains to standardization, achievable through industrial processes and mass production.

However, commodity fetishism only works when it mediates social interaction amid other consumer processes. It takes on a plethora of forms, as it does varieties of potential emotional connections luring customers to buy, which can be hastened for immediate gratification, or consumption in the now. Kaufman criticizes this emotionally driven consumption: "Living in a society dominated by capitalism, we inhabit a world where pleasure is increasingly structured as something to be bought. Fulfillment is conceived as something to be attained through the consumption of commodities."[52] However, to create such relationships and alleged emotional connections with objects or commodities takes time. How could advertisers quickly transfer this concept to mass-produced products? They achieve this in constructing narratives surrounding products.

Ideally, for commodity fetishism to work its "magic" (or "mystical character," as Marx indicates) and translate into desired eternally reproducible consumption through perceptions of value, purchase of the commodity should replicate similar sensations for consumers as receiving gifts from individuals with strongly positive shared emotional connections. To increase consumption and longings to perpetuate it, Japanese companies and advertisers have discovered ways to impart a gift's patina into the commodity, with three things required to prompt combined feelings of rarity and familiarity: limited editions, seasonal items (*kisetsu gentei*), and "traditional" Japanese flavors. In *The Gift*, a 1925 study on social solidarity in premodern cultures, sociologist Marcel Mauss (1872–1950) investigates how exchanges of objects impact social relations, and posits that gift-giving and reciprocity strengthen these to benefit group social dynamics.[53] Into contemporary times, Japanese society regularly engages in gift-giving and subscribes to notions of reciprocity, with givers desiring to foster or maintain positive social relationships.[54] Unsurprisingly, commodities actually cannot give back, but such reciprocity can be imagined in the possible emotional fulfillment products promise to share with consumers: a process potentially stimulating the masturbatory pleasure of shopping, requiring regular performance to garner satisfaction.

In Japan, popular writer Nakamura Usagi (b. 1958) detailed her problematic fascination with buying luxury goods in the book *Shoppingu no joō* (Shopping Queen, 2001),[55] and in *Shūkan bunshun* (Weekly Literary Spring) she wrote a weekly column by the same name where she unapologetically consumed name brands and luxury goods, often only because she liked the brands. Nakamura titled her book's first section *Watashi wa kaimono izonshō* (I'm addicted to shopping)[56] and confessed her craze for shopping both when stress built up and when it didn't, but also when she had money or spent it all—in other words, any occasion was a good time to shop![57] Additionally, she wrote four books on host clubs—establishments beginning in 1966 in

Japan, where, in exchange for increasingly higher amounts of money, heterosexual women can drink and chat with male hosts proffering them attention and flattery like celebrities, in a business model based on early postwar hostess clubs originally created for men.[58]

Most notably, Usagi published the evocatively titled *Ai to shihonshugi* (Love and Capitalism, 2002), where "love" is a commodity available for purchase at host clubs, and through more informal arrangements like compensated companionship.[59] Since the late 1990s, compensated dating (*enjo kōsai*) between teen girls and middle-aged men involving exchange of name-brand goods for companionship, and possibly sex, has been a hot topic in Japan's media,[60] and arguably, has resulted in moral panic.[61] Film scholar Nicholas de Villiers, citing journalist and former "webcam girl" Melissa Gira Grant's (b. 1978) exposé of sex work in analyzing Hideaki Anno's film *Love and Pop* (1998) about compensated dating, emphasizes how it "frequently acts as a metonym that condenses our anxieties and ambivalence about capitalism, materialism, and the national economy."[62]

Beginning in mid-2001, Nakamura spent fourteen months immersed in a Kabuki-chō host club in Tokyo's Shinjuku ward, where she paid a staggering fifteen million yen on her favorite host. In a 2003 *Japan Times* interview, Nakamura said, "When all our desires are satisfied, what's left is to pay for something we can't see—and it all comes down to illusions. And the ultimate illusions exist in human relationships."[63] Her experience represents capitalism's endpoint, where physical commodities no longer exist, but as substituted forms through emotional fetishism, where fake (paid) relationships substitute for real relationships, and instead of fetishized material objects, consumers seek desire itself. Here, the fake relationship *is* the commodity, or, more precisely, the labor that goes into producing this fake relationship.[64] However, while consuming these purchasable fake relationships, Nakamura understood that she still kept buying brand-name luxury goods to validate her identity as a woman in late capitalism, and "through the rhetoric of the deserving consumer" even proudly admitted her spending as sustaining Japan's capitalistic society.[65] Anthropologist Daniel Miller's *A Theory of Shopping* posits acts of purchasing as "treat" and leisure activity, yet, inspired by Georges Bataille's (1897–1962) notions of sacrificial ritual, Miller also perceives consumption within a sacrificial framework resonating with Nakamura's self-revelatory confessions of spending.[66]

Holocaust survivor and controversial Canadian addiction specialist Gabor Maté's award-winning *In the Realm of the Hungry Ghosts*[67] provides a compelling glimpse into commodity fetishism's extreme endpoint, where consumers pursue endless, insatiable desires to purchase ever more commodities to achieve (fleeting) sensations of emotional fulfillment to substitute for real human relationships. Because consumption is capitalism's engine, advertisers seek to tap into commodities' addictive properties, attractively portrayed to create narratives of emotional satisfaction. Maté himself suffers from self-confessed addiction to online shopping, and he believes that childhood traumas like his own lead to addictive behaviors in late capitalist societies. He uses as allegory Buddhist concepts of souls in limbo due to karmic misdeeds before death, where the living must feed their insatiable phantom appetites to prevent mayhem: "The inhabitants of the Hungry Ghost Realm are depicted as creatures with scrawny necks, small mouths, emaciated limbs and large, bloated, empty bellies. This is the domain of addiction, where we constantly seek something outside ourselves to curb an insatiable yearning for relief or fulfillment. The aching emptiness is perpetual because the substances, objects, or pursuits we hope will soothe it are not what we really need."[68]

As business historian David McNally suggests, Marx employed a plethora of monster metaphors approaching gothic horror genres.[69] In Marx's writings, amid what might be considered commodity *fetishization,* objects take on quasi-religious qualities like idols for European capitalists,[70] and consumers "[bow] down before something spectral."[71] In a late-twentieth-century Japanese context, through brand names, Nakamura definitely fell in thrall of commodities exerting supernatural power over her to manipulate endless purchasing. Certainly, Marx expressed moral condemnation of such capitalist processes dehumanizing both workers and consumers in courses of events that Hungarian Marxist philosopher Georg Lukacs (1885–1971) termed "reification."[72] The commodity's unnatural power is obviously artificially constructed through discourse, but within new social relations spawned by capitalism, it takes on a (horrifying) life of its own.

A possible antidote to such forms of reification might be what I term "manufactured artisanality," potentially applied to products in a simulated harkening back to earlier times before industrialization's detrimental impact on human relations, in a controlled return of a repressed premodernity attempting to dispel the magical (but inherently fake, and substituted) life-force of fetishized commodities. The reimputing of labor into products could add a human, rather than mystical, or supernatural element, to commodities, which theoretically would displace their own proper agencies onto those of consumers. However, as simulacra of handcrafted articles, products "luxuriated" by application of manufactured artisanality might still serve as substitutes for fetishized commodities in their own version of commodity fetishism. Instead of ruminating upon the purpose of this seemingly reiterative process, historians might ask, why now? And, why was a kind of manufactured artisanality inherent to Japanese business and advertising models since the nascence of large, seemingly depersonalized conglomerates in the late nineteenth century?

MANUFACTURED ARTISANALITY: FROM COMMODITY FETISHISM TO FETISHIZATION OF LABOR

In a US Chamber of Commerce Foundation blog, Michael Hendrix's 2012 article "The Artisanal Manufacturing Revolution" uses the term "artisanal manufacturing" to refer to an American trend emerging from the Occupy Movement (2011–2012)[73] amid efforts to reclaim labor from impersonal corporate factories. Today, such portrayals of manufacturing might be described as what I term "hipster artisanality," or even "hipster capitalism," which now exists on a global scale and allegedly endures due to consumer demand. "Hipster," a word related to jazz originating in the late 1930s,[74] now refers to a contemporary subculture composed of new generations of millennial young people, mostly Caucasian and middle-class, but also prevalent in large urban centers in Japan, Europe, Latin America, and elsewhere, who desire returning to times when handicrafts and personalized labor mattered, and which unironically manifests itself in popularity of canning, prominent beards, braids, craft brews, handmade leather goods, vintage denim, and other contemporary fads.[75] Unsurprisingly, these are all trendy preoccupations requiring time, money, and certain privileges. Yet, amid a preponderance of hipsters and associated trappings lurks a certain critique of capitalism very much representing an era.

Whereas the commodity fetishism examined earlier hides labor, its antidote would seemingly be to reveal, or reinvent, labor. Essentially, imagined artisans would replace anonymous laborers engaged in mass production in far-off factories elsewhere. For example, consumers can easily envision skilled artisans in Kumano, a traditional

Introduction   19

Japanese brush-purveying region, making Shiseidō brushes by hand rather than in manufacturing dependent upon machines serviced by industrial workers' bodies trained to perform one step in a cumulative process, as pioneered by American industrialist Henry Ford (1863–1947), in assembly lines to speed efficiency. This now-commonplace notion of invented artisanal labor is quite recent, and perhaps even invented by Japanese.

Thus, within a Japanese context, in manufactured artisanality, consumers' potential relationships with commodities are hastened and made more immediate by crafted nostalgia for a prelapsarian artisanal past harkening back to Tokugawa times and before, projected onto products whose allure, despite mass production, must be manufactured artificially and framed by construction of compelling narratives leading consumers to buy. In this study, subsequent chapters explore my concept of manufactured artisanality to characterize Japanese products' allure. Therein, artisanality is revealed as *invented* artisanal manufacturing. A glimpse into Japan's history of advertising and brand-name products discloses that Japanese pioneered a version of such value-added commodity fetishization now so popular in the United States and worldwide. American and global anticapitalist critique among millennials, along with rising hipster tropes, have contributed to preferred product types and narratives created around them to effectuate "wholesome" or "ethical" consumption; yet, this still falls under Marx's premise of commodity fetishism, laden with forms of purely manufactured enchantment for products "crafted" within certain narratives. Basically, in all of capitalism's stages, and especially late capitalism, commodity fetishism is unavoidable and inescapable, and it becomes ever stronger in worsening addictions leading to greater consumer compulsions.

How Japanese companies frame their history and imbue their (new, scientifically developed) products with manufactured artisanality also mirrors Marx's idea of reification (*verdinglichung*—making into things), where social relations are imbued into a commodity. The commodity becomes a subject with its own agency, and the consumer an object, an idea further developed by Lukacs. Intricately tied to commodity fetishism, Japanese name brands in their very nature cite invented histories of artisanship and reference "invisible" craftspeople through assigned craftsmanship allegedly going into every mass-produced product. A lucrative assumption is that consumers desire to know about comfortingly long histories behind products, or an "invented tradition"[76] of craftsmanship to ensure quality. Curiously, certain

20 *Introduction*

narratives crafted via advertising harken back to the product's alleged origins (or artisanal manufacturing) during the premodern and Tokugawa eras, often just before Japan's 1854 "opening" to the West, or even a throwback to Japan's Genroku (1688–1704) cultural "golden age," in a seminal Freudian point of return before the opening's primal scene or during Edo's flourishing culture to reference "authentic" and allegedly undiluted Japanese traditions. Yet, this kind of quality (resembling that of handcrafted articles) was also framed as accessible to all consumers, when Japan was increasingly democratizing its political system in the late nineteenth century, and once again, in the postwar period after imperial defeat in 1945.

Within a product's fictive history, one thus consumes the human relations inherent within the product: essentially, "hipster capitalism," which asserts nostalgia for a seemingly golden past where careful craftsmanship created every product, or for a time before the commodity *was* a commodity. Here, labor's very concept is consumed; an assumption of painstaking effort is applied to production of certain products with unique traits. Ironically, what can be called "fetishization of labor" naturally assumes creation of luxury products (because of high labor costs involved) or masks conditions of exploitation.

Such notions of fetishization of labor appear in earlier antecedents of Japan's more recent prewar past. Most notably, 1968 Nobel Prize winner in literature, Kawabata Yasunari (1899–1972), whose award consideration partially stemmed from his novella *Yukiguni* (Snow Country, 1934/1937), fetishizes complicated and laborious processes whereby Niigata "maidens" produced *chijimi* textiles by hand, with cloth dyed and bleached on snow.[77] This product, through its handicraft production and rarity, resists mass manufacturing and assumes complex interconnected relationships to gain access, while concurrently, a declining market with less consumer demand threatens continued production. However, intellectuals amid Imperial Japan's domestic industrial saturation issued forth literary nostalgia for artisanal labor. As intellectuals, Japanese writers possessed uncanny abilities to mirror their society's broader, unarticulated preoccupations.

Kawabata, though an establishment writer, often echoed proletarian themes in his work. Nostalgia for authentic articles rather than manufactured simulacra painfully reveals how human relations between producers and consumers were severed in an increasingly industrial society. Kawabata projects such yearnings and nostalgia upon the mental

Introduction 21

perambulations of his protagonist Shimamura as he returns to a fictional Yuzawa located between Gunma and Niigata Prefectures to consume young women's labor and their bodies seemingly stuck in developmental time warps, apparently untouched by capitalism's ravages, but ironically still forced to sell sex to make ends meet.[78] Their sexual exploitation is aestheticized when the women themselves become commodities like the provincial geisha Shimamura patronizes, since the luxury commodity that they once made now seems a wasted effort due to declining demand and extravagant expense.[79] *Snow Country* thus reveals capitalism's destruction of community amid aestheticized landscapes of the writer's imagination. Ironically, when Kawabata wrote his iconic piece, Imperial Japan embarked upon Manchuria's control and colonization, in a utopian experiment meant to protect workers and farmers from capitalism's depredations under the Japanese-led fascist state's paternalistic care. Formerly leftwing domestic Japanese adherents were attracted to this cause, like once-proletarian activist Yamada Seizaburō (1896–1987), and even Kawabata himself, in extensive travels throughout Manchukuo and promotion of literary activities.[80]

Yet, contrasting this seemingly anachronistic example from prewar Japanese literature, contemporary fetishization of labor also appears in current concepts of manufactured artisanality worldwide. For example, in the present United States, the cashmere sweater firm Lingua Franca specializes in hand-embroidering political slogans, hip-hop lyrics, and pop-cultural sayings with mild countercultural edginess on luxury knits mass-produced in China. In 2016 Rachel Hrushka, the brand's designer, began embroidering sweaters to reduce anxiety upon her psychiatrist's recommendations, and then conceived a business plan offering this product.[81] Handiwork is now performed by five women, referred to by name in the company's periodic email newsletters, which advertise Lingua Franca as "a line of sustainably-sourced, fair trade luxury cashmere sweaters, all hand-stitched by women in NYC."[82] Obviously, the sweaters themselves are not exclusive at all, with cashmere gluts in the global market spawned by Chinese oversupply in the past two decades.[83] Rather, these products are "luxuriated" by the addition of value-added American labor in the privileged Bleeker Street location of a Lingua Franca atelier, which allows sale at prices ranging from $380 to $525, depending on message lengths. Here, phrases stitched in thread form the commodity's appeal, where messages (including activist political slogans and pop-cultural memes) are literally themselves commodified,

22   *Introduction*

and consumers assume their purchases will improve the world by generating awareness of social issues, with the firm's cut of profits (usually $100 from each sweater) donated to charity.[84]

Some of these issues surrounding manufactured artisanality will be revisited in later discussions of brand names Issey Miyake and Comme des Garçons during the 1960s and 1970s. Basically, when artisanality is manufactured, products are luxuriated and intentionally divorced from inescapably industrial origins, in a new and fashionable commodity fetishism developed in late Meiji Japan, and which also enjoyed its moment in postwar Japan during the height of the Japanese economic miracle.

WHAT DOES LUXURY MEAN IN MODERN JAPAN?

A study of democratization of luxury for Japanese companies (and products) merits discussion of what luxury means in Japan, and how it might actually prevent, rather than spur, consumption; therefore, "luxury" needs to be manufactured through a certain set of qualities for the product. One of these is advertising's activation of commodity fetishism, citing premodern Japanese antecedents in a Shintō-inspired popular belief system. Another is manufactured artisanality, where imputed craftsmanship luxuriates products. According to the *Oxford English Dictionary*'s online website, "luxury" in English has three nuanced meanings: "1. A state of great comfort or elegance, especially when involving great expense; 2. An inessential, desirable item which is expensive or difficult to obtain; and 3. A pleasure obtained only rarely."[85] Its contemporary origins date from the mid-seventeenth century, whereas the word originally denoted lechery in Middle English, which stems from "Old French *luxurie, luxure,* from Latin *luxuria,* from *luxus* 'excess.'"[86] In contrast, luxury (*zeitaku*) in Japanese harbors meanings of profligacy or waste; thus, moralists or government officials often deemed it preferably eliminated by society or the state. So, in Japanese contexts, what does it mean to consume luxury? Indeed, a product (*shōhin*) consumed (*shōka shiteru*) by a consumer (*shōhisha*) somewhat resembles processes of "digestion" or bodily function.

Until the early twentieth century, when indoor plumbing became ubiquitous, to eliminate bodily wastes, rural and urban Japanese relied on latrines serviced daily by night soil collectors. Due to varied and often more nutritious diets, city dwellers produced richer human manure than their rural counterparts. Thus, different grades of night

Introduction 23

soil developed because of varied consumption patterns of urbanites and peasants in their diets. Additionally, higher quality, or "special edition," excrement with luxury connotations appeared as a seasonal commodity, according to frequencies of rich banqueting throughout the year, such as *bōnenkai* (end-of-year celebrations) bookending the New Year. David Howell indicates that night soil became such an important commodity in Tokugawa-era Osaka and Edo that it generated bitter mercantile competition for the best (and most economically priced) product[87]—exactly a problem that the shogunate wished to avoid in battles against luxury.

In the mid-Tokugawa era, shogunal officials viewed luxury as wasteful and profligate, initiating the Kansei Reforms (1789–1793) to combat it, even curtailing proto-capitalization and associated urbanization by encouraging reagrarianization. As the shogun's senior councillor, Confucian moralist Matsudaira Sadanobu (1759–1829) supported these financial reforms to resist state excesses. Sadanobu's story is not unique for Tokugawa Japan, where burgeoning *chōnin* (merchant class) mercantile energies threatened to generate unseemly disparities between ruling elites and merchants, viewed as the Confucian moral hierarchy's lowest status group. Despite official condemnation of profligacy, and popular enjoyment in shunning (or envying) extravagant lifestyles of the merchant classes and pleasure quarters, these groups developed distinct characteristics largely formed during the Genroku period, developing what many today understand as distinctly Japanese culture: geisha, woodblock prints, Noh plays, and Kabuki theater.

Essentially, for capitalism to function in Japan, expansion of consumption involved promotion in a nation where overconsumption was impossible or warned against. Therefore, mass consumption during industrial capitalism's nascence from early Meiji beginnings onward always required portrayal as "democratizing" to stave off connotations of elite excess and hedonism—qualities often applied to luxury—while, alternately, consumers needed persuasion to overcome the "shame" of consumption. Thus, in Japanese contexts, markets developed that privileged quality over quantity, a tenet actually opposing many standard notions of Western capitalism. Indeed, in Japan, the "special edition," though not as expensive as some luxury products, allowed for controlled mass quantities still enrobed in a veneer of exclusivity through limited availability. Japanese companies also create luxury in offering the allegedly scarce "limited edition" or items labeled *kisetsu gentei* (seasonally limited) sold at premium prices, to

24 *Introduction*

heighten interest in the company's more ordinary products, available at cheaper prices.[88] Here, limited edition or seasonal products serve to circumvent a particularly Japanese "allergy" to consumption. Clearly, some postwar individuals like Nakamura had few problems consuming, but despite allegedly hedonistic 1980s-era mass consumption during unprecedented prosperity, overconsumption has never been a particularly Japanese trait. Amid modern Japan's quotidian middle-class frugality, advertising often rearticulates women's economic power in keenly focusing upon women as likely purchasers of luxury products or commodities acquiring luxury as seasonal items, limited editions, or in manufactured artisanality based on invented traditions citing premodernity.

Democratizing Luxury: Genealogy of a Term

In the United States during the Occupy Movement (2011–2012), versions of "manufactured artisanality" and "democratizing luxury" arrived as marketable concepts, and they flourished while adherents of both left- and right-leaning political economics desired state intervention in capitalism. However, as successive chapters reveal, Japan expressed derivations of these phenomena first—sometimes as much as decades to a century before appearing in the West. More recently, these trends were expanded in the United States by advertisers and companies to stimulate consumption among millennials (born 1981–1996)[89] likely expressing anticapitalist leanings spurred by coming of age during the Great Recession (December 2007 to June 2009) following the subprime mortgage crisis. Inspired by former presidential candidate Bernie Sanders (2015–2020, b. 1941), around 50 percent of US millennials and Gen-Xers (born 1965–1980)[90] expressed political orientations favorable to redistributive forms of socialism strongly regulating wealth, with almost half of millennials viewing capitalism negatively,[91] while younger people generally desired left-leaning solutions to economic problems and appeared amenable to state intervention in capitalism. Despite denials by conservative commentators, President Donald Trump's 2019 expansion of trade tariffs and agricultural subsidies also pointed to acceptance of limited state guidance in corporate enterprise by right-leaning Americans who feared Chinese market dominance—largely due to Chinese manufacturing of American name-brand luxury goods. However, 1930s-era fascist regimes (who adopted rightwing versions of socialism in corporatism, along with certain dis-

Introduction 25

courses of left-oriented socialism without the actual policies) also maintained corporatist approaches to capital and to certain industries; consider Manchukuo, Imperial Japan, Nazi Germany, and now, arguably, Xi Jinping's (b. 1953) China. Here, state intervention in capitalism in a Chinese context also translated into anticorruption measures meant to combat conspicuous wealth initially flaunted in the late 1990s and attacked use of luxury name-brand goods as bribes.

In the late twentieth and early twenty-first centuries, spanning economic fluctuations from the US-based dotcom bust (1999–2000) to the subprime mortgage crisis (2007–2009) that plagued world economies, new technologies grew exponentially and expanded global access into new markets. This arose amid greater efficiency for global supply chain management and online purchasing facilitated by smartphones (with nearly omnipresent Apple iPhones available since 2007, after which competitors like Samsung also joined the market), while Chinese and Eastern European markets developed robustly alongside greater individual purchasing power. Consequently, from the millennium onward, increasing levels of accessibility to luxury appeared globally. However, over a century ago, Japanese companies pioneered a certain model for the near-mass access to luxury so ubiquitous today. Terms for this massification of quality products, which I call "democratizing luxury," have abounded in Western scholarship of the past two decades.

Among US researchers publishing during the global recession, antecedents to "democratizing luxury" include the less appealing term "populence," coined by Elad Granot and Thomas Brashear, meaning "popular opulence," where "new luxury" (versus "old luxury," articulated in 1899 by American economist Thorstein Veblen [1857–1929]) now "includes products for mass-market appeal to consumers across various income and social classes."[92] Their study found that "populent" goods were consumed for "overall superiority (high quality), fashionable and 'cool' ('demonstrating sophistication, discerning abilities, and success'), moonshooting and bottom-barreling (paying premiums for goods with 'high perceived quality, performance, and emotional engagement' while seeking bargains for all others), signaling (attracting friends and mates for a sense of belonging), self-catering, exploring, and inconspicuous consumption (high quality, expensive, but without conspicuous brand elements)."[93] Populence also refers to "mass production and distribution of premium goods and services,"[94] where products cater to emotional needs; by activating a product's appeal through commodity fetishism, demand could even circumvent a sluggish economy and attract midrange consumers.[95] Here similarities intersect with Japan's past three decades. Also, Granot, Russell, and Brashear-Alejandro found that women primarily account for recent growth of new luxury goods constituting populence,[96] where experiences and emotional connections are key, which I argue appeared in Japan from the late nineteenth century onward, when middle- and upper-class women controlled household finances and desired products looking modern and conferring social capital.

As a term first appearing in English-language scholarly research, "democratizing luxury" was initially used by Polish business professor Klaudia Plazyk in 2013, inspired by earlier work in Poland by E. Sek, who coined the phrase (in Polish) in 2004. Sek showed how this phenomenon arose around the millennium, when companies sought to increase customer bases to improve financial indicators to satisfy investors, and more wealthy young people could afford luxury goods.[97] Beginning in the early 1990s, and following emergence of new markets in postcommunist societies like Poland (and arguably, Mainland China), Plazyk perceives luxury goods markets evolving with greater access to global mass markets. In addition, Deng Xiaoping's 1992 Southern Tour both attempted to deflect from Mainland China's post-Tiananmen political crackdown and jump-start Special Economic Zones like Shenzhen and Shanghai's Pudong area. Plazyk also indicates that by 2013, high-net-worth individuals in Asia-Pacific areas and North America each reached 4.3 million, with Europe numbering 3.8 million.[98] Essentially, Asia-Pacific markets for luxury goods were just as important as American ones due to high numbers of individuals potentially able to purchase these luxury items. For many Japanese, the most commonly associated characteristic for luxury is that it is "expensive."[99] However, as my study shows, this is more commonly associated with foreign luxury goods (like Louis Vuitton) and not domestically manufactured ones, which began as substitutes for high-end imports in the late nineteenth century.

In the United States, "democratizing luxury" first started appearing as an industry-specific term around 2016, when marketing experts attempted to formulate ideas for American companies to spur greater consumption. This originated when Jeremy Goldman, CEO of marketing and branding consultancy Firebrand Group, which published the ebook *20.16 Big Ideas for 2016*, interviewed Alexa von Tobel, who heads LearnVest, a company creating apps to aid financial literacy tar-

Introduction 27

geted to younger millennials.[100] She claimed "democratizing luxury" as her Big Idea, whereby corporations used technology like apps to access mass markets beyond the 1 percent for luxury goods and services. Thus, she believed more users could allow companies to deliver high-quality products at lower prices.

However, Japanese consumers of domestic luxury goods cite "high quality" as their greatest reason for purchases "based on craftsmanship, style, and service."[101] Japanese women, in particular, rate these factors highly for luxury goods. They also likely "prefer in-store shopping experiences," which deliver more personalized forms of consumption.[102] Careful deliberation is more often practiced by Japanese in brick-and-mortar stores than online, where companies promise immediate sales and easy returns. Generally, Japanese belong to a nation of reticent consumers with long histories of government anxiety about personal consumption—too little spending harms the economy, while too much encourages debt and dissipation of family assets.

Because 60 percent of Japan's total GDP is composed of private consumption, the Bank of Japan (BOJ) (Japan's leading government central financial institution like the Federal Reserve) researches and compiles consumption statistics to form data termed the Consumption Activity Index, which assesses the Japanese economy's health.[103] As of June 2019, most recent BOJ data indicate that Japanese consumers rate most highly the following factors (with three possible choices from a list of fourteen categories) determining which goods and services they will spend money on in the next year: low price (54.1 percent), safety (47 percent), durability (41.3 percent), reliability (39.2 percent), and functionality (30.7 percent).[104] Brand reputation (2.1 percent) and design (7.4 percent) were curiously among the lowest categories in importance. Additionally, these factors point to increasing frugality among Japanese consumers, who seemingly exhibit tendencies to choose items and services with long-term durability, which basically prevents further consumption growth. Wholesomeness was another middling characteristic, appearing at 17.6 percent. In opinion surveys since 1996, the BOJ also uses "bustle of shopping streets and amusement quarters" as an indicator to assess economic conditions. For Japanese consumers, foodstuffs, daily commodities, and clothing comprise the greatest spending, and therefore, such prices matter most.

Incidentally, these are also categories describing products examined in subsequent chapters, and arguably, through which luxury is appreciated on a quotidian basis in daily consumption. *Democratizing*

28 *Introduction*

Luxury will examine shifting meanings of this term in modern Japanese contexts over a period of roughly 150 years.

In the late nineteenth century, Western-connoted consumer products produced by several of Japan's now iconic global corporations enabled striking business successes for the aspirational luxuries they promised to customers. Amid a society that valued frugality, these products allowed consumers to feel proud of their purchases produced by Japanese companies and secure in their efficacy. Growth of newspapers and print capitalism stimulated consuming communities, with women a particularly important target group for new Japanese corporations' advertisements due to their control over household finances. With slow extinction of artisanal manufacturing amid supplanting by mass production came an artificially created commodity fetishism imposed by advertising to emphasize infinitely reproducible products' alleged uniqueness. The next chapter further examines this "manufactured artisanality," which reinforces nostalgia for absent craftspeople whose handicraft was only recently replaced by modern manufacturing.

Chapter One

CRAFTSMANSHIP AND PROTO-BRANDING IN THE TOKUGAWA ERA

In the ancient Asiatic and other ancient modes of production, we find that the conversion of products into commodities, and therefore the conversion of men into producers of commodities, holds a subordinate place, which, however, increases in importance as the primitive communities approach nearer and nearer to their dissolution.[1]

—*Karl Marx*, Capital, *vol. 1*

Japanese capitalism's particular nature in its rapid late nineteenth-century formation, coupled with preexisting proto-capitalist practices beginning as early as the Muromachi (1336–1573) and Tokugawa (1603–1868) periods, combined with specific cultural aspects to create unique modern business environments that ultimately engendered what I call "democratizing luxury." Tokugawa proto-industries, such as sake and soy sauce brewing, set the stage for Japan's Meiji-era industrialization and provided a basis for promoting domestic consumption and taste arbitration through product placement and logos in woodblock prints. In Japan, social practices surrounding capitalism suffused both shopping and advertising, and companies arising during the early Meiji period took cues from Tokugawa-era *kamon* (family crests) to create logos encapsulating these practices.

To understand advertising's relationship to larger consumption structures and notions of luxury, it is crucial to briefly examine Japanese capitalism's origins and name brand development's prehistory. This chapter examines unique aspects of a particularly Japanese form of capitalism and consumption in Japanese contexts. However, how

30 *Chapter 1*

consumers understood quality and value developed over time amid solid foundations of products produced by guilds of highly organized artisans, recognized as a separate class in the Tokugawa social order. Apprenticeships and guilds provided frameworks for standardized quality dissemination, and even design models, while shops and proto-industries created their own logos. The logo emerged at this time, where such symbols showcased certain values expressed by products. So began a particularly Japanese iconography of luxury, where women became increasingly important arbiters in purchasing household items—initially through itinerant sellers or sending household retainers to shops.

THE NATURE OF JAPANESE CAPITALISM: CAPITALISM AS A SET OF SOCIAL PRACTICES

Notably, capitalism is not simply the interplay of "market forces" or an independent process occurring as a result of historical factors leading up to a natural evolution toward industrial development, as past scholarship and more recent political economy commentary often characterized the 1867–1868 Meiji revolution and Japan's associated industrialization. Rather, as Cynthia Kaufman emphasizes, capitalism reproduces itself in individual social practices: "Capitalism can be understood in a similar way: a set of practices that begin in a particular historical moment and then develop into patterned structures. Capitalism is better understood as a contingent, or historically accidental, set of interrelated practices rather than as an organism or a machine. . . . We can think about capitalism as embodied in and perpetuated by the projects of a variety of agents."[2] She also asserts that "capitalism has developed as a social formation"[3] and "operates as a discourse."[4] Such social formations or discourses include generating consuming communities via newspaper advertisements, which subsequent chapters investigate in greater detail.

First, one must ask, what is unique (or similar) in Japanese conditions fostering capitalism that translates into how mass-produced products are later represented and advertised? How can capitalism's rise in Japan be linked with the growth of Japanese media and consuming communities? Before answering these questions, a short examination of Japanese capitalism's greater structures is necessary to show how social practices embedded within certain economic structures influenced its development.

Japan's independent nascence of capitalism was prescient and, in certain ways, followed similar patterns as Western European and American "models," as briefly described below. However, key differences were the country's largely hereditary Confucian-based class structure and limiting of external trade during late feudal times, contrasting with Europe's overseas trade expansion.[5] Additionally, Japan was only involved in a very short trans-Asian slave trade run by Portugal from the mid-to-late sixteenth century, which lacked scope to engender similar wealth and capital formation as Europe's relationship to Africa and the Americas via the slave-based Atlantic economy. While Japan's example reveals slavery was not a necessary precondition for modern capitalism's successful evolution, African slavery certainly fueled global capitalism, as transatlantic slave trades provided primitive accumulation necessary for its worldwide expansion.

Throughout its history, feudal Japan was engaged in trade with Chinese and Koreans, and by the mid-sixteenth century, first with Portuguese, and then with Spaniards via the Philippines, and with the British from 1613 until 1639. For nearly five decades, Portugal also ran a lucrative firearms and gunpowder trade with a Japan wracked by internecine warfare, and in exchange, bought domestic captives resulting from Sengoku-period disturbances (1467–1600), and, additionally, purchased captured Koreans after warlord Toyotomi Hideyoshi's (1537–1598) 1592 invasion of the Korean Peninsula, when thousands were brought to Japan for sale.[6] In 1595, when Hideyoshi prohibited slave trading with Portugal over concern for large numbers of Japanese sold, other forms of commerce continued.

However, Portuguese missionaries and their empire's political concerns also arrived with traders, and laws against propagating Christianity initiated by Hideyoshi in 1587 were strengthened in the early seventeenth century, which led to the country's partial closing to European powers in what historians anachronistically call *sakoku* (closed country) edicts (1623–1651).[7] By 1639, with Portugal's expulsion, trade in the port of Nagasaki proceeded largely between Japanese and Chinese, and it flourished on the city's artificial island, Deshima, with Europeans who traded under the Dutch East India Company flag, whose less threatening Protestant Christianity and practical acceptance of trade limitations allowed the shogunate to continue commercial relations.[8] After conditions stabilized following late sixteenth-century Japanese invasions, Korean trade continued as usual, regulated by Sō clan daimyō

32   *Chapter 1*

(feudal lords) administrating Tsushima Island, and trade with the Ryūkyūs proceeded through retainers of the Shimazu clan daimyō in Satsuma domain.

To some extent, limiting external trade also prevented the potentially destabilizing leaching of silver wealth outside of Japan, while it permitted the shogunate to focus concerns upon hard-won internal cohesion and state formation following the key 1600 Battle of Sekigahara between supporters of Hideyoshi's heir and Tokugawa Ieyasu (1543–1616), the Tokugawa shogunal lineage's (1603–1868) founder. From the 1630s to 1640s, the shogun, or military ruler, Tokugawa Iemitsu (1604–1651) initiated the *sankin kōtai* (alternate attendance) policy, requiring daimyō to periodically travel to and spend intervals in Edo (contemporary Tokyo) to attend the shogun, where they left behind families as hostages upon return to their respective domains. This policy was intended to dissipate domains' excess wealth to prevent funding warfare. Nevertheless, it stimulated commercial growth and inns along several famous roads, including the Tōkaidō and Nakasendō, with eventual spread of regional economic activities and continued development of castle towns agglomerating near former *shōin* (untaxed private estates run by nobles or religious institutions). This additionally established Edo as an important political, cultural, and economic center, with popular cultural forms arising from pleasure quarters and among the merchant class.

Within the Tokugawa state's Confucian-inspired social order, merchants—despite their economic importance—ranked at the bottom of four status designations, with samurai, or warrior-bureaucrats, on top, followed by peasants and artisans. Of course, entire groups of people existed outside this social order, including the nobility, clergy, entertainers, and outcastes (*eta*, "polluted ones": leather tanners or animal skinners), sometimes called *hinin* ("non-human": certain performers, gardeners, undertakers, and beggars, including former criminals and the diseased or disabled).[9] At the social pyramid's apex, the shogunate, or *bakufu* (tent government), supported samurai families by rice stipends, measured in *koku* (about 4.5 rice bushels, or a man's yearly rice consumption), with rice cultivated by the peasantry. Money lenders converted these rice measures into usable cash, which contributed to monetization. In exchange for cash, artisans provided implements, objects, building materials, and other items requiring skilled labor. Thus, merchants, or *chōnin*, were viewed as ranking lowest in the Tokugawa social order because they allegedly failed to contribute to production of virtue like samurai, food like peasants, or goods like artisans, while commerce and profit-seeking were assumed to be self-serving. Because merchants needed to justify social value amid this Confucian-based political structure, business practices became enwrapped in virtue through social exchange in teachings of merchant academies like Osaka's Kaitokudō,[10] and many envisioned "work as ethical practice."[11] Prior to state-led capitalization, ordinary people joined cooperatives, or *kō*, to advance credit and loans for business endeavors and helped one another succeed through mutual aid associations.[12]

However, by the mid-Tokugawa era, the *bakufu*'s fairly stable social and economic system began to crumble, with nearly 25 percent of samurai unemployed and without official stipends.[13] Thus, they were forced to acquire jobs beyond their social station as farmers, artisans, or merchants engaging in commercial activities for economic survival. Low-ranking samurai Katsu Kōkichi (1802–1850), in his 1843 autobiography serving as his descendants' cautionary tale, laments: "I continued to report regularly to the commissioner's residence. I also had to make ends meet, so I tried my hand at dealing in swords and other military accouterments. . . . I was anxious to find official employment. But I also had to dash about making money."[14] Both "declassed" samurai[15] and merchants perceived chances for success within conceptions of enlightened capitalism, inspired by reinterpretations of neo-Confucian values blended with Western business concepts arising after the late nineteenth-century Meiji revolution. Like in the West, Japanese capitalism's early foundations rested upon a popular base of self-reliance, which meshed well with Western narratives of entrepreneurial attempts at self-made education such as Scottish journalist Samuel Smiles' didactic and anecdotal *Self Help* (1859). In 1871, Nakamura Masanao (Keiu) (1832–1891), a Confucian scholar formerly attached to the Tokugawa family who studied in England from 1866 to 1868, translated this as *Saikoku risshi hen* (Compilation of advice on establishing intentions), which became requisite reading for entire generations of entrepreneurs emerging from the old samurai class who appreciated Smiles' message of frugality, perseverance, diligence, and moral thrift.[16]

This brief historical background reveals how commercial elites and producers joined the government to take advantage of preexisting socioeconomic structures allowing rapid expansion into "true" capitalism with global reach as Japan acquired an empire. However, if large-scale production is used as a marker for determining this development, Japan's capitalist origins likely began as early as the mid-to-late Tokugawa

34 *Chapter 1*

period. In the late eighteenth to nineteenth centuries, proto-industries including sake and soy sauce brewing arose in Japan's countryside, alongside smaller-scale artisanal production of implements and material goods in local, regional, and urban workshops. Osaka, then known as Japan's "kitchen," became a place of exchange and monetization, where rice stipends were converted into money and samurai sent retainers to purchase household items. Scholars including David Howell argue that late Tokugawa-era proto-capitalist underpinnings allowed flourishing of relatively rapid industrialization in the early Meiji period (1868–1912),[17] beginning with textile industries like in the West and soon evolving into light and heavy industries. Precursors "included paper-making, sake and soy sauce brewing, iron and other metalworking, and the processing of agricultural and marine products, such as tea, indigo, sugar, wax, vegetable oil, whale by-products, and a variety of fertilizers."[18] By investigating a Hokkaidō fishery as a case study, Howell believes that rural industry provided a crucial step in bridging Tokugawa rural economies with later factory-based Meiji industrialization.[19]

Capitalism's development in Japan followed similar lines as in the West, though occurring in a much-compressed late nineteenth-century time frame following the opening of large-scale foreign trade in 1858 after the US-initiated Harris Treaty of Amity and Commerce was signed. However, Marxian scholars also note early Meiji-period "primitive accumulation" (1868–1872) whereby former daimyō received large government payoffs to start what later became large corporations. After divesting them (and lower-ranked samurai) of feudal status and stipends in 1872, Meiji Emperor Mutsuhito (1852–1912) accorded some aristocratic titles akin to Western European hereditary elites. For example, later viscount Shibusawa Eiichi (1840–1931), known as the "father of Japanese capitalism," was instrumental in initiating banks after his brief early 1870s stint leading the Ministry of Finance.[20] The Matsukata Deflation, early 1880s policies prompting fiscal restraint enacted by finance minister Matsukata Masayoshi (1835–1924) to address inflation arising from banks flooding the economy with paper money,[21] also prompted conditions where zaibatsu—large-scale conglomerates—arose to purchase land and smaller businesses, often forming from preexisting family businesses like Mitsui and Sumitomo.[22] The capitalist class began from this reassignation of government capital into hands of private ownership under government regulatory sponsorship.

Interestingly, in 1873, a year after the Meiji state abolished status categories, Christianity was again permitted amid state support of national industrialization. In *Capital,* Marx's concepts of capital formation differ from Asian societies by privileging Christianity's impact on social relations. For scholars like Max Weber (1864–1920), Christianity, namely Protestantism, served as an engine of capitalism's rise. Weber argued that the Protestant Ethic's tenets favored industrialization because of their impacts on economic structures.[23] The Japanese example contradicts Weber's obviously Eurocentric thesis; in Japan, Christianity, and especially Protestantism, was unessential to capitalism's development. Although no direct correlation exists in Japan, some Japanese capitalists did convert to Christianity due to the religion's perceived modernity and linkages with Western business networks, while the rise of the nation-state and state-supported capitalization also played important roles.

Even though late Tokugawa antecedents in rural industry and regional or urban workshops run by artisanal guilds failed to generate new demographic patterns, early twentieth-century urban industrialization soon displaced large countryside populations, which moved into the cities for employment. Concurrently, traditional social structures where paternalistic landlords functioned as quasi-welfare nets for imperiled landless farmers transformed into conditions where urban-based absentee landlords stopped providing tenants security. This pattern hastened the movement of rural populations into cities when economically hard-pressed parents sold daughters to procurers for textile factories or even brothels while young men ventured into work involving hard physical labor, including mining and heavy industries.

Highlighting the preponderance of working-class suffering, early twentieth-century Japanese literature evinces themes of rural distress and labor hardships. Proletarian writer Kobayashi Takiji's (1903–1933) *Fuzai jinushi* (Absentee Landlords) (1929) captures tenant farmers' struggles amid abandonment by paternalistic landlords' traditional safety nets, while his *Kani kōsen* (The Factory Ship), published the same year, details the harsh working conditions of men on a crab-canning ship, where the state ended a strike at the story's conclusion by sending out the Imperial Japanese Navy.[24] Along with increased inequalities between wealthy property owners and rural or urban working classes, the late nineteenth and early twentieth centuries saw the growth of a new Japanese middle class, with emerging concentrations of capital in large cities and burgeoning suburban rings, while secondary metropolises like Kanazawa, Niigata, Okayama, and Sapporo also contributed to the circulation and cross-fertilization of commerce and ideas.[25] By the 1920s, with the advent of Fordism, Taylorization, and rationalization (*gōrika*) in industrial production, companies promoted their commodities' ubiquitous salability and created new markets throughout Japan and its empire.

From the late 1920s into the 1930s, Japanese capitalism's true nature was bitterly disputed by left-oriented *Kōza-ha* (lecture faction) intellectuals, who upheld the 1927 Soviet Comintern theses advocating two-staged proletarian, and then bourgeois, revolution due to Japan's alleged underdevelopment, and the *Rōnō-ha* (labor-farmer faction), which pressed for single-staged immediate socialist revolution.[26] These debates occurred during economic uncertainty and increasing Japanese incursions into China and Manchuria, whose resultant press jingoism and economic ramifications partially offset domestic perceptions of crisis. Political scientist Germaine A. Hoston believes "the debate, if presented in its original terms, can explain important aspects of Japan's capitalistic development, because the debate itself constituted a response to a particular stage in the development process."[27]

These two intellectual factions' Marxist-inspired thought also later influenced Western luminaries, including Canadian diplomat-scholar E. H. Norman (1909–1957) and even British historian William G. Beasley (1919–2006). Their classic English-language texts still inform contemporary students on scholarly discourses in Japanese studies. In refuting these factions, Beasley believed that the West was solely responsible for Japan's arising nationalism that generated a top-down Meiji revolution.[28] In contrast, while supporting ideas concerning feudal remnants and incomplete bourgeois revolution staged by economically distressed lower-level samurai, Norman propounded that some aspects precipitated Imperial Japan's path toward fascism, itself a state-supported corporatist structure for capital.[29] While fascism's political premises disappeared after defeat, amid late-1980s postwar economic successes, Japanese scholars such as Yoshimi Yoshiaki viewed Japan as still practicing imperial democracy, where fascist elements lay dormant but periodically effloresced into ethnic nationalism or particularism.[30]

Such discourses evince tensions amid state intervention into Japan's particular form of capitalism by driving or curbing consumption, and by promoting corporate drives for expansion that paralleled prewar imperial or postwar democratic impulses. For example, these appear in Japan's postwar role as a responsible developmental actor espousing what later developed into neoliberalism when former East Asian and Southeast Asian colonies rebuilt their economies. Additionally, historian Sheldon Garon asserts that Japanese state savings campaigns tempered twentieth-century consumption, while thrift and frugality merged with "Asian values" of a common Confucian heritage in other countries.[31] Japan's independent Tokugawa-era nascence of capitalism presciently followed similar patterns as Western European and American "models." Yet, these historical developments evince larger structures, which require elucidation to generate an understanding of how capitalism flourished in Japan, with uniquely Japanese characteristics and certain global similarities.

A Brief History of Premodern Japanese Artisan and Trade Associations

Marxist historian Amino Yoshihiko asserts that the post-Kamakura era (1185–1333) fourteenth-century transitionary period was essential for laying down early capitalism's foundations with monetization, rising commerce in castle towns, and credit extension.[32] In feudal Japan, and particularly in the twelfth to sixteenth centuries, pre-modern *za*, which scholars translate as "guilds" or "brotherhoods,[33] arose from associations of merchants, manufacturers, and individuals engaging in related businesses in the growing towns and cities; these medieval associations were groups dealing in similar products like oil, medicines, and fish, or even performances like Noh. Most prominent in and around Kyoto and Nara, with handicraft associations composed of producers specializing in one product for entire towns or villages,[34] they also included performers and entertainers under protection of noble patrons or religious institutions.[35] Actually, the word *za* came from the distinctive platforms these associations erected near temples and/or shrines to perform or display their wares. From the premodern into the Tokugawa eras, artisans produced handicrafts of particular products located in certain villages or towns that often banded together in *za*. These associations also helped establish certain standards, measures, and uniform appearances for products within broader scopes of individual buyers and merchants assuming specific quality from those locations. Such structures intimate the organization behind Tokugawa-era mercantile transactions and how some trade associations already standardized measurements and quality within quasi-monopolistic structures.

Regarding political protection for these emerging social organizations engaged in economic activities during eras of endemic internecine conflict, historian Kenneth Alan Grosberg asserts that in the Muromachi period, guild-like *za* helped protect artisans' and merchants' economic activities through licensed monopolies and state patronage.[36] However, this patronage also strengthened the Ashikaga shogunate's control over the national economy and built tax revenues.[37] *Za* sold items under protection of patrons from local warrior elites or religious institutions, and as members, craftspeople possessed rights to use designated workshops under the association's name.[38] Passage for unassociated merchants through certain areas (*sekisho*, or barriers) entailed a toll, but patronage in a *za* under a lord's or shogun's protection also helped alleviate this potentially detrimental economic impact and aided commerce. Mary Louise Nagata explains the complex political interplay of mutually beneficial social relations prompted by economic activities of medieval *za*, whose organization benefited members and patrons for political and economic gain:

> The income of the nobility naturally depended on their own ability to give brotherhoods legal and political protection to ensure their access to markets and to safeguard their privileges, which would in turn attract other brotherhoods keen to have them as patrons. Patrons were in competition with each other, as well as with the clergy, and the growing warrior class. So it was that brotherhoods did not protect merchants and artisans from the demands of political authorities, but rather political authorities protected brotherhoods from attacks and competition from other brotherhoods, and assisted them in gaining advantages in supply, road access, and market positions vis-à-vis other brotherhoods. In return, patrons gained support in the form of dues and services, as well as the means to establish and improve their political status by providing protection and assistance.[39]

Outside castle towns, rural *za* also developed, with concentrations in certain regions and localities in the Kansai (near contemporary Kyoto) and Kantō (near contemporary Tokyo) areas, and by the late fifteenth century they became more independent of patrons, whether individuals or institutions, and attained greater monopolistic character. The Ōnin War (1467–1477) precipitated unattached merchants, whose activities began threatening the hold of *za*.[40]

In the late sixteenth century, under Oda Nobunaga (1534–1582), many such associations became known as *rakuza*, with more relaxed structures. Within growing numbers of castle towns, daimyō sometimes allowed merchants to engage freely in business within their boundaries.[41] However, coupled with a land survey conducted to help unify Japan, Hideyoshi abolished *za* under shrines, temples, and noble patronage[42] and instead established a "free trade" policy.[43] Nagata asserts that during unification, these leaders abolished *za* to promote such free trade, a policy maintained by subsequent Tokugawa rulers deep into the seventeenth century, which initially allowed the unifiers to remove competing centers of political and economic authority from noble patrons and religious institutions.[44] However, merchants and producers soon created groups resembling *za*, like trade associations. In the early Tokugawa period under shogunal patronage, these became known as *nakama* (trade associations) or *kabu-nakama* (chartered trade associations or stock societies). Nagata asserts that these new kinds of *za* allowed the Tokugawa shogunate more leverage over economic activities and functioned "to centralize control of certain key industries, to centralize state economic power, and to create the necessary framework for national markets."[45] With state patronage, such *za* "were granted monopolies for the purpose of state control rather than for personal profit. That allowed the state to control certain aspects of international trade, the monetary system, and national standards of measurement."[46]

After what was retroactively known as the Sakoku Edicts, when feudal Japan was closed to foreign trade with most Western nations, except limited trade with the Dutch, individuals began banding together in secret *nakama* to prevent undue domestic competition. However, in 1721 the shogunate required all merchants and manufacturers to join *nakama* to prevent free trade.[47] Nagata explains that "in the eighteenth century the state found the dues and taxes paid by stock societies to be a convenient source of revenue, but that concern was probably secondary to their policing and economic management functions. The stock societies, therefore, provided trust and regulation necessary in a rapidly growing national market set in a decentralized political and legal environment."[48]

40   *Chapter 1*

The shogunal capital Edo (contemporary Tokyo) also harbored *toiya* or *tonya* (trade brokers), who ran warehouses and shops. Factors, brokers, and exchange brokers were the most powerful, along with dyers, weavers, and sake producers.[49] Those belonging to *kabu-nakama* holding certain business contracts soon standardized measurements, weights, and qualities of products, such as cotton.[50] In the mid-eighteenth century, *ie*, or trading houses, also emerged, and resembled workshops or factors who worked with putting-in systems presaging modern factories during a proto-capitalist era. Interestingly, Japan's largest contemporary companies, Mitsui and Sumitomo, both began this way. Nagata views *za* as an important step within early Japanese capitalism's foundations, where state patronage of business activities was important and mutually benefited producers and merchants: "The Japanese organization was a private exercise of political authority and in many ways was a private exchange of goods and services for private privilege, and semi-public political support for mutual benefit and exchange being an important part of the Japanese system."[51]

As the nineteenth century approached, further economic transformations led to fractalized associations with greater parts, which persisted until the early Meiji period.[52] Toyoda Takeshi believes that these developments characterized Japanese capitalism's late feudal mechanisms. With the 1854 Treaty of Kanagawa's political impetus, opening two ports to Western trade, and with the 1858 Harris Treaty of Amity and Commerce's corresponding arrival of relatively unfettered foreign trade, trading houses were further reorganized into *sōgō shōsha*, or general trading companies, whose activities significantly impacted Japan's emergence of modern capitalism until the early twentieth century. In prewar times, these were further consolidated into the aforementioned zaibatsu, and after postwar reconstruction of industries in the late 1940s and early 1950s, appeared as *keiretsu* (companies linked by shareholdings). An investigation into the histories of these early Japanese business associations allows scholars to view the historical interactions between state and business interests and how they contributed to social formations later surrounding corporations and consumers of their products. However, it is crucial to first look at how goods arrived in consumers' hands, and the spaces showcasing them amid social practices framing their acquisition.

Delivering the Goods: The Social Life of Shopping in Late Tokugawa Japan

Shopping in late Tokugawa Japan radically differed from today's spectacular consumption of myriad products in swanky department store aisles in Tokyo's big-name flagships Mitsukoshi and Matsuzakaya, themselves late-Meiji-era creations. Today's seemingly aimless, yet entertaining, window-shopping and urban *flannerie*, initially described by early twentieth-century urban ethnographer Kon Wajirō (1888–1973) as *Ginbura* (Ginza cruising—with Ginza being Tokyo's fanciest commercial area),[53] began in the 1910s or mid-1920s, when shod customers now wandered freely through vast store floors. This new social practice, where customers no longer needed to remove shoes, allowed anyone to enter stores, and it democratized the shopping experience without compulsory purchasing obligations. In contrast, during the Tokugawa period, vendors brought goods directly to homes, and toward the late seventeenth century, small stores arose where customers could purchase items with money. In 1673, the Mitsui family formed Echigoya, Mitsukoshi department store's Tokugawa-era precursor, with a retail location opening in 1683 in Edo's Nihonbashi area where customers directly purchased kimono cloth on-site.

Certainly, use of money predicated the existence of a stable monetary system and opportunities to reliably convert rice stipends into cash for samurai and merchant customers who could afford goods. A monetary economy's beginnings, where exchanges of cash ensured the absence of debt upon payment, also developed in parallel to extant social practices underlying these commercial relations. The growth of a cash economy flourished alongside existing use of credit and other exchange forms, with trading of favors and gifts, while offers of sustenance, aid, or objects as moral obligations facilitated such exchanges beyond debt, as illuminated by anthropologist David Graeber's *Debt: The First 5,000 Years*,[54] which argues that human relations are arranged along "baseline communism"[55] beyond economic transactions or expectations of return, while Marcel Mauss' notions of reciprocity are based on social exchanges where gifts imply continuing relationships.[56]

As concrete expressions of such social phenomena, one must first examine social spaces framing shopping encounters in their physical, architectural form. Originally, shopping from itinerant vendors, or *mono-uri*, kept transactions within spaces of streets or residences' rear gates, expanding in the Muromachi period and flourishing as important

42   *Chapter 1*

components of urban and local landscapes in Tokugawa times.[57] By contrast, fixed physical stores provided precursors to more modern settings in the selling practices and social relationships cultivated between buyers and sellers within.

Oftentimes, before entering shops, customers were beckoned by beautifully carved signs, or *kanban,* which served as advertisements for items sold within through characteristic shapes denoting artisanal objects—combs, *geta* (wooden sandals), pipes, and so on—or functioned as painted placards carved with calligraphic wording featuring store names and wares.[58] These signboards, besides helping consumers find shops amid tiny warrens of businesses, also helped illiterate people, including non-samurai women, understand by shape what they sold; thus, the *kanban*'s readily apparent signification often resembled prototypical logos later adopted by larger businesses, with proprietors' names sometimes appearing as *mon* (family crests).[59]

In early fixed stores, like Echigoya, strict spatial divisions circumscribed shopping experiences, with limited access to increasingly enclosed interiors. In these premodern shops, after customers identified needs when hailed by signs, they first stooped under cloth curtain flaps, or *noren,* to slide open *shōji* (rice-paper paneled doors). Entrances into mercantile spaces then led into a *genkan,* either dirt or stone, and shoes were removed and placed on a wooden-slatted platform, whereupon a shopkeeper's attendant greeted customers and switched the shoes' direction. Then, customers—usually men with accompanying retainers or servants who waited in the entrance—climbed onto the raised, tatami-matted platform toward the shop's front, and then slowly stooped toward an antechamber, where purveyors scurried back and forth bringing out wares by creeping forth from a *sōko* (warehouse) behind it. After polite discussion and serving of adequate-quality tea in appropriate dishes according to customers' perceived ranks, shopkeepers' attendants brought out purchasable artisanally made items for scrutiny.

The entire process took time, but resembling modern eras, the longer customers remained in the shops, the more they bought; thus, in Japanese shops, where any business transaction first assumed extensions of hospitality to customers, potential consumers' very entrance implied their intent to buy. Therefore, shopkeepers first built relationships with customers, in fortuitous linkages known as *en,* which in Japanese culture refer to business or personal ties. These were cultivated with small gifts and carefully gauged hospitality aiming for end results where customers, in subsequent purchases, eventually paid off debts (and more) for entertaining costs spent to establish hopefully enduring bonds, which in modern times are expressed as *omotenashi*. Mauss calls such exchanges operating before the existence of markets in premodern societies as a "system of total services" where the "gift" always presupposes something in return, because it embodies the giver's spiritual essence, and therefore, is not "free."[60] According to Mauss, such a gift presumes inherent reciprocity: "The most important feature among these spiritual mechanisms is clearly one that obliges a person to reciprocate the present that has been received."[61] Of course, parallel continuance of such gift-based reciprocity alongside commercial transactions, embedded within nuanced calculations of exchange, also entrenched customers within subtle gradations of debt. However, Graeber's baseline communism also emerges, wherein human encounters encompassing a certain conviviality also require some form of refreshment to extend potential relationships.

Hence, smooth social relations fostering commerce between purveyors and clients rested on keen understandings of prevailing social norms imposed by the Tokugawa shogunate, where merchants were viewed as socially inferior to samurai and others higher up on the officially sanctioned neo-Confucian-inspired status ladder. However, many individual lived experiences actually ran counter to these expectations, especially within commercial transactions, which were highly performative. High-ranking samurai customers sent either male retainers or well-positioned servants bringing other lower-ranking individuals who intimately knew their tastes and predilections in wares. In the merchant classes, where strict gender roles were relaxed (or scarcely regarded), women ran households and supported businesses, and they also came in person for purchases, usually accompanied by domestic servants to carry wares and increase the encounter's congeniality—which even led shopkeepers to purchase goods or services from their own clients. In the 1870s, abolishment of feudal class structures initially helped "democratize" shopping experiences, formerly circumscribed by strict demarcations of physical and social space. The next development supporting this end was early twentieth-century department stores allowing customers to enter without removing their shoes.

More recently, unique contemporary business models capitalizing on Tokugawa-era conceptions of space and surroundings built by artisans and craftsmen have conferred aspects of manufactured artisanality to retail spaces themselves, a trope expressed in exclusive Kyoto artisanal boutiques and, increasingly, in Tokyo. Issey Miyake's high-end Kyoto-based fashion boutique designed by Fukasawa Naoto cites this unique history in a framed simulacrum of space mimicking elite Tokugawa shopping experiences.[62] A former warehouse behind the *machiya* (townhouse) building is now an art gallery, called Kura, which means "storehouse." Both the renovated building and attached gallery frame the brand firmly within Tokugawa history and traditional artistic elegance citing *wabi-sabi* in "a beautiful and peaceful environment which fuses tradition and innovation," featuring a dark gray wash resembling *sumi* (traditional charcoal ink) over its stucco exterior.[63] The gallery, once a merchant storehouse, is only accessible by a leisurely stroll through the shop, while its free access also connotes democratic enjoyment of luxury without predicating purchase.[64]

Of course, art galleries attached to boutiques or department stores are nothing new in Japan; they have existed since at least the early twentieth century on the upper floors of department stores like Mitsukoshi. More recently, retail spaces themselves have become artistic

Figure 1.1. Issey Miyake-Kyoto, Tsuchiya-chō boutique back garden in a former merchant warehouse, 2019. https://www.isseymiyake.com/en/stores/562, accessed July 25, 2021.

Craftsmanship and Proto-branding 45

spaces, meant to circumvent vulgar industrial connotations of the mass-produced products featured, fetishizing these commodities' properties through invented traditions of manufactured artisanality that heighten value and create luxury.

ARBITRATION OF QUALITY AND VALUE FROM THE PREMODERN PERIOD INTO THE INDUSTRIAL PERIOD

How exactly, at the consumer level, did premodern Japanese society understand value and quality? And how is such value created? Is this exclusively related to Western capitalist societies? Graeber's work on indigenous and colonial societies provides interesting clues.[65] Regardless of geographical location or era, Graeber perceives value as "social power" revealing how humans make meaning. In late capitalism, he argues that value can be understood through commodity fetishism, which marks all industrialized, commodity-based societies.[66] However, value as essential to formations of social relations also existed in Tokugawa times, with material status markers announced in clothing, objects used, and myriad other things. How did individuals in the Tokugawa period understand quality? And how can one understand linkages of artisanship to premodern ideas of value and quality?

Social quality, or "social capital" in modern times following Pierre Bourdieu's characterization, was then determined by the highly stratified Tokugawa class system, wherein certain behaviors, clothing, and even speech connoted where one stood in the four-tiered status system of samurai, peasant, artisan, or merchant. According to Bourdieu, "Social capital is the aggregate of the actual or potential resources which are linked to possession of a durable network of more or less institutionalized relationships of mutual acquaintance and recognition."[67] Thus, social class was also highly performative, potentially spilling outside codified categories, which became increasingly porous by the early nineteenth century due to dwindling official positions for samurai, uncertain economic conditions, and growth of a powerful merchant class. Just like today, lower-status individuals took on airs and assumed behaviors of their "betters," as in Ihara Saikaku's (1642–1693) comic novels set in the "Floating World" (ukiyō, a euphemism referencing fleeting encounters and experiences in pleasure quarters composed of brothels and theaters amid merchants). Here, with comedic effects, stiff and formal samurai attempted to appear cognizant of unspoken behavioral norms, while vulgar merchants with

46   *Chapter 1*

wealth navigated successfully through thickets of parallel social conventions.

In this alternative reality contesting the rules and regulations of purportedly virtuous shogunal power, and among the Confucian-based sociopolitical order's allegedly lowest status group, performers and entertainers set rules of style and initiated trends filtering upward through the social ranks—even moderately adopted by samurai wives in hairstyles and kimono linings.[68] Negotiating this complex arena of parallel social behaviors mirroring refined society required immense acquired skills of socialization and disposable income. In the Tokugawa period, style afficionados were called *tsū*, or "connoisseurs," where *tsūjin* (*hommes au courant*) were well-versed in matters involving exchanges of money and sex within pleasure quarters. In this space, "quality" in social relations, or certain understandings of popular fashions, literary styles, or entertainment forms, was purchasable. Not necessarily always sexual, much entertainment with geisha (courtesans) consisted solely of enjoying their presence while drinking, telling stories, and watching dances, amid ranked grades of entertainment provided by beautifully dressed, well-comported women and adolescent boys hired for an evening's portion.

How about premodern notions of quality for objects? Pre-industrial determinants of value and quality before mass production assumed each object's or item's uniqueness due to handicraft manufacture by artisans—literally their own class—who were further grouped into guild-like organizations called *za* or trading associations like *kabu-nakama*, which helped ensure certain shared characteristics or qualities of their "products." These items were all artisanally created in processes often requiring years of training under masters, who sometimes belonged to guilds or trade associations, and whose wares were not mass-produced; thus, individual producers, or masters, mattered greatly, while additional value was added later through their use, with corresponding attachment of narratives. Artisans' interactions with merchants who sold handmade items, and strong Floating World relationships, also imbued manufactured objects with value as mediators of social relations. Certain objects like hairpins or *netsuke* (obi sash toggles) sometimes assumed proto-commodity status in pleasure-quarter settings, driving fashion and style, similar to how kimonos of particular fabrics, prints, and colors became trendy after appearing on courtesans depicted in woodblock prints by celebrated artists like Kitagawa Utamaro (c. 1753–1806), renowned for *bijin-ga* (images of beauties) and kabuki actor prints. While artists signed or left individual seals on paintings or prints, artisans sometimes engraved their names' characters upon object surfaces, like tea bowl bases; yet, if producers' names lacked cachet, such products were usually endowed with defining local or regional characteristics. In premodern times, most ordinary objects possessed highly regional natures, with certain city quarters specializing in utensils or tools, like Osaka for kitchen implements and Seto (in contemporary Aichi Prefecture) for pottery and tea bowls. An item's provenance might also indicate allegedly high (or lower) quality.

In Tokugawa times and before, narratives crafted around origins and uses of artisanally made products increased their distinction. In the tea ceremony, determinants of value for utilized objects involved retellings of their stories, including suppositions of age and provenance, but most importantly, narratives crafted around their original production, and then, who later owned and used them. Also, these objects' geographical and social proximities to political power centers mattered. Therefore, what was considered "luxury" in premodern eras (and today, to some extent, for artisanal objects) was continuously crafted anew in a "democratic" narrative process emphasizing requisite sharing with others to assume and maintain value via stories told and retold about their use. According to historian Morgan Pitelka, "Tea practitioners collect and use tea utensils to display wealth and taste, to demonstrate personal connections, and to engage in non-verbal conversations with other tea practitioner *cognoscenti*."[69] Essentially, though tea utensils and bowls were safely maintained in boxes for lengthy times, they were purposefully and periodically (perhaps seasonally) revealed for their spectacular value, or value arising from being seen and who did the seeing. Pitelka dubs such connoisseurship in accumulating high-value objects as "spectacular accumulation," a term he borrowed from earlier studies on art collecting in seventeenth-century Antwerp and pre-1997 Asian Economic Crisis Indonesia's "Wild West frontier culture"; he defines his usage as "the practice of hoarding symbolically significant things and aggressively displaying and deploying them for cultural and political gain."[70] In premodern Japan, this included tea bowls and utensils, pottery items, and, during the Sengoku period (1467–1600), even preserved heads of enemies captured in battle.

Crucially, for artisanal objects during premodern eras, and for brand-name commodified products in industrial times, is their value

48 *Chapter 1*

in potentially serving as mediators of social relations in conferring status, or social quality, upon their owners. Contrasting with artisanally produced items, mass-produced products are defined by reproducibility; as standardized products created from patented factory processes staffed by replaceable workers, they can be produced or purchased literally anywhere and still offer similar quality. Thus, in modern times, value and guaranteed quality must be assured by brand names legally protected by patented trademarks. As subsequent chapters show, limited-edition mass-produced brand-name items sometimes circumvented mass production's "commonness" with value growing over time due to rarity and subsequent narratives acquired, like being used or worn by notable individuals.[71]

In the postwar period, value for brand-name goods constitutes what Eric King Watts and Mark P. Orbe term "spectacular consumption," or "a process through which the relations among cultural forms, the culture industry, and the lived experiences of persons are shaped by public consumption."[72] Though their study focuses on a Budweiser ad featuring African American men enjoying beer and hailing another in an allegedly culturally specific manner—airing during the 2000 Super Bowl and receiving a Grand Prix and Golden Lion prize in Cannes—one can perceive similar connections with Japanese name brands. The American television advertisement's quotidian "othering" of the group enjoying the product, despite Bud's majority white male consumers, and its representative "manufacturing (of) authenticity"[73] for supposed male Afro-sociability, also resonates with postwar Japan's luxury brand advertising. In Japanese magazine ads, posters, and television spots, white women (or men) consume or wear products ranging from makeup and watches to liquor, in settings appearing "authentically" Western to viewers, and accessed by wider publics, possibly on television or large digital screens in urban *sakariba* (bustling places) like Tokyo's famous Shibuya crossing. Likewise, 1970s-era Suntory television ads featured Western male actors like Peter Lawford lauding the whisky's attributes, and in 2003, *Crouching Tiger, Hidden Dragon* (Ang Lee, 2000) actress Zhang Ziyi boasted preternaturally shiny black tresses in Japanese television commercials touting Kaō Corporation's scientifically manufactured Asience shampoo containing traditional East Asian medicinals like ginseng. By gazing at and desiring authentically Japanese, purportedly high-quality products consumed by racial or ethnic others, Japanese consumers engaged in spectacular consumption by vicariously imbibing a mascu-

Craftsmanship and Proto-branding   49

line Anglo-American atmosphere or enjoying distinctly "Asian" shiny hair like the Chinese actress.

If, in premodern times, spectacular accumulation helped garner social capital and ascribed political and social value to artisanally made objects, then in postmodernity, spectacular consumption achieved both aims through mass-produced brand-name products. Both forms of what I call "spectacularity" allowed mediation of social relations to create value for consumable objects. This process has now been embodied within certain brand names evolving to connote quality, with value conferred within the social cachet proffered by consuming them. Value is also tied to luxury, considered high value (and often, high-priced), but which only maintains airs of exclusivity because its success is based upon mass consumption. In late industrial capitalism's modern globalized world, "specialness" and uniqueness are artificially ascribed via advertising to absolutely non-unique mass-produced products. Essentially, advertising in print and electronic media via commercials and interactive websites reintroduces a certain allure or aura to products, corresponding to addictive commodity fetishism packaged as an "idea" or "lifestyle" that they embody.

German philosopher Walter Benjamin (1892–1940), in his influential 1935 essay "The Work of Art in the Age of Its Technological Reproducibility," persuasively asserts that, for mechanically reproduced art objects, "the authenticity of a thing is the quintessence of all that is transmissible in it from its origin on, ranging from its physical duration to the historical testimony relating to it. Since the historical testimony is founded on the physical duration, the former, too, is jeopardized by reproduction, in which the physical duration plays no part. And what is really jeopardized when the historical testimony is affected is the authority of the object, the weight it derives from tradition."[74] Benjamin's suppositions can also pertain to mechanically reproduced objects, or commodities created by mass production, which basically lost their artisanality and aura of long traditions of craftsmanship, along with narratives attached to production on an individual human scale, because "the uniqueness of the work of art is identical to its embeddedness in the context of tradition."[75] Arrival of technologies permitting creation of large numbers of mechanically reproduced objects detached these products from essential uniqueness, and lent themselves to mass scale, which also developed in accelerated paces once objects, people, and even moving scenery became reproduceable as images where only surface depictions remained, now deracinated from a sole human creator's authenticity, and issuing infinitely from a machine or projector, like film. Georg Lukacs also noted the insidiousness of industrial rationalization and Taylorization as erasing the humanity (and artisanality) of artisans now transformed into workers tasked with mechanical reproduction within mass production processes: "If we follow the path taken by labour in its development from the handicrafts via cooperation and manufacture to machine industry we can see a continuous trend towards greater rationalization, the progressive elimination of the qualitative, human and individual attributes of the worker. On the one hand, the process of labor is progressively broken down into abstract, rational, specialized operations so that the worker loses contact with the finished product and his work is reduced to the mechanical repetition of a specialized set of actions."[76]

Writing when Fordism, Taylorization, and rationalization were already established industrial practices in commodity production, Benjamin convinces his readers to consider infinitely reproducible images' impacts upon cultural production, where depictions no longer held original artworks' aura (or embedded "tradition") but were simulacra consumed on mass levels, with clear political effects. He perceived aestheticization of politics as characterizing fascist regimes, which motivated mass sentiments toward populism respecting private property (or acquisition of more mass-produced objects), while communists responded by "politicizing art," or, like Marcel Duchamp (1887–1968), created "ready-mades" by allegedly re-endowing an *objet* with an artificial aura cast upon a mass-produced object alienated from earlier artisanality.[77] When Benjamin developed his theories, making visible the labor put into creation of objects or products, contributing to their "surplus value," was a tenet of working-class proletarian revolution. However, in contemporary times, with socioeconomic structures marked by late capitalism, fetishization of labor in allegedly artisanal, but still mass-produced, products became a powerful marketing tool in "manufacturing artisanality"—an advertising scheme pioneered in Japan but now adopted ubiquitously in advanced global economies following the anticapitalist Occupy Movement initiated in the United States.[78]

In Benjamin's time, warnings about mechanical reproduction's potential sensory and political consequences embedded in his notable essay were also clarion calls against succumbing to fascism's emotional allure. For Benjamin, infinite reproducibility of National Socialism's symbols and messages not surprisingly sounds like a brand name's successful functioning in advertising. Ironically, Adolf Hitler (1889–1945) was a failed artist whose paintings never progressed beyond lowbrow kitsch decorating early twentieth-century German living rooms; yet, he was masterful at manipulating film and radio for their power to capture (and infinitely reproduce) his populist message of National Socialism to large mass audiences with easily identifiable symbols and phrases. Ensuring such messaging's effectiveness, Benjamin asserted that ideas, or perceived social or political value, required communication in images adopting easily identifiable symbols, much like *kamon* (samurai or noble family crests) announcing particular attributes of feudal Japan's clans, or how brand-name logos displayed standardized quality in industrialized countries beginning in the late nineteenth century.

As a German theorist, Benjamin likely meant the swastika or *hakenkreuz* (hooked cross), an ancient Eurasian symbol diverging from earlier historical patterns by curiously revolving rightward when adopted by National Socialists in 1920, and becoming ubiquitous after Hitler's 1933 ascent to power.[79] Nazi abuse of the swastika between 1920 and 1945, and by contemporary European and American neo-Nazi sympathizers, reveals the dangers in appropriating and infinitely reproducing a once-positive Eastern religious symbol for populist movements based on emotionalism and tribalized hatreds. In Japan, a thick *manji* (swastika) surrounded by a circle remains the *kamon* of the nearly extinct Hachisuka clan dating from the fourteenth century, while it also connotes locations of Buddhist temples on Japanese maps, and thus still serves as a neutral symbol of familial or religious connotations.

Basically, the swastika's meanings, when viewed as a logo or easily recognizable sign generating quickly extracted meaning or value, hold entirely different cultural connotations for Euro-American and

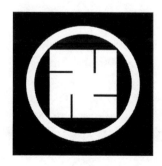

Figure 1.2. Hachisuka clan emblem. https://en.wikipedia.org/wiki/Hachisuka_clan, accessed July 25, 2021.

52 *Chapter 1*

Japanese viewers—(usually) entirely negative in the West and most likely positive in Japan. Jacques Derrida's concept of an unstable, and potentially infinite, signifier is relevant here,[80] as is Roland Barthes' notion of signs as potentially laden with cultural connotations.[81] Through a logo, these emotionally charged values—whether connoting a distinguished family's long historical lineage, certain political movement, or company's potential moral obligations under a brand name—can be quickly communicated and distilled. Like past Japanese samurai families who adopted easily identifiable, culturally specific symbols as signs of clans' provenance or character, current brand names in Japan (and elsewhere) apply similar symbols to communicate products' quality, and even values, through a logo.

Therefore, it is useful to briefly examine how these logos developed, and their connections to trademarks.

Japanese Luxury's Early Iconography—Samurai *Mon*

In contemporary times, brand names with associated logos are quick ways for companies to connote manufactured value to consumers, and thus create artificial notions of value and ensure homogeneous high quality. Essentially, many Japanese company logos now associated with particular businesses are based on samurai *kamon,* while feudal-era merchants and artisanal guilds in the *za* system also created *mon.* Until 1872, Japan maintained a hereditary class-based system whose samurai class neared 6–8 percent of the total population, which surpassed numbers of Europe's aristocracy. However, despite high status, to ensure decorum and moral propriety, the shogunate subjected samurai and their families to multiple sumptuary laws limiting ostentatious expressions of luxury viewed as endemic to the merchant class. Samurai social qualities thus merged with ascetic conceptions of taste for acquired objects and clothing, and combined to create notions of meticulously cultivated refined shabbiness arising from frugality.

Ideas of restrained elegance, conveyed by high-quality artisanal manufacture designed to last for frugal consumers, developed into particularly Japanese forms of luxury still extant today. Notably, in Bank of Japan surveys, contemporary Japanese consumers still rate low prices, durability, reliability, and functionality as favored qualities in consumer purchases, ranking much higher than brand reputation and design.[82] These aspects of Japanese consumer behaviors also translate into long-term use of high-quality products until absolutely necessary

Craftsmanship and Proto-branding 53

replacement—a practice unbeneficial to economic growth or further capital expansion. Historical reasons also exist for such preferences.

Some American consumers of Japanese products first encountered allegedly traditional concepts of *wabi* ("witheredness"; flawed imperfection) and *sabi* ("loneliness"; ascetic refuge in nature) through US designer Leonard Koren's (b. 1948) quasi-Orientalist lens in *Wabi-Sabi for Artists, Designers, Poets, and Philosophers* (1994), to "explain" Japanese aesthetic ideals to Westerners.[83] However, these ideals were indeed firmly embedded in samurai values of restraint and moral forbearance. Since premodern times, profligacy and extravagance were frowned upon, while imperfections and loneliness were believed to hone character. These qualities' origins stem from Zen Buddhist traditions, which expanded among commoners in feudal Japan amid Kamakura-period political disturbances, and acquired acclaim within precarious warrior classes during the Muromachi period. For these groups, the Zen-inspired tea ceremony capitalized on *wabi-sabi*–inspired values, where celebrated, though imperfect, artisanally created objects grew in social and political value through use, and acquired legendary qualities in narratives reproduced about their provenance with continued owner-curated appreciation.[84]

In the modern industrial era, such refined qualities of artisanal objects made by hand, that literally fetishize their creators' flawed humanity, are impossible to reproduce mechanically. Instead, *mon* used by certain Japanese product manufacturers and companies could re-impart to mass-produced products what Benjamin calls a lost "aura" or "tradition," and to certain extents, be conveyed upon commodities through "manufactured artisanality" harkening back to an allegedly mythic past. This is very much a uniquely Japanese version of luxury pioneered in Japan for mass consumers still "remembering" artisanal production after a very short compressed industrialization, who may feel a certain nostalgia for craftsmanship by hand. For example, in 1907, as one of Japan's first real department stores following construction of a three-story Western building in Tokyo's Imagawa-bashi area, Matsuya Gofukuten (Matsuya Piece Goods Store) abolished its original trademark and utilized the *shōkaku* (pine crane) logo of a stylized crane in a circle resembling a *mon*.[85] In 1978, this mark was replaced with the current Westernized all-capital-letter MATSUYA logo, and in 1989, the Ginza store adopted a logo of a stacked M and G, a seeming hybrid of Western and Japanese-style logos.[86] Matsuya's 1907 stylized logo signifies late Meiji-period reassertions of Japanese identity amid

54 Chapter 1

political climates rethinking national identity, while its late-1970s romanized logo reflects a renewed fascination with Western-style brand names amid increasing travel abroad by middle-class Japanese. The Ginza store's early Heisei-era (1989–2019) iteration reveals interest in American initialization of lower-priced famous designer-line logos, like DKNY for Donna Karan and CK for Calvin Klein, amid growing economic uncertainty. Here, two traditions merge to claim both signifiers.

Notably, in 1913 Matsuya Department Store compiled 4,260 illustrations of *mon*, which it called "heraldic crests."[87] This manual originally served as a reference book for shop clerks processing orders for crests screened onto kimono silks. However, when notability of family names began diminishing in importance with growing urban anonymity and a new middle class, Matsuya also cataloged these crests' diversity (and numerousness), with families once borrowing stylized images from nature, like animals, plants, and natural features, to compose meaningful symbols for their clans. Existing family crests were also consulted to create new company logos, with this book likely serving as a design manual for early twentieth-century Japanese commercial designers. In 1915, when Fukuhara Shinzō (1883–1948) developed the Shiseidō Company's camellia logo,[88] its pattern curiously resembled a *mon*. Shiseidō's ultimate contemporary expression of symbolic prestige creation inspired by traditional samurai symbols was reproducing its corporate logo into an allegedly artisanally produced face brush, discussed later.

The most famous Japanese logos today include those of big conglomerates, which often propagate online their long corporate histories (occasionally dating from early Tokugawa times). However, the practice of writing company histories (*shashi*) stems from the Meiji period, when during significant anniversaries, like the tenth, fiftieth, or even hundredth year of operation, companies published literature detailing their activities. Carefully detailed *shashi*, sometimes appearing each decade, emphasize the corporation's development, growth, and new products or initiatives in self-congratulatory or reflexive tones. Efforts to connect the contemporary late-capitalist present with a premodern, preindustrial past of allegedly unbroken commercial activity also emerged in late nineteenth-century Japanese corporations' early adoption of *mon*-like logos, which for some, continues until the present. One, the Mitsui group, including Mitsukoshi department stores and other industrial concerns, still maintains its unique *mon-*

Craftsmanship and Proto-branding

like logo designed with three parallel lines in a diamond-shaped frame resembling a wooden tray. According to business scholars Pantea Foroudi, T. C. Melewar, and Suraksha Gupta, logos should be easily identifiable and express corporations' values:

> The corporate logo is the official graphical design for a company and the uniqueness of the design requires significant creativity, which must match a firm's strategy and identity: it should be unique and creative in its design. When the strategy is recognized, the corporate visual identity makes the organization memorable and well-known through its corporate logo. . . . In addition, a favorable design can engage an audience by asking them to visually interrelate with the logo. Well-known organizations with a favorable reputation gradually adapt their corporate logo in a way that is barely visible to the audience. The corporate logo as a visual expression is a significant tangible asset of the organization.[89]

An interesting example revealing how logos recently evolved in East Asian countries with even more compressed industrialization than Japan is found in neighboring Mainland China. For contemporary logo creation, Timothy Parent, a China fashion consultant and *WeAr Magazine*'s editor, asserts that "symmetry is more attractive to people in general, so usually logos have some sort of symmetry."[90] Based on studies of street style and nearly 100,000 photos of fashion design in China over the past decade, Parent believes that

> Many Chinese logos feature Chinese characters, and as they are pictographs (similar to Japanese *kanji*), they can be rendered to more closely reflect what the word is expressing (i.e. Chinese typography for logos in either ancient Chinese, for more traditional brands, or calligraphy-style font). A new wave of graphic design in China favors Western minimalism in logo design. Some Chinese brands omit Chinese characters so as to appear more international. Different demographics go for drastically different styles, and given that there are many different types of logos in China, it is easy to see a brand's ideology and aesthetic values from their logos.[91]

Like in Japan, Chinese logos in the decades following Deng Xiaoping's (1904–1997) 1979 Opening and Reforms also initially harkened to traditional pasts, with some firms later adopting Western fonts to seem more modern.

56 *Chapter 1*

Naomi Klein's best-selling turn-of-the-millennium book *No Logo*—whose critiques against corporate power and untrammeled consumerism inspired antiglobalization proponents and, later, Occupy Movement activists—argues that brand names appeared simultaneously with the factory, which manufactured "uniform mass-produced products," whose nascence began amid industrialization.[92] In the United States, she pinpoints the late nineteenth century for early brand names, with Heinz pickles, Quaker Oats, and Campbell's soup becoming popularly recognized brand-name products with logos connoting artificially manufactured familiarity.[93] Klein argues that the brand is "the core meaning of the modern corporation," with "advertisement as one vehicle used to convey that meaning to the world."[94] While "manufactured sameness" took root with factory standardization, advertisements educating consumers about products soon transformed into "building an image around a particular brand name version of a product."[95]

Although Japanese corporations adopted brand names nearly synchronously with Western ones, they needed to go beyond merely creating iconic products, and so they endeavored through advertising to ascribe unique attributes to heighten the effects of commercially beneficial commodity fetishism. Here, tendencies toward democratizing luxury, along with communicating manufactured artisanality, were unique aspects of modern Japanese marketing models for consumer products.

Manufactured Artisanality as a Selling Point

On the Shiseidō cosmetic company's 2021 English-language website, the Japanese corporation engages in contemporary framing of its history to global consumers: "The history of Shiseido is not merely a story about products and services; it is a story of a company taking a broader perspective to also consider aspects of culture and lifestyle, and seeking always to create new value. This is the true history of Shiseido."[96] Certainly, representing for consumers long histories of brand-name recognition and associated qualities is not new, nor is it exclusively Japanese. However, creating "new value" within longer corporate histories and presenting "history" like a product resembles Marx's idea of reification, a term further developed by Lukacs. In the commodity structure, social relations are imbued into a commodity, and thus, the commodity becomes a subject with its own agency when relations between people take on characteristics of objects expressing "phantom objectivity," with the consumer transforming into an object "chosen" by the commodity.[97] As this corporate description promises, Shiseidō's customers directly consume a history embedded within the company's (new) mass-produced products and thereby access a constructed artisanality, or "manufactured artisanality." It is this artificial relationship between consumers and (fictitious) individual producers, now commodified within products, that becomes a selling point. Essentially, manufactured artisanality itself becomes a commodity to increase the product's value, just like commodified labor adds value to commodities depending on its type and length—as in Kawabata's descriptions of *chijimi* cloth.

Shiseidō's online presence reveals the corporation's efforts to distance itself from industrial capitalism's obvious mass production, in which product advertising now approaches the realm of commodity fetishism. The brief online infomercial (running late summer 2019) for the new Hanatsubaki Hake polishing face brush, modeled after Shiseidō's iconic camellia flower logo, touts it as "handcrafted by Kumano artisans" and "made in Japan with legendary quality and craftsmanship," while featuring an attractive light-skinned Afro-European model.[98] Here, consumers literally use the company's stylized logo as a brush to smooth out makeup and beautify their faces. In addition, its materials of "high performance fibers," promised as "100% animal free," are combined with "Hidden Core" technology to provide a smooth and comfortable makeup experience. The product actually combines *four* brush heads (a new concept) embedded into a thick black lacquer-like ceramic base, further citing the product's Japaneseness, along with characters for *Tokyo Ginza* on the box's bottom. Internally protected by a disposable clear plastic case, it is hulled within

Figure 1.3. Shiseidō Hanatsubaki Hake polishing face brush, 2019. https://www.shiseido.com/us/en/hanatsubaki--hake-polishing-face-brush-0729238161368.html?cgid=brushes, accessed July 25, 2021.

58   *Chapter 1*

an opaquely translucent, elegant, gray outer plastic box resembling those enrobing art museum products.

Kumano brush artisans' early history well-represents premodern Japan's proto-industrialization model, which has recently approached artisanal mass production due to popular demand. Around 1840, faced with seasonal unemployment following rice harvests, farmers in Hiroshima Prefecture's Kumano region, who had traded city-bought brushes locally, began making them themselves.[99] Nearly two hundred years later, 1,500 artisans allegedly churn out an impressive fifteen million brushes yearly, which, as described by Chief Cabinet Secretary Yukio Edano in 2011, "showcase Japan's traditional craftsmanship and brand power."[100]

Such manufactured artisanality has become an important aspect of Japanese products, and many advertisements craft narratives of uniquely Japanese quality, personal attention to products, and careful craftsmanship.

CONCLUSION

Beginning with Japanese capitalism's proto-history, this chapter explores premodern artisanship and *za* as precursors to product standardization, and then examines early development of company logos as symbols of product quality for important Tokugawa-era merchant families. Logos for such businesses (not yet "true" companies) were inspired by samurai crests, or *mon*, because of social capital acquired from that high-status distinction. An interesting example is the Mitsui family logo, whose three lines within a four-edged diamond-shaped box cite three wells in their name. Here, the logo comprises a manufactured, constructed status distinction, where the proto-company functions as family enterprise, and instead of hereditary status, familial belonging is conferred by business activities and associated trade operations. Logos now refer to large corporations, but in the premodern past, they also connoted individual businesses and trade associations, whose organizational structures allowed a basis for social practices from whence Japan's early capitalism arose.

Logos, and later, brand names, deeply signify specific social spaces demarcated as places of commerce punctuated by highly performative ritualized norms of exchange. Indeed, manufactured artisanality itself is performative in its fetishization of labor and how it is publicized and "explained" through displays and advertisements retaining performative elements. Shopping encounters' high performativity in layers of politeness and implied reciprocity remain characteristics of Japanese shopping models and are even embedded in companies' signifiers in logos and advertisements like the Shiseidō Corporation's camellia. This symbol, or sign, representative of the tea plant *Camellia sinensis,* embodies Shiseidō's concept of *omotenashi* (literally, "no outside/exterior/surface," translated as "hospitality"), where clients or customers are treated as insiders or guests. Erasure of clearly delineated social boundaries between outsider and insider in Japanese customer and purveyor relationships began in an early twentieth-century practice permitting customers to wear shoes in stores, where the outside was literally brought in. The next chapter describes how artisanal production merged into mass-produced manufacturing with growth of shops into companies, and correspondingly, how small shops selling a particular item expanded into department stores with multiple sections purveying myriad products.

Chapter Two

COMMODIFYING WESTERN MODERNITY, NEW JAPANESE CORPORATIONS, AND THE DEPARTMENT STORE

The late nineteenth century saw the formation of a plethora of successful companies producing accessible luxury consumer products: Shiseidō (1872) and Kaō (1887) manufactured cosmetics and soaps; Seikō (1881), pocket watches, and later, wristwatches; and Kotobukiya (later, Suntory) (1899), spirits. The Western-style maquillages, timepieces, soaps, and liquors they created represented a new modern age, with luxury now mass-produced industrially, and relatively inexpensively. Consumers did not require wealth to purchase smaller items representative of more expensive aspirational products—a strategy that Japanese companies even now employ to perfection. Newspaper advertisements began marketing these aspirations toward modernity, enwrapped in the successes of Imperial Japan, while women's magazines also displayed depictions of bourgeois women surrounded by "necessary" accouterments of modernity: all available for sale. Department store display cases rendered products of varying price points newly accessible to all shod consumers in emporia resembling spectacular museums of consumption.

THE BOURGEOISIFICATION OF SPACE: FROM PUBLIC TO PRIVATE CONSUMPTION

Philosopher Michel de Certeau's notion of the "practice of everyday life" resonates strongly with Japanese society's profound transformations just before the twentieth century.[1] While Japan's government certainly hoped to influence subjects' behaviors via propaganda initiatives to aggrandize the nation, corporations also entered the fray by using advertising to engender greater profits by creating products and promoting certain lifestyles to effectuate this. National and corporate interests thus intersected, but they never quite monopolized Japanese consumers' fickle habits, which were most strongly influenced by changing notions of space propelled by modernization. As the Meiji era transitioned into the Taishō period (1912–1926), Japan saw a profound shift from what one might view as public to private consumption. This coincided with growth of two popular institutions: the museum (*hakubutsukan*, literally "hall of myriad things") and department store (*hyakkaten*, literally "store of hundreds of commodities"), where consumers went to either consume knowledge for edifying national purposes or purchase products for personal reasons, and thus, "acquire" modernity. This form of modernity is aptly described as an inherently hybrid "imperial modernity" originally inspired by the desire to catch up to Western powers and influenced by the effects of Japan's military incursions onto the continent, which was neither exclusively Western nor Asian but, rather, a combination of these elements.[2] Indeed, department stores transformed into new museums of a capitalist and imperialist age containing a bricolage of commodities. In addition, notions of public and private began developing with the rise of a national bourgeoisie and conceptions of private property along with ownership. This also corresponded to urbanization and large population shifts away from rural regions. With the growth of Taishō-era *bunka jūtaku* (culture houses), separate discrete spaces, like bedrooms, living rooms, kitchens, and bathrooms, emerged within homes for specific purposes, as in the West. Hence, for a growing Japanese middle class, consumption of food, drink, and bathing moved from public, communal spaces to private, bourgeois spaces denoted by function.

Indeed, the regimentation of bodies, personal movement, and individual activities in public, along with state discipline encroaching into domestic spaces of the home, became characteristics of imperial regimes embraced by middle-class subjects. Historian Timothy Burke indicates how, in Europe, social norms of hygiene, cleanliness, and dress became tied to ideals of civilization and respectability, coupled with ideas of racial superiority later imposed on colonial peoples in Africa and elsewhere.[3] Similarly, anthropologist Hildi Hindrickson notes how "Africa and the West are mutually engaged in a semiotic web" in characterizing how body surfaces in late to early twentieth-century African history were understood by colonial regimes and colonized peoples themselves,

62   *Chapter 2*

which she views as indicating the "constructedness and the interconnectedness of cultural systems."[4] Though Japan only experienced semicolonial status under the unequal treaty system after 1858, the Meiji government soon embarked on reforms evidencing desired parity with the West, including those concerning personal appearance. For example, in 1872, in Tokyo, the Japanese government imposed the Misdemeanor Law (*Ishiki kaii jōrei*), which banned all forms of nudity and undress, along with mixed-gender bathing at public bathhouses, and by 1873 this law extended into provincial areas. According to anthropologist Satsuki Kawano, "As a result of the state's intervention, ordinary people's bodies became the objects of intense sartorial surveillance as new rules for displaying bodies, in and out of clothing, came into effect."[5] Such scrutiny also penetrated deeply into homes, merging with already transforming social practices, determined by the interplay between imposition of state norms, consumer desires, and creation of new markets.

Hence, this key time period experienced shifts where cosmetics, soap, watches, and spirits[6] morphed from Western-connoted luxury items to necessities crucial to modern life. To be modern meant being Western, and being Western also meant possessing and using various Western-style commodities amid an atmosphere of modernity in Japan. Additionally, these commodities reshaped Japanese quotidian life and privileged individuals over the communal; hence, life became more individualized and commodity-driven. Manufactured by corporations including Kaō, bar soap, initially uncommon in Japan, became associated with notions of (compulsory) personal hygiene, cleanliness, and respectability, while cosmetics produced by companies like Shiseidō became tied to feminine beauty and middle-class refinement.

Along with ideas of propriety and appropriate forms of dress, modernity and capitalism required punctuality for all imperial subjects. Thus, watches by Seikō came to mean acceptance of up-to-the-minute standardized time, and they reflected public virtues of punctuality in a society where daily rhythms were no longer dictated by agricultural calendars, seasons, or the sun's position. This included regimentation of time even for leisure activities, where social calls became more predictable with the widespread arrival of timepieces for the middle classes. Even refreshments reflected Japan's hybrid new modernity. As alternate forms of hospitality to Japanese green tea and rice crackers, Kotobukiya's spirits could be served with Western-style biscuits and jam procured from Fūgetsudō (a chain of shops selling cookies and candies incorporated by Yonezu Matsuzō in 1872)[7] or Meidiya (a provisioner of imported pantry items founded by Isono Hikaru in 1885 and initially associated with international shipping).[8] With new social practices, modern life required such provisioning of various commodities, also symbolizing broader social transformations even mirrored in Imperial Japan's political culture.

Japanese women played important roles in spreading imperial modernity through their commodity choices due to growing economic power as bourgeois consumers, coupled with control over household management and domestic space. Hence, advertisers throughout Japan's empire targeted bourgeois women as a market for these new products because they increasingly determined household purchases and managed domestic affairs. In Juliann Sivulka's study of American advertising, parallels emerge with Imperial Japan in advertisers appealing to women: "For the mass national market targeted by marketers, the ideal consumer had always been female. Techniques such as market segmentation and targeted promotions emerged at the same times as this conception of the consumers as largely female. As a result, those marketers, who understood that the woman's market could be developed, also shaped the idea of *consumption as a feminine activity.*"[9]

In the early twentieth century, a rising East Asian consumer culture generated by women paralleled extensions of Japanese imperialism, and also revealed how corporate and state aims intersected. Interestingly, the Japanese companies now most strongly associated with accessible luxury name brands were incorporated during this time of immense social, economic, and political transformations, and they built their roots amid this heady atmosphere of imperial modernity.

Japan's First Corporations and Mass-Produced Personal Luxury Commodities

The founding of Japan's most iconic companies coincided with key historical national events in the early Meiji period that seemingly promised an increasingly democratic political atmosphere: the 1872 abolishment of the samurai class and associated status distinctions, appeasement of the increasingly violent People's Rights Movement (Minken undō, 1879–1881) with the Meiji government's 1881 promise of a constitution to assuage individuals desiring codified rights including voting rights, and the emperor's 1889 gift of a constitution to Japanese subjects after an eight-year-long research and drafting process.

Steps toward democratization of the new nation's political environment coincided with Japan's accelerated industrialization alongside democratization of consumer experiences, with new means of producing and selling commodities in new spaces less defined by class and wealth distinctions. This meant that more people could afford and access commodities than ever before, which only the upper classes had once consumed, like pharmaceuticals and beauty products, hygiene items, timepieces, and Western liquors. Some companies were initially inspired by Western incarnations in Europe and the United States, but their founders soon discovered how to properly accommodate business and advertising models to the specific needs of Japanese customers.

Companies like Shiseidō, Seikōsha, Kaō, and Kotobukiya began in this atmosphere, and they attempted to create products to offer similar quality as Western counterparts—and then later surpassed them, so customers even preferred Japanese-manufactured commodities. These companies' early histories seem dominated by their largely male founders' hagiographic stories, as innovators devoted to superior craftsmanship and exemplary quality competing on equal levels as the West. Thus, their purpose mirrors the Meiji state's desire to achieve parity with the revision of the unequal treaties imposed upon Japan, a goal achieved in 1899 with the original European signatories of the 1858 Harris Treaty of Amity and Commerce, but not until 1911 with the United States. Company literature and online websites immortalize these men's stories, detailing their histories in larger-than-life descriptions as benevolent fathers of capitalism, and selfless, devoted entrepreneurs aiming to improve consumer lives with high-quality products.[10] These hence appear as hagiographies of entrepreneurship, linking intrepid, innovative figures with the state's self-help philosophy so representative of the late Meiji era. They also exemplify the period's *risshin-shusse* ("go out into the world to make one's name") philosophy that the Japanese government so desired to impart to imperial subjects and lend glory to the nation.

However, the beginnings of these companies focusing on comestibles and small technology items like watches were not always smooth, and consumers needed to be convinced that buying these products would vastly improve their lives—or at least make them seem more "modern." Not only did they aspire to create products of high quality, they also sought to surpass Western counterparts, but with greater accessibility and lower prices. Hence, these companies began business with early concepts of democratizing luxury, making all individuals

Commodifying Western Modernity 65

"worthy" consumers of products. By triumphantly appropriating state discourses, they sold pride in Japan's economic and industrial "prowess" and thus led consumers to actually prefer Japanese-made products over imported ones. The quintessential Meiji-era entrepreneur remains Shibusawa Ei'ichi (1840–1931), but others also entered a select pantheon of individuals reflecting Imperial Japan's growing mercantile presence.

Pharmaceuticals and Cosmetics in Culturally Hybrid Settings — Shiseidō (1872)

In 1872, Fukuhara Arinobu (1848–1924), former chief pharmacist to the Japanese Navy's earliest incarnation, began the Shiseidō Company's precursor as a pharmacy introducing improved hygiene and Western-style medical practices to Japan. Its name's Chinese characters, or "hall of life[-giving] resources," a phrase inspired by the Chinese divinatory text Yijing ("Book of Changes," aka I Ching), held an exotic appeal that positioned the business as a purveyor of traditional Chinese medicine. However, instead of an experience where customers entered a shop and needed to wait for apothecaries to mix customized blends of herbs, they could now purchase already prepared packages produced according to scientific principles in hygienic environments boasting high-quality standards.

For example, in 1888, Shiseidō was the first Japanese pharmacy to produce modern toothpaste.[11] Its earliest product popular among consumers was Fukuhara Sanitary Tooth Powder, retailing at 25 *sen* (a hundredth of a Japanese yen), or nearly ten times more costly than rival products running at 2 to 3 *sen* due to value-added ingredients. Though expensive, the highly effective tooth powder combated tartar and halitosis, and it contained milder ingredients than the harsh salts and powdered limestone usually added by competitors, which contributed to its popularity.[12] Several years later, the company additionally began focusing on beauty products and cosmetics. Developed in 1897, Shiseidō introduced Eudermine, its first, and now iconic, cosmetic product, derived from the Greek words for "good skin," which served as a skin softener prior to application of moisturizer and powder. This product is still sold today, in distinctive retro red glass bottles designed in 1997 by French creative director Serge Lutens (b. 1942), who in 2000 began to produce his own brand for a cosmetics and makeup line. The current bottle evokes angular art deco splendor and Orientalist exoticism with its carved rectangular shape topped by a small circular stopper with round base perched on a crimson glass bottle. In the late nineteenth century, the tonic-shaped red bottle with its round, crystal-ball-like stopper and ribbon around its neck imitated similar Anglo-American perfume containers, and it boasted a sticker with yellow, pink, and light blue roses and the product's name. The original product contained rosewater, while its current incarnation is "subtly perfumed with an accent of rain-washed peony that seems to relax your entire being. Skin radiates, its softness evoking that of a flower petal."[13] Hence, the company used assertions of scientific efficacy, product innovation, and impeccable design to publicize products in a purported commitment to quality continuing until the present.

Another notable corporate aspect was customer outreach with refreshments while shopping. After visiting the 1900 Paris Expo, Fukuhara returned home via New York City, becoming enamored of American drugstores where people could sip fountain drinks and linger. He envisioned similar snack counters in Japan, inspiring him to create an American-style soda fountain with counters selling sodas and ice cream alongside a pharmacy and cosmetics retail shop, which his son Fukuhara Shinzō (1883–1948) instituted in 1902 in the pharmacy's fashionable Tokyo Ginza area location. Its earliest customers were geisha attracted from the nearby Shimbashi district, encouraged to enjoy fountain drinks with free gifts including an Eudermine bottle with every soda purchase—an excellent marketing ploy drawing in mass customers by offering glimpses of Japan's classic and highly esteemed entertainers sipping American-style drinks, and thereby linking cosmetics to high quality.[14] Here, the Western drink's modernity combined with embodiments of traditional Japanese artistry in tableaux of consumption by high-class geisha. This also revealed Shiseidō's democratizing luxury, where ordinary customers enjoyed observing high-class artists in relaxed settings while consuming New York–inspired sodas. Citing this history, Shiseidō Parlour's contemporary website touts its founder's relentless quest for authenticity and exemplary quality: "Arinobu's policy was always to go after the real thing—everything he used, not just the soda machines, but the glasses, spoons, and even syrup, was imported from the USA. His attitude of pursuing 'new values,' 'high quality,' and 'the real thing' is still carried on as the policy of Shiseido Parlour."[15] The counter later served Western-style meals, including beef stew and now-iconic *omuraisu* (omelet-rice); a victim of the 1923 Great Kantō Earthquake's conflagrations, the eatery was rebuilt in 1928 as a freestanding adjacent restaurant called Shiseidō Parlour.

Subsequently, Fukuhara Shinzō took over his father's business, later forming a corporation in 1927. He conceived of Shiseidō as a hybrid creation merging his father's original aims to purvey remedies with a modern pharmacy modeled on Western retail stores' convenience and selection. In 1908, Shinzō followed paternal footsteps and traveled to New York to study pharmacology at Columbia University, and he spent 1909 to 1913 in the United States, Paris, and traveling through Europe. He was briefly employed by the popular Yonkers-based pharmacy Burroughs and Wellcome, whose president, William Gallagher, presented him with a farewell gift of product samplings composed of a line up of well-known American pharmaceuticals, which Shiseidō later used as archival resources.[16] After returning to Japan, Shinzō "was determined to reinvent Shiseidō in the image of the finest makers of luxury cosmetics he had encountered in Paris and New York."[17] In the late 1910s, Shiseidō products in beautifully designed packaging with high-quality formulations enthralled Japanese consumers.

Joining the roster of Shiseidō's earlier best-selling Fukuhara sanitary toothpaste (1888) and Eudermine facial toner (1897), products redesigned and reformulated by the company—such as Seven Colors face powder (featuring pastels beyond the usual white to blend imperfections, 1917), Hanatsubaki perfume (Japan's first mass-produced perfume, 1917), and Cold Cream (a makeup remover and moisturizer, 1918)[18]—soon became staples of up-and-coming households throughout Japan's archipelago. They also revealed changing Japanese attitudes toward notions of hygiene and spatial usage for toiletry purposes. These products all assumed the premise that owners possessed spaces to put and store products—on dressers or in bathrooms, in bottles or jars beautiful enough to display—and enjoyed ample leisure devoted to preparing their toilettes. In addition, they presupposed certain ideas of personal grooming and cleanliness.

JAPANESE BATHING CULTURE

By the early twentieth century, the Meiji state successfully convinced its subjects that they needed to be "clean" in various methods imposing public hygiene concepts,[19] despite popular bathing habits existing long before the early Tokugawa era's intensely social bathhouse culture.[20] Historian Lee Butler notes that commercial baths began flourishing in

68 *Chapter 2*

the Muromachi period, when no less than twenty public baths were referenced by Kyoto-based writers.[21] Yet, they were relatively expensive and functioned as luxurious forms of recreation rather than primarily serving cleansing purposes; in a 1471 diary entry, an aristocratic Yamashina family retainer mentioned that bathhouse entrance cost each man of his party 8 *mon,* or equivalent to a liter of rice.[22] During the Meiji era, however, costs to use bathhouses, or *sentō,* were strongly regulated to ensure use by all social classes. Thus, many ordinary Japanese began their day gossiping and washing at public bathhouses, and might end their day similarly. Bathhouses became important community loci and disseminators of local and regional news while individuals performed ablutions in steam-heated underground spring water, and scrubbed off the evening's sweat or day's dust and grime.

This tradition of government control over *sentō* prices continues today; since October 1 of the Reiwa era (2019–present), entrance costs a relatively inexpensive 470 yen for adults (about the price of coffee in Tokyo cafés), 180 yen for kids ages six to twelve, and 80 yen for children under age six.[23] Although bathhouses continue their existence into contemporary times, many Japanese view them as "retro" relics enjoyed by hipsters and tourists, or nostalgic elderly. In fact, Stéphanie Crohin-Kishigami, a French scholar married to a Japanese and now living in Japan, was even named Japan's official "Sentō Ambassador"; recently, she published a book featuring the pleasures of Japanese bathing culture, which she hopes to help revive.[24] There are also medical benefits to relaxing in the bath. Dr. Hayasaka Shinya, a medical researcher focusing on medicinal properties of daily bathing and hot springs, postulates that daily soaking in Japanese-style baths reduces anxiety, improves circulation, ameliorates sleep, and benefits heart conditions.[25] Yet, for Japan's turn-of-the-century bourgeoisie, bathing soon moved into private domains, which reduced its largely social element, though *onsen* (hot springs) tourism increased with the expansion of rail lines.[26]

In the late nineteenth century, indoor plumbing and Western-style bathrooms became status symbols for aspiring Japanese middle-class consumers in an atmosphere rife with comparisons to Western countries. Wealthier Japanese built baths into their homes, though located in less accessible areas nearer the kitchen and garden. However, until the mid-twentieth century, ordinary people still utilized public bathhouses along with chamber pots and outhouses attached to homes. In some Tokyo quarters underserved by sewer pipes and public sanitation services, this practice continued until the early 1960s, while such "improvements" were only completed due to the 1964 Tokyo Olympics' impending arrival, when Japan once again fell under discerning foreign scrutiny nearly two decades after World War II's end. Deep into the Meiji period and beyond, "nightsoil" collection was so efficient that "it defied replacement by modern sewage and water supply systems even in newly expanded urban areas of Japan."[27] Historian David Howell notes that from the Tokugawa into Meiji periods, excrement was sold as a useful commodity for fertilizer, and was graded according to quality based on the wealth of city quarters where it was collected.[28] In the celebrated writer Mishima Yukio's (1925–1970) 1949 semi-autobiographical *Kamen no kokuhaku* (Confessions of a Mask),[29] the young narrator as a toddler in the late 1920s retrospectively fantasizes about the daily neighborhood spectacle of the somewhat-tragic nightsoil collector in his alluringly tight blue cotton thigh-high pants.[30] As a remnant of Edo culture, this laborer made his rounds with buckets on a yoke, evocatively described by Mishima as a "ladler of excrement."[31]

In the early twentieth century, some literati even eulogized traditional Japanese toilets on the verge of extinction. The 1933 essay *In'ei raisan* (In Praise of Shadows) by popular writer Tanizaki Jun'ichirō (1886–1965) begins by describing Japanese architecture, including indigenous aesthetics under threat of disappearance. Tanizaki even extolled Japanese toilets' aesthetic virtues, featuring murky darkness lurking in corners, comfortingly pungent aromas, and natural wood and straw construction, contrasting with the West's sterile antisepticism.[32] Such cultural preoccupations roiling below a rapidly modernizing Japan's surfaces indicated deep social traumas amid rapid technological transformation and pointed to social and private spaces immensely in flux. The plethora of products created for Meiji and Taishō consumers certainly reflected these aspirations, aspersions, and anxieties.

MILLED SOAPS AND HYGIENE PRODUCTS: LUXURY CLEANSING FOR EVERYONE — KAŌ (1887)

When Nagase Tomirō (1863–1911) founded the Kaō (Flower King) Soap Company in 1887, few Japanese routinely employed separate cleansers to remove dirt and detritus from their bodies; instead, they used *nuku-bukuro* (dirt-extracting bags)—bran-filled linen bags resembling sloughing sponges—prior to bathing.[33] According to Basil Hall

70   *Chapter 2*

Chamberlain (1840–1935), a British professor of Japanese at Tokyo Imperial University and author of *Things Japanese* (1890), soap usage was not popular until the late 1880s.[34] In the 1870s, Japanese pharmacies began selling imported Western fat-based soaps, with the Kaō Company later initiating its vocation for specializing in personal hygiene products—namely bar soap, then shampoo, and later still, laundry detergents. Thus, the company attempted to make its name by purveying high-quality soaps and skin-care products with greater accessibility and lower cost than Western manufacturers. These were sold in pharmacies, and later, in department stores. In 1890, the company launched its iconic product Kaō sekken (Kao soap), and in 1931 it introduced an improved formula with a cheaper price.

Further chapters will expand on Kaō's product lines, but during its early developmental stage the company built a niche in producing cleansing and skin-care products affordable to frugal middle-class housewives, imparting confidence in their quality by advertising that products were "worth" the price to support families' health. When Kaō bar soap came onto the market, soap was still very Western-connoted and considered an expensive luxury; thus, the company's Japanese-produced version was viewed as easier to access and significantly less expensive. However, frugal Japanese consumers still needed a special impetus convincing them to justify the extra cost. Usually, women made the family purchases and held the domestic purse strings, and thus they served as gate keepers for household accounting—a role the Meiji state encouraged, where, according to Naoko Komori, "Women were expected to contribute to the nation's savings for investment in modern industry by practising frugal household management."[35] Essentially, much of Imperial Japan's economic and financial well-being rested in women's hands, along with individual families' physical health. Yet, the state also returned the favor by boosting subjects' national pride and offering women a sense of agency in impacting Japan's future through their actions, whether by shopping or saving.

Like many companies initiated during the Meiji era, the Kaō Soap Company (and later, Kaō Corporation) fully capitalized on the triumphant new Japanese state's perceived successes, also reflected in product packaging and even soap bar wrappers. For example, an 1890 wrapper for Kwa-ō soap indicated on the product's label its use by Japan's army and navy, thus aligning the product with Japanese imperialism. Moreover, next to this endorsement was one by Tokyo Imperial University's Medical Department, indicating that the nation's

Commodifying Western Modernity 71

Figure 2.1. "Kwa-ō" soap wrapper, 1890. Courtesy of Kaō Corporation.

future doctors trusted the soap's efficacy to fully eradicate germs when used by medical professionals in teaching, research, or medical settings. Therefore, housewives reading the label before purchase were assured of high quality, while using it could also engender patriotic feelings in simultaneously consuming the same product as the imperial military and empire's top medical institution. Reflected in packaging and advertisements, such forms of vicarious patriotic consumption and state paternalism toward consumers presaged shifts toward fashionable celebrity product endorsements from the 1920s to 1930s. Certainly, the state's "good wife, wise mother" paradigms likewise adopted by corporations played a role in attracting frugal Japanese middle-class women consumers who felt they could best serve families' needs and budgets with such allegedly reliable products.

Here, "luxury" meant high quality and efficacy. The product came wrapped in a paper hull and label, sealed with a red sticker, and decorated with yellow camellias flush with green leaves, the company's signature moon logo, and arabesque Art Nouveau designs discreetly decorating corners. Below a smiling crescent moon, a small, ribbon-like banner indicates Nagase Company's production of the product, as part of Kaō Corporation. Beneath it, "MADE IN JAPAN" prominently appears in English capital letters, which implied the soap's possible export—whether throughout Japan's empire or even Hawaiʻi for patriotic Japanese immigrant consumers. Here, the superior, domestically manufactured product has supplanted Euro-American imports, and the label proudly exclaims Japanese provenance. In choosing to

Figure 2.2. Late nineteenth-century soap wrapper indicating trademark quality. Courtesy of Kaō Corporation.

purchase Kaō's items over products made by the British Lever Brothers or American Procter and Gamble corporations, Japanese consumers helped pioneer this shift.

The labels of other early soap products produced by Kaō also indicate concerns for promoting its trademark, and warn of corresponding "inauthenticity" for any competitor's formula. Kaō's signature trademark of a sphere with a cross inside placed within a golden star-like crest appears to mirror Western trademark symbols, and diverges from typical stylized *mon* reproduced by earlier Japanese businesses as logos. Text in English and Japanese indicates that Kaō glycerin soap was "authentic," with high quality assuring luxury. Use of a roman font and English language conferred simulacra of Western modernity and authenticity upon the product. The label also trumpets the soap's alleged "world renown" or global repute following Meiji Japan's success on the world stage in defeating China during the Sino-Japanese War (1894–1895), and later Russia, following the empire's 1905 victory in the Russo-Japanese War (1904–1905). The refined quality of Kaō products, compared to other "coarse" ones, purportedly conferred higher-class status to consumers.

In her research on Meiji-era patent medicines, historian Susan Burns reveals similar contemporaneous preoccupations for manufacturers.[36] Because no central government agency proofed quality for pharmaceuticals or personal hygiene products, companies needed to convince customers that products were effective, safe, and reliable. Certain Japanese trade guilds, under a central authority with government-appointed officers, did attempt to improve business practices and transform production. Amid mass production and increasingly scientific forms of management, such desired attributes were more easily attainable. However, as late as 1919, a British publication announced pitfalls in Japanese imported goods' reputed lack of standardization and hinted that uniform quality for most Japanese commodities was still a work in progress: "Complaints from importers of Japanese manufactures are numerous in respect to lack of uniformity in quality and regularity in output, due chiefly to the fact that so often large orders are sublet to various smaller concerns, each making the goods according to his own lights. Doubtless, with further supervision and increase of efficiency, Japanese goods will eventually attain a reputation for standard quality and hold their own in the trade markets of the world."[37] These concerns about uneven quality and company outsourcing to cheaper suppliers curiously mimic Western complaints about manufacturers in developing markets, more recently in China, whose manufactured wares have attained high quality in mere decades. Apparently, for prewar Japan, such concerns also permeated international business environments, while patent medicines and soaps were among Japan's largest exported commodities.[38] Therefore, it is unsurprising that Kaō's product advertising emphasized excellent quality and effectiveness, with broad appeal.

Like Shiseidō, the company soon ventured into personal care products and cosmetics. Another popular Kaō product was Nihachisui (Two Eight Water), a moisturizer inaugurated in 1900 and advertised in newspapers as *kōtōkeshō-yō*, or usable as a "high-class cosmetic" and purportedly "fine product," or *kahin*, that both "ladies and gentlemen" would love. Presumably cheaper and unisex, Nihachisui entered the market roughly three years after Eudermine's initiation, and flowers on the product's label and its neck ribbon bore some similarities to Shiseidō's best-seller as a competing skin "softener." Kaō thus attempted to broaden the market for a product popularized earlier by a rival company.

Through rhetoric in government pronouncements, along with efforts of corporations like Shiseidō and Kaō, which produced multiple new toiletry products, personal hygiene and grooming soon became aspects of a thoroughly modern Meiji Japanese lifestyle. This advertised

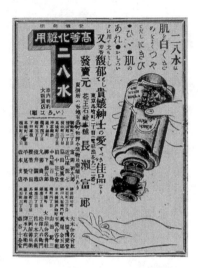

Figure 2.3. Nihachisui moisturizer newspaper advertisement, early 1900s. https://www.kao.com/global/en/about/outline/history/products-history/, accessed July 25, 2021.

regulation of the body and its surfaces through cleansing and toning also mirrored other aspects of an increasingly regimented industrial modernity, including conceptions of time.

High-Quality Affordable Watches for the Masses—Seikō (1881)

Notions of regimented time arrived in Japan as early as the late sixteenth century with the importation of mechanical clocks from western Europe, but these remained curiosities for the wealthy, and few adopted measured allocations of time to regulate their lives. Actually, from the late medieval period deep into Tokugawa-era Japan, castles, temples, and other political and religious centers controlled time as a public good: drums or bells only intermittently announced a "'variable-hour' time allotment system" based on the seasonally influenced Chinese-inspired zodiac rather than "fixed-hour time" characterizing imported mechanical European timepieces.[39] Historian Uchida Hoshimi notes that "what distinguishes timepieces from other consumer goods is that the time they display is defined by a unified societal time system, thus making them what could be called devices of 'social information.'"[40] Basically, all "watches must tell the same time," while "the standard that defines the correct time is a public timepiece in the possession of a political or religious authority."[41] The use of standardized time began in the late nineteenth century with a series of reforms initiated by a progressive Meiji government intent upon a modernization program raising Japan to Western standards.

Following the 1868 Meiji Restoration and Emperor Mutsuhito's (1852–1912) ascension to political power, and concurrent to the early 1870s institution of universal elementary education and compulsory military service for young men, Japan's new imperial government engaged in top-down calendar reform in 1872 to conform to Western practices, unilaterally switching from the East Asian lunar calendar to the Gregorian calendar. For many Japanese, this government-imposed development without explanation was so confusing that education reformer and entrepreneur Fukuzawa Yukichi (1835–1901), who founded Keio University's precursor in 1858, was moved to write *Kairekiben* (Exposition on the Changing of the Calendar).[42] In an essay allegedly composed in six hours upon his floor amid bitter December cold, and published in early 1873, he detailed reasons for the changes, and urged people to educate themselves; some prefectures even created an ordinance recommending its reading by the general public.[43]

Yet, "true" concepts of time were not instituted in Japan's school system until the 1880s;[44] such time consciousness also inculcated pupils' obedience and disciplining as imperial subjects. Following the early 1880s Matsukata Deflation caused by fiscal restraint policies stabilizing Japan's economy amid global recession,[45] Japanese industry also began flourishing in the textile and railroad sectors.[46] Both factories and railroads were soon bound to strict timetables regulating either production or transportation. Wealthier landowners also absorbed smaller farms suffering from debt, which dispossessed farmers and ensured rural exodus for individuals who began populating urban mills as workers. Hence, rapid growth in industrialization in late nineteenth-century Japan began to correspondingly impart ideas among all social classes that time could be monetized.

In his 1944 antiwar essay, "The Tyranny of the Clock," Canadian political philosopher and anarchist thinker George Woodcock (1912–1995) evocatively reveals how commodification of time arose from industrial capitalism, and ultimately, precipitated exploitative conditions:

> Modern, Western man, however lives in a world which runs according to the mechanical and mathematical symbols of clock time. The clock dictates his movements and inhibits his actions. The clock turns time

76   *Chapter 2*

from a process of nature into a commodity that can be measured and bought and sold like soap or sultanas. And because, without some means of exact time keeping, industrial capitalism could never have developed and could not continue to exploit the workers, the clock represents an element of mechanical tyranny in the lives of modern men more potent than any individual exploiter or any other machine.[47]

In Meiji Japan and elsewhere, rural workers began forcibly acclimating themselves to relentless factory rhythms overshadowed by clocks, while white-collar professionals learned to read timetables of trams and trains for commutes and paced their activities hourly during workdays. To keep track of time as an increasingly valuable commodity, personal timepieces also became essential commodities as well as valuable possessions for modern individuals, and thus, transformed from premodern luxuries into necessities. Hence, the more communal clock moved from public spaces into workplaces and private homes; yet, it also migrated into pockets, and subsequently, onto the wrists of the bourgeoisie, and later still, hung from workers' necks or rested in their pockets. Similar processes occurred in late nineteenth-century Japan, which, like the West, experienced industrial acceleration due to imperial wars.

Yet, similar to the companies featured here, much of the technology for Japanese watchmaking was initially acquired from the United States amid a course of foreign tutelage soon supplanted by indigenous innovation. In 1881, Seikō's history began with the opening of a watch- and clock-repair shop in central Tokyo's Ginza area by its founder, Hattori Kintarō (1860–1934), who also sold timepieces.[48] The company achieved several notable milestones in its early years: in 1892, Hattori set up the Seikōsha factory and began producing wall clocks, and in 1895, pocket watches were added to its roster of manufactured goods.[49] The Time Keeper, Seikō's first pocket watch, issued in 1895, boasted a Japanese-made silver case, but most of its 22-ligne movement was actually imported from Switzerland.[50] In addition, much technology for mass production of watches in Japan first came from the United States, when "in 1894, the Osaka Tokei Manufacturing Company introduced machinery for factory production from a U.S. company and under the instruction and watchful eye of an American engineer, began manufacturing pocket watches with lever escapements."[51] This adopted new invention spread quickly and allowed for the rapid expansion of Japan's watchmaking industry, which Seikō soon dominated; it provided for production of a more affordable product, which led to the eventual democratization of access to watches for ordinary people.

In 1899, Hattori, like Shiseidō's founder, Fukuhara Arinobu, benefited from a trip to the West to observe watchmaking in factories abroad, investigating the implements they used, and then acquiring or designing his own for Japanese technicians. By 1901, Seikō had emerged as Japan's largest retailer of watches and clocks, and in 1905 it expanded sales overseas into Shanghai and Hong Kong through individual purveyors.[52] In 1909, Seikō initiated a pocket-watch line fittingly called "Empire," whose more rapid manufacture benefited from the company's development of an ingenious "automatic pinion lathe . . . dramatically enhancing productivity."[53] According to the Japan Clock and Watch Association (JCWA), due to innovators like Hattori, "By the end of the Meiji Era, there were more than twenty factories throughout Japan turning out about 3.8 million timepieces annually."[54] Seikō watches were still created by hand with mass-produced artisanal manufacturing; the JCWA notes that this failed to impede large-scale production: "Although the Japanese horological industry was typically handcrafted manufacturing, technical skills improved due to the dexterity of the workers, which would serve as a driving force in future development."[55] Nevertheless, these advances helped diffuse clock and watch ownership throughout Japan: Uchida estimates that by 1907, 72.3 percent of households owned a clock, and 10 percent of all Japanese owned a pocket watch—about one in four adult males.[56] Clearly, a market formed very rapidly in the early twentieth century.

Seikō also ventured into production of a relatively new consumer timepiece: the wristwatch. In 1913, Hattori created Japan's first wristwatch, the Laurel. Initially, only thirty to fifty were produced per day,[57] but they were soon issued to Imperial Army officers as a more practical timepiece than pocket watches.[58] Production increases spurred increased foreign trade, especially for consumers on the United States' West Coast, which boasted sizable Japanese immigrant and Japanese American populations. A January 16, 1918, article in the *Jeweler's Circular,* an important weekly American trade publication, notes how a Japanese producer of watch parts, including crystals, traveled to the United States to scout locations for two envisioned US offices: "K. Kouishi, president of the Kouishi Kotakubo & Co., manufacturers of watch crystals, Tokio, Japan, visited the foreign trade office of the Seattle Chamber of Commerce and Commercial Club recently."[59]

78   *Chapter 2*

The article also indicated that Mr. Kouishi proudly reported how "the watch crystal industry . . . was formerly in the hands of the Germans and Americans. Now Japanese are strong contenders in this market."[60] In 1924, Hattori produced the first Seikō-brand wristwatch, which exploded in popularity, and thus secured a bright future for his company.[61] When the first Seikō-labeled wristwatch arrived on the market, the company intended it as a cheaper alternative to Western models, like the American Rolex, while Seikō designers worked hard to make their products preferred over such watchmakers in price, quality, and appearance. Interestingly, such concern with high-quality manufacturing is built into the Japanese characters of Seikōsha's name, meaning "exquisite manufacture," which implies manufactured artisanality, while its homophones *seikō* (exquisite; also "clear-skilled" or "mental acuity," if its *kanji* are read separately) and *seikō* (success) also reference desirable qualities.

Yet, in the early Taishō period, competing watch producers from the United States and Switzerland also paid for advertisements in *sōgō zasshi* (integrated intellectual magazines) like *Chūō kōron* (Central Review), one of Japan's most popular monthly literary magazines, initiated in January 1887 as *Hanseikai zasshi* (Reflection Society Magazine) and renamed in 1899.[62] Such publications disseminated contemporary literary trends and communicated the latest currents in modern Japan's intellectual thought. They were also read by largely bourgeois male readerships potentially in the market to purchase watches.

For example, a 1914 advertisement on the magazine's back cover displays three different watches as commodities sold in Mitsukoshi department stores—venues detailed later in this chapter. The American men's Elgin wristwatch appears to the right of a women's pocket watch from Japan, the smaller Steady appearing above the larger Swiss men's Jouvenia. This advertisement was seen at an important transitionary moment, when consumers began switching from pocket watches to wristwatches, which still retained some characteristics of their precursors. Wristwatches were originally developed for women in the late nineteenth century, but by the early twentieth century were adopted by militaries and aviators, who coveted their practicality; the jeweler Cartier created the Santos-Dumont wristwatch in 1904 for celebrated Brazilian pilot Alberto Santos-Dumont (1873–1932).[63] By 1911 there were 3,989 retail watch and clock stores in Japan, with 605 in Tokyo alone.[64] Smaller retailers specialized in watches, but new department stores like Mitsukoshi also sold them, which allowed more people to

Commodifying Western Modernity 79

Figure 2.4. 1914 Mitsukoshi advertisement for watches, *Chūō kōron* back cover. Courtesy of Perkins-Bostock Library, Duke University.

access them in a less intimidating purchasing atmosphere, enabling "window shopping" through glass vitrines. By the Taishō period, wristwatches took off in popularity as the bourgeoisie readily adopted regimentation of time attached to their person, now embodied as a fashionable new consumer item.

With hours rigidly demarcated by minutes and seconds, amid a new human condition that Woodcock so eloquently described as the "tyranny of the clock," the new bourgeoisie ensconced in offices sought new, modern means to unwind at home and in public spaces. This included sampling Western-style alcoholic beverages.

Western-Style Wines and Liquors for Broader Japanese Audiences — Kotobukiya (Suntory) (1899)

Due to its initially expensive and "exotic" foreign reputation, Western-style liquor, including fortified sweet wine and whisky, was imbibed as a luxury product in new modern cafés, like Café Raion (Lion), a "Western-style salon" that opened in 1911 with waitresses known as

80   *Chapter 2*

jokyū (female servers), demurely coiffed like Gibson Girls and dressed in white aprons over traditional kimonos.[65] By the mid-1920s, these cafés had lost their elite connotations and instead became quotidian meeting places for a largely male clientele enjoying relaxed drinking opportunities amid friends and flirtatious waitresses working for tips; the number of cafés in Tokyo's fashionable Ginza area more than doubled, "from 20 in 1922 to 50 in 1929."[66] In addition to these new drinking establishments, just like in the Anglo-American world, sweet wines and whisky were increasingly imbibed in private homes to lubricate human relations and extend hospitality. Until the early twentieth century, these particular drinks were imported by large-scale purveyors of foreign groceries and spirits like Meidiya, and they commanded steep prices. Smaller stores in large Japanese cities also specialized in Western consumables, including wines and liquors, to make them more accessible to bourgeois customers in Japan.

In 1899, after serving as apprentice to a pharmaceuticals shop, Osaka businessman Torii Shinjirō (1879–1962) founded such a store, which he called Torii Shoten (Torii's Store), a wine-producing and distributing business serving as precursor to the Suntory Company. Torii not only sold various wines but also harbored ambitions to create wines on par with Europe. Interestingly, the contemporary framing of Suntory's history on its English-language website paints Torii as a craftsman with allegedly traditional Japanese qualities of *ganbari* (unceasing effort) and paternal benevolence toward employees: "Shinjiro had the dreams and pride of a true craftsman, and dedicated his life to creating good products, working untiringly and sparing no effort to improve their quality. . . . He was not content to be simply a tradesman, producing whisky to make a profit, but strove all his life to make a contribution to society."[67] A purportedly benevolent founding patriarch obsessed with high quality and craftsmanship is an important trope for many Japanese companies built upon premises of modeling, and then surpassing, the West in product manufacturing and selling modes. Here, for Torii, corporate values intersected with his hagiography as company founder, akin to narratives popularized in Meiji-era serialized novels published in newspapers where main characters overcame numerous hardships to reach success, and concurrently, also examined their inner selves. Literary scholar Janet A. Walker views such literature as a means for readers to reflect upon their own individuality, which the nation then strongly promoted as a component of success and economic growth.[68] Such late-Meiji reading and consuming communities of frugal middle-class consumers were initially those who supported the company's growth, of whom many were housewives purchasing drinks for husbands and guests. In other words, Torii's business catered to the tastes of a growing bourgeois Japanese audience who desired sampling Western alcoholic libations but balked at the prices of imported variants.

Notably, 1907 marked the creation of Akadama Port Wine (renamed Akadama Sweet Wine in 1973), which became the foundation of the business's early Japanese market. The wine, produced from grapes grown in Yamanashi Prefecture, initially sold for a reasonable price of 38 *sen* per bottle, rising in price to 55 *sen* in 1927 and to 1 yen 30 *sen* in 1935; in 1945, marked by wartime scarcity, its price mounted to 5 yen 50 *sen* per bottle.[69] This honeyed, fortified wine resembled port, a sweet red wine with a high level of alcohol, popular among Southern Europeans and the British, which stored well without refrigeration despite Japan's seasonally humid and often warm climate. In 1921, Torii founded Kotobukiya Limited as an agent to bottle and handle his wine trade, including Akadama Port Wine, which as its first popular product dominated 60 percent of Japan's wine market that year.[70] Western-style sweet wines also more likely appealed to women, who favored them over drier varieties of sake (rice wine) and shōchū (Japanese vodka) largely preferred by men, which was soon challenged by Western liquors like whisky. In turn-of-the-century Japan, husbands or single *salarymen* (businessmen in growing numbers by the early twentieth century) asked for certain liquors at local bars or *izakaya* (pubs), along with a growing number of cafés.

In 1922, the new company's most iconic ad for Akadama Port Wine featured a sepia-toned photograph of a nude young Japanese woman daringly gazing into the camera, luring male customers to imbibe the sweet drink, with the words *bimi* (delicious), *jiyō* (nourishing), and *budōshū* (grape liquor) directly below.[71] While holding the small glass of deep red liquid, she also appears elaborately coiffed in a respectable style, with a modest chain necklace around her neck and a prominent gold ring on her left middle finger and gold bangle around her left arm—possibly indicating her status as a young bride serving wine to her husband anticipating their nuptial bed. These small details potentially tempered the poster's racy connotations. Kotobukiya's innovative, bold advertisement, designed by Kataoka Toshiro and

82   *Chapter 2*

Inoue Mokuda, and featuring singer Matsushima Emiko (d. 1983), was also Japan's first nude female poster, which won first place at the 1922 Werbe-Kunst-Schau [Commercial Art] Exposition in Nuremberg, Germany.[72]

Certainly eye-catching, the poster appeared amid great contemporary interest in sociological norms and public hygiene, where sexual matters were an important component. Historian Sabine Frühstück indicates an early 1920s explosion of journals on sexology with a preponderance of "the urge to investigate, speak, and confess about sexual matters" in popular journals and magazines, including newspapers like *Yomiuri Shimbun.*[73] Advertising Akadama wine as "nourishing," with an appealing, healthy looking young nude model, revealed that Japanese began viewing sex, preferably in marital relationships, as essential to everyday health, and revealed commercial artists incorporating such ideas into their work. Concurrently, more Japanese men enjoyed sweet wine and stronger drinks in the growing number of cafés known for attractive and witty waitresses working for gratuities instead of salaries.[74] Less expensive and more accessible than drinking with highly trained geisha, these waitresses engaged in what historian Elise K. Tipton terms "pink collar work," where they sometimes intimated sexual favors to earn more tips in a curated space emphasizing freer mingling between the sexes.[75] Advertising posters for Kotobukiya's products certainly circulated in such atmospheres, and helped them gain greater name recognition among male consumers.

By the early 1920s, Torii's company began commanding a significant portion of the market, and by the decade's end, he started using the Suntory name for certain products. In 1923, he fostered the development of its first whisky, initially based on those of Scotland, by using Japanese water and unique distilling techniques in the new Yamazaki distillery near Kyoto, which brought the corporation into a new era—production began in late 1924. In 1929, Kotobukiya created its first "genuine" single-malt Japanese whisky, called Suntory Shirofuda, or "white label."[76] While individual purveyors continued selling Kotobukiya's products as high-quality cheaper versions of Western sweet wines and liquors, they were also increasingly found in popular modern venues: department store basements, which also sold high-end groceries and foreign canned or boxed items. These enormous shopping emporia combined myriad new products under one roof and allowed customers to view (and touch) numerous comestible items.

Shrines of Consumption: The Birth of Department Stores

To understand environments selling Japanese luxury commodities including whisky, and key loci where companies drew their customers, it is crucial to investigate the role of department stores, originally mid-nineteenth-century inventions pioneered in France and England. These were consumption spaces with a vast emporia of goods acquired from various empires, along with newly mass-produced commodities and the latest fashions. In a Japanese context, historian Noriko Aso terms customers of department stores, along with Tokyo-based national museums and other collections, as "consuming publics," who from the late nineteenth century until wartime defeat were attracted to institutions holding public exhibits, which also disciplined individuals in how to look and act in spaces intimately tied to their nation and society.[77] Consumers not only observed or bought items but also familiarized themselves with the vast modern spaces where they were contained or purchased, symbolizing industrial capitalism's successes amid birth of new commodities and new social practices within imperial nations.

Japanese marketing historian Kazuo Usui characterizes consumers as "social beings," whose consumption patterns are informed by decision-making where "the act of consumption—selection, purchase, use, maintenance and disposal of goods and services—shows a particular pattern in a particular historical time and place."[78] In department stores, commodities were housed like rare objects, despite infinite reproducibility due to industrial mass production. Shiseidō and Kaō featured special counters and vitrines displaying commodities like artifacts under glass in museums. Beyond value-added displays on attractive pedestals or in glass vitrines, their qualities were touted as unique or alluring by advertisers. In advertising, commodities targeted specific "consuming communities" like bourgeois housewives or young men.

Not surprisingly, the first department stores began several decades after nations embarked on their industrial revolutions, beginning with textile industries, which provided mass-produced raw materials for clothing and fashions, and progressed into heavy industry, which popularized steel-and-glass construction clad with brick or stone masonry often used in building the first department stores' atria. In England, this industrializing process began in the late eighteenth century, while France and the United States industrialized in the early

84 *Chapter 2*

nineteenth century, and Japan engaged in rapidly compressed industrialization in the late nineteenth century. Industrial capitalism thus allowed for the quick proliferation of massive numbers of new products, often sold in vast quantities at cheaper prices. Therefore, spaces
that showcased them grew in importance to add cachet or "value" to
these commodities, whose companies producing them also used trademarks to ensure quality, while advertising propagated name brands
for quick consumer recognition.

In 1838, Au Bon Marché, the world's first department store,
opened in France on Paris' Left Bank, with many of its current marketing practices initiated in 1852 by owner Aristide-Jacques Boucicaut
(1810–1877), who encouraged high sales volume on low margins with
fixed prices on discount, while allowing exchanges and refunds, and
who also introduced store advertising, along with paying employees
on commission. These new practices led to phenomenal sales growth
"in the years 1852 to 1863, (that) rose from 450,000 to 7 million
francs."[79] Housed in a multistory galleria with a glass atrium designed
partially by Alexandre-Gustav Eiffel (1832–1923), the store encouraged leisurely browsing and attracted customers from all social classes.

In Britain, Harrods was the first stockist of factory-made canned
foodstuffs and exotic goods, but in 1849 it diverged from its earlier
model as grocery purveyor and opened a multileveled shop in its now
iconic London Knightsbridge location. With its inclusive motto Om-
nia Omnibus Ubique, or "All Things for All People, Everywhere,"[80]
the store is currently Europe's largest, and it still provides unusual and
ultra-luxe commodities amid an Orientalist atmosphere citing Ancient
Egypt and the Middle East. As European cultural critic Walter Benjamin posited, "The first department stores appear to be modeled on
oriental bazaars," with balustrades draped in tapestries.[81] This exotic
flavor was no accident; it was likely part of store marketing tactics that
were later adopted worldwide.

Liberty of London (established in 1875) began selling textiles and
items from Japan and East Asia within its basement, renamed the Eastern Bazaar, in 1885, offering carpets and furnishings, while Selfridges
(founded in 1908) seduced customers with silk-curtained window displays unveiling new fashions like theater shows.[82] Selfridges' current
website, showcasing the store's history in colorful images and text, features its American founder, Henry Gordon Selfridge (1858–1947),
who emphasized that "a store should be a social center, not merely a
place for shopping," and advocated five marketing facets: "making

beauty big business, making a spectacle, championing women's rights, the theater of retail, and tuning in."[83] Further descriptions emphasize that stores were "social spaces, not just shops. They're environments in which you can enjoy extraordinary experiences that you can't find elsewhere."[84] Characteristics of department stores as social spaces and "experiences" developed early in their histories and now seem ubiquitous worldwide as business models.

In the United States, Philadelphia-based Wanamaker's "Grand Depot," built for the 1876 American Centennial Exposition, featured a Moorish façade, constructed overlaying the former Pennsylvania Railroad Station, subject to complete redesign in 1877 as the nation's first real department store. Lit by electric lights since 1878 and connected by telephone since 1879, the store lured customers into 129 concentric counters of men's and women's clothing styles, with dry goods arranged around a central circular counter. Its current edifice dates from 1910, built by Chicago architect Daniel H. Burnham (1846–1912), who designed the 1893 World's Columbian Exposition and other notable Second City buildings; now owned by Macy's, the store's signature Great Organ and Eagle sculpture still grace its Grand Court.

Like its European and American counterparts, Japan's first full-fledged Tokyo-based department store was Mitsukoshi, founded in 1904 as a store selling formal wear (kimonos), and then as an emporium "promising customers greater spatial freedom, social knowledge, and participation in a visual spectacle."[85] In 1914, its still-extant neo-classical facade with internal European-inspired architecture was built in Nihonbashi. After the 1923 Great Kantō Earthquake's fires destroyed its interior, the store was reconstructed in 1925, emerging with a revolutionary new practice modeled after Western counterparts: customers no longer needed to remove their shoes, as was customary for Japanese business establishments until the early twentieth century.[86] In 1932, customers enjoyed access to convenient transportation networks via a basement subway station. Designated an important "national cultural property" in 2016, the store still flourishes today, with subsidiaries in Ginza and Shibuya.[87] In 2008, Mitsukoshi's stores merged into the Isetan group (including the Isetan department store) to form Isetan Mitsubishi Holdings Ltd., a *keiretsu* (corporate network) mirroring the structures of most large Japanese companies, like Mitsui and Company.

To draw customers, department stores in Western Europe, the United States, and Japan constructed vast buildings framing halls of

86   *Chapter 2*

incomparable size with imposing steel-girded construction clad in marble and granite, housing massive displays of goods and products. Department stores thus framed new experiences of immediate on-site consumption, with owners applying models of virtue to possibly deceptive practices of buying and selling, where consumers flocked to their destination in quasi-pilgrimages to a "temple" or shrine of consumption luring them to browse. In such consumption spaces framed within usually secular narratives of buying and selling—whether in late nineteenth to early twentieth-century Europe, United States, or Japan—department stores' atmospheres harbored a quasi-religious charm, where customers entered brightly lit interiors boasting shining marble or granite floors, with feelings of reverence resembling pilgrimages to purchase fleeting fulfillment through mass-produced commodities.

In the United States, religious historian Nicole C. Kirk argues that Philadelphia department store owner John Wanamaker (1838–1922) viewed retail as a religious mission; in 1911, he even declared the department store a "temple":

> Wanamaker aimed not only to shape the budding American retail experience, but also to evangelize his customers and employees, creating model middle-class Protestants. Wanamaker saw his retail empire not as separate from religion but as an instrument of it, as a means of achieving moral reform in business, in the city, and in individuals' lives. Wanamaker, like many others during this period, developed a new way to deliver "old time religion." He harnessed the material world and aesthetics for his ministry, seeking to influence and define the moral order of the urban milieu through architecture, material goods, and public religious and civic events.[88]

As a Protestant moral reform movement proponent and friend of influential evangelist Dwight Moody (1837–1899), Wanamaker intended for Christian principles to suffuse his business practices: advertisements sharing homespun wisdom were based on fact, product quality was guaranteed, sales gave fixed prices with generous return policies, and his company offered employees free medical care and pension benefits.[89]

This paralleled practices of retailers in the United States, Europe, and Japan, which similarly constructed purportedly wholesome, modern spaces suffused by ethical practices, including their owners' religious principles or characteristics. Notably, Paul Lerner's study of Jewish-owned German department stores from 1880 until 1940 depicts them as "consuming temple[s]."[90] His interdisciplinary approach examining literature, popular media, and advertising reveals how department stores in Germany celebrated modernity and urbanism, plus incited popular anxieties, while they reflected and shaped German culture as snapshots into contemporaneous society. Interestingly, Lerner frames German department stores as particularly "Jewish" arenas of monetary exchanges for goods, composed of bricolages of alluring items, where consumers congregated to observe and purchase objects symbolizing cosmopolitan and new modernities in spaces also conspicuously selling Kosher food and Jewish books, advertising with Jewish religious symbols, and closing for Jewish Sabbaths within a broader culture often expressing anti-Semitism. Lerner indicates that in late nineteenth and early twentieth-century Germany, "Jews held, or at least started, the overwhelming majority of department stores and clothing and fashion houses throughout the country"[91] and thus maintained important roles in offering consumers myriad products at all price points. He posits that "both the German department store's 'Jewishness' and its magical qualities intersected with a discourse that represented the department store as an ersatz church, a secular temple or indeed a cathedral of commerce."[92] Essentially, Lerner views prewar German department stores as most closely expressing consumption as a religion.

In describing the late nineteenth-century department store's quasi-religious thrall, Lerner cites Zola's description of Au Bon Marché in *Au Bonheur des Dames* (The Ladies' Paradise), an 1883 story of a locus where "money and commodities were replacing the divine as objects of worship" and "commodity worship was filling a gap left by the waning of traditional religious devotion amidst modernity's secularizing tug."[93] For Europeans, the commodity's allure within department stores' social spaces seemingly surpassed comparable potential spiritual and social fulfillment found in actual temples or churches. In "Arcades, Magasins de Nouveautés," within his 1930s-era Convolutes, or sheaves of notes, Benjamin indicates that "on Baudelaire's 'religious intoxication of great cities': the department stores are temples consecrated to this intoxication."[94] Commodity fetishism, as enshrined in the department store's museum-like seasonally curated collections, endows objects with overwhelming charm and renders them irresistible to consumers.

Notably, Benjamin begins his 1935 essay on "Paris, the Capital of the Nineteenth Century" within *The Arcades Project* with a discussion of *magasins de nouveautés* (literally, "shops for new items" or

88 *Chapter 2*

"fancy goods stores"), precursors to modern department stores in Parisian arcades built in the early nineteenth century. He writes about stores' social spaces and new business practices: "The customers perceive themselves as a mass; they are confronted with an assortment of goods; they take in all the floors at a glance; they pay fixed prices; they can make exchanges."[95] In his addenda notes, discussing the dialectic of the commodity, Benjamin posits a "theory of the collector" engaged in "elevation of the commodity to the status of allegory,"[96] where he sees spiritual connections between shopping and owning products, now imbued with symbolic attributes comprising commodities. Throughout his writings, Benjamin laments the world's disenchantment, where commodities as objects re-enchant amid relentless capitalism.

However, Japan never experienced a corresponding secularization like that emerging from the Enlightenment amid Western industrial capitalization; long-standing Shintō practices endowed objects with specific spiritual qualities depending on particular usages, rarity, or geographical provenance. Religion, in the syncretic manner expressed in Japan, was integral to daily practice without compartmentalization; it was never artificially rendered separate from professional activities. This included the mercantile world. The merchant classes enjoyed long-term connections with certain Buddhist temples and Shintō shrines, while families kept *butsudan* (Buddhist altars) or *kamidana* (Shintō household shrines) with offerings of fruit, rice, tea, water, or sake in homes and businesses. Smaller household cupboards or niches were often associated with local religious entities or owners' professions, while also honoring ancestors and local deities.

Since the Tokugawa period, Japan's merchant class profited from historical Shintō connections, with small shrines protecting shoppers along with their families and staff engaged in commerce. For example, the Mitsui family, who owned the Mitsui conglomerate, began commercial activities in 1673 with a small kimono fabric store founded by Mitsui Taketoshi, who moved it in 1683 to the present Mitsukoshi department store's location; he also engaged in money-lending, a common practice among successful merchants. In 1904, the Mitsui family's ancestral deity was enshrined in the Nihonbashi Mitsukoshi main store's rooftop garden. On September 21, 1914, the store's first Western building began hosting a rooftop offshoot of the Mimeguri Shrine, housing the Mitsui family's guardian deity, who since Tokugawa times resided in Mukojima, now Tokyo's Sumida ward located near the Asakusa temple and entertainment area.[97] *Mimeguri* means "protecting three wells," and it cites the Mitsui family name.[98] That year, the store's publicity magazine *Mitsukoshi* featured the shrine's image, advertising it to customers.[99]

In the postwar period, this spiritually infused atmosphere of a temple or shrine might still be familiar to Japanese shoppers patronizing the original Tokyo-based Mitsukoshi Nihonbashi-area store. Since 1960 it has been graced by a massive four-story-high statue of a "Heavenly Maiden [Goddess] of Sincerity," or *Tennyo magokoro*, which resembles Kannon Boddhisatva (the goddess of mercy), in a central ground floor hall, towering over expensive jewelry and luxury bauble displays. A 1973 *New York Times* article featured the remarkable statue in a "Resorts and Travel" section series on Christmas shopping in England, Japan, and Iran.[100] Before its 1960 installation, craftsman Satō Gengen spent ten years carving it from a 500-year-old cypress wood block from the Kifune Shrine's forested precincts near Kyoto, and painted it in light green, blue, white, and red clay pigments, along with gold and platinum decorations.[101] The statue's vast expense and decades of embodied labor provide a perfect example of uncommodifiable artisanality (and fetishization of artisanal labor) towering over a shrine of consumption dedicated to selling multiple mass-produced commodities alongside artisanally manufactured ones.

Appearing during the Japanese economic miracle's early years, the statue holds important nationalistic connotations beyond notability to domestic and foreign tourists; the protective qualities of the shrine's wood are significant due to a purportedly 1,600-year history, where the *kami* Tamayorihime-no-mikoto, mother of Japan's first emperor, Jimmu, allegedly appeared to order local nobility to build Kifune Shrine ("Yellow Boat Shrine") to honor water spirits near the origin of rivulets flowing from Kibune River into Kamo River and then into Osaka Bay.[102] Kifune Kami is also believed to be descended from Japan's national progenitor gods; according to *Nihon Shoki* (Chronicles of Japan), Izanagi-no-mikoto, enraged by his wife Izanami-no-mikoto's death from birthing the fire god, cut him up into three pieces with his sword, where one became Taka-okami, or the rain god.[103] Hence, the statue allegedly also protects Mitsukoshi against fire, which indeed destroyed the store in 1923.

Most significantly, the "Goddess of Sincerity" undeniably symbolizes Japan's economic strength rendered in feminine form, resurrected after fires from earthquakes and wartime Allied bombings, and conveys desired ethical principles and cosmopolitan modernity combined with

90   *Chapter 2*

traditions ostensibly infusing Japanese business practices in Japan's flagship department store housed in its political and economic capital—once the Japanese empire's center. These same aspects are also mirrored by innovative Japanese companies producing luxury consumer products long showcased in Japan's top department stores. Nowadays, Shiseidō, Kaō, Seikō, and Suntory are all name brands highly sought after by consumers worldwide who seek affordable yet high-quality products promised by Japanese corporations built upon reliability and value. However, complex consumer environments underpin their lengthy histories, where sociopolitical phenomena informed advertising reflecting modern Japan's shadows of imperialism, war, and nationalism.

CONCLUSION

In the early Meiji period, new Japanese companies created iconic products to rival overseas Western counterparts in quality and design. Such consumer products were not mere imitations, but added innovations taking into account cultural and national specificities. These included innovations in advertising, purveying, distribution, and even ingredients, where Japanese producers manufactured once out-of-reach luxury consumer products like cosmetics, soap, watches, and alcoholic beverages at relatively affordable prices, and strove to retain similar connotations of luxury once assumed by Western-made items. Japanese companies also created a particular form of capitalism unique to Japan that spoke of paternalistic benevolence to customers built upon corresponding growth of potentially long-term relationships promising affordable high quality, imputed craftsmanship, and respect. Hence, this reputed care toward individual consumers led to increasing numbers of frugal bourgeois housewives contributing to populating their homes with these products, whose use surpassed mere function and extended into transformations of social practices. In late Meiji to Taishō Japan, soap, cosmetics, wristwatches, and liquors all added important components to spatial bourgeoisification, which involved regimentations of hygiene, beauty, time, and even leisure, which benefited both corporations and the state. Consequently, Kaō, Shiseidō, Seikō, and Suntory all included components involving specific Japanese national identity in their advertisements.

Although many products were initially purveyed in unique retail spaces developed by companies, like Shiseidō's Parlour, or by distributors like Kotobukiya for Suntory's precursor, they truly benefited from late Meiji-era department store proliferation. Here, products were displayed in glass cases, and customers window-shopped both outside and inside stores. Department stores additionally "luxuriated" goods within, showcasing them in privileged positions behind glass and on pedestals like tantalizing museum objects, both alluring *and* conveniently purchasable. Later, these Japanese products expanded throughout Japan's empire into Taiwan, Korea, and Manchuria, where they began connoting quality and luxury amid reputations of imperial power. Though many consumer products could appeal to both men and women, companies began tailoring retail and advertising specifically to women consumers. This approach continued into the interwar period and revealed women's growing decision-making power in holding family purse-strings as housewives or, increasingly, earning salaries within new white-collar professions welcoming women. By then, Shiseidō, Kaō, Seikō, and Suntory were firmly established as reputable name brands connoting particularly Japanese forms of high-quality affordable luxury.

Chapter Three

MODERN GIRLS AND SALARYMEN CONSUMING THE WEST

During the pivotal interwar period, Imperial Japan experienced numerous influential developments marking a new age of political and cultural modernity, which scholars refer to as emblematic of "Taishō Democracy," contemporaneous to the evolution of new currents of literary and artistic modernism, which also influenced advertising. During the reign of the less-charismatic, mentally and physically disabled Emperor Yoshihito (1879–1926) overlapping the Taishō era (1912–1926), this important time period was bookended by the end of World War I (1914–1918) and Manchukuo's 1932 establishment, just before Prime Minister Inukai Tsuyoshi's (1855–1932) assassination. These key years heralded growth in democratic institutions concurrent with expansion of state power and rising militarism amid growing technological innovation and urbanization celebrating modernity and consumerism. These elements translated into media landscapes where state and business interests often dialogued, attempting to influence the masses while steering consumption.

Initiated by rising inflation after World War I, the 1918 Rice Riots revealed Japanese women's informal political power, especially housewives impacted by economic fluctuations, who joined political protests and urged beneficial change. The state viewed women controlling household finances as less threatening than so-called modern girls (*moga*) who displayed hedonistic consumerist tendencies without desiring marriage or who consorted with leftist "Marx boys." Despite such contradictions, alluring images of modern girls appeared in countless advertisements cajoling readers into consuming products from department stores and other retailers. Advertisements attracted young, educated working women and housewives to these venues, though their target seemed archetypal "modern girls" with untrammeled spending habits.

After Imperial Japan's wars absorbed Taiwan (1895) and Korea (1910) into the empire, Japanese companies extended products throughout Japan and its colonies, framed within department-store vitrines displaying the metropole's advancements and bourgeois aspirations. Though the 1923 Great Kantō Earthquake wreaked destruction on Imperial Japan's capital and left countless dead, it also ushered in an era of rebuilding marked by creativity, innovation, and accelerated technological progress amid adoption of multifaceted modernist forms of cultural production. The rise of mass media fostered political environments characterized by mass politics and new political parties on both the left and right, while leftwing cultural producers developed a new proletarian culture believed to challenge capitalist excess. In 1925, the arrival of universal male suffrage was tempered by the Peace Preservation Law limiting rights of free speech and assembly. The Japanese state issued this "safeguard" to target groups or individuals allegedly disavowing private property or proposing anarchism. Nevertheless, proletarian arts and literature encompassed porous categories of modernist expression, incorporating leftist writers who also wrote ad copy, and proletarian artists who created commercial art, in an interesting symbiosis where corporations co-opted messages propagated by the mass media to sell products.

Concurrently, companies promoted bourgeois cachet for their commodities in magazines for loyal customers touting high-class (*haikara*) modern lifestyles and new leisure pursuits like skiing and hiking, also featuring current events and broader global developments. In the 1920s and 1930s, Shiseidō and other companies created magazines and customer loyalty clubs for consumers to join and receive bonus items or discover new products, which appealed to frugal professionals or homemakers. *Shiseidō geppō* (Shiseidō Monthly) and later *Hanatsubaki* (Camellia) magazine provided women and their families glimpses into modern "cultured" life, or *bunka seikatsu,* featuring hybrid Japanese and Western modernities, while Kotobukiya (Suntory's precursor) disseminated postcards equating its liquors with an alluring urban world's newfound desires. Company advertising featured products consumed or displayed in aesthetically appealing interiors featuring women, some clearly "modern girls" or resembling Western

94 *Chapter 3*

actresses. Seasonally produced or limited-edition products represented aspirational luxuries in Westernized, largely urban settings: Japanese advertising strategies still feature these key characteristics. Efflorescence of new forms of modernity in mass media, politics, and cultural arenas marked the interwar period—deeply impacting Imperial Japan's consumerism.

Seikō: Timely Innovations Regimenting Modern Life

The early twentieth century featured vigorous flows of commodities, people, and ideas within and beyond domestic Japan and its growing empire, whose effects permeated national mass media and sociocultural environments. Individuals became keenly aware of simultaneous developments in their homelands and beyond, through new forms of communication and transportation prompting increased social interactions and informational flows. Intellectual historian Harry D. Harootunian asserts "the narrative that dominated Japanese sensibility between the wars was distinguished by a consciousness that oscillated furiously between recognizing the peril of being overcome by modernity and the impossible imperative of overcoming it."[1] With rapid advances in transportation, industry, and technology in everyday life, Japanese subjects were constantly confronted by dramatic interplays between synchronous and asynchronous modernities. This mind-set coincided with radical breakages between new modernities ushered in by cataclysmic disaster striking the imperial capital with seismic implications for Japan and its empire.

In 1923, on September 1 around noon, the Great Kantō Earthquake, estimated at 7.9 magnitude, struck Tokyo's environs,[2] damaging buildings and igniting fires that generated over 130 large-scale blazes[3] contributing to a massive death toll of 108,858 people, with 13,275 classified as missing, according to 1930 statistics.[4] The earthquake's further destruction included *jikeidan* ("self-defense groups" or vigilantes) brutally killing around 6,661 Koreans allegedly poisoning wells, along with suspected leftists and others with nonstandard, regional Japanese accents.[5] Anthropologist Sonia Ryang asserts that the atrocity arose from a political climate whereby ethnic Koreans were denied inclusion into Japan's national sovereignty, and whose status as unassimilable outsiders led to vicious targeting by Japanese vigilantes encouraged by authorities amid disaster.[6] The massacre coincided with police and military violence inflicted by officials including Captain Amakasu Masahiko (1891–1945), responsible for the extrajudicial killings of anarchist Ōsugi Sakae (b. 1885); Ōsugi's common-law wife, feminist writer Itō Noe (b. 1895); and their young Japanese American nephew, Tachibana Munekazu (b. 1917), during arrests amid martial law purportedly instituted to protect Japanese citizens.[7] The assassination nevertheless occasioned widespread condemnation, and for a half-decade, the government expressed freer latitude toward leftist cultural production and activism, permitting development of new forms of proletarian art and modernism.[8] Yet, the earthquake's largest impact was cultural, influencing modernist art, literature, and film, with currents like Constructivism developed by the avant-garde Mavo group led by Maruyama Tomoyoshi (1901–1977), which included commercial artists like Yanase Masamu (1900–1945),[9] while new cultural trends developed alongside the proliferation of businesses and corporations reemerging with greater innovations.

Conflagrations also destroyed the stores, headquarters, and factory of Seikōsha, Japan's premier watch manufacturer, which all needed rebuilding. Nevertheless, the company viewed this calamity as an opportunity to rebuild with greater technological innovation, and remarkably, it restarted operations in November 1923.[10] In a bold, unprecedented move, the company implemented no-cost replacement with newly produced watches for all timepieces customers had returned for repairs but lost in the fires, "thereby gaining the firm trust of the public."[11] Certainly, this helped seal brand loyalty while earning Seikōsha positive publicity at a precarious time.

Rapid rebuilding of factories and renewed customer confidence allowed the corporation's quick introduction onto the market of the first watch produced with Seikō's brand name in December 1924.[12] Featuring a thin black leather band, relatively large winding apparatus, and a much smaller second dial in the watch face's lower part, it was described by the company as an important "milestone model" to "introduc[e] to the world for the first time the brand name [Seikō] that was later to become synonymous with precision and accuracy, innovation and refinement."[13] Its relatively thin 24.2-millimeter case was made of nickel and featured a 9-ligne, seven-jewel movement with standard seconds subdial, and it was the first watch to feature Seikō's name as counterpoint to dominant Western watch manufacturers.[14] Here, a Japanese watch producer consciously promoted itself as commensurate

96   *Chapter 3*

in quality with comparable Swiss or German manufacturers. National institutions, including Japan's premier transportation network, recognized this high-level craftsmanship and international quality.

In 1929, Japan's Ministry of Railways designated Seikōsha's domestically produced pocket watch as its official timepiece, with the company now its official watch supplier.[15] This 1929 model Type 19 was first branded Seikōsha, and in 1931, its successor, with a unique knurled interior case design, was officially branded the Seikōsha Railway Watch.[16] The company's website notes that "train drivers often made wooden cut-outs on their consoles where the approved pocket watch would sit in line of sight as they drove their trains."[17] Certainly, trains required exceptional timing accuracy and exposed passengers and businesses to highly defined time consciousness, where railways' influence extended beyond original transport functions. Historian Louise Young's *Beyond the Metropolis* underlines the importance of Japan's provincial cities and considers how interwar growth of so-called second-tier metropolises with associated telecommunications and transportation networks impacted broader social interconnectedness within the nation and imperial peripheries.[18] Aided by clocks in public locations like train stations and workplaces, along with increasingly prevalent personal timepieces like pocket- and wristwatches, time-consciousness predicated upon accuracy and exact time regimentation spread throughout Imperial Japan and became a symbol of modernity.[19]

In 1932, Seikōsha constructed the still-extant neo-Renaissance-style Hattori Clock Tower (named for company founder Hattori Kintarō) in Tokyo's swanky Ginza 4-*chōme* [number four city block] area.[20] This eye-catching new signpost soon became a potent symbol of modernity and the prominent high-fashion district's emblem of modern luxury; it was also the first monument that commuters noticed when detraining at the Ginza stop on the Tokyo Metro Ginza Line (operating between Ginza and Asakusa, a popular entertainment area) that began service on December 30, 1927.[21] The clock tower survived wartime air raids and is now an important historic landmark in one of Tokyo's most popular consumer centers, with its concentration of high-end boutiques and department stores that includes Mikimoto, Louis Vuitton, Issey Miyake, Mitsukoshi, and Takashimaya. Interestingly, the clock tower building still houses the Seikō corporation's Wako Store, a large, elegant boutique purveying luxury and limited-edition Seikō watches and other brands.[22]

When built, the clock was also an omnipresent modern symbol of time's power in ordering middle-class Japanese society according to rational principles resembling the factory in industrial capitalism. For Imperial Japan's bourgeoisie, the office was an important locus for business and government matters regimented by the relentless march of time in carefully ordered increments. Philosopher George Woodcock, also a former railway clerk, proposed how time consciousness permeated capitalist society with artificial regularity: "The influence of the clock imposed a regularity on the lives of the majority of men which had previously been known only in the monastery. Men actually became like clocks, acting with a repetitive regularity which had no resemblance to the rhythmic life of a natural being. . . . Out of this slavish dependence on mechanical time which spread insidiously into every class in the nineteenth century there grew up the demoralising regimentation of life which characterises factory work today."[23] Not everyone in Japan's empire experienced time or "modernity" similarly, where extension of exact time followed transportation and communications networks and workplaces integrated into capitalist time conceptions. Concurrently, technological innovation, popular culture, and other indices of the modern progressed at different rates and led to a prevalence of asynchronous modernities during the interwar period.

Japanese intellectuals and cultural producers took notice of this phenomenon and expressed it in their works, especially in the relatively new medium of film, lending itself to perceived immediacy and realism despite featuring constructed realities as an artwork. Harry Harootunian posits that "thinkers and writers responded to Japan's modernity by describing it as a *doubling* that imprinted a difference between the new demands of capitalism and the market and the force of received forms of history and cultural patterns."[24] Certainly, this condition, which Kyoto School philosopher Watsuji Tetsurō (1889–1960) termed *nijū seikatsu* (double life), is not unique to Japan; Harootunian cites German thinker Ernst Bloch (1885–1977), who described 1930s-era Germany, another capitalist late-developer like Japan, as exhibiting "synchronicity of the non-synchronous, the simultaneity of the non-contemporaneous."[25] Contemporaneous films also expressed these concepts.

In Mizoguchi Kenji's (1898–1956) 1929 silent film *Tōkyō kōshinkyoku* (Tokyo March), based on Kikuchi Kan's (1888–1948) popular novel, much of the melodrama revolves around shots of the main character's somewhat-outmoded pocket watch. By the 1920s,

Figure 3.1. A still frame from the film *Tōkyō kōshinkyoku*, 1929. IMDb website, https://www.imdb.com/title/tt0020510/mediaviewer/rm782254336/, accessed July 12, 2021.

timepieces were considered essential wardrobe items for the middle-class *sarariman* (salaryman), and they represented growth of a *sarariman* culture so entrenched that watches regularly appeared in motion pictures as encapsulations of time and modernity. Mizoguchi's film, considered by American film critic Donald Richie (1924–2013) as an early Shōwa era (1926–1989) version of Expressionism with "[social] criticism at the core,"[26] revolves around Fujimoto Yoshiki, a bank employee and wealthy businessman's scion, and his love for Michiyo, also known by her geisha name Orie. Represented by the pocket watch, Yoshiki appears caught in a liminal space between asynchronous modernities.

The film was released when pocket watches were rapidly being replaced for the convenience and stylishness of more modern wristwatches. Notably, the film shows how a company employee used a prized pocket watch, possibly an earlier Roman-numeral model like Seikōsha's Empire (1909), worn by his father's generation,[27] and how this possession could store a beloved's precious photo, in this case Michiyo/Orie—an intriguing juxtaposition of an attractive working-class woman with the strict ordering of time. Yoshiki seems trapped between traditional and modern—a position enhanced by his high-quality, yet clearly outmoded, vest harboring his pocket watch, and circulation between the geisha house and the more fashionable café where he pursues Michiyo/Orie, engaging in what the philosopher Watsuji calls a "double life."[28] Not only did the pocket watch symbolize time's passage, but it also denoted punctuality for bank employees in a business devoted to exact calculation (and protection) of finances with absolute accuracy.

Tokyo March, in roughly 30 minutes of extant footage from an originally 110-minute reel, opens with an evocative text panel noting "Tokyo . . . city of culture and progress . . . but also capital of vice and debauchery"[29] and reveals montage-like scenes of trains, roads, and the red-brick Western-style Marounouchi business district near Tokyo station—fully displaying the imperial capital as a bustling site of commercial labor and incessant transport of people and goods. Immediately afterward, the camera focuses on a scene of weekend leisure, where a panel indicates "Sunday. . . . The wealthy youth busy themselves with their favorite sport above the poor areas."[30] Yoshiki plays tennis, a newly popular Western sport, with friends dressed in tennis whites. He hits a ball badly and it lands in an alley onto working-class quarters below the court. Michiyo, a working-class factory girl, attempts to retrieve the ball and futilely throws it against a net intended to keep balls in but also protects players from streets below in a symbolic scene emphasizing contemporaneous barriers preventing interactions between Japan's higher and lower social classes. However, Yoshiki finds the attractive young woman's determination charming and takes her photo, which he later affixes within his watch's cover. At work in the bank the next day, Yoshiki takes out his pocket watch attached to a chain clipped to his vest pocket, and glances longingly at Michiyo's photograph, which he then shows to his friend Sakuma.[31]

The same night, while the men went drinking, Michiyo reappears on a darkened street with her friend, returning from their factory workplace, and proceeds to her aunt and uncle's lodgings, where she discovers that her aunt just lost her own factory job and immediately considered employing Michiyo as a geisha like her sister, the girl's mother. Michiyo later consents, and begins work as Orie, only to discover that Yoshiki and his father, Fujimoto, along with Yoshiki's best friend, Sakuma, all fell in love with her; Orie's shy and lugubrious demeanor, born from loss, orphanhood, and perceived futility in a patriarchal culture where she little decides her fate, causes her to unwittingly turn her neck away and hide her melancholic face within her sleeves—both gestures believed particularly erotic to men in the geisha

100   *Chapter 3*

world. During her employment, Orie wears her dead mother's ring, which Fujimoto later recognized as one he presented to a past geisha with whom he consorted. Michiyo eventually leaves the geisha house after Fujimoto buys out her employment from her female boss and she begins working for a Western-style café serving drinks, where she also encounters Yoshiki and Sakuma. Later, Yoshiki is devastated when he discovers Michiyo is his half-sister, but he gives Sakuma his blessing to marry her instead. The unhappy couple—both weeping because Michiyo felt cajoled into an arranged marriage against her will, and Sakuma felt guilty for abandoning his best friend—soon leaves Japan for a honeymoon on a ship heading for the United States.

Mizuguchi's repeated shots featuring Yoshiki's pocket watch reveal the anthropomorphic power of this now somewhat-outmoded object in mediating social interactions between Sakuma and Yoshiki, and Yoshiki and Orie (Michiyo), through commodity fetishism. In a particularly poignant scene midway through the extant film, Orie caresses the watch that Yoshiki shows her, displacing her affection onto the object.[32] At the film's conclusion, Yoshiki gives his prized pocket watch to Sakuma, symbolizing their indelible friendship.[33] For petit-bourgeois Japanese families in the 1920s and 1930s, a Seikō watch was considered a relatively affordable "frugal luxury" when even middle-class men's office labor became harshly regimented by capitalism, along with the labor of working-class women in factories and elsewhere. "Modern girls" now working in new professions like elevator attendant, trolley operator, switchboard operator, department store clerk, taxi dancer, or café waitress were also greatly subjected to commodification of time.[34] In the film, as a geisha, Orie's labor is regimented, too, considering her time spent with Fujimoto and Yoshiki, for which they paid the geisha house.

Mizoguchi poignantly highlights contemporaneous popularized proletarian themes while also revealing issues surrounding social class and gender, along with glimpses into the lives of contemporary middle-class salarymen at work and play juxtaposed against those of the working classes. Like in *Tokyo March,* amid a capitalist system now governed by regimented and monetized conceptions of time, white-collar workers unwound by imbibing spirits seemingly making time slow down—certainly in geisha houses for traditionalists, but also in bars and cafés proliferating after the 1923 Great Kantō Earthquake.

Suntory Whisky: A Modern Drink Blending Scottish Know-how with Japanese Craftsmanship

Since the late nineteenth century, urban Japanese began enjoying whisky in the country's first indoor Western-style drinking establishments, such as the Kamiya Bar, opened by Japanese brewer Kamiya Denbei in Tokyo's Asakusa entertainment area.[35] However, growth in café culture truly began after the Great Kantō Earthquake, with fifty cafés existing on the Ginza area's main street alone while around 15,500 waitresses (*jokyū*) were employed in Tokyo by 1929.[36] Historian Elise Tipton describes establishments like Café Raion (Lion) as providing important locales for young men to drink spirits like whisky to decompress, accompanied by attractive young waitresses paid by tips in a venue symbolically "in between the home and the workplace."[37] These cafés were initially inspired by European and American cultural forms but, over time, developed their own uniquely Japanese attributes with a particular cosmopolitan art deco look featuring exterior neon lights, dim interiors, and potted foliage framing waitresses' manufactured flirtations modeled upon modern girls to garner more tips for their labor.

Interestingly, the 1929 release of the first whisky distilled entirely in Japan coincided with the popularity of cafés, and it soon developed its own following in such drinking establishments.[38] The well-received spirit resulted from a decade-long process of trial and error. This first "true" Japanese whisky, manufactured by Kotobukiya, Suntory Company's precursor, boasted genuine roots in Scotland. Taketsuru Masataka (1894–1979), the so-called "father of Japanese whisky," was a sake brewer's son from a family hailing from Takehara City in Hiroshima Prefecture. Taketsuru traveled to Scotland in late 1918 to study organic chemistry at the University of Glasgow. He took lodgings with a recently deceased doctor's family who accepted boarders to make ends meet: there, he met Jessie Roberta "Rita" Cowen (1896–1961), the Scottish woman who eventually became his wife and primary business partner.[39] In summer 1919, Taketsuru enrolled in a chemistry course taught by Thomas Stewart Patterson (1872–1949), the university's first Gardiner Professor of Chemistry.[40] Intent on mastering traditional Scottish distillation techniques, Taketsuru soon apprenticed at Longmorn Distillery (now Glenlivet) in Speyside and then at Hazelburn Distillery in Campbeltown. On January 8, 1920, despite the Cowen family's disapproval, Taketsuru and Rita married; the couple returned to Japan with plans to establish a distillery.[41]

In 1923, Taketsuru was hired by Torii Shinjirō, founder of Kotobukiya, later known as Suntory, to establish a distillery in Yamazaki, located between Osaka and Kyoto in a region known for its water's legendary purity. Developing whisky, an initially quite costly and laborious process, requires nearly five years from a distillery's initiation to the final product—including setting up the operation's technical aspects, creating wooden barrels and smoking peat, and careful blending—or merely aging if a single malt.[42] In the meantime, the company produced other Western-style products, including toiletries and seasonings, some that became quite popular, like Smoker toothpaste, Palm Curry, Tory's Sauce, and Tory's Black Tea.[43] Hence, in 1929, under Taketsuru's direction, Kotobukiya finally produced its first true Japanese-made whisky, known as Suntory Shirofuda (Suntory White Label) for its paper label's signature color.[44]

An early advertisement introducing Suntory Shirofuda ran on January 13, 1930, in the widely read *Asahi Shimbun*, which boasted a fairly highbrow readership with a taste for Western-style liquors, judging by the prominence and frequency of such ads.[45] However, arriving right during the early global Great Depression (1929–1939), when few could prognosticate the economic downturn's length, the

Figure 3.2. Advertisement for Suntory Shirofuda in *Asahi Shimbun*, January 13, 1930, 6.

slightly more affordable, domestically made whisky also attracted the newspaper's frugal, middle-class readers.[46] The large advertisement in the lower left-hand corner took up a fifth of a page. Here, two stone *koma-inu* (lion dogs)[47] frame both sides of copious text to dwarf a small bottle labeled "Suntory Scotch" in English within an elegant stone gate bordered in stylized Western floral and leaf designs evoking European Art Nouveau motifs. They metaphorically lure customers to pass through the gate as a next step in purchasing and sampling the entirely Japanese-made product. The whole advertisement thus appears as an invitation to imbibe in hospitality implied by entrance to a luxurious residence resembling those of Japan's aristocracy.

The ad copy's first sentence announces the product as a genuine "pot-still" whisky, complete with a concluding exclamation point for emphasis.[48] Such high-energy multisentence pronouncements combine to create an exhaustively long hyped description that reveals a surprisingly laborious near-decade-long process of "scientific" preparation and production for a high-quality Japanese product. At its very top, appearing above *katakana* script for Suntory Whisky, proudly ran the phrase *Danjite harukai wo yōsezu* ("Absolutely no need for importation"), which appealed to contemporary readers' growing nationalistic feelings.[49] The advertisement clarifies that Japanese no longer needed reliance upon imports for high-quality whisky.

Nevertheless, despite its homegrown appeal, Suntory Shirofuda was initially unpopular among domestic consumers. Mike Miyamoto, Suntory Whisky's current global brand ambassador, noted that compared with today's softer, and more floral, fragrant whiskies, Shirofuda "was disastrous. It was too smoky. . . . People didn't like it at all."[50] Japan's first whisky too closely resembled scotch's peaty, smoky flavors, to which Japanese consumers were unaccustomed. Yet, despite setbacks, following the 1931 Manchurian Incident, which heralded the aggressive Japanese colonization of Manchuria and China, Suntory Whisky was sold overseas in these foreign markets and was even exported to the United States in 1934 after Prohibition's lifting.[51] Suntory Shirofuda soon acquired a reputation in Japan as a Western-style connoisseur's libation, while proliferation of this relatively more affordable Japanese whisky in its early heyday was also hailed as a component of modern life.

However, due to differences in opinion with Torii on distilling processes and taste, Taketsuru soon left Kotobukiya. In July 1934, he opened his own company, Dai Nippon Kajū Kabushikigaisha (Great

104 *Chapter 3*

Japan Juice Company) in Yoichi on Hokkaidō, Japan's northernmost island, whose climate resembles Scotland's and harbors natural peat bogs along the Ishikari River, where the distillery was completed in October near Sapporo, an important commercial center.[52] Because at least three years are required following a distillery's initiation to actually produce marketable whisky, the company began selling apple juice from Hokkaidō's abundant apple trees to gain revenue during the wait. Whisky distilling finally began in 1936, but the Yoichi distillery did not market its first whisky until 1940; Taketsuru's main product was known as Nikka whisky, Suntory's strong competitor.[53] Soon after its introduction, Nikka whisky fell under wartime government procurement, as will be discussed in chapter 4.

Imperial Japan's early twentieth-century capitalism was marked by growth of new products like whisky, offering small luxuries to consumers of all classes. The Great Japan Juice Company and Kotobukiya profited from an era when bars and cafés proliferated, while various drinks became associated with new leisure concepts developing after the Great Kantō Earthquake amid increased capitalist regimentation of time and labor for both the *sarariman* and factory worker. This included working-class café waitresses who served the men, likely middle-class company employees, within a system compensating labor according to their appeal and time spent entertaining. Such café service contributed to the modern girl's image as flirtatious, sexually available, and likely to spend her earnings on luxuries.[54]

THE MODERN GIRL AS "IDEAL" CONSUMER

Arising in the early twentieth century, the "new woman" predated the modern girl concept and was directly linked to women's increasing mobility through growing opportunities for higher education, political participation (an 1890 ban on attending political meetings was rescinded in 1922), and calls for women's suffrage (not garnered until 1946 in the postwar period). Though it seemed as if more opportunities opened for women in white-collar jobs, women's participation in clerical work was statistically insignificant and dwarfed by the numbers and percentages of women in factory jobs.[55] Middle-class publications like *Women's Review* and *Housewife's Friend,* boasting circulations of around three million, supported women's suffrage[56] while also hosting discussions of contemporary debates, popular novels, and

Modern Girls and Salarymen

more mundane topics on beauty and household management. Historian Sharon Nolte notes that "the rising importance of education and the growth of the urban middle class encouraged reconsideration of the importance of women as knowledgeable homemakers and active citizens."[57] But, elite women were also consumers, with access to family finances to purchase food and other household items. They engaged in certain aspirational purchasing, sometimes showcasing new freedoms for women, which contemporaneous advertisers recognized. In reality, compared to showy modern girls, housewives were actually the most consistent purchasers of household consumer items. Nevertheless, by the 1920s a new *moga* trope emerged, which alternately titillated and threatened consumers and corporations alike with allegedly untrammeled shopping habits for fashionable clothing and an outrageous search for pleasure and luxury in consuming everything from Western cuisine, liquor, and tobacco to popular media. Plus, she was incorrigibly flirtatious without consummation of her bold sexuality.

In 1929, according to *Housewife's World,* a respectable women's magazine geared toward a largely middle-class housewife clientele, there were "Ten Qualifications for Being a Moga":

1. Strength, the "enemy" of conventional femininity
2. Conspicuous consumption of Western food and drink
3. Devotion to jazz records, dancing, and smoking Golden Bat cigarettes from a metal cigarette holder
4. Knowledge of the types of Western liquor and a willingness to flirt to get them for free
5. Devotion to fashion from Paris and Hollywood as seen in foreign fashion magazines
6. Devotion to cinema
7. Real or feigned interest in dance halls as a way to show off one's ostensible decadence to *mobō* (modern boys)
8. Strolling in the Ginza every Saturday and Sunday night
9. Pawning things to get money to buy new clothes for each season
10. Offering one's lips to any man who is useful, even if he is bald or ugly, but keeping one's chastity because "infringement of chastity" lawsuits are out of style.[58]

These attributes consisted of knowing Western fashions, products, and consumption habits, and involved lifestyles centered around consuming

106   *Chapter 3*

food, drink, fashion, and one unmentioned aspect: beauty products and cosmetics. Historian Barbara Sato views the modern girl as arising in media images and advertisements following the 1923 earthquake and as a "representation of consumer culture" and "quintessential icon of consumerism."[59]

However, by the mid-1920s, the modern girl became cause for alarm among journalists writing in Tokyo newspapers. Stories about her, like in famous writer Tanizaki Jun'ichirō's novel *Naomi,* first serialized in Osaka *Asahi Shimbun* and set in Tokyo and its suburbs, were hugely popular, but they endured selective censorship due to the main character Naomi's unregulated sexuality and voracious consumption of modern, trendy items. Few readers noted a critique of capitalism in Tanizaki's work, but the story revealed both how objects failed to buy a person happiness or satisfaction and how traditional gender roles were not suitable for a modern consumer society based on desires over necessities. The novel's more conservative reading revealed how a husband's strong hand in marriage was needed to restrain a wife's untrammeled spending and sensation-seeking if unsaddled by children. The modern girl thus confronted normative ideas about marriage and family, and her "selfish" approach to rampant mass consumption made her both a darling of advertisers and bugbear of the government, which desired social stability amid scares of chaotic left-wing-inspired "free love" and shirking of arranged marriages. Even worse was the modern girl's unnatural avoidance of childbirth, so threatening to the fabric of national families during the rising current of militarism after the 1931 Manchurian Incident.

Historian Miriam Silverberg notes how the modern girl challenged existing sociopolitical conceptions, while her newfound economic power made her less dependent upon men in a new mass culture celebrating consumption.[60] The modern girl trope, beginning as a later offshoot of the Taishō-era "new woman," was largely an imaginary media construct but became ubiquitous as an image symbolizing new consumer cultures. Though modern girls were not necessarily more likely to purchase or use Shiseidō cosmetics, Kaō soaps, or Suntory drinks, they were often depicted in advertisements as alluring, desirable counterpoints to largely housewife consumers who usually bought products.

Japan's Beauty Empire: The Lure of Overseas Japanese Department Stores and Brand-Name Products

As Japanese business interests extended their reach into northeast Asia in the early twentieth century following the expansion of Imperial Japan's colonies, department stores began representing visual trappings of the empire's successes that could be purchased and enjoyed in the domestic space.[61] Women consumers were important in this process, and they delighted in their rising purchasing power with the growth of urban bourgeoisies in East Asian cities. In particular, they increasingly consumed small luxury items including cosmetics and toiletries. Notably, Tokyo-based flagship department stores, including Mitsukoshi and Takashimaya, carried products by companies like Kotobukiya, Seikō, Shiseidō, and Kaō, and expanded throughout the Japanese empire into trade centers near port cities with railroad links, including Seoul in Korea and Dairen in Manchuria.[62] For example, Mitsukoshi incorporated in Seoul (1906) and Dairen (1928), with both locations becoming full-fledged branches in 1929.[63] Incidentally, in August 1929, a Shiseidō chain store also opened in Seoul, the same year that popular Japanese graphic designer Sugiura Hisui (1879–1965) became design department chair for Tokyo's Imperial School of Fine Arts; he designed advertising posters for Mitsukoshi, including its Seoul branch.[64]

Publicity for this newly opened branch reveals colorful modernist aesthetics emphasizing colonial modernity and a highly cosmopolitan flavor, while showcasing a notable presence of fashionable women shoppers. As a representative Tokyo-based commercial artist, Sugiura in a cutting-edge advertising poster for Seoul's Mitsukoshi branch displays two couples identifiable as Japanese through the women's kimonos, who stroll in a cityscape with three women easily recognizable as "modern girls" wearing Western clothing featuring fur-collared coats and cloche hats. The women sport red lipstick, and presumably, white face powder (both possibly manufactured by Shiseidō), and the store's corner rises prominently behind them like a ship's prow, mimicking the Osaka branch in Japan's traditional commercial center. Mitsukoshi's colonial Seoul outpost thus represented familiarity to Japanese customers encountering a similar building back home. Hence, they possibly associated its architecture with the comforting experience of consuming Japanese name brands, which promised standard levels of

Figure 3.3. Poster of the newly completed branch of Mitsukoshi department store in Seoul, Korea, 1929. Public Domain Museum, https://en.600dpi.net/sugiura-hisui-0004276/, accessed August 4, 2021.

high quality and communicated a luxurious lifestyle emphasizing elevated social status, but also quotidian reliability.

Such venerable Japanese department stores, like Mitsukoshi and Takashimaya headquartered in Tokyo, thus spread the empire's goods throughout areas colonized by Japan in emporia celebrating veritable spectacles of consumption mimicking museums where all items on display were for sale. These imperial commercial outposts also harbored their own Shiseidō counters, where Japanese and Korean or Chinese colonial subjects could purchase favored products while assured of high Japanese quality intimated by the empire's scientific progress. Companies like Shiseido and Kaō even created special brands for Chinese and Korean customers that advertisers believed would appeal to them besides products solely marketed in domestic Japan. In outlets found in less-famous department stores or smaller shops, consumers throughout Japan's colonies or spheres of influence found versions of Shiseidō's popular face powder geared specifically toward their market.

According to the company's official website, Shiseidō started doing "full-fledged international business" as early as 1931, when it began exporting Rose Cosmetics to Southeast Asian countries.[65] Shiseidō also created a new Blue Bird line (*Seichō* in Japanese, *Qingniao pai* in Chinese) specifically for Chinese customers. In 1932, coinciding with Manchukuo's establishment as Imperial Japan's client state, the Mitsui Company started exporting Shiseidō's Blue Bird line of cosmetics, soaps, detergents, and toothpaste for "Manchurian" customers in Japanese-occupied northeast China. Since the time of the Russo-Japanese War (1904–1905), Mitsui had purveyed items for Japan's military along with consumer products. Northeast China, known as "Manchuria" in English prior to its 1931 Japanese takeover, had enjoyed economic connections to Japan since the aforementioned war's end, and the Shiseidō Corporation expanded its commercial operations in 1932 when Japan's imperial presence solidified into tutelary statehood. In 1935, a Shiseidō sales branch opened in Shenyang, and it soon began to publish the informational magazine *Chieinsutoa kenkyū* (The Chainstore Research). By 1938, Shiseidō had ventured into other Asian countries after opening sales branches in northern Chinese cities with strong Japanese political influence, including Shinkyō (contemporary Changchun), Harbin, Dairen, Tumen, Tianjin, Shanghai, and Qingdao, along with other cities in Japan's empire, including Seoul, Pusan, and Taipei.[66]

110   *Chapter 3*

In the 1930s, Shiseidō also targeted marketing strategies specifically to colonial Japanese and "Manchurian" consumers, with Blue Bird's signature yellow boxes featuring Japanese script instead of the usual English to communicate specifically Japanese modernity and luxury. In a Shiseidō outlet opening in Mitsukoshi's Dairen branch in 1931, consumers could buy Blue Bird Face Powder, a product developed for the "Continent." Its packaging consisted of an elegant yellowish-gold round cardboard box designed by Japanese commercial artist Maeda Mitsugu in 1932. Packaging graphics created for greater Asian markets featured a brunette woman with bobbed hair in the fashion of American actress Louise Brooks (1906–1985), in a simpler pattern than Yamana Ayao's (1897–1980) Japan-oriented design created that same year featuring a Western blonde woman with longer hair, signature Shiseidō camellia, and perm, juxtaposed against a rayed yellow-and-black background with stripes on the box's side. Clearly, these two Tokyo-based Japanese designers wished to create subtle differences between Western and Asian modernities in varieties of luxury communicated by each "model," color scheme, and design.[67]

In stylized graphics by Yamana and others, Caucasian women generally appeared in advertisements geared toward domestic Japan, while women with Asian appearances dominated publicity for the "Continental" market. Here, the Shiseidō company attempted to specifically link itself with scientific, Western (Parisian and New York) fashion-oriented luxury modernity in Japan, whereas in Asian markets from the early 1930s onward it highlighted Asian—and specifically Japanese—modernity. In such contexts, "Japanese" meant up-to-date, modern, and scientific as Asia's "rightful" leader in fashion and beauty fields. Shiseidō thus expressed Japan's imperial modernity, emphasizing hybrid forms of aesthetics that certainly echoed official Japanese propaganda slogans of "harmony" coupled with the collaborationist rhetoric of the later Greater East Asia Co-Prosperity Sphere's (1940–1945) multiethnic and multicultural aims.[68] Historian Naoki Sakai posits that contemporaneous Japanese cosmopolitanism lent itself to this ideology.[69]

Imperial Japan's connections with its empire, and particularly with Manchukuo (designated as "empire" in 1934), were lauded in various media, like the women's magazine *Housewife's Friend.* In March 1934, *Housewife's Friend* published a colorized photo of Manchu Empress Wanrong (Western name Elizabeth, 1906–1946), wife of Manchukuo's "puppet" emperor, Aisin Gioro Pu Yi (1906–1967), whose framed photograph appears to her upper left. She resembles Shiseidō models with her white powdered face and bright red lips, while a red background surrounding her face evokes Imperial Japan's flag colors; her golden yellow chair references Pu Yi's abdicated imperial throne following the 1911 Xinhai Revolution that initiated China's Republic (1912–1949).

Important Manchukuo women's images clearly influenced advertisements created by Japanese companies. With a similar ostrich-plumed fan, popular actress Yamaguchi Yoshiko (1920–2014), masquerading as a Chinese woman named Ri Kōran (Li Xianglan), also appeared in Shiseidō advertisements. In 1941, Shiseidō hired this famous Manchukuo-based actress to advertise cosmetics and soap (her 1940 film *Shina no yoru* [China Nights] had popularized her on-screen image). Such media reveal how Japanese imperial modernity and control increasingly displaced Chinese modernity during the Asia-Pacific War (1931–1945).

Paralleling the spread of Japanese imperial modernity, Shiseidō, and its competitor, Kaō Corporation, marketed Japanese luxury goods at all price points to customers throughout the empire in commercial

Figure 3.4. Wanrong (Elizabeth), Empress of Manchukuo, as photographed for *Shufu no tomo* in March 1934. Courtesy of *Shufu no tomo* archives, Tokyo, Japan.

112   *Chapter 3*

venues like department stores and chain stores. Kaō marketed products in China using strategies allowing consumers access to affordable luxury while also offering higher quality than rivals to justify slightly higher prices. Concurrently, Japanese companies capitalized on allegedly superior scientific modernity, which these beauty product companies continue to employ today. Then, as in drugstores now, to highlight their prescriptive and "scientific" nature, cosmetics were displayed near patent medicines in see-through glass cases, while exclusive high-end department stores like Mitsukoshi and Takashimaya lent high-class cachet to beauty products purveyed there. Most importantly, customers were reassured of Shiseidō products' effectiveness when company "beauty consultants" wrote them individualized prescriptions to address specific concerns—a practice still currently available.

However, "brick and mortar" retailers like Mitsukoshi were not the only way Shiseidō products were disseminated throughout Japan and its empire. "Miss Shiseidō" mobile beauty salons (*Biyō idō saron*) arrived in 1935 following the selection of a second group of Miss Shiseidō representatives originally intended to staff larger department stores. Beginning in Tokyo, and then extending into domestic Japan's other regions, these new Miss Shiseidōs, armed with pens and prescription pads, instructed women how to scientifically manage modern beauty regimens. According to Michiko Shimamori, editor-in-chief of *Kōkoku hihyo* (Advertising Critique), these encounters empowered female consumers: "Miss Shiseido was, indeed, a beauty messenger carrying the media of self-expression to Japanese women."[70] Only two years later, mobile beauty salons expanded throughout Japan's empire to appear at department and chain stores in areas colonized by Japan, like Korea, Manchuria, and Taiwan[71]—paralleling Japanese military incursions into China after 1937. In addition, Miss Shiseidōs made special visits to local "Camellia Club" meetings for the company's customer loyalty program.[72] Called "beauty missionaries" by Shimamori, they were "taught cosmetic techniques and science, and dermatology; they were also educated in theater, music, Western painting, and other cultural activities. Rather than simply selling cosmetics in stores, they introduced the latest fashion trends."[73] These representatives thus embodied Japanese imperial modernity, fashion, and scientific practices applied to beauty, which strongly correlated with forms of cultural capital and high levels of cultural education. Essentially, through appealing charm extended toward clients, Miss

Shiseidōs actively embodied a Japanese civilizing mission where their methods represented advanced beauty practices emanating from the imperial center.

Theorist Pierre Bourdieu's concept of "cultural capital"[74] as a means of enhancing social mobility certainly applied to Chinese and other East Asian consumers' use of Shiseidō cosmetics like facial powder to acquire fashionable pallor, and seeking to educate themselves about brand-name products' benefits. Clearly, demand by imperial consumers supported Shiseidō's success, aided by expanding distribution in chain stores and smaller shops aside from larger department stores. For Japanese and colonial consumers, these mobile beauty salons represented both embodied and objectified capital, which also attained institutionalized components through the company's reputation for Japanese luxury. The women chosen to represent the company as Miss Shiseidōs possessed idealized forms of beauty. They enjoyed naturally pale skin and graceful physiques enhanced by Western dress—qualities representing embodied capital—while cosmetics used to enrich this inherent, "natural" beauty were a form of objectified capital. Thus, Shiseidō's "beauty missionaries" embodied the company's Japanese imperial modernity, with its incursions into domestic and imperial markets in concert with the Japanese empire's political power.

Here, as in other colonial endeavors, Japanese companies and their representatives led in developing specific images of imperial womanhood for areas under Japan's political, economic, and cultural domination or influence. Clearly, domestic Japanese, and Japan's imperial subjects in colonized China, Taiwan, and Korea, avidly consumed Shiseidō cosmetics despite possible negative political connotations and welcomed the luminous pallor they promised, along with luxurious Western-inspired modernity, including hybrid elements unique to Asia through imperial modernity. However, as Eugenia Lean notes, until the late 1930s, Chinese innovators like cosmetics tycoon Chen Diexian (1879–1940) also offered alternatives: homegrown products adapted from foreign models using local ingredients with advertising emphasizing China's literati culture.[75] Nevertheless, during potentially precarious economic times, Shiseidō adopted a key business strategy marketing Japanese imperial modernity in the colonies.

114   *Chapter 3*

Glimpses into Modern Luxury: Shiseidō's Company Magazines

Precipitated by both natural disaster and human-created economic depressions, in the 1920s, Japanese companies developed innovative strategies to promote business and showcase products to broader population segments. These included more efficient distribution channels and free publications for consumers. Following the devastating 1923 Great Kantō Earthquake in Tokyo that eventually stimulated cultural and economic innovation, the Shiseidō Company initiated a voluntary chain store system where retailers were guaranteed 20 percent of profits if they upheld the corporation's set prices and devoted exclusive spaces to its products.[76] Thus, consumers could shop at any chain store knowing prices for Shiseidō's products were the same everywhere, a practice that helped the company achieve popularity. Consequently, seven thousand chain stores throughout Japan's archipelago soon carried Shiseidō products and purveyed them to a growing middle class of women consumers.[77] As a bonus, customers received a free monthly magazine highlighting the company's commodities amid luxurious modern lifestyles.

With its initial November 1924 edition, Shiseidō established *Shiseidō geppō* (Shiseidō Monthly) as the first such magazine in Japan's cosmetics industry. Any Shiseidō chain store throughout Japan proffered to consumers this company-published journal intended for larger customer segments.[78] Consumers could now satisfy their fascination for Shiseidō products at home in a publication promising useful cosmetic tips and envision exciting modern leisured lifestyles while enhancing their own beauty. Following the 1927 financial crisis that plunged Japan into an economic recession preceding the global Great Depression (1929–1939), Shiseidō pioneered new distribution channels within Japan to stop competitive price-cutting by smaller retailers. This strategy proved successful. In 1929, before the Great Depression's devastating impact, and just prior to its increasingly international moment, Shiseidō boasted a respectable $0.9 million in domestic sales of skin-care products and color cosmetics.[79]

In 1933, the monthly magazine's name changed to *Shiseidō gurafu* (Shiseido Graph),[80] mirroring contemporaneous growth of commonly available pictorials adopting high-quality color printing technologies since the late nineteenth-century advent of chromolithography. Beginning in the 1920s, and based on understanding photography's potentially positive impacts on consumer culture, advertisers in both Japan and the United States started printing in color.[81] Market surveys by Harvard School of Business professor Daniel Starch, author of *The Principles of Advertising* (1923), even revealed that vibrant color advertisements promoted more business.[82] Such colorful snapshots of life enhanced by Shiseidō products made the magazine's commodities appear more "real" to consumers, and thus translated into greater consumption.

The Shiseidō Company published this in-house journal for customers to feature cosmetics and beauty in a lifestyle publication showcasing luxurious, leisured, and Western-inspired aspirational living, often termed *bunka seikatsu* (culture life). Thus, even if consumers could not afford activities enjoyed by "modern girls" and bourgeois families depicted as skiing in the Nagano Alps, playing golf, and enjoying city outings, they could sample them vicariously in photographs displaying "culture life." Consumers might instead purchase lipstick or face powder to resemble the magazine's models, and directly partake in its colorful modern dreams constructed within. The magazine ran until November 1936, at which point it was renamed *Hanatsubaki* (Camellia) to signify the company's logo;[83] around 1937, it began featuring nationalistic covers corresponding to Imperial Japan's invasion of China.

In the 1920s and 1930s, *Shiseidō Monthly* and *Shiseidō Graph* ushered in pictorial glimpses of new, modern lifestyles for women consumers to emulate and follow vicariously, even if the depicted leisure activities were financially infeasible. Thus, Shiseidō's cosmetics became powerful indices of luxurious new modernities for its customers, mostly housewives rather than the media's alluring "modern girls." While domestic labor and household management roles persisted, middle-class Japanese women could treat themselves by using high-quality cleansers and adopting a practical new hairstyle increasingly prevalent in various media, including Shiseidō's.

Everyday Hygiene for Skin and Hair: Luxury Soap and Shampoo for Modern Life

In 1929, Shiseidō's only leading Japanese competitor, Kaō Corporation, specializing in toiletries (for bath and body, along with shaving cream), boasted over twice Shiseidō's revenues at $2 million in total.[84] As was noted earlier, Kaō initially gained repute in the soap industry, establishing itself as purveyor of high-quality Japanese alternatives to

Figure 3.5. Newspaper advertisement for newly formulated Kaō soap, March 1931. Depicted in Gennifer Weisenfeld, "'From Baby's First Bath': Kaō Soap and Modern Japanese Commercial Design," *The Art Bulletin* 86, no. 3 (September 2004): 582.

Western luxury soaps. These midrange cosmetic products grew in the early 1930s with price reductions, while maintaining superior quality, in product lines that expanded to attract broader customer ranges.

Shot by modernist photographer Kanamaru Shigene (1900–1977), a full-page documentary-style March 1931 newspaper adver-

Modern Girls and Salarymen 117

tisement published in leading Japanese newspapers inaugurated Kaō's campaign for its latest product—a newly formulated soap.[85] Kanamaru opened Kinreisha, Japan's first commercial advertising photography studio, in 1926, and he later covered the 1936 Berlin Olympic Games for the Japan Newspaper Photography Association.[86] In 1932, he published the seminal manual *Shinkō shashin no tsukurikata* (The Making of Modern Photography), which included photography from influential Western avant-garde photographers such as Lazlo Moholy-Nagy (1895–1946), Man Ray (1890–1976), and Albert Renger-Patzsch (1897–1966), whose works respectively represented Bauhaus, Surrealism, and New Objectivity.[87] Their influence also appeared in Kanamaru's commercial photography.

The advertisement's text characters run horizontally from left to right in a Western-style reading layout to publicize the day that *shinsei Kaō sekken* (newly formulated Kaō soap) arrived on the market, announcing at the top, *Iyoiyo honjitsu shinsei Kaō no hi* (Today at Last, the Day of New Formula Kaō!).[88] Below this, similarly sized script indicates its 99.4 percent purity and 10 *sen* price, while near the lower right-hand corner, a soap bar floats in space, featuring new modernist packaging and script designed by the parvenue graphic design student Hara Hiromu (1903–1986), who won the company's 1930 art contest.[89] The advertisement features busy montages of workers enthusiastically greeting the arrival of Kaō soap's new formulation before its delivery on trucks to retailers, which resembles a collective military victory celebration. In its upper right-hand corner, several male workers look like soldiers raising their arms in *banzai* ("long live") gestures, while women workers in white aprons throng the streets and trucks with banners announcing the new formulation. Here, the soap is prepared for a great welcome by the masses by a company issuing the new product. Utilizing nationalism as a trope, the advertisement was meant to appeal to broad segments of potential customers from all classes by democratizing a once-unaffordable luxury product. Art historian Gennifer Weisenfeld asserts that "Kaō targeted several consumer groups, with upper- and middle-class urban women initially constituting the major portion of the company's national consumer base. In the process of democratization, the target clientele was expanded to include blue-collar women and their families."[90]

Beginning in the Taishō era, such imagery was influenced by broader currents of what contemporary commentators termed "massification" (*taishūka*) within mass media and mass culture, and even

118   *Chapter 3*

political landscapes, where elements of the state, consumerism, and mass media conjoined to create a sense of simultaneous consumption of modern life, broadened among different social classes and adherents of new political ideologies.[91] In *Taishō bunka, 1905–1927* (Culture in the Taishō Period), social psychologist Minami Hiroshi (1914–2001) proposed a growth of liberalism and democracy as characterizing the era, which nevertheless merged into totalitarianism by the mid-to-late 1930s amid interplay between mass culture and the state.[92] Intriguingly, while democratic institutions grew to encompass more individuals, state control over new rights also increased due to government fears of anticapitalist and communist organizations allegedly threatening Imperial Japan's existing social and economic order. In 1925, the House of Representatives Election Law extended the right to vote to all able-bodied men ages twenty-five and above without records of incompetency, bankruptcy, homelessness, public assistance, or prison sentencing—still marginalizing many working-class men.[93] This was coupled with the 1925 Peace Preservation Law, which severely limited free speech and right of association, thus stifling press criticism, labor unions, calls for socialism, and other forms of leftwing protest, with threatened imprisonment of "groups whose goal is to deny the system of private property or to change our national essence (*Kokutai*, literally "national body")."[94] By the 1928 election featuring (still-limited) universal male suffrage, left-oriented "proletarian" parties had captured only 5 percent of popular votes, which nevertheless frightened authorities and led to massive crackdowns on suspected leftists in March 1928.[95] Advertisements evincing Imperial Japan's tilt toward a fascistic political system also reflected a relationship blurring mass media and state interests.

On September 24, 1931, another smaller, though still noticeable, Kaō advertisement ran in *Asahi Shimbun* six days after the Manchurian Incident, whereby Japan's Kantō Army invaded northeast China.[96] In the days and months that followed, American and British condemnations prompted Japan's government to distance itself from the Anglo-American world, a tendency expressed subtly in commercial advertisements in apparent dialogue with the news. Here, an eye-catching ad—roughly one-sixth the page's size in the "household" (*katei*) section below an article on "new autumn vegetable dishes" and a women's advice column on whitening skin—features a large, steel-girded bridge framing a modern factory complex, completely void of people, resembling many post–Manchurian Incident modernist photographs.[97] The

Modern Girls and Salarymen 119

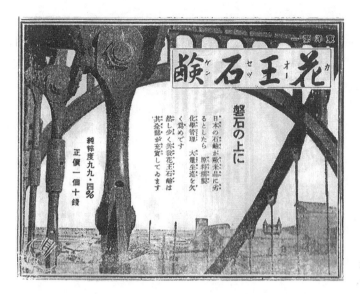

Figure 3.6. Advertisement for Kaō soap in *Asahi Shimbun,* September 24, 1931.

factory itself replaced absent, potentially anticapitalist revolutionary masses, while descriptions of the superior commodity's exemplary properties reaffirmed a Japanese capitalism equaling the Anglo-American West. Horizontal bold black characters for *Kaō sekken* (Kaō soap) (read right to left) appear in a rectangular white box at the advertisement's upper right-hand corner, with *Tōyō dai'ichi* (First in the Orient) in smaller characters directly above.[98] The ad's approximate center hosts the vertical phrase *Banjaku no ue ni* (Upon the monolith), followed by smaller vertical script at left, indicating, "If Japanese soap is inferior to Western products, it is because it lacks the refining of raw materials, chemical [quality] control, and mass production. But at least our Kaō soap is enriched with all of these [aspects]."[99] Here, Kaō places its product on a monumental pedestal above others, with "99.4% purity rate, actual price 10 *sen* each" at the far left—echoing earlier advertisements with advertising copy now entirely in Japanese-style reading layout.[100] Conscious adoption of a nationalistic tone and a more traditional text layout convention represent a growing patriotic tenor suffusing Japanese advertisements amid economic uncertainty at a pivotal political moment of rising nationalism.

In the early 1930s, besides offering reasonably priced luxury soap for budget-minded consumers, Kaō began producing other high-quality cleansers and detergents. Opportunities for increased profit arrived with changing fashion trends favoring certain hairstyles. The short bobs increasingly worn by prewar Japanese women, or the *mimikake* (ear-hiding) hairdos designed to mimic them, spotlighted limp hair, and thus necessitated changes in personal care habits to maintain the new fashion. A decade earlier, longer hair dressed in complicated chignons evoking the new woman, or traditional buns favored by older women, benefited from carefully combed oilier hair that allowed coiffures to remain in place longer. For this purpose, women purchased hair oils such as Shiseidō's Camellia Oil. Yet, without frequent washing, the trendy shorter hairstyles appeared flat, unkempt, or dirty on thick, straight dark hair, despite saving grooming time. With a growing feminine preference for bobbed hair—a mainstay for Japanese girls since the early twentieth century, but now increasingly adopted by trendy, practical, young working women—the company launched a new product.

In April 1932, Kaō shampoo came onto the market, and according to the company's online history, it allegedly caused "'shampoo' to become an everyday word, changing Japanese hairwashing habits."[101] Kaō shampoo's packaging featured the stylized profile of a pale-skinned, dark-haired Western woman, without specific nationality, firmly citing hair-washing as a modern Western practice. In the early Shōwa period, Japanese women washed their hair infrequently, so the product required careful instructions for customers to adopt new hygienic and consumption practices promoted by the company.

However, distinction as Japan's first shampoo, appearing in 1926, rests with Kuzuhara Kōgyō's (Kuzuhara Industries) Modan Shanpū (Modern shampoo) powder, whose formula included antiseptic borax and pH-regulating soda ash.[102] As a boxed shampoo powder, Kaō shampoo also contained similar ingredients but added kaolin and bentonite clarifying clays that bind with oils to neutralize them. From 1938 onward, the shampoo was formulated into a user-friendly liquid with high-quality alcohol, and unlike powder, the bottled shampoo attained higher status in retail locations as a cosmetic instead of an ordinary variety- or drugstore item.[103] Clearly, when small indulgences were increasingly curtailed amid Imperial Japan's burgeoning war in China, the new beautifully bottled formula also made Kaō's signature shampoo appear more luxurious.

Contrasting with the box's initial exterior design, from 1932 onward, Kaō shampoo advertisement posters featured the profile of a long-necked geisha dressed in a traditional red kimono with light-blue underlining and a black obi, along with red lettering announcing the product's price. Notably, the geisha's hairstyle is a modified *takashimada* (high topknot) more reminiscent of newly married Tokugawa-era women. Geisha and others adopting this style originally fixed their hair weekly in an elaborate hairdo hardened with egg whites, and during sleep, laid their necks upon specially crafted wooden or ceramic pillows to maintain the heavy coiffure's neatness: this image highlights the woman's pale white neck as fetishized by traditional Japanese artists and writers. The poster's right foreground hosts the shampoo box, situating modernity in close proximity to tradition, as if the women in the poster and box were conversing.

In Japan, shampoo distinct from soap was a comparatively new innovation, and thus a consumer luxury product, worded in *katakana* used for foreign loan words, while *kamiarai* (hair wash) appears in smaller type near the geisha to clarify the product's intended use. At five *sen,* or one-twentieth of a yen, the shampoo box was relatively inexpensive as an affordable luxury for most middle-class consumers.

Like shampoos geared toward frequent hair-washing, companies formulated new products concurrently with modern lifestyle changes, as growing popularity of scientifically proven methods of cleaning revealed. Advertisements and promotional literature or journals produced by Japanese corporations intimated that potentially "dirty" spaces inhabited by consumers also benefited from "modern" cleansers. Housecleaning was newly framed as "science," and so housewives and servants required educating about correct procedures and proper products. Here, large corporations began replacing the state as purveyors of

Figure 3.7. Poster for Kaō shampoo, 1932. "About the Kao Group: Product Introductions," Kaō corporate website, https://www.kao.com/global/en/about/outline/history/products-history/, accessed July 16, 2021.

122   *Chapter 3*

useful knowledge for regulating and managing domestic matters. These concepts developed into scientific housewifery, an allegedly logical, rational form of household management based on systematic approaches to dirt and order.[104]

In 1934, the Kaō Corporation founded the Housework Science Laboratory, renamed Nagase Housework Science Laboratory in 1937; the postwar Kaō Housework Science Laboratory reappeared in 1954.[105] The company also published the *Science of Housework Magazine* (*Kaji no kagaku*) to support these initiatives. According to Kaō's website, "From 1934 until 1940, the laboratory held 4,536 workshops for a total of 1.5 million participants."[106] Run by male scientists for housewives to rationalize housework, they improved household labor efficiency amid new public health concepts. This paralleled corporations adopting *gorika* (rationalization) to produce more items and extract greater labor from workers in factories or offices. Interestingly, such capitalist regimentation experienced by workers, along with frugality routinely practiced by housewives, greatly benefited the nation as Japan's empire headed into wartime.

CONCLUSION

Following the Great Kantō Earthquake, interwar Japan heralded the embrace of new forms of modernity along with the arrival of myriad new commodities connoting modern life. This included capitalist regimentation of time in workplaces, for which timepieces became necessities; yet, growth of new leisure pastimes for Imperial Japan's middle class balanced this development. Whether drinking spirits at home or in the proliferating cafés staffed by female servers, the *sarariman* could relax while imbibing favored intoxicants. Both factory workers and businessmen at work or play became fodder for an increasing number of films featuring proletarian social issues arising from Japanese capitalism's critical examination.

For women, aspirational lifestyles were widely depicted in varied publications. Even if new sports like skiing or tennis were unaffordable, bourgeois housewives vicariously enjoyed depictions of upperclass leisure activities in women's magazines, including free company publications like *Shiseidō Monthly* and the colorful, image-filled *Shiseidō Graph*. Though modern girls were popularly believed to fuel women's luxury consumption, housewives purchased most consumer items for middle-class households. Advertisers also most often targeted this group.

Newspaper advertisements revealed contemporaneous political trends by evoking nationalism and mass culture, while Japanese companies increasingly offered versions of Western-style luxury in Japan-made products. Their iconic modernist imagery, including photographic modernism, appealed to customers equating such forms with imperial modernity specific to technologically progressive and scientific Japan—a trope also appealing to consumers in Imperial Japan's colonies. Nevertheless, in advertisements and overseas business into East Asia, Japanese corporations soon exhibited close relationships between commercial and imperial expansion after the Manchurian Incident, resulting in intimate connections during wartime.

Chapter Four

FRUGALITY, PATRIOTIC CONSUMPTION, AND THE MILITARY

By the early 1930s into the 1940s, war fever surrounding successive military incursions into Manchuria, China proper, and then Southeast Asia suffused product advertisements—especially for items potentially deemed nonessential luxuries like makeup, liquors, and watches. In July 1940, the Japanese government initiated the frugality campaign "Regulations Restricting the Manufacture and Sale of Luxury Goods."[1] Soon enough, *zeitaku wa teki da* (luxury is the enemy) appeared in advertisements and popular media to incite consumers to save for the nation. Historian Barak Kushner proposes that this phrase was actually coined around 1938 by Miyazaki Takashi, who edited *Kōkokukai* (Advertising World), a magazine covering advertising agency trends[2]—indicating considerable lag time before advertising professionals' key audiences learned of these concerns. After 1940, corporations producing small comestibles like makeup, liquors, and other items likely considered luxuries engaged in various strategies to remain profitable and sustain business. These included patriotic advertising, military procurements, and substitutions for increasingly scarce materials.

As the Asia-Pacific War progressed, advertising featured preparation of troop care packages (*imon bukuro*, or "comfort bags") and intimated how patriotic consumption supported the empire. In particular, women, and sometimes children, were targeted as consumers and convinced that purchasing products could improve their menfolk's morale at war even amid domestic curtailment. When wartime strictures threatened consumer product sales, Japanese companies obtained military contracts for products like soap for Kaō, whisky for Kotobu-kiya (Suntory brand), and perfumes for Shiseidō. Toward the war's end, with intensification of Allied bombings of factories after 1944, consumption of most newly manufactured commodities nearly stopped, with aspirations for survival surpassing luxury and prompting ersatz goods and barter in an ascetic lifestyle allegedly inspired by imperial troops.[3]

Consuming the War: War Fever in Advertisements, 1937–1941

Historian Benjamin Uchiyama's *Japan's Carnival War: Mass Culture on the Home Front, 1937–1945*[4] illuminates the celebratory atmosphere surrounding the 1937 outbreak of war with China, followed by subsequent attacks on the Republican-era Chinese capital (1912–1938) of Nanjing (1937–1938) and the US naval base at Pearl Harbor, Hawai'i (1941), which heralded a "dynamic, improvisational dimension to total war mobilization."[5] He asserts that popular tropes emerged within the mass media and then were consumed as mass culture icons: "the thrill-seeking reporter, the mischievous munitions worker, the tragic soldier, the elusive movie star, and the glamorous youth aviator."[6] These figures motivated enthusiastic publics to follow their exploits in newspapers, films, and posters, forming a thrilling and exciting new sense of wartime nationhood at times otherwise potentially filled with gloom. Some tropes, including soldiers and movie stars, also appeared in wartime advertisements for soap, cosmetics, drinks, and comestibles.

Interestingly, during the Second Sino-Japanese War (1937–1945) and beyond, newspaper advertisements in Japan's leading newspapers like *Asahi Shimbun* communicated strong connections with broader international events, also supported by the nation's business and entertainment establishments. This juxtaposition of news and commercialism intensified during the pivotal Battle of Shanghai (August 13 to November 26, 1937), which revealed heavy Chinese military resistance in the key Yangtze River region in a soon-extended war preceding a mid-November Japanese advance toward Nanjing to hasten China's anticipated capitulation.

On November 7, 1937, the day after Italy joined the Anti-Comintern Pact, an alliance initially signed with Germany on November 25, 1936, as a protection against the Soviet Union, the foreign

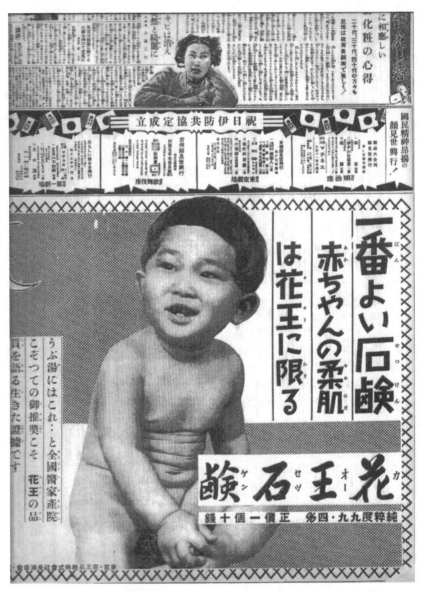

Figure 4.1. Kaō soap advertisement in *Asahi Shimbun,* November 7, 1937. Tokyo: Japan Publications Trading Company, 2008, 104.

Frugality, Patriotic Consumption, and the Military   127

grocery purveyor Meidiya and popular theaters Tokyo Gekijō (Tokyo Theater), Kabuki-za (Kabuki Theater), and Dai-ichi Gekijō (First Theater) ran advertisements congratulating the pact.[7] This endorsement by Tokyo's flagship commercial and entertainment institutions depicts a prominent central banner commemorating this international alliance, complete with Japanese and (fascist) Italian flags festooning both sides and spanning the newspaper's width near the page top.[8]

The announcement also appears directly under an article in the *Katei biyō* (Household Beauty) column on age-appropriate makeup techniques for women in their twenties, thirties, and forties, which begins by mentioning weddings and other occasions arising in the upcoming New Year's season.[9] The column imparts knowledge on how women can look their best at any age, where makeup can conceal acne, freshen appearances, and cause wrinkles to disappear while whitening the face—allegedly, for a good impression at numerous social engagements, and perhaps, to generate interest from potential marriage partners.[10] Though products by Shiseidō or Kaō are not explicitly referenced, as Japan's most popular cosmetic and toiletry companies, their creams, whitening powders, soaps, and toothpastes were particularly sought after by women consumers. Incidentally, a carefully made-up, wistful-looking modern girl with short, permed hair rests upon her arms in the column's midst, seemingly perched over the laudatory Anti-Comintern announcement, while touching behind her neck as if contemplating recent events.[11] Below her photo appears a large photograph of a baby boy.

Intriguingly, the bottom two-thirds of this page is a Kaō soap advertisement displaying a plump, healthy, naked baby boy sitting up happily and smiling at readers.[12] Such imagery mirrors the state's growing pro-natalist policies as Imperial Japan began miring itself in protracted war with China. Like many industrializing countries, 1930s Japan experienced a steep birthrate decrease, which concerned the government for demographic reasons and the need to replenish future soldiers: in 1930, the state prohibited the sale of all birth control devices except condoms, and in 1937 it prohibited birth-control-related publications, while police began hassling activists and doctors imparting related information or performing procedures like abortions.[13] Here, the baby boy is eye-catchingly displayed like an attractive commodity, with the advertisement exhorting "The best soap! Only Kaō for baby's soft skin."[14] Underneath it appears "Kaō soap" in large

128 *Chapter 4*

characters, with smaller words below indicating "purity 99.4%, actual price each piece 10 *sen.*"[15] Just like in Kaō's early twentieth-century advertisements, the company emphasizes high quality at reasonable prices, or affordable luxury for a precious infant son, all supported by endorsements from Japan's medical establishment. To the left of the photo is the corporation's benevolent-looking moon logo smiling at the child, with text below instructing consumers that "[Only] this for baby's first bath—recommended by all the nation's doctors and maternity hospitals. Living proof that speaks of Kaō's quality."[16] Though this particular advertisement never explicitly references war, its placement amid a flurry of war-related news and announcements implicitly connects it to broader national developments.

Curiously, congratulatory advertisements merging commercialism and national news also reflected popular enthusiasm for war during both the Imperial Japanese military's attacks on China's capital in December 1937 and the US Pearl Harbor naval base in December 1941—though by 1941, advertisements were smaller and appeared toward the page bottom. When I began researching *Asahi Shimbun* wartime Japanese advertisements in 2014, I was shocked to discover images of Japanese soldiers with broad smiles marching in lantern parades celebrating the "Nanking Victory" in mid-December 1937. Such images even appeared in toiletry endorsements, for products with scant wartime connections.

An eye-catching, full-page December 11, 1937, Lion toothpaste advertisement, with its upper half composed of a map of Imperial Japan's recent military triumphs in eastern China, featured a soldier and sailor in the ad below gazing happily at four lanterns festooned with "Long live the imperial military!"[17] Between them loomed the phrase "The field which transmits our country's might," while to their left, another message asserted that "Health protects the country."[18] Smaller type urged consumers to thank the Imperial Japanese military and explained toothpaste's patriotic, health-promoting effects, supposedly supporting Japanese-led victory.[19] Lanterns evoked contemporaneous celebratory parades held in Tokyo, which also appeared in other advertisements communicating a jauntily patriotic atmosphere. Notably, this scene featured a cartography of the Imperial Army's westward march along the famous Yangtze River's eastern stretches toward the Chinese capital, Nanjing.[20] In such newspaper advertisements, maps of the Imperial Army's conquered areas in China appeared amid products hawked, highlighting how domestic consumers could use the

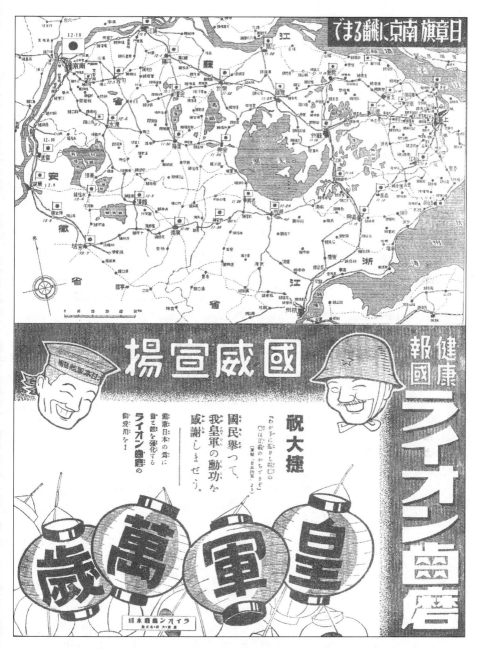

Figure 4.2. Lion toothpaste advertisement in *Asahi Shimbun*, December 11, 1937. Tokyo: Japan Publications Trading Company, 2008, 165.

130   *Chapter 4*

same products as their heroic troops, and thus allowed consumers to feel simultaneous connections to battlefield victories while at home.

Such advertisements certainly reflected a "thrilling" democratization of still vicarious experiences of a far-off war. Since imperial troops at these key moments were engaged in military incursions in distant places, consumers perceived war as little impacting their lives except as spectacular consumption, whereby Imperial Japan's alleged battle successes inspired viewers and readers with the military's triumphant exploits and "honorable" deeds. Advertisements gained a nationalistic flavor where shoppers literally consumed the same products as the army or navy and acquired synchronous pleasure associated with military battles, while sending such products overseas to troops in care packages. As the Asia-Pacific War opened up multiple fronts after 1940, consumers increasingly engaged in patriotic consumption, where purchasing products functioned to express patriotism.[21] More importantly, when products were meant for comfort bags, shoppers gained pleasure in believing that soldiers or sailors consumed them with rising morale allegedly helping to win battles.

PATRIOTIC CONSUMPTION AND DISSEMINATION OF *IMON BUKURO*

Originally developed by educator Yajima Kajiko (1833–1925) during the Russo-Japanese War, *imon bukuro* enjoyed a four-decade-long history of commercialism infused with patriotism from 1904 until the Asia-Pacific War's conclusion.[22] Though English-language scholarship, including mine, usually translates *imon* as "comfort," *imon* literally means "consolation" or expressions of sympathy, condolence, or commiseration—this differs from *ian* ("solace" or "recreation [enabling] peace"), which during wartime, within *ianfu,* translates as "comfort woman," and referred to women recruited or forced into sexual labor for Japanese military brothels.[23] Both words applied to common Japanese civilian (and imperial government) expectations that soldiers and sailors at war required either material or physical purveyance of "comfort" for battle effectiveness. The comfort bag was a roughly shoebox-sized natural cotton drawstring bag printed with simple seasonal patterns and affixed with an address and mailing instructions, later filled with *imonpin* (comfort items), various small, comestible items sent to battlefields as memories of home: candy, cigarettes, toiletries, lipstick, and even tiny handmade dolls. Essentially, small, tangible items of comfort placed into the bag expressed civilians' sympathetic sentiments while not physically present on battlefields with their loved ones. Yet, comfort bags rarely reached their intended individual recipients, and rather, became expressions of generalized comfort, and even luxury amid ascetic battlefield rigors.

However, postcards intended for troops, or *imon ehagaki* (comfort postcards), did allow individuals to express more personalized sentiments to certain soldiers or sailors, and they sometimes appeared as appendices within popular media, like *Shōnen kurabu* (Boys Club), a journal for boys published from 1914 until 1962. *Boys Club* targeted primary- and middle-school boys still forming their identities and viewpoints; the magazine enjoyed vast popularity, with 750,000 copies sold in 1935.[24]

One postcard, attached to a special New Year's *Boys Club* edition dated between early 1938 and 1943, during the military care package practice's greatest prevalence, was captioned "The Military Care Package Is Loaded with Sincerity" and appealed to adolescent male senders with an illustration by Satō Namiko, an artist associated with the magazine.[25] The postcard shows a preteen middle-school girl in a Western-style sailor school uniform, packing a bag and sitting next

Figure 4.3. "The Military Care Package Is Loaded with Sincerity" postcard. East Asia Image Collections, Skillman Library, Lafayette College. https://ldr.lafayette.edu/concern/images/fb494944d, accessed July 2, 2021.

132   *Chapter 4*

to her older sister, who knits a sweater. The young woman wears a colorful floral kimono featuring blue, red, yellow, and white designs, with *furisode* (swinging sleeves) indicating she is a twenty-year-old unmarried woman during *Seijin no hi* (Coming-of-Age Day), a Japanese celebration traditionally held on the second Monday of January. Indeed, during New Year's festivities at home, the postcard's further descriptive text evokes sacrifices of Imperial Japan's "heroes" (*yūshi*) amid a foreign snow-covered plain and contrasts their harsh surroundings with this interior scene of feminine warmth and choice comfort items included in a package prepared by two sisters. The image also reinforces how, in prewar and wartime Japan, providing comfort was a traditionally feminine activity—especially during the holidays. Perhaps, the older girl will soon marry a soldier upon his return, while she also portrays an idealized woman that younger male readers might desire while growing up.

According to Gijae Seo, a wartime Japanese literature scholar, "The editorial department [of *Boys Club*] did not forcibly instill ideas and ideologies into children, but framed a way for children themselves to discover and learn from the magazine."[26] This included the magazine's dynamic use of various media, including appendices with "comfort postcards" or maps, along with exciting stories and cartoons. Echoing Uchiyama, Seo asserts that in consuming *Boys Club*, "Children could prepare themselves as soldiers for the future through the romanticizing of war. Through such efforts, war could be transformed into something that could inspire them with cheer and excitement."[27] Children's ideological mobilization, arguably, turned them into consumers, and it also urged parents to make purchases to express growing patriotism and admiration for troops. Here, mass media functioned to increase consumption even among children, but also extended state power by obfuscating clear distinctions between state and society in the public sphere.[28] Because men were increasingly drafted into Imperial Japan's war machine, targeting women and children on the home front became necessary for corporations to maintain profits after the state deemed many consumer items "luxuries."

This premise also appeared in newspaper advertisements for *imonpin*, like candy, otherwise viewed a luxury with Imperial Japan mired in the burgeoning war with China. On November 10, 1937, in an *Asahi Shimbun* advertisement for Morinaga caramels, a cartoon boy in a soldier's uniform salutes readers, cheerfully exhorting "Let's thank Mr. Soldier!"[29] Smaller print above directs, "Let's give caramels to the

Frugality, Patriotic Consumption, and the Military 133

Figure 4.4. Morinaga caramel ad, *Asahi Shimbun,* November 10, 1937. Tokyo: Japan Publications Trading Company, 2008, 148.

soldiers in a care package to increase their spirit [*genki*]."[30] Here, boys were convinced that although they could only play costumed soldiers on the home front, their purchases would arrive on the battlefield to provide troops with bursts of energy promoting final victory. As fighting progressed, with Japan's military nearing Nanjing while battling Chinese forces from December 1 until complete capitulation on December 13, advertisements expressed a heightened patriotic tenor attempting to attract more customers during a potentially shaky economic time.

On December 12, 1937, a massive half-page *Asahi Shimbun* advertisement announced a congratulatory sale held until 9:00 p.m., including a lottery (*dai-fukubiki*) celebrating Nanjing's fall with free giveaways, held at the Matsuzakaya department store's Ueno branch in Tokyo amid military "victory."[31] Certainly, the sale occurred prior to New Year's festivities, when families traditionally bought gifts, but now, the store prominently indicated availability of comfort items.[32] The image shows the store's entrance to the left, with a determined woman shopper in a chic black coat and hat gazing at the ad's print, while a traditional housewife in a kimono and *haori* (thigh-length jacket) stands behind her, with occasional men in hats and coats amid the crowd. The women depicted in Western-style clothing and traditional Japanese kimono indicate that, regardless of dress and related aspects of class or politics, all women were expected to perform patriotic consumption duties. Here, despite some men accompanying the women, shopping is clearly framed as a "feminine" activity—including purchasing comfort items.

This commercial phenomenon with nationalistic overtones reveals strong connections between popular media like *Boys Club*, mass news media including *Asahi Shimbun*, and Japan's imperial government, in relationships where state and business interests closely intertwine.[33] Such relationships are common in fascism, where the

Figure 4.5. Advertisement announcing a congratulatory sale at Matsuzakaya department store in celebration of Nanjing's fall, *Asahi Shimbun,* December 12, 1937. Tokyo: Japan Publications Trading Company, 2008, 179.

Frugality, Patriotic Consumption, and the Military 135

bourgeoisie and state ally to mold working classes and others into following its designs. The comfort bag phenomenon reached its apex in 1937 to 1945—and particularly flourished from mid-1937 until early 1938, coinciding with the Second Sino-Japanese War's early battles.[34] In *Asahi Shimbun* and other newspapers, articles on *imonpin* for comfort bags instructed women, children, and elderly consumers on what to purchase for troops abroad, while department store advertisements revealed where to buy them. However, not only general media but also employee publications featured comfort bags.

This included company publications like Shiseidō's *Chieinsutoa kenkyū* (The Chainstore Research), a publicity magazine created for Shiseidō company employees that was published from 1935 to 1939.[35] Certainly, company workers, including many women, read the magazine and chose to pattern their actions upon its depicted imagery, like engaging in the popular comfort bag preparation practice, also featured on *The Chainstore Research*'s cover several months following the outbreak of war with China. The phenomenon manifested earlier, following the 1931 Manchurian Incident, where battles to conquer northeast China lasted until 1933, so Japanese women were already familiar with comfort bags and perceived them as boosting morale for soldiers overseas.

The October 1937 cover of *The Chainstore Research* reveals a young woman in a short-sleeved Western-style black dress packing a comfort bag with Shiseidō products such as soap and toothpaste.[36] Clearly, this positive expression of patriotism was also expected of the corporation's female staff. A Japanese *hinomaru* (rising sun) flag appears at the top right, along with four warplane silhouettes framing her gaze into the distance, seemingly considering aviators engaged in aerial bombardment in the Second Sino-Japanese War's early stages. This cinematic scene directly juxtaposes the home front and battlefield without differentiation, and the message intimates that domestic Japan's war efforts are equally important as Japanese planes claiming enemy skies. Here, the publication reveals that even employees at a cosmetics corporation believed they could beneficially affect wartime outcomes. Such media represented the expansion of troop care packages into workplaces of large corporations and news companies, including *Asahi Shimbun*, which sponsored drives or became dropping-off points for comfort bags.

By 1938, preparing comfort bags became an entrenched social practice engaging individuals at all Japanese social levels, including the

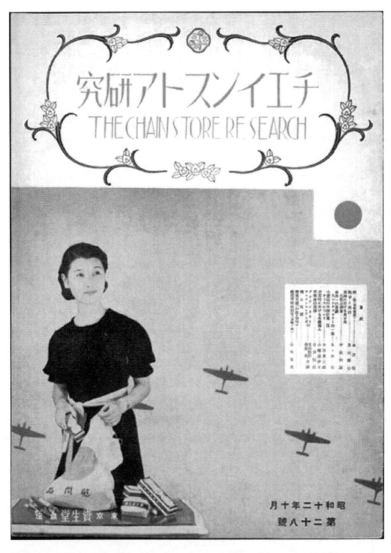

Figure 4.6. Cover of a Shiseidō company magazine with woman packing a comfort bag, October 1, 1937. MIT Visualizing Cultures website, "Selling Shiseido: Cosmetics Advertising and Design in Early Twentieth Century Japan—Visual Narratives: Commercial Advertising and the War," https://visualizingcultures.mit.edu/shiseido_02/sh_visnav07.html, accessed May 21, 2021.

prime minister and the Imperial Household Agency.[37] In early 1939, troop care packages reached mass production peaks, when on January 21, *Asahi Shimbun* reported its office received an unprecedented two million comfort bags in only twenty-five days.[38] Into the early 1940s, comfort bags experienced popularity as indelible components of the commercial landscape. Yet, by early 1944, mass enthusiasm surrounding comfort bags began abating. Civilians continued sending them to continental Asian fronts, but Allied bombing raids on Japan's Pacific sea lanes hindered transport to imperial troops on ships or islands. On January 25, the *Asahi Shimbun* Tokyo morning edition noted that the Imperial Navy declined to accept comfort bags,[39] and the next day in its evening edition, it requested readers to send money instead.[40] Notably, the commercial frenzy surrounding mass production of Japanese military comfort bags by civilians revealed intersections of commercial and business interests promoting Imperial Japan's wartime national interests.

HANATSUBAKI KURABU AND MOTIVATING LOYAL CUSTOMERS WITH INCENTIVE BUYING, 1937–1940

Besides benefiting financially from the comfort bag phenomenon, extending even to toiletries and cosmetics, the Shiseidō Company instituted other measures to ensure modest profitability during wartime. The contemporary experience of periodically buying certain cosmetics in order to receive special-occasion bonus products or limited-edition seasonal gifts is well-established worldwide. As was noted earlier, this business practice began in Japan in the 1930s by companies like Shiseidō purveying consumer products, where a year of customer loyalty and careful coupon collection earned shoppers an exclusive luxury gift. This helped motivate frequent purchases and aided in circumventing long-term national frugality trends, encouraged by both the state and Japanese bourgeois cultural norms.[41]

In November 1937, when the "China Incident" became a fully entrenched war, Shiseidō initiated the *Hanatsubaki kurabu* (Camellia Club) based on incentive buying. The company published a pamphlet explaining each year's reward, which included sections for customers to paste coupons collected with each purchase, and issued a free magazine for shoppers to generate enthusiasm for modern lifestyles featuring Shiseidō's products. In 1938, Japan's government instituted a 10 percent consumption tax on luxury products like cosmetics, so the

138   *Chapter 4*

Camellia Club ingeniously allowed Shiseidō to maintain profits despite greater consumer frugality.[42]

Shiseidō's Corporate Museum and Archives still displays in sleek glass cases perfectly preserved models of elegant "gifts" Shiseidō customers received each year after remitting a complete book of coupons earned with total purchases.[43] All "free" commemorative products were high-quality artisanal luxury items, featuring excellent artisanal craftsmanship of local Japanese metalwork, weaving, or lacquerware in modern designs complementing fashionable women's Shiseidō cosmetics use. Accrued only through purposeful and steady yearly consumption of mass-produced cosmetics, these limited-edition artisanally produced incentive products also generated their own commodity fetishism. When women drew attention to themselves by using these exclusive products in theater or department store powder rooms—new public venues where women freshened up their toilettes—other patrons might ask them about these chic items, and thus, the objects helped advertise themselves. Here, commodities mediate social interaction, an important element of commodity fetishism, while the gifts' additional intent seems to be publicity via spontaneously generated conversations surrounding Shiseidō products.

These Western-style gifts with traditional Japanese elements were only offered yearly, requiring loyal customer practices of repeated purchases over time, which increased their allure and value. Though all were free giveaways, each promotional item was of exceptional collectible quality: the 1937 gift featured a black-enameled art deco silver metal vanity case; 1938 saw a pink brocade clutch purse graced by a camellia and octagonal border; 1939 unveiled a ceramic *obitome* (kimono sash fastener) by Tomimoto Kenkichi (1886–1963), and 1940 marked the advent of a rose-decorated, red-lacquered folding mirror crafted in Shizuoka Prefecture.[44] After 1940, no more incentive products appeared, with luxury now targeted as "enemy," though artisanal or craft items were exempt from regulations prohibiting manufacture of certain luxury goods.[45]

Shiseidō's yearly giveaways even became coveted collectors' items, like Tomimoto's kimono sash fastener. Named a "Living National Treasure" in 1955, Tomimoto received the emperor's "Order of Culture" designation in 1961.[46] From 1908 until 1910, the ceramic artist studied interior design in England; after his return to Japan, he befriended expatriate British potter Bernard Leach (1887–1979), even translating Leach's interactions with *Shirakaba-ha* (White Birch

Group) writers and artists.[47] Originally influenced by William Morris (1834–1896) and the Arts and Crafts Movement, in the 1920s Tomimoto admired the *Mingei undō* (Folk Craft Movement) popularized by philosopher Yanagi Sōetsu (1889–1961).[48] In the early twentieth century, both movements in England and Japan emphasized ordinary people's artisanality and use of natural materials to counter increasingly ubiquitous Taylorization and standardized industrial products[49]— exactly what permitted mass production and large Japanese companies' success like Shiseidō. Wartime incentive gifts offered Shiseidō's loyal customers increasingly rare artisanality following frequent consumption of industrially produced products.

This special club for consumer fans also echoed the company magazine *Shiseidō Gurafu*'s (Shiseidō Graph) 1936 renaming as *Hanatsubaki* (Camellia), described as a "medium at the forefront of the times."[50] *Hanatsubaki,* like its predecessor, was published by Shiseidō as a free pictorial for women customers focusing on cosmetics and beauty, while sharing fashion tips and featuring the arts.[51] The magazine initially promoted products and modern lifestyles and, after late 1937, also drew attention to its new incentive buying club amid wartime frugality.

As the war lingered, magazine covers became increasingly patriotic and nationalistic, emphasizing militaristic themes. Magazine content began to reflect the empire's broader political trends and developments, revealing that Shiseidō understood how modern Japanese women yearned for news featuring current events. *Hanatsubaki* especially depicted women's lives throughout the empire, like in Manchukuo, and even connected their roles to larger propaganda aims. A November 1938 *Hanatsubaki* cover features a resourceful rural Japanese woman whose kimono, obi, and apron reflect the Manchukuo flag's colors. While the cover model's slightly tanned face likely lacked powder or cosmetics, women readers could admire the strength and dignity of "authentic" *tairiku yome* (continental brides) flocking to Manchukuo to marry Japanese settlers in a mission to spread Japan's settlements throughout occupied northeast China.[52]

Other covers reveal more obvious wartime themes. The August 1939 cover showcases a nearly monochrome blue-washed black-and-white photograph of a three-warship flotilla right before World War II's (1939–1945) European outbreak. The lightly colorized January 1940 cover shows a much-revered Mt. Fuji at dawn, indicating the year "2600" to commemorate Japan's mythical 660 BCE founding by

140   *Chapter 4*

the legendary Emperor Jimmu (711–585 BCE). The May 1940 cover reveals two warships, and a black, yellow, blue, and red flag in the bottom right-hand corner referencing the famed battleship *Mikasa,* from which Admiral Tōgo Heihachirō (1848–1934) victoriously fought in the Russo-Japanese War, again with the date 2600. In contrast, the June 1940 cover displays a stylized aerial scene with an airplane shadow imprinted over the landscape, referencing China's inland bombing and prefiguring Indochina's September invasion.[53] The magazine's last issue appeared in August 1940, at which point it succumbed to wartime strictures limiting paper and color usage, and only reemerging in June 1950.

Luckily for Shiseidō, an alluring new celebrity arrived to advertise products domestically and in overseas Japanese colonies and satellite states. Here, association of a popular entertainer with a Japanese company helped "luxuriate" and sell products in a practice resuming in postwar times.

SHISEIDŌ'S ADVERTISING ICON FROM MANCHUKUO: THE ACTRESS AND SINGER RI KŌRAN

In the wartime media of the late 1930s and early 1940s, glamorous models and movie stars embodying Japan's imperial modernity advertised cosmetics to lure frugal Japanese customers during commercially precarious times.[54] Their product endorsements communicated a prewar luxury now increasingly unattainable for domestic consumers while also circulating in exotic realms beyond customers' ordinary experiences. The most famous celebrity was Fushun-born and Beijing-educated Japanese entertainer Yamaguchi Yoshiko, known by her Chinese name Ri Kōran, and also known as Li Xianglan, who played in propaganda films (*kokusaku-eiga*), or *tairiku-eiga* (continental films) produced by the Manshū eiga kyōkai (Manchurian Film Association, or *Man'ei*), including the blockbuster *China Nights* (1940). Appearing onscreen in Chinese dress, Li's Japanese identity was an "open secret,"[55] with Chinese audiences interpreting her films differently than Japanese ones.[56] Japanese viewers first experienced Li as a beguiling new rising talent who appeared in vaudeville actor Enoken's (Enomoto Ken'ichi, 1904–1970) stage show and films like *China Nights,* where she starred with Hasegawa Kazuō (1908–1984). Most Japanese audiences then assumed she was Chinese.

Frugality, Patriotic Consumption, and the Military   141

In 1941, Li's national identity was finally revealed as Japanese, but fans in Japan continued lavishing praise upon the cosmopolitan actress: "Your bewitching continental looks and beautiful voice are just as popular now as when you debuted as a Manchurian actress. Your personality and looks perfectly suit Manchurian, Chinese, Korean, or even Western clothes, depending on how one looks at you."[57] Though Li hailed from a bourgeois Japanese settler family supported by the semigovernmental South Manchuria Railways Company, Chinese audiences were captivated by Li's alluring voice and stunning looks showcasing soft pale white skin. Nevertheless, they were unimpressed by her on-screen presence in roles sympathetic to Japan, and more appreciated her sonorous songs while strongly associating her image with appealing tunes.[58] *China Nights'* signature song, "*Shina no yoru*" (China Nights), was so catchy that Chinese viewers thought of Li more as a singer than an actress, while the song remained popular in Tokyo long after the war, including among American Occupation-era expatriates.[59] According to historian Norman Smith, Li "established a formidable career as a singer, popularizing several of the most beloved Chinese songs of the twentieth century,"[60] which included "*He ri jun zai lai?*" (When Will My Love Return?), "*Mai tang ge*" (The Candy Selling Song), and "*Ye lai xiang*" (Night Fragrance).[61] These songs also became popular in Japan with the star's 1941 Tokyo performances.

In the early 1940s, Shiseidō capitalized on Li's burgeoning success as an actress and singer by hiring her as an advertising icon with easy name recognition and a desirable feminine appearance. Her superior skin quality exemplified Japanese women's allegedly pure-white flawless skin, and her appearances in Shiseidō advertisements symbolized an imperial modernity that consumers throughout the empire could emulate by using the Japanese corporation's cosmetics. In June 1940, Manchuria Shiseidō Company, Ltd. was established as an overseas subsidiary;[62] the company wished to increase market shares among local Chinese populations and Japanese settlers by featuring Li in a commercial poster series as an archetypal Chinese modern girl with a permed bob. Historian Rebecca Nickerson highlights Li's importance as the company's visual "face" during its expansion into northeast Asia: "The message that these ads conveyed was that by using Shiseidō products Chinese women could become 'modern,' even if they could not, as Li/Yamaguchi could if she chose, become 'Japanese.'"[63] Actresses in early twentieth-century China held reputations as style arbiters, and in

142   *Chapter 4*

the commercial public sphere they symbolized a modicum of "liberation" for women—so their images, including those of courtesans, influenced female consumer behavior.[64] The same was true in Japan, where Li's celebrity status truly skyrocketed after a key early 1941 performance series in Tokyo.

On February 11, 1941, held on the yearly anniversary of Japan's mythical 660 BCE founding date, Li performed in three special shows held at Nippon Gekijō in Tokyo's Yūrakuchō ward to honor "Japan-Manchukuo Friendship," where she sang hit songs from *China Nights* and an earlier film, *Sōshū yakkyoku* (Evening Song in Suzhou, 1940). These demanding performances solidified her image as ambassadress of Imperial Japan's intimate relationship with its Manchukuo client state. Her popularity prompted several thousand fans, unable to purchase tickets for any of the three shows, to swarm the theater premises, demanding entrance.[65] Remarkably, between Li's three exhausting singing appearances highlighting Japan-Manchukuo friendship, she posed for Shiseidō's photographers, who used her images for at least two advertising posters later that year geared toward Chinese markets in Imperial Japan's occupied areas.[66] In early twentieth-century East Asia, and especially China, where few women attained literacy, advertising posters were useful in reaching consumers by portraying products and popular celebrities demonstrating their efficacy.[67] Most likely, urban Chinese women with some literacy read advertisements, while literate men certainly purchased products for illiterate spouses; nevertheless, a commodity's visual representation juxtaposed with a famous actress' image allowed broad consumer groups to recognize products displayed in department stores or Shiseidō chain stores.

Such celebrity endorsements included a poster advertising Shiseidō soap that featured Li glancing provocatively at viewers, dressed as a red-lipstick-wearing (Chinese) modern girl framed by a pink ostrich feather fan—a familiar trope in contemporary posters evoking China or Manchuria.[68] The feathers suggest her skin's ethereal softness attained by using Shiseidō products, including luxury soap, and situate her image within a broader context of early twentieth-century publicity for Shanghainese actresses. Covers of the Chinese women's pictorial *Liangyou* (Young Companion), published in Shanghai from 1927 to 1937, often depicted actresses in such poses.

In an advertising poster for *Xuehua gao* (Snowflake Cream), a whitening face cream produced by Shiseidō, described as *Zishengtang laopai* (the Shiseidō "long-standing brand"), Li wears jade earrings and a dark blue silk *qipao* (a modified traditional Chinese women's dress featuring a thigh-high slit) with pink trim, while holding a bouquet of yellow, pink, and light-red carnations interspersed with light pink chrysanthemums.[69] Such flowers intimated multifaceted meanings to Chinese viewers; carnations evoke happy occasions and frequently appear in wedding bouquets. Though traditional Chinese literati couplets once eulogized chrysanthemums as signifying autumn or winter, pink chrysanthemums specifically reference Japan's imperial family, which lends a syncretic, imperialist flavor. Both posters

Figure 4.7. Shiseidō soap ad featuring actress and singer Yamaguchi Yoshiko, known by her Chinese name Ri Kōran, 1941. In Gennifer Weisenfeld, "Marketing Beauty in a Time of War: Ads and Posters, 1937–1941," *Selling Shiseidō II—Cosmetics Advertising and Design in Early 20th-Century Japan: Visual Narratives,* 1941 [sho5_1941_bk177a_soap], https://visualizingcultures.mit.edu/shiseido_02/sh_visnav03.html, accessed July 6, 2021.

144   *Chapter 4*

show a forced-winter peony decorating Li's coiffure—revealing the photographs' shooting during the Chinese New Year holiday, since the flower symbolizes prosperity, good fortune, and love.[70]

In both advertisements, Li models as "Chinese," or as a Japanese star referencing simulated Chinese or Shanghainese on-screen elegance, symbolically placing her within loci now occupied by Imperial Japan—whether Manchukuo or the port cities of Suzhou and Shanghai that were referenced in her films. Clearly, Shiseidō's in-house photographers consciously portrayed her in fashions emphasizing common tropes Chinese viewers associated with glamorous actresses—her fan, direct gaze, short permed hair, flowers, and high-collared *qipao*. According to art historian Ikeda Shinobu, this artistic decision stemmed from assimilationist impulses deriving from Japanese imperialism: "The image of a Japanese woman in Chinese dress signified . . . a hybrid 'China' that Japan sought to disengage from the West and to appropriate as part of the Japanese empire."[71] However, the posters also simultaneously invoke Shiseidō's Tokyo headquarters in displaying a round-cornered diamond-shaped camellia logo with "GINZA" and "TOKYO" written below in capital roman letters, which cites the firm's clearly "superior" Japanese origins.

Thus, the posters' composition alludes to Japanese imperial modernity emphasizing a still-hierarchical cosmopolitanism interwoven with obvious messages of exoticism, which literary scholar Sarah Frederick views as a "possible way to move away from East-West narratives and categories of Orientalism and colonialism as the only factors at work," where "from the Japanese perspective, she (Li) is modern and Chinese, and Japanese."[72] Hence, chimera-like aspects of Li's media presence allowed her to become an important symbol of Manchukuo's hybridity touted in state propaganda featuring alleged *minzoku kyōwa,* or "harmony of the (five) races."[73] In these ephemeral advertisements, as a "Chinese" actress, she helped to sell an exotic vision of continental beauty to Japanese and Chinese customers in Manchukuo and China proper, while purveying Japanese imperial modernity as an entertainer representing both Japan and a Japanese company.

Notably, during my July 2012 interviews with Shiseidō's Tokyo Corporate Culture Division, company representatives indicated they found no other extant advertisements for Shiseidō, nor any involving Li, appearing in Manchuria, Manchukuo, or Shanghai.[74] They also mentioned that art historian Gennifer Weisenfeld had asked them a

Frugality, Patriotic Consumption, and the Military   145

similar question some years before. Most likely, Shiseidō advertisements ran in other Japanese-oriented newspapers and pictorials in northeast China; yet, further research is required by scholars of media like the Chinese-language, Japanese-run *Shengjing shibao* (Shenyang News).[75] Intriguingly, Li's face was found to appear in several Chinese advertisements for her films.[76] Shiseidō posters featuring the actress besides the two referenced above possibly exist in Chinese historical archives or were lost during wartime turmoil and the Cultural Revolution (1966–1976). Shiseidō's official exchanges with two American scholars indicate potential tensions between the company's desire to assist researchers while remaining protective of the firm's colonial past during expansion into then-emerging markets like Mainland China and South Korea, where "history issues" related to wartime Imperial Japan often negatively influence sales—a topic I explore in chapter 6. Li's public disavowal of her role in creating Manchukuo propaganda possibly also contributed, with Shiseidō respecting her wishes to break ties with what she viewed as a shameful past.

Yamaguchi's film career lasted two decades, from 1938 to 1958, when she married diplomat Otaka Hiroshi (1928–2001) and lived briefly in Southeast Asia.[77] Following 1960s-era stints as a news anchorwoman and television host, she served as a pioneering female politician in the Japanese Diet's upper house from 1974 until 1992.[78] In recent years, as the Asian Women's Fund's vice president, she vocally advocated compensating victims of Imperial Japan's wartime military sexual slavery. Feeling "great guilt for having played a Chinese woman useful for Japanese purposes," Yamaguchi indicated acceptance of culpability in acting in films once promoting the Manchukuo regime as sustained by the Japanese Kantō Army's shadow presence.[79] Played by an ethnically Japanese actress in a Chinese woman's guise, her characters were simulacra of how contemporaneous Japanese imperialists believed colonized Chinese women should act and dress. As a prominent Japanese company with imperial overseas markets, Shiseidō provided her cosmetics.

Clearly, Yamaguchi's 1941 advertisements for the corporation were based on Shiseidō's pragmatic strategy to also increase sales of beauty products in occupied Chinese territories lacking wartime Japan's business restrictions. In comparison, domestic Japan was beset by rationing, increased consumption taxes, and draconian prohibitions against luxury item production.

146   *Chapter 4*

Wartime Strictures Transform Luxury in Domestic Japan

In 1938, a 10 percent consumption tax on luxury items dampened sales for high-ticket or nonessential products in wartime Japan. In response, in mid-June 1938, Shiseidō began selling products in overseas territories utilizing Japan's yen, including the Liaodong Peninsula's Kantō district, Manchukuo, and Chinese cities under Japanese occupation.[80] Additionally, the corporation established factories in the port city of Shanghai and in Fushun in occupied northeast China, and it distributed products to local subsidiaries for selling.[81] However, business conditions continued to worsen domestically.

In July 1940, the Japanese government's Ministry of Commerce and Industry and Ministry of Agriculture, Forestry, and Fisheries issued *Shashihintō seizō hanbai seigen kisoku* (Regulations Restricting the Manufacture and Sale of Luxury Goods) in tandem with national mobilization laws; the regulations were intended to shift civilian consumption toward purchasing war bonds.[82] In accordance with the regulations, Shiseidō had to cease manufacturing within Japan twenty-three products labeled "luxury items" (*zeitaku-hin*).[83] Even though makeup could be construed as an unnecessary luxury and thus an "enemy" following rationing's onset and component scarcities, lipstick remained a popular consumer item until the war's end. Despite potential luxury connotations, red lipstick continued selling well during wartime, with its packaging eventually changed to wooden tubes as companies like Shiseidō spared metal for battle necessities.[84] On the domestic home front, urban women considered lipstick an essential beauty item, so quotidian ubiquity among women in towns and urban centers maintained its popularity. In addition, women in large Japanese cities potentially targeted for Allied bombing campaigns even believed that, if properly made up, their corpses were more likely to be treated with respect if they were killed in an air raid.[85]

Lipstick also became a favored item in military care packages. In patriotic consumption intended to boost morale, Japanese women continued to purchase it for themselves, and for menfolk at war as *imon bukuro* contents. Japanese soldiers on battlefields used lipstick to "reward" *ianfu*, or "comfort women," in the empire's comfort stations providing sexual services,[86] and cosmetics also helped "improve" civilian relations, as an adult equivalent to candy for children. Often, lipstick was bartered for difficult-to-obtain commodities like cigarettes or other necessities, and therefore it was extremely valuable for military care packages.

Interestingly, lipstick escaped the government's designation as a prohibited luxury item because of possibly negative effects upon morale and expected women consumers' outcry. Women volunteers in munitions factories, likely targets of Allied bombing campaigns reaching Japan by November 1944, even received special rations of Shiseidō's signature red lipstick, allegedly to maintain positive spirits and attract productive volunteers. In 1944, wood supplanted aluminum lipstick containers, though Marumo Toshiyuki, curator of Shiseidō's Corporate Archives, asserts that lipstick formulations remained identical despite its humbler packaging.[87]

Limited access to strategic materials, including steel, aluminum, and glass, engendered packaging innovations that somewhat eroded Shiseidō's name-brand luxury reputation. Bakelite or cardboard replaced the metals previously used for cans, containers, and boxes, and ceramics replaced glass. In 1938, Shiseidō had instituted an innovative recycling program to support the war effort. In August 1940, *Hanatsubaki* fan magazine articles encouraged Camellia Club members to return empty bottles to collection boxes in urban or regional chain stores and outlets festooned with the slogan, "Even one bottle [is] a resource for the rise of Asia."[88] This campaign incidentally coincided with the magazine's last issue, circulating in Tokyo, Osaka, and other large Japanese cities, while the company expanded advertising strategies abroad.

By 1940, wartime strictures had affected most aspects of Shiseidō's production, leading the corporation to recalibrate its attention to daily-use pharmacy items over luxury products—producing toothpaste in 1940, manufacturing Isabistin laxatives in 1941, and developing Hifumoto salve in 1942, while a luxuriously named Ginza *sappon* (*savon,* or "soap" in French) joined Japan's nationwide rationing system, thus democratizing luxury during wartime.[89] However, in 1943, the 10 percent wartime luxury consumption tax increased to an astonishing 120 percent, which essentially halted cosmetics production; all beauty salons also were required to close.[90] Besides creating products like soap for Japan's government rationing program, Shiseidō remained afloat in 1945 through state procurements. Other companies producing toiletries, such as Kaō, experienced a similar trajectory.

148 *Chapter 4*

Luxury Products for the Military and Government: Procurement Contracts for Japanese Companies

In July 2012, I was warmly welcomed to the Kaō Corporation's museum and archives in Tokyo's Sumida ward, where corporate representatives kindly placed a small American flag on a table by the reception desk.[91] This subsidiary is separate from the corporation's global headquarters, currently located in the Nihonbashi-Kayaba-chō area of Tokyo's Chūō ward. Later, I observed exhibits at the attached public access corporate museum portraying how the company publicized its history to general audiences.

I was hosted by public relations specialist Machida Saori, who courteously ushered me into a small meeting room featuring archivists and staff pleased to share their corporation's history with me. Amid their presence, I viewed a promotional video about Kaō's history, and then, while wearing the provided white kid gloves, I enthusiastically perused prewar documents and product labels. Company employees later scanned several into a CD for my use. However, they also warned that the multiple soap formulas and labels indicating the company's extensive operations in occupied Nanking after 1937 could not be scanned, because if they were published, Kaō's China-based sales could be negatively impacted.

Nevertheless, the company representatives extended great kindness and hospitality, and they seemed delighted that a researcher would give their corporation free, and hopefully, positive publicity. However, they politely requested that I not publish aspects of the company's wartime history. Clearly, Kaō Corporation boasts a long history of military soap and toiletry production, beginning when Japan's navy began to purchase Kaō soap in 1890—endorsements appeared on labels for the same soap produced for civilians. In 1938, during the so-called China Conflict, Kaō unsurprisingly procured military contracts from Japan's government, and it produced soaps in Nanking after the city's brutal defeat and occupation by the Imperial Army.[92]

Due to my previous research on Manchukuo, company representatives mentioned a Kaō soap factory in Shenyang, then known in Japanese as Hōten (Fengtian in Chinese, Mukden in English), where foreign prisoners, including Americans, were given the "opportunity" to work, which potentially saved their lives, as POWs' fates could spell death in Imperial Japan's harsh prison camps or controversial biological weapons research Unit 731 near Harbin.[93] My hosts framed the

Kaō Corporation as Manchukuo's "Schindler"—referencing Nazi Party member Oskar Schindler (1908–1974), who saved Polish Jews employed in his factory during the Holocaust.[94] There are indeed some similarities.

Hirai Hirokazu, an economic historian, indicates that in December 1937, Manchukuo's government issued a new law where prisoners' work incomes covered prison expenditures rather than taxes, and under this new public accounting system, Mukden Number Two Prison (designated for foreigners, likely Chinese and Allied prisoners of war) later became Manchuria's largest soap manufacturing facility in cooperation with Kaō.[95] In 1940, at the Manchukuo government's "request," Kaō Corporation set up Manshū Kaō (Manchuria Kaō) in Hōten to produce soap and other products.[96] Here, soap production by this Japanese company used local and regional materials, like Manchurian hardened soybean oil and Korean hardened fish oil.[97] According to economist Sunaga Noritake, Mukden Number Two Prison Soap Factory (Hōten Dai-ni Kangoku Sekken Kōjō), managed by the Manchuria Kaō Soap Company, used prison labor to supply nearly all of Manchukuo's demand for cosmetic soap production.[98] Notably, he revealed that luxury soaps were produced by POW labor for a Japanese company to maintain wartime profitability.

In Japan proper, the wartime Japanese government also pressed the Shiseidō Corporation into service for strategic purposes. In the early 1940s, Prince Konoe Fumimarō's (1891–1945) cabinet enacted public-private corporations, called *eidan* (management foundations), during wartime mass-mobilization to more effectively manage government resources in corporatist structures loosely resembling Italian fascism.[99] In autumn 1944, Japan's Trade Corps (Kōeki Eidan) emerged under the Ministry of Commerce during wartime mass-mobilization. It soon tasked Shiseidō to produce large amounts of high-quality perfumes, lotions, creams, and makeup products in a little-known secret government project hiring temporary workers amid men's drafting to battlefields and young women's compulsory factory work.[100]

These high-quality export perfumes and other products were ostensibly sold at high prices (with relatively low volume) in exchange for strategically useful materials, like tungsten, valuable for alloys and weaponry, and copper, an important component of electronics, communications, and metal alloys. In areas bordering Japan's empire, China and Russia harbored global tungsten[101] and copper[102] reserves, with a neutral Soviet Union as a likely market for expensive foreign

150   *Chapter 4*

perfumes despite authoritarian communist rule under Joseph Stalin
(1878–1953). Shiseidō's perfumes produced in 1945 included amber-
colored Fantasy and Deluxe scents: a tall, masculine bottle wrapped
in a parchment-paper-like box, and a wider-based, feminine flask with
a ball stopper and small gold-ribboned neck.[103] After defeat, other
Japanese companies relabeled products commandeered by the Trade
Corps and, under command of American Occupation authorities under
General Headquarters (GHQ), sold them all in barely a month on the
open market.[104] Clearly, wartime privations caused pent-up demand
during peacetime, when Japanese consumers again desired small luxuries amid brightening economic and social climates.

　　Nevertheless, wartime procurements for soaps and other toiletries aided the Kaō and Shiseidō corporations in remaining economically viable—and arguably, even allowed them to quickly revive after
the war due to almost-continuous production. Other industries producing luxury products also benefited from these practices, including
whisky manufacturers.

Drinking Away One's Troubles: Whisky during Wartime, 1937–1945

During the Asia-Pacific War, Imperial Japan's two largest manufacturers of whisky were Kotobukiya, producing Suntory whisky, and Dai
Nippon Kajū Kabushikigaisha (Great Japan Juice Company, known
as Nikka Whisky Distilling Company after 1952), which began offering Nikka whisky in 1940. The wartime climate deeply influenced both
companies as important military suppliers. Bottled whisky, unlike beer
or sake, fortuitously survived long voyages, vigorous jostling, and extreme temperature fluctuations en route to battlefields or battleships,
for troops to enjoy this useful comfort.

　　A long-standing tradition persisted in supplying Japan's Imperial
Navy with a similar "rum ration" as Great Britain, which provided
an initial model for Japan. The British Navy's rum ration existed since
the mid-seventeenth century following the 1655 capture of the
Caribbean island of Jamaica; however, by the Edwardian period
(1901–1910), English naval reformers viewed it as a "barrier to opti-
mal crew efficiency."[105] Hence, this daily ration served at dinnertime
in a "tot" glass was reduced to "one eighth of a pint of spirit," or a
relatively modest two ounces diluted with six ounces of water.[106] During the Sino-Japanese War, Japan's navy received three ounces of sake

Frugality, Patriotic Consumption, and the Military 151

(15–16 percent alcohol) or other higher-alcohol substitutes (rum and whisky, 40 percent alcohol) per day.[107]

In the early twentieth century, the navy's head physician, Admiral Baron Saneyoshi Yasuzumi (1848–1932), traveled throughout Great Britain and Europe to observe Western medical practices and wrote a treatise on naval medical techniques perfected during the previous war[108] that highly praised liquor's benefits: "For, in exposure to severe cold, or heavy rain, the use of spirits stimulates the action of the skin and is a great preventative against catching cold; after severe labour, it recreates strength; when the digestive power is dull during the hot season and the heart gets weakened, it is a stimulant. It also raises the spirits and gives hilarity when on lonely expeditions; and many other benefits can be obtained from the use of liquors."[109] He advocated additional spirit rations whenever sailors experienced certain conditions: "During the voyage in stormy weather, after rowing in rough water, coaling, fighting, and in severe cold below freezing point, and at the time of sentinel duty in the dead of winter, 6 ounces of Japanese *sake*, or one ounce of spirits (rum, brandy, or Japanese *shōchū* diluted with water) was officially given."[110] This extra alcohol amount was further supplemented by gifts from friends or purchases at the ship's canteen of up to six ounces for personal evening consumption, plus more on Sundays and holidays.[111] As recommended by Admiral Saneyoshi, Japan's early Meiji navy began following a merit-based liquor incentive policy believed to support wartime good health and morale. Hence, liquor was not viewed as a luxury, but as a necessity, from the very beginning of modern Japanese success in naval warfare. Such convictions continued into the Second Sino-Japanese War with military procurement of whisky, now increasingly popular among male drinkers.[112]

Though Suntory's precursor company, Kotobukiya, unveiled Japan's first whisky, Shirofuda (White Label) in 1929, it was initially unpopular among consumers due to its smoky, peaty flavors. Success arrived nearly a decade later, coinciding with Japan's midsummer 1937 invasion of north China. In 1937, a few years after Suntory's distiller Taketsuru Masataka (1894–1979) left to create his own distillery, Torii Shinjirō (1879–1962) adjusted the peat's burning, fine-tuned various blends, and finally developed his masterful Suntory Whisky Kakubin (Square Bottle), Japan's first authentic whisky with a consumer following.[113] Soldiers, and men soon drafted into the military, developed a taste for the increasingly popular Kakubin, and yearned for its

152   *Chapter 4*

smooth taste and high alcohol content everywhere they went. The next year, the company unveiled Suntory Whisky Kakubin-pokketo (Pocket-Sized Square Bottle), the popular spirit's smaller-sized and conveniently portable version.[114] While available records omit corroborating this claim, easier battlefield transport may likely have prompted a smaller bottle's release.

In 1939, Kotobukiya began producing whisky specifically for troops as Imon-yō Santorii Uisukii ("Comfort-Use" Suntory Whisky).[115] This was followed by Old Suntory Whisky Kuromaru (Black Ship) in 1940,[116] referencing US Commodore Matthew C. Perry's (1794–1858) steam-belching "black ships" employed for "Gunboat Diplomacy" forcing open Tokugawa-era Japan, that also brought the nation's first gifts of whisky on March 13, 1854.[117] However, after the outbreak of the Pacific War in 1941, Kotobukiya experienced the Imperial Navy's requisitioning of its main factories for aviation fuel production, including the Osaka factory and Akadama wine-making facility. Limited commercial access to whisky was further hampered after the navy requisitioned the Yamazaki Distillery and provided barley for Ikari [Anchor] brand Suntory whisky specifically produced for naval officers in 1943.[118] The cream-colored bottle label, framed in a yellow Western-style crenellated border, unsurprisingly featured an anchor atop the whisky's signature red dot logo bisected by white *katakana* (phonetic Japanese script for foreign words) lettering for Suntory.[119]

Although Suntory's Hokkaidō-based competitor, Dai Nippon Kajū Kabushikigaisha, steadily lost money until 1938, the company soon garnered military supplier status and favorable rationing for coal and other supplies, allowing it to earn massive profits until the empire's defeat.[120] Nikka whisky, first produced in 1940, was specifically allocated to army officers, but limited amounts also appeared on the commercial market. Advertisements by celebrated modernist woodblock print artist Okuyama Gihachirō (1907–1981) included a Hokkaidō black bear in profile with a red scarf tied around his neck, cradling a whisky bottle with a bear stopper.[121] Okuyama also completed woodblock prints in 1939 depicting a heroic statue of company founder Taketsuru, and a 1943 woodblock series of five prints showing the Yoichi Nikka whisky distillery's nearly deserted placid northern scenery, where a single laborer shovels coal into stills and another rolls a barrel; other prints show gray stone buildings evoking foreboding monumentality.[122] After the Yoichi facility bottled the whisky, it arrived at the Army Transportation Department's shipping unit, or Akatsuki (Dawn) Unit in Otaru, once Hokkaidō's busiest trading port with the Anglo-American world. In summer 1942, with Japan's Aleutian Islands invasion and occupation, the whisky even traveled to North America after the military placed its order, which the company now conveniently bottled in unbreakable cans labeled *hige-uisukii* ("beard whisky"),[123] possibly referencing the military's lack of time for shaving during battles.

The war also impacted other aspects of Japanese whisky production, curiously imparting industry benefits. After 1941, with the Pacific War's intensification, foreign oak from the enemy United States and Great Britain was no longer imported for casks; hence, Japanese-made whisky thereafter was imbued with specifically "Japanese" flavors from barrels of *mizunara* (*Quercus crispulus,* Japanese oak) used to age the liquor.[124] Interestingly, this special wartime measure by Japanese whisky producers made a future impact on contemporary whisky sales as a rare luxury item. If aged in barrels now running at $6,000 per cask of *mizunara,* a resinous wood from trees over two hundred years old used for building temples and incense production, contemporary Japanese whisky commands a steep price due to the wood's rarity and celebrated "complex notes of sandalwood, coconut, spice, and Japanese incense."[125] Originally designated to comfort Japan's military amid imported oak scarcities, this unique indigenous wood-imbued whisky is now a highly coveted luxury commodity.

The 1944 to 1945 Allied bombing campaigns on the Japanese mainland negatively impacted production and led to survival measures by the two major whisky producers. The Yamazaki Distillery's promotional website states that Kotobukiya's owner Torii "brought his barley and whisky into a bomb shelter to protect it from air raids"[126] and posits, "If he hadn't saved the whisky, it would have been impossible to resume production immediately after the end of WWII."[127] A special bomb shelter was dug in the Yamazaki valley to stash precious reserved barley and aging whisky barrels under bamboo and vegetation to hide them from looters.[128] Nevertheless, Allied fire bombings completely destroyed the company's Osaka facility, including the Akadama sweet wine factory. The Yoichi Distillery in Hokkaidō escaped destruction but suffered barley shortages and logistical challenges getting whisky to the navy when the victorious Allies increasingly dominated shipping channels.

However, alcoholic beverages were not the only necessary "luxury" commodities produced for Japan's military during wartime; timepieces were also deemed essential. In 1940, when watches fell under

154 *Chapter 4*

the state's luxury prohibitions, the Japanese watch industry welcomed this survival measure.

Seikō's Military Watches, 1940–1945

In 1938, during the early Second Sino-Japanese War, the Seikō company produced a staggering 1.2 million timepieces per year.[129] A year later, Japan's entire watch industry manufactured over five million units at its peak before scarcities of metals and strategic materials began cannibalizing production.[130] The July 1940 "Regulations Restricting the Manufacture and Sales of Luxury Goods" made illegal the sale of wristwatches priced over 50 yen.[131] According to labor historian Chimoto Akiko, Japanese government officials earned average monthly salaries of 104.20 yen in 1939 to 1940, and 115.37 yen in 1940 to 1941,[132] so such wristwatches then cost nearly half of a middle-class family's monthly income. This was a considerable expenditure when the government exhorted to Japanese that "luxury is the enemy" and steered them toward higher savings rates and war bond purchases.[133] Nevertheless, when watch companies were hampered from producing high-end products, the industry's most successful leader responded by enthusiastically purveying timepieces and other instruments for the military.

Because Seikōsha was Japan's largest, and best-equipped, watch company, in 1938 it had garnered an exclusive contract to manufacture watches for the military while increasingly producing precision instruments for airplanes and other wartime conveyances.[134] These chrome-plated watches resembled civilian counterparts with a "manually wound calibre, small second, 24-hour dial with Arabic numerals and a chrome case"[135] but differed in decoration. For each branch, watches "had either an anchor (navy), a star (army) or a cherry blossom (air force)," while models for pilots "featured radium hands and dial for better visibility during night flights."[136] Though comparable in size to other nations' military watches, these Seikō-produced wristwatches were relatively small and functional, but not adapted for special conditions beyond usual durability and reasonable accuracy.[137]

The war's intensification and progression over larger portions of neighboring China and wider Asian continental swathes also spelled greater demand for aerial bombers. Hence, Seikōsha's watch manufacturing evolved to meet specifications for aviators, portrayed as heroes in popular media. In 1940, the company unveiled the Tensoku (*Tentai kansoku,* "astronomical observation") *tokei* (watch), a huge, functional 48.5-millimeter-wide watch with a large radium dial used by Japanese aviators to navigate.[138] The Tensoku was inspired by the German Luftwaffe's 55-millimeter watch, conceived in 1935 and perfected in the late 1930s, called the *Beobachtungsuhr* (observation watch),[139] or B-Uhr, supplied to the Luftwaffe by one Swiss and four German manufacturers during World War II, including A. Lange & Söhne, Wempe, and Lacher & Co. (Laco).[140] The Japanese military's version perfected by Daini Seikōsha (Second Seikō Company) in its 1937-built factory[141] contained special innovations. Nickel-coated to save valuable steel for war efforts, the aluminum-case watches were initially calibrated from pocket watches, included an extra-large onion-shaped winding knob suitable for gloved hands, and contained the same high-quality 19-ligne movements as pocket watches; however, these high-quality specifications were downgraded as wartime progressed.[142]

Due to the Tensoku's size, pilots wore it around their thighs for convenience, or around their necks, and sometimes stashed it into a small receptacle in iconic Mitsubishi A6 M "Zero" fighter planes, found near the instrument dial's upper left-hand side.[143] Interestingly, this purported association with the Zero recently caused the Tensoku watch to skyrocket in value as a "kamikaze watch" in contemporary collectors' circles, despite not being specifically issued to special attack force pilots.[144] These particular watches were (and still are) scarce, since most pilots actually used pocket watches hung around their necks. Few surviving Japanese aviators might have believed that over seven decades later, these watches would become coveted luxury items in global auctions: at the November 2018 Geneva Watch Auction, one sold for 23,750 Swiss francs, or 26,483.20 US dollars—*twice* its anticipated price.[145]

Such military procurements helped Seikōsha stay afloat as a Japanese watch manufacturer while the government cracked down on "unnecessary" luxuries, including common consumer goods like watches. Nevertheless, fear of the war's progression onto Japan's four main home islands prompted several key watch companies to move their manufacturing facilities to Nagano Prefecture's Japanese Alps. In 1943, Seikō opened a factory run by Daiwa Kōgyō (Daiwa Industries, Ltd.), a cooperative company of Daini Seikōsha (later, a joint venture company),[146] which was a watch-parts supplier established in

156   *Chapter 4*

1942 by a former Seikō employee in Suwa within the Nagano Alps.[147] The Citizen Watch Company also opened a Nagano-based production facility in Iida City. These were wise moves, as Allied bombing raids destroyed Citizen's and Seikō's Tokyo-based factories.[148] Interestingly, these relatively remote factories allowed both companies to rapidly revive postwar business when economic conditions began improving by the late 1940s.

PRODUCTION FACILITIES, PURVEYORS, AND DEPARTMENT STORES TAKE A HIT, 1944–1945

Although Japanese already suffered from wartime exigencies intensifying with the Pacific War's arrival, it was not until 1944 that the war's destruction truly impacted domestic Japan's infrastructure and quickly eroded civilian morale. Beginning in June 1944, bombing campaigns conducted by B-29 Superfortress aircraft under the US Army Air Corps XX Bomber Command led by Brigadier General Kenneth Bonner Wolfe (1896–1971) brought the war's battlefront to mainland Japan and slowly began destroying industrial production. According to the *United States Strategic Bombing Survey*, when American planes flew at an average of 30,000 feet over Japan, less than 10 percent of bombs reached their intended strategic targets; even so, they brought widespread destruction to infrastructure and the lives of Japanese civilians.[149] This posed problems for the US military, which desired accurate, precision bombing to hasten the Pacific War's conclusion.

In late August 1944, General Curtis LeMay (1906–1990) arrived to take charge. After months of little success with high-altitude bombardment using conventional bombs, he switched to a strategy based on low-altitude nighttime bombing with napalm-containing firebombs and incendiaries, whose ensuing fires soon decimated urban production while causing massive civilian death tolls. LeMay understood that a mid-February 1944 evening attack on Germany's city of Dresden effectively killed tens of thousands of people (more recently determined by historians as 25,000 dead in several Allied raids) in one military operation using this new ordnance, while considerable residential areas were also destroyed in ensuing firestorms.[150] Concurrently, US troops were mired in protracted battles with Imperial Japan's army for the strategically important island Iwo Jima, intended as an American bombing base upon victory. This hastened more Allied bombing incursions into the domestic archipelago.

Frugality, Patriotic Consumption, and the Military

In early March 1945, the XXI Bomber Command's raids under LeMay's leadership began inflicting major damage upon Japan's urban centers to erode the Japanese government's persistence in fighting.[151] Late on March 9 and early on March 10, American planes exacted what LeMay arrogantly called "the most devastating raid in the history of aerial warfare" upon Tokyo, with lethal napalm-enhanced ordnance destroying 25 percent of the city and leaving over 84,000 dead and 90,000 wounded[152] (185,000 total casualties, according to the *United States Strategic Bombing Survey*).[153] Amid the steady hail of 1,665 tons of bombs, including "500-pound E-46 napalm-carrying M-69 incendiary bombs," over a million Tokyo inhabitants lost their homes, while 270,000 buildings succumbed to destruction.[154] Notably, on May 23 and 24, LeMay again initiated two devastating full-scale attacks on Imperial Japan's capital city; here, 502 B-29 Superfortress bombers engaged in two of the war's worst Allied firebombing attacks on central Tokyo, further destroying over 44 square kilometers with incendiary bombs.[155] Similar to catastrophic firestorms following earlier American and British raids on Berlin and Dresden, these burning maelstroms caused by napalm-fueled incendiary bombs spun out of control throughout the city and sucked oxygen from sheltered pockets as mile-high raging fires rendered the nighttime sky bright as day.

In the war's last two years, Allied bombs devastated most of Japan's manufacturing facilities and factories as particularly sought-after targets. The Kaō Corporation's wartime fate reveals Allied impacts on production. The company's first factory, built in Tokyo's Azuma area after the 1923 Great Kantō Earthquake, was completely destroyed in 1944. The corporation's original iconic modernist Tokyo headquarters dating from January 1931 also succumbed to the flames. In late 1944, seven out of twenty-six factories specializing in fatty acid production were damaged, harming 22.5 percent of 123,630 production tons, with fourteen out of forty-six soap factories impacted, and 38.3 percent of 161,310 tons of soap lost.[156] By 1945 the Kaō Corporation's highest rate of soap production was only 24,000 tons, or a mere 9 percent of 1939 peak production levels.[157] At the war's conclusion, Allied bombing campaigns had clearly decimated production.

In this atmosphere of ever-encroaching destruction and growing anxiety spurred by air-raid sirens announcing impending attack, Japanese civilians were increasingly prompted by survival concerns, rather than purchasing small luxuries to enhance personal or troop

158   *Chapter 4*

morale. Any consumption diminished starkly—whether for necessities or even food. Amid multifaceted severe circumstances alongside heightened danger, ordinary Japanese became more distrustful of government pronouncements. According to the *United States Strategic Bombing Survey*, "Progressively lowered morale was characterized by loss of faith in both military and civilian leaders, loss of confidence in Japan's military might and increasing distrust of government news releases and propaganda."[158] Personal attitudes reflected this, revealing progressively more stressful experiences of war: "People became short-tempered and more outspoken in their criticism of the government, the war and affairs in general."[159] Nevertheless, vocalization of personal distress never coalesced into organized resistance as the citizenry generally complied with government rules despite increased grumbling.[160]

Exhibits in Tokyo's Shōwa Museum strikingly reveal wartime's anxious climate as experienced by ordinary Japanese in mainland Japan. During June 2014 and July 2018 research visits, I examined exhibits and interacted with contemporaneous material objects in a national museum dedicated to preserving the wartime period's public history in promoting government agendas for peace.[161] A museum docent kindly allowed me to "experience" the war in donning an air-raid hood, personal protection gear still used by Japanese children from preschool onward to protect against falling objects and flames during fire-generating earthquakes.[162] In an exhibit on wartime schoolchildren, I particularly noticed the *hinomaru-bentō* (Japanese flag lunchbox), a patriotic meal resembling the Japanese flag composed of white rice and one *umeboshi* (salted preserved plum) voluntarily eaten by schoolchildren and others sympathizing with troops fighting overseas, newly popularized after September 1939 following the Nomonhan Incident (May 11 to September 12, 1939).[163] Most Japanese troops in the field were provisioned with rice, but no *okazu* (side dishes), and needed to forage, requisition, or seize food in areas they invaded.[164] By 1942, even rice, a usual staple for middle-class to upper-class Japanese, became a luxurious commodity exclusively enjoyed by high-ranking military members, the wealthy, and rural farmers.[165]

Lack of adequate food compounded wartime stressors, with the war's final two years revealing particular hardships for Japanese civilians. Historian Samuel Yamashita, the first scholar writing extensively in English about the effects of diminished food sources on ordinary Japanese during the Pacific War, named a book chapter "No Luxuries until the War Is Done" in alluding to a popular wartime phrase.[166] In

1940, the Japanese government began exerting control over food distribution, with sugar and dairy products in Yokohama, Nagoya, Kyoto, and Kobe voluntarily rationed in July, prices for forty vegetable types fixed everywhere in the same month, seafood prices limited starting in September, and government control over rice production initiated in October.[167] April 1941 saw food distribution systems begin in Japan's six largest cities based on ration coupons for "daily necessities,"[168] while that September, allotments for most daily staples were set at monthly per-person rations for meat, fish, miso, salt, soy sauce, and cooking oil—with these, especially rice rations, falling precipitously as the war continued.[169] By 1944, most Japanese consumed a stringent 1,900 calories per day, which dropped to only 1,600 by summer 1945, although heavy industry and coal mine workers were allotted slightly higher rations.[170]

Just procuring food expended much energy in a task falling to middle-aged married women or children, since most men between the ages of fifteen and forty-five had been drafted, with young women tasked with factory work to compensate for lost manpower. A 1942 government survey indicated that "a family of five spent an average of four and a half hours a day standing in line for food," while "by 1944 Tokyo 'had lines of about a hundred people' in front of food shops."[171] Largely self-sufficient rural families growing food fared better, while urban working and middle classes were often forced to rely on the black market or barter heirlooms for food with farmers from the countryside. Poor nutrition, along with laborious means to acquire rations, took a toll on consumers and dampened desires to shop for anything beyond food.

Clearly, Imperial Japan's multifront war in China, Southeast Asia, and the Pacific caused dreadful circumstances for Japanese subjects and companies amid a burgeoning state rationing system supported by national and personal desires to shirk even small luxuries in sympathy with troops far afield or afloat. According to business historian Rika Fujioka, Japanese commercial endeavors withered considerably in domestic Japan, where wartime impacts constituted formidable obstacles to commerce: "sales amounted to 886 million yen in 1941, but plummeted to nearly half of this level within four years— to 462 million yen in 1945."[172]

During the war, a plethora of unsurmountable challenges particularly plagued domestic department stores while providing opportunities for those in Japanese colonies. Mitsukoshi, Japan's largest department

160   *Chapter 4*

store, lost sales due to declining inventory, shifting demand, and uncertainty from wartime conditions, including damage by Allied bombings after 1944. However, Imperial Japan's colonies in Manchuria (Dairen) and Korea, which benefited from relative political stability and few direct wartime impacts, helped recoup lost revenues. Hence, Mitsukoshi's overseas subsidiaries in Seoul and Dairen, whose floor space of approximately 7,500 square meters resembled Sapporo's branch, performed stunningly during wartime, when "sales in the Seoul branch amounted to 11 million yen in 1943, compared with 6.8 million yen at the Dalian branch, and only 2.9 million yen at the Japan-based Sapporo branch."[173] Other department stores, such as Takashimaya, also remained viable through overseas branches and became on-site purveyors of clothing and furnishings for Japan's military. As a result, Fujioka notes that "sales in the overseas branches accounted for 67.1 percent of its total sales in the second half of 1944," when Takashimaya's profits nearly reached top prewar sales revenues.[174] In conclusion, Fujioka asserts that Japanese department stores' overseas branches "mirrored the Japanese government's war policy by capitalizing on Japan's expansion of territory, although their internationalization only constituted spatial expansion, and not functional expansion."[175] Such department stores were essentially viewed as specifically "Japanese," as were their products, and thus, after Japan's defeat, they acquired negative connotations in Korea and northeast China after liberation from Japanese colonial control.

War's intensification with the arrival of Allied bombings, food rationing, and overall hardships endured by Japan's civilian population led many to voluntarily shirk any luxuries by 1945, even if meant for troops. Japan's urban landscapes were riddled with ruins, and lack of caloric intake diminished individual morale as everyday lives were consumed with the harsh tasks of personal survival.

CONCLUSION

Initially, the Sino-Japanese War had little impact on Japan's population, who consumed their news avidly in media including *Asahi Shimbun,* in which companies ran advertisements for consumer products portraying victorious troops to capitalize on wartime. Such spectacular consumption allowed consumers to experience warfare's vicarious "thrills" and later inspired purchases of small luxury items for troop comfort bags. After 1938, when the imperial government began exhorting higher savings rates and urging war bond purchases, Japanese companies intensified earlier strategies to inspire consumption among likely customers, such as loyalty clubs offering free merchandise, advertising products for troop care packages, and marketing commodities amid military victories or militaristic themes. Here, consumers were made to believe that they engaged in patriotic consumption beneficial to the state. Between 1938 and 1940, Japan's government also enacted a series of luxury regulations and consumption taxes on certain products. As war intensified on the continent, Japanese corporations were enlisted into military procurement for products like soap, whisky, watches, and even perfumes, which helped them remain economically viable despite wartime government strictures. In the early 1940s, popular celebrities, like Japanese actress and singer Yamaguchi Yoshiko, known in Chinese as Li Xianglan or Ri Kōran by contemporaneous audiences, advertised Shiseidō's beauty products in Manchukuo and Japanese-occupied China when luxury regulations began harming cosmetics profits in domestic Japan.

However, after Imperial Japan's late 1941 initiation of the Pacific War with its attack on Pearl Harbor in the US territory of Hawai'i, conditions for companies and consumers began worsening as the empire further mired itself in total war. The smaller size and less conspicuous placement of newspaper advertisements near page bottom also revealed the curtailing of consumption and dampened commercial presences of corporations involved in producing consumer products. By late 1944, Allied bombing campaigns targeted Japanese cities, knocking out production facilities and creating uncertainty in basic survival for ordinary Japanese, who saw their homes burn down while lacking enough food. Even the Imperial Navy now refused accepting comfort bags, urging civilians to send money instead. When the war ended in mid-August 1945, many Japanese greeted the emperor's announcement with acute relief and looked forward to hopefully brighter days ahead.

Chapter Five

CONSUMING THE BRIGHT LIFE

For the rest of Japan the people who have been able to become
salary men are symbols of the *akarui seikatsu* (bright new life), the
life with leisure time, travel and recreation, and few binding obligations and formalities. Because he has security from the firm he may
steadily acquire the new consumer goods without fear of being
without income and going into debt. For the person who aspires to
be a salary man, the bright new life is indeed a rosy picture. For the
salaried family each glamourous new purchase is the result of careful
planning and many sacrifices. To an affluent American, the bright
new life appears orderly but ascetic, and he finds it hard to share the
anticipation with which the Japanese salaried family awaits each
new acquisition.[1]

—*Ezra Vogel (1963)*

Defeat seemed a welcome respite after fifteen years of continental
war in Asia devoured Japan's population, ravaged the archipelago with Allied firebombings and atomic weapons, and stripped a
godlike emperor of divinity. Nearly eight years of the US-led occupation from 1945 until 1952 also influenced the Japanese to consume
American popular culture and styles, echoing a 1920s-era fascination.
In the postwar era, the United States was held up as a standard, while
after rebuilding, Japanese mass production slowly returned in light industries featuring toys and small electronics. "Democracy" became a
symbol of reemerging political and economic choices, and soon translated into consumer environments. Following the Occupation, Suntory's precursor Kotobukiya, which initially created a whisky to rival
foreign ones from Scotland and the United States, began purveying a

more affordable product accessible to ordinary consumers in the growing number of bars franchised to the company. The innovative yet inexpensive wares of Casio (1946) and Sanrio (1960) boasting vast choices for product designs arose during this moment, and bookended contesting political currents prior to Japan's economic miracle and Liberal Democratic Party (LDP) dominance. Born during Prime Minister Ikeda Hayato's (1899–1965) "Income Doubling" Plan initiated in 1960, Sanrio Corporation's precursor purveyed products reflecting postwar optimism and abundance, while children and youth emerged as important consumers for previously unattainable toys and small electronics. Whereas exported Japanese products were initially denigrated as "cheap," the early postwar years represented domestic market saturation and a steep elevation in product quality.

Recovering from Defeat: Allied Occupation (1945–1952) and the Korean War (1950–1953)

Not surprisingly, the immediate postwar period initially hampered big business. Dirt on city streets blackened shoes and ankles as wartime rubble persisted against complete clearing, while *rus in urbus* landscapes developed from hastily constructed shanties on burned lots. This bleak environment was marked by scarcity, which led urban dwellers throughout Japan to pawn valuable remaining belongings for provisions and other necessities and rely on unauthorized street markets, known as the black market (*yami-ichi*). Architectural historians Hatsuda Kōsei, Murakami Shihori, and Ishigure Masakazu estimate that *yami-ichi* existed in most Japanese cities with over 45,000 inhabitants.[2] Unemployment was also rampant, with Japan's Ministry of Welfare estimating between five and six million unemployed in 1946, though media speculations circulated of ten to fifteen million without work.[3] These conditions led ordinary Japanese to buy and sell in these unregulated markets serving as postwar Japan's first free markets permitting individuals to survive and revive businesses.

Not everyone patronized or approved of *yami-ichi*. In October 1947, Yamaguchi Yoshitada, a Tokyo district court judge, chose to starve to death while succumbing to tuberculosis in gruesome activism rather than break the Food Control Law by buying on the black market to supplement his family's meager government rations.[4] This pathos-filled story even appeared in an American *Time* magazine article, "Japan: Wages of Sinlessness," where Yamaguchi's widow bitterly

164 *Chapter 5*

remarked, "It is horrible these days to be married to an honest man."[5] Although the Occupation government officially banned *yami-ichi*, according to Hatsuda and sociologist Hashimoto Ken'ichi, these spaces were economic safety nets for often-marginalized people: war widows, former colonial subjects, orphans, and others rendered destitute or displaced by the war.[6]

While cities were slowly cleared of rubble, and people regained future-oriented optimism, toy industries and small electronics, including watch making, recovered quickly, due to subsidiaries moving to inland or mountainous rural areas during wartime. Small toy trucks ingeniously produced from rubber bands and tin cans discarded by the US military caught the eye of GIs, who alerted Occupation officials to opportunities for furnishing potentially popular toys to American children.[7] On August 15, 1947, US authorities deemed that toys were Japan's first commodity for legal export, which required labeling as "Made in Occupied Japan."[8] Ironically, a plebian plaything originally meant to bring joy to Japanese children helped save the defeated nation's economy. Anthropologist Anne Allison argues that "the Japanese toy industry . . . played a major role in rebuilding the national economy," where "export revenues in the toy industry came to 322 million yen in 1948, more than tripled by 1949 (to 1 billion yen), and reached 8 billion yen by 1955."[9] Since the war, no "official" exchange rate existed; however, on April 25, 1949, authorities with the Supreme Commander of the Allied Powers (SCAP) established an exchange rate of 360 yen to one US dollar, which put the 1949 figure at an impressive $2,777,777.77 ($31,418,650.71 in mid-2021).[10] Though companies producing small consumer goods like toys and watches slowly began recapturing domestic markets, they also contended with quality-control issues that caused negative reception of Japanese-made products overseas from the late 1940s into the 1950s.

Concurrently, the Occupation government levied prohibitive domestic consumption taxes to restrain purchases of consumer products beyond necessities or those harboring luxury connotations. Such actions comprised SCAP's initially severe program of democratization. In April 1948, economist Henry Shavell (1918–2007), working as SCAP's taxation and economic advisor, who served as "principal architect of the modern Japanese Tax Code,"[11] publicized his mission in Japan in an article in the prestigious University of Chicago–based *Journal of Political Economy*.[12] The Occupation undertook its most radical tax reforms between September 1946 and March 1947, with

Consuming the Bright Life

tax rates sometimes increasing up to 90 percent to cut wartime debt.[13] Shavell notes how "indirect taxes were increased upon luxury and sumptuous goods, while those on more essential cost-of-living goods were lowered."[14] Individuals also faced increased taxation, where personal direct taxes were meant to precipitate wealth redistribution. For corporations, taxes were intended to prohibit excess wealth concentration like that contributing to prewar formation of zaibatsu (conglomerates). The rationale for the Occupation's draconian tax imposition was that measures "were explicitly designed to favor a social climate more conducive to the growth of democratic institutions."[15] Also, they aimed to curb rising inflation starting in late 1946.[16] Unsurprisingly, consumer confidence dwindled, and Japan plunged into recession. Corporations thus redefined their corporate missions as supporting the fledgling democracy and advertised products as essential commodities instead of luxuries—like Casio's metal-ring quellazaire allowing hard-to-obtain cigarettes to be smoked down to their nubs.

Concurrently, 1947–1948 "Reverse Course" economic policies and the 1949 "Dodge Line" advocated by SCAP economic advisor Joseph Dodge (1890–1964)[17] were based on premises by George Kennan (1904–2005), then directing the State Department's Policy Planning Staff, proposing that Japan could serve as East Asia's industrial manufacturing base and that its economic growth might stem rising threats of communism. SCAP soon initiated stricter political measures to ensure these conditions. General Douglas MacArthur's (1880–1964) orders broke up a February 1947 general strike. Though leftist parties like the Communists and Socialists, who garnered majority votes in the April election, were allowed to reemerge,[18] they were defanged as the "lovable communist party of Japan" or diminished in impact.[19] From the late 1940s onward, amid Mainland China's already likely Communist takeover, which in October 1949 became the People's Republic of China (PRC) led by Mao Zedong (1893–1976), Japan was viewed as an important anticommunist bulwark.

In this climate, and expressing Kennan's support for containment policies, the United States became involved in the Korean War (1950–1953) when the northern Democratic Republic of Korea invaded the Republic of Korea in June 1950. After 1945, both the Soviets and Americans occupied northern and southern portions of Japan's former colony as these decolonizing parts coalesced into new countries each loyal to their latest occupiers; they were soon absorbed into the emerging Cold War (1945–1991) politics developing between the two

166   *Chapter 5*

postwar superpowers.[20] While Japan hosted staging areas for American operations in Korea, the United States also purchased military procurements from Japanese companies with newly reconstructed factories. Hence, Prime Minister Yoshida Shigeru (1878–1967), in office from 1948 until 1954, styled this economic windfall as a "gift of the gods."[21]

As Cold War allies, the United States and Japan both signed the 1951 Treaty of San Francisco to officially end occupation by 1952, followed by the Sōgo Kyōryoku Oyobi Anzen Hoshō Jōyaku (Treaty of Mutual Cooperation and Security between the United States and Japan), widely known as the Anpō Treaty, which initiated the US-Japan military alliance and guaranteed Japan's security with American military bases under a "nuclear umbrella," while Japan's diplomacy now emphasized economic relationships with the broader world.

Nearly a decade later, despite economic optimism and revived commercial ties with the United States, the Anpō Treaty's impending renewal was overwhelmingly unpopular, especially among the nation's youth and trade unions, since it seemingly linked Japan's fate too closely with American "patronage." On January 19, 1960, the United States and Japan nonetheless renewed their Occupation-era mutual security treaty, permitting American military bases to remain in Japan. Its ratification on May 20 sparked huge protests, which prevented US president Dwight D. Eisenhower from a three-day visit to Tokyo and the Nikkō Shrine beginning on June 15.[22] Historian Nick Kapur asserts that near-majorities of Japan's public participated in these mass protests: "For a period of fifteen months, from March 1959 through June 1960, an estimated 30 million people from across the archipelago—approximately one-third of Japan's population of 92.5 million—participated in protest activities of some kind."[23] Excepting the mid-to-late 1960s student protests at mainly Tokyo-based universities, the 1959 to 1960 mass protests were a last gasp of popular challenges to a relatively stable LDP-dominated political system continuing until the early 1990s.

During Yoshida's tenure, Japan adopted a strategy later named the Yoshida Doctrine in 1977 by political scientist Nishihara Masashi (b. 1937), which marked US-Japan relations for decades thereafter.[24] Due to US military protection and defense spending limits to below 1 percent of GDP, Japan now flourished economically, with efforts to "develop the country as a trading nation."[25] Interestingly, Yoshida's finance minister was Ikeda Hayato, who later served as prime minister during one of Japan's highest economic growth periods (1960–1964). The rise of a middle class in a thriving democracy was thus tied to greater disposable income and economic consumption.

THE BRIGHT 1960S AND JAPAN'S "NEW MIDDLE CLASS"

Aside from the initial post–Korean War boom, Japan's so-called postwar economic miracle (1955–1991) was inextricably tied to political consensus under the center-right LDP, lending itself to economic stability supporting steady high growth amid government measures sustaining corporate development. Additionally, postwar Japan's initially US-imposed democracy flourished: a postwar constitution promulgated in November 1946 and enacted in March 1947 promised women and all adult citizens voting rights and included Article Nine, a clause renouncing projectable military power while curtailing defense spending. This freed government revenues to help rebuild the nation. In 1960, Prime Minister Ikeda unveiled his Income Doubling Plan, which promised to double Japanese incomes within a decade. This goal was indeed realized by 1970, with optimistic predictions fairly characteristic of the Japanese economic miracle bolstered by political stability ensured by continued LDP successes and further American military procurements during the Vietnam War (1965–1975). Such developments translated positively into political, economic, and social benefits.

By the late 1950s, influenced by Cold War perspectives, scholars including sociologist Ezra Vogel (1930–2020) equated democracy with Japan's postwar middle-class consumer society. Here, measures of equality appeared within economic prosperity available for growing numbers of Japanese, along with rights to decide one's political fate through voting. With a rising yen, consumers also "voted" for favorite products amid new economic success following a decade-long process of political, social, and economic reconstruction initiated by the Allied Occupation to help Japanese become more like Americans. These individuals coalesced into a favored new class largely defined by employee loyalty to companies and personal devotion to consumer products. However, despite rapid growth of consumer cultures targeting the middle class, in the early 1960s, middle-class status was still aspirational for many Japanese, and steeply rising in subsequent decades. According to sociologists Tamio Hattori and Tsuruyo Funatsu, "In Japan, 'professional, technical, managerial and clerical workers' who

168   *Chapter 5*

constitute the 'new middle class' came to exceed 20% of the total labor force in 1965, surpassed 30% in 1985, and reached 35% in 1995."[26] What exactly characterized Japan's "new middle class," and how did they view luxury and personal consumption patterns?

From 1958 to 1960, Vogel and his wife Suzanne lived in central Tokyo, next door to Japanese psychologist Takeo Doi (1920–2009—later celebrated in the United States for his seminal research on social interactions in Japan[27]—and then moved for fieldwork to an eastern Tokyo suburb named Mamachi.[28] Assisted by Suzanne, and certainly inspired by informal discussions with Doi, Vogel completed his pivotal research on the growth of a new Japanese middle class, and through "salaryman" archetypes he outlined Japanese consumption patterns by tracing buying habits of "typical" Japanese families in a representative Tokyo suburb. These findings became his still-influential 1963 study *Japan's New Middle Class: The Salary Man and His Family in a Tokyo Suburb,* which included the chapter "The Consumer's 'Bright New Life.'"[29] Vogel discovered that when middle-class Japanese families desired aspirational products connoting status and success, they playfully called them three "Imperial Regalia"—a phrase referencing the Japanese imperial family's traditional premodern symbols: mirror, sword, and jewel. In Vogel's late 1950s study, his informants noted these were usually appliances, like an "electric refrigerator or washing machine or perhaps a vacuum cleaner,"[30] which connoted status and success for most middle-class Japanese. Essentially, these commodities invoked manifestations of commodity fetishism in a nation of aspirants ravenous for new products.

Electric appliances, or *denki yōhin* (electronic goods—literally, "electrical necessities"), were first seen as aspirational luxury items but, as decades progressed, became necessities easing housewives' labor as husbands and children spent increasingly longer periods outside their homes working and studying. Larger purchases requiring huge savings also prompted smaller indulgences of increasingly affordable luxuries like now-ubiquitous domestically produced whisky and Japanese-made watches, which rewarded Japan's sacrificial salarymen whose efforts had bolstered the economic miracle. As incomes rose, children were treated with toys and cute products by companies like Sanrio, which later pioneered the *kawaii* (cute) phenomenon. This bright, hopeful new economic climate encouraging families who yearned to shed wartime darkness and deprivation became a perfect setting for

Japan's new middle-class consumer society in a stronger revival of the consumer capitalism that had developed in 1920s Japan.[31]

WHISKY'S DEMOCRATIZATION: TORYS BARS AND UNCLE TORYS (1950s–1960s)

When war ended, Kotobukiya and its rival Dai Nippon Kajū Kabushikigaisha (Great Japan Juice Company) continued fulfilling military contracts for whisky—this time, for thirsty Allied conquerors desiring easy intoxication by day's end who preferred whisky and beer over rice wine. In October 1945, the two companies began brewing and distilling anew, and used cached stock for blends. This initial impetus helped revive both producers' businesses. In 1946, Kotobukiya re-released Torys Whisky as a standardized-quality, more affordable domestic liquor than imports. In 1952, Dai Nippon Kajū Kabushikigaisha modernized its image to focus exclusively on whisky and changed its name to Nikka Whisky Distilling Company.[32] Though Japanese bars serving liquor revived during the Allied Occupation, Kotobukiya decided to create a franchised whisky bar providing high-quality liquor in a desirable setting, a business approach also followed by Nikka.

The hardscrabble postwar years prompted proliferation of questionable liquor sources in makeshift surroundings patrolled by lackeys of reemerging yakuza (organized criminal) bands. Yakuza also ran urban Japan's black markets, where liquor often came straight from the US Army Post Exchange (PX), where it was purchased and then resold by American soldiers or Japanese *panpan* "girls" (women exchanging sexual services for resellable "gifts") who were given PX goods as compensation.[33] After the Occupation ended and Japan began experiencing stable economic growth, anthropologist Anne Allison notes a corresponding rise in hostess bars, where women served salarymen drinks and offered sexually charged attention in spaces permitting "opening up" and "relieving tension" after work.[34]

By contrast, in 1955, Kotobukiya's founder Torii Shinjirō created the respectable Torys Bar to feature his company's reputable Japanese-made products and further advertise the brand in a desirable setting emphasizing male camaraderie. This allowed more people to afford good-quality domestic whisky, which slowly relinquished its reputation as a luxury product associated with the American conquerors' near-unattainable bounty. Over 1,500 such Torys Bar establishments opened

170   *Chapter 5*

from the late 1950s to the mid-1960s; these franchises with standard-ized products offered the hard-working *sarariman* relaxation and cama-raderie after a tough workday.

Such curated unwinding often included entertainment from a dex-terous and skillful bartender. Originally, ice carving—learned in pre-war times from British and American bartenders and initially enjoyed by Japan's wealthy aristocracy, who could afford iceboxes or refrig-eration by the late 1920s and early 1930s—was a veritable performance art resurrected in Japanese bars beginning in the 1950s and continu-ing until today in higher-end establishments whose bartenders main-tain the art.[35] In 2003, before a memorable meal with Takanarita Tōru and his wife Megumi in a celebrated sushi restaurant near the famed Tsukiji Fish Market, the former *Asahi Shimbun* bureau chief in Wash-ington, DC, took me to a bar in Tokyo's exclusive Ginza area with his assistant. Several years before, I had worked for him in the DC bu-reau, and Mr. Takanarita wanted to celebrate my doctoral candidacy at the University of Chicago while I was in Japan for pre-dissertation research. In the small but elegant Ginza bar, the bartender removed a large ice block from a tiny freezer below the counter and sliced off a tranche. He expertly shaped the tranche into a block, and after care-ful ministrations, two perfectly shaped hexagonal cubes fit exactly into a pair of traditional whisky glasses. These provided the sculpturesque base for a high-end aged Suntory single-malt Hibiki whisky. Several patrons, including Mr. Takanarita, kept private bottles stashed in the bar, so it was a great honor to share one belonging to my former boss. However, at the time, whiskies were no longer popular among young people; my host hailed from a generational cohort of postwar Baby Boomers whose coming of age coincided with the mid-to-late 1960s when hard-working and -imbibing salarymen ushered in Japan's eco-nomic success while Suntory Whisky's fortune exploded.

Establishments like franchised Torys Bars also began featuring a more refreshing, lighter drink than a shot of whisky on the rocks. From the late 1950s into the 1960s, to assist Japan's whisky industry and the new bars he developed, Torii initiated the practice of *mizuwari* (literally, "cut with water," or diluting whisky with water), which developed into Japan's highball drinking culture.[36] Japanese had discovered the "high-ball," whisky mixed with club soda and ice (often called *wistan* for its soda water, or *tansan*, mixed within), back in the 1920s. Tradition-ally, Scotch whiskies, similar to their later Japanese cousins, were drunk neat or on the rocks—adding water like the flamboyant Victorian-era (1837–1901) Scottish distiller Tommy Dewar (1864–1930) or the late nineteenth-century American bars in Manhattan pioneering the drink would disturb their peaty flavors.[37] However, like American ones, Japanese whiskies are lighter and fruitier, and since the 1950s, Japanese bartenders have mixed one ounce of whisky with four ounces of water or club soda, though in the United States and Great Britain, alcohol content "increases" by diminishing water to three ounces.[38] By the early 1960s, according to Saji Keizō (1919–1999), son of Kotobukiya founder Torii, "whisky highballs, together with beer, became the beverage of choice among professional workers, dominating professional 'salaryman' drinking culture."[39] Though *mizuwari* service for whisky and highballs certainly helped popularize Japanese whisky in postwar times, another important development expanded the Suntory Whisky brand throughout Japan: a "lovable" cartoon mascot.

In 1954, Kotobukiya hired illustrator Yanagihara Ryōhei (1931–2015) to work in its advertising department, and in 1956 he began editing *Yōshū tengoku* (Liquor Heaven), a free magazine placed in Torys Bars for customer enjoyment.[40] Just like Shiseidō's company publication *Hanatsubaki,* this promotional periodical promoted certain lifestyles and touted Kotobukiya products. It was then that he created Japan's most iconic mascot for the Torys Bar and its signature whisky[41]—"Uncle Torys," a rotund, bald, cigar-chomping, middle-aged Anglo-American man with shadowed eyes in a green tweed blazer and blue-striped tie.

In most of the ads created by Yanagihara, Uncle Torys did anything to imbibe his favorite drink, ignoring others and even family to favor drinking. Rather than viewing him as an irredeemably self-centered alcoholic, Japanese male consumers perceived him as expressing personal desires to decompress at all costs from surrounding pressures. In consideration of Japanese advertising campaigns featuring non-Japanese nationals, anthropologist Millie Creighton explains that "foreigners often provide a mechanism for expressing selfish sentiments in a culture which has long frowned on Wagamama, or self-centered concerns."[42] As a social geographer, Alastair Bonnett proposes yet another intriguing understanding of Uncle Torys's import in late 1950s and early 1960s commercials and advertisements: "A kind of knowing game is enacted that allows the pleasures of selfish consumerism to become all the more tantalising by being cast as, simultaneously, foreign, transgressive and entirely available . . . the *gaijin* [foreigner]; his/her body and his/her rhetoric of selfishness are less likely to be read as an imposition from outside than as reflective of

172   *Chapter 5*

Japanese agency, as products of Japanese priorities, a Japanese manipulation of the identities available within capitalism."[43]

Here, Uncle Torys appears as a particularly Japanese manifestation of a new capitalistic identity countering men's self-sacrifice demanded by companies and families. As an uber-ordinary antihero, Uncle Torys thus appealed to Japanese men increasingly grateful for an easily attainable means to unwind after work and represented the now-ubiquitous *sarariman* focusing occupational energies toward corporate success. However, anthropologist Amy Borovy also notes the toll on married Japanese women managing their husbands' drunken behavior and all household tasks in relationships marked by codependency.[44]

Numerous comical ads reveal permissive (even hyperbolic) attitudes toward liquor by this wannabe bon vivant who, in contemporary contexts, might be viewed as a raving alcoholic preferring to remain drunk. In one of Uncle Torys's first television commercials produced by TCJ Animation Center in 1958, he drags himself into a bar after a long evening at work, and while imbibing two shots, his deflated, or *shiboreta* (wrung out—a popular expression among professionals after a long day's toil), expression re-expands as his face reddens following eight more highball drinks.[45] Curiously happy and refreshed instead of stone-cold drunk, Uncle Torys then hops and skips out of his namesake bar holding his briefcase and smoking a cigarette. Through an easily recognizable cartoon, Yanagihara's character promoted a relatively inexpensive Torys Whisky (300 yen per bottle) and popularized a once luxurious Western drink to growing masses of white-collar men needing quick decompression after work. According to Sapporo Beer Company statistics, a large bottled beer cost 125 yen in 1955 and 115 yen in 1963, while a typical bottle of "quality" (or imported) whisky sold for 730 yen in 1953 and 750 yen in 1962; bankers earned an average of 5,600 yen per month in 1956 and 21,000 per month in 1963.[46] Hence, Torys Whisky cost only twice as much as beer and half as much as imported whisky, thus democratizing whisky as a now-accessible luxury product.

Not only was Torys Whisky affordable, it also served as a valued gift or "bribe" for discerning male recipients, whether bosses or family members. A clever 1959 television commercial shows Uncle Torys using a bottle of Torys Whisky to placate a tiny visiting alien who knocks on his door at night and refuses to leave; only after the small bipedal squid-headed creature refuses bananas, a tuba, and a sombrero as tribute, he accepts Uncle Torys' proffered bottle, implying the whisky is "out of this world."[47] A 1960s cartoon TV commercial capitalizing on the popularity of Westerns in Japan shows a traditional Japanese festival hawker brokering peace between American cowboys and "Indians" by imbibing a Torys Whisky bottle, while the chief winks at viewers.[48] Here, too, the whisky brings conviviality between people at odds, like "Indians" and their foes, or employees and bosses, at a time when American popular culture enthralled Japanese audiences.

The 1960s were pivotal to Japanese whisky expansion. Honoring Kotobukiya's sixtieth anniversary in 1960, Torii unveiled high-end Suntory Royal Whisky to increase its corporate repertoire. A year later Torii hired his son Saji Keizō, initially Kotobukiya's managing director, as its second president to catapult Suntory Whisky into mass markets. In 1961, Saji initiated innovative ways to promote products, including opening the Suntory Museum of Art, which allowed ordinary people to view and enjoy fine art exhibitions, along with the influential "Let's Drink Torys and Go to Hawai'i" campaign, which brought overseas travel to America's newest state within reach for one hundred lucky winners.[49] This campaign, held until December 10, 1961, with winners announced in early January 1962 coinciding with New Year's (*Oshōgatsu*) celebrations, was publicized by a television commercial replete with surfing, hula dances, sunny beaches, and swaying palm trees.[50] First prize featured a certificate of deposit totaling enough cash for a Hawai'i trip for one hundred winners in an era when such a trip was the height of luxury for middle-class Japanese, with consolation prizes of 15,000 yen ($681.11 in mid-2021) for four hundred winners and 1.5 million cans of Torys Wistan (whisky soda) for other consumers.[51] According to contemporary ad posters, customers received two prize tickets for each large or deluxe bottle, and one ticket for a pocket-sized bottle.[52] In 1961, Suntory Whisky also "became the first Japanese whisky to be approved for registration in the United States,"[53] so the company featuring Hawai'i was a timely enterprise for expanding Japanese tourism and name brands onto American soil. In Saji's obituary, *New York Times* financial journalist Nick Ravo indicated that before his 1999 death, "Mr. Saji, as president of Suntory for 29 years, was instrumental in changing Japan's drinking habits,"[54] and arguably, those of the Anglo-American world.

In 1963, recognizing Suntory Whisky products' importance, Saji changed Kotobukiya Company's name to Suntory,[55] originally composed by using "san," meaning "mister" in Japanese, and founder Torii Shinjirō's last name, in a more Westernized combination.[56] This

Figure 5.1. Advertisement for the 1961 "*Torisu o nonde Hawaii e ikō!*" campaign. Courtesy of Suntory Holdings Limited, copyright Suntory Holdings.

name change further profited from the by-now beloved Uncle Torys character, who continued appearing in advertisements where he insouciantly persisted in choosing to drink Suntory Whisky above other activities—including in an autumn 1964 print ad during the Tokyo Olympics where he preferred to serve himself whisky in a highball glass while turning away from the television showing three Japanese flags at different heights—implying gold, silver, and bronze medalists in an event.[57] Even his unimpressed dog fails to mind the televised spectacle, with these captions:

Tōyō no majo wa	Oriental sorceresses
Kin medaru ni yoi	Get drunk on gold medals.
Banshūka wa	Collectors of myriad things
Kinen no nanto ka yoi	Get drunk on all sorts of mementos.
Purei gāru wa	Play girls are
Gaijin-kyaku ni yotteru	Getting drunk on their foreign clients.
Orinpikku ni	I who can't get drunk
Yoenai ore wa	on the Olympics
Torisu o nomu!	Am drinking Torys![58]

Consuming the Bright Life 175

One late 1964 advertisement never featured the character, but instead depicted a single dark-complexioned Japanese *sarariman* relaxing in long underwear while forced to iron pants. Contemporary readers understood that he lived alone, since otherwise his mother, girlfriend, or wife would perform these onerous duties for him to maintain a professional appearance at work. His comically disheveled hair appears amid a carefully hung elegant white shirt, askew blazer, and jaunty bowler hat. The Uncle Torys presence was implied, since the man mitigated domestic drudgery in a fashion honoring the iconic character: ironing suit pants with his right hand while balancing a whisky glass in his left, while ogling a pornographic magazine catering to broad tastes by showing a woman in lingerie on one spread facing a man's naked butt on another. The righthand caption ironically states:

"Bōchū Torisu ari"	"Torys amid (the) busyness"
Kanzen naru shinshi no	
tame no supirittsu!	Spirits for a perfect gentleman!

An advertisement appearing in early January 1965 for the New Year's season shows a rare glimpse of Uncle Torys's family life, as he ignores his irate wife and disappointed daughter in formal kimono playing *sugoroku* (double-six), a traditional Japanese board game for *Oshōgatsu*, and spends the time drinking Torys Whisky while so inebriated he lies on his side.[59] The hilarious caption describes the scene:

Oshōgatsu no asobi no naka de,	Amid the fun of New Year's,
ichiban tanoshii no wa,	the most enjoyable is that,
sugoroku yatte,	during *sugoroku*,
ikkai yasumi ga detta toki,	whenever a pause comes up
Torisu ga,	it's because Torys
yukkuri tanoshimeru kara ne.	can slowly be enjoyed.[60]

In Yanagihara's ingenious composition, the eye meanders from the prose-poem–like righthand caption, to the mother and daughter, and then to the board game, landing upon a prone Uncle Torys, whose elbow points to the whisky bottle, and after following his spindly arrow-like legs, finally rests upon a larger Torys bottle with product information including pricing.[61]

Such memorable, humorous, and informally effective illustrations by Yanagihara, coupled with a transgressive cartoon character's appeal

176   *Chapter 5*

in casually rebelling against domestic or social duties, helped catapult the product's popularity among rising middle-classes, and also ensured Suntory's brand name recognition. By the 1970s, Uncle Torys even appeared on limited-edition collectible promotional "goods" like proto-bobblehead toothpick holders, including one advertising Suntory Whisky Red, where he sported a signature red blazer, white shirt, thin black tie, and white camellia boutonnière, all while holding a Suntory Whisky bottle in his right hand and pistol in his left![62] Widespread popularity of gangster films and spy-flics featuring James Bond likely prompted this prop, whereby Uncle Torys acquired "dangerous" and mysterious aspects to his character as man-about-town. The toothpick holder's backside, or Uncle Torys' head, stated "Bottom's up!" in a cartoon bubble, while the brand "Suntory Whisky 'Red'" appeared behind his blazer. Such limited-edition items helped augment brand visibility as they sat on living room *kōtatsu* (heated tables) or dinner tables before family and guests, and prompted customers to collect tickets by purchasing whisky and thereby ensured brand loyalty by inculcating a frequent purchasing habit.

As a product of his era, Uncle Torys, while a comical character, revealed the toll of economic success on ordinary Japanese male office workers who drank to relieve stress and rewarded themselves with liquid relaxation after busy days at their companies. Despite an initially cheaper price than foreign imports, Suntory Whisky began as a scarcely affordable luxury item that became increasingly accessible to customers by the 1950s and 1960s. Japanese watches also followed suit as essential high-quality accessories for *sarariman* attire. The ability to accurately keep track of time soon became essential for punctuality at business meetings and workplace arrival and departure times.

CASIO (1946) AND SEIKŌ: PIONEERS IN AFFORDABLE ACCURACY

The Japan Clock and Watch Association's (JCWA) compilation of a timeline of important postwar dates reveals a quick revival for Japan's watch industry and associated regulatory organizations amid a near-decade of challenging economic conditions. Some urban timepiece companies recovered from the war more quickly, including Seikō and Citizen, which had moved their production facilities from Tokyo to mountainous areas in Nagano Prefecture less targeted by Allied bomb-

Consuming the Bright Life   177

ings.[63] However, the Occupation government imposed an astonishingly high commodity tax of 60 percent on watches until March 1947, when it was lowered to 50 percent until July 1948; at that point the tax dropped to 30 percent.[64] In 1947, to mitigate domestic hardships, Japanese timepiece-makers initiated exports to areas using the British pound, yet they suffered setbacks with the pound's September 1949 devaluation.[65] Moreover, the JCWA, founded in April 1948 to domestically promote the horological industry and lobby for favorable business conditions, indicated that "in April 1949, the two rates for timepieces (pocket watches, alarm clocks—¥430, wristwatches, table clocks, wall clocks—¥410) were changed to a uniform high-yen exchange rate of ¥360."[66] That same year, two organizations arose to aid retailing practices and assure uniform high quality—especially if exports were to flourish: the All Japan Watch and Clock Retail Association, and the first Council for Quality Inspection of the Japan-Made Watch and Clock, followed by a second council in 1950. Yet, it was not until 1951 that relief came when the commodity tax exemption rate was raised and the Korean War mitigated the Dodge Plan's harsh policies.[67] Additionally, 1954 saw the founding of the Japan Watch and Clock Inspection Institute, further consolidating uniform quality standards.[68] Despite external regulatory measures initiated as by-products of SCAP's early democratization initiatives where watches were deemed a "luxury," and strict quality-control regulations imposed by industry associations, Japan's watch industry persisted, and welcome new players soon emerged.

Amid this atmosphere of hard-scrabble survival in the difficult early peacetime years, what became one of Japan's best-known (and most ubiquitous) watchmakers originally began as a tooling parts purveyor. In 1946, Waseda University–educated lathe operator Kashio Tadao (1917–1993) founded Kashio Seisakujo (Casio Manufacturing Company), which manufactured machinery parts in Tokyo's suburban Mitaka area. Originally from a working-class background and born in what is now Nakoku City in Kōchi Prefecture, Tadao and his family moved to Tokyo for opportunities involving its reconstruction following the 1923 earthquake. After completing a high school education, Tadao apprenticed with a lathe operator and later processed parts as a subcontractor while studying at Waseda University with the factory owner's support.[69] Clearly, Tadao's genius, work ethic, and determination paid off to ensure his company's success, along with the combined talents of three younger brothers, Toshio (1925–2012), an inventor

178 *Chapter 5*

using digital technology; Kazuo (1929–2018), a sales and marketing innovator; and Yukio (b. 1930), a design engineer.[70] Following Japan's defeat, one of Casio's first successful products was the *yubiwa* (finger ring) pipe, allowing smokers to glean minute tobacco remnants from a filter-less cigarette—incredibly useful during tobacco shortages.[71]

In 1957, the company was renamed Casio Computer Company. Corresponding to this change, that June, Kashio Toshio "invented the 14-A, the world's first compact all-electric calculator small enough to be used in an office setting," which fit onto a standard-sized office desk.[72] According to the online Casio Museum, "The name 14-A indicates that the computer has a capacity of 14 digits and that it is the first product, from [beginning] where [sic] the first letter of the alphabet."[73] In production until September 1959, the product cost a staggering 485,000 yen[74]—about 2,900,000 yen or $26,658 in 2021.[75] In comparison, IBM's 610 Auto-Point Computer, which included calculating functions, then cost a whopping $55,000 ($1,150 for office and $460 for academic monthly rental)—or $516,061 in 2021.[76] The pared-down Japanese model was economical and user-friendly when compared to its American competitor. After producing calculators, Casio progressed to computers, followed by musical keyboards, and finally, in 1974, produced one of its most successful products: digital watches, discussed in chapter 7.

Like Casio, the Seikō Corporation also benefited from production catalysts from the Korean and Vietnam Wars, with corresponding postwar sales growth, to emerge by the 1960s as a global watch-making leader. This accomplishment was highlighted in Seikō's honor of being chosen as the 1964 Tokyo Olympics' official timekeeper, for which the company issued 1,200 units of stopwatches for timing athletes. To commemorate this historic Olympics on Japanese soil, a version of this stopwatch was designed as a watch in the stainless-steel Seikō Crown Chronograph, Japan's first chronograph boasting a "monopusher system."[77]

In 1969, Seikō upended the horology world when it introduced the world's first quartz watch—the Astron. Freeing consumers from constant winding for mechanical watches or routinely assuring movement while attached to wrists for automatic self-winding watches, quartz also boasted greater accuracy than previous mechanisms. Quartz's accuracy was previously something only owners of high-end luxury watches could expect, and even those only held accuracy to several minutes each month. Though Americans accomplished a human lunar landing that year, Japanese achieved astonishing results in timekeeping: near-perfect accuracy. True perfection was only achieved by Seikō more than four decades later with the Seikō Astron GPS Solar Watch, released onto the market in 2012, and continually synched via up to four satellites at once to triangulate accurately to the atomic clock in all the world's thirty-nine time zones, literally anywhere.[78] Despite initially high prices of $2,300 to $3,850 with a limited-edition release of only 2,500 pieces in steel or titanium, the watch contained unique features usually only available in watches twice its cost, including an ultra-low power consumption quartz movement and solar power.[79] Japan thus pioneered the world's first quartz watches and continued perfecting them by adding features and selling them at prices ordinary middle-class consumers could afford. These were then sold throughout the world in an extraordinary democratization of luxury for millions of grateful consumers.

Moreover, the world's most popular digital wristwatch also came from Japan, produced by Seikō's competitor Casio, previously achieving success in consumer technology by selling affordable calculators and computers. Resembling a small computer worn on the wrist, the country's first digital LCD wristwatch with an automatic calendar, the Casiotron, hit markets in November 1974. Although this model was not the earliest—Intel Corporation's Microma held that honor in 1972, a year also marking Hamilton's first mass-produced digital watch, the Pulsar P-1—it still became the most popular globally.[80] In comparison, the Pulsar P-1, famously worn by actor Roger Moore's (1927–2017) James Bond in *Live and Let Die* (1973), initially sold for $2,100 and boasted a solid gold case, while later versions sold for $275.[81] Though the Casiotron was originally expensive at 58,000 to 65,000 yen (around $533 in contemporary US dollars), it acquired a following due to several innovative features: a buttonless LED display showing hours, minutes, and seconds, and a calendar function including months and days.[82] The Casiotron's still-reasonable cost made consumers view it as an affordable luxury with impeccable quality flaunting its features when high-tech gadgetry became popular amid Cold War superpower scientific competition and the space race.

By the mid-1970s, Japanese watches and other products finally attained reputations for superior high quality, technological sophistication, and name-brand recognition prefiguring the 1980s-era pop-cultural products that provided a foundation for "Cool Japan." However, what truly accelerated global expansion for products like

180   *Chapter 5*

the Astron and Casiotron was the Tokyo Olympics' branding impact, which helped spread Japanese products into foreign markets with Japan's triumphant return to the global scene in a high-impact, peaceful competition of international athletes. While showcasing Japan's technological expertise, this sports event broadcast positive scenes of the country and its unique culture to the world.

Selling Japaneseness: The Tokyo Olympics and Shiseidō's Forays into American Markets (1964)

By the early 1960s, as Japan achieved near-complete reconstruction and economic revival harkened great international promise, its future appeared bright indeed. Another closely interrelated element of national pride was garnering the summer Olympic Games, slated for Tokyo in 1940 but derailed by war. This would also be the first Olympics held in Asia, a historic honor chosen by the International Olympic Committee on May 26, 1959.[83] In 1964, Japan finally hosted the Tokyo Summer Olympics, with the event delayed to autumn (October 10–24) to benefit from mild weather while avoiding the humidity, high heat, and frequent typhoons typical of Japanese summers.[84] In *Tōkyō Orinpikku* (Tokyo Olympiad), a brilliant documentary of the city and its sporting events, producer Ichikawa Kon (1915–2008) revealed reconstructed infrastructure showcasing the nation's renewed physical body through remarkable displays of Japan's athletes, who won twenty-nine medals (sixteen gold, five silver, and eight bronze), with several winning swimming and track-and-field events.[85] Track runner Sakai Yoshinori (1945–2014), born in Hiroshima in the year that Americans detonated the wartime atomic bomb, brought the Olympic torch into Yoyogi Stadium for the torch relay's historic final lap as a poignant message of peace and resurrection to the international scene.

The Olympics also trained Western eyes onto Japan, and in particular, Americans, who by the early 1960s harbored conceptions of Japan beyond simple wartime memories of a formidable enemy. This included the Zen Buddhism craze, initiated in the 1950s among the Beat Generation. In the United States, Anglo-American philosopher Alan Watts (1915–1973) initially popularized Zen Buddhism through his influential *The Way of Zen* (1957)[86] and weekly radio broadcasts on Berkeley, California's KPFA station, including "Way beyond the West," and numerous lectures in San Francisco and elsewhere from the late 1950s into the 1960s.[87] Styling himself as "philosophical entertainer" rather than scholar,[88] Watts gained multitudes of "converts" to new ways of thinking about religion and art influenced by Japan. Zen Buddhism was also skillfully "defanged" of wartime martial elements,[89] and in American minds it now represented peaceful contemplation and altruistic seeking of social harmony during the turbulent domestic times characterized by John F. Kennedy's (1917–1963) 1963 assassination, civil unrest, and emerging political protests. Japan, whose 1947 postwar constitution renounced war, represented ideals of peace and harmony that the United States seemingly lost during the Cold War, amid American curiosity about a new postwar ally and rising economic contender. Certain impressions of Zen popularized by US proponents joined aspects of this new peaceful image cultivated by Japan.

The Shiseidō Corporation wisely capitalized on this connection, and in 1964 named its first specifically American-oriented perfume "Zen," ostensibly "for a religious philosophy well known in the West and often associated with the essence of Japanese culture."[90] Zen was designed by American perfumer Josephine Catapano (1918–2012), who in 1953 created Estée Lauder's first perfume, Youth Dew, a bestselling brown-colored amber-spicy fragrance redolent of scents evoking late fall and winter, elegantly housed in an hour-glass bottle tied with gold ribbon and topped with a gold cap.[91] *Fragrantica,* a widely read international fragrance blog, describes Shiseidō's Zen perfume as a "chypre fragrance" with an "intensive floral scent" featuring "hyacinth, orange blossom, jasmine, mimosa, daffodil, violet and woody-musky base" and evoking sandalwood incense in its base notes.[92]

Zen came in an elegant vase-like bottle suggesting black lacquer, topped with a round black glass stopper, and luxuriously gilded with floral motifs resembling *Kodaiji-makie* (Kodai Temple sprinkled images—powdered gold leaf sprinkled upon images painted in lacquer].[93] The bottle's flowers and grasses allude to the temple's celebrated cached Warring States' Era (1467–1615) ten-drawered poetry-writing box.[94] The exquisite bottle cites superior Japanese craftsmanship, intimating this depository of Japan's national treasures. Established in 1608 by Kita-no-Mandokoro (1548–1624), or "Nene," widow of Toyotomi Hideyoshi (1537–1598) and Japan's second "Great Unifier," Kōdaiji is one of the Zen religious tradition's foremost Kyoto-based temples, boasting numerous halls designated as "cultural treasures" along with other rare objects.[95]

The temple favors Rinzai Zen traditions, emphasizing sudden enlightenment spurred by intense *zazen* (seated meditation) practices

182 *Chapter 5*

and *kōan* (complex riddle) study; Rinzai was, incidentally, the first Zen school to arrive on American shores, thanks to Sasaki Shigetsu (1882–1945), or Sōkei-an, who in 1931 initiated the Buddhist Society of America, later named the First Zen Institute of America.[96] After Sasaki's death, his wife, Ruth Fuller Sasaki (1892–1967), Alan Watts' mother-in-law and Beat poet Gary Snyder's (b. 1930) mentor, who taught Japanese Studies scholars like Burton Watson (1925–2017), became the first American woman to achieve full-fledged Rinzai priestess status at the Kyoto-based Daitokuji (Daitoku Temple) in 1958; thereafter, Fuller popularized Zen on the East Coast at the institute Sōkei-an had founded.[97] Thus, in evoking gilt designs originally from Kōdaiji, initially run by Hideyoshi's widow Kita-no-Mandokoro, the bottle also cited Zen traditions that Americans possibly recognized. Hence, consumers could vicariously consume Japan's luxurious national treasures and now-fashionable religious traditions, while reassured by a US perfumer's expertise, whose skill already produced numerous best-selling scents resonating with American tastes. Intriguingly, the scent and its bottle were thus a unique Japanese-American coproduction with important symbolic value, just like Sakai's triumphant final leg of the Olympic torch relay.

Not long after launching this perfume, Shiseidō opened a US subsidiary in 1965. During the 1960s, the corporation experienced phenomenal domestic successes, due to pent-up consumer demand for quality products at reasonable prices, but also from the accessible luxury promised by these commodities. According to University of Tokyo economist Kazuyuki Motohashi, "This strong growth is attributed to its business model, which consisted of voluntary chain stores built over a resale system in which stores were obligated to sell products in their retail stores at set prices."[98] Such new prosperity also translated into greater confidence in risk-taking, and coincided with the company's first expansion overseas into markets with sizable Japanese populations or partial Japanese ancestry: Shiseidō's "first overseas sales were in Taiwan in 1957, followed by . . . product launches in the United States, with Hawaii in 1962, New York and other cities in 1965."[99] Such forays into East Asian and then American markets characterized the trajectory of many Japanese companies producing consumer products. Now that Japan built a reputation for quality manufacturing and marketed renewed cultural traditions eliding colonial pasts, purchasing Japaneseness appealed to consumers of Japanese products. The future Sanrio Corporation, whose iconic cartoon character

Consuming the Bright Life

Hello Kitty took the world by storm in the mid-1970s, arrived at this time.

SANRIO: CAPITALIZING ON "CUTE" (1960–PRESENT)

One of the most successful marketing stories where a Japanese company capitalized on its uniquely Japanese origins was Sanrio's 1974 development of Hello Kitty. Though Shiseidō and other companies increasingly purveyed products internationally representing Japanese forms of luxury or high quality, Hello Kitty truly became a global phenomenon with generations of loyal fans worldwide. Sanrio goods were well-made, yet affordable, so young women and even children could buy them frequently to create collections demonstrating in commodity form the "bright life" once promised by 1950s-era Japanese government officials. However, while hints of Hello Kitty's appeal and that of other cartoon friends appeared in early products, the company's initial history revealed glimpses of future inroads among diverse global fans.

Founded on August 10, 1960, by Tsuji Shintarō (b. 1927) as the Yamanashi Silk Company, Sanrio's (established in 1974) corporate precursor arrived during Prime Minister Ikeda's pivotal Income Doubling Plan. Tsuji's company's name referenced the bucolic, mountainous wine- and fruit-producing area where he was born outside Tokyo, and initially provided Japanese women consumers with much-needed domestically produced cloth to sew kimonos. In the postwar period, new clothing allowed Japanese to finally express brighter and more hopeful attitudes when economic hardships were increasingly viewed as past events. Thus, as individual incomes rose, people enjoyed more disposable income to purchase items to brighten their lives beyond bare necessities. Postwar Japanese experiencing decades of war and straitened circumstances were wary of luxury but allowed themselves increasingly more small-scale indulgences. These included gifts for family, relatives, friends, and work companions, initially purchased for altruistic reasons to bring joy to individuals on special occasions when personal splurges were still frowned upon.

Daniel Miller, in ethnographical work on shopping among seventy-six ordinary working- to middle-class multiethnic households in mid-1990s North London,[100] characterized shopping as "a primary technology of love within modern relationships"[101] primarily expressed as "daily provisioning of everyday goods."[102] Here, mainly housewives

184   *Chapter 5*

purchased necessary items for family members, with occasional treats bought to express tender feelings and devotion toward individuals amid generally frugal conceptions based on thrift. These "treats" were small, still affordable luxuries that revealed domestic sacrifices performed amid quotidian household management. Gifts of small, high-quality yet affordable manufactured products thus served to activate what Sanrio's founder Tsuji called "social communication," or "expression of respect and love" toward another through the mediation of objects.[103] Interestingly, Miller's theory of shopping strongly resonates with how Tsuji recently defined his company's philosophy based on purveying products representing "social communication":

> In order to get along with one another, we need to respect and to love. And the expression of respect and love is the basis of Sanrio's "Social Communication" business. Ever since Sanrio's establishment in 1960, this philosophy has been the core of our business, which ranges from the design and sale of social communications gifts and greeting cards, to publishing, production and distribution of the Strawberry Newspaper, to the planning and operation of theme parks. The common thread running through all our various business is the idea of giving "from the heart" and "of the heart." Whether one is sad, down, happy or whatever . . . we want to help people share their important feelings with one another.[104]

Here, Sanrio's products usefully mediate social relations by stimulating emotional ties through objects, potentially showing recipients givers' wishes to convey respect and love—and especially, demonstrate sincere feelings toward others. Essentially, this is a classic example of commodity fetishism.

Sociologist Marcel Mauss's 1925 study *The Gift* proposes that exchanges of objects deeply influence social relations, further strengthened through gift-giving and reciprocity to benefit group social dynamics.[105] Indeed, Miller's later study *The Comfort of Things*, which examined how people related to objects in their homes and others around them, discovered that "relationships . . . flow constantly between people and things."[106] Individuals attach specific narratives to dearly held objects, often because they were given by a beloved person or acquired while accompanying those with whom they felt strong emotional connections. However, if commodities themselves could generate such feelings without intermediaries, then amid consumer

Consuming the Bright Life
185

capitalism's bounds, companies could succeed in developing winning products.

Developed in 1867, Karl Marx's concept of commodity fetishism proposes that commodities mediate social relations, where labor producing the commodity is hidden, while the commodity's abstract and subjective value becomes perceived as concrete and objective.[107] Hence, the commodity's use value or *perceived* use value becomes the most important aspect of its existence on the market. Thus, commodity fetishism only works when it mediates social interaction. This appears in the Yamanashi Silk Company's trajectory from cloth purveyor to seller of gift items or greeting cards "luxuriated" with cheerful patterns communicating bright optimism to make recipients feel "respect and love" "from the heart" and "of the heart."[108]

In 1962, this cheery optimism was expressed in the first pair of rubber sandals Tsuji decorated with flowers; the company soon began producing a line of gift items with a strawberry pattern, all commodities known as *fanshii guzzu,* or "fancy goods" in English.[109] Later, Sanrio encapsulated this notion in iconic cartoons developed for wildly popular goods in subsequent decades, beginning with Hello Kitty in 1974. Media scholar Sharon Kinsella defines "fancy goods" as small, desirable gift items referencing Western-style foreign flavors in a Japanese context.[110] Indeed, "fancy" implies Occidentalist exoticism, often with imagined Anglo-American or French provenances, where the ordinary acquires airs of luxury due to allegedly Western origins or imitating Western products connoting hospitality or personal courtesy, like tea sets or stationery materials offered by the company. In 1962, noting his discovery that flowers or strawberries decorating a commodity increased its popularity, Tsuji reportedly said, "If you attach added value or design to the product, they sell in a completely different way."[111] Interestingly, the flowers, patterns, and then characters that Tsuji placed onto products were exactly what created their value or "luxuriated" goods by creating greater value.

To synthesize sociopolitical, economic, and cultural notions of value, anthropologist David Graeber argues in *Towards an Anthropological Theory of Value*[112] "that value will necessarily be a key issue if we see social worlds not just as a collection of persons and things but rather as a project of mutual creation, as something collectively made and remade."[113] For Tsuji's "social communications business," his pattern- and flower-enhanced "fancy goods" allowed remaking an

186   *Chapter 5*

idealized social world based on "respect and love," where individuals gave gifts and exchanged items to solidify relationships among both closest contacts and workplace colleagues. Of course, if one considers specifically Japanese notions of reciprocity where gifts require exchanges of slightly less valuable items than the giver's, or a future social obligation, this model where consumers and fans favor a certain character (or set) thus allows for repeated purchasing and infinite reproduction of such social relations within consumer capitalism's monetized setting. Fancy goods are "valued" not because of the amount or quality of labor producing them—a split-second decal stamp or colors imprinted upon plastic surfaces—but because of the product's commodification in ways that fetishize its value.

Clearly, the mid-1960s expansion of this new business method spelled an important evolution for Tsuji's company, when he instituted key changes to propel it into its current powerhouse. In 1968, the Yamanashi Silk Company received a license to produce products featuring Snoopy, American cartoonist Charles M. Schulz's (1922–2000) beloved beagle character from the long-running Peanuts comic strip (1950–2000).[114] These products' popularity revealed how Japanese consumers adored items adorned with well-received American cartoon animals or characters. In 1969, Tsuji developed the Sanrio Greetings Company, Ltd. Allegedly, Tsuji took "San," meaning "saint" in Spanish, from the names of Southern California cities like San Diego and San Francisco, and added "rio," Spanish for "river," as an homage to the US state harboring his idol Walt Disney's (1901–1966) home.[115] Other sources indicate that "Sanri" came from Chinese-style (*onyomi*) readings of Japanese characters for Yamanashi, Tsuji's birthplace, with "o" as the sound excited consumers made when receiving his desirable products.[116] In 1971, the first Sanrio "Gift Gate" shop opened in Tokyo's popular Shinjuku shopping hub.[117] In April 1973, the Yamanashi Silk Company changed its name to Sanrio Company, and its corporate headquarters were moved to the Gotanda area of Tokyo's Shinagawa ward, an important transportation network.[118]

From 1974 to 1976, illustrator Shimizu Yuko (b. 1946) developed and drew the Hello Kitty character, also known as "Lady Kitty"; her full name was Kitty White, born in London's suburbs, who enjoyed her mother's apple pie and possessed Blood Type A (most common for Japanese and northern Europeans).[119] British provenance for the company's first character was sparked by late 1960s and mid-1970s Anglophilia, inspired by the Beatles' 1966 Tokyo tour, Emperor Hirohito's 1971 visit to England after fifty years, and Queen Elizabeth II's 1975 reciprocal visit. In decorating "fancy goods," Hello Kitty first appeared in 1975 on a coin purse, with her popularity skyrocketing.[120] Hello Kitty–related goods were sold in the United States starting in 1976, in Europe in 1978, and elsewhere in Asia in 1990; by the early 2000s, Sanrio products were most popular in Japan (and elsewhere) among adult women ages eighteen to forty.[121]

In *Pink Globalization: Hello Kitty's Trek across the Pacific,* anthropologist Christine Yano provides a feminist critique of the global Hello Kitty phenomenon and its development, along with associated *kawaii* (cute) cultures, and analyses this mouthless, and arguably, voiceless, character's mystique. Yano describes a compelling market success story; while admiring Kitty-*chan*'s tenacity, she questions her allure as an icon seemingly representing female passivity. In a July 17, 2020, opinion piece in *Nikkei Asia,* a global business newspaper, Nobuko Kobayashi, managing director of transaction advisory services for the accounting firm Ernst & Young Japan, viewed *kawaii* culture as harmful to Japanese businesswomen by detracting from their workplace success with still-engrained stereotypes of gendered behavior.[122] Regardless of whether certain fandoms perpetuated detrimental gender norms, they also permitted valuable identity markers for individuals reticent about self-expression.

This is particularly true of teens. In the late 1990s, as a junior high school English teacher at eight Nagoya suburban schools in the Japan Exchange and Teaching program, I noticed that shyer girls and boys enthusiastically conversed with me when I asked about their cellphone charms or school-bag toggles featuring Hello Kitty, Bad Batsumaru (a Sanrio penguin character), Doraemon (a blue robot), Kyorochan (a candy company's small bird character), and others.[123] At liminal developmental stages, middle schoolers identified with *kawaii* culture, while a pantheon of characters helped them navigate growing responsibilities as comforting protective talismans from childhood. For Japanese (and others) childhood itself is luxurious, as individuals enjoy soon-to-be-rare moments of complete freedom from financial, social, and emotional responsibilities—which only wealthy adults potentially circumvent by outsourcing responsibilities to others paid to handle them. Hence, in quotidian manipulation by their owners' hands, these tangible characters provide immediate access to extraordinary symbolic realms. Undoubtedly, numerous women fans feel similarly.

Here, Yano agrees with Anne Allison's analysis of *kyarakutā* (characters) as "enchanted commodities" bringing "enchantment and fun as well as intimacy and identity,"[124] yet she asserts that while *kyarakutā* are often associated with children, they also "transform the adult world—fraught with responsibilities, dangers, and global matters—into a haven of play and nostalgized childhood."[125] She cautions consumers to look beyond products' allure, and urges realistic perceptions of *kyarakutā* as "commodities" that "circulate through capitalist realms of exchange and social relations of consumption"[126] where "the commodity fetishism of Hello Kitty lives in and through excess."[127] This seemingly infinite material abundance decorated by characters includes clothing, cosmetics, blankets, and household objects like Hello Kitty rice cookers, thermoses, rice bowls, and even "massagers."[128] Yano argues that all Hello Kitty's incarnations remain commodities "attributed with special powers derived in part through the multiple manifestations of late-capitalist excess."[129] In a Benjaminian sense, Hello Kitty thus becomes a material object involved in the world's "re-enchantment" within societies shaped by late industrial capitalism's alienating processes. Imbuing of magical properties into Sanrio characters resembling cute neotenous animals or extraordinary household items, especially talking food (egg yolks, salmon filets, or burned bean-paste rolls), has accelerated in recent years.

Contemporary characters like Gudetama (initiated in 2013),[130] a lazy egg too apathetic to dance for his Twitter followers, are designed to appeal to overworked Millennials, while Aggretsuko (initiated in 2015),[131] a harried red panda working amiably as an accounting company "office lady" who decompresses with heavy metal karaoke, caters to Generation Z workers' frustrations. Interestingly, Gudetama won a 2016 fan contest over Kirimi, a cooked salted Chilean salmon filet slice (a common Japanese side dish) sporting a fish sausage (*kamaboko*) on her head; both feature handless pink plush arms and legs.[132] Born August 31, 2013, as a character, Kirimi literally exists to be consumed: "She's best friends with Kamaboko. When cut into slices, she hopes she tastes good. . . . This is Kirimi's reason for being. She's waiting to be eaten together with all her friends at the table."[133] While Kirimi's passivity and vulnerable cuteness enamor some consumers, Gudetama's childlike refusal, curmudgeonly apathy, bizarrely sexual rear, and plump yolk-like body attracts fans of all ages and genders, judging by his preponderance of merchandise.[134] Both Gudetama and Aggretsuko provide edgier alternatives to "cuteness" communicated by the relatively innocuous Hello Kitty character, and they represent Sanrio's responsiveness to conditions today's consumers more readily relate to. If a new (or rediscovered) character becomes popular, encouraged by the company's yearly ranking contests, Sanrio produces more "goods" for consumers to purchase and collect. But some afficionados are unsatisfied with merely purchasing products; for them, personally "meeting" characters appeases their cultish enthusiasm.

For Sanrio fans, similar to American, Japanese, and other foreign tourists heading to Disneyland in Anaheim, California, to see Mickey Mouse "in person," a trip to meet favorite characters near Tokyo allows them to experience entire manufactured worlds peopled by cartoons and *kawaii* luxury based on nostalgic Western exoticism.[135] Here, luxury is situational and locational, and it must be located within certain spaces or moments. Tama New Town on Tokyo's outskirts hosts one of Japan's most popular attractions, Sanrio Puroland (*Piyūro Rando;* Pure Land), more popularly known as "Hello Kitty Land," an indoor theme park attracting over 1.5 million visitors yearly before the 2020–2022 global pandemic. Opening in early December 1990, it lost money for three years during Japan's burst economic bubble, but later revived with domestic and international popularity for Hello Kitty's brand.[136] Currently, entrance to Sanrio Puroland costs a reasonable 3,300 yen ($29.96 in mid-2021) for adults and 2,500 yen ($22.70) for children and seniors for a weekday pass, with slightly higher weekend prices (3,900 yen [$35.41] and 2,800 yen [$25.42]) and lower afternoon prices[137]—affordable compared to the larger US-based Disneyland, running at $124–$154 for a daily adult entrance and $117–$146 for children.[138] Puroland's business plan correlates with models ensuring repeat customers, frequent souvenir and "goods" purchases in strategic locations, and luring multigenerational domestic and foreign tourists.

Puroland now savvily markets to multiple age groups and consumer needs, with curated visits or *tanoshimeru o-susume puran* (recommended enjoyment plans) for grandparents, families, friends, or couples.[139] In July 2020, ninety-two-year-old Sanrio founder Tsuji Shintarō appointed his thirty-one-year-old grandson Tsuji Tomokuni as chief executive, coinciding with plans to increase revenue following the pandemic, including expanding consumer bases for all ages and nationalities.[140] Enjoying accessibility for strollers or wheelchairs, tourists generally visit attractions, including Lady Kitty House, Mymero-addrive (train ride), Sanrio Character Boat Ride, Twinkling Twin tour,

Fuwafuwa (Fluffy) Kids Land, Hello Kitty love bell, seasonal shows, and parades, while stopping at souvenir booths, shops, and character photo opportunities. The park is composed of a two-floor Sanrio Town and Puroland Village, containing most attractions, and is topped by Rainbow Land's two additional floors offering restaurants.[141] Because bringing food into Puroland is banned, except for religious or dietary restrictions, visitors can eat at any of six restaurants, including Character Food Court, Sweet Parlor, Restaurant Yakata, Sanrio Rainbow World Restaurant, and Cinnamoroll Dream Cafe.

The park's flagship Occidentalist fine-dining buffet, Yakata no Resutoran (Mansion Restaurant), provides families a kid-friendly luxury experience where elegance and glamour props invite customers to enjoy their surroundings without exclusivity. In Japan, only high-end hotels usually offer Western-style buffets, and costs typically discourage families. A British-style fake white limestone-and-brick building beckons with potted cedars and comforting lights framing a faux marble–tiled hallway entrance framed by iron grillwork. A discreet clock looms, reminding customers of the permitted dining hour, with ten additional minutes for families' stroller- or wheelchair-encumbered departures with children and grandparents.

Besides consuming "British" food from Lady Kitty's country, fans dine at Restaurant Yakata to meet six different Sanrio characters, including Hello Kitty, Dear Daniel (Kitty's male cat friend), Cinnamoroll (a long-eared, green-eyed white lapin), My Melody, Pompompurin (a yellow French dog), and Wish Me Mell (a white rabbit with pink polka-dot ears). Fans can hug, pet, compliment, and converse with characters coming to their table in exclusive one-on-one encounters. Most visitors understand that the characters are costumed employees playing roles, as in Disneyland, but pretending the imaginary, "enchanted" world is real augments their enjoyment as they see past-purchased products come to life.

Another treat is sampling expensive meat- and dairy-centric Western cuisine at reasonable prices for ordinary Japanese (in Japan, meat and dairy products cost more than in the United States, Great Britain, or Australia). Before the pandemic, the affordable buffet cost 2,900 yen ($26.60 in early 2020) for adults, 1,500 yen ($13.76) for elementary schoolers, and 1,100 yen ($10.09) for children age three to school age; it provided consumers "exotic," hearty Anglo-American cuisine resembling mid-twentieth-century British department store cafeterias.[142] Ordinarily, Puroland's English-language website promises a buffet of "40 menu items including a featured menu of deluxe roast chicken, deluxe roast pork, home-made beef tongue stew, and the chef's recommended apple cake, as well as salad, dessert, and more! All-you-can-drink soft drinks are also included."[143] Pandemic safety modifications converted the buffet into a weekend-only operation, where patrons junior high age and above received trays of four main dishes, three sides, rice, salad, soup, soft drink, and ice cream for 2,420 yen ($21.99 in mid-2021), while three-year-olds to elementary schoolers enjoyed three kid-friendly bite-sized Western main dishes featuring a chicken nugget, fries, and hot dog, Hello Kitty–shaped rice with pickled radish, salad, soup, and soft-serve ice cream in a tiny Pompompurin (Pompom Pudding) mug for 1,540 yen ($13.99).[144] This luxurious bounty of all-one-can-eat roasted meats, gratins, and stews, complete with dinner rolls, salad, and soft drinks, represented an affordable splurge for middle-class families, which Covid-19 safety measures had tempered during the pandemic.

Puroland customers could also reserve a nearby well-appointed Hello Kitty–themed hotel room. Global popularity of Japan's *kawaii* culture and rising fandoms prompted two Tokyo-area luxury hotels from Keio Plaza's elite hotel line to design several themed rooms. From 2014 to 2019, when it was discontinued, Keio Plaza Hotel in Tokyo's bustling Shinjuku area offered hotel guests four Princess Kitty rooms and four Kitty Town rooms, featuring a take-home Hello Kitty doll, pouch, slippers, stationery, skin-care set, key book, and bottled water.[145] The luxurious rooms featured character color schemes, Princess Kitty *en-relief* plastic murals, shoelike chairs, Hello Kitty framed prints, themed appliances, and other amenities generating pleasurable encirclement by the value-added character.

Unsurprisingly, this luxurious experience was pricey: in 2017, the Shinjuku-based hotel charged two guests 66,528 yen ($603.41) and 74,056 yen ($671.69) including breakfast.[146] A beautifully presented multicourse breakfast with drink carafes prolonged the Hello Kitty–charged atmosphere with character-shaped foods and elegant Western-style white tablecloth dining.[147] In January 2019, the Shinjuku-based rooms reverted to ordinary guestrooms, while that June, Keio Plaza Hotel-Tama, proximate to Puroland, added four Sanrio character-themed rooms to existing ones from 2014,[148] including Hello Kitty, My Melody, and Little Twin Stars (Kiki and Lala).[149] Currently, they

192   *Chapter 5*

cost 60,500 yen ($549.03 in mid-2021) for two adults.[150] Here, Hello Kitty "luxuriated" hotel lodgings, or, like Sanrio's president Tsuji has indicated, "attached added value" to the product to create more value.

Realistically, value for Sanrio characters and curated experiences lay within in-person purchases, which failed to transfer into online marketplaces: in June 2020, during social distancing, Sanrio suffered massive revenue losses. The global news network CNN noted that "for the year ended March, net profits plunged 95% from the previous year to 191 million yen ($1.8 million), due largely to a drop in merchandise sales and the closure of its theme parks. Sales fell 6.5%."[151]

Adding value by applying popular characters like Hello Kitty to products and experiences, whether in theme parks, hotel rooms, or airplane exteriors to attract consumers, much resembles designer goods' brand-name logos. In the 1970s, consumers of Hello Kitty and other *kiyarakutā* prefigured skyrocketing Japanese (and near-global) obsessions with brand names and logos in the affluent 1980s.[152] Thus, Hello Kitty (or another Sanrio character) was an initial step for girls and young women fanatical about cute culture and its affordable fandom, while their quest for the latest, most popular "goods" featuring favorite characters resembled slightly older professional women craving European high-fashion leather goods. Contemporary practices of applying cartoon characters to fashion are expanding; in 2020, Paris-based luxe fashion brand Balenciaga designed the Hello Kitty Medium Ville Top Handle bag, selling for $2,590 in the United States.[153] Due to growing overlapping fandoms, it is surprising that official coproductions between the Hello Kitty brand and luxe French label Louis Vuitton (LV) have not yet appeared.

However, "unofficial" homages to Hello Kitty and LV have earned great acclaim. In 2021, Los Angeles–based American street fashion designer Sheron Barber (b. 1981), creator of the military/police-inspired "tactical-fashion" brand DR14, developed bespoke deconstructed designs from LV bucket bags and purses decorated with Italian leather Hello Kitty–like accents to honor the cute Japanese character.[154] In 2019, Barber pioneered a unique process reassembling high-fashion luxury leather goods like LV, and sewing together components of other designer purses like Hermès to create larger, more functionable pieces attaining sublime luxury.[155] Barber hails from a New Jersey working-class background, where high-priced, high-quality used fashion pieces are shared for years between family members and friends rather than purchased new; Barber's creativity was sparked by ingeniously retailoring vintage LV items to develop new, more fashionable designs still lasting a lifetime.[156]

These bespoke pieces hosting Barber's name brand, due to value-added artisanal labor by himself and his craftspeople, brought him design-world critical acclaim rather than legal trouble. A *Forbes* cover article on Bernard Arnault (b. 1949), head of Möet Hennessy Louis Vuitton, quotes Barber citing Arnault as inspiring his success.[157] Though possibly inspired by Balenciaga's product, Barber initially created Hello Kitty purses to treat his young daughter, who adored the character.[158] An innovator like Tsuji, the American designer conceived lucrative new business opportunities by using a licensed character to create greater value.

Handmade as individual retooled designer works by Barber's own craftspeople, these remarkable pieces now command ultra-luxury prices to select buyers, and are thus usually purchased by celebrities and entertainers like Chris Brown, Drake, Rihanna, Quavo, Young Thug, and 21 Savage, among others.[159] This initially "renegade" appropriation of LV and the iconic Hello Kitty pattern, blended with the refashioned "base" of a highly recognizable French logo, reveals how entrenched the Japanese cartoon emblem has become in global luxury fashion worlds, where Kitty White is now celebrated in hip-hop music circles to symbolically transcend racial lines.

Chapter 7 covers street fashion (both its democratization and "luxification") in more detail and investigates issues related to consuming communities and collecting, whether of character goods or name-brand products from certain Japanese companies.

CONCLUSION

Roughly a decade after Japan's Allied Occupation ended, the country entered a remarkable economic expansion sustained by political stability. Japan's ties to the United States through the US-Japan Alliance, enshrined in the 1951 Treaty of San Francisco, allowed for a swift economic revival bolstered by American procurements of domestically manufactured materiel during the Korean and Vietnam Wars. Postwar rapid manufacturing growth also allowed prosperity's filtering throughout Japan's social ranks, where a majority considered themselves "middle class" by the early 1970s. Nevertheless, memories of wartime hardship and potential shame associated with profligacy haunted consumption, where many still believed "luxury is the enemy"

194 *Chapter 5*

and consumers carefully weighed value for purchases before buying. Hence, high quality became an expected aspect of products demanded by consumers—even if they were initially considered indulgences, including once heavily taxed commodities like watches and whisky. Kotobukiya's Torys Whisky, first advertised by the delightfully selfish heavy-drinking Uncle Torys cartoon in 1958, soon became an affordable, domestically produced whisky appealing to the harried *sarariman* at bar franchises throughout Japan.

Corporations like Seikō, Shiseidō, and Casio geared their marketing tactics toward economic conditions and enjoyed steady domestic growth as Japan prepared to host the 1964 Tokyo Olympics and showcase the newly reconstructed nation to the world. To further expand, these companies set their sights overseas and successfully ventured into the United States, Europe, and East Asian countries to market specific versions of Japaneseness associated with their products—a trend flourishing in the 1970s and 1980s, explored in the next chapter. One of Japanese popular culture's most successful overseas projections was Hello Kitty, which developed as a value-added character in the mid-1970s to appeal to consumers desiring "cute" products reminding them of carefree childhoods. Originally, young Japanese consumers embraced Hello Kitty as a British character from London whose exotic whiteness heightened her appeal, while in the contemporary United States, she is now celebrated for Japanese cuteness. Even in mass-produced consumer items sold overseas and domestically, Japanese companies insisted on maintaining high quality, while retaining aspects of manufactured artisanality and periodically producing limited-edition products in innovative business models continuing until today.

Chapter Six

CONSUMING JAPANESENESS AND GLOBAL BRAND-NAME RECOGNITION

A mid global counterculture revolutions contesting restrictive Cold War social norms and politics leading to a disastrous Vietnam War, Japanese consumers rejected the generic Western modernities celebrated in prewar times, along with American popular culture once admired in the 1920s and 1950s, and sought a return to "authentic" Japanese roots. After a short social upheaval, conservative forces reestablished themselves, and the 1970s represented a reversion to general reacceptance of consumer capitalism, where Japanese uniqueness became a leitmotif also increasingly "sold" in product marketing abroad. Concurrently, Anglo-American celebrity endorsements of the time showed domestic consumers that Japanese design and high quality were superior to comparable Western standards. By the 1980s, such beliefs intersected with culturally based *Nihonjinron* (discourse on Japaneseness) ideologies, which signaled Japanese exceptionalism seemingly explaining national economic success through allegedly superior culture.

Fashion companies Comme des Garçons (1969), featuring clothing, art, and high fashion, and Issey Miyake (1970), purveying fashion and then perfume, enthralled the global fashion scene by attracting consumers with gender-neutral, quality designs evoking premodern Japanese styles and craftsmanship with artistic flair. As these companies globalized in the 1980s, they highlighted their brands' specifically Japanese provenance and cited premodern styles. Japanese high fashion's relatively affordable and less intimidating aspects increased appeal

195

196   *Chapter 6*

overseas and domestically, while other companies provided cheaper Japanese alternatives to higher-priced Western cosmetics, beauty products, beverages, and timepieces. In the late 1970s and early 1980s, American actors promoting products for companies like Suntory signaled growing use of foreign spokespeople to increase product visibility and manufacture authenticity: foreigners promoted "higher-quality" Japanese-made products as "superior" to Western originals.

As economic fortune prompted more Japanese to consume and release their long-standing luxury aversions, advertising slogans of middle-class-oriented department stores like Seibu, first opening in Tokyo's humble Ikebukuro ward as Musashino Department Store in 1940 and acquiring its present name in 1949,[1] exhorted customers to embrace a "delicious life" (*oishii seikatsu*)—essentially, an indulgent, "luxurious" life. Additionally, the contemporaneous economic revival of East Asian neighbors saw Japanese companies' repenetration of the Korean and Chinese markets that were so important in prewar times. Like Japanese counterparts, Chinese and Korean consumers discovered the less expensive high-quality luxury of Japanese products competing with similar Western name brands. Shiseidō and Kaō particularly marketed products to former Japanese colonies, rekindling specifically Japanese modernity in women customers' imaginations. By the 1980s, a brand's Japaneseness became a selling point at home and abroad.

Midcentury Counterculture Protest, Art, and Style

To understand the socioeconomic and cultural climates amid Japan's remarkable consumer society developing from the 1960s into the 1980s, clues appear in key midcentury sociopolitical transformations within a Japan keenly seeking national redefinition. Prior to the 1960 Anpō Treaty, numerous Japanese citizens protested perceived quotidian normalization of political complacency amid renewal of the 1951 Treaty of San Francisco enabling continued US military protection of Japanese security, which Japan's government eventually strong-armed through the National Diet, or legislature. This included writers and artists, who responded with avant-garde performance art called "anti-events" by art critic Tōno Yoshiaki (1930–2005), and created provocative art objects from consumer waste detritus and discarded building supplies referencing the war and the rapid reconstruction afterward.[2]

In 1958, the groundbreaking Tokyo-based *Yomiuri Indépendent* exhibition pioneered new art forms and inspired later art trends.[3] Here, artist Arakawa Shūsaku (1936–2010) exhibited a piece from his controversial late 1950s "Coffin Series"; he moved to New York City in 1961 to learn from Marcel Duchamp (1887–1968) and joined the Neo-Dadaism Organizers group (active from 1960 to 1963).[4] His series featured stained wooden boxes lined with faded silk futons (cotton-filled bedding) harboring embryo-like globules of cement amalgamating fur and hair, with some in cotton wrapping, which American critics perceived as grotesquely evoking human corpses perishing in Allied bombing raids or US atomic attacks.[5] The artist named some pieces for famous scientists, "referencing science fiction and surrealism and evoking the recent memory of war."[6] Having experienced childhood air raids, Arakawa sought ways to cheat death through art, including living space. Five years before his sudden 2010 death, I toured his 2005 Reversible Destiny Lofts in Tokyo's Mitaka suburb. He seemed delighted when I called him "Japan's surrealist architect," referencing his use of biomorphous forms, riotous juxtapositions of shapes and colors, and uneven, bumpy floors intended to challenge and develop the senses to create lived experiences like children or elderly persons in cognitive flux.[7]

Described as an important artistic "crucible" by Arakawa's Neo-Dadaist colleague Akasegawa (Katsuhiko) Genpei (1937–2014), the unjuried yearly *Yomiuri Indépendent* exhibition was held in the Tokyo Metropolitan Museum of Art and enjoyed sponsorship by the politically right-leaning *Yomiuri Shimbun* from 1949 to 1963, when it was suddenly canceled, anticipating the 1964 Tokyo Olympics.[8] The *Yomiuri* originally used this yearly exhibition to reveal the newspaper's support of modernity and democratization during the Occupation, but it soon evolved into a venue for truly experimental and radical art, even presaging the punk movement's general tenor. Yet, the increasingly conservative Japanese government began to perceive some of its art as dangerous.

Akasegawa and others in the leftist-sounding Dadaist "Hi-Red Center" art collective, formed in 1963 under Yoshimura Masunobu (1931–2011), were viewed as ideologically threatening, even though their group's name arose from "English translations of the first character of the family names of its three primary members, Takamatsu Jirō, Akasegawa Genpei, and Nakanishi Natsuyuki."[9] In November 1965,

198 *Chapter 6*

Akasegawa was indicted for the "crime" of reproducing a thousand-yen bill (about \$39.50 in mid-2021 currency) for his 1963 art series *Morphology of Revenge,* which he called "modeling" (*mōkei sen'en satsu;* "model" thousand yen bill); he soon turned the lengthy court trial (1966–1970) into performance art, where artist friends testified, merging art objects, photographs, documents, and other testimonies into his exhibit.[10] From the mid-to-late 1960s, Hi-Red Center artists thus playfully questioned values for money and art in capitalist society, and protested against a government seemingly unable to differentiate between counterfeiting and artistic interpretation—generating important art world debates on authenticity.

Akasegawa and his colleagues also objected to how a supposedly democratic nation allegedly shirking its fascist past treated marginalized people in Japan, and highlighted their activities against a backdrop where Japan soon reentered the global arena. According to art historian Taro Nettleson, in mid-October during the Tokyo Olympics, Hi-Red Center performers cleaned swanky Ginza shopping area streets with dish detergent "as a critique of the fervor with which the state had cleansed the streets of Tokyo, not only of trash and debris but also of unwanted citizens such as the homeless and *shisōteki henshitsusha* or 'thought perverts', in an effort, which many described as 'war-like', to present Japan to foreign visitors in the best light possible."[11] Ironically, Ginza was also Japanese luxury product consumption's epicenter; hence, the artists critiqued consumer capitalism's detrimental effects where the poor were unwelcome except as low-paid workers.

Historian William Marotti believes that through such performance art "happenings" and in concrete artworks, Akasegawa "affirmed the potential of a radical art to create 'moments' disclosing the 'dictatorial system of "everydayness,"' loosening the grasp of a naturalized world of 'real things,' and allowing its transformation to become conceivable."[12] Essentially, Akasegawa and his cohort desired breaking destructive cycles of commodity fetishism so firmly entrenched in their society, including money's sacrosanct position. Neo-Dadaist use of found objects, molding detritus into artworks, and spontaneously generating "happenings" and art events by Arakawa, Akasegawa, and others in the early to mid-1960s presaged the radical dynamism suffusing late 1960s and early 1970s art scenes in Japan and the United States.[13] The so-called 1969 generation benefited from these artists' works and actions in movements a decade prior, prefiguring Vietnam War–era protests and countercultural youth movements issuing from popular challenges to the state and society. These aspects also reappeared in global punk currents in the 1970s and beyond.

In the self-reflective semi-autobiographical 1987 novel *69*, writer Murakami Ryū (b. 1952) details middle-class Japanese high school students' lives near an American military base in Sasebo, Kyūshū, and their subtle transformations in liberating a hedonism contradicting their increasingly conformist society.[14] Previously, Murakami gained domestic and international fame for decadent novels depicting drug use and characters refusing Japan's largely middle-class, intensely consumerist society. These included *Kagirinaku tōmei ni chikai burū* (Almost Transparent Blue), a fiercely descriptive sketch of edgy youth exploring society's margins, winning the Gunzō Prize for New Writers and the highly coveted Akutagawa Prize in 1976.[15] Though *69*'s teenaged main character, Yazaki Kensuke, and his friends only peripherally participate in the larger student protests rocking Japan, they personally encountered issues with their proximity to Sasebo, a US military forward base for Vietnam War operations. They occupied the roof of "Northern High . . . known for getting the best *college entrance* results,"[16] from which Kensuke never graduated, and espoused ideals mimicking American hippies, shaken by similar counterculture and civil rights protests. In this short, lighthearted romp contrasting darker, surrealist works exploring modern Japan's underbelly, Murakami depicts a story possibly recognized by contemporary American youth. In 1969, Kensuke wryly noted that "Zenkyoto, the Joint Campus Action movement, had already begun to run out of steam, but it had at least managed to keep Tokyo University from functioning for a while. Naively, we all hoped that something might actually change."[17] In chasing impossible dreams of fame with a garage band that never performed publicly, and quoting foreign philosophers' vaguely understood ideas, Kensuke focused on fun over studying, shirking a *sarariman*'s future reproducing Japan's national aspirations for middle-class economic success. For him, "there was a convenient tendency to describe people who studied for college entrance exams as *capitalist lackeys*."[18] Published during Japan's late 1980s economic apex, *69* was Murakami's literary examination of key moments when youth questioned society's expectations of education as replicating a homogenizing social system based on consumerism.

The student protests and radical art of the 1960s also highlighted that, while the Japanese Economic Miracle (1955–1991) brought greater consumer buying power, it also increased social alienation for

200　　　　　　　　　　　　　　　*Chapter 6*

working classes and urban middle classes. Bifurcated gender roles ensured that men experienced increasingly longer working hours, coupled with married women's greater household management roles, amid nationwide cultures of productivity that brutally molded youth into competitive students aiming to pass numerous schooling and employment tests. In Japan, the pursuit and attainment of material wealth within standardized life courses for the middle classes appeared to be a Faustian bargain exchanged for personal freedom.

RETURN TO NORMALCY: CONSUMER CAPITALISM AND JAPANESE EXCEPTIONALISM

In the early 1970s, Japan experienced an episode of economic uncertainty and slow growth following the Nixon shock (1970–1971), when US president Richard Nixon (1913–1994) initiated a foreign exchange reserves crisis in decoupling the dollar from the gold standard, imposed textile quotas, and accepted invitations to visit Mainland China without consulting Japan or its allies; this was compounded by the impacts of the OPEC oil crisis (1973).[19] The Japanese economy nevertheless quickly rebounded from near-recession, which could have prolonged late 1960s social protests, but instead, conservative forces began resurfacing in the mid-1970s. Japanese youth were reabsorbed into a larger socioeconomic system promising material wealth in exchange for social conformity. In the über-competitive 1970s and 1980s, such stereotypical characteristics of Japan's society became more widespread and even penetrated working-class lives when few Japanese described themselves as anything but middle class. Such perceptions were built on myths of cultural and ethnic homogeneity.

Unsurprisingly, this time period corresponded with popular *Nihonjinron* cultural ideologies. Though discourses on Japanese uniqueness had existed since the Tokugawa-era rise of *Kokugaku* (national learning), a nativist philosophy setting Japan apart from neighboring China that focused on Japanese classics and thought,[20] beliefs that Japan succeeded economically and politically following the war due to a unique culture, language, and social values began flourishing in the mid-1970s. However, according to popular culture scholar Ishikawa Satomi, after the Pacific War, "the urgent task for these *nihonjinron* authors was to persuade the Japanese people of their superiority to the West and thereby enhance its integrity"; hence, ideas about "traditional culture" developed, following introspection over democratization and civil society by political theorists like Maruyama Masao (1914–1996).[21] In the 1970s, technological innovation and Japanese-style management principles were added to these allegedly unique aspects of Japanese identity.[22] In his 1980 study *Nihonjinron no keifu* (The Genealogy of a Discourse of Japaneseness), evolving from crystallizations of public lectures, Japanese social psychologist Minami Hiroshi (1914–2001) first critically examined and codified a plethora of ideas morphing into this discourse.[23]

Concurrently, American researchers were equally interested in Japanese "uniqueness." In 1979, US sociologist Ezra Vogel published his influential book *Japan as Number One: Lessons for America.*[24] After extensive research in late 1950s Japan with yearly returns, he argued that Japan should serve as a model for a declining America: "The more I observed Japan's success in a variety of fields, the more I became convinced that given its limited resources, Japan has dealt more successfully with more of the basic problems of postindustrial society than any other country. It is in this sense, I have come to believe, that the Japanese are number one. Astounded by recent Japanese successes, I found myself wondering why Japan, without natural resources, was making substantial progress in dealing with problems which seemed so intractable in America."[25] For Vogel, Japan offered numerous models potentially beneficial to the United States, then believed to be threatened by Japanese success built upon trade expansion and economic prowess.

Almost two decades later, the Japanese national identity's allegedly inherent facets were examined by American political philosopher Seymour M. Lipset (1922–2006) in his 1996 book *American Exceptionalism: A Double-Edged Sword.* In the chapter "American Exceptionalism—Japanese Uniqueness,"[26] Lipset compares American and Japanese concepts encapsulating national identity and laments aspects of how the United States differs from Japan.[27] He believed that for Americans, "exceptionalism is a double-edged concept. . . . We are the worst, as well as the best, depending on which quality is addressed."[28] For Japan, Lipset refers to Japanologist Scott Flanagan's studies of 1963 and Japanese government-administered National Character Surveys in 1988 indicating value changes, where a general embrace of "modernity" transformed into desires to return to "tradition" by the mid-1970s.[29] Lipset also found "evidence for the continued strength of traditional values" in studies beyond Flanagan's, along with "higher self-esteem" seemingly tied to national success.[30]

202   *Chapter 6*

Clearly, for Japanese and American social scientists, *Nihonjinron* supported perceptions of nationalism based on economic success and a mythological unique identity in Japan's ability to quickly rise from wartime ashes, conveniently forgotten to embrace a postwar mass consumer society based on a now-democratized commodity fetishism accessible to all.[31] Unsurprisingly, when middle-class Japanese families referred to aspirational products they desired as the "three imperial treasures," they cited the imperial family's traditional premodern regalia: mirror, sword, and jewel. In Vogel's late 1950s research, compiled in *Japan's New Middle Class* (1963), these were initially appliances, like an "electric refrigerator or washing machine or perhaps a vacuum cleaner."[32] By the 1960s, Japanese began coveting "'three Cs or Ks'—*kaa*, *kūrā* and *karā terebi* (car, air-conditioner and colour television)," and in the early 1970s yearned for the "'three Js'—*jūeru*, *jetto* and *jūtaku* (jewels, overseas vacation and house)."[33] Midcentury postwar Japan, experiencing similar postwar late capitalism as Europe and the United States, enjoyed unprecedented prosperity that allowed consumers to purchase a wide variety of desired products that conferred social capital. Yet, aspects of social and cultural critiques posed by 1960s-era Japanese artists and writers suffused consumers' cultural environments, and uncannily returned as uneasily repressed elements in fashion scenes.

COMME DES GARÇONS (1969): PUNK AND FETISHIZATION OF *WABI-SABI* IN ARTFUL DESTRUCTION AND PURPOSEFUL WEAR

Sociologist and fashion scholar Ruth Rubinstein, in her pivotal 1995 study *Dress Codes*, reveals how certain styles and fashions communicate the wearer's authority and cultural values.[34] In 2000, she developed a "semiotics of dress" in American contexts.[35] Yet, Rubinstein's assumption of absolute individual agency in clothing choices, where personas are carefully crafted through garments, presupposes certain factors. A semiotics of dress assumes the time, money, and privileged social position ensuring power to allow such consumer positioning. Here, political, social, and economic environments intersect to foster a semiotics of dress based on wearers' freedom for personal choice. Such a system privileges individuality and liberation from top-down political or social dictates imposed on dress.

The opposite to this spectrum is the "fashion victim" trope, where consumers fall prey to conflicting fashion dictates, and serves as a hyperbolic cautionary tale about commodity fetishism's excesses expressed in certain name brands or clothing articles, or wearing several similar clothing items simultaneously, to acquire a product's social capital. Modern consumers are sometimes depicted as unable to make sound fashion choices and are assumed to be naive. Generally, "fashion" in the United States and Japan is situated between the poles of pure consumer choice and slavish imitation, and consumers wear clothing at personal levels of affordability, comfort, and social capital, while designers often cite political and social movements when creating their products. Essentially, the semiotics of dress is an intriguing way to investigate fashions by Kawakubo Rei (b. 1942) and Miyake Issei (1938–2022), whose designs consistently remain avant-garde.

In the late 1960s, these now iconic Japanese designers achieved renown by developing unique garments with artistic styling challenging high-fashion dictates in allowing the democratization of body shape, fostering wearability, permitting fluidity of gender norms, and costing less than European or American counterparts. Building reputations in the mid-1970s into the 1980s with a preponderance of black amid profuse color in designs, and for artful distressing or craftsmanlike working of fabrics or other unusual materials rarely applied to clothing, they presented humbler, refreshing, and artistic alternatives to French and American designers' ornate opulence during unprecedented global prosperity. However, sociologist Lise Skov argues that Kawakubo and Miyake arrived at a moment when the international fashion press viewed Japanese designers as representing their nation, perpetuating an Orientalist discourse.[36]

In reality, the two designers were inspired more by Anglo-American punk currents than their own culture. Japan's most radical fashion designers arrived on the fashion scene inspired by waves of global counterculture movements also reaching Japanese shores, but whose impact soon issued outward from Japan, hitting California's Pacific Coast and reverberating to New York, then spreading across the Atlantic into London and Paris. Such cosmopolitan appropriations of global styles blended with interpretations of traditional Japanese elements while emphasizing artistic edginess. Once punk arrived in the mid-1970s global music arena,[37] its rebellious clothing by band members and fans inspired artists and carried lasting influences among Japanese designers like

204   Chapter 6

Kawakubo and Miyake, whose brands acquired cult status by the late 1980s or early 1990s in the United States and Japan.

These developments correspond to my personal experiences of these artistic currents' intersections with fashion. In the early 1990s, New York City's Lower East Side, or East Village, boasted the twentieth century's last authentic Jewish delis and several underground hardcore punk music clubs—close to the country's cutting-edge art galleries and not far from the original 1970s Greenwich Village birthplace of punk.[38] While discussing writings by Marx and Kropotkin, my friend well-versed in newer derivations of older punk scenes took me to a club ensconced within a crumbling, one-story warehouse-type brick building hosting a hidden basement venue, where strident screams were amplified by microphone-tempered metallic noise. Several long-haired Japanese men, in metal-studded black leather jackets, torn jeans, and safety pins piercing white T-shirts, lips, and ears, immersed themselves in the music, wearing outfits in homage to the Ramones (1974–1996) and other bands.[39] Their women companions were clad entirely in asymmetrical black, similar to "black crows," devotees of Kawakubo's early 1980s designs,[40] while a blaringly physical sonic wall aided momentary dissolution of self. Musician Greg Ginn (b. 1954), of the Black Flag punk band (1976–1986), discusses New York's origins for these young men's looks, which resurfaced in London and evolved into high fashion: "Richard Hell [b. 1949] was spotted in the East Village in ripped shirts held together by safety pins. Malcolm McLaren [1946–2010], then working with the Dolls, took that image in his head back to London, and with designer-wife Vivienne Westwood [b. 1941], stylized punk-fringe-Downtown-junkie-artist-squalor to high fashion and pop culture."[41] In the East Village, the buildings' November bleakness striated with black-and-white graffiti indicated liminal spaces where youth, including Japanese and American tourists like us, sought comforting oblivion in a city often too concerned with outer appearances—where DIY punk clothing and Kawakubo's couture could coexist.

The next day, our brief foray into the neo-punk scene led to a Bleeker Street thrift shop where I purchased a bargain-priced navy peacoat near the Greenwich Village atelier of Arakawa and his partner Madeline Gins (1941–2014). Thus attired, in a creative city section that attracted numerous Japanese artists like Arakawa, I advanced into avant-garde art gallery areas near New York's famous SoHo (south of Houston Street), where one gallery featured a roaming donkey under a chandelier overshadowing a polished wooden floor festooned with the animal's excrement. Amused by the spectacle of an animal clearly oblivious to pretentious critics hovering around, we left to shop and sightsee.

Struck by a display of long woolen coats suspended from wire strings, I wandered into a nearby SoHo atelier. There, a soft army-green boiled wool form-fitting cashmere coat beckoned me to try it on, feeling light and warm while flattering my swimmer's physique. The Comme des Garçons boutique's airy, minimalist atmosphere with glass windows filtering light upon blond wooden floors highlighted clothing like honored guests in a welcoming setting, radically opposed to stuffy, exclusivist European couture. Here, I could try on as many clothes as I liked despite my obvious cash-strapped youth. This high-end boutique represented Kawakubo's designs alongside antifashion elements amid New York City's now hip ruins during early 1990s gentrification and a modest nationwide economic recession. By the late 1990s, the area would host vibrant boutiques of another avant-garde Japanese designer, Miyake Issei: Pleats Please opened on Prince Street in May 1998, and Issey Miyake, designed by architect Frank Gehry (b. 1929), launched in Tribeca on Hudson Street in 2001.[42]

In 1969, when Kawakubo branched out from stylist work to design a clothing line, her stunning success was initially unanticipated; inspiration came from the modest loose-fitting traditional garb of Japanese peasants and fishermen whose look quickly became popular among fans attuned to luxury fashion.[43] In 1973, she incorporated Comme des Garçons in Tokyo, which soon grew into an international sensation, with designs that *New Yorker* staff writer Judith Thurman called "clothing as wearable abstraction" showing in Paris, London, and New York City fashion weeks.[44] In its initially monochromatic palette, with artfully distressed clothing featuring asymmetry and the ubiquitous black, Kawakubo's work and attitude cited Zen Buddhism's anti-authoritarianism, coupled with the punk movement's activist artistic roots still evident in New York's art world over two decades later. Fashion luminaries including Karl Lagerfeld (1933–2019) praised Kawakubo's daring, where "she gave a new sense of beauty to the standard idea of what was considered 'beautiful' in the world of fashion," while contemporary artist Cindy Sherman (b. 1954), who collaborated with her as a 1990s-era model, noted that "she doesn't answer to anyone, doesn't care if her designs are wearable or functional, much less salable."[45]

206   *Chapter 6*

For the now-iconic Holes collection (fall/winter 1982–1983), the Comme des Garçons brand became known for Kawakubo's designs of ingeniously loomed sweaters with intentional holes, which she created by "programming the loom to create a fabric with randomly placed holes."[46] Interestingly, the company artificially manufactured what many young (and frugal) adherents of punk looks either affected by wearing worn vintage clothing or intentionally hand-distressed to achieve particularly edgy appearances. Anthropologist Dorinne Kondo views this collection as Kawakubo aiming "to introduce the surprise of the imperfect, the trace of the handmade, into the process of mechanical reproduction."[47] Here, the designer imparts consciously manufactured artisanality into a mass-produced clothing line to make each piece unique as an irreproducible luxury emblem.

In an April 2017 *New York Times* article published during the height of Kawakubo's success, which coincided with an unprecedented exhibition of her work, fashion critic Alexander Fury posits, "More broadly, isn't the entire spiky, confrontational identity of Comme des Garçons peculiarly punk?"[48] Kawakubo's collections consistently cited punk themes for over three decades, pointing to long-standing inspiration: Destroy, featured on Paris runways (1982), Adult Punk (fall/winter 1997–1998), Hard and Forceful (fall/winter 2000), and 18th-Century Punk (fall/winter 2016–2017). Fury also highlights the designer's lack of pretentiousness and egalitarianism: "In an age of designer-celebrity-saturation and overexposure, the fact Kawakubo has refused to bow at the end of any of her shows for decades is, possibly, the most punk gesture of all."[49] Essentially, Kawakubo forcibly sought to shift the focus onto her clothing and its unique artistic qualities emphasizing wearers' individuality instead of amplifying her designer persona like many Europeans or Americans.

At the time, Fury's article helped publicize the much-anticipated New York Metropolitan Museum of Art's historic 2017 exhibit *Rei Kawakubo / Comme des Garçons: Art of the In-Between,* one of only two living designers' fashion exhibitions, with French couturier Yves Saint Laurent (1936–2008) as the first. The exhibition catalog of Kawakubo's work rhapsodically lists "strategies that recur in Kawakubo's collections—fusion, imbalance, the unfinished, elimination, and design without design" and notes that "these modes of expression, [are] all rooted in a Zen Buddhist aesthetic principle known as wabi-sabi"[50] in a commentary fetishizing the sublime clothing's "Japaneseness" also likened to avant-garde art. In the catalog, the museum's curators thus characterized Kawakubo's sculptural monochrome contributions, arguably exoticizing and orientalizing the pieces and historicizing them to viewers: "The expressions of mu, ma, and wabi-sabi in her early 1980s collections, unfamiliar to most Western audiences, were interpreted by some observers as grotesque or offensive. An iconic black sweater pierced with holes from 1982 exemplifies what many critics called Kawakubo's 'ugly aesthetic.' She dubbed it her 'lace'" sweater, clarifying: 'To me they're not tears. Those are openings that give the fabric another dimension. The cutout might be considered another form of lace.'"[51]

Andrew Bolton, who curated *Rei Kawakubo / Comme des Garçons: Art of the In-Between,* believes that Kawakubo's work is understandable through the lens of Zen *kōan,* which she once disclosed in an interview describing her creative process.[52] Certainly, Zen Buddhist concepts are easily perceived in her choices of materials, including purposefully knit holes ("nothingness"), boiled wool (playful use of "space"), and fetishization of time and wear ("wabi-sabi") in Comme des Garçons' clothing articles. Additionally, Kawakubo's simple patterns brutally deny high fashion's ostentatiousness with artfully distressed, deeply colored boiled wool pieces and increasingly iconic black sweaters with enloomed holes. These highly sculpturesque creations initially remained acquired tastes for Westerners that specifically challenged opulent 1980s high fashion and beauty's exacting dictates but, by the millennium's second decade, were enshrined within New York's Metropolitan Museum of Art's hallowed halls.

More than ten years earlier, Kawakubo indicated that she was fascinated by how consumers might approach her clothes in a mass market where fashion became democratized, an interest that prompted her to collaborate with Swedish "fast fashion" purveyor H&M.[53] Jörgen Anderssen, the company's contemporaneous global marketing director, discussed how he cautiously approached Kawakubo in 2008 for their brief partnership: "We went to her with the word 'Contradiction,'" and wondered, "Could you be as artistic, highly creative as she is and still be commercial?"[54] In an April 2008 press release issued by the Swedish clothing company, Kawakubo indicated her own reasons for collaborating: "I have always been interested in the balance between creation and business. It is a dilemma, although for me creation has always been the first priority. It is a fascinating challenge to work with H&M since it is a chance to take the dilemma to its extreme, and try to solve it."[55] Honoring H&M's second Tokyo-based

208 *Chapter 6*

store, opening in November 2008 in Harajuku—a district known for innovative street fashions (detailed in chapter 7)—Kawakubo created fifty reasonably priced pieces featuring cleverly artistic and easily wearable articles for an autumn 2008 collection that included clothing for women, men, and some children's items, along with accessories and a unisex fragrance.[56] Nevertheless, Kawakubo later returned to more luxury-oriented design platforms.

In a 2012 *Asahi Shimbun* interview, Kawakubo asserted that "because good things [*īmono*] require human hands, time and effort, they are invariably expensive."[57] Yet, she also expressed fears that too many people forgot clothing's potential anti-establishment or radical messages. Many Japanese framed Comme des Garçons as "anti-logo," while the French name, translated as "like the boys," seemingly negated fickle dictates of "traditional" haute couture women's fashion dominated by Paris while embracing genderless anti-chic. Moreover, the clothing's artful craftsmanship was intended to represent itself rather than co-opt a brand or logo's allure. Kawakubo indicated that creative work is "not just about clothes. People these days are okay with passing their time even if they don't have strong, cool, or new things. Passion, excitement, anger, and the motivation to break through the status quo are diminishing. I'm worried about that trend."[58] Hence, her residual yearning to retain clothing as a form of social contestation reflected an earlier aspiration for clothing's essentiality to social protest and individuality in a society increasingly valuing conformity.

However, like designers for many Japanese name brands, Kawakubo later sought ultra-luxe venues for her fashionable creations, and she also luxuriated her fashions with the limited-edition concept long popular in Japan. For the 2014 Icons and Iconoclasts: Celebrating Monogram collection of the French fashion house Louis Vuitton, she collaborated to create six limited-edition purses; citing previous themes, each was called "Bag with Holes." In February 2021 these were reissued, with a limited number of high-end handbags sold by lottery for potential customers at Tokyo's Louis Vuitton shop along Shibuya ward's elegant Jingumae avenue.[59] Here, Kawakubo ventured far beyond her avant-garde roots. But, in adding artfully large, asymmetrical holes to handbags in seemingly random locations, she still partially subverted these pieces' alleged high-quality perfection usually too elegant to be redone as punk. The path from punk to luxe into the millennium also resembled Vivienne Westwood, once Kawakubo's 1970s inspiration and now a UK fashion icon.[60]

Despite such embraces of high-end mass luxury by designers like Kawakubo, aspects of late 1960s utopian desires expressed by Japanese artists remained constant inspirations for many and continued beyond the 1990s. Japanese designers expressed these themes in avant-garde fashions revealing a sense of egalitarianism where their clothing allegedly destroyed gender and class hierarchies with androgenous, gender-neutral clothing often in only one size or draped around the body.

Issey Miyake (1970): Passionate about Pleats

Contemporaneous to Kawakubo's bold designs challenging high fashion's premises, much of Issey Miyake's (1938–2022) work promised a return to Tokugawa-era elegance and craftsmanship combined with avant-garde art elements. Even today, Issey Miyake's Kyoto shop harkens to artisanal traditions of Japan's past cloth merchants, situated in a former *machiya* (traditional wooden "townhouse"). The *kura* (warehouse) behind the shop also mimics Tokugawa-era shopping layouts, receiving customers in the front and bringing goods from storage in back. Here, the *machiya* is refashioned as a modern art gallery enrobed in a traditional framework, featuring clothing instead of artworks, with products hanging against the walls like art and displayed in vitrines like rare treasures. Such an environment luxuriates products and enhances their manufactured artisanality while also evoking Miyake's deeply rooted symbiotic transnational connections between the Japanese and American contemporary art worlds.

To understand Miyake's role first as artist, and then as designer, along with contemporary environments where his higher-end and mass consumer–oriented designs are sold, it is illuminating to follow the designer's creative trajectory. As an artist, Miyake initially melded cosmopolitan cultural elements into his work and then began to "recover" and aggressively market his clothing's allegedly traditionally Japanese aspects within contemporary art contexts. The Hiroshima-born designer graduated from Tokyo's Tama University in 1964 and originally planned to become a commercial artist. However, his interest in fashion propelled him in 1965 to enter the Paris-based École de la Chambre Syndicale de la Couture Parisienne (School of the Union[ized] Chamber of Parisian Couture), learning essentials of fashion design drawing, creating cloth patterns, and sewing clothing; soon afterward, he began apprenticing with couturier Guy Laroche (1921–1989) and assisted

Figure 6.1. Issey Miyake Kyoto boutique, 2018. "ISSEY MIYAKE KYOTO: Opening on Saturday, March 17th" (March 17, 2018), Issey Miyake, Inc., corporate website, https://www.isseymiyake.com/en/news/1875, accessed June 28, 2021.

Hubert de Givenchy (1927–2018).[61] By 1969, perceptions of rigidity in the French couture fashion world led Miyake to spend half a year in New York, where he worked for Geoffrey Beene (1924–2004) and met iconoclastic artists like Abstract-Expressionist Robert Rauschenberg (1925–2008).[62]

In 1970, the designer returned to Tokyo to initiate the Miyake Design Studio, where he departed from France's fashion world to revisit his Japanese roots, while resisting others' labeling as particularly "Japanese."[63] In certain coal-black, almost distressed fashions, Miyake rendered dark homages to his wartime Hiroshima youth,[64] when Japanese kimono (literally, "wear(able) thing") were still plentiful for women, which more practical clothing increasingly replaced, like *monpe* (homemade trousers made from kimono bottom halves): "I learned about the space between the body and the fabric from the traditional kimono . . . not the style, but the space."[65] Because kimono are always made from a certain number of rectangular panels in a set ratio, they fit people of any shape and size, and can be unstitched and resewn in practical modifications like *monpe*.

While attracting cosmopolitan fashion-conscious Japanese consumers, Miyake's garments also slowly began intriguing New Yorkers. In 1971, he created a collection specifically for the city that so fascinated and welcomed him, including a pioneering handmade one-size-fits-all polyester piece prefiguring later fashions, and soon garnered retailing space in Bloomingdale's, Manhattan's flagship department store.[66] The designer gained a niche among New York City's most influential fashion elites with unique, allegedly "Japanese" avant-garde styles. The cover of a 1978 "coffee-table" early retrospective of the artist's past and contemporary work featured Miyake's muse, Somali-American model Iman (b. 1955), in black garments draping her body and blurring into a dark background, highlighting the deep crimson, wide, pleated obi-like belt around her waist that mirrored her red lips.[67] Other garments presage 1990s street fashion, including a baggy beige silk mechanic's suit likely citing those worn by Americans during the Occupation; a hooded black cape over black sweat pants; and a cotton oversized cinch-waisted windbreaker with a baseball cap–wearing model.[68] Former *Harper's Bazaar* and *Vogue* fashion columnist Diana Vreeland (1903–1989), then serving as Costume Institute consultant to the Metropolitan Museum of Art, where she organized fashion exhibitions,[69] provided a foreword for the book and underlined Miyake's entrenchment in this fickle world.[70]

The designer gained worldwide attention with his provocative autumn/winter 1980–1981 formfitting Bodyworks collection,[71] which toured internationally from 1983 to 1985.[72] In the 1983 traveling exhibition's catalog, Japanese and American luminaries from literary and art worlds wore Miyake's clothing, including celebrated writer and Tendai Buddhist nun Setouchi Jakuchō (1922–2021) cheerfully wearing a black *ruana* (cape) over her habit, and American celebrity pop artist Andy Warhol (1928–1987) sporting a black, kimono-like jacket.[73] Although one piece was a plastic resin bustier molding to the body, amid other torso-covering garments of resin, wire, and rattan,[74] Miyake's creations usually hang loosely over the body to allow wearers to drape and wrap garments into sculpturesque, wearable art. Other iconic pieces now housed in New York's venerable Metropolitan Museum of Art include his 1985 gray "Seashell" knit coat, featuring internal ribbing of red, lavender, and pink;[75] a black 1989 knit dress from the Cicada Pleats collection, resembling Kawakubo's creations;[76] and a spring/summer 1990 collection yellow-and-maroon draped dress displaying an early version of his APOC (A Piece of Cloth) concept prefiguring the Pleats Please brand.[77] These garments featured unique techniques like heat embossing, texturing, and artisanally

212   *Chapter 6*

generated pleats and bumps added after manufacturing. Miyake asserted that his clothes "become part of someone, part of them physically."[78]

This quasi-biomorphous melding to wearers' bodies or harmonious sculptural effects involving bodies supporting draped cloth would become Miyake's main selling points in democratizing luxury fashions at accessible price points. In 1988, he developed Pleats Please, an industrially manufactured line of polyester-made fashions emerging as its own brand in 1993. Contrasting earlier designs, it featured mass-produced fabrics in synthetic materials where articles of clothing held pleats almost indefinitely and allowed lower costs more affordable to average consumers.[79] In the 1970s and early 1980s, Miyake's first pleated creations were perfected in rayon and silk, and they required particularly laborious processes to care for them, whereby wearers needed to carefully wash garments and roll up fabric for drying to maintain pleats. Over time, the manufactured pleats' sharpness wore down and softened, with colors slowly fading, lending an elegant worn look to Miyake's garments echoing *wabi-sabi* ideals lauded by American fashion critics in Kawakubo's designs. However, these unique pleated fashions brought the designer his greatest acclaim and celebrity status, and advanced greater popular consumption of Pleats Please fashions after the mid-1990s.

Garments in the Pleats Please line and brand were cut two-and-a-half to three times larger than finished products for later pleating; this generous cloth allocation permitted a refreshing democratization of form and wearable accessibility, whereby any body type (or gender) could wear the pleated, form-flattering sheaths and pants. Miyake's creations in washable synthetic fabrics also maintained color-fastness and wrapped clients' bodies in still highly practical, beautifully wearable art. During the designer's 2016 National Art Center retrospective in Tokyo,[80] running almost concurrently with New York's Metropolitan Museum of Art Costume Institute exhibit,[81] British fashion journalist Tamsin Blanchard proposed that Miyake's "universal clothing product" achieved international appeal because "these are clothes that are made from polyester and can be machine washed, rolled up in a suitcase and unpacked to look as crisp and springy as they did when you packed them; they are light, ageless, trans-seasonal, cross-cultural, ambisexual . . . and don't cost a fortune."[82]

Echoing Blanchard, the company's English-language global website touts the Pleats Please brand concept as featuring convenient and versatile clothing permitting consumers unique experiences of luxurious high fashion integrated into everyday life: "These clothes combine functionality—they're light and wrinkle-proof, they don't need to be dry-cleaned, and they can be folded to a compact size for easy storage and carrying—with a versatility that makes them suitable for all settings in your daily life. Comfortable and beautiful too, these clothes have become deeply entrenched in the daily lives of modern women. This brand reflects Issey Miyake's fundamental concept that "'design is not for philosophy, but for life,' and continues to evolve today."[83] The Japanese website, geared toward customers in Japan and Japanese-speaking diasporas, highlights similar information, yet Miyake's original quote *Kurashi no naka de ikite koso, dezain no sonzai kachi ga aru* (Living one's daily life is the very point [or value] of design's existence)[84] is translated slightly differently in English (above) and Mandarin Chinese (*jianti-zi,* simplified characters indicating Mainland Chinese audiences—Taiwan, Hong Kong, and Southeast Asian Chinese diasporas use traditional characters, or *fanti-zi*) as *Sheji bushi weile zhexue er cunzai, ershi weile shenghuo* (Design does not exist for the sake of philosophy, but is for life).[85] Slight nuances in translating *kachi* (value, or point, meaning inclination) more broadly as "philosophy" reflect cultural inclinations and how Miyake's clothing line is marketed differently to Anglo-American and Chinese consumers.

However, how might consumers tangibly experience Pleats Please as both shopper and customer? During Japan's brutally hot July 2018, I decided to personally experience Miyake's Pleats Please design venture's branding and strolled into the Roppongi Hills boutique in Tokyo's swankiest shopping area. Situated in a mall resembling Chicago's Michigan Avenue emporia with multiple floors in soothing beige-toned oak flooring around a subtly lit central atrium, the store's white light beckoned with white walls, shiny white tile flooring, and flattering illumination highlighting the attractive, brightly colored clothing on display. Just like Issey Miyake's signature original products, the boutique featured garments in various seasonal colors and patterns in polyester serrated with tiny pleats flowing against the body into elegantly round amorphous waves. I was then eight months pregnant with my third child, and technically not seeking clothing unable to fit after her birth. Yet, the dresses' gorgeous colors and sculpturesque forms, in light, cool fabrics dispelling the summer heat, enticed me. An attentive salesman discreetly imparted that Issey Miyake's usual sizes of 1, 2, and 3 relate to length, not width, so I chose a size

214   *Chapter 6*

3 long pearl-gray sheath, which, true to his recommendations, was still elegantly wearable months (and years) later.

Miyake's less expensive line offered consumers luxury designs in an artistic, relaxed shopping environment with conscientious salespeople. Even if customers could not afford my simple Pleats Please ankle-length dress costing 25,000 yen (around $220 in 2018), those desiring luxury at affordable prices could still purchase the line's least expensive product: pleated bags in blue shades, costing only 5,000 yen (around $47 in 2018).[86] With long handles for tying into a more compact purse, these blue handbags referenced traditional Japanese indigo *furoshiki* (cloth squares tied into handheld parcels), while pleats allowed considerable size expansion to carry extra items. Basically, Pleats Please was an affordable, practical, artistic, and versatile alternative to couture fashion due to innovative mass-produced polyester pleating featured in multiple products.

However, Miyake's now-iconic pleat was not a new invention, whose "discovery" both he and a famous US designer claimed. In the 1980s, Miyake and Mary McFadden (b. 1938) allegedly simultaneously reinvented the refined Fortuny pleat developed in early twentieth-century Venice. Initially created by Spanish designer Mariano Fortuny y Madrazo (1871–1949) and his wife, costume designer Henriette Nagrin (1877–1965), classical Greek designs inspired signature Fortuny pleating and characterized their revolutionary form-flowing Delphos gown, produced from 1907 until 1950.[87] By the 1970s, Fortuny designs also became popular in the American vintage trade, with actress Lauren Bacall (1924–2014) wearing a red Delphos gown to the 1978 Oscars, which possibly showcased the pleat for Miyake and McFadden.

McFadden, like Miyake, gained fame in the 1970s and 1980s for designs citing classical and multicultural heritages. She claimed inspiration for her pleated dresses in premodern Japanese techniques, when only early processing and dying of Australian-made synthetic polyester charmeuse fabric took place there, with final signature pleating processes completed in the United States. Through a lens of cultural appropriation, McFadden thus explains the creation of her fabrics' iconic pleating: "It was Lily who developed the technique of cutting the Marii pleated silk pinned on paper patterns. Later, I found the polyester satin-back fiber in Australia that falls like liquid gold on the body, as if it were ancient Chinese silk. The fabric was always converted and dyed in Japan, according to the inspiration of each collection, then sent back to the U.S. for the heat transfer pleating process. . . . I named the technique 'Marii' pleating, a Japanese version of my name, Mary."[88] Mirroring 1980s-era American fascination with Japan amid Japanese prosperity and rivalries with the United States, in 1988 McFadden designed an Orientalist collection inspired by eleventh-century novelist Murasaki Shikibu's Heian period (794–1185) classic, *The Tale of Genji*, following completion of her yearlong 1987 close textual reading after presenting a fashion show in Japan. Her collection was "comprised of almost a hundred gowns, patterned with Japanese motifs rendered naturalistically or symbolically. Chrysanthemums, wisteria, plum blossoms, and lotus flowers were woven or painted on skirts and sleeves. Thunderbolts, waves, and golden clouds conveyed other aspects of the Japanese reverence for nature."[89] Essentially, McFadden's dresses provided canvases for her own vision of traditional Japanese motifs, exoticizing Japanese affinities for the natural world. No doubt, Miyake engaged in similar cultural appropriation amid integration into New York's art world, within interpretations of street fashions worn by Black and Latinx youth walking the city's streets and visiting his exhibitions.

Here, the global high fashion design world's porousness, where Japan remains integral, surfaces in cultural appropriations, transfers, and exchanges, evidenced when an American designer echoed a Japanese innovator's fashions inspired by a near-century-old European trend. By the 1980s, Japan and the United States were enmeshed in key essentialist cultural dialogues amid growing trade frictions, where designers and companies evoked each country's cultural "exoticism" to appeal to consumers. Such symbiotic capitalistic cultural exchange also appeared in the commercial lives of other products besides fashion, including Japanese whisky.

BEFORE BILL MURRAY: SUNTORY'S AMERICAN CELEBRITY ENDORSEMENTS

In a memorable scene from the Academy Award–winning American Hollywood film *Lost in Translation* (2003), actor Bill Murray's (b. 1950) jaded character Bob Harris, an aging film star, sits at the Shinjuku Park Hyatt bar to relax after a Suntory whisky commercial shoot. He soon meets Charlotte, a fresh-faced, jet-lagged, slightly lost young American woman played by Scarlett Johansson (b. 1984). Her bemused Orientalist interactions with Japanese in Tokyo, and Murray's frustrated attitude toward Japanese film crews while promoting whisky,

216 *Chapter 6*

lampooned cultural differences highlighted in encounters between Americans and Japanese still extant after the millennium. Critics asked director Sophia Coppola (b. 1971) if she based her film on personal experience of a 1990s Tokyo fashion shoot.[90] When faced with allegations of racism in an interview with *The Independent,* a British newspaper, Coppola clearly was uncomfortable: "'I can see why people might think that but I know I'm not racist. I think if everything's based on truth, you can make fun, have a little laugh, but also be respectful of a culture. I just love Tokyo and I'm not mean spirited,' she continues, beginning to sound slightly panicked. 'Even on our daily call sheets they would mix up the "rs" and the "ls"—all that was from experience, it's not made up.'"[91] Despite her refutations, the film is laden with racist tropes reflecting a long history of Western stereotypes of Japanese. Certainly, as director, Coppola essentialized and exoticized prior experiences, informing the film's similarly aged Charlotte, while Suntory's Japanese advertisers understood a Western foreigner's appeal in a familiar environment that to him seemed alien.

Though Bob's overpaid Suntory cameo possibly seemed novel to *Lost in Translation*'s viewers, such celebrity endorsements were not a new phenomenon; rather, they were popularized in late 1970s Japan, when Anglo-American approval of Japanese products highlighted alleged superior quality and lent them an Occidentalist allure. According to communications scholar Noriko Huruse, "Commercials presented by the celebrity-authority accounted for 24 percent of the total number of Japanese commercials. This finding indicates that use of fame is an effective strategy in Japanese commercials, and is the embodiment of the good repute of a product."[92] Findings were based on her comparative study of "50 television commercials [that] were selected respectively from 114 Japanese television commercials and 78 American television commercials videotaped during the hours between 5:00 and 9:00 p.m. on Friday, May 13, 1977."[93] These appeared in prime time, with viewers most familiar with products relying on celebrities, including Hollywood actors, to vouch for exceptional quality.

One of Japan's first foreign celebrity endorsers was British-born former "Rat Pack" member, actor Peter Lawford (1923–1984), whose first wife (1954–1966), Patricia Kennedy (1924–2006), was sister to former president John F. Kennedy (1917–1963) and senators Robert "Bobby" F. Kennedy (1925–1968) and Edward "Ted" Kennedy (1932–2009). Therefore, Lawford's 1978 Suntory Royal ad endorsement was an important achievement for the company, since he was both an established actor and immersed in elite American political and social circles. One of Japan's most celebrated directors, known overseas primarily for samurai films, Akira Kurosawa (1910–1988), shot television commercials for Suntory featuring Lawford and also filmed actors Sean Connery (1930–2020) and Peter Falk (1927–2011) in commercials. Kurosawa's participation, and well-known foreign actors like Lawford, Connery, and Falk, thus "established strong credibility" for the brand.[94]

Kurosawa hired on with Suntory to finance his iconic 1980 samurai film *Kagemusha* (Shadow Warrior), which won a Palme d'Or at the Cannes Film Festival that year. For *Kagemusha*'s international version, Francis Ford Coppola (b. 1939), flush with victory from his critically acclaimed Vietnam War film *Apocalypse Now* (1979), and George Lucas (b. 1944), director of the fabulously popular *Star Wars* (1979) and *The Empire Strikes Back* (1980), both inspired by Kurosawa's samurai epics, served as *Kagemusha*'s executive producers, and amid Tōhō Studio's budget shortfall, lobbied for Twentieth Century Fox's financing in exchange for exclusive international distribution rights.[95]

Sofia Coppola's father, Francis Ford Coppola, also appeared in a 1980 Suntory Reserve television ad with Kurosawa.[96] Coppola arrived onscreen after shooting *Kagemusha* amid armored feudal horsemen galloping through a stream recreating the 1575 Battle of Nagashino, a scene utilizing five thousand extras and taking nine months to complete; an older male narrator states in Japanese, "Now, the world's gaze is fixed upon these two men as on nobody else," and then indicates, "There's no stronger friendship than that between these two men." The commercial ends by featuring the product, then selling for 3,200 yen—though pricey, still less expensive than rare British Isle–produced whiskies.[97] Another ad features only Kurosawa amid actors in Sengoku-era garb, where a Japanese-speaking male narrator praises his "taking up the [epic film's] challenge" and concludes with Kurosawa reverently holding a black lacquer samurai helmet, placing it so another helmet frames the whisky bottle amid a voiceover of "passion knows no limits."[98]

The same year, celebrated art director Asaba Katsumi (b. 1940) began creating Suntory advertisements, including the acclaimed *Yume kaidō* (Dream Road) series (1980) featuring China's quasi-legendary Silk Road for the first time in Japanese advertisement history.[99] In one ad, a caravan and mounted horsemen's ahistorical black-and-white images communicated timeless qualities and inserted Suntory into a

218 *Chapter 6*

long history of liquor production spanning East and West in the apocryphal road linking Xi'an (the capital during the Tang Dynasty [618–907]) and Rome. Asaba likely echoed Kurosawa's television ad featuring Asian mounted horsemen. Yet, whereas Kurosawa's citing of Japan's past is dynamic and celebratory of contemporary economic strength with samurai helmets placed next to Suntory whisky, the *sarariman*'s favored drink, Asaba presents Suntory's product in a China seemingly rooted in traditions and the past, despite its rapid economic awakening with Deng Xiaoping's (1904–1997) 1979 Opening and Reform Policy. That year, Suntory first initiated whisky exports to China, and in 1981 it sponsored the Beijing International Marathon, the country's first; 1984 marked the opening of China's first beer joint venture company in Shanghai, with Suntory also investing in Jiangsu Suntory Food Co., Ltd.[100]

Perhaps Asaba intimated that China, too, would soon embark on remarkable economic expansion connected to trade, intimated by citing the Silk Road linking East and West. While no celebrity appears in Dream Road publicity, these advertisements provide interesting framing of a neighboring country for an alcoholic beverage brand that consumers increasingly began associating with lifestyles involving business success and hard-earned leisure for men seeking luxury and life's finer aspects.

JAPAN'S PROSPEROUS 1980S AND WOODY ALLEN'S "DELICIOUS LIFE"

In the early 1970s, after late 1960s protests and youth movements waned, a mass consumer society subsumed the energies generated from Japanese youths' political anxieties. By the late 1970s and into the early 1980s, many young Japanese matured into lives defined by jobs and family in a society where arranged marriages and life goals for specific age groups were increasingly normalized. Domesticated by social expectations, they were placed into a consumer society absorbing their aspirations, and a new consumer fascination with luxury developed, lacking the stigma of earlier times. Concurrently, more women entered workplaces, delaying marriage while living at home with parents and rewarding themselves with brand-name products. Popular contemporary advertisements reflected these preoccupations and showcased future optimism. Especially for women consumers, historians Jan Bardsley and Hiroko Hirakawa assert that "self-expression has

Consuming Japaneseness 219

replaced self-sacrifice as the new orthodoxy and permits a certain degree of self-indulgence as well, especially when it's in service of developing a sophisticated palate."[101] Beginning in the 1970s and into the heady 1980s, popular novels and magazine short stories featured as characters "enlightened career wom[e]n" who indulged themselves with brand-name goods and lavish gourmet restaurant meals after working hard.[102] A print culture explosion expanded these tropes, where advertisements celebrated the enjoyment of economic success through consumption of commodities, both durable and edible.

Such concepts appear in a 1982 Seibu Department Store advertisement series by Asaba, who founded the influential Katsumi Asaba Design Studio in 1975. It highlighted the festive phrase *oishii seikatsu* (delicious life), coined by advertising copywriter Itoi Shigesato (b. 1948), a major force in Japan's late postwar advertising world, who later directed writing for Studio Ghibli animation.[103] Itoi was likely inspired by jazz musician and popular singer Yano Akiko's (b. 1955) same-named popular song from her 1982 album *Ai ga nakucha ne* (Even though We Haven't Got Love).[104] Yano's freshly enunciated lyrics amid snappy jazz beats resemble advertising copy, and they cite shopping and consumption in lyrics like "sold-out weather" and "new white shirts" along with the song's titular "delicious life."[105] She celebrates vastly plentiful consumable items, where consumers revel in myriad material options to purchase when true love proves elusive—either from lack of opportunity or still-common arranged marriage customs. Literary scholar Yoshihiro Yasuhara believes that "delicious life" more broadly characterizes an era to "represent the economic euphoria that captured the general public's fresh sense of reality in Japan's 1980s."[106] The phrase's indulgent flavor soon became a figurative leitmotif when Japan's early 1980s economic power extended beyond the Pacific and began challenging US global economic dominance.

American comedians like Woody Allen (b. 1935) were subsumed and assimilated into Japan's popular culture in an irresistible commercially sponsored wave of Japaneseness. Japanese moviegoers first became enamored of the comedically awkward Allen and his signature New York City–inspired humor in his now-classic 1979 film *Annie Hall,* starring Diane Keaton (b. 1946). As a popular entertainer, Allen joined a new Japanese trend where Anglo-American actors advertised everything from Suntory liquors to Nissin Cup Noodles. In one ad based on a still from a similar television commercial, he incongruously wears a traditional Japanese men's kimono while seated on a velvet cushion like a *rakugo* (comic narration) performer, and holds a long white scroll of calligraphy practice paper with the Japanese phrase "delicious life" inexpertly brushed in black ink by the comedian himself.[107] Script to Allen's left indicates *Sennen mo bannen mo* (Even a thousand years or ten thousand years . . .), and ends with the concluding phrase, *Seibu wa kyō mo, zuuuuto saki mo, otetsudai suru tokoro aru desu* ("Seibu is now and everrrrmore the place helping [you achieve this]"); Seibu's poster thus confidently invites consumers to enjoy eternal "good life" as 1982 fades into the 1983 New Year, while progressing toward the twenty-first century. The advertisement promises that within Seibu, a fulfilling life, like a meal or eternal banquet, is purchasable by all consumers. Allen, a comedian known for trenchant humor, is "Japanized" within the satirical trappings of *rakugo*, a traditional Japanese art form dating from Tokugawa times, which often captured sardonic pronouncements on contemporary society and current trends.

In another print ad in the series also featured as a television commercial, the seemingly bored actor sits at a desk behind a name plate stating his role as *Oishii seikatsu sōdan-in* (Delicious Life Consultant), while a small fan blows air into his face and pens sit ready at his left, in a hilarious parody of Allen as bureaucrat.[108] The "joke" arises where, nearly four decades after the war ended, Japanese consumers clearly don't need to economize or rely on outside help (or foreign intervention) for instructions on how to live a good life. Yet, traces of long-term frugality once zealously promoted by prewar and wartime governments remained for Japanese consumers. Historian Sheldon Garon, known for his research on Japanese spending habits, indicates that a 1977 government poll surveying Japanese households on "savings behavior and savings consciousness" discovered how "fully 42 percent 'somewhat agreed' or 'strongly agreed' that luxury is the enemy."[109] He explains that "'luxury is the enemy' was one of the best-remembered slogans of wartime Japan" and notes that its support only fell to 28 percent two decades later (in 1997).[110] Hence, this Seibu Department Store advertisement poking fun at bureaucrats, who couldn't possibly understand how to exhort ordinary people's enjoyment, might strongly resonate with readers. Allen's comic role endorsing Seibu's wares as a symbolic "gatekeeper" for consumer enjoyment likely created a noteworthy image. According to advertising historian Namba Kōji, such ads exhibiting *Seibu rashisa* (Seibu-ishness) helped rehabilitate the department store's image to transform it from "stuffy" to stylish in potential customers' minds.[111]

As part of a series running from 1989 to 1991 in television and print, Asaba's similarly memorable 1989 celebrity endorsement ad for Nissin Cup Noodles displayed a black-and-white photograph of Austrian American bodybuilder and action-film actor Arnold Schwarzenegger (b. 1947), casually holding a convertible on his shoulder like a surfboard, with script indicating that "Schwarzenegger eats [them]."[112] Hence, the advertisement revealed how Nissin's convenient snack products acquired delicious cachet even beyond the Pacific, and even spread in popularity to Hollywood and Malibu, where Japanese-produced instant ramen noodles connoted strength like a Schwarzenegger, photographed with a vintage Alfa Romeo.[113] Hence, Asaba's ad reinforced a message that relatively inexpensive Japanese noodles could be enjoyed anywhere as tasty, convenient, and nourishing snacks, which implicitly connoted Japanese economic strength.

Unsurprisingly, after achieving notable success with clever advertising for numerous commodities sold by department stores and corporations, Asaba extended his reach beyond consumer products. In 1998, he designed a logo for the Democratic Party of Japan (DPJ, or Minshutō) featuring a red sun dipping into water mirroring its reflection, and a poster for that year's Nagano Winter Olympics.[114] Here, Asaba's melding of advertising and propaganda becomes evident in government publicity, both conflated in Japanese as *senden*. In 2013, citing interest in the Weimar-era (1919–1933) German Bauhaus Movement, Asaba designed the art deco–inspired logo for Homme Plissé Issey Miyake (a new men's line similar to Pleats Please).[115] That year, Asaba finally received recognition from Japan's government by receiving the Order of the Rising Sun (Gold Rays with Rosette) to commemorate his influential achievements in Japanese marketing's competitive landscape.[116] Clearly, Asaba's eye-catching advertisements marked the early 1980s into the 2010s, and achieved their purpose by heightening brand-name recognition for commercial products, clothing designers, sporting events, and even a political party. In terms of their historical merit, they also communicated valuable social ideas—like how "delicious life" served as a reflection of 1980s Japan.

One of Japan's most influential commentators on the advertising business also adopted such an approach. Amano Yūkichi (1933–2013), editor in chief of *Kōkoku hihyō* [Ad Criticism], an important trade

222   *Chapter 6*

magazine for the advertising industry, attempted to theorize Japanese advertising by reinterpreting Canadian communications philosopher Marshall McLuhan's (1911–1980) theory of media through the lens of 1980s Japan.[117] In often informal-appearing columns and writings, like McLuhan, he urged attention to "the medium as the message" and was fascinated by "the cultural meaning of an ad—how it reflected social attitudes at that particular time."[118] *Japan Times* journalist Philip Brasor once asked Amano why different companies sometimes employed the same celebrity to endorse products; he responded that timely "freshness" was crucial to the advertising business, which viewed advertisements as purely utilitarian in potentially leading to tangible results, or increased consumption if a featured entertainer was popular.[119] This certainly described Allen and Coppola along with Kurosawa, who appeared in multiple early 1980s advertisements. Amano's *Kōkoku hihyō* tenure began in 1979, when television advertising reached a critical period of media influence in Japan, but in 2009 he decided to terminate the publication, noting transformations in mass media due to the role of Internet advertising.[120] Now, other influential factors have arrived, including complex algorithms barraging consumers with ads tailored to particular tastes.

Both Asaba and Amano existed in symbiotic relationships whereby each played an important role in connecting media messages to the public and advertising industry decisionmakers—their important work defined an era where Japanese consumer goods exploded onto a scene where consumers, inspired by celebrities, now vicariously enjoyed a good life through commodities. Essentially, celebrity spokespeople in Japan enabled powerful commodity fetishism in lending their fame, mystique, or genius to particular companies. This prefigured a cosmetic company's hiring of a French photographer and design consultant who soon became an advertising expert and beauty celebrity.

SHISEIDŌ AND SERGE LUTENS: JAPANESE LUXURY THROUGH A (FRENCH) ART DECO LENS

By the 1960s, once Shiseidō consolidated a sizable portion of Japan's consumer market for luxury cosmetics with what University of Tokyo economist Kazuyuki Motohashi calls "soaring sales in its domestic market," it began overseas expansion.[121] This included US subsidiaries opening in August 1965, and in Italy in August 1968, while the company further penetrated European markets in July 1980 with the creation of Shiseido Deutschland (Germany) and Shiseido France.[122] In a January 2005 talk at London's Japan Society, Yutaka Goto, director general of Shiseidō Communications Centre for Europe, noted that marketing strategies appealing to Japan's largely middle-class society failed to succeed in a more socially stratified Western Europe.[123] As a high-quality brand offering wide product ranges at multiple price points in Japan, whose domestic strategy followed the democratization of luxury, the company instead "decided to adopt a prestige brand as its overseas strategy, and targeted the upper class. Instead of aiming for recognition by the general public, Shiseidō directed its efforts in pursuing the prestigious customer."[124] After 1980, luxuriation of Shiseidō's image in France with the company's emphasis on "prestige" reactivated preexisting Orientalist ideas of Japan prevalent in French museum cultures and cultural critique.

Such notions partially stemmed from French theorist Roland Barthes' (1915–1980) influential *L'Empire des Signes* (Empire of Signs, 1970),[125] instrumental in France, Japan, and the United States for "explaining" Japaneseness to foreign audiences.[126] Upon cultural anthropologist Maurice Pinguet's (1929–1991)[127] 1966 invitation, Barthes traveled to Tokyo to teach a semester at L'Institut Franco-Japonais, returning twice that year, where he composed a portion of his iconic text.[128] According to Barthes, who found Japan's allegedly Zen-like simplicity and ascetic design sparseness inspirational and refreshing, when compared to France's colonial baroqueness: "The West moistens everything with meaning, like an authoritarian religion which imposes baptism on entire peoples."[129] Essentially, he interpreted Japan through exoticized preoccupations with Zen, a religious tradition adopted from China during the late Heian period (794–1185), which he viewed as a domestic philosophy with distinct aesthetics. Interestingly, much of Barthes' knowledge about Zen Buddhism was inspired by Anglo-American philosopher Alan Watts' *The Way of Zen* (1957),[130] which popularized Zen among Americans and Westerners and energized an emergent 1960s hippie movement.[131] *Empire of Signs* effuses that "the whole of Zen wages a war against the prevarication of meaning"[132] and revels in the "thusness" or seeming facticity of objects, gestures, and actions in Japan.[133]

Comparative literature scholar Diana Knight views Barthes' Orientalist characterization of Japan as an uncomplicated "fantasized utopian civilization" posited as counterpoint against postcolonial

224 *Chapter 6*

Morocco, where he lived from 1968 until 1969 while composing most of the text.[134] As a Frenchman whose understanding of Japanese was opaque at best, Barthes comprehended little spoken to him, despite extensive note-taking, forcing him into a meditative-like fugue where he focused intensely on people and things or relied upon a translator's subjective interpretations. Hence, in Japan, he remained steeped in a heightened atmosphere where the environment itself exuded a strange significatory luxury where even ordinary objects projected precious allure: "From the slope of the mountains to the neighborhood intersection, here everything is habitat, and I am always in the most luxurious room of this habitat: this luxury (which is elsewhere that of the kiosks, of corridors, of fanciful structures, collectors' cabinets, of private libraries) is created by the fact that the place has no other limit than its carpet of living sensations, of brilliant signs (flowers, windows, foliage, pictures, books . . .)."[135] For Barthes, "brilliant signs" characterized Japan as an abundant, democratically available "carpet of living sensations," whose very "Japanness" exuded luxury. By the late 1970s, the French theorist's high literary stature elevated his pronouncements to sublime levels, creating a mysterious allure that Japanese companies soon learned to capitalize on in realizations that exoticism sells—especially when filtered through French lenses.

This strikingly appears in Shiseidō's 1980 signing on of French designer Serge Lutens (b. 1942), who earlier gained renown as art director of makeup development for the classic Parisian fashion house Christian Dior.[136] Initially, the Shiseidō Corporation's in-house Advertisement Creation Department's Japanese directors grumbled that a Frenchman was hired to lead overseas business strategies, but this shrewd investment soon paid off.[137] Lutens ingeniously melded his version of traditional Japanese aesthetics with cosmopolitan ideals of luxury referencing the Art Deco movement to rival anything produced domestically by the French; such an approach strongly boosted company sales. Instead of simply creating a simulacrum of Frenchness for a French market already saturated with luxury fashions issuing from Paris, the designer channeled a particular Orientalized version of Japan that brilliantly translated into packaging and advertising of Shiseidō's products.

The Shiseidō Corporation asserts that in Lutens' first advertisements geared toward overseas audiences, he appropriated as "sign" an iconic round circle motif connoting Japan in a nod to Barthes.[138]

Yet, Goto notes that conservative Japan-based company representatives perceived Lutens' initial designs as too avant-garde:

> In the center is the red sphere representing the red sun of the Japanese flag, with an image of a woman. We were shocked when we first saw this design, but we had to acknowledge that it brilliantly symbolized the essence of Shiseido. The design was Japanese to French eyes while it was French to Japanese eyes. Rather than depicting outright Japanism with straightforward Japanese images, it set out to establish a more universal image. This image superbly represented the fusion of the East and the West that has been the aim of Shiseido since its foundation.[139]

This alleged East-West fusion proved a continuing leitmotif for Shiseidō in overseas markets profiting on selling the products' Japanese origins, even if not entirely produced in Japan.

A foreign corporation's penetration of an elusive French beauty market also meant developing a foothold in the perfume industry. In 1981, Lutens designed Shiseidō's first European-oriented perfume, Nombre Noir (Black Number); contemporary Serge Lutens company representatives indicate its name references Lutens' pun on harmony in *nombre d'or* (the golden ratio) added to *noir* (black), his favorite color, along with clever inclusion of *ombre* (shadow), since he viewed himself as "the man of the shadow."[140] An early perfume ad shows Lutens sitting pensively at a white cloth–bedecked table hosting tiny fragrance samples and a small lamp against an art deco–inspired background with the French caption, "I think of those for whom the unique is quotidian."[141] Here, luxury is democratized much like Barthes perceived Japan: Lutens' very surroundings become signs of luxury in a lush habitat of olfactory consumption.

Another advertisement for Nombre Noir displays a European woman in black, with her skirt's pleats prefiguring a design popularized by Issey Miyake arrayed around her gracefully bent figure caressing its origami-like folds, situated above a poetry-like caption: "The rose. The jasmine. The Chinese Osmanthus. The ylang-ylang of Nossi-bé [Madagascar]. The pale iris of Tuscany. Exhaling since dawn. Black Number in its black widow's garb of night. The perfume created by Serge Lutens for Shiseidō."[142] This litany of exotic floral scents seemingly enwraps the woman in an olfactory mist amid an expansive gesture highlighting her black skirt; for Japanese, black connotes formality and elegance,

226 *Chapter 6*

while for Westerners, the color imparts a funereal seriousness and avant-garde chic. The black pathos of mourning is thus tempered by the widow's slightly dangerous sexuality, where alluring rose scents hide painful thorns potentially tearing skin while the nose draws in fragrance.

This complex, unique "amber woody" perfume chemically formulated by perfumer Jean-Yves Leroy was composed of several expensive ingredients prompting three layers (top, middle, and base notes) of a remarkable twenty scent notes with two stand-outs: large amounts of ephemeral synthetic rose damascones and pure rare Osmanthus extract, whose scent resembles apricots or peaches.[143] In France, the Damask rose (*Rosa damascena*) blooms from June to July, while in China and Japan, Osmanthus bushes flower in late autumn, so this product was truly a harmonization of characteristically Western and Eastern scents as well as seasons. Currently, Nombre Noir's most likely contemporary "clone" might be Lutens' La Fille de Berlin, a pared-down "amber-floral" fragrance with only six notes dominated by rose accords that Lutens developed in 2013 with British perfumer Christopher Sheldrake.[144]

The original perfume's 1982 market arrival was well-received, but due to expensive ingredients, a high-quality, elegant box featuring origami silk, and a black hexagonal art deco glass bottle, it actually cost the company more to produce than recover with sales revenues.[145] Unfortunately, certain bottles leaked and caused customer complaints. These reasons prompted Shiseidō's mid-1980s recall; current perfume blogs still rave about it as "the world's rarest perfume" and fetishize its scarcity. A tiny original flacon of 15 milliliters of parfum (containing 15–40 percent fragrance concentrations, with 20–30 percent on average) ran for $2,800 in spring 2021.[146] Nevertheless, the perfume consecrated Lutens' fate as a noteworthy scent designer. Additionally, it helped publicize Shiseidō products in France and elsewhere as a prestige brand.

In 1992, Shiseidō opened its first high-end store at the prestigious eighteenth-century Palais Royal address in Paris' exclusive *première arrondissement* (first circle), whose interior Lutens designed, and displayed his signature bell jars for perfumes. Eight years later, the designer took over the luxe boutique with Shiseidō's blessing. A 2015 Shiseidō press release indicated that "confident of his own experience in perfumery and supported by the Shiseidō group, Serge Lutens decided to create his own brand [in 2000]: Parfums Beauté Serge Lutens, later renamed as 'Serge Lutens' for Serge Lutens perfumes."[147] Currently, the Palais Royal showroom offers special hour-and-a-half appointments for *une recontre privilégiée* (a privileged encounter), exclusively marketed as *prix variable selon prestations* (prices vary according to services).[148]

Yet, in late 2015, Shiseidō (re)purchased Parfums Beauté Serge Lutens to control its trademark while still maintaining Lutens as brand director to retain its "rare and luxe" concept.[149] Brand expert Jean-Noël Kapferer and luxury marketing consultant Vincent Bastien, former CEO of Yves Saint Laurent Parfum, predicted several years earlier that Serge Lutens could benefit from a strategy of "'mass-premiumization' of couture perfumes," similar to how the originally small family businesses of Louis Vuitton and Chanel became luxe global brands.[150] Such a "premiumization" approach, defined by marketing experts Glyn Atwal and Douglas Bryson as "borrowing characteristics associated with upper-class consumerism and lifestyle and attaching them to mass or lower priced brands, upgrading their value, and making them more desirable or distinct,"[151] approximates Japanese companies' "democratization of luxury" proffered for decades. More recently, Serge Lutens has offered seasonal incentives for customers who purchase a certain product price level,[152] provides beautifully packaged miniature sets and discovery collections at affordable prices,[153] and maintains a growing discrete online presence.[154] Though Lutens initially only designed perfumes for Shiseidō, he also created cosmetics for his new firm, including lipstick, foundation, and nail polish in art deco colors echoing his 1980s commercial advertisement posters for the company. Cosmetics packaging also cited Lutens' fascination for Japan and perfumes.

My own March 2021 purchase of Serge Lutens nail polish, packaged in elegant black-and-peach paper like a high-end perfume box, when opened revealed a "Made in Japan" sticker on its base. The rectangular glass jar resembled a tiny perfume bottle from the prestigious bespoke Di Ser brand, whose Hokkaidō-based chemist-owner, Shinohara Yasuyuki, allegedly manufactures perfumes by hand from essences distilled from traditional Japanese woods, herbs, and flowers in Sapporo.[155] Most likely, Shiseidō produced the nail polish in Japan, while its jar possibly shared Di Ser's same supplier. Even though the product was marketed by a French company, a glass produced in Japan mirrored imperfections of traditional Japanese *wabi-sabi* aesthetics, where the receptacle reveals a slightly asymmetrical inner rectangle holding the polish within. This "flaw" represents one of Bastien's "24

228 *Chapter 6*

Anti-Laws of Marketing" for luxury products, where his second law asks, "Does your product have enough flaws to give it soul?"[156] In the high-fashion world, including cosmetics and perfume, Japan itself, and associated ideas of *wabi-sabi,* are now strongly connoted with luxury.

Essentially, as a Japanese company capitalizing on its Japanese provenance, Shiseidō has enjoyed a long and intimate relationship with Lutens in encouraging his endeavors, and thus, seeks to protect his image. Lutens, in turn, by using his Paris-based brand's chic French identity, promotes "rare and luxe"[157] encounters with scents created in collaboration with his perfumer, Christopher Sheldrake.[158] Additionally, Shiseidō and Lutens' symbiotic relationship continues with the company manufacturing cosmetics, and now perfumes, for his Serge Lutens prestige brand.[159] Here, Japanese and French luxury combine in an elegant coproduction, which allows Serge Lutens to sell steadily in France, Japan, and North America, but with greatest growth in the EMEA (Europe, Middle East, and Africa) region, where Shiseidō's fragrance brands, including Serge Lutens, Issey Miyake, and Elie Saab, recorded stunning 12 percent growth in 2019.[160] However, Shiseidō's greatest success remains its phenomenal capturing of strong consumer bases in China.

Shiseidō: Japanese Luxury for Chinese Consumers

On its corporate website highlighting company history, the Shiseidō Corporation indicates how it began selling products in Taiwan in 1957, while its first Mainland China venture was in 1981, when the company initially sold cosmetics in Beijing; in 1983, it even signed a tech tie-up agreement with China's capital city.[161] These forays into the Chinese market were possibly also the corporation's survival measure. Economist Kazuyuki Motohashi notes that Shiseidō's inroads into China coincided with a domestic slump in business following Japan's burst economic bubble and "a long period of stagnation for the company, coinciding with further diversification of consumer preferences, buying patterns, sales channels, and pricing."[162] These challenges were met by the application of several innovative approaches for both domestic and overseas markets.

In 1982, within Japan, the company took its usual broad product line and segmented it into five age groups to allow targeted marketing, while "stores were organized into subspecialties targeted at specific markets" to tap into consumer tastes in different retail venues.[163]

Additionally, in the 1990s, steady growth of discount stores and informal shopping venues were popularized when the economic recession began chipping away at corporate profits. Department stores and retailers carefully cultivating their client base for years once largely generated these. Shiseidō now needed to create products reaching customers in humbler spaces more attractive to frugal consumers who still desired high quality and occasional small luxuries.

Motohashi emphasizes the impacts of difficult economic conditions in Japan, which the 1997 Asian financial crisis further exacerbated, when a cosmetic resale system was discontinued, thus initiating a price war.[164] In response, Shiseidō mired itself in a "vicious cycle of introducing numerous new products, dispersing marketing investments, reducing the power of their brand, and experiencing poor sales."[165] These measures failed to combat sluggish growth, and the company reverted back to smaller brand numbers, nevertheless failing to sustain themselves amid a deflationary economy supporting thrift. Motohashi notes that in early 2005 Shiseidō enacted management reforms "to expand overseas profits and create a post-resale domestic business model."[166] This included embracing discount stores for higher-quality products originally retailed in department stores needing to be quickly circulated into sales, along with expanding further into China, where in the 1990s, the company opened up joint ventures in Beijing and Shanghai.

Remnants of the company's late 1990s and early 2000s measures welcomed by frugal consumers continue into the present, along with its powerful Chinese marketing approach. Shiseidō is well-known for layered skin-care approaches, where one first cleanses the face, then applies a softener, followed by a serum, skin cream along with eye cream, and sunscreen, sometimes blended into skin cream. However, purchasing each component to create a daily-use set is expensive, so in Japan, for entry-level customers, discount stores sell Shiseidō and other cosmetic brands reaching the end of recommended shelf lives in department stores, along with lower-end mini versions of larger luxury products. In the early 2000s, these discounted off-season bottles or jars of Shiseidō products produced in Japan soon became coveted purchases for Chinese friends and business connections finding these luxury items unaffordable in their own country. My own experiences corroborate this.

In 2005, while in Japan on a Fulbright Research Fellowship at Waseda University, I packed numerous bottles of Shiseidō skin softeners

230   *Chapter 6*

and whitening products to mail to Chinese friends of my then-husband. These luxury "gifts," though still affordable to middle-class Japanese consumers, represented out-of-reach splurges for Chinese consumers, and thus facilitated maintaining important overseas business contacts, or *guanxi* (connections), for businessmen and their wives. The same year, American investigative journalist Sheridan Prasso shopped in Shanghai's upscale Plaza 66 Mall, where she discovered a jar of Japanese-made face cream from Shiseidō's luxury line Clé de Peau (Key to Skin) selling for a prohibitive $500 for only thirty grams.[167] Such prices revealed the premiums Chinese women then paid for foreign luxury products to perfect their complexions and whiten skin. However, while few might afford imported Clé de Peau products, less wealthy Chinese women in regional cities could still purchase affordable Shiseidō products produced by two Chinese joint ventures marketing under Za, Uno, and Fitit brands in 4,172 small retail outlets and 700 freestanding stores.[168] In China, Shiseidō "chainstores" arrived in 2004, and interestingly, mirrored strategies that the company pioneered in domestic Japan of the 1920s and 1930s. This constituted a wise business decision where Shiseidō democratized products symbolizing Japanese luxury, even if only limited numbers sold in China were of the highly coveted "Made in Japan" provenance so yearned for by Chinese friends. In 2005, Prasso noted that "some 90 million urban women in China spend 10% or more of their income on face cream, lipstick, mascara, and the like, particularly in fashionable Shanghai, where women spend 50 times more per capita on cosmetics than women nationwide."[169] Unsurprisingly, during trips to Japan, Chinese tourists head to Shiseidō and associated Clé de Peau counters in famous Tokyo department stores like Isetan and Mitsukoshi, or seek cheaper discounters in Shinjuku and Ikebukurō.

In 2008, when returning to Japan for a short research trip, and hoping to keep belongings light, I ventured into Daikokoku Drug, a Shinjuku-based discount drugstore, where I purchased a trial-sized set of Shiseidō-made products in sky-blue plastic bottles encased in a clear plastic pouch. Japanese youth and young Chinese tourists thronged the store, where customers filled their baskets with numerous sale products during the store's weekly discount. However, to my chagrin, these entry-level products seemed to be diluted versions of richer products I used in the United States; plus, they emitted insistent "freshness" akin to popular Japanese laundry detergents evoking melon and mint fragrances. Such a set was likely a lower-cost formulation targeted to youth markets.

Only in June 2017 did the Shiseidō Corporation specifically introduce a new skin-care line called WASO; in a press release "targeting Millennials," the company outlined its motives as "empowering Millennials to feel beautiful in their own skin whatever their gender, nationality, age or status."[170] In this line initially offered in Japan, China, and the United States, Shiseidō engaged in the further democratizing of its products by offering cheaper versions of its standard and luxury lines, now enhanced with extracts of Japanese herbs and plants, where "the range has been crafted with authenticity at its core"[171] to appeal to this particular consumer generation worldwide.

In late 2021, five skin-care elements from Shiseidō's standard high-quality line advertised as "the Japanese beauty skincare ritual" in the United States were now conveniently sold online in limited-edition trial kits at more reasonable prices than buying all five full-sized products—one kit emphasizes skin vitality (Essential Energy) while another focuses on wrinkle smoothing (Benefiance).[172] In this marketing approach, Shiseidō hoped that these sample-sized vials in beautifully designed plastic jars would serve as gateway purchases ensuring consumers' greater satisfaction through frugal apportionment of fairly pricey products with repeated purchases. Theoretically, if skin responded favorably to the kit's prescribed regimen, then consumers might be tempted to invest in a purchase of the larger products.

Until the COVID-19 pandemic's seismic effects began influencing sales in 2020, the US market represented steady growth for Shiseidō; compared with 2019, one year later the company experienced sales losses of 20 to 30 percent in every region except China, which saw 11 percent growth, while profits fell 18.8 percent in the Americas but rose 3.2 percent in domestic Japan and exceeded double that in China, with 7.8 percent profit growth.[173] Such purchases, either in person or online, were by younger consumers increasingly acquiring luxury items amid a new image embracing high quality and elite lifestyle choices emphasizing craftsmanship and natural products.

Much such demand still comes from the United States, with China close behind. In 2017, according to the China E-Commerce report from Secoo, Asia's largest high-end e-commerce platform, and Tencent, the largest data company in China, the United States composed 22 percent of the global luxury market, while China captured nearly

232 *Chapter 6*

21 percent.[174] Also, 48 percent of Chinese luxury shoppers were surprisingly young—under thirty years of age.[175] Interestingly, in 2015 China's Millennials and Generation Z accounted for 34 percent of the country's discretionary disposable income, predicted to increase to 50 percent by 2025.[176] While following celebrities on social media sites like Weibo who communicate positive and negative product reviews,[177] these young Chinese consumers more importantly are also self-aware netizens highly attuned to political issues between China and Japan possibly affecting sales.[178] Hence, the China market provides both opportunities and challenges to Japanese corporations.

SHISEIDŌ AND KAŌ: JAPANESE COMPANIES NEGOTIATING CHINESE MARKETS

During my July 2012 visit to Kaō Corporation's museum and archives, I was warmly hosted by public relations specialist Machida Saori.[179] The company's building, constructed in the 1950s and 1960s during the Economic Miracle, resembled others housing "traditional" postwar Japanese corporations, complete with an excellent employee cafeteria at inexpensive, subsidized prices prompting staff to chat over meals together instead of venturing outside alone for refreshment. After accompanying me to meet with company archivists, Ms. Machida brought me to dine on traditional home-style Japanese comfort food with an iced coffee fortified with white creamer and liquid sugar. Because we both studied abroad in Paris during college, we spoke some French over lunch.

In retrospect, Machida possibly attempted to discover my approach to her company's history—especially considering my interest in wartime history and astonishment when its curators showed me materials from the Nanjing-based Kaō factory established after Imperial Japan's military occupation of China's Republican capital. Japanese companies are well-known for jealously guarding trade secrets and fiercely protecting national and international reputations—survival measures in a cut-throat business with potentially loyal, though fickle, consumer bases. Nevertheless, Machida had little cause for concern, since I intended to focus on Shiseidō's marketing, sales, and strategies to make luxury accessible.

In contemporary East Asia, past Japanese imperialism is still a haunting specter, with a rising China demanding respect as modern, scientific, and powerful—much like late nineteenth- to early twentieth-century Japan. Chinese women now use skin whiteners to raise their social capital, just as 1930s-era Japanese and colonial women did when Imperial Japan's power grew and Japanese companies expanded commercial roles throughout East Asia with clever advertising. In 2005, 2011, and briefly, in 2012, what the international media calls "history issues" led to Chinese boycotts of Japanese goods to potentially endanger huge and profitable markets. While this term is oversimplified and trite, journalists, television anchors, and political scientists use it as shorthand to reference numerous unresolved issues surrounding Japan's past imperial aggression in China and northeast Asia. These tensions point to vocal cohorts of Chinese citizens confronting (and using) their nation's past to gain political advantages and rectify Imperial Japan's past abuses. China's government allows a modicum of publicly expressed dissatisfaction to engender greater internal political cohesion during disruptive socioeconomic change, and popular nationalism also serves state interests in achieving unity against a common outside "enemy." Regardless of the Chinese government's role, protests against Japan and boycotts of Japanese goods point to the growing consumer power of China's rising middle class, with greater agency in personal consumption and national responses to issues relating to Japan's imperial past.

Now, as in the 1930s, despite political views and increasingly vocal public opinions, young Chinese women still value white skin, often equated with stylish Japanese women along with Chinese upper-class status and high educational achievement; their purchases account for Shiseidō's success in urban China. Throughout Asia, $7.5 billion went toward skin lightening products in 2020 despite a pandemic and global reflections against racism,[180] down from a 2010 peak of $18 billion.[181]

In late 2005, amid a postwar anniversary year of particularly bitter Chinese protests against Japan, Saitō Tadakatsu, Shiseidō's China operations chairman, noted his company's growing success with whiteners and pale-toned foundation creams. He indicated, "Chinese people ask for [an] even whiter tone than what is selling well in Japan," and added "when we try to sell them their exact color, they say, 'Too dark. Do you have anything lighter, brighter?'"[182] Other Shiseidō executives in areas formerly within Japan's empire, like Taiwan, also noted similar obsessions with white skin. In 2009, Nydia Lin, a Taiwanese Shiseidō senior executive, emphasized that "we promote the idea of whitening . . . the Chinese say, 'You can cover all your defective parts if you are white.'"[183] However, whiteness is advertised differently

234 *Chapter 6*

based on regional markets. In the 1980s and 1990s, Shiseidō's marketing strategies in Asian markets like China and Japan began emphasizing whitening, while in the United States, the company focused on blocking damaging sun rays for UV protection with health and anti-aging effects.[184] Each market initially used local models to appeal to its customer base.[185] In contemporary times, as in prewar (and even wartime) eras, Chinese and Asian consumers employ scientific, modern methods to achieve whiteness by using bleaching creams and concealing cosmetics to reach certain beauty ideals, and Shiseidō performs an important role in supplying this demand.

Since the 1990s, two production factories have existed in Mainland China, which support Shiseidō's "strengthening of [a] global production structure," while in May 2010, the company acquired Hong Kong–based Dah Chong Hong Cosmetics company as part of its "strengthening of [a] business scheme."[186] In 2008, Shiseidō pulled ahead of Kaō with $7.011 billion beauty product revenues amid $7.220 billion total corporate revenues, covering globally accessible products including skin care, fragrances, color cosmetics, toiletries, and hair care.[187] In 2010 the corporation garnered 20 percent of revenues outside its home region—including Europe, the United States, and Asia.[188] That year, China became the fourth-largest global market for beauty products, with $17.7 billion in revenues, of which a large portion went toward skin care—primarily skin lightening products.[189] Quite understandably, sizable business in the Chinese market still prompts the Shiseidō Corporation and other companies like Kaō to act protectively about their colonial past to ensure steady consumer demand for vast arrays of products.[190]

CONCLUSION

The early 1960s issued in avant-garde artistic movements resulting from mass protests against renewing an unpopular US-Japan joint security treaty. Echoes of these Dada-like expressions reappeared in Japan's fashion world from iconic designers who later embraced aspects of 1970s global punk movements. However, radical art spawned in the 1960s failed to achieve lasting effects upon Japan's broader society, which by the 1970s accepted political stability and economic growth at the cost of personal freedom constrained by social conformity. Strong economic success also led to expressions of Japanese uniqueness, termed *Nihonjinron*, lauded by two influential American academics, and appearing as leitmotifs in advertisements and consumer products.

The 1970s and 1980s clearly spelled a heady time of expansion and experimentation for many Japanese companies, and the decades coincided with the development of overseas subsidiaries—especially in complex markets like France and Mainland China. Here, by the 1990s, Japaneseness also became a main selling point, where either Japan's traditional arts and culture were fetishized in product design or Japanese manufacturing promised commodities' high quality and effectiveness. In Japanese companies' globalization, each market demanded fresh new approaches now recognizing particular desires of national consumer bases and even political ideologies. Regardless of how these corporations advertised and marketed products, their Japanese provenance became essential to the commercial fetishization of commodities purveyed—an important aspect continuing into the present.

Chapter Seven

THE RISE OF "COOL JAPAN" AND JAPANESE LUXURY-CONSUMING COMMUNITIES IN THE VIRTUAL WORLD

It is the deepest enchantment of the collector to enclose the particular item within a magic circle, where, as a last shudder runs through it (the shudder of being acquired), it turns to stone. Everything remembered, everything thought, everything conscious becomes socle, frame, pedestal, seal of his possession.[1]

—*Walter Benjamin, "The Collector,"* in The Arcades Project

With the late 1980s burst of Japan's economic bubble, consumers rethought conspicuous consumption and returned to affordable staples. Japanese and Americans flocked online with the Internet's concurrent growth and consumed another's street fashions, like Bathing Ape (1993) and other brands, originally inspired by Japanese reinterpretations of 1950s American popular culture termed *Ametora* or "American traditional." The World Wide Web's expansion, along with popular Japanese anime (animated films) and manga (comics and graphic novels), enabled male-dominated *otaku* (enthusiasts) and other consumers of Tokyo / Los Angeles / New York Black and Latinx fashions (now problematically called "streetwear" or "street fashion" with luxury connotations)[2] to form online consuming communities. Toward the millennium's end and onward, originally inexpensive Japanese wares were "luxuriated" by assigning rare or ephemeral qualities to hard-to-find limited editions with purportedly high-quality craftsmanship. Seikō and Casio aficionados dissected product qualities in social media posts, company website reviews, and watch fora where emergent *otaku* markets began (re)capturing largely young male consumers.

236

The Rise of "Cool Japan"   237

Japanese product advertising, including Shiseidō's, reclaimed notions of Tokugawa-era quality and craftsmanship, and evoked a global movement driven by so-called hipsters and millennials favoring artisanality over mass production. Contemporary consumption of these companies' products derives from fetishization of allegedly unique Japanese high quality or traditional essences connoting luxury in comestible items. Though mass-produced, their manufactured artisanality thus retains aspirational qualities amid mild anti-capitalist critique.

American Captivation with Japanese Popular Culture (1950s–Present)

Fascination with Japanese culture flourishes in the United States and has even become quotidian. In January 2020 the upscale grocer Trader Joe's featured Japanese specialty items like *binchōtan* (white charcoal)-infused cotton washcloths, along with food products containing matcha (powdered green tea), seaweed, and sweet soy sauce, like rice crackers. The washcloth's colors cite symbolism from Murasaki Shikibu's classical Heian-era novel *The Tale of Genji,* including lavender (*Murasaki,* Prince Genji's second Fujiwara clan wife), gray (clerics), and light orange (royalty, autumn). While the latter food products gained acceptance during the American 1980s-era sushi craze, now completely domesticated in supermarket counters, recent additions of artisanally connoted Japanese products with alleged Tokugawa origins intersect with contemporary American (and global) obsessions with craftsmanship, especially among younger consumers. Current hipster trends favoring Japaneseness echo earlier 1950s crazes, including haiku (3-line, 17-syllable poems of 5, 7, and 5 syllables), also recently festooning Japanese green tea bottles by Itō-en and other companies.

Postwar global fascination for Japanese popular culture began in the 1950s-era United States, when American GIs returned home with an appreciation for Japanese art, design styles, literature, and even religion (primarily Zen Buddhism) experienced during the Occupation, while emigrating increasing numbers of Japanese wives.[3] These women, and some men, created cultural groups showcasing traditional Japanese art forms, where they generously shared cultural knowledge of Japan after arrival, and often developed careers teaching ikebana (flower-arranging) methods or became bonsai (exquisitely pruned potted tree) practitioners. Thus, formerly carefully controlled Japanese cultural forms cultivated by elites were "democratized"

238   *Chapter 7*

beyond strict schools headed by (usually male) masters, where interested students could pay to join classes or freely experience staged demonstrations for mixed Japanese and American audiences of women and men. US historian Meghan Mettler views this phenomenon as contributing to Japan's informal diplomacy, establishing Japan as a peaceful postwar "cultural" force.[4]

In the 1950s, ikebana and haiku percolated into white American middle-class culture. Bearded counterculture beatniks espousing Zen and Japanese-inspired literary pursuits were even hired as extras lending "interest" to elite parties and social events.[5] New York City photographer Fred W. McDarrah (1926–2007) initiated a legitimate business from a tongue-in-cheek 1959 "Rent-a-Beatnik" ad in the *Village Voice* promising "genuine BEATNIKS: badly groomed but brilliant (male and female)" at $40 per night.[6] Beatniks allegedly performed themselves, representing an exotic subculture alien to the largely politically conservative, go-getting guests, though still WASPs of reassuringly similar class and ethnic backgrounds. These poetry-consuming or -producing unshaven, denim-clad young men (and sometimes, women) from educated, privileged backgrounds resemble contemporary hipsters, whose most serious adherents nowadays purchase jeans fashioned from hard-to-obtain cloth milled in Osaka, like Kapital, based on original late nineteenth-century Levi's looms. In the 1950s, elite Japanese cultural forms democratically expanded into certain realms, while the twenty-first century's older teenagers and twentysomethings luxuriated them in other contexts.

The Japanese-influenced beatnik craze was only one aspect of how postwar Americans experienced Japanese cultural products. By the mid-1950s, Japan began exporting films, beginning with *kaijū* (monster) movies featuring Godzilla, a gigantic prehistoric irradiated reptile crossed with a gorilla (*gorira*) and whale (*kujira*). In 1954, the first monster flick featuring Godzilla, directed by Honda Ishirō (1911–1993) and filmed at Tōhō Studios, arrived on Japanese screens; it also reinvigorated specters of nuclear radiation from the 1945 US atomic bombings of Hiroshima and Nagasaki, coinciding with the 1954 Lucky Dragon incident where a Pacific-based American nuclear weapons test rained fallout upon a Japanese fishing boat by that same name. In 1956, the movie crossed the Pacific to the United States as an adaptation codirected by Honda and Terry O. Morse (1906–1984). *Godzilla: King of the Monsters* featured fictional American reporter Steve Martin's personal experience of the monster's devastation. In 2015, commemorating the film's success as an enduring cultural phenomenon and foreign tourism promoter, Godzilla was named "tourism ambassador," with honorary citizenship in Tokyo's Shinjuku ward, a major shopping and university hub; incidentally, he destroyed this popular area in all three films.[7] In response, an American critic sarcastically tweeted "its [sic] easier for fictional monsters to get citizenship than migrants in (the) US."[8]

Beyond Godzilla, Japanese monsters menacing and cute remain lasting pop cultural trends in the United States and globally. Anthropologist Anne Allison pinpoints the Power Rangers' 1990s US television expansion as crucial in spreading Japanese popular culture among American kids.[9] Fascination with Pokémon (formed from "pocket" and "monster") began concurrently, appearing in ubiquitous, cheap small plastic or rubber goods with appealingly jaunty colors and cute packaging. In the millennium's mid-teens, Pokémon coalesced into the massively popular virtual game Pokémon Go, where players searched invisible Pokémon on smartphones in virtual spaces overlaying actual physical geographies of towns and cities. Though small, these affordable, addictive consumer items encouraged collecting, enshrined in their "gotta catch them all" advertising slogan. Pokémon characters have retained an important global pop-cultural presence, still crucial for Japan's global projection of "soft power," while maintaining economic competitiveness.

In the late 1980s, Harvard University Kennedy School professor Joseph Nye developed the "soft power" concept,[10] popularized in the millennium's first decade as an international relations theory often linked to American influence.[11] He explains: "What is soft power? It is the ability to get what you want through attraction and rather than coercion or payments. It arises from the attractiveness of a country's culture, political ideals, and policies."[12] Nevertheless, political scientist Matsuda Takeshi criticizes Japan's soft power as linked to dependence upon the United States.[13] For Japan, the 1 percent cap on total gross domestic product for defense expenditures kept government spending low, while the United States maintains military bases in Japan and foots nearly half their cost. This allowed Japan's government to allocate funds to other sectors while retaining a stable economy, excepting the "Lost Decade," beginning with the bubble economy's early 1990s burst and further exacerbated by the 1997 Asian economic crisis. Yet, economic vicissitudes aside, "democratization" of such goods emerging from appeal for Japanese manga and anime greatly

240   *Chapter 7*

advertised Japan as a brand, while projecting the country as a fashionable "flavor" to consume for buyers with cool taste. Here, Japan's soft power was as much about profit as diplomacy.

Branding "Cool Japan"

Unsurprisingly, like any slow-moving bureaucracy, Japan's government was late in articulating and encapsulating this phenomenon to its advantage. According to historian Nancy Stalker, whose analysis echoes Nye's, "Government agencies began to realize the power of the 'Cool Japan' brand in the early twenty-first century and created numerous programs to promote popular culture as a key component of Japan's 'soft power.'"[14] Not until 2010 did the Ministry of Economy, Trade and Industry (METI) open the Creative Industries Promotion Office, when officials felt that only large companies produced the global marketplace's iconic Japanese products. In November 2013, to help smaller Japanese companies purveying goods exemplifying "Cool Japan" expand overseas investments, METI officials launched a 60 billion yen fund, with 50 billion yen financed by the government and 10 billion yen stemming from private banks and corporations.[15] The Cool Japan Fund bills itself as "a public-private fund with the aim of supporting and promoting the development of demand overseas for excellent Japanese products and services. Cool Japan Fund aims to commercialize the 'Cool Japan' and increase overseas demand by providing risk capital for businesses across a variety of areas, including media & content, food & services, fashion & lifestyle and inbound."[16]

However, like any cultural phenomena that governments attempt to steer and moralistically leverage into national publicity machines, the fund quickly encountered difficulties. In 2017, sexual harassment accusations were levied against senior management, and in 2018 *Nikkei Asian Review* journalists deemed it underperforming. In business or political worlds, seemingly excellent ideas failing to meet expectations often get blamed on poor leadership. Thus, in 2018, the fund's new president and CEO Kitagawa Naoki was hired, after his predecessor, Ota Nobuyuki, Issey Miyake brand's former CEO, stepped down. Projects linked to Ota and chairman Iijima Kazunobu's business ties to former companies were especially deemed underperforming.[17]

Kitagawa, as Sony Music Associated Records' ex-president and Sony Music Entertainment's former corporate advisor, thus explains the

Cool Japan Fund's mission statement: "We would like to contribute even more to industrial development in the field of Cool Japan by promoting excellent Japanese products and services that we are proud of and passionate about while accurately judging the ever-changing world market. We hope that numerous companies will be with us to take on the world."[18]

The fund's promotional website states its aim to expand Japanese businesses marketing and profiting from Japan's allegedly unique culture: "For Japan to achieve a dynamic economic growth, Japanese businesses must actively expand and capture overseas markets. The government of Japan is focusing on increasing inbound and outbound demand by developing Japanese businesses that draw on the unique added value embedded in Japanese culture and lifestyle."[19] Of course, in such initiatives surrounding "J-Cool," its bureaucratic side was initiated much later than actual trend development or growth and expansion of dynamic consuming communities.

For example, in planning for the (later postponed) 2020 Tokyo Olympics, the ASICS corporation attempted to capitalize on a long extant J-Cool phenomenon in Japanese and American markets. Beginning in 2002, heritage brand Onitsuka Tiger (now part of ASICS) ventured into global markets (overwhelmingly represented by the United States) and began reissuing vintage Japanese track shoes; since 2008, it has offered a "Nippon Made" sneaker selection whose allegedly superior craftsmanship and costlier materials purportedly allow wearers greater luxury at higher prices.[20] For the Japanese market, ASICs also offered several 2020 limited editions, like the 1983 Point-getter, a retro high-top basketball shoe intended as a fashion statement. Its online advertisement portrays a model wearing madras pants resembling a 1960s "Take Ivy" throwback (a youth fashion trend discussed further below), standing on brown brick stairs against a brown stucco laminate paint background fronting a building likely constructed to anticipate the 1964 Tokyo Olympics.[21] The shoe subtly incorporates stitching from Tokyo Olympics colors: turquoise, yellow, and red, with black for ASICS' signature stripes.

For the US market, honoring the postponed 2020 Tokyo Olympics, ASICS unveiled its Edo Era Tribute Pack running shoe series, informing potential consumers about its newest product line's ecological ingenuity rooted in Japanese "tradition." According to ASICS, "Now known as Tokyo, Edo was one of the first cities in the world to

242   *Chapter 7*

follow sustainable practices, so we were inspired to create the Edo Era Tribute pack and pay homage to the ASICS Japanese heritage."[22] The online advertisement touts recycling 300,000 PET bottles to produce this collection, thus linking the shoe with premodern Japan's supposedly long history of sustainability. Showcasing scenes from Japan's most celebrated city, the promotional video shows a barefoot person walking on tatami matting; then, they run in the featured shoe amid Tokugawa-era storefronts, a bamboo forest, vintage vending machines, an old Tokyo bridge, and subway train, followed by a sprint through Akihabara, a nightclub, and seafront near Tokyo's largest bridge; finally, they remove the shoes to enter an old building, perhaps a temple. The product's logo, citing a Tokugawa-era *mon* with a brush-stroked circle enclosing a bottle shadow, subtly references the recycled bottles composing the shoe's nylon fabric. The closing scene notes: "As the city has evolved, so have we. Inspired by the sustainable culture of Edo."[23]

Additionally, the shoes feature traditionally Japanese black coloring from charred cedar wood, or *shōsugi-ban,* where panels are burnt to preserve wood for fire- and pest-proofing with techniques pioneered in Tokugawa (Edo) times. Their black and graphite gray nylon mesh is cleverly printed with Japanese characters for Tokyo and its wards, like Shinjuku, while "Tokyo" appears in yellow print on black laces, with a yellow dot on the tongues with Tokyo written within. Here, black and yellow colors symbolize the ASICS Tiger shoe's "tiger" heritage, citing Onitsuka Tiger brand-name track shoes developed in 1949, later absorbed into the ASICS corporation (formed in 1977).[24] In Japan, the Edo Era Tribute Pack collection featured the Metaride, equivalent to the American Glideride, and boasted a special bridge-shaped sole, selling for 29,700 yen ($278.62 USD) versus $150 in the United States. Clearly, Japan's hosting the Olympics, prior to its postponement, allowed companies like ASICS to design, produce, and project Japanese-connoted value-added qualities upon products, and capitalize on J-Cool's global moment.[25]

Initially, much of Cool Japan's trope was not government-sponsored, having developed organically among globe-trotting Japanese and American youth through Black and Latinx street fashions amid burgeoning worldwide consumption of anime and manga in the 1990s. To truly penetrate J-Cool's dialectical history in dialogue with US-Japan relations, one must examine its early 1960s American origins.

The Rise of "Cool Japan" 243

JAPANESE STREET FASHIONS: FROM PREPPY STYLE TO HIP-HOP (1960s–1990s)

After a year serving as an assistant language teacher in Seto City with the Japan Exchange and Teaching Program in the late 1990s, I entered a master's program at Harvard University, aiming for a globe-trotting journalism career. When I arrived on campus, instead of the preppy garb allegedly expected at Ivy League institutions, I wore Japanese "street" clothing inspired by fashions I encountered in Nagoya-based working-class youth-clothing shops, and which I admired when worn by my neighbors' son, who presumably belonged to a motorcycle gang. My then–graduate advisor Akira Iriye, a prominent historian of US–East Asia relations, to his credit never blinked at my possibly inappropriate clothing choices, with artfully washed Japanese-made denim button-front jeans and T-shirts featuring phrases like "Oriental Mood Product," complemented by blue rubber flip-flops. My inadvisable, but not-so-unique, early twenties' sartorial predilections referenced larger, global trends hitting the West Coast before penetrating bastions of East Coast privilege like Harvard. Back then, imported "authentic" made-in-Japan street fashions were costly, or required extensive overseas travel to Tokyo and other Japanese cities. Though decidedly casual, prior to high fashion's recent normalization of Black and Latinx hip-hop and urban fashions that, through processes of commodification and appropriation, came to be known as "streetwear," these conferred upon American wearers value-added luxury based on privileged access to overseas work and study opportunities, or wealth for travel to visit relatives and friends in Japan.

Notably, these cross-cultural transfers of Japanese and American street fashions share long histories, with contemporary pop-culture luminaries in the United States praising Japanese counterparts for referencing their own unique styles. Los Angeles–based Mexican American graffiti and tattoo artist Mr. Cartoon (Mark Machado, b. 1970), who works as a logo designer for top brands like Nike, indicates "the Japanese have been lowriding and simulating West Coast culture since the late '80s."[26] Reggie Casual, an Afro-Latinx fashion consultant and former Los Angeles corporate marketing expert working in Tokyo since 2016, positively affirms contemporary Japanese street fashion's appreciation of American styles based on Black and Latinx urban youth:

244   *Chapter 7*

> I believe that culture is meant to be shared and if we're able to share culture with each other, we'll understand each other more. Instead of arguing about what is cultural appropriation,[27] we should be fighting for cultural equality. . . . As an American with Afro-Latino heritage, I can see how seeing Japanese people in black or Latino styles is offensive to people. But I think more than anything, it validates our culture. It shows how impactful other cultures have been, not only in Japan but also around the world. This culture came all over from the Caribbean, Africa, America, etc., and there are Japanese people that see that and emulate that and incorporate that into their personalities.[28]

Casual views the 1990s as a key moment when Japanese street fashions "went global" and created their own discourse under prominent luminaries.[29] These include Fujiwara Hiroshi (b. 1964), an influential deejay known as Ura-Harajuku (Harajuku back[street]) fashion's "godfather,"[30] who founded the brands Good Enough and Fragment Design as an early adopter of Black hip-hop styles and music after an early 1980s trip to New York City,[31] along with Nigō (Nagao Tomoaki, b. 1970),[32] Bathing Ape's progenitor, and Takahashi Jun (b. 1969), brand creator of Undercover, who in 1993 with Nigō launched the Harajuku-based shop Nowhere to sell their clothing.[33] Philip Santiago, Nigō's former Los Angeles–based brand consultant, notes that, for the man financing their endeavors, Fujiwara was *ichigō*, or "number one" in Tokyo's Harajuku area, while Nigō's name meant "number two"; they created numerous brands soon publicized by Japan's press, which enjoyed symbiotic relationships with them in popularizing their fashions.[34] Thus, both designers helped generate nearby Ōmotesandō Avenue's revival as a mainstream high-fashion center in Tokyo.[35]

In the late 1990s into the early 2000s, some American street fashions were inspired by awareness of youth casual wear in Japan expanded by these designers, along with interpretations of looks purportedly worn in Harajuku's backstreets, a trend US singers and celebrities also capitalized upon.[36] By the turn of the millennium, trendy hipsters in the United States "discovered" Japanese selvedge denim, like Kapital, Supreme, and other brands, with fabrics referencing vintage American shuttle looms and historical sewing techniques, while Fujiwara even teamed with Nike, the United States' most well-known sneaker brand, to create the HTM.[37] In Japan, these trends, originally inspired by certain images of Americana or US urban fashions, dialogued with another in a quasi-dialectical pendulum of repeated cultural borrowing, appropriation, and assimilation.

In 1998, Suzuki Daiki (b. 1962), a former 1970s-era Woolrich product buyer for Japanese suppliers, created the Engineered Garments line for his New York City–based boutique NEPENTHES (a 1996 offshoot of the original Aoyama-district Tokyo boutique opening in 1988). He ran this shop with Shimizu Keizō (b. 1958), who partnered with the original Tokyo-based NEPENTHES venture and became fascinated by American vintage clothing as a youth and briefly sold US-inspired VAN products in Isetan Department Store's men's section prior to enrolling in Bunka Fashion College.[38] In 2002, Engineered Garments became a full-fledged brand, which trend website Hypebeast describes as a look that "strikes a balance between vintage prep and blue-collar workwear."[39] Interestingly, from 2006 to 2010, Suzuki designed for the US-based Woolrich company, whose fashions he once emulated.[40] Shimizu likewise created brands like NEEDLES, which reinterpreted and manufactured in Japan the American vintage styles he once procured in the United States. Here, a particular evolving style involving quotidian fashions ran full circle through a dynamic cultural transference between Japan and the United States.

However, in the 1950s and 1960s, Japanese street fashions were based on those allegedly found in the United States, with wearers, and then designers, reimagining American preparatory school outfits or 1950s-era Ivy League fashions. These became like a uniform, with extensive discussions of "rules" in growing numbers of postwar fashion magazines. Japanese fashion historian W. David Marx notes how, in the early 1960s, the first Japanese men's fashion magazines like *Men's Club* promoted maniacal attention to detail, where "homosocial one-upmanship brought fashion—previously belittled as a 'feminine' pursuit—closer to technical 'masculine' hobbies such as car repair and sports."[41] *Men's Club,* connected to the VAN Jacket brand initiated in 1951 by men's clothier Ishizu Kensuke (1911–2005), instructed readers on how to properly affect American Ivy League styles to appear nonchalantly well-dressed in sartorial trappings of privilege.

The designer gained inspiration for this "Ivy" look from a US Marine lieutenant and Princeton University graduate befriended in postwar Allied-occupied Shanghai. In 1949, VAN Jacket's Osaka-based precursor was christened Ishizu Shōten (Ishizu Shop), and by the 1950s into the early 1960s, Ishizu developed a niche in ready-to-wear clothing, cheaper than tailored originals. Barely a decade following

246   *Chapter 7*

Japan's US-led Allied Occupation, an enduring Japanese trend called *Ametora* ("American traditional" abbreviated) arrived, reflecting Japan's rising prosperity and democratization of American luxury through a Japanese lens. *Heibon Punch* exploded this trend into Japanese youth culture's mainstream. Launched on April 28, 1964, its cover featured four boys "chatting to another boy in a red sports car" wearing "blazers, short cotton pants, loafers, (and) sharply parted Kennedy haircuts"; it sold 620,000 copies and reached one million in circulation by 1968.[42]

Young Japanese who adopted *Ametora* could vicariously emulate high-class American elite youth in a clothing fad that nonetheless threatened government authorities believing their sartorial affectations meant gang membership; by the early 1960s, it acquired a rebellious flavor, when the so-called Miyuki Tribe, teenagers fascinated by casual dress styles purportedly copied from American Ivy League universities, flocked to shopping areas like Ginza on weekends. In September 1964, just before Japan's summer Olympic Games,[43] historian Marx notes that for contemporaneous Japanese authorities, "fashion . . . was a matter for law enforcement" because high school and college students were expected to wear plain, dark school uniforms, and Tokyo police believed "only unrepentant rebels experimented with American looks like Hawaiian shirts and MacArthur sunglasses."[44] Though most Miyuki Tribe youth came from influential, well-to-do families, student elites at Waseda and Tokyo Universities were also more likely to engage in antigovernment protests at the time. Japan's top two private and public universities, respectively, attracted sons, and now, daughters, of wealthy families who could afford overseas travel to purchase preppy clothing in the United States, arrange for delivery to Japan, or buy from emerging designers like Ishizu who copied the trend.

However, this once-rebellious fashion fad soon filtered into all social sectors of the largely middle-class Japanese society. This mid-1960s craze also influenced ordinary middle-class adults with its new look, connoting casual American success from a democratic country that helped reshape postwar political structures with a new constitution, and which jumpstarted the economic miracle through procurements for the ensuing Korean and Vietnam Wars. By 1964, many Americans and Japanese viewed Japan as fully recovered from the war, with a thriving democracy, and thus worthy of worldwide showcasing via the summer Olympics.

The 1964 film *Tōkyō Orinpikku* (Tokyo Olympiad) by producer Ichikawa Kon (1915–2008) envisioned a restored cityscape in Japan's capital city. Notably, it also showcased well-dressed Japanese masses attending sports events and ceremonies. In concluding scenes where marathon runners pass through Tokyo streets near a water station, garments of ordinary Japanese spectators and race officials reveal contemporary snapshots of dress and hairstyles.[45] Relatively formal vestments remain de rigeur, along with some aging veterans wearing military uniforms and children largely in school uniforms. Like the Opening Ceremony's Japanese athletes in "white cotton pants/skirts, navy/red striped ties, white hats and shoes, and three-button red jackets,"[46] officials doling out water and wet sponges were carefully dressed in Ishizu's designs, featuring blue sport coats, white shirts, red ties, gray pants or skirts, and white-banded straw hats—mimicking Ishizu's new American-inspired *Ametora* style promoted for his VAN Jacket clothing company in his *Men's Club* publication.

After the Tokyo Olympics showcased this reinterpreted trend, and following success of Ishizu's accessible style, the designer felt he needed to codify what "Ivy" meant. On May 23, 1965, Ishizu sent his son Shōsuke and VAN Jacket staff to travel for two weeks to all eight American Ivy League institutions to create the documentary *Take Ivy* (1965).[47] Despite their ambitions, Cornell University and University of Pennsylvania were omitted, with footage largely gathered at Dartmouth College, whose campus was most welcoming, owing to spring semester "Japan Week."[48] The two-hour film, where only eight minutes are now widely available, was named after the Dave Brubeck (1920–2012) quartet's jazz piece *Take Five,* and premiered on August 20, 1965, at the swanky Akasaka Prince Hotel.[49] Following the film's success, a book version was published to complement its scenes of casually clad bicycle riders on campus streets, brick and white clapboard buildings, young men walking with books, seminar rooms featuring professors in coats and ties, and a crew team rowing near Dartmouth.

The subsequent book *Take Ivy* (1965), written by Ishizu's son Shōsuke, VAN Jacket sales promoter Kurosu Toshiyuki, and company public relations representative Hasegawa Hajime, with shots by *Men's Club* photographer Hayashida Teruyoshi, evolved from photos and notes gathered while hunting for "authentic" preppy garb to codify on screen. Its introduction trumpets: "Not only does the name Ivy

League sound prestigious, American students are attracted to college life at Ivy League universities for their long history and glorious traditions."[50] Unsurprisingly, the writers also contextualized American Ivy League experiences within Japanese elite reverence for University of Tokyo (Tōdai), Japan's top public university. Far from an ethnography, *Take Ivy* was nonetheless consulted by Americans and Japanese as a snapshot into a unique elite subculture, whose relaxed yet privileged-looking style was easily adopted with proper clothing.[51] The book has since become a cult classic in both Japan and the United States: notably, Japanese first codified what "preppy" meant and where it was found—democratizing originally elite fashion sensibilities representing a select group from a powerful foreign ally.

This alleged "exposé" of American elite fashion seems ironic, or reminiscent of a specific subculture amid slow decline, by focusing on surfaces of casual privilege worn by white American society's scions amid desegregation and struggles for equality sparked by the contemporaneous civil rights movement and 1964 Civil Rights Act. Hayashida's photos seem arrested in time by portraying almost no women or people of color, contradicting brewing societal changes. In 1963, Radcliffe College began allowing women students to receive Harvard degrees, and four years later Yale and Princeton both admitted women. Kent Garrett, in his 2020 memoir of his experiences as a Black man in Harvard's class of 1963, notes how his eighteen Black classmates "constituted 1.595 percent of the entering class, more than any Harvard freshman class had included since the institution's founding in 1636,"[52] while it was the last time official school records disparagingly referred to him and fellow Black students as "negro."[53] Until recently, students of color have remained rarities in the Ivy League, where nearly half (or more) of students still self-identify as white, so the style's persistent associations with white young American men is unsurprising.[54]

Fifteen years later, US writer Lisa Birnbach's *The Preppy Handbook* (1980) further demystified and democratized American preppy culture, and increased its domestic (and later global) popularity.[55] As *Take Ivy* inspired Japanese youths' imitations of an "exotic" elite culture, *The Preppy Handbook* revealed that, while few could access this impenetrable elite culture, as long as one dressed (and acted) like a preppy, then anyone could "be" a preppy. However, after the 1980s, shifts from preppy clothing to styles inspired by US urban trends marked transformations in class and racial inspiration for both Japanese and Americans. Whereas preppy styles were based on clothing worn at Ivy

The Rise of "Cool Japan"   249

League institutions by mostly white bourgeois men, inspiration now came from working-class Black and Latinx youths. Interestingly, this shift arrived amid declining Japanese economic power, with Japan's burst economic bubble following its Economic Miracle and a mild US recession after high Cold War expenditures and rising military engagement in the Middle East.

Amid larger economic contexts tempering consumption, in early 1990s Japan, new casual wear seemingly mimicked late 1970s and early 1980s American street clothes worn by Black and Latinx working-class teenagers in certain areas of New York City, Los Angeles, and even Chicago connoting hip-hop fandom, gang signs, or membership in subcultures like *cholo* or goth.[56] Before widespread appropriation throughout global fashion worlds, these clothing choices maintained a slightly marginal edge of cheap utilitarianism and even criminality. In the United States, these so-called streetwear fashions then assimilated interpretations of late 1980s California surfer culture exemplified by the brand Stüssy, before they crossed the Pacific through critical masses of Japanese aficionados seemingly obsessed with the look.[57] Japanese tastemakers like Fujiwara, an early champion of Black hip-hop street fashions, also teamed up with Sean Stussy to promote US-inspired surfer styles.[58] Baseball caps, "trucker hats," T-shirts, denim, sneakers, sweatsuits, and the now archetypal "hoodie" (hooded sweatshirt) composed the style, while NBA stars and rappers mainstreamed fashions originated by Black and Latinx working-class youth in urban areas.[59]

By the 1990s, hip-hop fashion, with signature baggy clothing, Timberland boots, plaid, dungarees, oversized T-shirts, denim, premium sportswear like Air Jordans, paisley bandanas, camo, puffy jackets, track suits, and preferred-brand hoodies including Champion, among other clothing indicating the trend, was fully entrenched in the United States amid street fashion enthusiasts of all ethnicities and social classes.[60] Gary Warnett (1978–2017), a British fashion journalist and cultural guru of hip-hop "streetwear" and sneaker trends, noted in a 2015 video on hoodie history shot in his swanky London Knightsbridge office that "at its best, the hooded sweatshirt is an incredibly democratic item."[61] He claimed that, ultimately, streetwear is integral to its utilitarian Black roots,[62] while Latinx contributions to street fashion trends issuing from Los Angeles and Chicago are also considerable.[63]

In Japan, amid economic uncertainty during the sociopolitically tenuous early 1990s, Nigō invented and founded A Bathing Ape (now

250   *Chapter 7*

BAPE) in 1993, based on personal interpretations of Los Angeles street fashion. The Bathing Ape concept's now apocryphal history comes from the Japanese expression "a bathing ape in lukewarm water," which means a blasé, overindulgent youth.[64] Nigō presciently anticipated his brand's popularity, but his designing work also intimates 1980s antecedents like clothing preferences described by the spoiled, style-conscious college student in Tanaka Yasuo's fictional brand-name consumerist manifesto *Somehow Crystal* (1981). Though BAPE's fashions were artificial reconstructions of fictitious Southern California styles, its designers actively maintained real US connections through Los Angeles–based insiders. Santiago, a Latinx former fashion consultant in Los Angeles working with Nigō to develop the brand's authentic "American-ness," remembers that, for its logo, Nigō was inspired by Cornelius in his favorite American film *Planet of the Apes* (1968) and early 1970s sequels, where he used stills from a marathon viewing session of the series.[65] Santiago believes that initial popularity fueling the brand stemmed from ideas of a brown culture taking over the dominant, white patriarchal culture as seen in the films.[66]

A Bathing Ape began as a "limited edition" fashion purveyor, and it first copied 1980s-era American rap artist Run DMC's puffy jackets.[67] Essentially, even Nigō recognized Black and Latinx contributions to streetwear's heritage. Though limited-edition items were mainstreamed in the past ten years, they still drew American and Japanese streetwear consumers two decades ago, while associations with marginalized groups lent the style a certain edge. Initially based in Harajuku in a shop called Nowhere, the company expanded into forty Japanese retail locations until 1998, when Nigō withdrew these into the original Tokyo location to maintain exclusivity.[68] Negative impacts of the 1997 Asian economic crisis and stagnating Japanese economy possibly also motivated his decision.

In an early 2000s interview with American journalist and Japanese pop culture scholar Roland Kelts, Nigō said, "Ten or fifteen years ago, the previous generation was happy just purchasing goods from the US or Europe. The influence was moving mostly in one direction. But my generation wants to be the creative center now. We want to make what's new right here in Tokyo, and we want to spread it to the world."[69] In 2003, Nigō teamed with hip-hop artist, producer, and fashion designer Pharell Williams (b. 1973) to create Billionaire Boys Club. This collaboration marked an important point of departure for Japanese streetwear brands, since rather than mimicking American fashions, Nigō now

The Rise of "Cool Japan"   251

joined forces with an established fashion leader. Thus, the early years of the new millennium were marked by great success, with Japanese street fashion's growing cult popularity among Black rappers and hip-hop artists. A Bathing Ape, or BAPE, is now known worldwide as one of the first (and foremost) street fashion brands in Japan and elsewhere.

In 2010, despite its success, Nigō sold the brand for only $2.8 million to Hong Kong fashion conglomerate I.T but remained as fashion consultant until 2013.[70] This changed BAPE's brand character, which originally featured small batches of limited editions but now was oriented toward mass production of limited iconic pieces. For two decades, Nigō designed for the brand, but in 2013 he switched to creating T-shirts for fast-fashion company Uniqlo's UT line.[71] Here, he felt he could truly democratize name-brand street fashion by selling it at low prices: "I thought I could be useful. . . . It was about the global reach of the company. . . . UT is streetwear, effectively. It's what people really wear on the street. It's interesting for me to be able to influence that."[72] Hence, *Japanese* streetwear is a unique fusion of American and Japanese casual styles allegedly worn by ordinary people on urban streets, boasting a long history dating three decades.

For many young Japanese, this easily accessible trend pioneered by people of color initially liberated them from couture fashion's high prices and stylistic constraints during economic recession. However, even this quotidian trend was later "luxuriated" amid great popularity as economic conditions improved. At the turn of the millennium and beyond, exclusive European name brands like Louis Vuitton, in hiring Japanese pop artist Takashi Murakami (b. 1962) for the 2002 Monogram Multicolor collection,[73] and Gucci, collaborating with gifted Harlem-based tailor and New York City fashion designer Dapper Dan (b. 1944) for a 2018 collection,[74] officially appropriated looks of hip-hop icons who in prior decades sported knockoffs and referenced Japanese youth styles.[75] Basically, what became global street fashion, informed by the US hip-hop phenomenon, was very much a US-Japan coproduction.

In an interesting 2019 juxtaposition of *Ametora* and BAPE harkening back to Nigō's limited-edition "tradition," the split BAPE/Levi's Ready Denim Heavy Collaborative Capsule trucker jacket appeared for a very short time, selling from December 5 until December 7.[76] This extremely limited-edition item, advertised online, hid its price from consumers (likely collectors and aficionados) until electronic

252 *Chapter 7*

checkout, and was sold exclusively via Dubai-based music and hip-hop culture promotion company SoleDXB.com's online marketplace. Its Instagram site describes this scarce commodity amid a longer history connecting midcentury Americana with Japan:

> Levi's® Type III Trucker Jacket, born in 1967, is an apparel icon. Now it's more than the sum of its parts. Levi's® x BAPE® Split Trucker Jacket has a full zip down the back so it can be zipped apart and zipped onto any other jacket in the collection. The first release of Levi's® x BAPE® is a limited edition Dubai version. It's made of 12-oz. indigo denim, features screen-printed Levi's® logos and "stitching" in a play on the famous BAPE® camo. Its 13-oz. black twill counterpart is lined with the famous BAPE® camo print in black, white, red and green—colors inspired by the United Arab Emirates.[77]

This American-Japanese street fashion collaboration, sold via a Dubai-based website, with UAE flag colors reproduced in the spliced jacket's BAPE side's camo pattern, truly transculturates West and East. The zipped-together split jacket was situated in a marketplace between the United States and Japan in the Middle East's most consumerist city-state remaining aloof from political conflicts by becoming a mecca of consumption. This piece, created to generate publicity hype, was likely absorbed into collectors' showcase stashes.

Worldwide collectors of street fashions and Japanese pop cultural products are largely driving Japan's economic strength, along with Japanese high quality's now-global reputation for other consumers. Deeper analyses of collecting cultures and their relationship to Japan is crucial to understanding Japanese name brands' popularity and comprehending their global moment's history.

THE COLLECTOR: *OTAKU* AND THE ULTIMATE IN COMMODITY FETISHISM

Earlier chapters briefly touched upon notions of collecting as a social practice tied to extreme forms of commodity fetishism, also exemplified by the Japanese name for collectors: *otaku*. In "The Collector" in his Convolutes, or sheaf of notes for his unfinished mid-1930s *The Arcades Project*, Walter Benjamin provides perhaps the best critical English-language definition of *otaku* yet in Western contexts. His sublime passage is worth quoting at length:

The Rise of "Cool Japan"   253

What is decisive in collecting is that the object is detached from all its original functions in order to enter into the closest conceivable relation to things of the same kind. This relation is the diametric opposite of any utility, and falls into the peculiar category of completeness. What is this "completeness"? It is a grand attempt to overcome the wholly irrational character of the object's mere presence at hand through its integration into a new, expressly devised historical system: the collection. And for the true collector, every single thing in this system becomes an encyclopedia of all knowledge of the epoch, the landscape, the industry, and the owner from which it comes. It is the deepest enchantment of the collector to enclose the particular item within a magic circle, where, as a last shudder runs through it (the shudder of being acquired), it turns to stone. Everything remembered, everything thought, everything conscious becomes socle, frame, pedestal, seal of his possession. . . . Collecting is a form of practical memory, and of all the profane manifestations of "nearness" it is the most binding. Thus, in a certain sense, the smallest act of political reflection makes for an epoch in the antiques business. We construct here an alarm clock that rouses the kitsch of the previous century to "assembly."[78]

Much of Benjamin's ideas also apply to contemporary Japan. As a socially informed writer attuned to contemporary trends, Benjamin highlights that, since the nineteenth century, collector's items "were produced industrially."[79] This certainly rings true for Japanese collectors favoring street fashions like BAPE, certain limited-edition watches from Seikō and Casio, and Sanrio goods. Benjamin also notes how collectors favor the "tactile" over visual, where items must periodically be held, touched or dusted, and shown to others sharing similar tastes or interests.[80] Ironically, such consumer products are hardly rare, since collections arise from carefully curated picking and choosing of readily available commodities, with fetishized appeal generated from limited-edition status or through manufactured artisanality. Rather, these democratized commodities are luxuriated with acquisition stories or as iconic products representing certain histories. Benjamin views this as "the elevation of the commodity to the status of allegory"[81] in a practice privileging "allegory and the fetish category of the commodity."[82]

Collections also serve to create personal histories curated through objects possessing certain categories or name brands. Benjamin summarizes this as forming a "whole magic encyclopedia" where collectors function as "physiognomist" with quasi-scientific approaches to

254   *Chapter 7*

categorizing things of certain types, much like scientific taxonomists categorize collections of bird specimens or butterflies arranged by phenotypes through systematics:

> One may start from the fact that the true collector detaches the object from its functional relations. . . . It must be kept in mind that, for the collector, the world is present, and indeed ordered, in each of his objects. Ordered, however, according to a surprising and, for the profane understanding, incomprehensible collection. This connection stands to the customary ordering and schematization of things something as their arrangement in the dictionary stands to a natural arrangement. We need only recall what importance a particular collector attaches not only to his object but also to its entire past, whether this concerns the origin and objective characteristics of the thing or the details of its ostensibly external history: previous owners, price of purchase, current value, and so on. All of these—the "objective" data together with the other—come together; for the true collector, in every single one of his possessions, to form a whole magic encyclopedia, a world order, whose outline is the fate of his object. Here, therefore, within this circumscribed field, we can understand how great physiognomists (and collectors are physiognomists of the world of things) become interpreters of fate. It suffices to observe just one collector as he handles the items in his showcase. No sooner does he hold them in his hand than he appears inspired by them and seems to look through them into their distance, like an augur.[83]

Collectors prize fanatical pursuit of data-based "objectivity," where an object's entire history is recounted when briefly taken from its collection to recapture its "place" within the whole, ensconced in a material world of things made magical by the commodity's fetish qualities. Ironically, other than possessing "magical" powers to enthrall observers, collected objects kept apart from the world in collections no longer serve their original intended functions. Collected watches are usually never worn and are kept "New in Box," clothing is hung in special vinyl bags, and character "goods" perch on shelves for collectors and friends to observe longingly, and occasionally, hold.

So, how are collectors viewed in Japan, and why did a culturally specific word develop to describe them amid early 1980s high prosperity? Were there darker aspects to an obsessional practice potentially isolating collectors from others if attention to amassing collections and curating objects became all-consuming and highly competitive? How about the potentially bankrupting effects of purchasing items for collections, like "shopping queen" and best-selling celebrity author Nakamura Usagi's thirst for name-brand luxury goods? A short history of so-called *otaku* culture and its provenance is useful in understanding Japanese collectors and others.

In 1983, essayist Nakamori Akio coined *otaku* ("your honor"— essentially, "honorable dwelling"), which lampooned excessive politeness for nerdy, largely male, manga and anime enthusiasts in online communities.[84] They often enjoyed and collected hypersexualized versions of children's cartoons as cultural products, featuring doe-eyed girls with gigantic breasts and wide hips over impossibly narrow waists and long legs like Sailor Moon, or jaunty-looking boys sporting wearable technology as in *Mobile Suit Gundam* and the robot sidekicks popularized by Doraemon. According to Japanese cultural critic Hiroki Azuma, "otaku culture in reality originated as a subculture imported from the United States after World War II from the 1950s to the 1970s. The history of otaku culture is one of adaptation—of how to 'domesticate' American culture."[85] Azuma thus echoes Japanese scholars like Matsuda in criticizing US dependency within Japanese "soft power." Citing Disney and Fleischer Studios' influence on Japanese popular media through manga and anime cartoons, he posits that "between otaku and Japan lies the United States."[86] Apparently, in postwar postmodern creative spaces, the United States was Japan's shadow-presence, a culture reproduced in simulacra fetishizing and making monstrous earlier copies.

At the turn of the millennium, when Azuma's book was published, he claimed that most Japanese *otaku* were men, born between the late 1950s and early 1960s, making them thirty to forty years old, or middle-aged.[87] The theorist thus indicated the fallacy that *otaku* culture is "youth culture," since consumers were actually mature adults in positions of responsibility.[88] Although these individuals never experienced wartime and were born during the Economic Miracle's early years, they still felt war's intergenerational trauma and rapid economic growth's dislocations generating urban-based anomie. According to sociologist Mathieu Deflem, in Emile Durkheim's understanding of sociology, where the term anomie was popularized, "morality is equated with social order, and any profound disturbance of the social order is captured under the heading anomie."[89] Media preoccupation with the *otaku* phenomenon clearly reveals this.

256   *Chapter 7*

In the late 1980s, *otaku* became a popular catchword with darker connotations after Miyazaki Tsutomu (1962–2008), a young man allegedly suffering from schizophrenia or split-personality disorder,[90] known as the notorious "Otaku Murderer" in Japan's press, was caught after his spate of killing young girls from August 1988 to June 1989. The perpetrator incited a moral panic against manga, anime, and horror films, which he viewed and collected en masse, with nearly six thousand tapes littering his tiny room.[91] In horrific acts defying description, he literally consumed victims, severing and collecting their hands and teeth, along with burning their bones into ashes; he sent one victim's ashes to her parents.[92] What apparently triggered his killing spree and worsened Miyazaki's mental health was his beloved grandfather's sudden death; he even ingested the man's ashes to process his grief. In a fugue logic prompted by mental illness, he consumed small portions of past and present, thus uniting two generations of Japanese within his own body. During Miyazaki's court trial, he blamed the cartoon figure Rat Man, or Nezumi-otoko, for inciting him to engage in killings, and sketched the figure incessantly during proceedings.[93] His actions in the courtroom and beyond spurred heated debates in the media and among intellectuals about *otaku* and allegedly insalubrious consumption of Japanese popular culture in comics and animated films.

Sinister connotations aside, a cartoon character similarly named as Miyazaki's obsession was created by cartoonist Mizuki Shigeru (1922–2015), a veteran of the Asia-Pacific War's New Guinea campaign who developed his drawing skills as a *kami-shibai* (paper play) performer in the mid- to late 1940s—despite wartime injuries that severed an arm. In the 1960s and later, Mizuki was known for episodic *yōkai* (monster or spirit) adventures, in fanciful depictions of the supernatural inspired by premodern folklore and a neighborhood grandmother's tales during childhood.[94] His comic, *GeGeGe no Kitarō*, about a one-eyed, half-human boy, was serialized in print and then television, starting in 1968, which catapulted him to fame.

In 1973, Mizuki published his quasi-autobiographical masterpiece *Sōin gyokusai seyo!* (Let's All "Shatter the Jewels" [Sacrifice Ourselves] Together!), translated into English as *Onward Towards Our Noble Deaths* (2011).[95] *Gyokusai* was a term appearing after 1944 in wartime Japanese media in descriptions of allegedly heroic doomed flights of kamikaze (divine wind) pilots and suicidal battle charges of troops surrounded by enemies.[96] Mizuki's manga consists of simply drawn characters amid graphically realistic scenery detailing a unit of soldiers on Rabaul in New Guinea left to fend for themselves under abusive superiors, battling faceless American enemies and elemental jungle swamps harboring quicksand and crocodiles. Soldiers huddle in pointy-hooded raincoats, waiting out antediluvian tropical deluges, whose appearance foreshadows Mizuki's eerie, yet beloved, Rat Man character.

In 1988 to 1989, while Miyazaki perpetrated monstrous crimes following his grandfather's impressionable loss, *yōkai* trickster Rat Man also appeared as a sardonic or unreliable narrator in Mizuki's eight-volume *Komikku Shōwa-shi* (A History of [the] Shōwa [Era] in Comics), translated into English as *Shōwa: A History of Japan*.[97] Rat Man tellingly slips in and out of Mizuki's pictorial narrative of an era, perhaps representing the artist's unconscious wartime trauma suffusing his epic transwar history detailing key events unfolding alongside personal experiences as a child and youth. The return of the repressed through Rat Man for both Mizuki and Miyazaki thus becomes a leitmotif for unconscious traumas. Notably, Azuma argues that war's hidden trauma and subsequent defeat is at the crux of *otaku* assertions of national and personal identity enwrapped in identifications with certain characters: "The obsession with Japan in otaku culture did not develop from Japanese tradition but rather emerged after this tradition had disappeared. To put it another way, the trauma of defeat—that is, the harsh reality that we had decisively lost any traditional identity—lies beneath the existence of otaku culture."[98]

Often, because of grief, individuals begin hoarding objects that remind them of the deceased, or which fill the void left by keen loss. Behavioral researchers Kiara R. Cromer, Norman B. Schmidt, and Dennis L. Murphey show a "robust" relationship between hoarding and traumatic life events, where "closer examination revealed that the clutter factor of compulsive hoarding (and not difficulty discarding or acquisitioning) was most strongly associated with having experienced a traumatic event."[99] While hoarding was studied in individual contexts where researchers discovered that the behavior is usually triggered by deep personal trauma, how might this present on national levels? Collecting seems a key *otaku* characteristic, but how does it appear in practice? And, what about collecting's positive aspects, if practiced in moderation, like stimulating the economy, and, to cite Marie Kondo, its ability to "spark joy" among collecting communities?

258 *Chapter 7*

Seiko and Casio: Masters of the Limited Edition

Clues to these questions emerge in examining online watch aficionado communities. Notably, Japanese watches are wildly popular and exemplify principles of mass production in triumphs of consumer capitalism. The popular online fashion trend site Gear Patrol notes that "Today, Japanese makers are some of the largest manufacturers of mechanical movements and of completed watches, and shipped some 65 million timepieces in 2017."[100] Such huge numbers of watches would otherwise saturate markets—since someone might only need a few watches to complete their wardrobe—so, greater appeal must be generated for consumers to desire more watches than needed. A symbiotic relationship mimicking fandom often appears between collectors and companies producing these items, like G-Shock aficionados, who write the Casio Corporation requesting desired models or colors; this even extends to hip young fashionistas.

For example, the women's Baby G line, smaller and less aggressively "manly," now features a Decora style in pastel case colors, based on Japanese *kawaii* culture, billed as "dressed up in colors that recall the Decora fashion Harajuku street styles that got their start back in late 1990s."[101] Here, Casio clearly capitalizes upon the global "J-Cool" phenomenon, now extending its appeal to women consumers whose "cute" timepieces still maintain sturdiness, whether at the gym, during strenuous outdoor activities, or as aspirational activity watches. Indeed, manufacturing products specifically for women, or *jōsei-mukei* (ladies-oriented), is a long-standing practice for Japanese companies introducing new tech items,[102] and represents a concerted strategy to broaden customer bases. Yet, how should one understand consumer behavior surrounding collecting among ever-growing enthusiasts?

Anthropologist William Kelly in *Fanning the Flames: Fans and Consumer Culture in Contemporary Japan* (2004) examines Japanese consumers' agency in building particular practices and communities through the lens of fandom. He indicates the importance of "communities of mutual concern and shared commitment" for fans, who he defines as "excessive consumers," setting them apart from ordinary individuals purchasing objects or entertainment.[103] These communities, or "fandoms," resemble consuming communities coalescing around certain companies through brand-name loyalty, but are distinct in overconsumption of particular sports, celebrity figures, pop-cultural products, vintage records, or, like Nakamura Usagi, brand-name luxury goods. Fans are usually also collectors, and thus they act as careful curators of information and minute details about their objects of fascination. Kelly cites anthropologist Ted Bestor in characterizing "modern Japan as a self-anointed 'information society' [that] has placed a premium on data gathering, processing, and examination that may well support the pursuit of the arcane and the data technologies of fandom."[104] Notably, watch *otaku* fora express predilections for minutely detailed statistics and esoteric information exclusive to their groups.

In contemporary times, Japanese and global fans of Casio and Seikō congregate in online communities. Some collect Grand Seiko timepieces, which even surpass certification standards of the Contrôle Officiel Suisse des Chronomètres (Official Swiss Chronometer Testing Institute).[105] In 1960, Seikō initiated the Grand Seiko line, originally intended as a top-of-the-line luxury product surpassing standard Seikō watches, yet still highly affordable compared to Swiss brands like Rolex or Omega and storied American brands like Hamilton.[106] More recently, to commemorate Seikō's anniversary, the company created an ultra-luxe limited-edition product to enflame enthusiasm for the Grand Seiko line—or inspire more frugal consumers to purchase cheaper lookalike versions.

In January 2021, the Grand Seiko website began advertising the new SGBZ005, an over-the-top luxury self-winding automatic watch with an 84-hour power reserve dubbed the Masterpiece Collection's "Kintaro Hattori 160th Anniversary Limited Edition," where only fifty were sold. This elegant timepiece was "powered by Caliber 9R02 which is assembled, adjusted and finished by hand by the craftsmen and women of the Micro Artist Studio."[107] Despite its intimidating $103,000 USD price tag, placing it in a similar league as other formidably expensive timepieces like Patek Philippe, and provenance from an elite master artisans workshop, the watch looks surprisingly understated, and slightly resembles Seikō's original 1967 44GS Grand Seiko model, billed as "everlasting value reflecting the Japanese sense of beauty."[108] Both the pioneering 44GS and new SGBZ005 contain "the nine enduring elements of Grand Seiko style," which include "1. Double-width index at 12 o'clock, 2. Multi-faceted rectangular markers, 3. Highly-polished bezel, 4. Highly-polished planes and two dimensional surface, 5. Half recessed crown, 6. Flat dial, 7. Multi-faceted hour and minute hands, 8. Curved sideline, and 9. Reverse slanted bezel wall and case side."[109] Besides the constellation-like clear reverse containing thirty-nine jewels, this anniversary watch's elegance

260 *Chapter 7*

arises from a simple black crocodile leather watchband and platinum 950 case *zaratsu*-polished (a German-made machine producing distortion-free and mirror-like surfaces) like other models. Clearly encouraged by elite investors' massive wealth accrued during the contemporaneous COVID-19 pandemic, the company produced a model outperforming the most demanding standards.

Many intrepid Seikō collectors also purposely pay more for quite "ordinary" Seikō watches compared to similar Swiss watches because of greater perceived use or exchange value. For example, a mass-produced 1970s-era automatic Seikō chronograph was the world's first automatic chronograph, and the first worn in space: the Seikō 5 Speed-Timer Caliber 6139 became available in mid-May 1969.[110] In another case, in 1973, Colonel William Pogue (1930–2014) brought a watch originally acquired at Ellington Air Force Base's PX on board NASA's Skylab. Although NASA neglected deeming it "flight-approved," he considered it more familiar than alternatives since he had trained with the timepiece six months prior. Pogue remembered that, despite lacking official approval, it performed flawlessly. In 2007, after examining an old photograph of Pogue in Skylab, a watch enthusiast noticed that the astronaut was wearing a Seikō 6139–6002; soon, appreciative buzz about the timepiece augmented its cost. In 2008, capitalizing on the watch's sudden popularity and price hikes on collectors' forums, Pogue sold his watch for $6,000 to donate proceeds to the Astronaut Scholarship Foundation.[111] The photograph in space and proof of provenance undoubtedly influenced the price for Pogue's Seikō, but even 6139-6002 and other 6139 model watches with more mundane histories sell above $2,000 on auction sites.

Hence, luxury can be value-added for more readily available limited-edition watch models made by Seikō or Casio, depending on scarcity, pristine condition, or even patina. Certain qualities of exclusivity and rarity are projected upon scarce items, whose value augments when models are suddenly discontinued, and rise further still if boxes and instructions are kept pristine (as carefully handled "New Old Stock" or completely untouched "New in Box"). The most expensive collectibles thus appear completely new and are kept in boxes unused, after which they are enjoyed only vicariously as ultimate commodity fetishes by avid connoisseurs, known with pride as *otaku* in Japan and, increasingly, worldwide. For others, watches with patina serve as ultimate purchases—a notion popularized more recently on sites frequented by watch *otaku*.

The Rise of "Cool Japan" 261

From 2010 until 2015, on "The WatchSite: The Seiko & Citizen Watch Forum," one of the oldest and largest sites for Japanese watches, much discussion developed around the Japanese *wabi* concept. Although the high-brow US art world had already embraced *wabi* two decades prior following Leonard Koren's 1994 writings,[112] watch site denizens discovered it during recovery from a deep worldwide economic recession. To an initial question about the term, an American responded that it meant "the perfection of imperfection" and stated that, for the Seikō collecting world, it referred to "the signs of honest use," while a Japanese forum member soon added that "*wabi*, as it applies in Japanese culture is the art of imperfections. . . . When applied to a watch, invariably it's wear and tear and damage—in some cases it may be attractive—a patina on old metal, a softening of lines and rounding of edges."[113] Such appearances for items clearly much-loved and used also lend value to commodities.

Watchuseek, billing itself as the largest global Internet watch forum, boasts thousands of members, and often features *wabi* in its threads. In a 2013 online conversation on *wabi* in vintage watches on Watchuseek's Seikō forum, a collector going by the name of TimeTracker explained that its discussion broadened his perspective and prompted him to consider wearing his "Mint in Box" watches: "As a westerner, I am sure I don't completely grasp the concept of Wabi Sabi. But I am starting to see how a well worn watch could be more beautiful (and desirable) than a NOS [New Old Stock] example. A collector keeping his watches 'Mint in box' is not natural and is definitely a temporary state. I should start wearing and enjoying my MIB watches."[114] As a true *otaku*, TimeTracker revealed how even he felt uncomfortable about his "not natural" and hopefully "temporary" passion for keeping his collection pristine.

For Japanese watches, international fora created spaces for even more extreme collecting. Essentially, they celebrate the Japaneseness of mass-produced commodities with a plethora of models, in a form of capitalism seemingly dedicated to unlimited versions of one item. Constant evolution of new products and new models, with endless quests for perfection, along with imputed craftsmanship, makes Japanese products unique, and also "luxuriates" them for enthusiasts. Alongside more affordable quality products, iconic Japanese companies now unveil fabulously expensive higher-end versions, and thus, appeal to commodity fetishism activated among fans already hooked on cheaper goods.

262   *Chapter 7*

CASIO: FROM MASS-PRODUCED TOP QUALITY TO LIMITED EDITION

Recently, online watch communities have exploded for Casio watches, especially for the popular G-Shock watch—a perfect example of democratizing luxury. G-Shock arrived amid positive consumer experiences of Casio digital watches since the mid-1970s, further democratizing access to such timepieces following the company's establishment of a solid reputation for high quality from a distinctively Japanese high-tech corporation. According to the Casio corporate website, "Positioning the G-SHOCK shock-resistant watch as a mainstay of the market, he [Kazuo Kashio] helped turn the conventional view of the wristwatch as a 'fragile, luxury item' on its head, leading the way for watches to play a role in many more scenarios."[115]

This watch, introduced in 1983, was developed by Ibe Kikue (b. 1952), who allegedly subjected it to 183 quality tests. Ensconced in rubber armor inspired by Ibe's observing a bouncing rubber ball, the G-Shock is an affordable yet high-quality watch, uniquely calibrated by robot-like machines, and which appears virtually indestructible. The watch enjoyed highly successful US sales while initially priced around $50, with a DW-4000, originally selling in 1983 for an 11,400-yen list price in Japan and $59.95 in the United States.[116] In the 1990s, G-Shocks expanded in popularity and forged inroads into street fashion, with more color and style options; the Baby-G women's line was added in 1994 with the DW-520. Thus, Casio's G-Shock product reoriented the sport watch genre, and soon, US companies like Timex began marketing versions of the now-iconic watch. Yet, after a massive 1997 sales spike, consumer enthusiasm quickly faded, so Casio started developing more analog versions to anticipate the 2010s analog shift after market saturation by preponderantly digital watches.[117]

With economic conditions brightening globally in the 2010s, further trends skewed toward luxuriating hot commodities, including wristwatches. Billed as a do-everything watch ideal for sport, Casio released limited-edition FIFA World Cup G-Shock editions for France in 1998 and Germany in 2006. Additionally, Casio began featuring collaborations with hip Japanese and European designers, like Murakami Takashi in 2010, Belgian designer Martin Margiela in 2013, and Japanese street clothing line BAPE in 2018. In an unprecedented company move, in March 2019, at Baselworld, designer Ushiyama Kazuta unveiled the "cleaner" and lighter Gravitymaster model

GWR-B1000X, intended for pilots and weighing 72 grams, then priced at a jaw-dropping 120,000 yen (roughly $1,000).[118] An extreme luxury version is G-Shock founder Ibe's late 2019 dream watch, materialized in the heavy G-Shock "Pure Gold" G-D 5000R-9JR limited-edition model (only thirty-five were produced), each featuring an all-gold case, bracelet, and screws, selling for $69,500 USD to celebrate the product's thirty-fifth anniversary.[119]

While the majority of G-Shock watch production moved to Korea, and then Thailand and China, high-end Casio watches today still come from Japan, designed in the Hamura-based research-and-development facility, and originate on the company's Yamagata-based "Premium Production Line." Their "Made in Japan" status provides value-added luxury for products coming from a land allegedly populated by finicky engineers obsessed with extreme quality control: here, assembly takes 3–4 days, with 5–7 more days of tests, including water-pressure testing and days in a blistering hot and then icy cold room to mirror extreme conditions the watch might encounter.[120] In addition to this harsh and rigorous testing regime, G-Shock timepieces contain numerous parts assembled by hand, along with computerized synchronization of watch hands guided by a production engineer as a final step. Hence, these almost indestructible timepieces produced in environments seemingly privileging craftsmanship over fully mechanized assembly assure wearers of relentless reliability, no matter the extreme conditions of use—making them favorites of the military (US Navy Seals were once issued G-Shock watches), public safety officers, construction workers, and outdoor enthusiasts, along with frugal, fashion-conscious millennials. Despite their relatively higher cost as "Made in Japan" goods, the watches are still comparatively more affordable than Swiss or European counterparts.

In 2018, nine million Casio G-Shock watches of all kinds were shipped from overseas factories, highlighting the product's plebian popularity among global consumers. By 2010, Casio produced most of its lower-end watches in China, but in 2019, due to then–US president Donald Trump's "List-4" tariffs, which imposed 15 percent increases on imported Chinese-made apparel items, the company transferred manufacturing to Thailand.[121] Some more technical midrange models, like the solar and atomic solar G-Shock watches, were already manufactured for over a decade in Thailand,[122] which hosted a newer, more technologically advanced factory, and thus, many collectors preferred them over Chinese-made products. A 2021 company news

264   *Chapter 7*

release for the GSTB100GC-1A model from the coveted G-Steel collection promised consumers that, like other G-Shock timepieces,
"Each watch encompasses the 7 elements; electric shock resistance,
gravity resistance, low temperature resistance, vibration resistance,
water resistance, shock resistance and toughness."[123] Basically, if a
more expensive Japanese model was unaffordable, consumers were
still assured of Japanese quality even in cheaper G-Shock timepieces
made elsewhere.

Since its 1983 inception, the G-Shock brand name was synonymous with almost preternatural indestructibility, and this reputation,
along with early adoption of new technologies like solar power for
watches and atomic models synchronized to signals sent by atomic
clock towers used by militaries and space agencies like NASA, rendered it a line of largely handcrafted timepieces bringing accessible
and masculinized luxury to the masses. This fetishization of craftsmanship in watches also extends to other products, including Japanese
whiskies.

Japanese Whisky: Suntory's Global Award-Winning Master Craftsmanship

The decades-old Suntory box lay in my parent's basement, sadly gathering dust. My father was not a whisky drinker, but his friend, CEO
of a global German company who headed its Chicago subsidiary, was
an aficionado often hosting Japanese clients. For the German executive, the bottle encased in its special box was too precious to drink,
and thus, it was carefully saved and stored for a special occasion: my
father's sixtieth birthday in 1992. This bottle contained the first release of a limited-edition twelve-year-old Suntory Yamazaki Pure Malt
Whisky, introduced to the United States in 1990 and imprinted with
Yamazaki's characters indicating its distillery—a treat that few Americans could enjoy at the time. In contrast, by mid-2021, during this
book's writing, any bottle containing whisky distilled in the late 1970s
or early 1980s fetched premium prices globally as a scarce luxury commodity. Even at Dan Murphey's, a large Australian liquor retailer
with over 220 stores in a country where Japanese whiskies are currently less fashionable than in the United States due to heavy liquor
tariffs increasing prices, one distilled in the 1980s cost A$2,999.00,
or about $2,312.40 USD.[124] When returning home to visit my family
in 2017 after completing this book's research, I liberated the bottle

The Rise of "Cool Japan"   265

and sampled it. Nearly forty years after distillation, this sublime whisky finally issued forth its oaky perfume, and evoked crisp, yet smooth, softness when imbibed on the rocks.

In the late 1970s when Suntory Yamazaki Pure Malt Whisky was first distilled, Japanese whisky had already reached its prime, but by the early 1990s, its popularity steeply declined in Japan after the bubble economy's bust, and popular opinion began perceiving this "salaryman's" drink as dated. However, Suntory's and Nikka's executives starting viewing global markets as alternatives, and they soon sent reserved whiskies into international competitions. In 2001, a surprise upset in the global whisky world occurred when Nikka's Yoichi ten-year single malt won *Whiskey Magazine*'s "Best of the Best" award in a blind tasting competing against Scottish legends.[125] In 2003, twelve-year-old Suntory Yamazaki Pure Malt Whisky, which I later sampled at home, won the International Spirits Challenge's gold medal, received a year later by another Suntory whisky, the Hibiki thirty-year.[126] Yet, not until 2010 would Japanese whisky again command worldwide attention, and earn particular American acclaim, with the US arrival of Hibiki, Suntory's first Japanese blended whisky to win the "World's Best Blended Whisky Award."[127] This initiated an upward trend helping the company regain ground after the difficult 1990s and early 2000s.

This initiative includes educating global consumers about Japanese whisky's high-quality and craftsman-like production—a marketing tool correlating with Japanese companies promoting manufactured artisanality. Mike Miyamoto, a former Suntory distiller and now Suntory's global brand ambassador tasked with expanding the company's global consumer presence, notes that, "To help people understand the true culture of Japanese whisky, we don't consider whisky just as production, but as an art" wherein Japanese craftsmanship is "very detailed and very precise."[128] This also resembles Suntory's competitor, Nikka Whisky Distilling Company. Sugimoto Jun'ichi, currently heading Nikka's original Yoichi Distillery, indicates that Japanese whisky's distinctive flavor comes from artisanal processes carefully managing temperatures of coal-fired stills, which Nikka still maintains: "It's not something that can be proven scientifically, but the fluctuations in the heat of the coal fire seem to have a complex effect on the whisky produced. Using the same pot stills from the time of our founding has allowed us to create whisky that is distinctive to Yoichi. So we're not likely to change this traditional approach in the years ahead."[129] This "traditional approach" served Nikka well, earning the company

266 *Chapter 7*

"Best Japanese Single Malt Whisky" for a bottle of Nikka Single Malt Yoichi (1987) twenty-year-old at the World Whiskies Awards in Glasgow, Scotland, in 2008.[130] However, Nikka's rival Suntory garnered "World's Best Blended Whisky" for a bottle of Hibiki thirty-year-old that same year.[131]

Other factors besides allegedly "traditional" craftsmanship make whiskies Japanese, like barley almost exclusively imported from Scotland, distilleries using peat from Japan's northern lowland rivers like Hokkaidō's Ishikari, and filtration with bamboo rather than charcoal. In travels throughout Japan, Scottish journalist Dave Broom, known for his writings on whisky and spirits, and who serves as Suntory's international consultant, marveled that Japanese whisky-makers were "master artisans dedicated to their craft. The way they approached whisky was imbued with the concept of *kaizen*—continuous incremental improvement."[132] Besides marketing artisanality in whisky production, *kaizen* (transform into goodness) also pertains to Suntory's rapid adjustment to global market conditions and approaches to recent trends.

Mixed drinks are big business in the contemporary United States, England, and Western Europe, so the Suntory Company began envisioning a whisky to widely penetrate this broad consumer base. For American and European consumers, Suntory resurrected a highball "tradition" in recent campaigns for Suntory Whisky Toki,[133] a lower-priced blended alternative to Yamazaki single-malt and Hibiki premium-blended whiskies that arrived in 2016 on the American market at the recommended price of $39.99,[134] and in summer 2018 appeared on shelves in the United Kingdom, France, and Germany.[135] In 2014, Suntory acquired the ailing American Jim Beam company, renamed the new global conglomerate Beam Suntory, and set up international headquarters in Deerfield, Illinois, near other Chicago-area Japanese international companies.[136] Toki evolved from this merger as a drink that corporate leaders hoped would reinvigorate the US whisky world, by making it cool *and* exotic. As a smooth blend of American white oak cask malt whiskies from the Hakushū and Yamazaki Distilleries mixed with Yamazaki Spanish oak cask malt whisky for flavor, and a heavy-grain whisky from Chita Peninsula in Japan's Aiichi Prefecture for depth, this crisper and fruitier Toki whisky is marketed to younger, urban Generation Z'ers and millennials aged twenty-five to thirty-four years old, a cohort that in 2017 drank a staggering 826 million gallons annually, compared with 948 gallons for older peers.[137]

What accounts for this large rise in consumption? Besides marketing's effects in prompting greater alcohol consumption, journalist Gabrielle Glaser, in *Her Best-Kept Secret* (2013), notes exponentially high growth in American professional women's drinking with increased stressors at work and home amid expectations to maintain equally high standards in professional lives and parenting[138]—a social dilemma common to other developed societies in industrial late capitalism. Though younger men still drink more than younger women, both genders are increasingly likely to drink more while going out or at home than several decades ago: a problem exacerbated by the 2020–2022 COVID-19 pandemic.[139] More positively, this young cohort also craves greater authenticity in social encounters and expects this on consumer levels when enjoying retro drinks like highballs and other products demanding artisanal craftsmanship.[140]

In 2019 promotional videos, leading Brooklyn and London bartenders showcased high-quality Japanese technological innovation by using Suntory's automatic highball machines imported from Japan, while Tokyo bartenders highlighted labor-intensive artisanal ice carving for highballs using Suntory whisky.[141] Here, both machines and manpower were fetishized as commodified performances now composing trendy new Suntory bar experiences with cool Japanese touches. These videos market an accessible, high-quality commodity only offered by a reputable Japanese name brand. In January 2021, the company announced a planned move from its Chicago-based global headquarters to New York by mid-2022 to profit from the Empire State's cachet among younger drinkers.[142] Time will tell exactly how popular Japanese whisky will become among British and American millennials,[143] but they currently support strong upward trends where foreign consumption reinvigorates Japan's spirit trade, while Japanese liquor companies capitalize on their "Made in Japan" cachet of high quality and superior craftsmanship.[144]

Kaō Asience Shampoo: Capitalizing on Asian Science

Not only Japanese high technology and artisanally distilled whiskies but also products containing natural East Asian plant extracts have become attractive to global consumers and are now synonymous with Japanese brand names. In 2003, Kaō Corporation released its new Asience hair-care product line, advertised as combining traditional East Asian medicinal and herbal extracts with Western science to produce

268   *Chapter 7*

superior products. The line's name is formed from "Asian" and "science," or Asian science—formulated by Asian (Japanese) scientists while produced by Asians in Japan with traditionally Asian ingredients (besides cleansing agents). These include licorice essence for the scalp, plus essences of lotus flower, Korean ginseng, camellia oil, pearl protein, and shell ginger leaf. Asience first emerged in Japan, and in the 2010s it spread throughout East and Southeast Asia into areas once part of Japan's empire. In a 2017 *Nikkei Asian Review* interview, Kaō CEO Sawada Michitaka noted strong consumption in China, with consumers purchasing the company's value-added products like diapers and skin-care items, which he interpreted as largely middle-class customers seeking highest-quality products.[145] Sawada mentioned that in Japan, 30 percent of shampoo sales were for higher-end 800-yen bottles (presumably including Asience).[146] Essentially, ordinary middle-class consumers in East Asia and Japan still sought luxury despite economic uncertainty—this reveals how Kaō even democratized luxury during economically challenging times.

Following its spread to Hong Kong and Taiwan, Asience's popularity reached Southeast Asia in Singapore, Thailand, and, especially, Malaysia, where it enjoyed strong profits after its April 2009 introduction.[147] Advertised online in Malaysia as specifically formulated for ethnically Asian hair, an educational diagram shows a scalp subjected to repeated hair-washing, allegedly common among Asians: "Because we shampoo every day, it is important to use a shampoo that cares for the scalp." Addressing a particular consuming community, the diagram shows cross sections of healthy and damaged hair, along with photos of light falling in a straight line on healthy straight hair as opposed to damaged hair.[148] Right above appears a photo of Nagase Shinobu, Kaō's Hair Beauty Research Laboratories chief researcher: wearing glasses, a white lab coat, white shirt, and conservative black-colored tie, the smiling, middle-aged Japanese scientist clearly means business.[149] In recent decades, Malaysians and others have viewed Japan as high-tech, and as generating the region's latest scientific discoveries, underlined in the advertising phrase "Our Hair Beautifying Technology."

Currently, Kaō applies a quasi-artisanal testing process to potential shampoo varieties before they are sold. A thousand different formulas are purportedly tested on researchers' own hands before a new shampoo's approval, in a process where researchers try several each day, noting the gel's feel and possible drying effects—essentially adding human elements of *ganbari* (tireless effort) to their work. In the company's online promotional website, Japanese labor is thus fetishized, and joins the commodity's narrative, where the scientists' perfectionism results in a first-rate, high-quality unparalleled product. This also resembles the care taken by Seikō and Casio in manufacturing watches, subjecting them to tests far beyond necessary for similar timepieces, along with Shiseidō's emphasis on continuous research and development of superior products appealing to diverse customer groups. Such commitment to exactitude and measurable results in relatively affordable products offers quality usually only found in luxury commodities.

Notably, Karl Marx postulated that commodity fetishism leads to occlusion of social labor involved in manufacturing commodities,[150] but for Japanese commodities, at least some aspects of labor dedicated to manufacture are instead highlighted and proudly presented in ways intended to sell more products. While the entirety of labor required to manufacture commodities like G-Shock watches or Ascience hair-care products remains hidden, Japanese labor leading to their creation is celebrated, and thus utilized to make these commodities more salable.

DEMOCRATIZING BEAUTY: EXPANDING SCOPES OF AGE, ETHNICITY, AND GENDER

Since their 1870s inception and beyond, Japanese companies have been pivotal in producing high-quality items at price points accessible to all. These products were initially meant to serve as domestic alternatives to imported Western ones, while later, corporations became so international that their Japanese origins (or those of their products) even became obscured. These trends toward internationalization, and increasing incorporation of foreign subsidiaries after the 1990s, meant serving an increasingly diverse customer population with multiple subsets. Foreign lines, especially in the United States, targeted increasingly diverse groups of people for makeup and foundation purchases. More recently, cosmetic products have been geared to specific age groups like children, middle-aged women, elders (so far, in Japan only), and men, so that all consumers can enjoy goods like those purchased by earlier consuming communities.

In the 2000s Shiseidō broadened its customer bases internationally by reaching out to ethnicities beyond Japanese and other East Asians. The corporation has progressed far since summer 2005, when

270 *Chapter 7*

it sought twenty-something Caucasian face models in Tokyo to formulate new foundations for people of European ethnicities—most likely, for emerging Russian markets. In 1999, Shiseidō began selling cosmetics in Russia through a distributor; these product tests anticipated plans for a subsidiary in May 2007, with products sold beginning in January 2008.[151]

To succeed in these new markets, Shiseidō undertook *ganbari* in Japan, and when new product lines were ready, the company recruited people with skin types and tones similar to those of potential customers. My own experience in Japan sheds light upon Shiseidō's research strategies. Prompted by a tip from a Tokyo Union Church parishioner, I ventured into Shiseidō's Meguro-based testing headquarters, where I was escorted into a large room filled with rows of light-bulb-illuminated mirrors perched on small white tables with chairs, given a white bib, and instructed to carefully wash my face with cleanser at a line of porcelain faucets near the front. When I returned, an assistant applied a toner, referred to as "softener," and other products in Shiseidō's five-step retinue of cleansers, toners, serums, moisturizers, and sunscreens. Then, a man in a white lab coat, possibly a chemist, tested several foundation colors on my skin to assess their tone. Japanese foundations catering to largely Asian customer bases have greenish tints to offset brown sunspots and other imperfections, while American light-skinned foundations tend toward pinkish or orange flesh tints to conform to Caucasian skin's cool or warm tones, and blend freckles and blemishes. After several applications and repeated cleansings, I was thanked for my work, handed a crisp white envelope of cash, and offered a trial cosmetic item from new product selections on a rear table, so I chose a contoured curve mascara—an innovation only reaching companies in US retail markets a decade later. My experience was undoubtedly repeated by hundreds of women (and some men) in following years to create realistic fair, light, medium, tan, and deep shades offered to expand available foundations to all Shiseidō customers.

Globally, in the past few decades, individual countries have experienced growth in multiethnic populations, necessitating the embrace of inclusive diversity by corporations seeking to expand their consumer base. In 2019, Shiseidō pioneered its Synchro Skin foundation line, with an initial thirteen shades for the now-discontinued Lasting Liquid foundation; in 2022, it featured thirty shades for its Radiant Lifting and Self-Refreshing foundations that purportedly resist water without transferring onto fabrics or other surfaces.[152] The product line also promises flawless evenness, smoothness, and radiance with twenty-four hours of hydration for any skin tone. On the Shiseidō website, female models ranging from their teens to twenties in multiple ethnicities and races—Caucasian, Asian, Hispanic, Indigenous, African, and multiethnic[153]—represent different shades, while young men occasionally appear in advertisements with women to represent makeup's gender diversity. (In 2004, Shiseidō introduced skin care for men, including shaving cream.)[154] Few elements of the company's Japanese origins appear within the foundation's description, except for Asian-connoted ingredients of pearl powder and mandarin peel extract. Rather, the website recommends its application with one of two artisanally mass-produced Japanese makeup brushes. This midrange makeup product sold in Japan and the United States contrasts with Shiseidō's current top-shelf skin-care products, which fully capitalize on notions of Japaneseness and alleged exoticism.

Tested on three dozen women in summer to fall 2019, Shiseidō's exclusive Future Solutions LX line currently promises that its "most luxurious and ultra-potent anti-aging formula revitalizes and restores complexions with Skingenecell Enmei Complex, Shiseidō's exclusive youth-prolonging ingredient."[155] Geared toward women in their fifties and beyond, advertisements feature taut-skinned Caucasian and Japanese models in their twenties, whose faces apparently represent aimed-for ideals of American consumers—likely high-earning professional women seeking to rejuvenate their appearances without surgery or injections. This contrasts with Shiseidō's Prior brand, a Japan-only product line targeting elderly women also featured in advertisements. In 2022, Shiseidō's most expensive Future Solutions LX product was a 50-ml face cream retailing at $540 USD, packaged in an elegant gold Japanese paper box tied in a traditional manner with golden cords. To justify its high cost, online descriptions fetishize its particularly high quality and craftsmanship as a "breakthrough in extending youthfulness" involving ingredients harvested by hand, evolving from seven years of rigorous scientific research with the product finally released in 2017.[156] Interestingly, its top six ingredients are quite humble: water, glycerin, butylene glycol (a conditioning agent preventing ingredient clumping), cetyl ethyhexanoate (a skin-smoothing emollient ester), niacinamide (anti-inflammatory vitamin B-3), and squalene (a biochemical

272   *Chapter 7*

precursor to steroids), with value-added rare plant extracts nearing the ingredient list's bottom third. The cream is apparently an emulsion containing small extract amounts, along with hydrolyzed silk.[157] The product's high cost and rare provenance are further luxuriated by elaborate application processes accentuating its emollient qualities.

As it did in the 1920s and 1930s, Shiseidō emphasizes beauty consultants' contributions in training consumers to properly apply its products—a role expanding virtually with the COVID-19 pandemic keeping consumers away from stores. According to a "Defy Time" webinar featuring products from the Future Solutions LX line that I attended in January 2021, Shiseidō "Brand Expert" Cyndi Buck, a creamy complexioned white woman approaching fifty and seemingly untouched by aging, indicated how one plant was harvested a few times yearly at night, highlighting its rarity and efficacy based on Japanese traditions coupled with science. In a livestream video replete with hearts emitted by enthused fans "sharing the love" for Legendary Enmei Ultimate Renewing Cream, Buck luxuriated in the product's smooth texture during application, and highlighted its uncanny luminescence on her skin after removing it from a pearlescent white glass jar.[158]

Similarly, on the English-language portion of Shiseidō's Japanese website geared toward retailers, in a promotional video titled "Gifts from an Ancient Source," a male commentator with a distinctly British accent discusses the aforementioned cream's ingredients. These include Enmei herb, "picked by hand" and harvested five days yearly on auspicious dates on Mount Koya near Kyoto, Japan's cultural capital, and treasured green silk, reaching rigorous standards attained by only "one millionth of the silk in all the world." The video ends with the man indicating how the product contains "blessings from Japan's forests. Ginza, Tokyo."[159] Clearly, silk comes from carefully tended cocoons, with trays of caterpillars fattened on cultivated mulberry leaves, and not randomly found in wild forests like the video's description of Japanese "oak moths" in "pristine mountains of Japan"; such images of fortuitously foraged wild ingredients and herbs increase the product's fetishistic allure, portrayed as a rare, highly prized commodity representing ultimate Japanese cosmetic luxury.

Just like for limited-edition G-Shock watches and highest-end Grand Seiko timepieces, recent trends show how Japanese companies "luxuriate" products initially designed to provide accessible high-quality alternatives to otherwise unaffordable European or American versions. Interestingly, for Americans and other foreign customers, such products' very Japaneseness or "Made in Japan" status now connotes luxury itself. For particularly high-end product lines like Future Solutions LX, Shiseidō is profiting from growing numbers of US Gen-Xers (born 1965–1980); in 2021, they reached ages of forty-one to fifty-six years and boasted the highest average post-tax yearly income of $88,794 for any American generation, and also spent the most on apparel and personal care (including cosmetics), at $3,378 yearly.[160] Yet, these aging American consumers postdate those earlier enticed by Shiseidō in Japan.

Targeting Japan's rapidly aging population, Shiseidō began marketing to older Japanese women consumers and created two new product lines in 2007 and 2015 to tap into these trends: according to World Bank data, Japan's over-sixty-five population numbered nearly 21 percent in 2007 and rose to 26 percent in 2015, while Japanese women over age sixty-five comprised 23.4 percent in 2007 and nearly 29 percent in 2015 of Japan's total female population.[161] Hence, in August 2007, Shiseidō initiated Integrate Gracy, an affordable yet elegantly packaged, fragrance-free line sold at ordinary drugstores, which includes various foundations and makeup products geared toward active women in their fifties and beyond.[162] Shiseidō's corporate site indicates that Gracy's "name comes from a fusion of 'Grace' and 'Elegance,' and offers high quality and ease of use" for products, which are clad in indigo blue with tiny, festive gold stars decorating tubes and compacts for foundations, powders, and mascaras, while lipsticks come in gold tubes.[163] These products were also slightly cheaper than their original department store progenitors but maintained Shiseidō's celebrated quality and attractive packaging design.

In January 2015 Shiseidō launched Prior, a similar non-elite line targeted to even older female populations, which includes wider selections of skin care, base makeup including BB (beauty balm) creams, "point makeup" (eyeshadow, eyeliner, mascara, eyebrow pencil, blusher, and lipstick), and hair care (shampoo and conditioner), also appearing in drugstores and on the company's online shop Watashi (Me) Plus.[164] Elderly customers unable to commute to Shiseidō counters at urban department stores (or whose restricted retirement incomes prohibited the cost) could still walk to relatively inexpensive local drugstores or small neighborhood pharmacies to purchase these products. The line promised to address the euphemistically termed *otona no shichi-nan* (seven difficulties for adults): large pores, shadows, coloring, dryness, sagging,

274   *Chapter 7*

ugliness (*mie-nikui*), and troublesome-ness (*okkui*).[165] Television advertisements on the line's promotional website featured "mature" female models (likely in their sixties) in colorful, flowing clothing styles preferred by elderly women, while a middle-aged male announcer hawked the product's efficacy at the end to lend products an authority familiar to older Japanese women customers.[166] According to a 2003 study by communications scholar Akie Arima, voice-overs in Japanese television commercials skew overwhelmingly male, especially in commercials for older adults;[167] while in 2017, Arima, Michael Prieler, Florian Kohlbacher, and Shigeru Hagiwara discovered that, in both 1997 and 2007, cosmetics and toiletries that were marketed to the elderly predominantly featured women, where "the strong association between females and cosmetics/toiletries emphasized the importance that society assigns to female beauty and contributes to their sexualization."[168] Clearly, elderly Japanese women assigned high value to beauty as they aged, and Prior products could help them meet stringent social expectations.

In addition to marketing strategies targeting older women, Prior was advertised as "easy beauty," where packages were easier to open, revealing that pumps and cases were smoothly manipulable for hands suffering from arthritis, and packaging contained detailed instructions with photographs to instruct consumers; the line received a 2018 IAUD gold medal Universal Design Award due to accessibility. In the innovative Prior line, Shiseidō luxury thus reached elderly women in easily accessible retail locations and even promised user-friendly packaging with uncomplicated product usage directions—tapping into appreciative elderly markets desiring attractive makeup and effective creams designed for their needs at affordable prices geared toward fixed incomes.

CONCLUSION

In the late twentieth century, Japanese style and innovation emerged at the forefront for numerous consumer products manufactured by Japanese companies readily available throughout the globe. The Japanese government later codified this phenomenon in early millennium efforts to promote "Cool Japan," and through various funding efforts targeting smaller companies, attempted to foster Japanese corporate penetration into global personal consumer product markets. However, much of this propaganda campaign and boosterism of particularly Japanese products was performed by consumers themselves, who believed that Japanese quality control and attention to detail amid manufactured artisanality made for better products. Initially, cheaper travel abroad, and then Internet sales, made these products easily accessible if not already sold outside Japan, as for street fashions. From the 1990s onward, collecting communities surrounding certain products began forming in Japan and elsewhere. These were active in areas like watch collecting communities involving Seikō and Casio products.

"Made in Japan" continues to serve as an important selling point and proffers less-expensive luxury predicated on imagined craftspeople and exacting quality measures—allegedly only offered by Japanese due to their assumed historical control of quasi-artisanal production processes. These very qualities are also fetishized and promoted as value-added characteristics in products marketed overseas as "exotic," though highly reliable, and which harbor innovations developed through extensive research and development. Such properties even entered the personal care and cosmetics worlds, for corporate giants like Kaō and Shiseidō extending their markets into more diverse customer bases throughout Asia along with Europe and the United States. Another important domestic and international market began emerging after the millennium for Japanese companies—aging Gen-Xers with historically high disposable incomes and growing numbers of frugal elderly Japanese who desired luxury but balked at high prices and difficult-to-open containers. All these consumer practices surrounded global interpretations of "J-Cool," now a firmly entrenched marketing phenomenon issuing from Japan.

CONCLUSION
Nihon-shiki *Commodity Fetishism*

Previous chapters explored the interplay between advertising and consumption in modern Japan by investigating how particular Japanese companies at key historical moments assigned value, or "luxury," to mass-produced products as an important business model. In certain eras, targeting of women, children, and young men revealed consumption's political values in its aspirational and often gendered nature. Luxury in a Japanese context thus emerges as a high-quality artisanality artificially assigned to mass-produced products, along with a particular sense of "place" tied to region or nation, despite alienation from interpersonal relationships of producers with their material or medium. Companies also created products at all price points to allow accessibility to more consumers, while starkly curtailing production for certain limited editions to increase desirability.

In postwar Japan, rise of a middle class in a thriving democracy was tied to greater disposable income and economic consumption, with the Three Imperial Regalia (household appliances and other items) denoting consumer aspirations. An artificial sense of nationalism arising out of economic success blended with myths of unique Japanese identity to create a postwar mass consumer society based on commodity fetishism with brand names widely accessible in Japan and globally. The postwar period also saw Japanese companies concerned with building a mass consumer base, but engaged in democratizing luxury by making it available to all at reasonable prices, while maintaining earlier business patterns of accessibility, high quality, and exemplary service. This study explored the origins of company histories,

Conclusion   277

and their strategies encouraging Japanese and global customers to consume a seemingly unique Japanese luxury.

Japanese luxury is now available online to everyone any time with high-speed Internet access. Large-scale purchasing websites like Amazon and eBay (specifically, with the "Buy It Now" feature) in the United States and globally, along with sites like Buyee in Japan, now allow consumers to compare prices and eliminate waiting to complete purchases in store lines and obviate travel to acquire products. Aided by companies employing algorithms, social media users are bombarded with onscreen blasts of products that they might consider purchasing, and feel haunted when items appear onscreen that they may have discussed with friends in the material world. Here, the solid and intangible appear to mesh in propelling ever more sales. In recent times, commodity fetishism itself appears to have adopted a supernatural life of its own, with modern humans turning into hungry ghosts of desire, where creative advertising generates insatiable appetites for even more objects.

However, despite darker aspects of this potential futurity, are there valuable lessons to be learned from the Japanese example of name brands, advertising, and consumption? What, if anything, is positive about democratizing luxury during a time that some scholars have dubbed the "Necrocene?" Within the Japanese model of consumption, might it instead be possible to circumvent relentless disposability cycles reminiscent of contemporary global "throwaway" culture?

Commodity Fetishism Japanese-Style? Nested Copies in the Age of the Necrocene

As revealed previously, in Japan from the Meiji period until the late 1930s, imitating European luxury and style was common for iconic companies desiring to enhance their products' luxury image. Japanese brands were still more affordable and accessible to domestic consumers and those throughout the empire than similar items from Paris, Europe's fashion capital. The Shiseidō Corporation's history and trajectory exemplifies these trends. In the late nineteenth century, this Japanese company began with a vision to approximate Western cosmetics and perfumes in Japan. Over a century later, these were then sold in 1980s Europe, aided for two decades by a French creative director's advertising skills, who in the new millennium created his own brand, which the same Japanese company purchased sixteen years later.

278   *Conclusion*

French designer and photographer Serge Lutens (1942), who worked for Shiseidō from 1980 until 2000, brought his own French stylistic acumen to Shiseidō's cosmetic packaging and advertisements, and in 2000 he branched out to form his own brand, Parfums Beauté Serge Lutens, later renamed Serge Lutens. Of course, Lutens is an outsider who benefited from past connections to Japan, just as the Shiseidō brand originally benefited from Lutens' connections to France during 1980s-era "internationalization." His relationship with Shiseidō began with this symbiosis, and continues, since products for the Serge Lutens' cosmetics and perfume brand are actually produced by Shiseidō in France, with some in Japan, like nail polish. In March 2015 Lutens signed a deal with Shiseidō to purchase his own trademark, which maintained his concept of "rare and lux," while allowing Shiseidō's deeper penetration into high-end luxury French cosmetics and perfume markets.[1] At present, while kept on as the Serge Lutens company's creative director, Lutens brings Japanese design elements to perfume bottles (superficially resembling Shiseidō's long-term iconic product Euderme) and to Paris-based retail shops citing an Orientalized art deco atmosphere—especially the flagship Rue St. Honoré boutique. In this case, far from democratizing luxury, Shiseidō actually further luxuriated a brand under its new ownership, with a French creative director whose vision the company had long nurtured. Shiseidō's circular trajectory in Lutens' career represents the success of cross-cultural fertilization for many Japanese companies in the design and business worlds.

A contemporary product example of this East-West cultural borrowing and literal appropriation of Japanese artisanal manufacturing for the European market is Lutens' "Ghost Train" (*Train Fantôme*) scarf, appearing in fall 2019. Selling at $400 retail online, it is made in Japan of silk using traditional batik techniques (originally brought to Japan from Indonesia with Dutch traders during the Tokugawa period), which the website calls *chidori maki*, promising that "each Serge Lutens scarf contains a little of its creator's obsession" where "each collection is a limited edition." The scarf, citing a constructed Japaneseness and "authenticity" because of its "Made in Japan" status, fully represents Japanese-style democratized luxury in that even if a customer cannot afford a Louis Vuitton bag or other more expensive emblems of French luxury, they can still revel in this piece's uniqueness promising superior craftsmanship, as well as its greater affordability than one made in Europe. Of course, it is labeled "limited edition," and that it is

"Japanese" lends it a profitable exoticism. As Elad Granot, Latoya Russell, and Thomas Brashear-Alejandro assert, the "new luxury" also promises emotional fulfillment—a trope wherein commodity fetishism gains its monstrous power.[2] Did Lutens learn of these advertising techniques during his two-decades-long tenure at Shiseidō? Most certainly, Lutens' signature cross-fertilization of European and Japanese style with art deco forms also developed then.

Thus, the *Train Fantôme* scarf perfectly illustrates a commodity's fetishistic allure in luring customers into making a purchase—if only for its hauntingly unique and unusual design. One is reminded of consumers falling for the addictive qualities of online shopping, which psychologist Gabor Maté parallels with hungry ghosts, and Karl

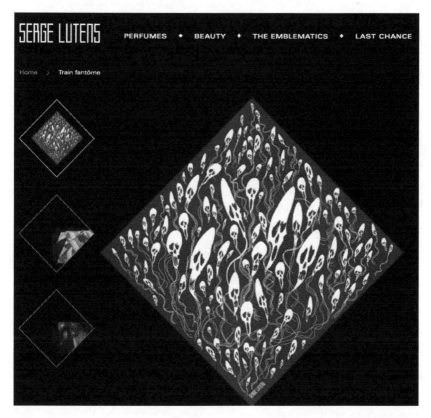

Figure C.1. Serge Lutens, *Train Fantôme* scarf, fall 2019. https://www.sergelutens.com/us/catalog/product/view/id/336/s/ghost-train-foulard-serge-lutens/category/84/, accessed July 25, 2021.

280   *Conclusion*

Marx's ascription of European idolatry to commodities. An advertising video for the piece shows a haunting parade of mask-like skulls with curiously squid-like appendages floating through a sea of darkness, which at certain angles look like jellyfish, spermatozoa, bulb-headed aliens in outer space, menacing fetuses, or deep-sea cephalopods.[3] Ominous musical notes reference impending doom, but then the orchestral music lifts and becomes a wondrous symphony to accompany the creatures as they agglomerate and approach their positions in a rectangular scarf upended on its points to resemble a diamond. In a symphony of purple and white, their shapes on silk look like Edvard Munch's *Scream* (*Der Schrei der Natur* [The Cry of Nature], 1893) or, more recently, the mask in the film *Scream* (1996).

More ominously, in the new millennium's second decade, few can argue against the fact that industrially based mass consumption contributes massively to environmental destruction. The earth's oceans now choke with plastic from packaging and disposable consumer goods, while their rise in temperature fosters jellyfish overpopulation—ironically, making oceans look eerily like the graceful harbingers of death intimated by Lutens' luxury silk scarf. In other words, commodity fetishism kills. As sociologist Jason Moore argues, exchanging chemist Paul Croutzen's term "Age of the Anthropocene" (the era of human-centered industrial control over the environment), coined in 2000, for the Capitalocene may be a more fitting term for global landscapes of revolution and radical changes in social relations engendered by capitalism since its mid-fifteenth-century rise.[4]

Yet, in *Between Earth and Empire*, philosopher John P. Clark posits that humankind is now more rightly positioned in the Necrocene, a "new era of death" amid mass extinction and "a reversal of the creative activity, the *poesis*, of the earth."[5] Clark blames an obsessive culture of mass consumption for generating short-term cravings only assuaged by acquisition.[6] As remedy, Clark proposes a spiritual solution: severing this endless cycle of attachment can heal both the earth and ourselves, liberating us from detrimental attachments to things, exactly what commodity fetishism does to haunted souls of consumers.[7] He hints that the only antidote to untrammeled capitalism's ills and its resultant commodity fetishisms appears to be a return to premodern ideas issuing from early Buddhism and Daoism, supported by communities of anarchistic free associations.

Not surprisingly, a gorgeous, silky-smooth scarf allegedly handcrafted with traditional Japanese artisanal practices accurately depicts

Conclusion   281

the "scream of nature"[8] in a rapidly warming and dying world. The meditation upon life and death that it promises serves like a mandala to ironically force onlookers to reflect upon deadly forms of consumption. As Walter Benjamin warns in his essay "The Collector": "With individuals as with societies, the need to accumulate is one of the signs of approaching death."[9] Here, the fetishized commodity calls out in a clarion cry to the consumer, ironically promising its own death.

While democratizing luxury and concomitant consumption may not be inherently evil, their effects could be sinister when adopted on a global scale and, coupled with penchants for hoarding, will be much precipitated by increases in global traumas generated by climate change and pollution: hurricanes, mass respiratory complications, co-morbidities (like heart disease and diabetes), and epidemics. As explained in the introduction, characters in the Japanese word for consumption, *shōhi*, cite disappearance, digestion, excretion, and expense, while those meaning luxury, *zeitaku*, inherently imply excess. One is reminded of cineaste Luis Buñuel's surrealist joke where colonists in the first scene of his 1930 film *L'Age d'Or* (Golden Age) can never aspire (or return) to a golden age and, instead, must begin their venture commemorated by an iconic pat of excrement laid upon the envisioned city's foundation stone,[10] the excreta of a future society of overconsumption choking in its own waste.

But, is this the story's veritable conclusion, or a realistic assessment of the future, and therefore, the potential "end of history"? Can we instead, by widespread adoption of ideas like Clark's, interestingly based on concepts with Japanese antecedents, find hope and remedy in this potential cautionary tale of a potential future not yet realized? Might not democratizing luxury have positive aspects to quell overconsumption and instead limit consumers to a few high-quality goods that they clearly need and can use for years?

Coda: A Return to Democratization of Luxury and Paths toward Healing

Rather than end this study on a pessimistic note, as a historian I genuinely believe that lessons in Japanese frugality and Japan's "traditional" allergy to consumption may have a place in greater global adoption. As indicated in my discussions of democratizing luxury in Japanese contexts, craftsmanship, precision, and high quality are precisely what can limit consumption, in that these qualities translate into

282 *Conclusion*

products with longer lives, and that also might generate greater appeal and "loyalty" in consumers, who could prefer to wear watches until the band wears out (and its mechanism; quartz watches last about twenty-five years) or finish every bit of their favorite Shiseidō powder, maintaining its beautiful case while periodically switching out cartridges with cosmetics inside. Likewise, the unisex, flowing clothing of Issey Miyake and other designers allows for long-term wear by any body type or gender with year-by-year shape fluctuations. In the past, luxury and quality of this caliber were only affordable to the rich, but Japanese pioneered its delivery to the masses and to middle-class audiences by eliminating the fussy formalism sometimes associated with luxury brands.

Moreover, due to experiencing some of the world's worst environmental catastrophes of the 1950s to 1970s, including the Minamata disaster, where the Chisso Corporation's mercury emissions poisoned the Inland Sea and associated fish populations (whose residues caused severe neurological damage in humans and animals consuming them), the Japanese now are keenly aware of the dire physical and mental suffering caused by pollution. Historian Brett Walker in his stunning exposé *Toxic Archipelago: A History of Industrial Disease in Japan* details the disaster's calamitous human and ecological consequences.[11] Learning from such past mistakes, Japanese are now viewed globally as excellent stewards of resources and leaders in conservation of birds and wildlife through organizations like Bird Life International. In addition, the recycling systems in Japanese cities are top-notch, with surprisingly trash-free city streets acclaimed the world over, while nonrecyclable items are burnt in high-tech ultra-clean incinerators reabsorbing particulates. Contemporary Japan has thus become a leader in green technologies involving waste handling and conservation.

In past decades, younger entrepreneurs like actor Iseya Yūsuke (b. 1976), brother of fashion designer Yamamoto Kansai (b. 1944) and a former Prada model, created businesses also addressing such problems in the fashion world, while making consumption more wholesome and sustainable through initiatives like the Rebirth Project, which hosts an umbrella of small businesses and boutiques.[12] The Rebirth Project's logo features the character *zai* for "again," written in white amid a field of black resembling embroidery or a computer pixel.[13] Such businesses, like Fact Fashion Laboratory, recycle materials from vintage clothing, fabrics, or bags, while others take visually flawed organic fruits and vegetables and deliver them to consumers (similar to Imperfect Foods, which began in Los Angeles and the Bay Area in the United States, billing itself as "Groceries on a Mission: grocery items that help reduce food waste"[14]). To support sustainable food production and consumption, Iseya also runs a Shibuya-based Tokyo pub serving delicacies like wild boar meat, where hunting of this now-invasive species helps cull its more disruptive members without natural predators to keep them from farmers' fields and municipal forests. Here, literal consumption made hip has a place even in wildlife conservation and environmental stewardship.

Instead of clearing closets of clutter and throwing out unnecessary items, and keeping only those that "spark joy"—taking a cue from Marie Kondo—perhaps consumers might consider purchasing only items that "spark joy" and using them until reaching points of maximum wear. Why not make proper stewardship of purchased consumer items an integral part of conservation? From its very beginnings, Japanese capitalism inherently spotlighted the invention of mass-produced items or comestibles, and wrapped them in narratives of manufactured artisanality to make their industrial production more palatable to consumers used to high levels of craftsmanship and artisanship in objects of daily use. Then, Japanese companies realized that democratizing luxury could allow traditionally frugal customers to overcome reticence, while still relying on expectations of high quality. I argue that both manufactured artisanality and democratized luxury might be qualities specific to Japanese capitalism that can help temper excessive consumption and steer it toward a more measured, sustainable consumption of only purchasing what is needed to ultimately bring long-term joy and environmental sustainability.

Notes

Preface

1. Anderson views the nation as "imagined political community," which Japanese newspaper advertisements also communicate to generate consumption. Benedict Anderson, *Imagined Communities: Reflections on the Origin and Spread of Nationalism* (London: Verso, 1996), 6.

2. See Jürgen Habermas, "From the Journalism of Private Men of Letters to the Public Consumer Services of the Mass Media: The Public Sphere as a Platform for Advertising," in Habermas, *The Structural Transformation of the Public Sphere: An Inquiry into a Category of Bourgeois Society,* trans. Thomas Burger (London: Polity Press, 1989), 181–196.

3. "The Japanese practice of selfless service. Bestowing compassion and empathy and showing the utmost respect." Shiseidō website, "What Is Omotenashi?," https://www.shiseido.com/us/en/exclusives/japanese-beauty/, accessed August 3, 2021.

4. Japanese companies periodically issue *Shashi* (company history) publications every ten years, including hundred-year histories if founded long ago.

5. Simon Partner, *Assembled in Japan: Electrical Goods and the Making of the Japanese Consumer* (Berkeley: University of California Press, 2000). Partner views Japan's economic revival as beginning in the 1950s with internally driven domestic consumer demand, which then spread to new markets.

6. Anne Allison, *Millennial Monsters: Japanese Toys and the Global Imagination* (Berkeley: University of California Press, 2006).

7. Christine Yano, *Pink Globalization: Hello Kitty's Trek across the Pacific* (Durham, NC: Duke University Press, 2013). Yano examines gender, consumption, and global marketing of a Japanese brand capitalizing on notions of femininity that both sustained and subverted gender norms in Japan and elsewhere.

8. Gennifer Weisenfeld, "Publicity and Propaganda in 1930s Japan: Modernism as Method," *Design Issues* 25, no. 4 (Autumn 2009): 13–28.

9. Annika A. Culver, "Shiseidō's 'Empire of Beauty': Marketing Japanese Modernity in Northeast Asia, 1932–1945," *Shashi—the Journal of Japanese*

286 *Notes to Pages xii–7*

Business and Company History 2, no. 2 (2013), https://shashi.pitt.edu/ojs/index
.php/shashi/article/view/16.

10. Sheldon Garon, "Luxury Is the Enemy: Mobilizing Savings and Popularizing Thrift in Wartime Japan," *Journal of Japanese Studies* 26, no. 1 (Winter 2000): 41–78; and *Beyond Our Means: Why America Spends while the World Saves* (Princeton, NJ: Princeton University Press, 2011).

Introduction

1. Benedict Anderson, *Imagined Communities: Reflections on the Origin and Spread of Nationalism,* rev. ed. (London: Verso, 1996), 43–46.

2. "Following the 129 Year Course of the Asahi Shimbun," 2012, http://www.asahi.com/shimbun/honsya/e/e-history.html.

3. Maurius Jansen, *The Making of Modern Japan* (Cambridge, MA: Harvard University Press, 2000), 415.

4. Sōseki quit his English teacher position at Tokyo Imperial University in 1907.

5. Tanizaki's story critiqued contemporary mid-1920s Japanese fascination for American culture in a parody where a young late-1920s salaryman, a respectable engineer named Jōji (Japanization of "George"), falls for a teenaged, Eurasian-looking working-class girl named Naomi. He attempts to mold her into the perfect Western wife, ending disastrously with selfish, rampant consumerism as she morphs into a sexually acquisitive "modern girl." A small suburban "culture house" with requisite middle-class accouterments failed to satiate her desires, so she began working in Tokyo dance halls, and eventually became a Yokohama-based courtesan to pay for an extravagant lifestyle whereby Jōji ironically becomes a kept man. See Tanizaki Jun'ichirō, *Naomi,* trans. Anthony Chambers (London: Vintage Books, 2001).

6. The Web Kanzaki: Music and Knowledge Sharing, "The History of Magazines in Japan, 1867–1988," https://www.kanzaki.com/jpress/mag-history.html, accessed November 13, 2019.

7. Maeshima Shiho, "Women's Magazines and the Democratization of Print and Reading Culture in Interwar Japan" (PhD dissertation, University of British Columbia, 2016), 108–146.

8. Maeshima, "Women's Magazines," 2.

9. Satoru Nakanishi and Tomoko Futaya, "Japanese Modernisation and the Changing Everyday Life of the Consumer: Evidence from Household Accounts," in *The Historical Consumer: Consumption and Everyday Life in Japan, 1850–2000,* ed. Penelope Francks (London: Palgrave Macmillan, 2012), 107–126.

10. Jordan Sand, *House and Home in Modern Japan: Architecture, Domestic Space, and Bourgeois Culture, 1880–1930* (Cambridge, MA: Harvard University Asia Center, 2003), 103.

11. Sand, *House and Home in Modern Japan,* 103.

Notes to Pages 7–9   287

12. Juliann Sivulka, *Soap, Sex, and Cigarettes: A Cultural History of American Advertising* (Belmont, CA: Wadsworth, 1998), 44.

13. Amy Bliss Marshall, *Magazines and the Making of Mass Culture in Japan* (Toronto: University of Toronto Press, 2019), 16.

14. Marshall, *Magazines and the Making of Mass Culture,* 169.

15. Brooke Erin Duffy, "Manufacturing Authenticity: The Rhetoric of 'Real' in Women's Magazines," *The Communication Review* 16, no. 3 (2013): 132–154.

16. Norma Field, *The Splendor of Longing in the Tale of Genji* (Princeton, NJ: Princeton University Press, 1987).

17. Tanaka Yasuo, *Nantonaku, kurisutaru* (Tokyo: Kawade shobō shinsha, 1981); and Tanaka Yasuo, *Somehow Crystal,* trans. Christopher Smith (Tokyo: Kurodahan Press, 2019).

18. Ministry of Internal Affairs and Communications, Statistics Bureau of Japan, *Statistical Handbook of Japan 2019,* https://www.stat.go.jp/english/data/handbook/c0117.html, accessed December 15, 2019.

19. See Ezra Vogel, *Japan as Number One: Lessons for America* (Cambridge, MA: Harvard University Press, 1979).

20. Karl Marx thus defines commodity fetishism: "A commodity is therefore a mysterious thing, simply because in it the social character of men's labour appears to them as an objective character stamped upon the product of that labour; because the relation of the producers to the sum total of their own labour is presented to them as a social relation, existing not between themselves, but between the products of their labour. This is the reason why the products of labour become commodities, social things whose qualities are at the same time perceptible and imperceptible by the senses. . . . But it is different with commodities. There, the existence of the things qua commodities, and the value relation between the products of labour which stamps them as commodities, have absolutely no connection with their physical properties and with the material relations arising therefrom. There it is a definite social relation between men, that assumes, in their eyes, the fantastic form of a relation between things. In order, therefore, to find an analogy, we must have recourse to the mist-enveloped regions of the religious world. In that world the productions of the human brain appear as independent beings endowed with life, and entering into relation both with one another and the human race. So it is in the world of commodities with the products of men's hands. This I call the Fetishism which attaches itself to the products of labour, so soon as they are produced as commodities, and which is therefore inseparable from the production of commodities." Karl Marx, "Section 4: The Fetishism of Commodities and the Secret Thereof," in *Capital,* vol. 1, https://www.marxists.org/archive/marx/works/1867-c1/ch01.htm#S4, accessed January 12, 2020.

21. Marx, "The Fetishism of Commodities."

22. Marx, "The Fetishism of Commodities."

288 *Notes to Pages 9–14*

23. William Pietz, "The Problem of the Fetish, I," *Anthropology and Aesthetics,* no. 9 (Spring 1985): 5.

24. Pietz, "The Problem of the Fetish, I," 5–6.

25. Pietz, "The Problem of the Fetish, I," 6.

26. William Pietz, "The Problem of the Fetish, II: The Origin of the Fetish," *Anthropology and Aesthetics,* no. 13 (Spring 1987): 23.

27. William Pietz, "The Problem of the Fetish, III: Bosman's Guinea and the Enlightenment Theory of Fetishism," *Anthropology and Aesthetics,* no. 16 (Autumn 1988): 119.

28. Pietz, "The Problem of the Fetish, III," 120.

29. Pietz, "The Problem of the Fetish, III," 116–117.

30. Pietz, "The Problem of the Fetish, I," 7.

31. Pietz, "The Problem of the Fetish, I," 9.

32. Pietz, "The Problem of the Fetish, I," 10.

33. Sigmund Freud, "Fetishism" (1927), in *Miscellaneous Papers, 1888–1938,* vol. 5 of *Collected Papers* (London: Hogarth and Institute of Psycho-Analysis, 1950), 202.

34. Louise J. Kaplan, "Unraveling Freud on Fetishism," in *Cultures of Fetishism* (New York: Palgrave Macmillan, 2006), 15–16.

35. Emily S. Apter, "Fetishism in Theory: Marx, Freud, Baudrillard," in *Feminizing the Fetish: Psychoanalysis and Narrative Obsession in Turn-of-the-Century France* (Ithaca, NY: Cornell University Press, 1991), 14.

36. Apter, "Fetishism in Theory," 14.

37. Marie Kondo, *The Life-Changing Magic of Tidying Up: The Japanese Art of Decluttering and Organizing* (Berkeley, CA: Ten Speed Press, 2014).

38. Kondo, *The Life-Changing Magic of Tidying Up,* 2–3.

39. Kondo, *The Life-Changing Magic of Tidying Up,* 4.

40. Kondo, *The Life-Changing Magic of Tidying Up,* 5.

41. "Hoarders Has Best Premiere Ever for A&E with Adults 18–49," *TV by the Numbers,* August 18, 2009, https://tvbythenumbers.zap2it.com/cable /hoarders-has-best-a-premiere-ever-for-ae-with-adults-18-49/25002/.

42. Randy Frost and Gail Steketee, *Stuff: Compulsive Hoarding and the Meaning of Things* (New York: Mariner Books, 2011).

43. Cynthia Kaufman, *Getting Past Capitalism: History, Vision, Hope* (Lanham, MD: Lexington Books, 2012), 75.

44. Helen Hardacre, *Shinto: A History* (London: Oxford University Press, 2016).

45. "Early Shinto," in *Sources of Japanese Tradition,* vol. 1, *From Earliest Times to 1600,* ed. William Theodore de Bary, Donald Keene, George Tanabe, and Paul Varley, 2nd ed. (New York: Columbia University Press, 2001), 17–18.

46. Angelika Kretschmer, "Mortuary Rites for Inanimate Objects: The Case of *Hari Kuyo," Japanese Journal of Religious Studies* 27, no. 3/4 (Fall 2000): 379.

47. Kretschmer, "Mortuary Rites for Inanimate Objects," 380.

Notes to Pages 14–16   289

48. Kretschmer, "Mortuary Rites for Inanimate Objects," 382–383.

49. Helen Hardacre, *Marketing the Menacing Fetus in Japan* (Berkeley: University of California Press, 1999).

50. "In the ancient Asiatic and other ancient modes of production, we find that the conversion of products into commodities, and therefore the conversion of men into producers of commodities, holds a subordinate place, which, however, increases in importance as the primitive communities approach nearer and nearer to their dissolution." Marx, "The Fetishism of Commodities."

51. Marx, "The Fetishism of Commodities."

52. Kaufman, *Getting Past Capitalism*, 73.

53. Marcel Mauss, *The Gift: The Form and Reason for Exchange in Archaic Societies*, trans. W. D. Halls (New York: W. W. Norton, 2000).

54. Joy Hedry, *Wrapping Culture: Politeness, Presentation, and Power in Japan and Other Societies* (Oxford: Clarendon Press, 1995).

55. Nakamura Usagi, *Shoppingu no joō* (Tokyo: Bunshun bunkō, 2001).

56. Nakamura, *Shoppingu no joō*, 11.

57. Nakamura, *Shoppingu no joō*, 12.

58. Akiko Takeyama, *Staged Seduction: Selling Dreams in a Tokyo Host Club* (Stanford, CA: Stanford University Press, 2016).

59. Nakamura Usagi, *Ai to shihonshugi* (Tokyo: Shinchōsha, 2002).

60. Chizuko Ueno, "Self-Determination on Sexuality? Commercialization of Sex among Teenage Girls in Japan," *Inter-Asia Cultural Studies* 4, no. 2 (2003): 319.

61. David Richard Leheny, *Think Global, Fear Local: Sex, Violence, and Anxiety in Contemporary Japan* (Ithaca, NY: Cornell University Press, 2006), 16–17.

62. Nicholas de Villiers, "Truth under the Uniform: Youth and Sexuality in Hideaki Anno's Love and Pop," in *Sexography: Sex Work in Documentary* (Minneapolis: University of Minnesota Press, 2017), 159.

63. Setsuko Kamiya, "Usagi Nakamura: Shopping Queen Shelves Host 'Illusion,'" *Japan Times*, January 12, 2003, https://www.japantimes.co.jp/community/2003/01/12/general/shopping-queen-shelves-host-illusion/#.XiYA2dZKiu4.

64. Commodified relationships occasionally harbor "real" emotional or romantic aspects. Russian sociologists Christopher S. Swader, Olga Strelkova, Alena Sutormina, Victoria Syomina, Volha Vysotskaya, and Irene Fedorova, in studying "gift-for-sex (GFS)" barters in a newly emergent postcommunist Russia, investigated GFS exchanges on a popular dating website. They examined "gender roles and inter-gender conflicts, the use of economic jargon, the link between luxury consumption and sexuality, and understandings of gift-giving and generosity, in order to show how GFS barters, despite being contractual, carry emotional and romantic content. As such, love is under a constant conversion process, through the medium of the contractual gift, into the fictitious commodity form." Christopher S. Swader, Olga Strelkova, Alena Sutormina, Victoria Syomina, Volha Vysotskaya, and Irene

290   *Notes to Pages 16–21*

Fedorova, "Love as a Fictitious Commodity: Gift-for-Sex Barters as Contractual Carriers of Intimacy," *Sexuality and Culture* 17, no. 4 (2013): 598.

65. Laura Miller and Jan Bardsley, eds., *Bad Girls of Japan* (New York: Springer, 2005), 118.

66. Daniel Miller, *A Theory of Shopping* (Ithaca, NY: Cornell University Press, 1998).

67. Gabor Maté, *In the Realm of the Hungry Ghosts: Close Encounters with Addiction* (Berkeley, CA: North Atlantic Books, 2008).

68. Maté, *In the Realm of the Hungry Ghosts,* 1.

69. David McNally, *Monsters of the Market: Zombies, Vampires and Global Capitalism* (Leiden: Koninklijke Brill, 2011).

70. McNally, *Monsters of the Market,* 127.

71. McNally, *Monsters of the Market,* 128.

72. Georg Lukacs, "Reification and the Consciousness of the Proletariat," in *History and Class Consciousness* (London: Merlin Press, 1967), https://www.marxists.org/archive/lukacs/works/history/hcc05.htm.

73. Michael Hendrix, "The Artisanal Manufacturing Revolution," US Chamber Foundation blog, March 12, 2012, https://www.uschamberfoundation.org/blog/post/artisanal-manufacturing-revolution/33661.

74. "What's the Origin of the Term Hipster?," https://www.dictionary.com/e/hipster/, accessed August 3, 2021.

75. Ico Maly and Piia Varis, "The 21st-Century Hipster: On Micropopulations in Times of Diversity," *European Journal of Cultural Studies,* August 18, 2015, https://journals.sagepub.com/doi/10.1177/1367549415597920.

76. "'Invented tradition' is taken to mean a set of practices, normally governed by overtly or tacitly accepted rules and of a ritual or symbolic nature, which seek to inculcate certain values and norms of behaviour by repetition, which automatically implies continuity with the past." Eric Hobsbawm, "Introduction: Inventing Traditions," in *The Invention of Tradition,* ed. Eric Hobsbawm, Hugh Trevor-Roper, Prys Morgan, David Cannadine, Bernard S. Cohn, and Terrence Ranger (Cambridge: Cambridge University Press, 1983), 1.

77. Kawabata Yasunari, *Snow Country,* trans. Edward G. Seidensticker (New York: Vintage Books, 1996), 150–151.

78. Miho Matsugu, "The Fusing of Labor and Love in *Snow Country,*" *Proceedings of the Midwest Association of Japanese Literary Studies* 5 (Summer 1999): 135.

79. Heather Bowen-Struyk, "Laborers of Love in *Snow Country:* The Fantasy of Capitalism," *Proceedings of the Midwest Association for Japanese Literary Studies* 5 (Summer 1999): 148.

80. Annika A. Culver, "Manchukuo and the Creation of a New Multi-Ethnic Literature: Kawabata Yasunari's Promotion of 'Manchurian' Culture, 1941–1942," in *Sino-Japanese Transculturation: Late Nineteenth Century to the End of the Pacific War,* ed. Richard King, Cody Poulton, and Katsuhiko Endo (Lanham,

MD: Lexington Books, 2012); Annika A. Culver, *Glorify the Empire: Japanese Avant-Garde Propaganda in Manchukuo* (Vancouver: University of British Columbia Press, 2013), 182–183; Hiromi Tsuchiya Dollase, "Kawabata's Wartime Message in *Beautiful Voyage*," in *Negotiating Censorship in Modern Japan,* ed. Rachael Hutchinson (New York: Routledge, 2013), 83–85.

81. Alexandra Macon, "Lingua Franca Opens a Store on Bleeker Street," *Vogue,* November 7, 2018, https://www.vogue.com/article/lingua-franca-store -opening-bleecker-street.

82. "About," Lingua Franca, https://linguafranca.nyc/pages/about-us, accessed September 25, 2019.

83. "Historic Cashmere Markets," *Capricorn Cashmere! Cashmere Goat Science Revealed* (blog), https://capcas.com/cashmere-history/historic-cashmere -markets/, accessed September 25, 2019.

84. Lingua Franca's home page reassures its white, upper-middle-class urban professional female consumers that purchases bring wholesome effects: "We're living in uncertain (and often scary) times. We don't have all the answers. But we try to listen and we try to learn. We're committed to fair trade, ethical labor practices, and the highest environmental standards. We're proud to pay our embroiderers, all local women in NYC, a living wage. Oh, and we're really into using our brand as a platform to inspire change—a portion of LF proceeds support the badass activists and organizations who are working for a better world." See "About," https://lingua franca.nyc/pages/about-us, accessed September 25, 2019.

85. Lexico, a dictionary search engine powered by a collaboration between Oxford University Press and Dictonary.com, https://www.lexico.com/en/definition /luxury, accessed November 4, 2019.

86. Lexico.

87. David L. Howell, "Fecal Matters: Prolegomenon to a History of Shit in Japan," in *Japan at Nature's Edge: The Environmental Context of a Global Power,* ed. Ian Jared Miller, Julia Adeney Thomas, and Brett L. Walker (Honolulu: University of Hawai'i Press, 2013), 137–151.

88. This is not exclusive to Japan, as it also appears in contemporary Europe—for example, Lindt creates seasonal chocolates (spring) and Nespresso offers limited-edition coffees like Cafecito de Cuba, Hawaiian Kona, and Liminha.

89. According to the Pew Research Group, the millennial generation is defined by persons with birthdates between 1981 and 1996. Michael Dimock, "Defining Generations: Where Millennials End and Generation Z Begins," January 17, 2019, https://www.pewresearch.org/fact-tank/2019/01/17/where-millennials-end-and -generation-z-begins/.

90. Generation X is defined by persons with birthdates between 1965 and 1980. Dimock, "Defining Generations."

91. Fifty percent of people ages 18–29 have very or somewhat positive views of socialism (and 52 percent have positive views of capitalism), while 47 percent of people ages 30–49 do (with 64 percent positive views of capitalism). "Stark

292   *Notes to Pages 25–27*

Partisan Divisions in Americans' Views of 'Socialism,' 'Capitalism': Half of Democratic Women—and Fewer than Half of Democrats under 30—Express Positive Views of Capitalism," Pew Research Center, June 25, 2019, https://www.pewre search.org/fact-tank/2019/06/25/stark-partisan-divisions-in-americans-views-of -socialism-capitalism/ft_19-06-25_socialism_half-of-democratic-women-express -positive-views-capitalism.

92. Elad Granot and Thomas Brashear, "From Luxury to Populence: Inconspicuous Consumption as Described by Female Consumers," *Advances in Consumer Research* 35 (2008): 991. The term was more formally proposed in Elad Granot, Latoya M. Russell, and Thomas G. Brashear-Alejandro, "Populence: Exploring Luxury for the Masses," *Journal of Marketing Theory and Practice* 21, no. 1 (Winter 2013): 32.

93. Granot and Brashear, "From Luxury to Populence," 991–992.

94. Granot, Russell, and Brashear-Alejandro, "Populence," 33.

95. Granot, Russell, and Brashear-Alejandro, "Populence," 32, 40.

96. In 2009, women made 73 percent of household purchases and made or influenced most high-end purchases, including homes. Granot, Russell, and Brashear-Alejandro, "Populence," 34.

97. E. Sek, "'Demokratyzacja luksusu': Czy moze doprowadzic do prezeorganizowania rynku dobr luksusowych," *Ekonomika i Organizacja Przedsiebiorstwa* 4, no. 651 (2004): 22–30.

98. Klaudia Plazyk, "The Democratization of Luxury: A New Form of Luxury," *Proceedings of the 9th International Scientific Conference for PhD Students and Young Scientists*, MERKÚR 2014, Faculty of Commerce, University of Economics in Bratislava, December 4–5, 2014, 162.

99. From B. Godey et al., "A Cross Cultural Exploratory Content Analysis of the Perception of Luxury from Six Countries," *Journal of Product and Brand Management* 3 (2013): 229–237. Quoted in Plazyk, "The Democratization of Luxury," 160.

100. Jeremy Goldman, "Why Brands Must Embrace the Democratization of Luxury in 2016: Alexa von Tobel Makes a Case for Embracing the Changing Face of Luxury, and Bringing It to Your Customers, in 2016," Inc., https://www .inc.com/jeremy-goldman/why-brands-must-embrace-the-democratization-of -luxury-in-2016.html, accessed October 3, 2019.

101. Sarah Ramirez, "Luxury Brands Can No Longer Overlook Japanese Consumers: Agility (Research)," *Luxury Daily,* July 2, 2018, https://www.luxury daily.com/luxury-brands-can-no-longer-overlook-japanese-consumers-agility/.

102. Sarah Ramirez, "Affluent Japanese, Korean Women Differ in Their Approach to Luxury," *Luxury Daily,* September 11, 2019, https://www.luxurydaily .com/affluent-japanese-south-korean-women-differ-in-their-approach-to-luxury/.

103. Consumption Activity Index, Bank of Japan, https://www.boj.or.jp/en /research/research_data/cai/index.htm/, accessed October 3, 2019.

Notes to Pages 27–33

104. The Japanese government survey received 2,050 responses from 4,000 questionnaires mailed to random national samples of adults aged 20 and above. "Results of the 78th Opinion Survey of the General Public's Views and Behaviors (June 2019 Survey)," Public Relations Department, Bank of Japan, July 5, 2019, 9, https://www.boj.or.jp/en/research/o_survey/data/ishiki1907.pdf.

CHAPTER 1: CRAFTSMANSHIP AND PROTO-BRANDING IN THE TOKUGAWA ERA

1. Karl Marx, "Section 4: The Fetishism of Commodities and the Secret Thereof," in *Capital*, vol. 1, https://www.marxists.org/archive/marx/works/1867 -c1/ch01.htm#S4, accessed October 11, 2019.

2. Cynthia Kaufman, *Getting Past Capitalism: History, Vision, Hope* (Lanham, MD: Lexington Books, 2012), 66.

3. Kaufman, *Getting Past Capitalism*, 70.

4. Kaufman, *Getting Past Capitalism*, 72.

5. Historians like Greg Grandin argue that the Atlantic slave trade strongly supported European capitalism's growth and expansion by fostering the Atlantic economy and corresponding penetration into North and South American colonies. Greg Grandin, *Empire of Necessity: Slavery, Freedom, and Deception in the New World* (New York: Henry Holt, 2014); and Alex Gourevitch, interviewer, "Capitalism and Slavery: An Interview with Greg Grandin," *Jacobin*, August 1, 2014, https://jacobinmag.com/2014/08/capitalism-and-slavery-an-interview-with-greg -grandin.

6. Kitahara Michio, *Portuguese Colonialism and Japanese Slaves* (Tokyo: Kadensha, 2013).

7. This word only became used with much frequency during the Bakumatsu period to describe the opposite of *kaikoku*, but first appeared in 1801 when Nagasaki interpreter Tadao Shizuki translated German doctor Engelbert Kaempfer's (1651–1716) *The History of Modern Japan* and called it *Sakoku-ron*. Kazui Tashiro, "Foreign Relations during the Edo Period: *Sakoku* Reexamined," trans. Susan Downing Videen, *Journal of Japanese Studies* 8, no. 2 (Summer 1982): 283–284.

8. See also Ronald P. Toby, "Reopening the Question of *Sakoku*: Diplomacy in the Legitimation of the Tokugawa Bakufu," *Journal of Japanese Studies* 3, no. 2 (Summer 1977): 323–363.

9. Gerald Groemer, "The Creation of the Edo Outcaste Order," *Journal of Japanese Studies* 27, no. 2 (Summer 2001): 263–293.

10. Tetsuo Najita, *Visions of Virtue in Tokugawa Japan: The Kaitokudō Merchant Academy of Osaka* (Honolulu: University of Hawai'i Press, 1987).

11. Tetsuo Najita, *Ordinary Economies in Japan: A Historical Perspective, 1750–1950* (Berkeley: University of California Press, 2009), 104–140.

12. Najita, *Ordinary Economies in Japan*, 64–87.

294 *Notes to Pages 33–36*

13. Katsu Kokichi, *Musui's Story: The Autobiography of a Tokugawa Samurai*, trans. Teruko Craig (Tucson: University of Arizona Press, 1991), xii–xiii..

14. Katsu, *Musui's Story,* 74.

15. Sometimes known as *ashigaru,* these former conscripted foot soldiers of the shogunate's feudal infantry prior to Tokugawa unification were the lowest-ranked samurai; thus, the Meiji Revolution most benefited them. William Beasley, *The Meiji Restoration* (Palo Alto, CA: Stanford University Press, 1972), 27–29.

16. Earl H. Kinmonth, "Nakamura Keiu and Samuel Smiles: A Victorian Confucian and a Confucian Victorian," *American Historical Review* 85, no. 3 (June 1980): 535–556.

17. David L. Howell, "Proto-industrial Origins of Japanese Capitalism," *Journal of Asian Studies* 51, no. 2 (May 1992): 269–286.

18. Howell, "Proto-industrial Origins," 275. See also Gary Leupp, "'One Drink from a Gourd': Servants, Shophands, and Laborers in the Cities of Tokugawa Japan" (PhD diss., University of Michigan, 1989), 500–545.

19. Howell, "Proto-industrial Origins," 270.

20. See Shimada Masakazu, *Shibusawa Ei'ichi—Shakai kigyō-ka no sendansha* (Tokyo: Iwanami shoten, 2011).

21. Steven J. Ericson, "The 'Matsukata Deflation' Reconsidered: Financial Stabilization and Japanese Exports in a Global Depression, 1881–85," *Journal of Japanese Studies* 40, no. 1 (Winter 2014): 1–2.

22. Maurius Jansen, *The Making of Modern Japan* (Cambridge, MA: Harvard University Press, 2002), 373, 376–377.

23. See Max Weber, *The Protestant Ethic and the Spirit of Capitalism* (New York: Norton Critical Editions, 2009).

24. In 2008, during the global financial crisis, this book became a Japanese best seller with over 500,000 copies sold. Kobayashi Takiji, *Kani kōsen* (Tokyo: Heibonsha, 1998). For an English translation, see Kobayashi Takiji, *The Factory Ship and the Absentee Landlord,* trans. Frank Motofuji (Seattle: University of Washington Press, 1973).

25. Louise Young, *Beyond the Metropolis: Second Cities and Modern Life in Interwar Japan* (Berkeley: University of California Press, 2013).

26. Germaine Hoston, *Marxism and the Crisis of Development in Prewar Japan* (Princeton, NJ: Princeton University Press, 1986), x.

27. Hoston, *Marxism and the Crisis of Development,* xiii.

28. Beasley, *The Meiji Restoration,* 241–272.

29. E. H. Norman, *Japan's Emergence of a Modern State: Political and Economic Problems of the Meiji Period* (New York: International Secretariat, Institute of Pacific Relations, 1940).

30. Yoshimi Yoshiaki, *Kusa no ne no fashizumu: Nihon minshū no sensō taiken (Atarashii seikaishi)* (Tokyo: Tokyo Daigaku shuppankai, 1987), and *Grassroots Fascism: The War Experience of the Japanese People,* trans. Ethan Mark (New York: Columbia University Press, 2015).

Notes to Pages 37–41 295

31. Sheldon Garon, "The Transnational Promotion of Savings in Asia: 'Asian Values' or the 'Japanese Model'?," in *The Ambivalent Consumer: Questioning Consumption in East Asia and the West,* ed. Sheldon Garon and Patricia McLaughlin (Ithaca, NY: Cornell University Press, 2006), 164.

32. Amino Yoshihiko, *Nihon no rekishi o yominaosu,* vols. 1 and 2 (Tokyo: Chikuma shobo, 1991 and 1993), and *Rethinking Japanese History,* trans. Alan S. Christy (Ann Arbor: Center for Japanese Studies, University of Michigan, 2012).

33. Mary Louise Nagata, "Brotherhoods and Stock Societies: Guilds in Pre-modern Japan," *IRSH* 53 (2008): 121–122.

34. Kenneth Alan Grosberg, *Japan's Renaissance: The Politics of the Muromachi Bakufu* (Ithaca, NY: Cornell University East Asia Program, 2001), 76.

35. Toyoda Takeshi, "Japanese Guilds," *Annals of the Hitotsubashi Academy* 5, no. 1 (October 1954): 75.

36. Grosberg, *Japan's Renaissance,* 48–49.

37. Grosberg, *Japan's Renaissance,* 77.

38. Toyoda, "Japanese Guilds," 76.

39. Nagata, "Brotherhoods and Stock Societies," 127.

40. Grosberg, *Japan's Renaissance,* 48.

41. Toyoda, "Japanese Guilds," 79.

42. Toyoda, "Japanese Guilds," 79.

43. Toyoda, "Japanese Guilds," 80.

44. Nagata, "Brotherhoods and Stock Societies," 129.

45. Nagata, "Brotherhoods and Stock Societies," 130.

46. Nagata, "Brotherhoods and Stock Societies," 130.

47. Toyoda, "Japanese Guilds," 80.

48. Nagata, "Brotherhoods and Stock Societies," 139.

49. Toyoda, "Japanese Guilds," 81–82.

50. Toyoda, "Japanese Guilds," 83.

51. Nagata, "Brotherhoods and Stock Societies," 129.

52. Toyoda, "Japanese Guilds," 84.

53. Miriam Silverberg, "Constructing the Japanese Ethnography of Modernity," *Journal of Asian Studies* 51, no. 1 (February 1992): 37–39.

54. David Graeber, *Debt: The First 5,000 Years* (New York: Melville House, 2011). See "The Myth of Barter," 21–42, and "A Brief Treatise on the Moral Grounds of Economic Relations," 89–126.

55. Far from characterizing a political system arranged around completely state-owned principles of property, Graeber defines "baseline communism" as "the understanding that, unless people consider themselves enemies, if the need is considered great enough, or the cost seemed reasonable enough, the principle of 'from each according to their abilities, to each according to their needs' will be assumed to apply." Graeber, *Debt,* 98.

56. Marcel Mauss, *The Gift: The Form and Reason for Exchange in Archaic Societies,* trans. W. D. Halls (New York: W. W. Norton, 2000), 6–7.

57. Matsumiya Saburō, *Edo no monouri* (Tokyo: Tōhō shobō, 1968); Elizabeth Kiritani, *Vanishing Japan: Traditions, Crafts, and Culture* (Rutland, VT: Charles E. Tuttle, 1995), 14–39.

58. In Japan, the Rittō History and Culture Museum exhibited Edo-period signage in 1992 and published a catalog: Rittō rekishi minzoku hakubutsukan, ed., *Edo no kanban: Moji no messeji* (Rittō, Japan: Rittō History and Culture Museum, 1992). More recently, examples of Tokugawa- and Meiji-era signs appeared in the San Diego–based Mingei International Museum's exhibition "Kanban: Traditional Shop Signs of Japan," curated by Alan Scott Pate, April 15–October 8, 2017. See also Alan Pate, *Kanban: Traditional Shop Signs of Japan* (Princeton, NJ: Princeton University Press, 2017).

59. See Matsumiya Saburō, *Edo no kanban* (Tokyo: Tokyo kanban kōgyō kyōtō kumiai, 1959), and *Edo kabuki no kōkoku* (Tokyo: Tōhō shobō, 1973).

60. Mauss indicates: "In the economic and legal systems that have preceded our own, one hardly ever finds a simple exchange of goods, wealth, and products in transactions concluded by individuals. First, it is not individuals but collectivities that impose obligations of exchange and contract upon each other. The contracting parties are legal entities: clans, tribes, and families who confront and oppose one another either in groups who meet face to face in one spot, or through their chiefs, or in both these ways at once. Moreover, what they exchange is not solely property and wealth, movable and immovable goods, and things economically useful. In particular, such exchanges are acts of politeness: banquets, rituals, military services, women, children, dances, festivals, and fairs, in which economic transaction is only one element, and in which the passing on of wealth is only one feature of a much more general and enduring contract. Finally, these total services and counter-services are committed to in a somewhat voluntary form by presents and gifts, although in the final analysis they are strictly compulsory, on pain of private or public warfare. We propose to call all this the system of total services." Mauss, *The Gift*, 6–7.

61. Mauss, *The Gift*, 9.

62. Issey Miyake Inc. website, https://www.isseymiyake.com/en/stores/562/, accessed October 1, 2019.

63. Issey Miyake Inc. website.

64. French high-end designer Louis Vuitton's boutique sponsors exhibitions in its boutiques, including on Tokyo's Omotesandō Boulevard.

65. David Graeber, *Towards an Anthropological Theory of Value: The False Coin of Our Own Dreams* (London: Palgrave Macmillan, 2001).

66. Graeber, "The False Coin of Our Own Dreams: Or the Problem of the Fetish, IIIb," in *Towards an Anthropological Theory of Value*, 229–261.

67. Pierre Bourdieu, "The Forms of Capital," in *Handbook of Theory and Research for the Sociology of Education*, ed. J. Richardson (Westport, CT: Greenwood Press, 1986), 241–258, https://www.marxists.org/reference/subject/philosophy/works/fr/bourdieu-forms-capital.htm, accessed March 12, 2020.

Notes to Pages 46–51

68. Timon Screech, *Sex and the Floating World: Erotic Images in Japan, 1700–1820* (Honolulu: University of Hawai'i Press, 1999), and *Shogun's Painted Culture: Fear and Creativity in the Japanese States, 1760–1829* (London: Reaktion Books, 2000).

69. Morgan Pitelka, "Introduction to Japanese Tea Culture," in *Japanese Tea Culture: Art, History, and Practice,* ed. Morgan Pitelka (New York: Routledge, 2003), 8.

70. Morgan Pitelka, *Spectacular Accumulation: Material Culture, Tokugawa Ieyasu, and Samurai Sociability* (Honolulu: University of Hawai'i Press, 2015), 6.

71. For example, cult status was conferred over time—especially among watch *otaku* communities in Japan—to versions of a rather modest Rolex Oyster Perpetual watch model (inspiring the more expensive Rolex Explorer) allegedly worn in 1953 by Sir Edmund Hillary to scale Mount Everest with his partner Tenzin Norgay, who actually wore it. Hillary actually sported a Smiths De Luxe watch. Produced in 1950 by Rolex, which sponsored the Nepal expedition, it was made in Switzerland to test the ascent's extreme climatic and geographic conditions, and required Hillary to return it afterward. "Found: The Rolex Sir Edmund Hillary Wore to the Peak of Mount Everest (Live Pics and Details)," *Hodinkee* (December 5, 2015), https://www.hodinkee.com/articles/found-the-ro lex-sir-edmund-hillary-wore-to-the-peak-of-mount-everest-live-pics-details.

72. Eric King Watts and Mark P. Orbe, "The Spectacular Consumption of 'True' African American Culture: 'Wassup' with the Budweiser Guys?," *Critical Studies in Media Communication* 19, no. 1 (March 2002): 1.

73. Term used by Brooke Erin Duffy, "Manufacturing Authenticity: The Rhetoric of 'Real' in Women's Magazines," *The Communication Review* 16, no. 3 (2013): 132–154.

74. Walter Benjamin, *Selected Writings,* vol. 3, *1935–1938,* ed. Howard Eiland and Michael W. Jennings, trans. Edmund Jephcott (Cambridge, MA: Belknap Press of Harvard University Press, 2002), 103. An earlier translation appears in Walter Benjamin, *Illuminations: Walter Benjamin, Essays and Reflections,* ed. Hannah Arendt, trans. Harry Zohn (New York: Schocken Books, 1969), 221.

75. Benjamin, *Selected Writings,* 105, and *Illuminations,* 223.

76. Lukacs, "Reification and the Consciousness of the Proletariat," https://www.marxists.org/archive/lukacs/works/history/hcc05.htm, accessed December 13, 2019.

77. Benjamin, *Selected Writings,* 121–122, and *Illuminations,* 242.

78. Naomi Klein's prescient turn-of-the-millennium *No Logo: Taking Aim at the Brand Bullies* (Toronto: Knopf Canada, 1999) became a quasi-handbook for antiglobalization adherents, plus the later Occupy Movement, whose protests she supported.

79. The United States Holocaust Memorial Museum, "The History of the Swastika," *Holocaust Encyclopedia,* https://encyclopedia.ushmm.org/content/en /article/history-of-the-swastika, accessed November 8, 2019.

80. See Jacques Derrida, *Writing and Difference,* trans. Alan Bass (Chicago: University of Chicago Press, 1978).

81. See Roland Barthes, *Mythologies* (New York: Hill and Wang, 1972), which expressed his ideas of a postwar French society ordered by bourgeois cultural myths. See also Barthes, *Empire of Signs* (New York: Hill and Wang, 1983). This study (first published in 1970) arose from Barthes' 1966 Japan visit, where he viewed Tokyo's center, containing the imperial palace, as "empty" and without transcendental significance. Amid Japan's postwar prosperity, few recalled the palace's prewar and wartime significance in everyday life.

82. "Results of the 78th Opinion Survey of the General Public's Views and Behaviors (June 2019 Survey)," Public Relations Department, Bank of Japan, July 5, 2019, 9, https://www.boj.or.jp/en/research/o_survey/data/ishiki1907.pdf.

83. See Leonard Koren, *Wabi-Sabi for Artists, Designers, Poets, and Philosophers* (1994; reprint, Point Reyes, CA: Imperfect Publishing, 2008). American audiences likely encountered *wabi-sabi* in a 2002 episode of Mike Judge's animated comedy *King of the Hill,* where Bobby cultivated a prize-winning rose lacking desired perfection, despite great effort. See *King of the Hill,* "The Son Also Roses," December 8, 2002, 23 minutes, animated television show. Created by Mike Judge and Greg Daniels. Directed by Dominic Polcino and Klay Hall.

84. Pitelka, *Spectacular Accumulation,* 19–22.

85. "History of Matsuya," http://www.matsuya.com/co/english/enkaku/; and "Matsuya no enkaku" (Matsuya's development), http://www.matsuya.com/co/enkaku/, accessed December 6, 2019.

86. "History of Matsuya."

87. See the reprint by Adachi Fumie, ed. and trans., *Japanese Design Motifs: 4260 Illustrations of Heraldic Crests Compiled by the Matsuya Piece-Goods Store* (New York: Dover, 1972).

88. "Shiseido Company Past," https://www.shiseidogroup.com/company/past/company-name/, accessed September 20, 2019.

89. Pantea Foroudi, T. C. Melewar, and Suraksha Gupta, "Corporate Logo: History, Definition, and Components," *International Studies of Management and Organization* 47, no. 2 (2017): 176–177.

90. Email correspondence with Timothy Parent, September 30, 2019.

91. Email correspondence with Timothy Parent. Some portions are edited for clarity.

92. Klein, *No Logo,* 27.

93. Klein, *No Logo,* 28.

94. Klein, *No Logo,* 27.

95. Klein, *No Logo,* 27.

96. https://corp.shiseido.com/en/company/history/, accessed April 21, 2023.

97. Georg Lukacs, "Reification and the Consciousness of the Proletariat," in *History and Class Consciousness* (London: Merlin Press, 1967), https://www.marxists.org/archive/lukacs/works/history/hcc05.htm.

Notes to Pages 57–62

98. Contrasting Shiseidō's largely Northern European and Japanese models two decades ago, its current embrace of multiethnic models reveals attempts to attract diverse global millennial and Generation Z markets. See https://www.shiseido.com/hanatsubaki--hake-polishing-face-brush-0729238161368.html?cgid=face-brushes, accessed September 20, 2019.

99. Steven John Powell, "Welcome to Kumano, Brush-Making Capital of Japan," *CNN Travel,* March 20, 2014, https://www.cnn.com/travel/article/kumano-brush-capital-of-japan/index.html.

100. Powell, "Welcome to Kumano."

Chapter 2: Commodifying Western Modernity, New Japanese Corporations, and the Department Store

1. De Certeau asserts that "A society is thus composed of certain foregrounded practices organizing its normative institutions *and* of innumerable other practices that remain 'minor,' always there but not organizing discourses and preserving the beginnings or remains of different (institutional, scientific) hypotheses for that society or for others. It is in this multifarious and silent 'reserve' of procedures that we should look for 'consumer' practices having the double characteristic, pointed out by Foucault, of being able to organize both spaces and languages, whether on a minute or a vast scale." Michel de Certeau, *The Practice of Everyday Life* (Berkeley: University of California Press, 1988), 48.

2. Differing slightly from a Japanese context (a subjectivity applied to certain aesthetics or objects connoting Japanese imperialism and modernity), the term "imperial modernity" was employed earlier by cultural studies scholars, like Nigel Joseph, who views it as a new modern subjectivity enslaved to consumerism or the state in imperial contexts. Nigel Joseph, "Robert Clive and Imperial Modernity," *CLCWeb: Comparative Literature and Culture* 12, no. 2 (2010), http://docs.lib.purdue.edu/clcweb/vol12/iss2/2.

3. Timothy Burke, *Lifebuoy Men, Luxe Women: Commodification, Consumption, and Cleanliness in Modern Zimbabwe* (Durham, NC: Duke University Press, 1996), 18–19.

4. Hildi Hindrickson, "Introduction," in *Clothing and Difference: Embodied Identities in Colonial and Post-Colonial Africa,* ed. Hildi Hindrickson (Durham, NC: Duke University Press, 1996), 1. In the same volume, see also Timothy Burke, "'Sunlight Soap Has Changed My Life': Hygiene, Commodification, and the Body in Colonial Zimbabwe," 189–212.

5. Satsuki Kawano, "Japanese Bodies and Western Ways of Seeing in the Late Nineteenth Century," in *Dirt, Undress, and Difference: Critical Perspectives on the Body's Surface,* ed. Adeline Masquelier (Bloomington: Indiana University Press, 2005), 150.

6. This includes "sweet wine," the English words the Japanese used to describe a port-like liqueur like Akadama Sweet Wine.

300 *Notes to Pages 63–68*

7. Tokyo Fūgetsudō website, Tōkyō Fūgetsudōno rekishi, https://www.to
kyo-fugetsudo.jp/about/history, accessed January 29, 2021.

8. Meidiya website, "Company Profile," http://www.meidi-ya.co.jp/en/com
pany/company.html, accessed January 29, 2021.

9. Juliann Sivulka, *Soap, Sex, and Cigarettes: A Cultural History of American Advertising,* 2nd ed. (Belmont, CA: Wadsworth, 2011), 44; emphasis added.

10. Family members sometimes self-publish these, like the biography of Nakada Kinkichi (1864–1926), Sumitomo's fourth corporate executive officer, known for his 1925 institution of an innovative retirement system. His grandson, Nakada Yoshinao, published his biography. Nakada Yoshinao, *Vita: Kinkichi Nakada* (San Francisco: Blurb.com, 2010).

11. Gennifer Weisenfeld, "Introduction: Selling Shiseidō: Cosmetics Advertising and Design in Early 20th-Century Japan," Visualizing Cultures, https://visual
izingcultures.mit.edu/shiseido_01/sh_essay01.html, accessed March 16, 2020.

12. Claudia Cusano, "Shiseido: The World's Oldest Cosmetics Company: Beauty of a Business," *Nuvo Magazine,* September 19, 2016, https://nuvomagazine
.com/magazine/autumn-2016/worlds-oldest-cosmetics-brand-shiseido.

13. Shiseidō Eudermine product sales website, https://www.shiseido.com/us
/en/eudermine-revitalizing-essence-0768614110019.html?gclid=CjwKCAjwq832
BRA5EiwACvCWscN5K-DFClDbhrzohVk-4eQupyqqkXuqWuHmohBVR
_0i66TgfBYR0xoCOggQAvD_BwE&gclsrc=aw.ds, accessed May 31, 2020.

14. Shiseidō Parlour, "History, Chapter One," https://parlour.shiseido.co.jp
/en/history/index.html, accessed March 20, 2020. Weisenfeld, "Introduction."

15. Shiseidō Parlour, "History, Chapter One."

16. Weisenfeld, "Introduction."

17. Rebecca Nickerson, "Imperial Designs: Fashion, Cosmetics, and Cultural Identity in Japan, 1931–1943" (PhD diss., University of Illinois at Urbana-Champaign, 2011), 99.

18. Shiseidō website, "About Us: History," https://corp.shiseido.com/en/com
pany/history/, accessed February 5, 2021.

19. See Jong-Chan Lee, "The Making of Hygienic Modernity in Meiji Japan, 1868–1905," *Uisahak: Korean Journal of Medical History* 12, no. 1 (June 2003): 34–53.

20. Lesley Wynn, "Self-Reflection in the Tub: Japanese Bathing Culture, Identity, and Cultural Nationalism," *Asia-Pacific Perspectives* 12, no. 2 (Spring/ Summer 2014): 70.

21. Lee Butler, "'Washing Off the Dust': Baths and Bathing in Late Medieval Japan," *Monumenta Nipponica* 60, no. 1 (Spring 2005): 20.

22. Butler, "'Washing Off the Dust,'" 21–22. Ordinary Japanese in the "Medieval" period could not afford rice and ate other grains like barley. This amount equaled what a well-to-do Kyoto man ate daily.

23. See *Tōkyō-to kōshū yujō nyūyu ryōkin tōsei kaku no gaitei jokyō,* in *Tonai no kōshū yokujō-sū oyobi nyūyoku ryōkin tōsei-kaku no suii,* https://

Notes to Pages 68–73   301

www.metro.tokyo.lg.jp/tosei/hodohappyo/press/2020/08/24/documents/04_01
.pdf, accessed January 29, 2021.

24. Stéphanie Crohin-Kishigami, *Furansu josei no Tōkyō sentō meguri* (Tokyo: Jībī, 2018), and *Sentō, l'art des bains japonais* (Vannes, France: Editions Sully, 2020).

25. Hayasaka Shinya, personal website, *Onsen ofurō no igaku kenkyūsha senmonka,* https://hayasakashi.wixsite.com/bath, accessed February 5, 2021. See also Japan Foundation webinar, "I Love Yu! Japanese Bath Houses, Hot Springs, and How to Soak Up the Benefits at Home," July 18, 2020, http://www.japan culture-nyc.com/japan-foundation-to-host-webinar-about-japanese-bathhouses -and-hot-springs/.

26. Along with visits to hot springs, similar to Western spas, all tourism began flourishing in late Meiji Japan. See W. Puck Brecher, "Contested Utopias: Civilization and Leisure in the Meiji Era," *Asian Ethnology* 77, no. 1/2 (2018): 46–48.

27. Anthony Walsh, "Economies of Excrement: Public Health and Urban Planning in Meiji Japan," *Historical Perspectives: Santa Clara University Undergraduate Journal of History, Series II,* 14, no. 9 (2009): 55.

28. David Howell, "Fecal Matters: Prolegomenon to a History of Shit in Japan," in *Japan at Nature's Edge: The Environmental Context of a Global Power,* ed. Ian Jared Miller, Julia Adeney Thomas, and Brett Walker (Honolulu: University of Hawai'i Press, 2013), 137–151.

29. Mishima Yukio, *Kamen no kokuhaku* (Tokyo: Kawade shobō, 1949).

30. Yukio Mishima, *Confessions of a Mask,* trans. Meredith Weatherby (Tokyo: Charles E. Tuttle, 1970), 8–9.

31. Mishima, *Confessions of a Mask,* 8.

32. Tanizaki Juni'chirō, *In Praise of Shadows* (New Haven, CT: Leete's Island Books, 1977), 3–5.

33. Basil Hall Chamberlain, "Bathing," in *Things Japanese* (London: John Murray, 1905), 61, found in "History of Japan: A Guide to Japan's Past and Present," https://www.historyofjapanguide.com/things-japanese-019.htm, accessed May 29, 2020.

34. Chamberlain, "Bathing," 61.

35. Naoko Komori, "The 'Hidden' History of Accounting in Japan: A Historical Examination of the Relationship between Japanese Women and Accounting," *Accounting History* 12, no. 3 (2007): 338.

36. Susan Burns, "The Japanese Patent Medicine Trade in East Asia: Women's Medicines and the Tensions of Empire," in *Gender, Health, and History in East Asia,* ed. Izumi Nakayama and Angela Leung (Hong Kong: Hong Kong University Press, 2017).

37. From W. H. Morton, *Present-Day Impressions of Japan: The History, People, Commerce, Industries and Resources of Japan and Japan's Colonial Empire, Kwantung, Chosen, Taiwan, Karafuto* (1919; reprint, Tokyo: Edition Synapse, 2008), 208.

302 *Notes to Pages 73–77*

38. Morton, *Present-Day Impressions of Japan*, 208.

39. Uchida Hoshimi, "The Spread of Timepieces in the Meiji Period," in "The Birth of Tardiness: The Formation of Time Consciousness in Modern Japan," special issue, *Nichibunken Japan Review: Journal of the International Research Center for Japanese Studies* 14 (January 1, 2002): 176–177.

40. Uchida, "The Spread of Timepieces," 176.

41. Uchida, "The Spread of Timepieces," 176.

42. Keio University Media Center Digital Collection, Digital Library of Yukichi Fukuzawa's Work, "Calendar Reform: *Kairekiben*," https://dcollections .lib.keio.ac.jp/en/fukuzawa/a18/67, accessed February 7, 2021.

43. "Calendar Reform."

44. The Seikō Museum (Ginza) website, Development of the Japanese Timepiece Industry Centered by Seikōsha, "The Fixed Time System and the Rise of the Timepiece in Commerce and Industry," https://museum.Seikō.co.jp/en /knowledge/relation_08/, accessed February 7, 2021.

45. See Steven J. Ericson, "The 'Matsukata Deflation' Reconsidered: Financial Stabilization and Japanese Exports in a Global Depression, 1881–1885," *Journal of Japanese Studies* 40, no. 1 (Winter 2014): 1–28.

46. Ericson, "The 'Matsukata Deflation' Reconsidered," 25.

47. George Woodcock, "The Tyranny of the Clock," *War Commentary—for Anarchism* (Mid-March 1944), http://www.spunk.org/texts/writers/woodcock/sp00 1734.html.

48. Seikō Watches, "Our Heritage," https://www.Seikōwatches.com/glob al-en/special/heritage/, accessed May 21, 2020.

49. Seikō Watches, "Our Heritage."

50. Mark Bernardo, "The History of Seikō through 12 Milestone Watches," WatchTime, January 20, 2021, https://www.watchtime.com/featured/timepiece -timeline-milestone-Seikō-watches/.

51. Japan Clock and Watch Association, "History of the Japanese Horological Industry," https://www.jcwa.or.jp/en/etc/history01.html, accessed November 22, 2019.

52. Japan Clock and Watch Association, "History of the Japanese Horological Industry."

53. Seikō Museum, "Kintaro Hattori: Chronological List," https://museum .Seikō.co.jp/en/Seikō_history/founder/founder/001/, accessed May 21, 2020.

54. Japan Clock and Watch Association, "History of the Japanese Horological Industry."

55. Japan Clock and Watch Association, "History of the Japanese Horological Industry."

56. Uchida, "The Spread of Timepieces," 189–190.

57. Seikō Watches, "Our Heritage."

58. Lorenzo Maillard, "WWII Japanese Military Watches," *Europa Star,* March 2019, https://www.europastar.com/archives/1004090826-wwii-japanese -military-watches.html.

Notes to Pages 77–82 303

59. *Jeweler's Circular* 75, no. 2 (January 16, 1918): 94.

60. *Jeweler's Circular,* 94.

61. Seikō Watches, "Our Heritage."

62. Kondo Motohiro, Nihon University Graduate School of Social and Cultural Studies, "The Development of Monthly Magazines in Japan," University of Michigan Winter Term Public Lecture Series, January 15, 2004, reprinted lecture, *Japan Science and Technology Promotion Agency Proceedings,* March 22, 2004, 2, https://www.jstage.jst.go.jp/article/gscs/1/1/1_1/_pdf.

63. David Belcher, "Wrist Watches: From Battlefield to Fashion Accessory," *New York Times,* October 23, 2013, https://www.nytimes.com/2013/10/23/fashion/wrist-watches-from-battlefield-to-fashion-accessory.html#:~:text=Wrist watches%20were%20worn%20only%20by,according%20to%20Guinness%20World%20Records.

64. Uchida, "The Spread of Timepieces," 185.

65. Elise K. Tipton, "Pink Collar Work: The Café Waitress in Early Twentieth Century Japan," *Intersections: Gender, History and Culture in the Asian Context* 7 (March 2002), http://intersections.anu.edu.au/issue7/tipton.html.

66. Tipton, "Pink Collar Work."

67. Torii famously stated, "You can advertise as much as you like, but it's no good if you don't have a good product. You can't be confident in advertising it, and if your customers start to say you're all talk, it's over. You have to start by making a really good product." Quoted in Sugimori Hisahide, *Bishu Ichidai: Torii Shinjirō Den. Nihon uisukii monogatari* (Tokyo: Mainichi Shimbunsha, 1966), cited in Suntory website, "History: Digest," https://www.suntory.com/about/history/index.html, accessed March 15, 2020.

68. See Janet A. Walker, *The Japanese Novel of the Meiji Period and the Ideal of Individualism* (Princeton, NJ: Princeton University Press, 1979).

69. Sun Ad Company, *Yatte minaware—Santorii no 70 nen (1)* (Tokyo: Suntory, 1969), 25.

70. Sun Ad Company, *Yatte minaware,* 25–26.

71. See Ad Museum Tokyo website, *Korekushon—Posutâ: Akadama pōto wainu,* https://www.admt.jp/collection/item/?item_id=83, accessed February 13, 2021.

72. Ad Museum Tokyo website, *Korekushon—Posutâ;* and Philbert Ono, "Japan's First Nude Poster," April 19, 2018, PhotoGuide Japan Blog, https://photojpn.org/news/2018/04/japans-first-nude-poster/.

73. Sabine Frühstück, "Managing the Truth of Sex in Imperial Japan," *Journal of Asian Studies* 59, no. 2 (May 2000): 344.

74. Elise K. Tipton, "The Café: Contested Space of Modernity in Interwar Japan," in *Being Modern in Japan: Culture and Society from the 1910s to the 1930s,* ed. Elise K. Tipton and John Clark (Honolulu: University of Hawai'i Press, 2000), 119–136.

75. Tipton, "Pink Collar Work."

304   *Notes to Pages 82–86*

76. Suntory website, "History: Timeline," https://www.suntory.com/about /history/timeline/, accessed February 13, 2021.

77. Noriko Aso, *Public Properties: Museums in Imperial Japan* (Durham, NC: Duke University Press, 2014), 169. Though chapter 5 is called "Consuming Publics," Aso never defines this term but notes that "Japanese department stores also positioned themselves alongside expositions and museums as cultural authorities, as generators and disseminators of social knowledge. In the process, their consumer publics, women and children included, merged with broader conceptions of society, nation, and empire." 183.

78. Kazuo Usui, *Marketing and Consumption in Modern Japan* (London: Routledge, 2014), 4.

79. Walter Benjamin, *The Arcades Project,* trans. Howard Eiland and Kevin McLaughlin, ed. Rolf Tiedemann (Cambridge, MA: Belknap Press of Harvard University Press, 1999), 58. Quoted in George d'Avenel, "Le Mécanisme de la Vie Moderne: Les Grands Magasins," *Revue des Deux Mondes* 124 (Paris, 1894): 335–336.

80. "History of Harrods Department Store: London Department Store Harrods Has Been Sold by Its Owner Mohammed Al Fayed to the Qatari Royal Family for £1.5 Billion," *BBC News,* May 8, 2010, https://www.bbc.com/news/10103783.

81. Benjamin, *The Arcades Project,* 48.

82. See Gordon Honeycombe, *Selfridges, Seventy-Five Years: The Story of the Store 1909–84* (London: Park Lane Press, 1984).

83. The online *Merriam-Webster Dictionary* defines this as "to associate oneself with what is happening or one's surroundings." *Merriam-Webster Dictionary,* "tune in," https://www.merriam-webster.com/dictionary/tune%20in, accessed February 25, 2021. "Tuning in" was also literal, because Selfridges was the first store to bring newly invented televisions to British consumers in 1925, and it broadcast live music from a department store rooftop radio in the prewar period. Selfridges website, "In Bloom: The Selfridges Story," https://www.selfridges.com /US/en/features/int/in-bloom-the-selfridgesstory/, accessed November 20, 2019.

84. Selfridges website, "In Bloom."

85. Aso, *Public Properties,* 169.

86. Mitsukoshi website, "Mitsukoshi's History," https://mitsukoshi.mistore .jp/store/nihombashi/foreign_customer/history/index.html, accessed November 14, 2019.

87. Mitsukoshi website, *Nihonbashi Mitsukoshi honten no rekishi saihakkan* (Rediscovering the History of the Nihonbashi Mitsukoshi Main Store), https://www.mitsukoshi.mistore.jp/nihombashi/column_list_all/nihombashi _history/index.html, accessed October 1, 2019.

88. Nicole C. Kirk, *Wanamaker's Temple: The Business of Religion in an Iconic Department Store* (New York: New York University Press, 2018), introduction, Kindle.

89. Kirk, *Wanamaker's Temple.*

Notes to Pages 87–94　　305

90. Paul Lerner, *The Consuming Temple: Jews, Department Stores, and the Consumer Revolution in Germany, 1880–1940* (Ithaca, NY: Cornell University Press, 2015).

91. Lerner, *The Consuming Temple,* 6.

92. Lerner, *The Consuming Temple,* 7.

93. Lerner, *The Consuming Temple,* 7.

94. Benjamin, *The Arcades Project,* 61.

95. Benjamin, *The Arcades Project,* 60.

96. "Materials for the Exposé of 1935," in Benjamin, *The Arcades Project,* 909.

97. Mitsukoshi website, *Mimeguri jinja* (Mimeguri Shrine), https://www.mitsukoshi.mistore.jp/nihombashi/column_list_all/nihombashi_history/list08.html, accessed October 1, 2019.

98. Mitsukoshi website.

99. Mitsukoshi website.

100. Richard Halloran, "A Goddess Watches Over 'Honorable Guests' at Tokyo's Mitsukoshi," *New York Times,* November 18, 1973, 567, https://www.nytimes.com/1973/11/18/archives/a-goddess-watches-over-the-honorable-guests-at-tokyos-mitsukoshi.html.

101. Maryann Adair, "Tennyo Magokoro—the Goddess of Sincerity," August 10, 2017, https://maryannadair.com/2017/08/10/tennyo-magokoro-the-goddess-of-sincerity/.

102. Kifune Shrine Official Website, "History," http://kifunejinja.jp/history-e.html#p2, accessed November 14, 2019.

103. Kifune Shrine Official Website, "Birth of the Kami of Kifune," http://kifunejinja.jp/history-e.html#p3, accessed November 14, 2019.

CHAPTER 3: MODERN GIRLS AND SALARYMEN CONSUMING THE WEST

1. Harry D. Harootunian, *Overcome by Modernity: History, Culture, and Community in Interwar Japan* (Princeton, NJ: Princeton University Press, 2000), x.

2. J. Charles Schenking, *The Great Kantō Earthquake and the Chimera of National Reconstruction in Japan* (New York: Columbia University Press, 2013), 16.

3. Schenking, *The Great Kantō Earthquake,* 130.

4. Schenking, *The Great Kantō Earthquake,* 38.

5. Sonia Ryang, "The Great Kanto Earthquake and the Massacre of Koreans in 1923: Notes on Japan's Modern National Sovereignty," *Anthropological Quarterly* 76, no. 4 (Autumn 2003): 746. See also Yoshiaki Ishiguro, "A Japanese National Crime: The Korean Massacre after the Great Kanto Earthquake of 1923," *Korea Journal* 38, no. 4 (Winter 1998): 331–354. For a perspective by "resident-Korean" (*Zai-Nichi*) scholars in Japan, see Tŏksang Kang and Pyŏngdong Kŭm, *Kantō daishinsai to Chōsenjin* (Tokyo: Misuzu Shobō, 1963); and by a Japanese

306   *Notes to Pages 94–96*

scholar, see Yamada Shōji, *Kantō daishinsai-ji no Chōsen-jin gyakusatsu to sono ato—gyakusatsu no kokka sekinin to minshū sekinin* (Tokyo: Shōshi-sha, 2011).

6. See Ryang, "The Great Kanto Earthquake," 731–748.

7. Asahi Shimbun Cultural Research Center, "Murder of an Anarchist Recalled: Suppression of News in the Wake of the 1923 Tokyo Earthquake," *Asia-Pacific Journal: Japan Focus* 5, no. 11 (November 3, 2007), https://apjjf.org/-The-Asahi-Shinbun-Cultural-Research-Center-/2569/article.html.

8. See William O. Gardner, "Anarchism and Imperialism: Hagiwara Kyōjirō's Danpen and Beyond," in *Advertising Tower: Japanese Modernism and Modernity in the 1920s* (Cambridge, MA: Harvard University Asia Center, 2006), 169–202.

9. Accounts differ for how Mavo's name developed. Most plausible is from Yanase's colleague, who in 1925 indicated that "m" stands for masse, "a" for "alpha," "v" for "vitesse," and "omega" for "end" to indicate time, space, and the entire universe. Gennifer Weisenfeld, *MAVO: Japanese Artists and the Avant-Garde, 1905–1931* (Berkeley: University of California Press, 2001), 64.

10. Seikō website, "About Our Group: History—Details," https://www.seiko.co.jp/en/group/history/chronology.html, accessed July 11, 2021.

11. Seikō website, "About Our Group."

12. Seikō website, "Our Heritage," https://www.seikowatches.com/global-en/special/heritage/, accessed July 11, 2021.

13. Seikō website, "About Our Group."

14. Previous models featured "Laurel" or "Empire" on the watch face. Mark Bernardo, "Timepiece Timeline: The History of Seiko through 12 Milestone Seiko Watches," WatchTime, January 20, 2021, https://www.watchtime.com/featured/timepiece-timeline-milestone-seiko-watches/.

15. Seiko website, "Our Heritage: History of the Only Manufacture with Every Watchmaking Expertise," https://www.seikowatches.com/global-en/special/heritage/, accessed February 17, 2021.

16. Anthony Kable, "Seiko Railway Watches," Plus9Time: Seiko, Citizen, and Other Japanese Watches, July 16, 2017, https://www.plus9time.com/blog/2017/7/16/seiko-railway-watches.

17. Seiko website, "Our Heritage."

18. Louise Young, *Beyond the Metropolis: Second Cities and Modern Life in Interwar Japan* (Berkeley: University of California Press, 2013), 7.

19. The wristwatch's spread among the Japanese middle class in the early twentieth century resembles the bicycle as a symbol of modernity in Porfirian Mexico (1876–1911). Historian William Beezley indicates that "Mexicans recognized the importance of progress, speed, and modernization through technology as they turned to bicycles. Cycling became the sport of the times." William H. Beezley, *Judas at the Jockey Club and Other Episodes of Porfirian Mexico* (Lincoln: University of Nebraska Press, 1987), 52.

20. Seiko website, "Our Heritage."

Notes to Pages 96–101   307

21. Tim Hornyak, "Heart of Gold: The Ginza Line Celebrates Its 90th Birthday," *Japan Times,* December 16, 2017, https://www.japantimes.co.jp/news/2017/12/16/national/history/heart-gold-ginza-line-celebrates-90th-birthday/.

22. John Goodall, *A Journey in Time: The Remarkable Story of Seiko* (Tokyo: Toppan Printing Company, 2003), 27.

23. George Woodcock, "The Tyranny of the Clock," *War Commentary—for Anarchism* (mid-March 1944), http://www.spunk.org/texts/writers/woodcock/sp001734.html, accessed July 20, 2021.

24. Harootunian, *Overcome by Modernity,* xvii.

25. Harootunian, *Overcome by Modernity,* xvii.

26. Donald Richie, "Expressionism in Film," *Richie Reader,* 5, prepared for the Tokyo–Berlin / Berlin–Tokyo Exhibition, Mori Art Museum, Tokyo, Japan (January 28–May 7, 2006), https://www.mori.art.museum/english/contents/tokyo-berlin/about/img/Expressionism.pdf, accessed July 13, 2021. For information on the exhibition, see https://www.mori.art.museum/english/contents/tokyo-berlin/index.html. See also Donald Richie, *The Donald Richie Reader: 50 Years of Writing on Japan* (Berkeley, CA: Stone Bridge Press, 2001).

27. For an image, see Seiko Museum Ginza website, "History of Seiko and Its Products: Stage 1 (1881–1920s)," "7. Popular Pocket Watch 'Empire,'" https://museum.seiko.co.jp/en/seiko_history/company/company/001/, accessed July 13, 2021.

28. Harootunian, *Overcome by Modernity,* xvii.

29. Ratcatcher, "Classic Cinema. *Tokyo March* (Kenji Mizoguchi, 1929)," at 1:28, https://www.youtube.com/watch?v=tsogNOUZfVw, accessed July 13, 2021.

30. Ratcatcher, "Classic Cinema," at 4:53.

31. Ratcatcher, "Classic Cinema," at 8:07–8:09. A still of the watch can be found at *Tōkyō kōshinkyoku* (Tokyo March), 1929, 1 hr., 41 min., IMDb website, https://www.imdb.com/title/tt0020510/mediaviewer/rm782254336/, July 12, 2021.

32. Ratcatcher, "Classic Cinema," at 14:34.

33. Ratcatcher, "Classic Cinema," at 27:33.

34. See "Part I: New Female Occupations," in *Modern Girls on the Go: Gender, Mobility, and Labor in Japan,* ed. Alyssa Freedman, Laura Miller, and Christine R. Yano (Stanford, CA: Stanford University Press, 2013), 21–84.

35. Jason Alexander, *Brewed in Japan: The Evolution of the Japanese Beer Industry* (Vancouver: University of British Columbia Press, 2013), 17.

36. Elise Tipton, "Pink Collar Work: The Café Waitress in Early Twentieth Century Japan," *Intersections: Gender, History and Culture in the Asian Context,* no. 7 (March 2002), http://intersections.anu.edu.au/issue7/tipton.html.

37. Tipton, "Pink Collar Work."

38. For an excellent background into Japan's whisky market and histories of top whisky producers, see Kaidō Mamoru, *Yōshū, biiru* (Tokyo: Jitsumu kyōiku shuppansha, 1989), 89–100 and 140–146.

308   *Notes to Pages 101–105*

39. Magnus Bennett, "The Scottish Mother of Japanese Whisky," *BBC World News,* January 11, 2015, https://www.bbc.com/news/uk-scotland-scotland-business-30682239.

40. University of Glasgow website, "University of Glasgow Story," "Masataka Taketsuru," https://universitystory.gla.ac.uk/biography/?id=WH24560&type=P, accessed May 27, 2021.

41. Bennett, "The Scottish Mother of Japanese Whisky."

42. See Brian Ashcraft with Yuji Kawasaki and Idzuhiko Ueda, "How Japanese Whisky Is Made," in *Japanese Whisky: The Ultimate Guide to the World's Most Desirable Spirit* (Tokyo: Tuttle, 2018), 29–34.

43. Mizu Kaoru, *Daini-wa: Kensan ga unda kessaku,* Suntory Whisky Museum website, https://www.suntory.co.jp/whisky/museum/mizukaoru/water_story2.html, accessed May 31, 2021.

44. Mizu, *Daini-wa.*

45. *Asahi Shimbun,* January 13, 1930, morning edition, 6.

46. It sold for around 4.5 yen a bottle, similar to well-known Scottish whiskies in Japan, but amounted to 10 percent of ordinary family monthly living expenses. Cited in Mizu, *Daini-wa.*

47. *Komainu* appear at entrance gates to Shintō shrines, aristocratic residences, and private homes in Japan, with protective, guardian-like functions, repelling evil spirits or bad luck. These statues also signaled to readers that this Japanese-made whisky was a luxury product served in elegant residences.

48. *Asahi Shimbun,* January 13, 1930, 6.

49. *Asahi Shimbun,* January 13, 1930, 6.

50. Jake Emin, "Why the World Is Hooked on Japanese Whisky," *Distiller* online magazine, March 30, 2019, https://distiller.com/articles/world-hooked-japanese-whisky.

51. Mizu, *Daini-wa.*

52. Nikka Whisky (English-language) European promotional website, "Nikka Story," https://www.nikkawhisky.eu/nikka-story/, accessed May 30, 2021.

53. "The Story of Japanese Whisky: Japan Distills a World-Class Whisky Tradition," Nippon.com online magazine, September 3, 2014, https://www.nippon.com/en/views/b04201/?pnum=2.

54. See Elise K. Tipton, "The Café: Contested Space of Modernity in Interwar Japan," in *Being Modern in Japan: Culture and Society from the 1910s to the 1930s,* edited by Elise K. Tipton and John Clark (Honolulu: University of Hawai'i Press, 2000), 119–136.

55. Sharon Nolte, "Women's Rights and Society's Needs: Japan's 1931 Suffrage Bill," *Comparative Studies in Society and History* 28, no. 4 (October 1986): 697.

56. Nolte, "Women's Rights and Society's Needs," 698.

57. Nolte, "Women's Rights and Society's Needs," 697.

Notes to Pages 105–110   309

58. See *Fujin sekai*, 1930. Also quoted in Stephen Sundberg, "The Modern Girl (and Modern Boy), c. 1930," http://www.oldtokyo.com/modern-girl-and -modern-boy-c-1930/, accessed October 7, 2019.

59. Barbara Sato, *The New Japanese Woman: Modernity, Media, and Women in Interwar Japan* (Durham, NC: Duke University Press, 2003), 45.

60. See Miriam Silverberg, "The Modern Girl as Militant," in *Recreating Japanese Women, 1600–1945*, ed. Gail Lee Bernstein (Berkeley: University of California Press, 1991), 239–266, and "The Modern Girl as Militant (Movement in the Streets)," in Miriam Silverberg, *Erotic Grotesque Nonsense: The Mass Culture of Japanese Modern Times* (Berkeley: University of California Press, 2006).

61. Short, edited excerpts of "Shiseidō's Asian Beauty Empire Then and Now" (11–13) and "The Role of Transnational Department Stores like Mitsukoshi" (13–15) are included here from my article "Shiseidō's 'Empire of Beauty': Marketing Japanese Modernity in Northeast Asia, 1932–1945," *Shashi: The Journal of Japanese Business and Company History* 2, no. 1 (2013): 6–21, https://shashi.pitt.edu/ojs/index.php/shashi/article/view/16/71. I thank the online journal's editor, Martha Chaiklin, for permission.

62. For photographs, construction data, and interior shots of Mitsukoshi's branches in Japan and its empire, see Mitsukoshi, *Dai Mitsukoshi rekishi shashin-chō: Sanseikō sōritsu nijū-nen kinen* (Tokyo: Toppan Printing Company, 1932), 143, 145; and Mitsukoshi, *Sangō kanji, Mitsukoshi shashin-chō* (Tokyo: 1941), unpaginated. These were donated by Waseda alumni who retired from the company and added their collections to Waseda University's Central Library.

63. Rika Fujioka, "The Pressures of Globalization in Retail: The Path of Japanese Department Stores, 1930s–1980s," in *Comparative Responses to Globalization: Experiences of British and Japanese Enterprises,* ed. Maki Umemura and Rika Fujioka (London: Palgrave Macmillan, 2013), 189.

64. For an image of Sugiura's ad for the Seoul Mitsukoshi branch, see Karasawa Masahiro, Kida Takuya, Naitō Yuko, and the National Museum of Modern Art, Tokyo, eds., *Kôkyôsuru Nihonjin: Kôgei-ka ga yume mita Ajia, 1910s– 1945* (Tokyo: National Museum of Modern Art, Tokyo, 2012), 119.

65. Shiseidō website, "Innovations in Aesthetics and Designs," in "About Shiseidō," http://www.my.shiseido.com/about/story/innovations/index.html, accessed July 21, 2013.

66. Adachi Mariko, "Luxury, Capital, and the Modern Girl: A Historical Study of Shiseidō Corporation," *Joseigaku kenkyū*, March 2005, 99.

67. For the image of the two boxes, see Nagai Kazumasa and Kaji Yūsuke, *Shiseidō kurieiteibu wâku* (Tokyo: Kyūryūdō, 1985), 131.

68. See Annika A. Culver, "Shiseidō's 'Empire of Beauty': Marketing Japanese Modernity in Northeast Asia, 1932–1945," *Shashi—the Journal of Japanese Business and Company History* 2, no. 2 (2013): 8.

310 *Notes to Pages 110–117*

69. Pheng Cheah and Bruce Robbins, eds., *Cosmopolitics: Thinking and Seeing beyond the Nation* (Minneapolis: University of Minnesota Press, 1998), 30. See also Naoki Sakai, "Asia as a Borrowing Index: Civilizational Transference and Colonial Modernity," *Border Crossings: The Journal of Japanese-Language Literary Studies* 8, no. 1 (June 2019): 21–37.

70. Michiko Shimamori quoted in Lynn Gumpert, ed., *Face to Face: Shiseido and the Manufacture of Beauty, 1900–2000* (New York: Grey Art Gallery, New York University, 1999), 84.

71. Shiseidō Corporate Culture Division, *Bi o tsutaeru hitotachi: Shiseidō byūtī konsarutanto shi* (Tokyo: Kyūryūdō, 2001), 27.

72. Shiseidō Corporate Culture Division, *Bi o tsutaeru hitotachi*, 27.

73. Shimamori, in Gumpert, *Face to Face*, 84.

74. Pierre Bourdieu, "The Forms of Capital," in *Handbook of Theory and Research for the Sociology of Education*, ed. J. Richardson (Westport, CT: Greenwood Press, 1986), 241–258.

75. See Eugenia Lean, *Vernacular Industrialism in China: Local Innovation and Translated Technologies in the Making of a Cosmetics Empire, 1900–1940* (New York: Columbia University Press, 2020).

76. Louisa Daria Rubinfien, "Commodity to National Brand: Manufacturers, Merchants, and the Development of the Consumer Market in Interwar Japan" (PhD diss., Harvard University, 1995), 238–248.

77. Rubinfien, "Commodity to National Brand," 238–248.

78. Ishikawa Yoshika and Satō Asami, eds., *Shiseidō monogatari: Shiseidō kigyō shiryōkan shūzōhin katarogu (1872–1946)* (Kakegawa: Shiseidō Corporate Museum, 1995), 29.

79. Geoffrey Jones, *Beauty Imagined: A History of the Global Beauty Industry* (New York: Oxford University Press, 2010), 368.

80. Ishikawa and Satō, *Shiseidō monogatari*, 44.

81. See Sally Stein, *The Rhetoric of the Colorful and the Colorless: American Photography and Material Culture between the Wars* (New Haven, CT: Yale University Press, 1991).

82. Melissa Banta, curator, Harvard Business School Historical Collections, *The High Art of Photographic Advertisement*, "The Challenge of Color," https://www.library.hbs.edu/hc/naai/05-challenge-of-color.html#fn9, accessed December 19, 2019.

83. Ishikawa and Satō, *Shiseidō monogatari*, 51.

84. Jones, *Beauty Imagined*, 368.

85. Gennifer Weisenfeld, "'From Baby's First Bath': Kaō Soap and Modern Japanese Commercial Design," *The Art Bulletin* 86, no. 3 (September 2004): 582.

86. Philbert Ono, "Kanamaru Shigene," *PhotoGuide Japan*, https://photoguide.jp/txt/KANAMARU_Shigene, accessed July 8, 2021.

87. See Kanamaru Shigene, *Shinkō shashin no tsukurikata* (Tokyo: Genkōsha, 1932).

Notes to Pages 117–122   311

88. Kaō Corporation, *Kaō-shi 100-nen (1890–1990 nen)* (Tokyo: Kaō Corporation Company History Editorial Office, 1998), 105.

89. Weisenfeld, "'From Baby's First Bath,'" 579.

90. Weisenfeld, "'From Baby's First Bath,'" 573.

91. Miriam Silverberg, "Constructing a New Cultural History of Prewar Japan," in "Japan in the World," special issue, *boundary 2* 18, no. 3 (Autumn 1991): 86.

92. See Minami Hiroshi, *Taishō bunka, 1905–1927* (Tokyo: Keisō shobō, 1965), and *Shōwa bunka* (Tokyo: Keisō shobō, 1987).

93. See James Huffman, "Universal Male Suffrage Law of 1925, *About Japan: A Teacher's Resource*, Japan Society, https://aboutjapan.japansociety.org /content.cfm/universal_male_suffrage_law_of_1925, accessed July 11, 2021. For the original, see *Kanpō*, May 5, 1925, in *Taishō nyūsu jiten*, vol. 7, ed. Uchikawa Yoshimi and Matsushima Eiichi (Tokyo: Mainichi Komiyunikēshiyon Shuppanbu, 1989), 293.

94. See James Huffman, "Peace Preservation Law of 1925," *About Japan: A Teacher's Resource*, Japan Society, https://aboutjapan.japansociety.org/content .cfm/peace_preservation_law_of_1925, accessed July 11, 2021. For the original, see *Tokyo Asahi Shimbun*, February 13, 1925, in Uchikawa and Matsushima, *Taishō nyūsu jiten*, vol. 7, 405.

95. Umeda Toshihide, "Posters from the 1930s: The Social Context," Ohara Memorabilia Collection, Ohara Institute for Social Research, https://oisr -org.ws.hosei.ac.jp/english/public/posters_social/, accessed July 11, 2021. See also Christopher Gerteis, "Political Protest in Interwar Japan: Part 1," *The Asia-Pacific Journal: Japan Focus* 12, issue 37, no. 1 (August 2014): 4.

96. *Asahi Shimbun shuku satsuban, Manshū jihen shashin gahō* (Manchurian Incident Pictorial Report), "Extra" (*Gōgai*) edition, September 24, 1931 (Tokyo: Japan Publications Trading Company, 2008), section 24, 14.

97. *Asahi Shimbun shuku satsuban, Manshū jihen shashin gahō*, 14.

98. *Asahi Shimbun shuku satsuban, Manshū jihen shashin gahō*, 14.

99. *Asahi Shimbun shuku satsuban, Manshū jihen shashin gahō*, 14.

100. *Asahi Shimbun shuku satsuban, Manshū jihen shashin gahō*, 14.

101. Kao Corporation, "Product Introductions," https://www.kao.com/glob al/en/about/outline/history/products-history/, accessed December 2, 2019.

102. Kaō Corporation, *Kaō-shi 100-nen (1890–1990 nen)*, 105.

103. Kaō Corporation, *Kaō-shi 100-nen (1890–1990 nen)*, 105.

104. For more on rationalization in the domestic sphere, see Kashiwagi Hiroshi, "On Rationalization and the National Lifestyle: Japanese Design of the 1920s and the 1930s," in Tipton, *Being Modern in Japan*, 61–74.

105. Kao Corporation, "Corporate History," https://www.kao.com/global /en/about/outline/history/company-history/, accessed November 12, 2019.

106. Kao Corporation, "The History of the Kao Group," https://www .kao.com/global/en/who-we-are/globalhistory/, accessed January 11, 2020.

312   *Notes to Pages 124–128*

CHAPTER 4: FRUGALITY, PATRIOTIC CONSUMPTION,
AND THE MILITARY

1. Sheldon Garon, "Luxury Is the Enemy: Mobilizing Savings and Popularizing Thrift in Wartime Japan," *Journal of Japanese Studies* 26, no. 1 (Winter 2000): 42.

2. Barak Kushner, "Advertising as Propaganda," in *The Thought War: Japanese Imperial Propaganda* (Honolulu: University of Hawai'i Press, 2006), 76.

3. Short portions of this chapter are adapted from Annika A. Culver, "For the Sake of the Nation: Mobilizing for War in Japanese Commercial Advertisements, 1937–1945," in *The Consumer on the Home Front: Second World War Civilian Consumption in Comparative Perspective,* ed. Hartmut Berghoff, Jan Logemann, and Felix Römer (New York: Oxford University Press, 2017), 145–174, https://global.oup.com/academic/product/the-consumer-on-the-home-front-978 0198784265?cc=us&lang=en&#; and Annika A. Culver, "Battlefield Comforts of Home: Gendered Commercialization of the Military Care Package in Wartime Japan," in *Defamiliarizing Japan's Asia-Pacific War,* ed. W. Puck Brecher and Michael W. Meyers (Honolulu: University of Hawai'i Press, 2019), 85–103. I thank Oxford University Press and University of Hawai'i Press for kind permission to use select heavily revised short passages from these chapters here.

4. Benjamin Uchiyama, *Japan's Carnival War: Mass Culture on the Home Front, 1937–1945* (Cambridge: Cambridge University Press, 2019), Kindle.

5. Uchiyama, *Japan's Carnival War,* introduction, Kindle.

6. Uchiyama, *Japan's Carnival War,* Kindle.

7. *Asahi Shimbun shuku satsuban,* November 7, 1937 (Tokyo: Japan Publications Trading Company, 2008), 104.

8. *Asahi Shimbun shuku satsuban,* November 7, 1937, 104.

9. *Asahi Shimbun shuku satsuban,* November 7, 1937, 104.

10. *Asahi Shimbun shuku satsuban,* November 7, 1937, 104.

11. *Asahi Shimbun shuku satsuban,* November 7, 1937, 104.

12. The baby is likely at least nine months old to be able to sit up alone. *Asahi Shimbun shuku satsuban,* November 7, 1937, 104.

13. With these measures and pro-natalist policies enacted in 1940, Japan's birthrate rose from a record low 26.5 births to 31.1 per 1,000 in population in 1941. Leonard Schoppa, "Demographics and the State," in *The Demographic Challenge: A Handbook About Japan,* ed. Florian Coulmas, Harald Conrad, Annette Schad-Seifert, and Gabriele Vogt (Leiden: Koninklijke Brill, 2008), 642.

14. *Asahi Shimbun shuku satsuban,* November 7, 1937, 104.

15. *Asahi Shimbun shuku satsuban,* November 7, 1937, 104.

16. *Asahi Shimbun shuku satsuban,* November 7, 1937, 104.

17. *Asahi Shimbun shuku satsuban,* December 11, 1937, 165.

18. *Asahi Shimbun shuku satsuban,* December 11, 1937, 165.

19. *Asahi Shimbun shuku satsuban,* December 11, 1937, 165.

Notes to Pages 128–137 313

20. *Asahi Shimbun shuku satsuban,* December 11, 1937, 165.

21. This practice was not exclusive to wartime Japan, even existing in the contemporary United States during the Great Recession (2007–2009). See Wan-Hsiu Sunny Tsai, "Patriotic Advertising and the Creation of the Citizen-Consumer," *Journal of Media and Communication Studies* 2, no. 3 (March 2010): 76–84.

22. Portions of this section appear in my earlier book chapter. See Culver, "Battlefield Comforts of Home," 85–103.

23. Sarah Soh, *The Comfort Women: Sexual Violence and Postcolonial Memory in Korea and Japan* (Chicago: University of Chicago Press, 2008). See especially chapter 3, "Japan's Military Comfort System as History," 107–142.

24. Gijae Seo, "*Shonen Kurabu* and the Japanese Attitude toward War," *Children's Literature in Education,* no. 52 (March 6, 2021): 49–67, https://link .springer.com/article/10.1007/s10583-020-09402-z.

25. East Asia Image Collections, Skillman Library, Lafayette College, "The Military Care Package Is Loaded with Sincerity," postcard, https://ldr.lafayette .edu/concern/images/fb494944d, accessed July 2, 2021.

26. Seo, "*Shonen Kurabu* and the Japanese Attitude toward War."

27. Seo, "*Shonen Kurabu* and the Japanese Attitude toward War."

28. See Jürgen Habermas, *The Structural Transformation of the Public Sphere: An Inquiry into a Category of Bourgeois Society,* trans. Thomas Burger and Frederick Lawrence (London: Polity Press, 1989).

29. *Asahi Shimbun shuku satsuban,* November 10, 1937, 148. Also discussed in Culver, "For the Sake of the Nation," 168.

30. Culver, "For the Sake of the Nation," 168.

31. *Asahi Shimbun shuku satsuban,* December 12, 1937, 179; Culver, "For the Sake of the Nation," 165–166.

32. A study by marketing scholars Yuko Minowa and Russell W. Belk examines how Japanese newspaper advertisements from 1937 to 1940 promote purchases of seasonal gift items using nationalism amid thrift and shortages. See Yuko Minowa and Russell W. Belk, "Gifts and Nationalism in Wartime Japan," *Journal of Macromarketing* 38, no. 3 (May 2018): 298–314.

33. Culver, "Battlefield Comforts of Home," 86.

34. Culver, "Battlefield Comforts of Home," 96–97.

35. Gennifer Weisenfeld, "Marketing Beauty: The Design Division, Marketing and Display," in "Selling Shiseidō: Cosmetics Advertising and Design in Early Twentieth-Century Japan," MIT Visualizing Cultures website, https://visu alizingcultures.mit.edu/shiseido_01/sh_essay03.html, accessed July 3, 2021.

36. Gennifer Weisenfeld, "Selling Shiseido: Cosmetics Advertising and Design in Early Twentieth Century Japan—Visual Narratives: Commercial Advertising and the War," MIT Visualizing Cultures website, https://visualizingcultures .mit.edu/shiseido_02/sh_visnav07.html, accessed May 21, 2021.

37. Culver, "Battlefield Comforts of Home," 96.

38. Culver, "Battlefield Comforts of Home," 97.

314   *Notes to Pages 137–140*

39. *Asahi Shimbun,* Tokyo morning edition, January 25, 1944, 3.

40. *Asahi Shimbun,* Tokyo evening edition, January 26, 1944, 2.

41. See Garon, "Luxury Is the Enemy," 41–78.

42. Culver, "For the Sake of the Nation," 171.

43. Existing sources are unclear on how many products customers had to purchase to receive these gifts, but customers completely filled Shiseidō's coupon book each year to redeem it for a premium giveaway. Likely, customers received a coupon for each purchase and then affixed it into a book to collect the coupons. Images of coupon books, and an explanatory pamphlet, appear in Weisenfeld, "Marketing Beauty."

44. Ishikawa Yoshika and Satō Asami, "Hanatsubaki-kai no hassoku," in *Shiseidō monogatari: Shiseidō kigyō shiryōkan shūzōhin katarogu (1872–1946),* ed. Ishikawa Yoshika and Satō Asami (Kakegawa: Shiseido Corporate Museum, 1995), 50.

45. Maeda Yasuyuki, "Zeitaku wa teki da: Sebiro, kamera, kikinzoku," in *Shōwa keizaishi,* ed. Arisawa Hiromi (Tokyo: Nihon keizai shimbunsha, 1976), 186–187.

46. "Tomimoto Kenkichi," National Museum of Asian Art, Smithsonian website, https://asia.si.edu/collections/new/acquisitions-2018/tomimoto-kenkichi/, accessed May 24, 2021. See also Tomimoto Kenkichi Kinenkan, Andō-machi website, June 1, 2012, https://archive.is/20120915060545/http://www.town.and o.nara.jp/contents_detail.php?co=cat&frmId=257&frmCd=3-6-0-0-0#selection -313.320-313.326.

47. Brian Moeran, *Lost Innocence: Folk Craft Potters of Onta, Japan* (Berkeley: University of California Press, 1984).

48. See Yanagi Sōetsu, *The Unknown Craftsman: A Japanese Insight into Beauty,* trans. Bernard Leach (Tokyo: Kodansha International, 1972).

49. For more on Yanagi's *Mingei* theory, see Yanagi Sōetsu, *Yanagi Sōetsu senshū (dai issen) shinpan: Kōgei no Michi* (Tōkyō: Nihon Mingeikan, 1955).

50. "Corporate Culture Magazine 'Hanatsubaki,'" Shiseido website, https:// corp.shiseido.com/en/sustainability/beauty-art/hanatsubaki.html, accessed May 24, 2021.

51. I thank Nakano Seishi, a retired Corporate Planning Division employee then volunteering at Shiseidō's Museum and Corporate Archives, for showing me these covers and arranging copies.

52. See Annika A. Culver, "Constructing a Rural Utopia: Propaganda Images of Japanese Settlers in Northern Manchuria, 1936–43," in *Empire and Environment in the Making of Manchuria,* ed. Norman Smith (Vancouver: University of British Columbia Press, 2017), 152–178.

53. Some appear in Gennifer Weisenfeld, "Commercial Advertising and the War: *Chain Store* and *Hanatsubaki,* 1936–1941," MIT Visualizing Cultures website, https://visualizingcultures.mit.edu/shiseido_02/sh_visnav07.html, accessed May 24, 2021.

Notes to Pages 140–142   315

54. This portion is loosely adapted from "Shiseidō's Advertising Icon from Manchukuo," a section in my article "Shiseidō's 'Empire of Beauty': Marketing Japanese Modernity in Northeast Asia, 1932–1945," in *Shashi: The Journal of Japanese Business and Company History* 2, no. 1 (2013): 16–20, https://shashi.pitt.edu/ojs/index.php/shashi/article/view/16. I thank Martha Chaiklin, *Shashi*'s editor, for permission to use this heavily edited excerpt.

55. Shelley Stephenson, "'Her Traces Are Found Everywhere': Shanghai, Li Xianglan, and the 'Greater East Asia Film Sphere,'" in *Cinema and Urban Culture in Shanghai, 1922–1943*, ed. Yingjin Zhang (Stanford, CA: Stanford University Press, 1999), 222–245.

56. Washidani Hana, "'Idō' to 'henshin'—Ri Kōran, 'Dai TōA kyōei-ken' wo," in *Ri Kōran to Higashi Ajia*, ed. Yomota Inuhiko (Tokyo: Seikōsha, 2001), 40–55.

57. Quoted in Michael Baskett, *The Attractive Empire: Transnational Film Culture in Imperial Japan* (Honolulu: University of Hawai'i Press, 2008), 78. See also Taguchi Masao, "Ri Kōran ni okuru kotoba," *Eiga no tomo* (June 1941): 98–99.

58. Norman Smith, *Intoxicating Manchuria: Alcohol, Opium, and Culture in China's Northeast* (Vancouver: University of British Columbia Press, 2012), 2.

59. Anthony Austin, interview by author, transcript and recording, Florida State University, Institute on World War II and the Human Experience Archives, November 12–14, 2013, 19.

60. Smith, *Intoxicating Manchuria*, 2.

61. Smith, *Intoxicating Manchuria*, 219n9.

62. Kao Soap Company, "Chronology: A 90 Year History of Kaō," October 1980, Shibusawa shashi dêta bêsu, https://shashi.shibusawa.or.jp/details_nenpyo.php?sid=3210&query=&class=&d=all&page=58.

63. Rebecca Nickerson, "Imperial Designs: Fashion, Cosmetics, and Cultural Identity in Japan, 1931–1943" (PhD diss., University of Illinois at Urbana-Champaign, 2011), 113.

64. Gail Hershatter, *Women and China's Revolutions* (Lanham, MD: Rowman and Littlefield, 2018), 115.

65. Ogura Mihō, a Shiseidō Corporate Culture Department representative, forwarded this information to me in email correspondence, May 10, 2013. She learned details from contacts at the Shiseidō Corporate Archives in Shizuoka. I thank Ms. Ogura, who I met in July 2012 at the Ginza Shiseidō headquarters in Tokyo, for finding this.

66. Mentioned to the author in email correspondence by Ogura Mihō, May 10, 2013.

67. In the 1930s agricultural missionary John Lossing Buck (1890–1975) surveyed rural Chinese and discovered that only 2 percent of girls ever attended school, and only 1 percent read Chinese characters. In 1982, a Chinese national census found that 95 percent of women over age sixty were illiterate. Cited in

316   *Notes to Pages 142–145*

William Lavely, Xiao Zhenyu, Li Bohua, and Ronald Freedman, "The Rise in Female Education in China: National and Regional Patterns," *China Quarterly,* no. 121 (March 1990): 64–65.

68. Adachi Mariko, "Luxury, Capital, and the Modern Girl: A Historical Study of Shiseidō Corporation," *Joseigaku kenkyū,* March 2005, 101, http://hdl .handle.net/10466/10100.

69. For an image, see Yabe Nobuhisa, *Shiseidō hyakunen-shi* (Tokyo: Shiseidō senden-bu, 1972), 107.

70. That year, beginning on January 27, 1941, Lunar New Year festivities lasted for fifteen days. Even today, Mainland China sustains large markets for "forced" winter peonies, where nearly a million potted peonies are cultivated each year to bloom for the New Year's Spring Festival. See "Forcing Peonies in Winter," Cricket Hill Garden, https://www.treepeony.com/pages/forcing-peonies-in-winter, accessed July 6, 2021.

71. Ikeda Shinobu, "The Allure of a 'Woman in Chinese Dress': Representation of the Other in Imperial Japan," in *Performing "Nation": Gender Politics in Literature, Theater, and the Visual Arts of China and Japan, 1880–1940,* ed. Doris Croissant, Catherine Vance Yeh, and Joshua Mostow (Leiden: Koninklijke Brill, 2008), 377–379.

72. Sarah Frederick, discussant's comments, "Corporate Histories" panel, "The Shiseidō Culture: Design, Fashion, Marketing," held on March 24, 2013, at the Association for Asian Studies (AAS) Annual Meeting in San Diego, California.

73. See Annika A. Culver, "Introduction: 'Manchukuo Perspectives' or 'Collaboration' as a Transcendence of Literary, National, and Chronological Boundaries," in *Manchukuo Perspectives: Transnational Approaches to Literary Production,* ed. Annika A. Culver and Norman Smith (Hong Kong: University of Hong Kong Press, 2019), 2.

74. Interview with Corporate Culture Division representatives, Shiseidō corporate headquarters, Shiodome, Tokyo, Japan, July 17, 2012.

75. This topic exceeds this book's scope. Further research is needed on related wartime media in northeast Asia (including northeast China, Korea, and even Taiwan) to explore such issues.

76. Email correspondence with Norman Smith, summer 2013.

77. For more on Yamaguchi's early life as actress, see Yamaguchi Yoshiko, *Ri Kōran: Watashi no hansei* (Tokyo: Shinchōsha, 1990).

78. For a summary of later events in Yamaguchi's life, see Roger Macy, "Yoshiko Yamaguchi Obituary: Actor and Singer Whose Japanese Nationality Saved Her from Execution by the Chinese Government," *Guardian,* September 22, 2014, https://www.theguardian.com/film/2014/sep/22/yoshiko-yamaguchi.

79. Otaka Yoshiko, "Looking Back on My Days as Ri Kōran (Li Xianglan)," trans. Melissa Wender, http://www.zcommunications.org/contents/42844 /print, 3. Originally published in *Sekai,* September 2003, 171–175.

Notes to Pages 146–149   317

80. Yabe, *Shiseidō hyakunen-shi,* 107.

81. Yabe, *Shiseidō hyakunen-shi,* 107.

82. Maeda, "Zeitaku wa teki da," 186.

83. Mentioned by Marumo Toshiyuki, curator of the Shiseidō Corporate Museum, in Kakegawa, Japan, during a tour with the author on June 19, 2014. Fieldwork notes.

84. For an image, see Shiseidō Corporate Museum, *Shiseidō monogatari: Shiseidō kigyō shiryōkan* (Kakegawa: Shiseidō Corporate Museum, 1995), 52.

85. Discussion with the museum curator, Marumo Toshiyuki, Kakegawa, Japan, July 2014.

86. Caroline Noma examines the comfort woman system and its early origins amid working-class Japanese sex workers who served Imperial Japan's military before its 1930s spread to include sexual slavery of women in colonies and Japanese-occupied territories. See Caroline Noma, *The Japanese Comfort Women and Sexual Slavery* (London: Bloomsbury Press, 2015).

87. Mentioned by Marumo Toshiyuki, curator of the Shiseidō Corporate Museum, in Kakegawa, Japan, during a tour on June 19, 2014. Fieldwork notes.

88. Yabe, *Shiseidō hyakunen-shi,* 109.

89. Culver, "For the Sake of the Nation," 172.

90. Culver, "For the Sake of the Nation," 172.

91. I thank Machida Saori, curator of the Kao Museum and Archives Corporate Culture and Literature Department, for hosting me during a July 13, 2012, visit.

92. Interview and meeting with curators, Kaō Corporation archives, Sumida ward, Tokyo, Japan, July 2012.

93. NARA staff, "Japanese War Crimes Records at the National Archives: Research Starting Points," in Edward Drea, Greg Bradsher, Robert Hanyok, James Lide, Michael Petersen, and Daqing Yang, *Researching Japanese War Crimes Records: Introductory Essays* (Washington, DC: Nazi War Crimes and Japanese Imperial Government Records Interagency Working Group, 2006), 92. See also Linda Goetz Holmes, *Unjust Enrichment: How Japan's Companies Built Postwar Fortunes Using American POWs* (Mechanicsburg, PA: Stackpole Books, 2001).

94. Interview and meeting with curators, Kaō Corporation archives.

95. Hirai Hirokazu, "'Manshūkoku' ippan kaikei mokuteki saishutsu yosan no dōkō: 1932–1942 nendō," *Keizai-gaku kenkyū* 52, no. 4 (March 11, 2003): 131.

96. Mine Takeshi, "Chūka jinmin kyōwa-koku ni keishō sareta Manshū kagaku kōgyō" (PhD diss., University of Tokyo, November 2007), 55.

97. Sunaga Noritake, "Manshū no kagaku kōjō—jō," *Rikkyō keizaigaku kenkyū* 59, no. 4 (2006): 143.

98. Sunaga, "Manshū no kagaku kōjō," 144.

99. See Uozumi Hirohisa, *Kō kigyō no seiritsu to tenkai: Senjiki. sengo fukkōki no eidan. kōdan. kōsha* (Tokyo: Iwanami shoten, 2009).

318   *Notes to Pages 149–152*

100. Nishino Seiji, Saitō Keisuke, and Satō Asami, eds., *Make-Up Tokyo—Shiseidō monogatari: Shiseidō kigyō shiryōkan shūzō katarogu (1946–1972)* (Kakegawa: Shiseidō Corporate Museum, 1996), 6.

101. Kim B. Shedd, "Tungsten," US Department of the Interior and US Geological Survey, *USGS 2017 Minerals Yearbook* (June 2020): 80.3–80.4.

102. "Global Copper Reserves as of 2020, by Country," Statistica, https://www.statista.com/statistics/273637/copper-reserves-by-country/#:~:text=Chile%20has%20the%20world's%20largest,metric%20tons%20as%20of%202020, accessed March 20, 2021.

103. Nishino et al., *Make-Up Tokyo*, 6.

104. Nishino et al., *Make-Up Tokyo*, 6.

105. Matthew S. Seligmann, *Rum, Sodomy, Prayers, and the Lash Revisited: Winston Churchill and Social Reform in the Royal Navy, 1900–1915* (Oxford: Oxford University Press, 2018), 42.

106. Seligmann, *Rum, Sodomy, Prayers, and the Lash Revisited*, 42–43.

107. Saneyoshi Yasuzumi, *The Surgical and Medical History of the Naval War between Japan and China during 1894–95*, trans. S. Suzuki (Tokyo: Tokio Publishing, 1901), 508.

108. See Saneyoshi, *The Surgical and Medical History*.

109. Saneyoshi, *The Surgical and Medical History*, 508.

110. Saneyoshi, *The Surgical and Medical History*, 514–515.

111. Saneyoshi, *The Surgical and Medical History*, 515.

112. Jeffrey W. Alexander, "Beer and Whiskey in Japanese Marketplaces," *Oxford Research Encyclopedias: Asian History*, September 26, 2017, https://oxfordre.com/asianhistory/view/10.1093/acrefore/9780190277727.001.0001/acrefore-9780190277727-e-176.

113. "Embrace Failure to Reach Success," in "Yamazaki Moments: I Am the Suntory Yamazaki Distillery—about Yamazaki," Suntory Yamazaki Distillery website, https://yamazaki-moments.com/about/, accessed May 26, 2021.

114. Sun Ad Company, *Yatte minaware—Santorii no 70 nen (1)* (Tokyo: Suntory, 1969), 260.

115. Sun Ad Company, *Yatte minaware*, 260.

116. Sun Ad Company, *Yatte minaware*, 260.

117. These included a whisky barrel for Japan's emperor and ninety gallons of whisky for his commissioner and councilors. The entire gift list appears in Roger Pineau, ed., *The Japan Expedition, 1852–1854: The Personal Journal of Commodore Matthew C. Perry* (Washington, DC: Smithsonian Institution Press, 1968). Images of the barrel and other gifts in woodblock prints appear in John W. Dower, "Black Ships and Samurai: Commodore Perry and the Opening of Japan (1853–1854)—Gifts," MIT Visualizing Cultures website, https://visualizingcultures.mit.edu/black_ships_and_samurai/bss_essay07.html, accessed May 30, 2021.

118. Sun Ad Company, *Yatte minaware*, 260.

Notes to Pages 152–154   319

119. For an image, see Mizu Kaoru, "Dai-sanwa: Gekidō no naka de no jukusei, Japanizu uisukii monogatari," Suntory Whisky Museum website, https://www.suntory.co.jp/whisky/museum/mizukaoru/water_story3.html#to_contents, accessed May 29, 2021.

120. Chris Bunting, "Japanese Whisky and War (1)," December 6, 2007, *Nonjatta* (blog), https://nonjatta.blogspot.com/2007/12/japanese-whisky-and -world-war.html. The exact figures can be found in *Dai Nippon kajū kabushiki gaisha, Son'eki keisansho* (Yoichi: Dai Nippon Kajū Kabushiki gaisha, 1988).

121. Miyoshi Hajime, *Nihon no posutā: Meiji, Taishō, Shōwa* (Tokyo: Shikō-sha, 2003), 53.

122. For images, see Okuyama Gihachirō, "Nikka uisukii Dai Nippon Kajū kabushiki gaisha," Yamada shoten online store, https://www.yamada-shoten.com /onlinestore/detail.php?item_id=41001, accessed May 30, 2021.

123. Yoichi Town Hall Public Relations Group, *Yoichi-shi machi de okotta konna hanashi, sono 109 "Sensō to Nikka,"* https://www.town.yoichi.hokkaido .jp/machi/yoichistory/2013/sono109.html, accessed May 30, 2021.

124. George Koutsakis, "What Is Japanese Mizunara Oak and Is It Worth It?," *Wine Enthusiast,* November 26, 2018, https://www.winemag.com/2018 /11/26/what-is-japanese-mizunara-oak-worth-it/.

125. In late 2019, the Matsui, a *mizunara* whisky produced by Tottori-based Kurayoshi Distillery, won the Best Japanese Single Malt Award in *Jim Murray's Whiskey Bible 2020,* with a 95/100 rating. *BBC Spirits,* November 20, 2019, https://bbcspirits.com/presse/the-matsui-mizunara-cask-won-a-new-medal -japanese-signle-malt-of-the-year-2020-in-murrays-whisky-bible/.

126. "Yamazaki Moments 6: I Am the Suntory Yamazaki Distillery," Yamazaki Distillery website, https://yamazaki-moments.com/about/, accessed May 28, 2021.

127. "Yamazaki Moments 6."

128. Mizu, *Dai-sanwa.*

129. Lorenzo Maillard, "WWII Japanese Military Watches," *Europa Star,* March 2019, https://www.europastar.com/archives/1004090826-wwii-japanese -military-watches.html.

130. *The Citizen Watch Story: How a Tokyo Jeweler's Experiment in Making Pocket Watches 84 Years Ago Led to the Creation of a Global Watch Colossus,* WatchTime, Spotlight: Citizen special edition, October 2013, 5, pamphlet archived at https://www.watchtime.com/wp-content/uploads/2013/10/WT_Spotlight_Citi zen.pdf.

131. Maeda, "Zeitaku wa teki da," 186–187. See also Owen Griffiths, "Need, Greed, and Protest in Japan's Black Market, 1938–1949," *Journal of Social History* 35, no. 4 (Summer 2002): 827.

132. Figures are indicated in Chimoto Akiko, "The Birth of the Full-Time Housewife in the Japanese Worker's Household as Seen through Family Budget

Surveys," trans. Diana Lynn Bethel, *U.S.-Japan Women's Journal. English Supplement*, no. 8 (1995): 58.

133. Garon, "Luxury Is the Enemy," 42.

134. Oren Hartov, "Military Watches of the World: Japan," Worn and Wound, October 14, 2020, https://wornandwound.com/military-watches-of-the-world-japan/.

135. Maillard, "WWII Japanese Military Watches."

136. Maillard, "WWII Japanese Military Watches."

137. Smaller wristwatches also denoted technical prowess because smaller gears and parts are harder to manufacture than larger parts for pocket watches.

138. The Seiko Museum's websites in Japanese and English curiously omit this timepiece, though recent watch forums express increasing interest generated by the 2018 high-profile Geneva Watch Auction. See "(Lot)196: Seikosha," Phillips Auction website, https://www.phillips.com/detail/seikosha/CH080218/196, accessed May 24, 2021.

139. Oren Hartov, "Military Watches of the World: Germany Part 1— 19th Century through World War II," Worn and Wound, December 7, 2018, https://wornandwound.com/military-watches-of-the-world-germany-part-1-19th-century-through-world-war-ii/.

140. Zen Love, "This Is the Seiko Watch Made for Japanese Pilots during WWII," Gear Patrol, September 12, 2019, https://www.gearpatrol.com/watches/a613700/watches-you-should-know-seikosha-tensoku-kamikaze/.

141. "About Our Group: History," Seikō company website, https://www.seiko.co.jp/en/group/history/, accessed July 11, 2021.

142. Love, "This Is the Seiko Watch."

143. Maillard, "WWII Japanese Military Watches."

144. Love, "This Is the Seiko Watch."

145. See "(Lot)196."

146. "About Our Group."

147. "Company History," Epson corporate website, https://epson.com/company-history, accessed April 22, 2021.

148. *The Citizen Watch Story*, 5.

149. *United States Strategic Bombing Survey (European War / Pacific War)* (Maxwell AFB, AL: Air University Press, October 1987), 84, https://web.archive.org/web/20080528051903/http://aupress.au.af.mil/Books/USSBS/USSBS.pdf.

150. Tony Reichhardt, "The Deadliest Air Raid in History: The Firebombing of Tokyo on March 9, 1945 Marked the Beginning of the End for Imperial Japan," *Air & Space Magazine*, March 9, 2015, https://www.airspacemag.com/daily-planet/deadliest-air-raid-history-180954512/.

151. Alexander B. Downes, *Targeting Civilians in War* (Ithaca, NY: Cornell University Press, 2008), 126.

152. Marine Guillaume, "Napalm in US Bombing Doctrine and Practice, 1942–1975," Mass Violence and Resistance, December 10, 2016, https://www

Notes to Pages 157–158 321

.sciencespo.fr/mass-violence-war-massacre-resistance/en/document/napalm-us
-bombing-doctrine-and-practice-1942–1975.html.

153. *United States Strategic Bombing Survey,* 92.

154. Robert Eldridge, "The March 1945 Firebombing of Tokyo and the Immorality of War," *Japan Times,* March 9, 2020, https://www.japantimes.co.jp/opinion/2020/03/09/commentary/japan-commentary/march-1945-firebombing-tokyo-immorality-war/.

155. Wesley Craven and James Cate, eds., *The Pacific: Matterhorn to Nagasaki. The Army Air Forces in World War II,* vol. 5 (Chicago: University of Chicago Press, 1953), 638–639.

156. *Kaō kabushiki gaisha shashi hensatsu shitsu, Kaō shi 100 nen (1890–1990 nen)* (Tokyo: Kaō Corporation, 1998), 162.

157. *Kaō kabushiki gaisha shashi hensatsu shitsu,* 163.

158. *United States Strategic Bombing Survey,* 96.

159. *United States Strategic Bombing Survey,* 96.

160. American postwar analyses attribute this to "Japanese" compliance rather than individuals rationalizing circumstances amid little choice: "Until the end, however, national traditions of obedience and conformity, reinforced by the police organization, remained effective in controlling the behavior of the population." *United States Strategic Bombing Survey,* 96. This assessment prefigures Yamashita's similar research findings. See "The Pacific War and Ordinary Japanese," in Samuel Yamashita, *Leaves in an Autumn of Emergencies: Selections from the Wartime Diaries of Ordinary Japanese* (Honolulu: University of Hawai'i Press, 2005), 3–50.

161. The Japanese government's Ministry of Education and Nippon Izokukai, a private group representing families of deceased Japanese Asia-Pacific War veterans, fund the National Shōwa Memorial Museum. While they present an antiwar orientation, they support visits to the controversial Yasukuni Shrine (across the street) to honor Imperial Japan's war dead.

162. In 2004, my then-four-year-old son was issued a similar orange fire-resistant treated padded cotton hood during enrollment at Tokyo's Toyama Preschool.

163. Author's fieldwork, photographs from wartime public history exhibit, *Senchū no gakudō gakuto,* in the *Shōwa-kan,* Tokyo, June 29, 2014.

164. In wartime diaries, Japanese servicemen noted how, by 1942, even unaccompanied rice became a valued meal. Aaron Moore, *Writing War: Soldiers Record the Japanese Empire* (Cambridge, MA: Harvard University Press, 2013), 212.

165. George Sekine Solt argues that in early twentieth-century Japan, "students, soldiers, shipyard workers, dock workers, train workers, and other industrial workers" generated strong demand for cheap Chinese-style noodle soup, or ramen, initially called *Shina soba* (Chinese thin wheat noodles) or *Shina udon* (Chinese thick wheat noodles). Noodle soup was a cheap (and fast) dish for working classes

322   *Notes to Pages 158–164*

and soon impacted rice's popularity during the interwar period. Rice consumption among Japan's entire population peaked in 1925 at 391 grams per person and fell to nearly half that by 1946. See George Sekine Solt, "Taking Ramen Seriously: Food, Labor, and Everyday Life in Modern Japan" (PhD diss., University of California at San Diego, 2009), 19, 62, 122.

166. Samuel Yamashita, *Daily Life in Wartime Japan, 1940–1945* (Lawrence: University of Kansas Press, 2015), 35–58.

167. Yamashita, *Daily Life in Wartime Japan,* 37.

168. Yamashita, *Daily Life in Wartime Japan,* 37.

169. Yamashita, *Daily Life in Wartime Japan,* 38–39.

170. *United States Strategic Bombing Survey,* 94.

171. Yamashita, *Daily Life in Wartime Japan,* 40.

172. Rika Fujioka, "The Pressures of Globalization in Retail: The Path of Japanese Department Stores, 1930s–1980s," in *Comparative Responses to Globalization: Experiences of British and Japanese Enterprises,* ed. Maki Umemura and Rika Fujioka (London: Palgrave Macmillan, 2013), 187.

173. Fujioka, "The Pressures of Globalization in Retail," 189.

174. Fujioka, "The Pressures of Globalization in Retail," 189.

175. Fujioka, "The Pressures of Globalization in Retail," 191.

CHAPTER 5: CONSUMING THE BRIGHT LIFE

1. Ezra Vogel, *Japan's New Middle Class: The Salary Man and His Family in a Tokyo Suburb* (Berkeley: University of California Press, 1963), 71.

2. Hatsuda Kōsei, Murakami Shihori, and Ishigure Masakazu, "The Nationwide Formation and Spread of *Yami-ichi* (Black Market) after World War II and Government's Involvements: Nationwide Survey of the Descriptions about *Yami-ichi* (Black Market) in Municipality Histories," *Journal of Architecture and Planning (Transactions of AIJ [Architectural Institute of Japan])* 82, no. 733 (March 2017): 805.

3. Owen Griffiths, "Need, Greed, and Protest in Japan's Black Market, 1938–1949," *Journal of Social History* 35, no. 4 (Summer 2002): 847.

4. Griffiths, "Need, Greed, and Protest," 858.

5. "JAPAN: Wages of Sinlessness," *Time,* November 17, 1947, http://content.time.com/time/subscriber/article/0,33009,887675,00.html.

6. See Hashimoto Ken'ichi and Hatsuda Kōsei, *Sakariba wa yami-ichi kara umareta* (Tokyo: Seikyū-sha, 2016).

7. Anne Allison, *Millennial Monsters: Japanese Toys and the Global Imagination* (Berkeley: University of California Press, 2006), 38.

8. Allison, *Millennial Monsters,* 38.

9. Allison, *Millennial Monsters,* 40.

10. Figure in International Monetary Fund Statistics Department, *International Financial Statistics: International Financial Statistics, August 1949, Vol. 2,*

Number 8 (Washington, DC: International Monetary Fund, 1949), 161. The current mid-2021 value of this amount was calculated using the CPI Inflation Calculator, https://www.in2013dollars.com/us/inflation/1949?amount=2777777.77, accessed June 26, 2021.

11. "Obituary: Shavell, Henry," *Boston Globe,* December 17, 2017, 33.

12. Henry Shavell, "Postwar Taxation in Japan," *Journal of Political Economy* 56, no. 2 (April 1948): 124–137.

13. Shavell, "Postwar Taxation in Japan," 124.

14. Shavell, "Postwar Taxation in Japan," 124.

15. Shavell, "Postwar Taxation in Japan," 124.

16. Henry Shavell, "Taxation Reform in Occupied Japan," *National Tax Journal* 1, no. 2 (June 1948): 127.

17. See Yoneyuki Sugita and Marie Thorsten, *Beyond the Line: Joseph Dodge and the Geometry of Power in US-Japan Relations, 1949–1952* (Tokyo: University Education Press, 1999); and Marie Thorsten and Yoneyuki Sugita, "Joseph Dodge and the Geometry of Power in US-Japan Relations," *Japanese Studies: 1981–2012* 19, no. 3 (1999): 297–314.

18. Eitarō Kishimoto, "Labour-Management Relations and the Trade Unions in Postwar Japan: Revival and Reestablishment of the Labour-Management Regulations Based on Seniority," *Kyoto University Economic Review* 38, no. 1 (April 1968): 10.

19. Deokhyo Choi, "Fighting the Korean War in Pacifist Japan: Korean and Japanese Leftist Solidarity and American Cold War Containment," *Critical Asian Studies* 49, no. 4 (2007): 546.

20. For more on the two postwar Koreas, see Bruce Cumings, *Korea's Place in the Sun: A Modern History* (New York: W. W. Norton, 2005).

21. Choi, "Fighting the Korean War in Pacifist Japan," 546.

22. Robert D. Eldridge, "How Eisenhower's June 1960 Trip to Okinawa Became a Catalyst for Reversion," *Japan Times,* June 17, 2020, https://www.japan times.co.jp/opinion/2020/06/17/commentary/japan-commentary/eisenhowers-june -1960-trip-okinawa-became-catalyst-reversion/.

23. Nick Kapur, *Japan at the Crossroads: Conflict and Compromise after Anpo* (Cambridge, MA: Harvard University Press, 2018), 1.

24. Yoneyuki Sugita, "The Yoshida Doctrine as a Myth," *Japanese Journal of American Studies,* no. 27 (2016): 123.

25. Sugita, "The Yoshida Doctrine as a Myth," 123.

26. Tamio Hattori and Tsuruyo Funatsu, "The Emergence of the Asian Middle Classes and Their Characteristics," *The Developing Economies* 41, no. 2 (June 2003): 152.

27. See Takeo Doi, "*Giri-ninjo*: An Interpretation," in *Aspects of Social Change in Modern Japan,* ed. R. P. Dore (Princeton, NJ: Princeton University Press, 1967), 327–336; *The Anatomy of Dependence: The Key Analysis of Japanese*

324 *Notes to Pages 168–170*

Behavior, trans. J. Bester (Tokyo: Kodansha International, 1973); and *The Anatomy of Self: The Individual versus Society,* trans. M. A. Harbison (Tokyo: Kodansha International, 1986).

28. William Kelly, foreword to Ezra Vogel, *Japan's Middle Class* (Lanham, MD: Rowman and Littlefield, 2013), xiv.

29. Ezra Vogel, *Japan's New Middle Class: The Salary Man and His Family in a Tokyo Suburb* (Berkeley: University of California Press, 1963).

30. Elise K. Tipton, *Modern Japan: A Social and Political History* (London: Taylor and Francis Routledge, 2002), 171.

31. Here, "transwar" means the time spanning prewar, wartime, and postwar eras. See Andrew Gordon, ed., *Postwar Japan as History* (Berkeley: University of California Press, 1993); *The Evolution of Labor Relations in Japan: Heavy Industry, 1853–1955* (Cambridge, MA: Harvard University Press, 1988); and *A Modern History of Japan: From Tokugawa Times to the Present* (New York: Oxford University Press, 2002). In his 2007 article "Consumption, Leisure, and the Middle Class in Transwar Japan," Gordon claims transwar continuity in historical study beyond politics: "This essay argues for the importance of a longer, but nevertheless bounded, era of 'transwar' transformation, and it seeks to extend the concept of a transwar process of change to realms of daily life, leisure and consumption. To speak of a transwar era in this sense is also distinct from a perspective linking pre- to postwar while leapfrogging the 'abnormal' dark valley of wartime." See Andrew Gordon, "Consumption, Leisure, and the Middle Class in Transwar Japan," *Social Science Japan Journal* 10, no. 1 (April 2007): 4. Historian Nakamura Masanori understands the transwar period as "persistence," especially of the emperor system and the imperial institution's ambiguous postwar metamorphosis. Nakamura uses *kansen-shi* ("persistent [traversing] war history") to refer to imperial continuities from the prewar into postwar periods. See Nakamura Masanori, *Sengoshi* (Tokyo: Iwanami shoten, 2005).

32. "Nikka Whisky History: History of Masataka Taketsuru and Nikka Whisky," Nikka Distilling Company website, https://www.nikka.com/eng/story/history/, accessed June 3, 2021.

33. Jesus Solis, "Japan's Black Market: *Yakuza,* SCAP, and the Culture of the *Yami'ichi*" (MA thesis, University of Colorado, 2012), 6, 14.

34. Anne Allison, *Nightwork: Sexuality, Pleasure, and Corporate Masculinity in a Tokyo Hostess Club* (Chicago: University of Chicago Press, 1994), 13.

35. For an interview with London-based Suntory Whisky brand ambassador Zoran Peric on the technique, see Annie Hayes, "In Focus: The Art of Japanese Ice Carving," *The Spirits Business,* May 20, 2017, https://www.thespiritsbusiness.com/2017/05/in-focus-the-art-of-japanese-ice-carving/. For videos of Japan's most well-known bartender and artisanal ice carver, see Corinne Mossati, "Hidetsugu Ueno: Bartending as an Art," Cocktails and Bars, October 3, 2018, http://www.cocktailsandbars.com/hidetsugu-ueno-san-bartending-as-an-art/.

Notes to Pages 170–173 325

36. "History: Revolutionizing the Way to Drink, 1955–1970," Suntory Company website, https://whisky.suntory.com/en/na/the-house/history#1955–1970, accessed June 3, 2021.

37. "Get to Know: The Perfect Scottish Highball," *Chilled* 2, no. 2 (2019): 89, https://issuu.com/chilledmagazine/docs/chilled_v12-i2_issuu/s/104961.

38. "Get to Know," 89.

39. Jeffrey W. Alexander, "Beer and Whisky in Japanese Marketplaces," *Oxford Research Encyclopedias*, September 26, 2017, 3.

40. Yanagihara Ryōhei, *Yanagihara Ryōhei no shigoto* (Tokyo: Genkōsha, 2015), frontispiece.

41. Neo Geo, "Animation: Ryohei Yanagihara (1931–2015)," Illustrators Lounge, December 20, 2016, https://illustratorslounge.com/animation/ryohei-yanagihara-1931-2015/.

42. Millie Creighton, "Imaging the Other in Japanese Advertising Campaigns," in *Occidentalism: Images of the West*, ed. James Carrier (Oxford: Oxford University Press, 1995), 146.

43. Alastair Bonnett, *White Identities: An Historical and International Introduction* (London: Routledge, 2018), 73.

44. See Amy Borovy, *The Too-Good Wife: Alcohol, Co-Dependency, and the Politics of Nurturance in Postwar Japan* (Berkeley: University of California Press, 2005).

45. tkodoh, "Suntory Torys Whisky Commercial (1960's)," May 1, 2006, https://www.youtube.com/watch?v=BbSk1s7hH50&list=PL6qz-D1hfrQ0SCHJvsBDjfQRZNqwyCi2i&index=2. See also viewers' comments.

46. Sapporo Biiru Kabushiki-gaisha, *Sapporo 120 nenshi* (Tokyo: Sapporo biiru kabushiki-gaisha, 1996), 380.

47. 03Tyke, *Santorī Torisu uisukī 2*, https://www.youtube.com/watch?v=CkOIHjK-JYM&list=PL6qz-D1hfrQ0SCHJvsBDjfQRZNqwyCi2i&index=3, accessed June 12, 2021.

48. Rocketjay, "Uncle Torys Cowboys and Indians," January 6, 2007, https://www.youtube.com/watch?v=YBHy4bNc0Yw&list=PL6qz-D1hfrQ0SCHJvsBDjfQRZNqwyCi2i&index=7.

49. "History: Timeline," Suntory Company website, https://www.suntory.com/about/history/timeline/, accessed April 25, 2023.

50. CISCO1812J, "Torisu de Hawai" [Hawai'i in Torys], May 24, 2008, https://www.youtube.com/watch?v=dnyOQEg4Rvc&list=PL6qz-D1hfrQ0SCHJvsBDjfQRZNqwyCi2i&index=1.

51. CISCO1812J, "Torisu de Hawai."

52. The poster appears in Kano Takuya, "The Story of Japanese Whisky: Whisky, a Spirit Imbued with Culture," *Nippon Magazine*, October 7, 2014, https://www.nippon.com/en/views/b04202/.

53. "History."

54. Nick Ravo, "Keizo Saji, 80, Who Headed Beverage Conglomerate, Dies," *New York Times,* November 6, 1999, A15, https://www.nytimes.com/1999/11/06/business/keizo-saji-80-who-headed-beverage-conglomerate-dies.html.

55. "History."

56. Due to Suntory's highball promotion, Japanese-style ice carving has entered mainstream, urban Anglo-American hip bar experiences.

57. See the ad in Yanagihara, *Yanagihara Ryōhei no shigoto,* 9.

58. My translation of the ad's captions in Yanagihara, *Yanagihara Ryōhei no shigoto,* 9.

59. See the ad in Yanagihara, *Yanagihara Ryōhei no shigoto,* 9.

60. My translation of the ad's caption in Yanagihara, *Yanagihara Ryōhei no shigoto,* 9.

61. See the ad in Yanagihara, *Yanagihara Ryōhei no shigoto,* 9.

62. At $49.99, this was a more reasonably priced Uncle Torys Suntory Whisky novelty promotional good. Anglo-American "hipster" markets recently developed for such collectibles, whose value increased in past years by being socially transgressive in representing antiquated gender norms and drinking habits while communicating a specifically Japanese provenance. See "Suntory Whisky Uncle Torys Toothpick Holder Red 1970s Ad Promo Figure Japan," https://www.ebay.com/itm/313528905766?hash=item48ffc77026:g:f7oAAOSw4Rxgnkzn, accessed June 11, 2021.

63. *The Citizen Watch Story: How a Tokyo Jeweler's Experiment in Making Pocket Watches 84 Years Ago Led to the Creation of a Global Watch Colossus,* WatchTime, Spotlight: Citizen special edition, October 2013, 5, pamphlet archived at https://www.watchtime.com/wp-content/uploads/2013/10/WT_Spotlight_Citizen.pdf.

64. "History of the Japanese Horological Industry," Japan Clock and Watch Association website, https://www.jcwa.or.jp/en/etc/history01.html, accessed November 22, 2019.

65. "History of the Japanese Horological Industry."

66. "History of the Japanese Horological Industry."

67. "Japanese Clock and Watch Industry," Japan Clock and Watch Association website, timeline found at https://www.jcwa.or.jp/en/etc/history02.html, accessed November 22, 2019.

68. "Japanese Clock and Watch Industry."

69. "History: April 1946: Kashio Seisakujo Founded in Mitaka, Tokyo," Casio Worldwide website, https://world.casio.com/corporate/history/#:~:text=1946,Apr.&text=The%20late%20Kashio%20Tadao%2C%20founder,of%20an%20uncle%20working%20there, accessed March 6, 2021.

70. "The Four Kashio Brothers," Casio Worldwide website, https://world.casio.com/corporate/brothers/, accessed April 16, 2021.

71. Vivian Morelli, "The Shock over Casio's New G-Shock," *New York Times,* March 20, 2019, fashion section, https://www.nytimes.com/2019/03/20/fashion/watches-casio-g-shock.html.

72. "The Four Kashio Brothers."

73. "Casio 14A," Casio Museum (online), http://www.casio-calculator .com/Museum/Pages/Numbers/14-A/14-A.html, accessed April 16, 2021.

74. "Casio 14A."

75. "Value of 1957 Japanese Yen Today," Inflation Tool website, https://www .inflationtool.com/japanese-yen/1957-to-present-value, accessed April 17, 2021.

76. "The IBM 610 Auto-Point Computer—the First 'Personal Computer,'" Columbia University Computing History, http://www.columbia.edu/cu /computinghistory/610.html, accessed April 16, 2021.

77. Mike Bernardo, "The History of Seiko through 12 Milestone Seiko Watches," January 20, 2021, https://www.watchtime.com/featured/timepiece-time line-milestone-seiko-watches/.

78. WatchTime editors, "Watch Review—Out of This World: Reviewing the Seiko Astron GPS Watch," WatchTime, June 8, 2016, https://www.watchtime .com/reviews/world-reviewing-seiko-astron-gps-watch/.

79. Ariel Adams, "Hands-On: Seiko Astron Solar GPS Hands-On," *A Blog to Watch,* March 25, 2012, https://www.ablogtowatch.com/seiko-astron-gps-solar -watch-hands-on/.

80. "The First Casio Digital Watch," Digital Watch Central, https:// digitalwatchcentral.com/the-first-casio-digital-watch/, accessed March 5, 2021.

81. Chaim Gartenberg, "Hamilton Is Bringing Back the Original Digital Wristwatch with an OLED Twist: In Honor of the 50th Anniversary of the Iconic Pulsar Wristwatch," *The Verge,* March 23, 2020, https://www.theverge.com/circuit breaker/2020/3/23/21191283/hamilton-psr-pulsar-digital-watch-price-50th-anni versary-remake-oled-lcd.

82. "The First Casio Digital Watch."

83. Ed Odevin, "A Look Back at When Tokyo Was Awarded 1964 Olympics," *Japan Times,* August 24, 2013, https://www.japantimes.co.jp/sports/2013 /08/24/olympics/a-look-back-at-when-tokyo-was-awarded-1964-olympics/.

84. "Cool Running: The Pleasant Temperatures of Japan's October 1964 Olympics," Nippon.com, October 21, 2019, https://www.nippon.com/en/japan -data/h00558/cool-running-the-pleasant-temperatures-of-japan%E2%80%99s -october-1964-olympics.html.

85. For a direct link to the film, see the International Olympic Committee, "Relive Kon Ichikawa's Iconic Film about the 1964 Games," Olympics website, October 16, 2019, https://olympics.com/en/news/relive-kon-ichikawa-s-iconic -film-about-the-1964-games.

86. See Alan W. Watts, *The Way of Zen* (New York: Pantheon Books, 1957).

87. "The Life of Alan Watts," Alan Watts website, https://alanwatts.org/life -of-alan-watts/, accessed April 13, 2021.

88. Scott Lowe, "Review of *Alan Watts—In the Academy: Essays and Lectures,* ed. by Peter J. Columbus and Donadrian L. Rice," *Nova Religio* 22, no. 3 (2019): 129.

328   *Notes to Pages 181–183*

89. See "The Incorporation of Buddhism into the Japanese War Machine (1913–1930)," 57–65, and "The Emergence of Imperial-State Zen and Soldier-Zen," 95–129, in Brian Daizen Victoria, *Zen at War,* 2nd ed. (Lanham, MD: Rowman and Littlefield, 2006). Though criticized for essentialist views of prewar Japan's military, Victoria's book reveals Zen Buddhism's connections to prewar and wartime Japanese military culture. Contrary to American conceptions of Zen as a "peaceful practice," Victoria as an ordained Sōtō Zen priest argues that his religious tradition once supported Imperial Japan's martial endeavors.

90. Shiseidō Corporate Museum website: products, "Introducing the Collection," http://group.shiseido.com/corporate-museum/preservation/item.html, accessed July 11, 2012.

91. "Estée Lauder Youth Dew for Women," *Fragrantica* perfume blog, https://www.fragrantica.com/perfume/Estee-Lauder/Youth-Dew-555.html, accessed April 12, 2021.

92. "Zen Original Shiseido for Women," *Fragrantica* perfume blog, https://www.fragrantica.com/perfume/Shiseido/Zen-Original-4837.html, accessed April 17, 2021.

93. "Kōdaiji makie," Kōdaiji website, https://www.kodaiji.com/makie.html, accessed April 17, 2021.

94. See the fourth image shown online in "Kōdaiji makie."

95. "Kōdaiji to kanren ji'in no takara-mono," Kōdaiji-shō Museum, https://www.kodaiji.com/museum/Treasure.html, accessed April 17, 2021.

96. See Janica Anderson and Steven Zahavi Schwartz, *Zen Odyssey: The Story of Sokei-an, Ruth Fuller Sasaki, and the Birth of Zen in America* (Somerville, MA: Wisdom Publications, 2018).

97. See Isabel Stirling, *The Life and Works of Ruth Fuller Sasaki* (Los Angeles: Counterpoint, 2006).

98. Kazuyuki Motohashi, "Shiseido Marketing in China," in *Global Business Strategy: Multinational Corporations Venturing into Emerging Markets* (New York: Springer, 2015), 155–171, https://link.springer.com/chapter/10.1007/978-4-431-55468-4_10.

99. Yutaka Goto, "How Shiseido Succeeded in Europe: History and International Strategy," talk at Japan Society of the United Kingdom, London, January 12, 2005; entire talk quoted in a thread by Mylene Famer, "How Shiseido Succeeded in Europe (SERGE LUTENS)," *Basenotes* perfume blog, December 2, 2005, https://www.basenotes.net/threads/180978-How-Shiseido-succeeded-in-Europe-(SERGE-LUTENS).

100. Miller is referring to a year-long mid-1990s study. See Daniel Miller, *A Theory of Shopping* (Ithaca, NY: Cornell University Press, 1998).

101. Quoted in Daniel Miller, *The Dialectics of Shopping* (Chicago: University of Chicago Press, 2001), 4.

102. Miller, *The Dialectics of Shopping*, 13.

Notes to Pages 184–187

103. "The Social Communication Business: A Message from Tsuji," Sanrio Company website, https://www.sanrio.co.jp/english/corporate/about_s/message/, accessed June 16, 2021.

104. "The Social Communication Business."

105. See Marcel Mauss, *The Gift: The Form and Reason for Exchange in Archaic Societies,* trans. W. D. Halls (New York: W. W. Norton, 2000).

106. Daniel Miller, *The Comfort of Things* (Cambridge: Polity Press, 2008).

107. Marx defines commodity fetishism in *Capital*'s first part: see my introduction. Karl Marx, "Section 4: The Fetishism of Commodities and the Secret Thereof," in *Capital*, vol. 1, https://www.marxists.org/archive/marx/works/1867-c1/ch01.htm#S4, accessed January 12, 2020.

108. See "The Social Communication Business."

109. Jonathon Greenall, "From Japan to New Horizons, the Complete History of Sanrio," Comic Book Resources, April 4, 2021, https://www.cbr.com/from-japan-to-new-horizons-the-complete-history-of-sanrio/.

110. Sharon Kinsella, "Cuties in Japan," in *Women, Media, and Consumption in Japan*, ed. Lise Skov and Brian Moeran (Honolulu: University of Hawai'i Press, 1995), 2.

111. Ken Belson and Brian Bremner, *Hello Kitty, The Remarkable Story of Sanrio and the Billion Dollar Feline Phenomenon* (Singapore: John Wiley and Sons, 2004), 39.

112. See David Graeber, *Towards an Anthropological Theory of Value: The False Coin of Our Own Dreams* (New York: Palgrave Macmillan, 2001).

113. David Graeber, "It Is Value That Brings Universes into Being," *HAU: Journal of Ethnographic Theory* 3, no. 2 (2013): 222.

114. "Natsukashi no kyarakutā-tachi—fuanshi guzu o furi kaeru," Midoru ejji [Middle Edge], November 10, 2015, https://middle-edge.jp/articles/I0002217.

115. Christine Reiko Yano, *Pink Globalization: Hello Kitty's Trek across the Pacific* (Durham, NC: Duke University Press, 2013), 15.

116. Greenall, "From Japan to New Horizons."

117. "Company History," Sanrio Company website, https://www.sanrio.co.jp/english/corporate/about_s/history/, accessed June 16, 2021.

118. "Company History."

119. "Hello Kitty," Characters, Sanrio website, https://www.sanrio.com/collections/hello-kitty, accessed June 17, 2021; "Hello Kitty," Profile, Sanrio website (Japan), https://www.sanrio.co.jp/character/hellokitty/#char_profile, accessed June 17, 2021.

120. "Company History."

121. Yano, *Pink Globalization*, 9–10.

122. Nobuko Kobayashi, "Opinion: Kawaii Culture Hurts Japanese Women in Business," July 17, 2021, https://asia.nikkei.com/Opinion/Kawaii-culture-hurts-Japanese-women-in-business.

330 *Notes to Pages 187–189*

123. Experiences noted during the author's teaching in Setō City, Japan, from July 1997 to July 1998.

124. Anne Allison, *Millennial Monsters: Japanese Toys and the Global Imagination* (Berkeley: University of California Press, 2006), 16–17. Quoted in Yano, *Pink Globalization,* 11.

125. Yano, *Pink Globalization,* 11.

126. Yano, *Pink Globalization,* 11.

127. Yano, *Pink Globalization,* 23.

128. Sanrio website, "Home & Kitchen," https://www.sanrio.com/collec tions/home, accessed June 16, 2021.

129. Yano, *Pink Globalization,* 23.

130. Alex Abad-Santos, "How Gudetama, a Lazy Egg Yolk with a Butt, Became an Unstoppable Cultural Phenomenon," *Vox,* April 18, 2017, https://www .vox.com/2017/4/3/14685348/gudetama-sanrio-hello-kitty-explained.

131. Sanrio Japan website, Character Profiles, *Aguresshibu retsuko,* https:// www.sanrio.co.jp/character/aggressiveretsuko/, accessed June 17, 2021.

132. *Sanrio kyarakutā daishō,* "Entry Number 011: *Kirimi-Chan,*" http://web .archive.org/web/20161014161227/http://sanriocharacterranking.com/characters /view/kirimichan, accessed June 18, 2021.

133. This is Sanrio's official English translation of basically similar information on the Japanese website. (The musical note is used as an emphasis mark in the sentence.) See "Characters: Kirimi," Puroland website, https://en.puroland.jp/char acter/kirimichan_en/, accessed June 16, 2021. For Kirimi's profile in Japanese, see Profile: *Kirimi-chan,* Sanrio website for Japan, https://www.sanrio.co.jp/character /kirimichan/#char_profile, accessed June 18, 2021.

134. For the US market, fifty-two different "goods" appear for Gudetama, including key chains, backpacks, pool sandals, Tamagotchi (egg-shaped electronic "pets"), binder clips, charms, baseball hats, a measuring tape, a piggy bank, and various apparel. No Kirimi items were available. See "Shop Gudetama," Sanrio English-language website, https://www.sanrio.com/collections/gudetama, accessed June 18, 2021. On the Japanese Sanrio website, Kirimi-chan appeared on the 2021 Sanrio Character Ranking contest for characters that fans wanted to see on a hairband (1,320 yen, or $11.98 in mid-2021) or as a neck pouch (1,650 yen, or $14.97)—presumably purchasable as limited-edition items in Sanrio stores throughout Japan. See Sanrio website in Japan, *2021-nen kyarakutā daishō dai san-dan,* https://www.sanrio.co.jp/goodsinfo/mx-ranking2021-03-202105/, accessed June 17, 2021.

135. To glimpse the park, with photographs and English commentary by a Japan-based Australian blogger, see "Sanrio Puroland: A Theme Park for Hello Kitty and Friends in Tokyo," *Appetite for Japan* (blog), January 26, 2017, https://appetiteforjapan.com/2017/01/26/sanrio-puroland/.

136. Yoshino Sakurai and Yoshihiro Hara, "Sanrio's 31-Year-Old CEO Looks beyond Hello Kitty," *Nikkei Asia,* September 26, 2020, https://asia.nikkei

Notes to Pages 189–192 331

.com/Business/Companies/Sanrio-s-31-year-old-CEO-looks-beyond-Hello
-Kitty.

137. For the English-language site, see "Ticket Price," Sanrio Puroland website, https://en.puroland.jp/?_ga=2.140286387.1812065907.1623697416-619186
700.1623697416, accessed June 15, 2021. For the Japanese-language site, see "Pasupōto," Sanrio Puroland website, https://www.puroland.jp/ticket/, accessed June 15, 2021.

138. "Admission: Tickets," Disneyland Resort website, https://disneyland
.disney.go.com/admission/tickets/dates/, accessed June 15, 2021.

139. Sanrio Puroland website, in Japanese, https://www.puroland.jp/, accessed June 14, 2021.

140. Toshihiro Sato and Yoshino Sakurai, "Hello Kitty Franchise Has First New Chief in 60-Year History," *Nikkei Asia*, June 11, 2020, https://asia
.nikkei.com/Business/Media-Entertainment/Hello-Kitty-franchise-has-first-new
-chief-in-60-year-history.

141. "Kan'nai mappu," Sanrio Puroland Japanese-language website, https://
www.puroland.jp/floor_guide/, accessed June 15, 2021.

142. "Restaurant Yakata," Sanrio Puroland English-language website, https://en.puroland.jp/shop/yakatarestaurant_en/, accessed June 14, 2021.

143. "Restaurant Yakata."

144. "Yakata no restoran," Sanrio Puroland Japanese-language website, https://
www.puroland.jp/facility/yakatarestaurant/?target=seasonal, accessed June 14, 2021.

145. For the Princess Kitty–themed hotel room, discontinued after January 3, 2019, see "Hello Kitty Hotel Room: Inside Keio Plaza Tokyo's Princess Kitty Room," *Appetite for Japan* (blog), January 15, 2021, https://appetiteforjapan.com
/2017/01/15/hello-kitty-hotel-room/.

146. "Hello Kitty Hotel Room."

147. "Hello Kitty Hotel Room."

148. "The Keio Plaza Hotel Tama Creates New 'Hello Kitty' Photographic Spot and Sanrio Characters Themed Rooms—'My Melody' and 'Little Twin Stars,' Keio Plaza Hotel Tokyo, December 3, 2018, https://www.keioplaza.com
/press/201812_03.html.

149. "Accommodation: Hello Kitty & Sanrio Room," Keio Plaza Hotel Tama website, October 2019, https://www.keioplaza.com/tama/sanrio/index.html.

150. "Accommodation."

151. Kaori Enjoji, "The 92-Year-Old Founder of Hello Kitty Is Handing the Business to His Grandson," CNN, June 15, 2020, https://www.cnn.com
/2020/06/15/business/sanrio-hello-kitty-ceo-intl-hnk/index.html.

152. Around 2000, Mainland Chinese consumers became designer and name-brand conscious.

153. Johannah Masters, "Balenciaga Unveils $2,590 Hello Kitty Bag," *New York Post*, January 10, 2020, https://nypost.com/2020/01/10/balenciaga
-unveils-2590-hello-kitty-bag/.

332   *Notes to Pages 192–197*

154. Karmen, "Hello Kitty Louis Vuitton Bags Upcycled by American Designer Sheron Barber," GirlStyle Singapore, May 9, 2021, https://girlstyle.com/sg/article/90373/hello-kitty-louis-vuitton-bags-sheron-barber.

155. Barber invited Instagram followers to critique his unique creative process: "I cut up a LV midnight eclipse garment bag and used two Hermès grade gators to construct this oversized (55CM) Birkin. It has original Louis Vuitton lock and hardware. What are your thoughts? Check out my story to see the process of how this bag was hand-constructed." Sheron Barber, Instagram, December 12, 2019, https://www.instagram.com/p/B5-4kU-JdXv/?hl=en.

156. "Drippin' in Leather and Full of Ideas: Portraits—Sheron Barber," Metcha, November 21, 2020, https://metcha.com/article/sheron-barber-roots-and-passion-into-custom-pieces.

157. Sheron Barber, Instagram, December 1, 2019, https://www.instagram.com/p/B5ioFjQpknj/?hl=en.

158. Karmen, "Hello Kitty Louis Vuitton Bags Upcycled by American Designer Sheron Barber."

159. "Bosses Who Lead and Inspire: Q and A with Sheron Barber," Parker XL, https://parkerxl.com/bosses-lead-inspire-qa-sheron-barber/, accessed June 1, 2021.

Chapter 6: Consuming Japaneseness and Global Brand-Name Recognition

1. "Enkaku, Kaisha jōhō," Seibu sōgō website, https://www.sogo-seibu.co.jp/info/history.html, accessed July 1, 2021.

2. "Early Works," Arakawa + Gins Reversible Destiny Foundation, http://www.reversibledestiny.org/art/early-works, accessed June 7, 2021.

3. For an excellent cultural history of postwar Japanese avant-garde art and politics, see Justin Jesty, *Art and Engagement in Early Postwar Japan* (Ithaca, NY: Cornell University Press, 2018). For an art historical approach, see Alexandra Munroe, *Scream against the Sky: Japanese Art after 1945* (New York: Harry N. Abrams, 1994).

4. Fumi Tsukahara, Director of the Aizu Museum, Waseda University, "Highlights of Shusaku Arakawa Exhibition—from Diagrams to Reversible Destiny and beyond," Waseda Online, 2014, https://yab.yomiuri.co.jp/adv/wol/dy/culture/140528.html.

5. Christopher Stephens, "Focus: Down with Death," *Artscape Japan,* May 2010, https://artscape.jp/artscape/eng/focus/1006_01.html; Ashley Rawlings, "Shusaku Arakawa," *Art Asia-Pacific Magazine,* July/August 2010, http://artasiapacific.com/Magazine/69/ShusakuArakawa19362010. Interestingly, Stephens was a member of the 1980s punk noise trio The Assholes.

6. "Early Works," Arakawa + Gins Reversible Destiny Foundation.

7. As a graduate student at Waseda University, I felt honored to hear Arakawa's lecture at Tokyo University in September 2004 and joined students on a 2005

Notes to Pages 197–201   333

tour of the Mitaka lofts. Arakawa passed away in 2010 in New York City; he and his partner Madeleine Gins (1941–2014) created art and architecture at their Greenwich Village office. Photographs of Mitaka apartment lofts, now rentable through AirBnB, appear online: "Reversible Destiny Lofts MITAKA—in Memory of Helen Keller," Arakawa + Gins Reversible Destiny Foundation, http://www.reversibledestiny.org /architecture/reversible-destiny-lofts-mitaka, accessed June 7, 2021.

8. William Marotti, *Money, Trains, and Guillotines: Art and Revolution in 1960s Japan* (Durham, NC: Duke University Press, 2013), 118.

9. Taro Nettleton, "Hi-Red Center's Shelter Plan (1964): The Uncanny Body in the Imperial Hotel," *Japanese Studies* 34, no. 1 (2014): 83.

10. Reiko Tomii, "State v. (Anti-)Art: Model 1,000 Yen Note Incident by Akasegawa Genpei and Company," *Positions: East Asia Cultures Critique* 10, no. 1 (Spring 2002): 144. For Akasegawa's artworks and exhibit featuring the trial, see *Sen'en satsu saiban no tenkai, Sakuhin shōkai, Akasegawa Katsuhiko,* Hiroshima City Museum of Contemporary Art, https://www.hiroshima-moca.jp /akasegawa/works/index.html https://www.hiroshima-moca.jp/akasegawa/works /index.html, accessed June 8, 2021.

11. Nettleson, "Hi-Red Center's Shelter Plan (1964)," 85–86.

12. Marotti, *Money, Trains, and Guillotines,* 7.

13. For Akasegawa's perspectives, see Akasegawa Genpei, *Objet o motta musansha* (Tokyo: Gendai shinchōsha, 1970) and *Hangeijutsu anpan* (Tokyo: Chikuma Shobo, 1994).

14. See Murakami Ryū, *69 Sikusutei nain* (Tokyo: Shueisha, 1987).

15. Tsuruya Makoto, "Murakami Ryū 'Kagirinaku tōmei ni chikai burū' no setsuna to jojō," *Mainichi Shimbun,* May 12, 2015, https://mainichi.jp/premier /business/articles/20151209/biz/00m/010/023000c.

16. Murakami, *69 Sikusutei nain,* 11.

17. Murakami Ryū, *69,* trans. Ralph F. McCarthy (Tokyo: Kodansha International, 1993), 9.

18. Murakami, *69,* 9.

19. See Max Frankel, "'Japan Inc' and 'Nixon Shocks,'" *New York Times,* November 25, 1971, 2; and Richard Douglas Partch, "The Nixon 'Shocks': Implications for Japan's Foreign Policy in the 1970s" (MA thesis, Portland State University, August 1972).

20. Philosopher Moto'ori Noringa (1730–1801) believed that Japan's culture was revealed in classics like Lady Murasaki's (973–1014) Heian-period (794–1185) novel *Genji Monogatari* (The Tale of Genji) and viewed *mono-no-aware,* or "evanescence of things," as the essence of Japanese cultural identity.

21. Satomi Ishikawa, *Seeking the Self: Individualism and Popular Culture in Japan* (Bern, Switzerland: Peter Lang, 2007), 174. Maruyama Masao is well-known for essays on Japan's prewar and wartime political thought. See Maruyama Masao, *Thought and Behaviour in Japanese Politics* (Oxford: University of Oxford Press, 1963).

334   *Notes to Pages 201–204*

22. Ishikawa, *Seeking the Self,* 174.

23. See Minami Hiroshi, *Nihonjinron no keifu* (Tokyo: Kōdansha, 1980). Minami also wrote *Nihonjin no shinri* (Tokyo: Iwanami shinsho, 1953), translated as *Psychology of the Japanese People* (Toronto: University of Toronto Press, 1972), which explained psychological aspects of postwar Japanese social behavior.

24. See Ezra Vogel, *Japan as Number One: Lessons for America* (Cambridge, MA: Harvard University Press, 1979).

25. "Preface," in Ezra Vogel, *Japan as Number One: Lessons for America* (1979; reprint, New York: Harper Colophon Books, 1980), vii.

26. Seymour J. Lipset, *American Exceptionalism: A Double-Edged Sword* (New York: W. W. Norton, 1996), 211–266.

27. Lipset defines the "American Creed" as "liberty, egalitarianism, individualism, populism, and laissez-faire." Lipset, *American Exceptionalism,* 19.

28. Lipset, *American Exceptionalism,* 18.

29. Lipset, *American Exceptionalism,* 221–222. Concepts like "modernity" versus "tradition" are deeply problematic, used by American (and Japanese) proponents of modernization theory, which viewed the United States as a positive global model for other nations.

30. Lipset, *American Exceptionalism,* 222–223.

31. Japanese and American critics of *Nihonjinron* began publishing critiques in the mid-1980s and 1990s. See Peter Dale, *The Myth of Japanese Uniqueness* (London: Routledge, 1986); and Yoshio Sugimoto, "Making Sense of *Nihonjinron,*" *Thesis Eleven* 57, no. 1 (May 1, 1999): 81–96.

32. Elise K. Tipton, *Modern Japan: A Social and Political History* (London: Taylor and Francis Routledge, 2002), 171. See also Vogel, *Japan's New Middle Class.*

33. Tipton, *Modern Japan,* 182.

34. See Ruth Rubinstein, *Dress Codes: Meanings and Messages in American Culture* (Emeryville, CA: Avalon Publishing, 1995).

35. Ruth Rubinstein, *Society's Child: Identity, Clothing, and Style* (Boulder, CO: Westview Press, 2000), 297.

36. Lise Skov, "Fashion Trends, Japonisme and Postmodernism: Or 'What Is so Japanese about Comme des Garçons?,'" *Theory, Culture, and Society* 13, no. 3 (1996): 130–131.

37. For a scholarly study of punk music history, DIY culture, and broader political significance, see Kevin Dunn, *Global Punk: Resistance and Rebellion in Everyday Life* (London: Bloomsbury, 2016).

38. For a concise history of the punk movement's origins in interviews with musicians, publicists, artists, and fans, including Joey Ramone, Richard Hell, Joy Rider, and Chris Stein, see Steven Blush, "New York Rock: The Birth of Punk, an Oral History: Joey Ramone, Richard Hell, Blondie and Others Describe the Organic 1970s Movement for Nonconformists with an FU Attitude," Cuepoint,

Notes to Pages 204–207 335

October 11, 2016, https://medium.com/cuepoint/new-york-rock-the-birth-of -punk-an-oral-history-63ed39b27dc6.

39. "Rip It to Shreds: A History of Punk and Style," Pitchfork, https:// pitchfork.com/features/from-our-partners/9943-rip-it-to-shreds-a-history-of -punk-and-style/, accessed June 29, 2021.

40. Véronique Hyland, "How Rei Kawakubo Spent Decades Defining the Avant-Garde," The Cut, April 18, 2017, https://www.thecut.com/2017/04/fashion -designer-rei-kawakubo-has-defined-the-avant-garde.html. For a Japanese article on how the "black crow tribe" began in the 1980s among fans of Comme des Garçons and Yohji Yamamoto (b. 1943), and suitable makeup, see "80-nendai no kuro no shōgeki 'karasu-zoku' no hajimari ha? Tokuchō ya kōde to shōkai," Furugisshon, November 19, 2020, https://furugishion.com/lifestyle/80s-karasuzoku/.

41. Quoted in Blush, "New York Rock."

42. "Issey Miyake, Inc.: Corporate History," https://www.isseymiyake.com /en/company/history/, accessed June 29, 2021.

43. Judith Thurman, "Profiles: The Misfit—Rei Kawakubo Is a Japanese Avant-Gardist of Few Words, and She Changed Women's Fashion," *New Yorker*, July 4, 2005, https://www.newyorker.com/magazine/2005/07/04/the-misfit.

44. Thurman, "Profiles."

45. Hyland, "How Rei Kawakubo Spent Decades."

46. Leonard Koren, *Wabi-Sabi for Artists, Designers, Poets, and Philosophers* (Point Reyes, CA: Imperfect Publishing, 2008), 63, 93.

47. Dorinne Kondo, *About Face: Performing Race in Fashion and Theater* (New York: Routledge, 1997), 64.

48. Alexander Fury, "7 Key Themes in Rei Kawakubo's Career," *New York Times,* April 28, 2017, https://www.nytimes.com/2017/04/28/t-magazine/fashion /rei-kawakubo-comme-des-garcons-themes.html.

49. Fury, "7 Key Themes in Rei Kawakubo's Career."

50. This guide accompanies the exhibition "Rei Kawakubo / Comme des Garçons: Art of the In-Between," Metropolitan Museum of Art, New York, May 4 to September 4, 2017. Rei Kawakubo, *Comme des Garçons: Art of the In-Between* (New York: MET, 2017), 4.

51. Kawakubo, *Comme des Garçons,* 14.

52. Steff Yotka, "Runway: Chief Curator Andrew Bolton Takes Us inside the Costume Institute's 'Rei Kawakubo / Comme des Garçons: Art of the In-Between' Exhibition," *Vogue,* May 1, 2017, https://www.vogue.com/article/rei -kawakubocomme-des-garcons-art-of-the-in-between-exhibit-andrew-bolton.

53. "Kawakubo Rei-san rongu intabyū," *Asahi Shimbun,* January 19, 2012, http://www.asahi.com/fashion/beauty/TKY201201180360.html.

54. Naomi West, "Rei Kawakubo of Comme des Garçons Designs for H & M," *Telegraph,* October 26, 2008, http://fashion.telegraph.co.uk/news-features/TMG 3365690/Rei-Kawakubo-of-Comme-des-Garcons-designs-for-HandM.html.

336   *Notes to Pages 207–211*

55. "Comme Des Garcons in Collaboration with H & M This Autumn," press release, H&M France, April 3, 2008, https://about.hm.com/fr_fr/news/342 788.html.

56. West, "Rei Kawakubo of Comme des Garçons Designs for H & M."

57. "Kawakubo Rei-san rongu intabyū—fuashon de mae ni susumu," *Asahi Shimbun*, January 19, 2012, http://www.asahi.com/fashion/beauty/TKY2012011 80360.html.

58. "Kawakubo Rei-san rongu intabyū."

59. Eric Brain, "Rei Kawakubo's Louis Vuitton 'Bag with Holes' Returns in Black," Hypebeast, February 26, 2021, https://hypebeast.com/2021/2/rei-kawakubo -louis-vuitton-bag-with-holes-icon-iconoclast-celebrating-monogram-reissue-2014.

60. Kawakubo admired fashions by British designer Vivienne Westwood, who designed outfits for the punk band The Sex Pistols, and whose 1970s-era clothing shop SEX Kawakubo visited in London. Kwame Adiyia, "Parallel Cultures: The Emergence of Punk Fashion," *Fashion Forward*, March 10, 2021, https://fashionmovesforward.com/articles/2021/2/parallel-cultures-the-emergence -of-punk-fashion.

61. Bonnie English, *Japanese Fashion Designers: The Work and Influence of Issey Miyake, Yohji Yamamoto, and Rei Kawakubo* (New York: Berg, 2011), 27–28.

62. English, *Japanese Fashion Designers*, 28.

63. English, *Japanese Fashion Designers*, 9.

64. Miyake limped because of childhood radiation-induced injuries from the US atomic bombing of Hiroshima. See the December 6, 2015, interview with Issey Miyake in *Yomiuri Shimbun*.

65. Quoted in English, *Japanese Fashion Designers*, 4.

66. English, *Japanese Fashion Designers*, 28–29.

67. Miyake Design Studio, *Issey Miyake: East Meets West* (Tokyo: Heibonsha, 1978), front cover.

68. Miyake Design Studio, *Issey Miyake,* unpaginated.

69. Bernardine Morris, "Review/Fashion: Celebrating the Flair that Was Vreeland," *New York Times,* December 7, 1993, https://www.nytimes.com/1993 /12/07/news/review-fashion-celebrating-the-flair-that-was-vreeland.html.

70. Miyake Design Study, *Issey Miyake,* foreword.

71. This softcover artbook features photographs of well-known Japanese and American cultural icons, captioned with the designer's statements in Japanese and English. See Issey Miyake, *Body Works* (Tokyo: Shogaku-kan, 1983).

72. "Bodice: Fall/Winter 1980–81, Issey Miyake," Masterworks: Unpacking Fashion, November 18, 2016–February 5, 2017, Metropolitan Museum of Art, New York City, https://www.metmuseum.org/art/collection/search/675703, accessed June 9, 2021.

73. Miyake, *Body Works,* unpaginated.

74. Metropolis editors, "The A to Z of Issey Miyake," *Metropolis Magazine,* May 10, 2016, https://www.metropolismag.com/design/the-a-to-z-of-issey-miyake/.

75. "Seashell: 1985, Issey Miyake," Masterworks: Unpacking Fashion, Metropolitan Museum of Art, New York, https://www.metmuseum.org/art/collection/search/87969.

76. "Dress: 1989, Issey Miyake," Masterworks: Unpacking Fashion, Metropolitan Museum of Art, New York, https://www.metmuseum.org/art/collection/search/87948.

77. "Dress: Spring/Summer 1990, Issey Miyake," Masterworks: Unpacking Fashion, Metropolitan Museum of Art, New York, https://www.metmuseum.org/art/collection/search/83329.

78. Metropolis editors, "The A to Z of Issey Miyake."

79. See Issey Miyake with Midori Kitamura, ed., *Issey Miyake: Pleats Please* (Berlin: Taschen, 2012).

80. The "MIYAKE ISSEY EXHIBITION: The Work of Miyake Issey" ran March 16 to June 13, 2016, at the Tokyo-based National Art Center and featured Miyake's work from 1970 until 2016; https://www.nact.jp/english/exhibitions/2016/miyake_issey/, accessed June 11, 2021.

81. The exhibition, in which Miyake was a featured designer, "explores how fashion designers are reconciling the handmade and the machine-made in the creation of haute couture and avant-garde ready-to-wear." MANUS × MACHINA: Fashion in an Age of Technology exhibition, Costume Institute, Metropolitan Museum of Art, May 5 to September 5, 2016, https://www.metmuseum.org/exhibitions/listings/2016/manus-x-machina, accessed June 11, 2021.

82. Tamsin Blanchard, "Issey Miyake: 45 Years at the Forefront of Fashion," *Guardian,* April 10, 2016, https://www.theguardian.com/fashion/2016/apr/10/issey-miyake-45-years-at-the-forefront-of-fashion.

83. "Pleats Please Brand: Concept," Issey Miyake company English website, https://www.isseymiyake.com/en/brands/pleatsplease, accessed June 9, 2021.

84. See the Japanese version, with basically the same information: "Pleats Please Issey Miyake: Concept," Issey Miyake Japanese website, https://www.isseymiyake.com/ja/brands/pleatsplease, accessed June 10, 2021.

85. "Pleats Please Issey Miyake: Concept," Issey Miyake Chinese website, https://www.isseymiyake.com/cn/brands/pleatsplease, accessed June 11, 2021.

86. Author's fieldwork, Pleats Please store, Roppongi Hills Mall, Tokyo, Japan, July 17, 2018.

87. Valerie Cumming, C. W. Cunnington, and P. E. Cunnington, *The Dictionary of Fashion History* (Oxford: Berg, 2010), 64.

88. Dyese Matthews, "Fashion Archeologist and Household Name: Mary McFadden," Textiles and Clothing Museum website, Iowa State University, https://textilesclothingmuseum.wordpress.com/2018/11/09/fashion-archeologist-and-household-name-mary-mcfadden/, accessed March 3, 2020.

338 *Notes to Pages 215–219*

89. Mary McFadden, *Mary McFadden: A Lifetime of Design, Collecting and Adventure* (New York: Rizzoli International Publications, 2012), 149.

90. Frank Toppel, "Sophia Coppola on *Lost in Translation*," *Screenwriter's Monthly Magazine*, March 11, 2004, http://www.screenwritersutopia.com/article/d154bf5f.

91. Fiona Morrow, "Sofia Coppola: Hollywood Princess," *Independent*, January 2, 2004, https://www.independent.co.uk/arts-entertainment/films/features/sofia-coppola-hollywood-princess-72526.html.

92. Noriko Huruse, "A Comparative Study of Communication Style in Japan and the United States as Revealed through Content Analysis of Television Commercials" (MA thesis, Portland State University, 1978), 78.

93. Huruse, "A Comparative Study of Communication Style," 88.

94. Bob Clark, "Suntory: The Advertising that Built a Powerful Japanese Brand," 24 K Marketing: Helping Businesses Unlock Growth, July 22, 2011, https://24kmarketing.com/2011/07/suntory-advertising-that-built-powerful.html.

95. Neil McGone, "Seventy Years of Cannes: *Kagemusha* in 1980," Criterion Collection, May 24, 2017, https://www.criterion.com/current/posts/4593-seventy-years-of-cannes-kagemusha-in-1980.

96. "Suntory Whiskey commercials Coppola & Kurosawa," https://www.youtube.com/watch?v=v-A2EH0vyd4, accessed March 3, 2021.

97. Captions in "Suntory Whiskey commercials Coppola & Kurosawa."

98. Captions in "Suntory Whiskey commercials Coppola & Kurosawa."

99. Tomoko Ishiguro, "Interview with Katsumi Asaba: Graphic Designer, Art Director," PLAT: Design Archive, June 19, 2018, https://npo-plat.org/asaba-katsumi-en.html

100. "Who We Are: History, An Unparalleled Legacy," Suntory China English-language website, https://www.suntory.cn/en/who_we_are/history/#:~:text=Suntory's%20history%20in%20China%20began%20in%201979%20with%20the%20export%20of%20whisky, accessed March 21, 2021.

101. Jan Bardsley and Hiroko Hirokawa, "Branded: Bad Girls Go Shopping," in *Bad Girls of Japan*, ed. Laura Miller and Jan Bardsley (London: Palgrave Macmillan, 2005), 112.

102. Bardsley and Hirakawa, "Branded," 112.

103. Lindsay, "Shigesato Itoi, the Copywriter: A Comprehensive Look," Yomuka!, February 6, 2011, https://yomuka.wordpress.com/2011/02/06/shigesato-itoi-the-copywriter-a-comprehensive-look/.

104. In performances, Yano also wore Miyake's pleated fashions.

105. For the song, see https://www.youtube.com/watch?v=zG7VUQZvFic, accessed January 28, 2020.

106. I thank Yoshihiro Yasuhara, associate professor of Japanese Studies at Carnegie Mellon University, for making me aware of Amano and Itoi's roles. Yoshihiro Yasuhara, "The Poetic Montage as Bodily Experience: Tanikawa Shuntarō's *Coca-Cola Lessons* and Amano Yūkichi's Theory of Advertising,"

Notes to Pages 220–223

Association for Japanese Literary Studies (AJLS) 2020 annual meeting, Inclusivity and Exclusivity in Japanese Literature, Emory University, January 25, 2020.

107. Itoi still hangs this scroll in his office. Lindsay, "Shigesato Itoi."

108. Ads from the "Delicious Life Campaign" appear in Lindsay, "Shigesato Itoi."

109. Sheldon Garon, "Luxury Is the Enemy: Mobilizing Savings and Popular Thrift in Wartime Japan," *Journal of Japanese Studies* 26, no. 1 (Winter 2000): 41.

110. Garon, "Luxury Is the Enemy," 41–42.

111. Namba Kōji, *Kōkoku no kuronorojī: Masu medeia no seiki o koete* (Tokyo: Seikai shisōsha, 2010), 174–175.

112. Ishiguro, "Interview with Katsumi Asaba."

113. For the television commercial, see Rusty Fish, "Arnold Schwarzenegger 1989–91 Nissin Cup Noodle Commercials," May 23, 2014, https://www.youtube.com/watch?v=XcH1v-VdAiA.

114. Dento House website, Katsumi Asaba, https://dento-house.com/fr/designer/, accessed January 28, 2020.

115. Semi-Permanent website, "Katsumi Asaba: Art Director, Katsumi Asaba Design Studio," https://www.semipermanent.com/profiles/katsumi-asaba, accessed January 28, 2020.

116. "Designers: Katsumi Asaba," Dento House, https://dento-house.com/en/designer/katsumi-asaba/, accessed March 6, 2021.

117. Amano's key works include Amano Yukichi, *Santorī jidai o kōkoku suru sekai o kōkoku suru* (Tokyo: Nihon iitsugyō shuppansha, 1977), *Motto omoshiroi kōkoku* (Tokyo: Daiwa shobō and Chikuma shobō, 1984), and *Kōkoku mitai-na hanashi* (Tokyo: Shinchōsha, 1987).

118. Philip Brasor, "Amano: Tracing Japan's Arc through Its Ads," *Japan Times*, November 16, 2013, https://www.japantimes.co.jp/news/2013/11/16/national/media-national/amano-tracing-japans-arc-through-its-ads/.

119. Brasor, "Amano."

120. MarkeZine Editorial Department, "Masu meidia chūshin no kōkoku no shūen, 'Kōkoku hihyō' ga sōkan 30 shūnen kinen-gō de kyūkan e," *MarkeZine News*, April 10, 2008, https://markezine.jp/article/detail/3236.

121. Kazuyuki Motohashi, "Shiseido Marketing in China," in *Global Business Strategy: Multinational Corporations Venturing into Emerging Markets* (New York: Springer, 2015), https://link.springer.com/chapter/10.1007/978-4-431-55468-4_10.

122. Motohashi, "Shiseido Marketing in China."

123. Referring to Shiseidō's Europe strategy, Goto remarked: "After World War II, Japan became a classless society. Most Japanese consider themselves in the middle class. Consequently, Shiseido never encountered any difficulty in selling an all-encompassing brand, which included everything from lower priced products to the upper end items. However, this type of marketing would not work in Europe."

340 *Notes to Pages 223–225*

Yutaka Goto, "How Shiseido Succeeded in Europe: History and International Strategy," Japan Society of the United Kingdom, London, January 12, 2005, entire presentation quoted in thread by Mylene Famer, "How Shiseido Succeeded in Europe (SERGE LUTENS)," *Basenotes* perfume blog, December 2, 2005, https://www.basenotes.net/threads/180978-How-Shiseido-succeeded-in-Europe-(SERGE -LUTENS).

124. Goto, "How Shiseido Succeeded in Europe."

125. Roland Barthes, *L'Empire des Signes* (Geneva: Skira, 1970).

126. Nishino Seiji, Saitō Keita, and Satō Asami, eds., *Shiseidō monogatari— Shiseidō kigyō shiryōkan shūzōhin katarogu (1972–1997)* 3 (Tokyo: Shiseidō Publicity Department, 1998), 16.

127. Barthes dedicated the book to Maurice Pinguet, who later wrote about suicide in Japan, including on writer Mishima Yukio's (1925–1970) death. See Maurice Pinguet, *La Mort Voluntaire au Japon* (Paris: Gallimard, 1984).

128. Colin Marshall, "Ways of Seeing Japan: Roland Barthes's Tokyo 50 Years Later," *Los Angeles Review of Books,* December 31, 2016, https://lareviewofbooks .org/article/ways-seeing-japan-roland-barthess-tokyo-50-years-later/1.

129. Roland Barthes, *Empire of Signs* (New York: Hill and Wang, 1982), 70.

130. Jay Prosser, "Buddha Barthes: What Barthes Saw in Photography (That He Didn't in Literature)," *Literature and Theology* 18, no. 2 (June 2004): 213.

131. See Alan W. Watts, *The Way of Zen* (New York: Pantheon Books, 1957).

132. Barthes, *Empire of Signs,* 73.

133. Barthes, *Empire of Signs,* 83.

134. Diana Knight, "Barthes and Orientalism," in "Textual Interrelations," special issue, *New Literary History* 24, no. 3 (Summer 1993): 625.

135. Barthes, *Empire of Signs*, 107.

136. Shiseidō Corporation press release, "Shiseido Signed for Purchasing Serge Lutens Trademark," December 22, 2015, https://corp.shiseido.com/en/news /detail.html?n=00000000000015.

137. Goto, "How Shiseido Succeeded in Europe."

138. Nishino, Saitō, and Satō, *Shiseidō monogatari*, 16.

139. Goto, "How Shiseido Succeeded in Europe."

140. Correspondence by Serge Lutens representatives with blog commentator SusanneS, "Nombre Noire Shiseido for Women," *Fragrantica* perfume blog, January 21, 2017, https://www.fragrantica.com/perfume/Shiseido/Nombre-Noir-29234 .html.

141. "Serge Lutens and Shiseido's Nombre Noire: The Legendary Unicorn," *Kafkaesque* perfume blog, November 28, 2016, https://kafkaesqueblog.com/2016 /11/28/shiseido-nombre-noir-serge-lutens-legendary-unicorn-serge-lutens/.

142. My translation. The advertisement appears in Neil A. Chapman, "Into the Labyrinth: Nombre Noire Perfume by Shiseido," *The Black Narcissus* perfume blog, September 19, 2016, https://theblacknarcissus.com/2016/09/19/into -the-labyrinth-nombre-noir-parfum-by-shiseido-i98i-2/.

Notes to Pages 226–228

143. "Nombre Noire Shiseido for Women."

144. "La Fille de Berlin Serge Lutens Fragrance for Women and Men," *Fragrantica* perfume blog, https://www.fragrantica.com/perfume/Serge-Lutens /La-Fille-de-Berlin-17162.html, accessed March 24, 2021.

145. "Serge Lutens and Shiseido's Nombre Noire."

146. Fragrance Vault online catalog, Nombre Noire, https://fragrancevault .net/products/copy-of-shiseido-vintage-nombre-noir-eau-de-parfum-4ml, accessed March 24, 2021.

147. "Shiseido Signed for Purchasing Serge Lutens Trademark," December 22, 2015, https://corp.shiseido.com/en/news/detail.html?n=00000000000015.

148. Serge Lutens Boutiques French website, Le Palais Royal, https://www .sergelutens.com/boutiques, accessed March 22, 2021.

149. "Shiseido Signed for Purchasing Serge Lutens Trademark."

150. Jean-Noël Kapferer and Vincent Bastien, *The Luxury Strategy: Break the Rules of Marketing to Build Luxury Brands* (London: Kogan Page, 2012), 335. Bastien encapsulates his luxury strategy for businesses offering luxury products: "The *luxury* strategy aims at creating the highest brand value and pricing power by leveraging all intangible elements of singularity—i.e. time, heritage, country of origin, craftsmanship, man-made, small series, prestigious clients, etc." See Vincent Bastien, "Marketing to a High-End Consumer, Using the Luxury Strategy," *Entrepreneur,* November 20, 2015, https://www.entrepreneur.com/article/250745.

151. Glyn Atwal and Douglas Bryson, *Luxury Brands in China and India* (London: Palgrave Macmillan, 2017), 50.

152. In summer 2021, for "A Summer in Bloom" promotion, Serge Lutens offered a complimentary hexagonal silver spray bottle for every $200-plus order in the US market. All orders offer four samples. Promotional email to the author, June 21, 2021.

153. See Miniature Set Collection Noire, four five-milliliter bottles of Lutens' iconic La Fille de Berlin, Nuit de Cellophane, La Vierge de Fer, and Ambre Sultan scents, offered for $55. Serge Lutens North American retail website, https://www .sergelutens.com/us/perfumes/miniature-set.html, accessed June 25, 2021; and see Discovery Set Collection Noire, eight four-milliliter vials arranged in rainbow color order, consisting of La Fille de Berlin, Nuit de Cellophane, Fils de Joie, Fleurs d'Oranger, Un Bois Vanille, Fémininité de Bois, L'Orpheline, and Ambre Sultan, https://www.sergelutens.com/us/perfumes/discovery-set-collection-noire.html, accessed June 25, 2021.

154. See the Serge Lutens North American website, https://www.sergelutens .com/us/, accessed June 25, 2021.

155. For the perfume bottles, see Di Ser's website, https://www.diser-parfum .com/en/index.html, accessed March 26, 2021.

156. Bastien, "Marketing to a High-End Consumer."

157. Branding language for Serge Lutens products quoted in "Shiseido Signed for Purchasing Serge Lutens Trademark."

342 *Notes to Pages 228–232*

158. "Christopher Sheldrake," *Fragrantica* perfume blog, https://www.fragrantica.com/noses/Christopher_Sheldrake.html, accessed June 9, 2021.

159. "Shiseido Signed for Purchasing Serge Lutens Trademark."

160. Sarah Ahssen, "Shiseido Grows 11.8% in EMEA Region, 5.7% Worldwide in 2019," *Fashion Network,* February 26, 2020, https://us.fashionnetwork.com/news/Shiseido-grows-11-8-in-emea-region-5-7-worldwide-in-2019,1191007.html.

161. "About Us: History," Shiseidō website, https://corp.shiseido.com/en/company/history/, accessed March 26, 2021.

162. Motohashi, "Shiseido Marketing in China."

163. "Shiseido Company, Limited," Reference for Business: Company History Index, https://www.referenceforbusiness.com/history2/14/Shiseido-Company-Limited.html, accessed April 11, 2021.

164. Motohashi, "Shiseido Marketing in China."

165. Motohashi, "Shiseido Marketing in China."

166. Motohashi, "Shiseido Marketing in China."

167. Sheridan Prasso, "Battle for the Face of China: L'Oréal, Shiseido, Estée Lauder—the World's Leading Cosmetics Companies Are Vying for a Piece of a Booming Market," *Fortune,* December 12, 2005, https://archive.fortune.com/magazines/fortune/fortune_archive/2005/12/12/8363110/index.htm.

168. Prasso, "Battle for the Face of China."

169. Prasso, "Battle for the Face of China."

170. Shiseidō press release, "Shiseido Launches New Skincare Line WASO Targeting Millennials," Shiseido corporate website, June 12, 2017, https://corp.shiseido.com/en/news/detail.html?n=00000000002206.

171. Shiseidō press release, "Shiseido Launches New Skincare Line."

172. Shiseidō online retail site; see https://www.shiseido.com/us/en/sets-and-travel/skincare-starter-kits/, accessed April 12, 2021. As of mid-2021, these were all sold out—revealing high popularity for "limited edition" status in the United States.

173. Shiseidō 2020 Annual Report, "Regional Overview: 2020 Results," https://corp.shiseido.com/report/en/2020/regional/?tab=1, accessed June 26, 2021.

174. These figures and statistics are quoted in "Beauty Buzz: These Consumers Will Dominate the Luxury Market," Beauty Packaging, January 26, 2018, https://www.beautypackaging.com/issues/2018-01-01/view_beauty-buzz/these-consumers-will-dominate-the-luxury-market-507101/.

175. "Beauty Buzz."

176. "Beauty Buzz."

177. Glyn and Bryson, *Luxury Brands in China and India,* 49–50.

178. Glyn and Bryson, *Luxury Brands in China and India,* 49–50.

179. This section contains a much-edited adaptation of small portions of my previously published work. See Annika A. Culver, "Shiseidō's 'Empire of Beauty': Marketing Japanese Modernity in Northeast Asia, 1932–1945," *Shashi—the Jour-*

Notes to Pages 233–236 343

nal of Japanese Business and Company History 2, no. 2 (2013): 11–12. I thank Martha Chaiklin, *Shashi*'s editor, for permission. Notes from author's July 2012 fieldwork in Tokyo, Japan.

180. Francesca Regalado, "Business Trends: Asia's Skin Whitening Market Reckons with Global Antiracist Push—Companies Including Johnson & Johnson and Unilever to Change Product Lineup," *Nikkei News,* June 1, 2020, https:// asia.nikkei.com/Business/Business-trends/Asia-s-skin-whitening-market-reckons -with-global-antiracist-push.

181. Phillip Martin, "Why White Skin Is All the Rage in Asia: From Pills to Lasers to Cream, What's Fueling the Boom in Skin Whitening Procedures across the Continent?," *Global Post,* November 25, 2009, http://www.globalpost.com /dispatch/china-and-its-neighbors/091123/asia-white-skin-treatments-risks.

182. Quoted in Prasso, "Battle for the Face of China."

183. Quoted in Martin, "Why White Skin Is All the Rage in Asia."

184. Masako Isa and Eric Kramer, "Adopting the Caucasian 'Look': Reorganizing the Minority Face," in *The Emerging Monoculture: Assimilation and the "Model Minority,"* ed. Eric Mark Kramer (Westport, CT: Praeger, 2003), 66.

185. Isa and Kramer, "Adopting the Caucasian 'Look.'"

186. Shiseidō news release, "Shiseidō to Introduce Corporate Culture and Promote Sales at Event in Russia," February 2011, https://corp.shiseido.com/en /releimg/1866-e.pdf.

187. Geoffrey Jones, *Beauty Imagined: A History of the Global Beauty Industry* (New York: Oxford University Press, 2010), 372.

188. Jones, *Beauty Imagined,* 272.

189. Shiseidō news release, "Shiseidō to Introduce Corporate Culture."

190. For details, see chapter 4.

Chapter 7: The Rise of "Cool Japan" and Japanese Luxury-Consuming Communities in the Virtual World

1. Walter Benjamin, *The Arcades Project,* trans. Howard Eiland and Kevin McLaughlin, ed. Rolf Tiedemann (Cambridge, MA: Belknap Press of Harvard University Press, 1999), 204–205.

2. This now-problematic term consciously erases Black and Latinx urban and hip-hop cultures giving rise to these fashion trends, and conflates with cultural appropriation. Priya Elan, the *Guardian*'s deputy fashion editor, quotes designer Nasir Mazar, "Why not just call it fashion," when asked to replace "streetwear." Columnist Micha Frazer-Caroll, a *Vogue* journalist, believes, "The popularisation of streetwear should be seen as appropriationist when designers and consumers don't pay due respect and, where appropriate, money to the style's roots." See Priya Elan, "Is Streetwear a Dismissive Term?," *Guardian,* February 2, 2016, https://www.theguardian.com/fashion/2016/feb/02/is-streetwear-a-racist-term, and Micha Frazer-Caroll, "Why We Need to Rethink the Term Streetwear," *Vogue,*

June 18, 2019, https://www.vogue.co.uk/article/is-the-term-streetwear-in-need-of-a
-makeover.

3. Meghan Warner Mettler, *How to Reach Japan by Subway: America's Fascination with Japanese Culture, 1945–1965* (Lincoln: University of Nebraska Press, 2018), 9.

4. Mettler, *How to Reach Japan by Subway,* 4–5.

5. Rich Weidman, *The Beat Generation FAQ: All That's Left to Know about the Angelheaded Hipsters* (Lanham, MD: Rowman and Littlefield, 2015), Kindle.

6. Weidman, *The Beat Generation FAQ.*

7. Heather Chen, "Godzilla Finally Gets Citizenship in Japan," *BBC News,* June 3, 2015, https://www.bbc.com/news/world-asia-32987622.

8. Chen, "Godzilla Finally Gets Citizenship in Japan."

9. Anne Allison, *Millennial Monsters: Japanese Toys and the Global Imagination* (Berkeley: University of California Press, 2006), 93–127.

10. Joseph Nye, *Bound to Lead: The Changing Nature of American Power* (London: Basic Books, 1990).

11. Joseph Nye, *Soft Power: The Means to Success in World Politics* (New York: PublicAffairs, 2004).

12. Nye, *Soft Power,* x.

13. Matsuda Takeshi, *Soft Power and Its Perils: US Cultural Policy in Early Postwar Japan and Permanent Dependency* (Washington, DC: Woodrow Wilson Center Press, 2007), *Sengo Nihon ni okeru Amerika no sofuto pawā: han'eikyūteki izon no kigen* (Tokyo: Iwanami shoten, 2008), and *Taibei izon no kigen: Amerika no sofuto pawā no senryaku* (Tokyo: Iwanami shoten, 2015).

14. Nancy Stalker, "'Cool Japan' as Cultural Superpower: 1980s–2010s," in *Japan: History and Culture from Classical to Cool* (Berkeley: University of California Press, 2018), 377.

15. Atsuko Fukase, "Tokyo Launches 'Cool Japan' Investment Fund," *Wall Street Journal,* November 18, 2013, https://blogs.wsj.com/japanrealtime /2013/11/18/tokyo-launches-cool-japan-investment-fund/.

16. Cool Japan Fund, "Message: President and CEO, Naoki Kitagawa," https://www.cj-fund.co.jp/en/about/cjfund.html, accessed January 15, 2020.

17. Karen Ressler, "Cool Japan Fund Appoints Sony Music Entertainment's Naoki Kitagawa as New CEO," Anime News Network, April 19, 2018, https:// www.animenewsnetwork.com/news/2018-04-19/cool-japan-fund-appoints -sony-music-entertainment-naoki-kitagawa-as-new-ceo/.130610.

18. Cool Japan Fund, "About," https://www.cj-fund.co.jp/en/about/message .html, accessed January 15, 2020.

19. Cool Japan Fund, "What Is Cool Japan Fund?," https://www.cj-fund.co .jp/en/about/cjfund.html, accessed January 15, 2020.

20. "History of ASICS," https://corp.asics.com/en/about_asics/history, ac-cessed May 14, 2020.

21. ASICS website, 1983 Pointgetter, https://www.asics.com/jp/ja-jp/mk/sportstyle/limited?car=gnavi-sportstyle, accessed May 14, 2020.

22. ASICS website, Glideride, https://www.asics.com/us/en-us/glideride/p/ANA_1012A930-001.html?size=9&width=Standard, accessed May 14, 2020.

23. ASICS website, Glideride.

24. ASICS website, Glideride.

25. For American markets, ASICS offers a Japanese-made line, ranging from $220 to $375. The website luxuriates the product's Japanese heritage and craftsmanship, while its leather comes from Kobe beef cattle. ASICS Japan Collection, ASICS website, https://www.asics.com/us/en-us/made-in-japan/c/aa90000037/, accessed February 28, 2021.

26. Keith Estiler, "The Influence of Chicano Culture in Fashion as Told by Leading Latino Pioneers in the Industry: Spanto of Born x Raised, Mister Cartoon and Willy Chavarria Relay Personal Insights," Hypebeast, February 20, 2017, https://hypebeast.com/2017/2/chicano-influence-in-fashion.

27. Scholars should consider key debates on cultural appropriation when examining cultural transference; however, these transcend my primary focus. See Patti Tamara Lenard and Peter Balint, "What Is (the Wrong of) Cultural Appropriation?," *Ethnicities* 20, no. 2 (April 1, 2020): 331–352. Lenard and Balint indicate that "we define cultural appropriation as the appropriation of something of cultural value, usually a symbol or a practice, to others. . . . Two additional conditions must be present to define an act of cultural appropriation: the presence of significant contestation around the act of appropriation, and the presence of knowledge (or negligent culpability) in the act of appropriation" (331).

28. Jamila Brown, "Randy Casual: 'Stop Mystifying Japan': Streetwear and Breaking into the Industry with the Fashion Youtuber," *Metropolis: Japan's No. 1 English Magazine*, October 24, 2019, https://metropolisjapan.com/reggie-casual/#:~:text=What%20is%20The%20Casual%3F,a%20part%20of%20the%20conversation.

29. Randy Casual, "The GOLDEN AGE of Japanese Street Fashion / The 90's," March 19, 2018, https://www.youtube.com/watch?v=eqskIlxj3dM.

30. Fujiwara scours the Internet and international fashion for developing trends and new artistic and cultural phenomena, describing his blog *Ring of Colour,* appearing in late 2015, as "a digital media collection of things worth knowing about," while international online trend magazine *High Snobiety* calls it "part Instagram feed, part Tumblr blog, part news site, it's a place where Fujiwara and likeminded peers can share discoveries, news, and tidbits." Gregk Foley, "How Hiroshi Fujiwara Changed Streetwear Forever," *High Snobiety,* https://www.highsnobiety.com/p/hiroshi-fujiwara-history/, accessed March 11, 2021. On May 29, 2016, Fujiwara posted the promotion video for my digital archive, The Oliver L. Austin Photographic Collection, featuring 1,000 rare color photographs of postwar Japan from 1946 to 1950. Fujiwara notes: "I watched on Facebook (a recent topic of conversation?) Harajuku 70 years ago.

346   *Notes to Pages 244–245*

It's photography from this person. . . . Similarly, there are lots of photographs of Tokyo. Invaluable." See Hiroshi Fujiwara, "A Brief Introduction to the Oliver L. Austin Collection," *Ring of Colour* (blog), May 29, 2016, https://ringofcolour.com/en/archives/18317.

31. Foley, "How Hiroshi Fujiwara Changed Streetwear Forever."

32. Philip Santiago, phone interview by author, August 3, 2021.

33. Luis Ruano, "NIGO and Jun Takahashi: NOWHERE," Hypebeast, September 28, 2009, https://hypebeast.com/2009/9/interview-nigo-jun-takahashi.

34. Santiago, phone interview with author.

35. Santiago, phone interview with author.

36. An egregious cultural appropriation of Japan's "Harajuku style" remains singer-celebrity Gwen Stefani's (b. 1969) 2004 album *Love. Angel. Music. Baby* and 2005 Harajuku Lovers tour, where she hired four Japanese American backup dancers named to match the album title, dressed in reimagined Japanese schoolgirl uniforms for her performances and videos and paid to follow her like fans. Criticized by notable Asian Americans, including comedian Margaret Cho (b. 1968), who in 2005 likened the performances to a "minstrel show" and the Japanese schoolgirl uniform to "blackface," Stefani still included two dancers in her 2021 comeback single "Let Me Reintroduce Myself." Margaret Cho, "Harajuku Girls," personal website, October 31, 2005, https://margaretcho.com/2005/10/31/harajuku-girls/; and Julia Emmanuele, "Gwen Stefani Still Doesn't Think Her 'Harajuku Girls' Era Was Cultural Appropriation," *Bustle,* November 20, 2019, https://www.bustle.com/p/gwen-stefani-says-her-harajuku-girls-era-wasnt-cultural-appropriation-19368917. In 2005, Stefani conceived the Harajuku Lovers perfume series, where twenty-eight fragrances were created from 2008 until 2014, referencing her dancers Love, Angel, Music, and Baby. "Harajuku Lovers Perfume and Cologne," *Fragrantica* perfume blog, https://www.fragrantica.com/designers/Harajuku-Lovers.html, accessed March 14, 2021.

37. Marc Richardson, "The Evolving Exchange between America and Japan," Grailed, January 17, 2019, https://www.grailed.com/drycleanonly/america-japan-style-relationship.

38. Hideki Goya, "Story of My Life: Interview with Keizō Shimizu—*Shimizu Keizō to Nepensu. Sono ashiato to korekara*," Nepenthes website, https://nepenthes.co.jp/bunker/feature/52/f52_2.html, accessed March 13, 2021.

39. "Daiki Suzuki," Hypebeast, https://hypebeast.com/tags/daiki-suzuki, accessed March 12, 2021; Thorsten Ingvaldsen, "NEPENTHES Founder Keizo Shimizu & Engineered Garments' Daiki Suzuki Talk Americana," Hypebeast, March 10, 2020, https://hypebeast.com/2020/3/nepenthes-needles-engineered-garments-keizo-shimizu-daiki-suzuki-ssense-interview.

40. Lucy Thorpe, "Uncovering Woolrich's 190-Year Legacy with Daiki Suzuki and Kara Jubin," *High Snobiety,* September 22, 2020, https://www.highsnobiety.com/p/woolrich-archive-kara-jubin-daiki-suzuki/.

Notes to Pages 245–249

41. W. David Marx, "The Climb of Ivy: The Styles of the American Ivy League Transform the Fashions of 1960s Japan," *Lapham's Quarterly* 8, no. 4 (Fall 2015), https://www.laphamsquarterly.org/fashion/climb-ivy.

42. Marx, "The Climb of Ivy."

43. The Olympics took place from October 10 until October 24, 1964.

44. W. David Marx, "Stalking the Wild Madras Wearers of the Ivy League," *New Yorker,* December 1, 2015, https://www.newyorker.com/culture/culture-desk/stalking-the-wild-madras-wearers-of-the-ivy-league.

45. "The Complete Tokyo 1964 Olympics Film / Olympic History," *Tōkyō orinpikku,* directed by Kon Ichikawa, https://www.youtube.com/watch?v=WHt0e AdCCns, accessed February 11, 2020.

46. Gunner Park, "Take Ivy: Kensuke Ishizu, the Godfather of Japanese Prep," Grailed, June 26, 2017, https://www.grailed.com/drycleanonly/kensuike-ishizu-master-class.

47. W. David Marx, "The Legendary *Take Ivy* Film," *Ivy Style,* November 27, 2011, http://www.ivy-style.com/the-legendary-take-ivy-film.html.

48. Marx, "The Legendary *Take Ivy* Film."

49. Park, "Take Ivy."

50. Ishizu Shōsuke, Kurosu Toshiyuki, and Hasegawa Hajime, with photographs by Hayashida Teruyoshi, *Take Ivy* (New York: Powerhouse Books, 2010).

51. I first saw *Take Ivy* at Chicago's Ralph Lauren store, which opened in the late 1990s. Powerhouse Books reprinted it in 2010; I was intrigued by its Japanese provenance, in a reprint emerging when Japan's government promoted "Cool Japan" as a national rebranding strategy.

52. Kent Garrett and Jeanne Ellsworth, "As the Nation Shifted from 'Negro' to Black," *Harvard Gazette,* February 7, 2020, https://news.harvard.edu/gazette/story/2020/02/last-negroes-at-harvard-traces-lives-class-of-1963/.

53. Kent Garrett and Jeanne Ellsworth, *The Last Negroes at Harvard: The Class of 1963 and the 18 Young Men Who Changed Harvard Forever* (New York: Houghton Mifflin Harcourt, 2020).

54. Tanya Dutta, "The Demographics of the Ivy League," *College Monk* (blog), October 13, 2020, https://www.thecollegemonk.com/blog/ivy-league-demographics.

55. Lisa Birnbach, *The Preppy Handbook* (New York: Workman, 1980).

56. Japanese casual fashion enthusiasts of cholo subcultures from East Los Angeles in Tokyo and Osaka created personal versions of the American trend. Omar Villegas, "Watch a Mini-Doc about Japan's 'Chicanos,'" *Mitú,* February 6, 2017, https://wearemitu.com/newsfeed/watch-a-mini-doc-about-japans-chicanos/.

57. Jian DeLeon, *The Incomplete: Highsnobiety Guide to Street Fashion and Culture* (Berlin: Die Gestalten Verlag, 2018).

58. Foley, "How Hiroshi Fujiwara Changed Streetwear Forever."

348   *Notes to Pages 249–252*

59. Jian DeLeon, "How Hip-Hop Left a Lasting Influence on Streetwear & Fashion," *Highsnobiety,* https://www.highsnobiety.com/p/hip-hop-streetwear-fashion-influence/, accessed March 4, 2021.

60. Gregk Foley, "The Trends and Brands That Defined '90s Hip-Hop Fashion," *Highsnobiety,* November 2020, https://www.highsnobiety.com/p/90s-hip-hop-fashion.

61. Gary Warnett, "The History of the Hoodie," September 18, 2015, https://www.youtube.com/watch?v=OKTR6kMs--8&t=10s.

62. Warnett, "The History of the Hoodie."

63. Maria Mora, "I Finally Feel Seen: What It's Like to Be Latinx in Streetwear Right Now," *Complex,* October 15, 2020, https://www.complex.com/style/latinx-in-streetwear-right-now.

64. Jonathan Sawyer, "Bape and Levis Debut Split Trucker Jackets: See Them Here," *Highsnobiety,* December 2, 2019, https://www.highsnobiety.com/tag/a-bathing-ape/.

65. Santiago, interview with author.

66. Santiago, interview with author.

67. Roland Kelts, *Japanamerica: How Japanese Pop Culture Has Invaded the US* (Basingstoke, UK: Palgrave Macmillan, 2006), 18.

68. "A Bathing Ape," *Highsnobiety,* https://www.highsnobiety.com/tag/a-bathing-ape/, accessed January 15, 2020.

69. Quoted in Kelts, *Japanamerica,* 18.

70. "A Bathing Ape."

71. Lauren Cochrane, "Nigo: 'Uniqlo Is Streetwear Too,'" *Guardian,* January 21, 2014, https://www.theguardian.com/fashion/2014/jan/21/nigo-uniqlo-streetwear-bathing-ape.

72. Cochrane, "Nigo."

73. Lines Murakami designed for Louis Vuitton include Cherry Blossom (2003), Panda (2004), Cerises (2005), MOCA Hands (2007, for a Museum of Contemporary Art Los Angeles exhibition), Monogramouflage (2008), and Cosmic Blossom (2010), while the much-beloved Monogram Multicolor collection was discontinued in 2015. See Haotian C., "A Colorful Reinterpretation of the Classic Monogram," Rebag, September 29, 2020, https://rebag.com/thevault/louis-vuitton-101-takashi-murakamis-monogram-multicolor-collection/.

74. Jian DeLeon, "How Hip-Hop Left a Lasting Influence on Streetwear & Fashion."

75. The 2002 novel *Shimotsuma Monogatari: Yankī-chan to Rōrita-chan,* made into a live-action drama in 2004, arrived in the United States in 2005 as *Kamikaze Girls.*

76. Jonathon Sawyer, "BAPE and Levi's Split Trucker Jackets Can Be Mixed and Matched," *Highsnobiety,* https://www.highsnobiety.com/p/bape-levis-split-trucker-jacket/, accessed January 15, 2020.

77. A Bathing Ape, Instagram, https://www.instagram.com/p/B5kpbB4hq22/?utm_source=ig_embed, accessed January 15, 2020.

Notes to Pages 253–257

78. Benjamin, *The Arcades Project,* 204–205.

79. Benjamin, *The Arcades Project,* 206.

80. Benjamin, *The Arcades Project,* 206.

81. Benjamin, *The Arcades Project,* 207.

82. Benjamin, *The Arcades Project,* 207.

83. Benjamin, *The Arcades Project,* 207.

84. Alex Martin, "Defining the Heisei Era: Part 7—Obsession: Examining the Rise of Otaku Culture," *Japan Times,* November 24, 2018, https://features.japantimes.co.jp/heisei-moments-part-7-obsession/.

85. Hiroki Azuma, *Otaku: Japan's Database Animals* (Minneapolis: University of Minnesota Press, 2009), 11; Azuma Hiroki, *Dōbutsuka suru posuto modan—otaku kara mita Nihon shakai* (Tokyo: Kōdansha, 2001).

86. Azuma, *Otaku,* 11.

87. Azuma, *Otaku,* 3.

88. Azuma, *Otaku,* 3.

89. Mathieu Deflem, "Anomie: History of the Concept," in *International Encyclopedia of the Social and Behavioral Sciences,* 2nd ed. (Amsterdam: Elsevier, 2015), 719.

90. Likely mentally ill, Miyazaki was judged "sane" by Tokyo's High Court and received the death penalty. "Court Rules Serial Killer Miyazaki Sane," *Japan Times,* June 29, 2001, https://www.japantimes.co.jp/news/2001/06/29/national/court-rules-serial-killer-miyazaki-sane/.

91. Karl Schoenberger, "Sordid Serial-Killing Exposes the Other Side of Innocence in Japan," *Los Angeles Times,* September 9, 1989, https://www.latimes.com/archives/la-xpm-1989-09-09-mn-1579-story.html.

92. Minoru Matsutani, "Serial Killer Miyazaki, Two Others Hanged—'80s Child Slayings Stunned Japan; Executions under Hatoyama Hit 13," *Japan Times,* June 18, 2008, https://www.japantimes.co.jp/news/2008/06/18/national/serial-killer-miyazaki-two-others-hanged/#.XldAyRNKg0o.

93. Wire Report, "Serial Child Killer Tsutomu Miyazaki, 2 Others Executed," *Japan Today,* June 17, 2008, https://japantoday.com/category/crime/serial-child-killer-tsutomu-miyazaki-executed.

94. Matt Alt, "Shigeru Mizuki's War-Haunted Art and Life," *New Yorker,* December 10, 2015, https://www.newyorker.com/culture/culture-desk/shigeru-mizukis-war-haunted-creatures.

95. Mizuki Shigeru, *Sōin gyokusai seyo!* (Tokyo: Kodansha, 1973), and *Onwards towards Our Noble Deaths,* trans. Jocelyne Allen (Montreal: Drawn and Quarterly, 2011).

96. Samuel Yamashita, *Leaves in an Autumn of Emergencies: Selections from the Wartime Diaries of Ordinary Japanese* (Honolulu: University of Hawai'i Press, 2005), 37–38.

97. Mizuki Shigeru, *Komikku Shōwa-shi* (Tokyo: Kōdansha, 1994), and *Shōwa: A History of Japan, 1939–1944* (Montreal: Drawn and Quarterly, 2014).

98. Azuma, *Otaku,* 15.

99. Kiara R. Cromer, Norman B. Schmidt, and Dennis L. Murphey, "Do Traumatic Events Influence the Clinical Expression of Compulsive Hoarding?," *Behaviour Research and Therapy* 45, no. 11 (November 2007): 2581–2592.

100. Chris Wright, "The Asian Watch Market: The Hidden History of Swiss Watchmaking's Biggest Rivals," Gear Patrol, February 12, 2019, https://gearpatrol.com/2019/02/12/best-watches-from-the-asian-market/.

101. G-Shock website, BABY-G line, Decora styles, BA110TM-7A, https://www.gshock.com/watches/baby-g/ba110tm-7a, accessed February 23, 2021.

102. As a graduate student in Tokyo, when in 2004 I purchased my handheld "mini" Casio EX-word floris XD-R970 (February 2003 release) electronic dictionary at Shinjuku's Bic Camera, I chose it to fit into a small purse, with a blue-lavender top and pearlescent gray keyboard. Its "cute" size and soothing colors allegedly rendered this high-technology item unintimidating and user-friendly to women consumers.

103. William Kelly, ed., *Fanning the Flames: Fans and Consumer Culture in Contemporary Japan* (Albany: State University of New York Press, 2004), 7.

104. Kelly, *Fanning the Flames,* 11.

105. Mark Bernardo, "The History of Seiko through 12 Milestone Seiko Watches," WatchTime, July 31, 2019, https://www.watchtime.com/featured/timepiece-timeline-milestone-seiko-watches/.

106. "Grand Seiko Collector's Guide," *The Spring Bar,* September 1, 2019, https://thespringbar.com/blogs/guides/grand-seiko-collectors-guide/.

107. Grand Seiko website, "Kintaro Hattori 160th Anniversary Limited Edition," https://www.grand-seiko.com/us-en/collections/sbgz005j, accessed February 23, 2021.

108. Grand Seiko website, "Design," https://www.grand-seiko.com/us-en/about/design, accessed February 23, 2021.

109. Grand Seiko website, "Design."

110. Gisbert Brunner, "Seiko: A Chronograph Chronology," WatchTime, November 17, 2020, https://www.watchtime.com/featured/seiko-a-chronograph-chronology/.

111. James Lambdin, "The 'Colonel Pogue' Seiko 6139," *DreamChrono* (blog), November 23, 2013, https://www.dreamchrono.com/2013/11/seiko-6139-pogue/.

112. Koren interpreted *wabi-sabi* in mid-1980s art and design publications, popularized in the mid-1990s in Leonard Koren, *Wabi-Sabi for Artists, Designers, Poets and Philosophers* (Berkeley, CA: Stone Bridge Press, 1994).

113. "Please Tell Me What *Wabi* Means," The WatchSite: The Seiko and Citizen Watch Forum, September 8, 2010, https://www.thewatchsite.com/threads/please-tell-me-what-wabi-means.7891/.

114. TimeTracker, Watchuseek website, Seiko Forum, "Wabi? This Is Wabi!," March 21, 2013, https://forums.watchuseek.com/f21/wabi-wabi-835390.html.

Notes to Pages 262–265 351

115. "The Four Kashio Brothers," Casio Worldwide website, https://world.casio.com/corporate/brothers/, accessed April 16, 2021.

116. "What Did the Original G-Shock Cost in 1983?," Casio G-Shock Forum, Watchseek, February 14, 2008, https://www.watchuseek.com/threads/what-did-the-original-g-shock-cost-in-1983.124775/#:~:text=Registered,-Joined%20Jun%204&text=The%20DW%2D5000%20cost%20%2459.95%20when%20new.

117. "The History of the Casio G-Shock Watch," *G-Central: The G-Shock Watch Fan Blog,* February 2021, https://www.g-central.com/g-shock-history/.

118. Vivian Morelli, "The Shock over Casio's New G-Shock," *New York Times,* March 20, 2019, https://www.nytimes.com/2019/03/20/fashion/watches-casio-g-shock.html.

119. Su Jiaxian, "Introducing the $70,000 G-Shock Limited Edition in 18K Yellow Gold," SJX, February 26, 2019, https://watchesbysjx.com/2019/02/g-shock-pure-gold-18k-yellow-gold.html.

120. Ariel Adams, "'Cool and Fun' Made in Japan: A Visit to G-Shock Watch Headquarters," *A Blog to Watch,* October 23, 2016, https://www.ablogtowatch.com/casio-g-shock-watch-headquarters-visit-made-japan-cool-fun/2.

121. G-Shock News, "Casio Is Shifting G-Shock Production from China to Thailand," *G-Central: The G-Shock Watch Fan Blog,* September 3, 2019, https://www.g-central.com/casio-is-shifting-g-shock-production-from-china-to-thailand/.

122. "Where Are G-Shocks Manufactured?," Watchuseek forum, June 12, 2010, https://www.watchuseek.com/threads/where-are-g-shocks-manufactured.411447/.

123. G-Shock press release, "G-SHOCK Unveils New, Two-Toned Colorway For Premium G-STEEL Collection," February 17, 2021, https://www.gshock.com/g-latest/news/g-shock-unveils-new-two-toned-colorway-for-premium-g-steel-collection.

124. "Suntory Whisky: The Yamazaki 12-Year-Old Pure Malt Special Edition 1980's Bottling 750mL," Dan Murphys, https://www.danmurphys.com.au/product/DM_ER_2000004020_YAM-12PM/suntory-whisky-the-yamazaki-12-year-old-pure-malt-special-edition-1980-s-bottling-750ml, accessed May 28, 2021.

125. Jim Frederick, "Japan's Whisky Rebellion," *Roads and Kingdoms,* February 26, 2014, https://roadsandkingdoms.com/travel-guide/tokyo/japans-whisky-rebellion/.

126. Frederick, "Japan's Whisky Rebellion."

127. Robert Simonson, "Japanese Whiskeys, Translated from the Scottish," *New York Times,* September 11, 2012, https://www.nytimes.com/2012/09/12/dining/japanese-whiskeys-gain-ground-in-america.html.

128. Jake Emin, "Why the World Is Hooked on Japanese Whisky," *Distiller,* March 30, 2019, https://distiller.com/articles/world-hooked-japanese-whisky.

352 *Notes to Pages 265–267*

129. "The Story of Japanese Whisky: Japan Distills a World-Class Whisky Tradition," *Nippon News,* September 3, 2014, https://www.nippon.com/en/views /b04201/?pnum=2.

130. "World Whiskies Award 2008," *A Wardrobe of Whisky* (blog), http:// www.awardrobeofwhisky.com/awards/World-Whiskies-Awards/2008# .YLpjfH1Kjeo, accessed June 3, 2021.

131. "World Whiskies Award 2008" and "Japan Distills a World-Class Whisky Tradition," *Nippon News,* September 3, 2014, https://www.nippon.com /en/views/b04201/.

132. Dave Broom, *The Way of Whisky: A Journey around Japanese Whisky* (London: Mitchell Beazley Publishers, 2017), 9.

133. Suntory describes the highball as originating in Japan. Suntory News Studio press release, "The History of the Highball: The Journey from Japan to the United States," August 23, 2019, http://us.suntory.com/news-studio/the-history-of -the-highball-the-journey-from-japan-to-the-united-states-1.html.

134. "Beam Suntory Releases Japanese Blended Whisky," *The Spirits Business,* June 10, 2016, https://www.thespiritsbusiness.com/2016/06/beam-suntory -releases-japanese-blended-whisky/.

135. Jack Rear, "Toki Whisky Could Finally Convince Millennials to Start Drinking the Spirit," Verdict, May 18, 2018, https://www.verdict.co.uk/toki-whis ky-japanese-high-ball.

136. "Suntory Holdings to Acquire Beam in $16 Billion Transaction," Beam Suntory website, January 13, 2014, https://www.beamsuntory.com/en/news /suntory-holdings-to-acquire-beam-in-16-billion-transaction#:~:text=OSAKA% 2C%20JAPAN%20and%20DEERFIELD%2C%20ILLINOIS,Holdings%20 Limited%20and%20Beam%20Inc.

137. Rear, "Toki Whisky Could Finally Convince Millennials to Start Drinking the Spirit."

138. Gabrielle Glaser, *Her Best-Kept Secret: Why Women Drink—and How They Can Regain Control* (New York: Simon and Schuster, 2013); and Caitlin Flanagan, "How Helicopter Parenting Can Cause Binge Drinking," *Atlantic,* September 2016, https://www.theatlantic.com/magazine/archive/2016/09/how -helicopter-parents-cause-binge-drinking/492722/, accessed June 3, 2021.

139. Kate Julian, "America Has a Drinking Problem," *Atlantic,* July/August 2021, https://www.theatlantic.com/magazine/archive/2021/07/america-drinking -alone-problem/619017/.

140. Metacake, an American online ecommerce marketing consulting firm, listed ways to approach this generation that "craves authenticity." See "Marketing to Millennials: The One Thing You Need to Sell to the Largest Generation," Metacake, April 18, 2018, https://metacake.com/marketing-millennials-one-thing-need -sell-largest-generation/.

141. "Rituals: Highball," videos entitled "Art of the Highball (Videos Filmed in London and Tokyo)," and "Toki Highball Craft (Filmed in NYC)," Suntory

Whisky website, https://whisky.suntory.com/en/global/products/toki#rituals, accessed June 3, 2021.

142. Niccola Carruthers, "Beam Suntory to Relocate HQ to New York City," *The Spirits Business,* January 27, 2021, https://www.thespiritsbusiness.com /2021/01/beam-suntory-to-relocate-hq-to-nyc/.

143. See Brian Ashcraft, Yuji Kawasaki, and Idzuhiko Ueda, *Japanese Whisky: The Ultimate Guide to the World's Most Desirable Spirit with Tasting Notes from Japan's Leading Whisky Blogger* (Tokyo: Charles Tuttle, 2018).

144. Like whisky, sake drinking is down in Japan, so Japanese companies aim to promote the drink abroad. In 2019, the United States was Japan's largest sake importer, with $63 million in products. Global sake markets are projected to rise from $9.3 billion to $13 billion in 2027. The Embassy of Japan even supported a sake promotional video targeting American consumers. Weston Konishi, President, Sake Brewers Association of North America, "Sake Diplomacy: The International Impact of Japan's National Alcohol," sponsored by YCAPS Getting to Know Japan Webinar Series and Japan Foundation's Center for Global Partnership, Zoom, June 1, 2021, https://www.ycaps.org/sake-diplomacy.

145. "Brace for Political Surprises, Economic Waves in 2017: Nikkei Panel— Experts Warn of US-China Friction, Upsets in Europe," *Nikkei Asian Review,* January 14, 2017, https://asia.nikkei.com/Economy/Brace-for-political-surprises-eco nomic-waves-in-2017-Nikkei-panel.

146. Kaō Company, Malaysia, website, "Asience: Science," https://web.kao .com/my/asience/science/, accessed October 4, 2019.

147. Kaō Company, Malaysia, website, "Awaken the Beauty within You with the New and Improved ASIENCE," March 1, 2010, https://www.kao.com /my/news_20100103.html.

148. Kaō Company, "Asience."

149. Kaō Company, "Asience."

150. Karl Marx, "Section 4: The Fetishism of Commodities and the Secret Thereof," in *Capital,* vol. 1, https://www.marxists.org/archive/marx/works/1867 -c1/ch01.htm#S4, accessed October 11, 2019.

151. Reuters Staff, "Japan's Shiseido Says to Set Up Unit in Russia," *Reuters: Consumer Products and Retail News,* April 18, 2007, https://www.reuters.com /article/idUST26196920070419.

152. See, for example, Synchro Skin Radiant Lifting Foundation SPF 30, https://www.shiseido.com/us/en/synchro-skin-radiant-lifting-foundation-spf-30 -9990000000208.html, accessed February 27, 2021.

153. Most scientists and historians agree "race" is a social construct, but it is still a useful category in examining popular discourses used by businesses. See Megan Gannon, "Race Is a Social Construct, Scientists Argue: Racial Categories Are Weak Proxies for Genetic Diversity and Need to Be Phased Out," *Scientific American,* February 5, 2016, https://www.scientificamerican.com/article/race-is-a -social-construct-scientists-argue/.

154. Graham Jones, "Shiseido: A Brief History," Ape to Gentleman, https://www.apetogentleman.com/shiseido-a-brief-history/, accessed February 29, 2021.

155. Shiseidō website, Future Solution LX line of products, https://www.shiseido.com/us/en/skincare/collections/future-solution-lx/, accessed February 26, 2021.

156. Shiseidō website, Future Solution LX, https://www.shiseido.id/en/lp-sfslx-legendary.html, accessed April 26, 2023.

157. Shiseidō website, Future Solution LX: Legendary Enmei Ultimate Renewing Crème, https://international.shiseido.co.jp/future-solution-lx-legendary-enmei-ultimate-renewing-cream-1011649930.html, accessed February 26, 2021.

158. Shiseidō "Defy Time" livestream event, https://www.shiseido.com/us/en/exclusives/livestream/, accessed February 27, 2021.

159. Shiseidō, Ginza, Japan website, "Legendary Enmei, Enriched with Sacred Energy," https://international.shiseido.co.jp/lp-sfslx-legendary.html, accessed February 26, 2021.

160. Stephanie Horan, "How Different Generations Spend Money," Smart Asset, January 16, 2020, https://smartasset.com/checking-account/how-different-generations-spend-money-2020.

161. "Population Ages 65 and above (% of Total Population)—Japan," and "Population Ages 65 and above, Female (% of Female Population)—Japan," World Bank online databank, https://data.worldbank.org/indicator/SP.POP.65UP.TO.ZS?locations=JP, accessed February 27, 2021.

162. PJ, "Brand Debut!!! Shiseido's Integrate Gracy," *A Touch of Blusher: Makeup, Skincare, Fragrance, and a Bit of Fashion* (blog), July 23, 2007, http://www.atouchofblusher.com/2007/07/brand-debut-shiseidos-integrate-gracy.html.

163. "Brands: Gracy," Shiseidō website, https://corp.shiseido.com/en/brands/gracy/, accessed February 27, 2021.

164. PJ, "New Japanese Beauty Line: Shiseido Prior," *A Touch of Blusher: Makeup, Skincare, Fragrance, and a Bit of Fashion* (blog), October 30, 2014, http://www.atouchofblusher.com/2014/10/new-japanese-beauty-line-shiseido-prior.html.

165. PRIOR, Shiseidō website (Japan), https://www.shiseido.co.jp/pr/about/, accessed February 27, 2021.

166. "TVCM," Prior promotional website, https://www.shiseido.co.jp/pr/cm/cm-11/, accessed February 27, 2021.

167. In 401 advertisements aired on a July 1996 weekday on NTV, a popular Japanese channel, roughly 335 had a male voice-over. Akie Arima, "Gender Stereotypes in Japanese Television Advertisements," *Sex Roles* 49, no. 1 (July 2003): 86.

168. Michael Prieler, Florian Kohlbacher, Shigeru Hagiwara, and Akie Arima, "Gender Portrayals of Older People in Japanese Television Advertisements: Continuity or Change?," *Asian Women* 33, no. 1 (March 2017): 32, 40.

CONCLUSION

1. Andrew McDougall, "Shiseido Completes Purchase of Serge Lutens Trademark," *Cosmetics Design-Europe,* January 5, 2016, https://www.cosmeticsdesign-europe.com/Article/2016/01/05/Shiseido-completes-purchase-of-Serge-Lutens-trademark.

2. Elad Granot, Latoya M. Russell, and Thomas G. Brashear-Alejandro, "Populence: Exploring Luxury for the Masses," *Journal of Marketing Theory and Practice* 21, no. 1 (Winter 2013): 31–44.

3. See the promotional video at https://www.youtube.com/watch?v=xz7sTz Tz0_k, accessed October 16, 2019.

4. Jason W. Moore, "Introduction: Anthropocene or Capitalocene? Nature, History, and the Crisis of Capitalism," in *Anthropocene or Capitalocene? Nature, History, and the Crisis of Capitalism,* ed. Jason W. Moore (Oakland, CA: PM Press, 2016), 6. Moore notes that in 2009 Andreas Malm first used the term, published in 2011 in radical economist David Ruccio's blog.

5. John P. Clark, *Between Earth and Empire: From the Necrocene to the Beloved Community* (Oakland, CA: PM Press, 2019), 317.

6. Clark, *Between Earth and Empire,* 20.

7. While writing this book, I desired products I researched, like the Shiseidō face brush. I refrained from purchasing the scarf, difficult after serially watching its haunting promotional video.

8. Clark cites a refrain from the song "Earth Died Screaming" (1992) by Indie rock musician Tom Waits: "[And] the earth died screaming While I lay dreaming." Clark, *Between Earth and Empire,* 11.

9. Walter Benjamin, *The Arcades Project,* trans. Howard Eiland and Kevin McLaughlin, ed. Rolf Tiedemann (Cambridge, MA: Belknap Press of Harvard University Press, 1999), 207–208.

10. Citing Luis Bunuel's surrealist film *L'Age D'Or* (Vicomte de Noailles, 1930).

11. Brett Walker, *Toxic Archipelago: A History of Industrial Disease in Japan* (Seattle: University of Washington Press, 2010).

12. Rebirth Project, https://www.rebirth-project.jp/, accessed April 22, 2020.

13. In 2020 Iseya was arrested for marijuana possession, a crime in Japan carrying substantial penalties, including jail. Following the incident, former partners accused him of domestic violence, prompting his resignation from the Rebirth Project's leadership. See "Former girlfriends accuse Iseya Yusuke of domestic violence, Iseya to resign from REBIRTH PROJECT," *Neo-Tokyo 2099,* September 10, 2020, https://neotokyo2099.com/2020/09/10/former-girlfriends-accuse-iseya-yusuke-of-domestic-violence/.

14. Imperfect Foods, https://www.imperfectfoods.com/, accessed April 22, 2020.

Bibliography

Note: For references to online articles and sources, please see the notes.

ARCHIVAL COLLECTIONS

Advertising Museum Tokyo (ADMT), Japan
Casio Museum online archive
East Asia Collection online archive, Lafayette College
Kikuzō bijyuaru, Asahi Shimbun digital collection
MIT Visualizing Cultures online archive
Nishigaki Collection, Central Library, Waseda University, Tokyo, Japan
Perkins-Bostock Library, Duke University, Durham, North Carolina
Shiseidō Corporate Archives and Museum, Kakagawa, Japan
Shiseidō Corporate Archives and Museum online archive
Shufu no tomo Women's Magazine Archives, Tokyo, Japan

INTERVIEWS AND FIELDWORK

Anthony Austin, interview by author, transcript and recording, Florida State University, Institute on World War II and the Human Experience Archives, November 12–14, 2013.

Kaō Corporation archives, company historians, interview by author, Sumida Ward, Tokyo, Japan, July 2012.

Machida Saori, curator, tour and discussion by author, Kao Museum and Archives Corporate Culture and Literature Department, Tokyo, Japan, July 13, 2012.

Marumo Toshiyuki, curator, tour and discussion with author, Shiseidō Corporate Museum, Kakegawa, Japan, June 19, 2014.

Nakano Seishi, retired Shiseidō Corporate Planning Division employee and Shiseidō Museum and Corporate Archives volunteer, discussion with author, July 2014.

Ogura Mihō, Shiseidō Corporate Culture Department representative, email correspondence with author, May 10, 2013.

Timothy Parent, former Shanghai-based fashion business consultant; *WeAR Magazine,* China editor; former president, Harvard Alumni for Fashion, Luxury and Retail, email correspondence with author, September 30, 2019.

358 *Bibliography*

Philip Santiago, brand developer, vintage clothing exporter to Japan, Nigō's former American collaborator, phone interview by author, August 3, 2021.

Pleats Please store, Roppongi Hills Mall, author's fieldwork notes, Tokyo, Japan, July 17, 2018.

Setō City Junior High Schools, author's fieldwork notes, Setō City, Japan, July 1997–July 1998.

Shiseido Corporate Headquarters, Corporate Culture representatives, interview with author, Shiodome, Tokyo, Japan, July 17, 2012.

Shōwa-kan, Senchū no gakudō.gakuto, author's fieldwork notes, Tokyo, Japan, June 29, 2014.

Norman Smith, email correspondence with author, summer 2013.

English-Language Periodicals

Asia Nikkei
BBC News
Boston Globe
Fortune
Guardian
Japan Times
Los Angeles Times
New Yorker
New York Times
Time
Vogue
Wall Street Journal

Japanese-Language Periodicals

Asahi Shimbun
Chieinsutoa kenkyū
Chūō kōron
Fujin kōron
Fujin sekai
Shiseidō geppō
Shiseidō gurafu

Other: Primary and Secondary Sources

Adachi, Fumie, ed. and trans. *Japanese Design Motifs: 4260 Illustrations of Heraldic Crests Compiled by the Matsuya Piece-Goods Store.* New York: Dover, 1972.

Adachi, Mariko. "Luxury, Capital, and the Modern Girl: A Historical Study of Shiseidō Corporation." *Joseigaku kenkyū,* March 2005, 88–106. http://hdl .handle.net/10466/10100.

Akasegawa, Genpei. *Hangeijutsu anpan.* Tokyo: Chikuma Shobo, 1994.

Bibliography 359

————. *Objet o motta musansha.* Tokyo: Gendai shinchōsha, 1970.

Alexander, Jason W. *Brewed in Japan: The Evolution of the Japanese Beer Industry.* Vancouver: University of British Columbia Press, 2013.

Allison, Anne. *Millennial Monsters: Japanese Toys and the Global Imagination.* Berkeley: University of California Press, 2006.

————. *Nightwork: Sexuality, Pleasure, and Corporate Masculinity in a Tokyo Hostess Club.* Chicago: University of Chicago Press, 1994.

Amano, Yukichi. *Kōkoku mitai-na hanashi.* Tokyo: Shinchōsha, 1987.

————. *Motto omoshiroi kōkoku.* Tokyo: Daiwa shobō and Chikuma shobō, 1984.

————. *Santorī jidai wo kōkoku suru sekai o kōkoku suru.* Tokyo: Nihon iitsugyō shuppansha, 1977.

Amino, Yoshihiko. *Nihon no rekishi o yominaosu.* Vols. 1 and 2. Tokyo: Chikuma shobō, 1991 and 1993.

————. *Rethinking Japanese History.* Translated by Alan S. Christy. Ann Arbor: Center for Japanese Studies, University of Michigan, 2012.

Anderson, Benedict. *Imagined Communities: Reflections on the Origin and Spread of Nationalism.* Rev. ed. London: Verso, 1996.

Anderson, Janica, and Steven Zahavi Schwartz. *Zen Odyssey: The Story of Sokei-an, Ruth Fuller Sasaki, and the Birth of Zen in America.* Somerville, MA: Wisdom Publications, 2018.

Apter, Emily S. "Fetishism in Theory: Marx, Freud, Baudrillard." In *Feminizing the Fetish: Psychoanalysis and Narrative Obsession in Turn-of-the-Century France,* 1–14. Ithaca, NY: Cornell University Press, 1991.

Arima, Akie. "Gender Stereotypes in Japanese Television Advertisements." *Sex Roles* 49, no. 1 (July 2003): 81–90.

Asahi Shimbun Cultural Research Center. "Murder of an Anarchist Recalled: Suppression of News in the Wake of the 1923 Tokyo Earthquake." *The Asia-Pacific Journal: Japan Focus* 5, no. 11 (November 3, 2007). https://apjjf.org/-The-Asahi-Shinbun-Cultural-Research-Center-/2569/article.html.

Asahi Shimbun shuku satsuban. Tokyo: Japan Publications Trading Company, 2008.

Ashcraft, Brian, with Yuji Kawasaki and Idzuhiko Ueda. *Japanese Whisky: The Ultimate Guide to the World's Most Desirable Spirit with Tasting Notes from Japan's Leading Whisky Blogger.* Tokyo: Charles Tuttle, 2018.

Aso, Noriko. *Public Properties: Museums in Imperial Japan.* Durham, NC: Duke University Press, 2014.

Atwal, Glyn, and Douglas Bryson. *Luxury Brands in China and India.* London: Palgrave Macmillan, 2017.

Azuma, Hiroki. *Dōbutsuka suru posuto modan—otaku kara mita Nihon shakai.* Tokyo: Kōdansha, 2001.

————. *Otaku: Japan's Database Animals.* Minneapolis: University of Minnesota Press, 2009.

Bardsley, Jan, and Hiroko Hirokawa. "Branded: Bad Girls Go Shopping." In *Bad Girls of Japan,* edited by Laura Miller and Jan Bardsley, 111–126. London: Palgrave Macmillan, 2005.

Barthes, Roland. *Empire of Signs.* New York: Hill and Wang, 1983.

———. *L'Empire des Signes.* Geneva: Skira, 1970.

———. *Mythologies.* New York: Hill and Wang, 1972.

Baskett, Michael. *The Attractive Empire: Transnational Film Culture in Imperial Japan.* Honolulu: University of Hawai'i Press, 2008.

Beasley, William G. *The Meiji Restoration.* Palo Alto, CA: Stanford University Press, 1972.

Beezley, William H. *Judas at the Jockey Club and Other Episodes of Porfirian Mexico.* Lincoln: University of Nebraska Press, 1987.

Belson, Ken, and Brian Bremner. *Hello Kitty, The Remarkable Story of Sanrio and the Billion Dollar Feline Phenomenon.* Singapore: John Wiley and Sons (Asia), 2004.

Benjamin, Walter. *The Arcades Project.* Translated by Howard Eiland and Kevin McLaughlin. Edited by Rolf Tiedemann. Cambridge, MA: Belknap Press of Harvard University Press, 1999.

———. *Illuminations: Essays and Reflections.* Edited by Hannah Arendt. Translated by Harry Zohn. New York: Schocken Books, 1969.

———. *Selected Writings.* Vol. 3, *1935–1938.* Edited by Howard Eiland and Michael W. Jennings. Translated by Edmund Jephcott. Cambridge, MA: Belknap Press of Harvard University Press, 2002.

Birnbach, Lisa. *The Preppy Handbook.* New York: Workman, 1980.

Bonnett, Alastair. *White Identities: An Historical and International Introduction.* London: Routledge, 2018.

Borovy, Amy. *The Too-Good Wife: Alcohol, Co-Dependency, and the Politics of Nurturance in Postwar Japan.* Berkeley: University of California Press, 2005.

Bourdieu, Pierre. "The Forms of Capital." In *Handbook of Theory and Research for the Sociology of Education,* edited by J. Richardson, 241–258. Westport, CT: Greenwood Press, 1986.

Bowen-Struyk, Heather. "Laborers of Love in *Snow Country:* The Fantasy of Capitalism." *Proceedings of the Midwest Association of Japanese Literary Studies 5* (Summer 1999): 144–154.

Brecher, W. Puck. "Contested Utopias: Civilization and Leisure in the Meiji Era." *Asian Ethnology* 77, no. 1/2 (2018): 33–56.

Broom, Dave. *The Way of Whisky: A Journey around Japanese Whisky.* London: Mitchell Beazley, 2017.

Burke, Timothy. *Lifebuoy Men, Luxe Women: Commodification, Consumption, and Cleanliness in Modern Zimbabwe.* Durham, NC: Duke University Press, 1996.

Burns, Susan. "The Japanese Patent Medicine Trade in East Asia: Women's Medicines and the Tensions of Empire." In *Gender, Health, and History in East*

Asia, edited by Izumi Nakayama and Angela Leung, 139–165. Hong Kong: Hong Kong University Press, 2017.

Butler, Lee. "'Washing off the Dust': Baths and Bathing in Late Medieval Japan." *Monumenta Nipponica* 60, no. 1 (Spring 2005): 1–41.

Chamberlain, Basil Hall. "Bathing." In *Things Japanese,* 61. London: John Murray, 1905. In "History of Japan: A Guide to Japan's Past and Present," https://www.historyofjapanguide.com/things-japanese-019.htm.

Cheah, Pheng, and Bruce Robbins, eds. *Cosmopolitics: Thinking and Seeing beyond the Nation.* Minneapolis: University of Minnesota Press, 1998.

Chimoto, Akiko. "The Birth of the Full-Time Housewife in the Japanese Worker's Household as Seen through Family Budget Surveys." Translated by Diana Lynn Bethel. *U.S.-Japan Women's Journal. English Supplement,* no. 8 (1995): 37–63.

Choi, Deokhyo. "Fighting the Korean War in Pacifist Japan: Korean and Japanese Leftist Solidarity and American Cold War Containment." *Critical Asian Studies* 49, no. 4 (2007): 546–568.

Clark, John P. *Between Earth and Empire: From the Necrocene to the Beloved Community.* Oakland, CA: PM Press, 2019.

Craven, Wesley, and James Cate, eds. *The Pacific: Matterhorn to Nagasaki. The Army Air Forces in World War II.* Vol. 5. Chicago: University of Chicago Press, 1953.

Creighton, Millie. "Imaging the Other in Japanese Advertising Campaigns." In *Occidentalism: Images of the West,* edited by James Carrier, 135–160. Oxford: Oxford University Press, 1995.

Crohin-Kishigami, Stéphanie. *Furansu josei no Tōkyō sentō meguri.* Tokyo: Jībī, 2018.

———. *Sentō, l'art des bains japonais.* Vannes, France: Editions Sully, 2020.

Cromer, Kiara R., Norman B. Schmidt, and Dennis L. Murphey. "Do Traumatic Events Influence the Clinical Expression of Compulsive Hoarding?" *Behaviour Research and Therapy* 45, no. 11 (November 2007): 2581–2592.

Culver, Annika A. "Battlefield Comforts of Home: Gendered Commercialization of the Military Care Package in Wartime Japan." In *Defamiliarizing Japan's Asia-Pacific War,* edited by W. Puck Brecher and Michael W. Meyers, 85–103. Honolulu: University of Hawai'i Press, 2019.

———. "Constructing a Rural Utopia: Propaganda Images of Japanese Settlers in Northern Manchuria, 1936–43." In *Empire and Environment in the Making of Manchuria,* edited by Norman Smith, 152–178. Vancouver: University of British Columbia Press, 2017.

———. "For the Sake of the Nation: Mobilizing for War in Japanese Commercial Advertisements, 1937–1945." In *The Consumer on the Home Front: Second World War Civilian Consumption in Comparative Perspective,* edited by Hartmut Berghoff, Jan Logemann, and Felix Römer, 145–174. New York: Oxford University Press, 2017.

362   *Bibliography*

———. *Glorify the Empire: Japanese Avant-Garde Propaganda in Manchukuo.* Vancouver: University of British Columbia Press, 2013.

———. "Introduction: 'Manchukuo Perspectives' or 'Collaboration' as a Transcendence of Literary, National, and Chronological Boundaries." In *Manchukuo Perspectives: Transnational Approaches to Literary Production,* edited by Annika A. Culver and Norman Smith, 1–12. Hong Kong: University of Hong Kong Press, 2019.

———. "Shiseidō's 'Empire of Beauty': Marketing Japanese Modernity in Northeast Asia, 1932–1945." *Shashi—the Journal of Japanese Business and Company History* 2, no. 2 (2013): 16–20.

Cumings, Bruce. *Korea's Place in the Sun: A Modern History.* New York: W. W. Norton, 2005.

Cumming, Valerie, C. W. Cunnington, and P. E. Cunnington. *The Dictionary of Fashion History.* Oxford: Berg, 2010.

Dai Nippon Kajū Kabushiki Gaisha. *Son'eki keisansho.* Yoichi, Japan: Dai Nippon Kajū Kabushiki Gaisha, 1988.

Dale, Peter. *The Myth of Japanese Uniqueness.* London: Routledge, 1986.

d'Avenel, George. "Le Mécanisme de la Vie Moderne: Les Grands Magasins." *Revue des Deux Mondes* 124 (Paris, 1894): 335–336.

de Bary, William Theodore, Donald Keene, George Tanabe, and Paul Varley, eds. *Sources of Japanese Tradition,* vol. 1, *From Earliest Times to 1600.* 2nd ed. New York: Columbia University Press, 2001.

de Certeau, Michel. *The Practice of Everyday Life.* Berkeley: University of California Press, 1988.

Deflem, Mathieu. "Anomie: History of the Concept." In *International Encyclopedia of the Social and Behavioral Sciences,* 719. 2nd ed. Amsterdam: Elsevier, 2015.

DeLeon, Jian. *The Incomplete: Highsnobiety Guide to Street Fashion and Culture.* Berlin: Die Gestalten Verlag, 2018.

Derrida, Jacques. *Writing and Difference.* Translated by Alan Bass. Chicago: University of Chicago Press, 1978.

de Villiers, Nicholas. *Sexography: Sex Work in Documentary.* Minneapolis: University of Minnesota Press, 2017.

Doi, Takeo. *The Anatomy of Dependence: The Key Analysis of Japanese Behavior.* Translated by J. Bester. Tokyo: Kodansha International, 1973.

———. *The Anatomy of Self: The Individual versus Society.* Translated by M. A. Harbison. Tokyo: Kodansha International, 1986.

———. "*Giri-ninjo*: An Interpretation." In *Aspects of Social Change in Modern Japan,* edited by R. P. Dore, 327–336. Princeton, NJ: Princeton University Press, 1967.

Downes, Alexander B. *Targeting Civilians in War.* Ithaca, NY: Cornell University Press, 2008.

Drea, Edward, Greg Bradsher, Robert Hanyok, James Lide, Michael Petersen, and Daqing Yang. *Researching Japanese War Crimes Records: Introductory Es-*

says. Washington, DC: Nazi War Crimes and Japanese Imperial Government Records Interagency Working Group, 2006.

Duffy, Brooke Erin. "Manufacturing Authenticity: The Rhetoric of 'Real' in Women's Magazines." *The Communication Review* 16, no. 3 (2013): 132–154.

Dunn, Kevin. *Global Punk: Resistance and Rebellion in Everyday Life.* London: Bloomsbury, 2016.

Eitarō, Kishimoto. "Labour-Management Relations and the Trade Unions in Postwar Japan: Revival and Reestablishment of the Labour-Management Regulations Based on Seniority." *Kyoto University Economic Review* 38, no. 1 (April 1968): 1–35.

English, Bonnie. *Japanese Fashion Designers: The Work and Influence of Issey Miyake, Yohji Yamamoto, and Rei Kawakubo.* New York: Berg, 2011.

Ericson, Steven J. "The 'Matsukata Deflation' Reconsidered: Financial Stabilization and Japanese Exports in a Global Depression, 1881–85." *Journal of Japanese Studies* 40, no. 1 (Winter 2014): 1–28.

Field, Norma. *The Splendor of Longing in the Tale of Genji.* Princeton, NJ: Princeton University Press, 1987.

Foroudi, Pantea, T. C. Melewar, and Suraksha Gupta. "Corporate Logo: History, Definition, and Components." *International Studies of Management and Organization* 47, no. 2 (2017): 176–196.

Francks, Penelope, ed. *The Historical Consumer: Consumption and Everyday Life in Japan, 1850–2000.* London: Palgrave Macmillan, 2012.

Freedman, Alyssa, Laura Miller, and Christine R. Yano, eds. *Modern Girls on the Go: Gender, Mobility, and Labor in Japan.* Stanford, CA: Stanford University Press, 2013.

Freud, Sigmund. "Fetishism" (1927). In *Miscellaneous Papers, 1888–1938,* vol. 5 of *Collected Papers,* 198–204. London: Hogarth and Institute of Psycho-Analysis, 1950.

Frost, Randy, and Gail Steketee. *Stuff: Compulsive Hoarding and the Meaning of Things.* New York: Mariner Books, 2011.

Frühstück, Sabine. "Managing the Truth of Sex in Imperial Japan." *Journal of Asian Studies* 59, no. 2 (May 2000): 332–358.

Fujioka, Rika. "The Pressures of Globalization in Retail: The Path of Japanese Department Stores, 1930s–1980s." In *Comparative Responses to Globalization: Experiences of British and Japanese Enterprises,* edited by Maki Umemura and Rika Fujioka, 181–203. London: Palgrave Macmillan, 2013.

Gardner, William O. *Advertising Tower: Japanese Modernism and Modernity in the 1920s.* Cambridge, MA: Harvard University Asia Center, 2006.

Garon, Sheldon. *Beyond Our Means: Why America Spends while the World Saves.* Princeton, NJ: Princeton University Press, 2011.

———. "Luxury Is the Enemy: Mobilizing Savings and Popularizing Thrift in Wartime Japan." *Journal of Japanese Studies* 26, no. 1 (Winter 2000): 41–78.

Garon, Sheldon, and Patricia McLaughlin, eds. *The Ambivalent Consumer: Questioning Consumption in East Asia and the West*. Ithaca, NY: Cornell University Press, 2006.

Garrett, Kent, and Jeanna Ellsworth. *The Last Negroes at Harvard: The Class of 1963 and the 18 Young Men Who Changed Harvard Forever*. New York: Houghton Mifflin Harcourt, 2020.

Gerteis, Christopher. "Political Protest in Interwar Japan: Part 1." *The Asia-Pacific Journal: Japan Focus* 12, issue 37, no. 1 (August 2014): 1–45.

Glaser, Gabrielle. *Her Best-Kept Secret: Why Women Drink—and How They Can Regain Control*. New York: Simon and Schuster, 2013.

Godey, Bruno, Daniele Pederzoli, Gaetano Aiello, Raffaele Donvito, Klaus-Peter Wiedmann, and Nadine Hennigs. "A Cross Cultural Exploratory Content Analysis of the Perception of Luxury from Six Countries." *Journal of Product and Brand Management* 3 (2013): 229–237.

Goodall, John. *A Journey in Time: The Remarkable Story of Seiko*. Tokyo: Toppan Printing Company, 2003.

Gordon, Andrew. "Consumption, Leisure, and the Middle Class in Transwar Japan." *Social Science Japan Journal* 10, no. 1 (April 2007): 1–21.

———. *The Evolution of Labor Relations in Japan: Heavy Industry, 1853–1955*. Cambridge, MA: Harvard University Press, 1988.

———. *A Modern History of Japan: From Tokugawa Times to the Present*. New York: Oxford University Press, 2002.

———, ed. *Postwar Japan as History*. Berkeley: University of California Press, 1993.

Graeber, David. *Debt: The First 5,000 Years*. New York: Melville House, 2011.

———. "It Is Value That Brings Universes into Being." *HAU: Journal of Ethnographic Theory* 3, no. 2 (2013): 219–243.

———. *Towards an Anthropological Theory of Value: The False Coin of Our Own Dreams*. London: Palgrave Macmillan, 2001.

Grandin, Greg. *Empire of Necessity: Slavery, Freedom, and Deception in the New World*. New York: Henry Holt, 2014.

Granot, Elad, and Thomas Brashear. "From Luxury to Populence: Inconspicuous Consumption as Described by Female Consumers." *Advances in Consumer Research* 35 (2008): 991–995.

Granot, Elad, Latoya M. Russell, and Thomas G. Brashear-Alejandro. "Populence: Exploring Luxury for the Masses." *Journal of Marketing Theory and Practice* 21, no. 1 (Winter 2013): 31–44.

Griffiths, Owen. "Need, Greed, and Protest in Japan's Black Market, 1938–1949." *Journal of Social History* 35, no. 4 (Summer 2002): 825–858.

Groemer, Gerald. "The Creation of the Edo Outcaste Order." *Journal of Japanese Studies* 27, no. 2 (Summer 2001): 263–293.

Grosberg, Kenneth Alan. *Japan's Renaissance: The Politics of the Muromachi Bakufu*. Ithaca, NY: Cornell University East Asia Program, 2001.

Bibliography 365

Gumpert, Lynn, ed. *Face to Face: Shiseido and the Manufacture of Beauty, 1900–2000*. New York: Grey Art Gallery, New York University, 1999.

Habermas, Juergen. *The Structural Transformation of the Public Sphere: An Inquiry into a Category of Bourgeois Society*. Translated by Thomas Burger and Frederick Lawrence. London: Polity Press, 1989.

Hardacre, Helen. *Marketing the Menacing Fetus in Japan*. Berkeley: University of California Press, 1999.

———. *Shinto: A History*. London: Oxford University Press, 2016.

Harootunian, Harry D. *Overcome by Modernity: History, Culture, and Community in Interwar Japan*. Princeton, NJ: Princeton University Press, 2000.

Hashimoto, Ken'ichi, and Hatsuda Kōsei. *Sakariba wa yami-ichi kara umareta*. Tokyo: Seikyū-sha, 2016.

Hatsuda, Kōsei, Shihori Murakami, and Masakazu Ishigure. "The Nationwide Formation and Spread of *Yami-ichi* (Black Market) after World War II and Government's Involvements: Nationwide Survey of the Descriptions about *Yami-ichi* (Black Market) in Municipality Histories." *Journal of Architecture and Planning (Transactions of AIJ [Architectural Institute of Japan])* 82, no. 733 (March 2017): 805–815.

Hattori, Tamio, and Funatsu Tsuruyo. "The Emergence of the Asian Middle Classes and Their Characteristics." *The Developing Economies* 41, no. 2 (June 2003): 140–160.

Hedry, Joy. *Wrapping Culture: Politeness, Presentation, and Power in Japan and Other Societies*. Oxford: Clarendon Press, 1995.

Hershatter, Gail. *Women and China's Revolutions*. Lanham, MD: Rowman and Littlefield, 2018.

Hindrickson, Hildi, ed. *Clothing and Difference: Embodied Identities in Colonial and Post-Colonial Africa*. Durham, NC: Duke University Press, 1996.

Hirai, Hirokazu. "'Manshūkoku' ippan kaikei mokuteki saishutsu yosan no dōkō: 1932–1942 nendo." *Keizai-gaku kenkyū* 52, no. 4 (March 11, 2003): 103–132.

Hobsbawm, Eric, Hugh Trevor-Roper, Prys Morgan, David Cannadine, Bernard S. Cohn, and Terrence Ranger, eds. *The Invention of Tradition*. Cambridge: Cambridge University Press, 1983.

Holmes, Linda Goetz. *Unjust Enrichment: How Japan's Companies Built Postwar Fortunes Using American POWs*. Mechanicsburg, PA: Stackpole Books, 2001.

Honeycombe, Gordon. *Selfridges, Seventy-Five Years: The Story of the Store 1909–84*. London: Park Lane Press, 1984.

Hoston, Germaine. *Marxism and the Crisis of Development in Prewar Japan*. Princeton, NJ: Princeton University Press, 1986.

Howell, David L. "Fecal Matters: Prolegomenon to a History of Shit in Japan." In *Japan at Nature's Edge: The Environmental Context of a Global Power*, edited by Ian Jared Miller, Julia Adeney Thomas, and Brett Walker, 137–151. Honolulu: University of Hawai'i Press, 2013.

366   *Bibliography*

———. "Proto-industrial Origins of Japanese Capitalism." *Journal of Asian Studies* 51, no. 2 (May 1992): 269–286.

Huruse, Noriko. "A Comparative Study of Communication Style in Japan and the United States as Revealed through Content Analysis of Television Commercials." MA thesis, Portland State University, 1978.

Hutchinson, Rachael, ed. *Negotiating Censorship in Modern Japan*. New York: Routledge, 2013.

Ikeda, Shinobu. "The Allure of a 'Woman in Chinese Dress': Representation of the Other in Imperial Japan." In *Performing "Nation": Gender Politics in Literature, Theater, and the Visual Arts of China and Japan, 1880–1940*, edited by Doris Croissant, Catherine Vance Yeh, and Joshua Mostow, 377–379. Leiden: Koninklijke Brill, 2008.

International Monetary Fund Statistics Department. *International Financial Statistics: International Financial Statistics, August 1949, Vol. 2, Number 8*. Washington, DC: International Monetary Fund, 1949.

Isa, Masako, and Eric Kramer. "Adopting the Caucasian 'Look': Reorganizing the Minority Face." In *The Emerging Monoculture: Assimilation and the "Model Minority,"* edited by Eric Mark Kramer, 41–74. Westport, CT: Praeger, 2003.

Ishiguro, Yoshiaki. "A Japanese National Crime: The Korean Massacre after the Great Kanto Earthquake of 1923." *Korea Journal* 38, no. 4 (Winter 1998): 331–354.

Ishikawa, Satomi. *Seeking the Self: Individualism and Popular Culture in Japan*. Bern: Peter Lang, 2007.

Ishikawa, Yoshika, and Satō Asami, eds. *Shiseidō monogatari: Shiseidō kigyō shiryōkan shūzōhin katarogu (1872–1946)*. Kakegawa: Shiseidō Corporate Museum, 1995.

Ishizu, Shōsuke, Toshiyuki Kurosu, and Hajime Hasegawa, with photographs by Teruyoshi Hayashida. *Take Ivy*. New York: Powerhouse Books, 2010.

Jansen, Maurius. *The Making of Modern Japan*. Cambridge, MA: Harvard University Press, 2002.

Jesty, Justin. *Art and Engagement in Early Postwar Japan*. Ithaca, NY: Cornell University Press, 2018.

Jeweler's Circular 75, no. 2 (January 16, 1918): 94.

Jones, Geoffrey. *Beauty Imagined: A History of the Global Beauty Industry*. New York: Oxford University Press, 2010.

Kaidō, Mamoru. *Yōshū, biiru*. Tokyo: Jitsumu kyōiku shuppansha, 1989.

Kanamaru, Shigene. *Shinkō shashin no tsukurikata*. Tokyo: Genkōsha, 1932.

Kang, Tŏksang, and Pyŏngdong Kŭm. *Kantō daishinsai to Chōsenjin*. Tokyo: Misuzu Shobō, 1963.

Kaō Corporation. *Kaō-shi 100-nen (1890–1990 nen)*. Tokyo: Kaō Corporation Company History Editorial Office, 1998.

Kaō kabushiki gaisha shashi hensatsu shitsu. Kaō shi 100 nen (1890–1990 nen). Tokyo: Kaō Corporation, 1998.

Bibliography

Kapferer, Jean-Noël, and Vincent Bastien. *The Luxury Strategy: Break the Rules of Marketing to Build Luxury Brand.* London: Kogan Page, 2012.

Kaplan, Louise. *Cultures of Fetishism.* New York: Palgrave Macmillan, 2006.

Kapur, Nick. *Japan at the Crossroads: Conflict and Compromise after Anpo.* Cambridge, MA: Harvard University Press, 2018.

Karasawa, Masahiro, Takuya Kida, Yuko Naitō, and the National Museum of Modern Art, Tokyo, eds. *Kōkyōsuru Nihonjin: Kōgei-ka ga yume mita Ajia, 1910s–1945.* Tokyo: National Museum of Modern Art, 2012.

Kashiwagi, Hiroshi. "On Rationalization and the National Lifestyle: Japanese Design of the 1920s and the 1930s." In *Being Modern in Japan,* edited by Elise K. Tipton and John Clark, 61–74. Honolulu: University of Hawai'i Press, 2000.

Katsu, Kokichi. *Musui's Story: The Autobiography of a Tokugawa Samurai.* Translated by Teruko Craig. Tucson: University of Arizona Press, 1991.

Kaufman, Cynthia. *Getting Past Capitalism: History, Vision, Hope.* Lanham, MD: Lexington Books, 2012.

Kawabata, Yasunari. *Snow Country.* Translated by Edward G. Seidensticker. New York: Vintage Books, 1996.

Kawakubo, Rei. *Comme des Garçons: Art of the In-Between.* New York: The MET, 2017.

Kawano, Satsuki. "Japanese Bodies and Western Ways of Seeing in the Late Nineteenth Century." In *Dirt, Undress, and Difference: Critical Perspectives on the Body's Surface,* edited by Adeline Masquelier, 149–167. Bloomington: Indiana University Press, 2005.

Kazui, Tashiro. "Foreign Relations during the Edo Period: *Sakoku* Reexamined." Translated by Susan Downing Videen. *Journal of Japanese Studies* 8, no. 2 (Summer 1982): 283–284.

Kelly, William. Foreword to Ezra Vogel, *Japan's Middle Class.* Lanham, MD: Rowman and Littlefield, 2013.

Kelly, William, ed. *Fanning the Flames: Fans and Consumer Culture in Contemporary Japan.* Albany: State University of New York Press, 2004.

Kelts, Roland. *Japanamerica: How Japanese Pop Culture Has Invaded the US.* Basingstoke, UK: Palgrave Macmillan, 2006.

King, Richard, Cody Poulton, and Katsuhiko Endo, eds. *Sino-Japanese Transculturation: Late Nineteenth Century to the End of the Pacific War.* Lanham, MD: Lexington Books, 2012.

Kinmonth, Earl H. "Nakamura Keiu and Samuel Smiles: A Victorian Confucian and a Confucian Victorian." *American Historical Review* 85, no. 3 (June 1980): 535–556.

Kinsella, Sharon. "Cuties in Japan." In *Women, Media, and Consumption in Japan,* edited by Lise Skov and Brian Moeran, 220–254. Honolulu: University of Hawai'i Press, 1995.

Kiritani, Elizabeth. *Vanishing Japan: Traditions, Crafts, and Culture.* Rutland, VT: Charles E. Tuttle, 1995.

368 *Bibliography*

Kirk, Nicole C. *Wanamaker's Temple: The Business of Religion in an Iconic Department Store.* New York: New York University Press, 2018.

Kitahara, Michio. *Portuguese Colonialism and Japanese Slaves.* Tokyo: Kadensha, 2013.

Klein, Naomi. *No Logo: Taking Aim at the Brand Bullies.* Toronto: Knopf Canada, 1999.

Knight, Diana. "Barthes and Orientalism." In "Textual Interrelations," special issue, *New Literary History* 24, no. 3 (Summer 1993): 617–633.

Kobayashi, Takiji. *The Factory Ship and the Absentee Landlord.* Translated by Frank Motofuji. Seattle: University of Washington Press, 1973.

———. *Kani kōsen.* Tokyo: Heibonsha, 1998.

Komori, Naoko. "The 'Hidden' History of Accounting in Japan: A Historical Examination of the Relationship between Japanese Women and Accounting." *Accounting History* 12, no. 3 (2007): 329–358.

Kondo, Dorinne. *About Face: Performing Race in Fashion and Theater.* New York: Routledge, 1997.

Kondo, Marie. *The Life-Changing Magic of Tidying Up: The Japanese Art of Decluttering and Organizing.* Berkeley, CA: Ten Speed Press, 2014.

Koren, Leonard. *Wabi-Sabi for Artists, Designers, Poets, and Philosophers.* 1994; reprint, Point Reyes, CA: Imperfect Publishing, 2008.

Kretschmer, Angelika. "Mortuary Rites for Inanimate Objects: The Case of Hari Kuyo." *Japanese Journal of Religious Studies* 27, no. 3/4 (Fall 2000): 379–404.

Kushner, Barak. *The Thought War: Japanese Imperial Propaganda.* Honolulu: University of Hawai'i Press, 2006.

Lavely, William, Xiao Zhenyu, Bohua Li, and Ronald Freedman. "The Rise in Female Education in China: National and Regional Patterns." *China Quarterly,* no. 121 (March 1990): 64–65.

Lean, Eugenia. *Vernacular Industrialism in China: Local Innovation and Translated Technologies in the Making of a Cosmetics Empire.* New York: Columbia University Press, 2020.

Lee, Jong-Chan. "The Making of Hygienic Modernity in Meiji Japan, 1868–1905." *Uisahak: Korean Journal of Medical History* 12, no. 1 (June 2003): 34–53.

Leheny, David Richard. *Think Global, Fear Local: Sex, Violence, and Anxiety in Contemporary Japan.* Ithaca, NY: Cornell University Press, 2006.

Lenard, Patti Tamara, and Peter Balint. "What Is (the Wrong of) Cultural Appropriation?" *Ethnicities* 20, no. 2 (April 1, 2020): 331–352.

Lerner, Paul. *The Consuming Temple: Jews, Department Stores, and the Consumer Revolution in Germany, 1880–1940.* Ithaca, NY: Cornell University Press, 2015.

Leupp, Gary. "'One Drink from a Gourd': Servants, Shophands, and Laborers in the Cities of Tokugawa Japan." PhD diss., University of Michigan, 1989.

Lipset, Seymour L. *American Exceptionalism: A Double-Edged Sword.* New York: W. W. Norton, 1996.

Lowe, Scott. "Review of *Alan Watts—In the Academy: Essays and Lectures,* edited by Peter J. Columbus and Donadrian L. Rice." *Nova Religio* 22, no. 3 (2019): 129–130.

Lukacs, Georg. *History and Class Consciousness.* London: Merlin Press, 1967.

Maeda, Yasuyuki. "Zeitaku wa teki da: Sebiro, kamera, kikinzoku." In *Shōwa keizaishi,* edited by Arisawa Hiromi, 186–187. Tokyo: Nihon keizai shimbunsha, 1976.

Maeshima, Shiho. "Women's Magazines and the Democratization of Print and Reading Culture in Interwar Japan." PhD diss., University of British Columbia, 2016.

Maly, Ico, and Piia Varis. "The 21st-Century Hipster: On Micropopulations in Times of Diversity." *European Journal of Cultural Studies,* August 18, 2015. https://journals.sagepub.com/doi/10.1177/1367549415597920.

Marotti, William. *Money, Trains, and Guillotines: Art and Revolution in 1960s Japan.* Durham, NC: Duke University Press, 2013.

Marshall, Amy Bliss. *Magazines and the Making of Mass Culture in Japan.* Toronto: University of Toronto Press, 2019.

Maruyama, Masao. *Thought and Behaviour in Japanese Politics.* Oxford: University of Oxford Press, 1963.

Marx, W. David. "The Climb of Ivy: The Styles of the American Ivy League Transform the Fashions of 1960s Japan." *Lapham's Quarterly* 8, no. 4 (Fall 2015). https://www.laphamsquarterly.org/fashion/climb-ivy.

Marx, Karl. *Capital: A Critique of Political Economy.* Volume 1, Book One, *The Process of Production of Capital.* Moscow: Progress Publishers, 1887.

———. "Section 4: The Fetishism of Commodities and the Secret Thereof." In *Capital,* vol. 1. https://www.marxists.org/archive/marx/works/1867-c1/ch01 .htm#S4, accessed October 11, 2019.

Maté, Gabor. *In the Realm of the Hungry Ghosts: Close Encounters with Addiction.* Berkeley, CA: North Atlantic Books, 2008.

Matsuda, Takeshi. *Sengo Nihon ni okeru Amerika no sofuto pawā: Han'eikyūteki izon no kigen.* Tokyo: Iwanami shoten, 2008.

———. *Soft Power and Its Perils: US Cultural Policy in Early Postwar Japan and Permanent Dependency.* Washington, DC: Woodrow Wilson Center Press, 2007.

———. *Taibei izon no kigen: Amerika no sofuto pawā no senryaku.* Tokyo: Iwanami shoten, 2015.

Matsugu, Miho. "The Fusing of Labor and Love in *Snow Country.*" *Proceedings of the Midwest Association of Japanese Literary Studies* 5 (Summer 1999): 135–143.

Matsumiya, Saburō. *Edo kabuki no kōkoku.* Tokyo: Tōhō shobō, 1973.

———. *Edo no kanban.* Tokyo: Tokyo kanban kōgyō kyōtō kumiai, 1959.

370 *Bibliography*

———. *Edo no monouri.* Tokyo: Tōhō shobō, 1968.

Mauss, Marcel. *The Gift: The Form and Reason for Exchange in Archaic Societies.* Translated by W. D. Halls. New York: W. W. Norton, 2000.

McFadden, Mary. *Mary McFadden: A Lifetime of Design, Collecting and Adventure.* New York: Rizzoli International Publications, 2012.

McNally, David. *Monsters of the Market: Zombies, Vampires and Global Capitalism.* Leiden: Koninklijke Brill, 2011.

Mettler, Meghan Warner. *How to Reach Japan by Subway: America's Fascination with Japanese Culture, 1945–1965.* Lincoln: University of Nebraska Press, 2018.

Miller, Daniel. *The Comfort of Things.* Cambridge: Polity Press, 2008.

———. *The Dialectics of Shopping.* Chicago: University of Chicago Press, 2001.

———. *A Theory of Shopping.* Ithaca, NY: Cornell University Press, 1998.

Miller, Ian Jared, Julia Adeney Thomas, and Brett L. Walker, eds. *Japan at Nature's Edge: The Environmental Context of a Global Power.* Honolulu: University of Hawai'i Press, 2013.

Miller, Laura, and Jan Bardsley, eds. *Bad Girls of Japan.* New York: Springer, 2005.

Minami, Hiroshi. *Nihonjin no shinri.* Tokyo: Iwanami shinsho, 1953.

———. *Nihonjinron no keifu.* Tokyo: Kōdansha, 1980.

———. *Psychology of the Japanese People.* Toronto: University of Toronto Press, 1972.

———. *Shōwa bunka.* Tokyo: Keisō shobō, 1987.

———. *Taishō bunka, 1905–1927.* Tokyo: Keisō shobō, 1965.

Mine, Takeshi. "Chūka jinmin kyōwa-koku ni keishō sareta Manshū kagaku kōgyō." PhD diss., University of Tokyo, November 2007.

Mishima, Yukio. *Confessions of a Mask.* Translated by Meredith Weatherby. Tokyo: Charles E. Tuttle, 1970.

———. *Kamen no kokuhaku.* Tokyo: Kawade shobō, 1949.

Mitsukoshi. *Dai Mitsukoshi rekishi shashin-chō: Sanseikō sōritsu nijū-nen kinen.* Tokyo: Toppan Printing Company, 1932.

———. *Sangō kanji, Mitsukoshi shashin-chō.* Tokyo: 1941.

Miyake, Issey. *Body Works.* Tokyo: Shogaku-kan, 1983.

Miyake, Issey, with Midori Kitamura, ed. *Issey Miyake: Pleats Please.* Berlin: Taschen, 2012.

Miyake Design Studio. *Issey Miyake: East Meets West.* Tokyo: Heibonsha, 1978.

Miyoshi, Hajime. *Nihon no posutā: Meiji, Taishō, Shōwa.* Tokyo: Shikō-sha, 2003.

Mizuki, Shigeru. *Komikku Shōwa-shi.* Tokyo: Kōdansha, 1994.

———. *Onwards towards Our Noble Deaths.* Translated by Jocelyne Allen. Introduction by Frederik L. Schodt. Montreal: Drawn and Quarterly, 2011.

———. *Shōwa: A History of Japan, 1939–1944.* Montreal: Drawn and Quarterly, 2014.

———. *Sōin gyokusai seyo!* Tokyo: Kodansha, 1973.

Bibliography 371

Moeran, Brian. *Lost Innocence: Folk Craft Potters of Onta, Japan*. Berkeley: University of California Press, 1984.

Moore, Aaron. *Writing War: Soldiers Record the Japanese Empire*. Cambridge, MA: Harvard University Press, 2013.

Moore, Jason W., ed. *Anthropocene or Capitalocene? Nature, History, and the Crisis of Capitalism*. Oakland, CA: PM Press, 2016.

Morton, W. H. *Present-Day Impressions of Japan: The History, People, Commerce, Industries and Resources of Japan and Japan's Colonial Empire, Kwantung, Chosen, Taiwan, Karafuto*. London: Globe Encyclopedia, 1919. Reprint, Tokyo: Edition Synapse, 2008.

Motohashi, Kazuyuki. "Shiseido Marketing in China." In *Global Business Strategy: Multinational Corporations Venturing into Emerging Markets*, 155–171. New York: Springer, 2015. https://link.springer.com/chapter/10.1007/978-4-431-55468-4_10.

Munroe, Alexandra. *Scream against the Sky: Japanese Art after 1945*. New York: Harry N. Abrams, 1994.

Murakami, Ryu. *69*. Translated by Ralph F. McCarthy. Tokyo: Kodansha International, 1993.

———. *69 Sikusutei nain*. Tokyo: Shueisha, 1987.

Nagai, Kazumasa, and Yūsuke Kaji. *Shiseidō kurieiteibu wāku*. Tokyo: Kyūryūdō, 1985.

Nagata, Mary Louise. "Brotherhoods and Stock Societies: Guilds in Pre-modern Japan." *IRSH (International Review of Social History)* 53 (2008): 121–142.

Najita, Tetsuo. *Ordinary Economies in Japan: A Historical Perspective, 1750–1950*. Berkeley: University of California Press, 2009.

———. *Visions of Virtue in Tokugawa Japan: The Kaitokudō Merchant Academy of Osaka*. Honolulu: University of Hawai'i Press, 1987.

Nakada, Yoshinao. *Vita: Kinkichi Nakada*. San Francisco: Blurb.com, 2010.

Nakamura, Masanori. *Sengoshi*. Tokyo: Iwanami shoten, 2005.

Nakamura, Usagi. *Ai to shihonshugi*. Tokyo: Shinchōsha, 2002.

———. *Shoppingu no joō*. Tokyo: Bunshun bunkō, 2001.

Namba, Kōji. *Kōkoku no kuronorojī: Masu medeia no seiki o koete*. Tokyo: Seikai shisōsha, 2010.

Nettleton, Taro. "Hi-Red Center's Shelter Plan (1964): The Uncanny Body in the Imperial Hotel." *Japanese Studies* 34, no. 1 (2014): 83–99.

Nickerson, Rebecca. "Imperial Designs: Fashion, Cosmetics, and Cultural Identity in Japan, 1931–1943." PhD diss., University of Illinois at Urbana-Champaign, 2011.

Nishino, Seiji, Keisuke Saitō, and Asami Satō, eds. *Make-Up Tokyo—Shiseidō monogatari: Shiseidō kigyō shiryōkan shūzō katarogu (1946–1972)*. Kakegawa: Shiseidō Corporate Museum, 1996.

———. *Shiseidō monogatari—Shiseidō kigyō shiryōkan shūzōhin katarogu (1972–1997) 3*. Tokyo: Shiseidō Publicity Department, 1998.

Bibliography

Nolte, Sharon. "Women's Rights and Society's Needs: Japan's 1931 Suffrage Bill." *Comparative Studies in Society and History* 28, no. 4 (October 1986): 690–714.

Noma, Caroline. *The Japanese Comfort Women and Sexual Slavery.* London: Bloomsbury, 2015.

Norman, E. H. *Japan's Emergence of a Modern State: Political and Economic Problems of the Meiji Period.* New York: International Secretariat, Institute of Pacific Relations, 1940.

Nye, Joseph. *Bound to Lead: The Changing Nature of American Power.* London: Basic Books, 1990.

———. *Soft Power: The Means to Success in World Politics.* New York: PublicAffairs, 2004.

Partch, Richard Douglas. "The Nixon 'Shocks': Implications for Japan's Foreign Policy in the 1970s." MA thesis, Portland State University, August 1972.

Partner, Simon. *Assembled in Japan: Electrical Goods and the Making of the Japanese Consumer.* Berkeley: University of California Press, 2000.

Pate, Alan Scott. *Kanban: Traditional Shop Signs of Japan.* Princeton, NJ: Princeton University Press, 2017.

Pietz, William. "The Problem of the Fetish, I." *Anthropology and Aesthetics,* no. 9 (Spring 1985): 5–17.

———. "The Problem of the Fetish, II: The Origin of the Fetish." *Anthropology and Aesthetics,* no. 13 (Spring 1987): 23–45.

———. "The Problem of the Fetish, III: Bosman's Guinea and the Enlightenment Theory of Fetishism." *Anthropology and Aesthetics,* no. 16 (Autumn 1988): 105–124.

Pineau, Roger, ed. *The Japan Expedition, 1852–1854: The Personal Journal of Commodore Matthew C. Perry.* Washington, DC: Smithsonian Institution Press, 1968.

Pinguet, Maurice. *La Mort Voluntaire au Japon.* Paris: Gallimard, 1984.

Pitelka, Morgan, ed. *Japanese Tea Culture: Art, History, and Practice.* New York: Routledge, 2003.

———. *Spectacular Accumulation: Material Culture, Tokugawa Ieyasu, and Samurai Sociability.* Honolulu: University of Hawai'i Press, 2015.

Prieler, Michael, Florian Kohlbacher, Shigeru Hagiwara, and Akie Arima. "Gender Portrayals of Older People in Japanese Television Advertisements: Continuity or Change?" *Asian Women* 33, no. 1 (March 2017): 25–47.

Prosser, Jay. "Buddha Barthes: What Barthes Saw in Photography (That He Didn't in Literature)." *Literature and Theology* 18, no. 2 (June 2004): 211–222.

Richie, Donald. *The Donald Richie Reader: 50 Years of Writing on Japan.* Berkeley, CA: Stone Bridge Press, 2001.

Rittō rekishi minzoku hakubutsukan, ed. *Edo no kanban: Moji no messeji.* Rittō, Japan: Rittō History and Culture Museum, 1992.

Bibliography 373

Rubinstein, Ruth. *Dress Codes: Meanings and Messages in American Culture.* Emeryville, CA: Avalon Publishing, 1995.

———. *Society's Child: Identity, Clothing, and Style.* Boulder, CO: Westview Press, 2000.

Rubinfien, Louisa Daria. "Commodity to National Brand: Manufacturers, Merchants, and the Development of the Consumer Market in Interwar Japan." PhD diss., Harvard University, 1995.

Ryang, Sonia. "The Great Kanto Earthquake and the Massacre of Koreans in 1923: Notes on Japan's Modern National Sovereignty." *Anthropological Quarterly* 76, no. 4 (Autumn 2003): 731–748.

Sakai, Naoki. "Asia as a Borrowing Index: Civilizational Transference and Colonial Modernity." *Border Crossings: The Journal of Japanese-Language Literary Studies* 8, no. 1 (June 2019): 21–37.

Sand, Jordan. *House and Home in Modern Japan: Architecture, Domestic Space, and Bourgeois Culture, 1880–1930.* Cambridge, MA: Harvard University Asia Center, 2003.

Saneyoshi, Yasuzumi. *The Surgical and Medical History of the Naval War between Japan and China during 1894–95.* Tokyo: Tokio Publishing, 1901.

Sapporo biiru kabushiki-gaisha. *Sapporo 120 nenshi.* Tokyo: Sapporo biiru kabushiki-gaisha, 1996.

Sato, Barbara. *The New Japanese Woman: Modernity, Media, and Women in Interwar Japan.* Durham, NC: Duke University Press, 2003.

Schenking, J. Charles. *The Great Kantō Earthquake and the Chimera of National Reconstruction in Japan.* New York: Columbia University Press, 2013.

Schoppa, Leonard. "Demographics and the State." In *The Demographic Challenge: A Handbook about Japan,* edited by Florian Coulmas, Harald Conrad, Annette Schad-Seifert, and Gabriele Vogt, 639–652. Leiden: Koninklijke Brill, 2008.

Screech, Timon. *Sex and the Floating World: Erotic Images in Japan, 1700–1820.* Honolulu: University of Hawai'i Press, 1999.

———. *The Shogun's Painted Culture: Fear and Creativity in the Japanese States, 1760–1829.* London: Reaktion Books, 2000.

Sek, E. "'Demokratyzacja luksusu': Czy moze doprowadzic do prezeorganizowania rynku dobr luksusowych." *Ekonomika i Organizacja Przedsiebiorstwa* 4, no. 651 (2004): 22–30.

Seligmann, Matthew S. *Rum, Sodomy, Prayers, and the Lash Revisited: Winston Churchill and Social Reform in the Royal Navy, 1900–1915.* Oxford: Oxford University Press, 2018.

Seo, Gijae. "*Shonen Kurabu* and the Japanese Attitude toward War." *Children's Literature in Education,* no. 52 (March 6, 2021): 49–67. https://link.springer.com/article/10.1007/s10583-020-09402-z.

Shavell, Henry. "Postwar Taxation in Japan." *Journal of Political Economy* 56, no. 2 (April 1948): 124–137.

374   *Bibliography*

——. "Taxation Reform in Occupied Japan." *National Tax Journal* 1, no. 2 (June 1948): 127–143.

Shedd, Kim B. "Tungsten." In *USGS 2017 Minerals Yearbook*, 80.3–80.4. Washington, DC: US Department of the Interior and US Geological Survey, June 2020.

Sheldon, Charles D. "Merchants and Society in Tokugawa Japan." *Modern Asian Studies* 17, no. 3 (1983): 477–488.

Shimada, Masakazu. *Shibusawa Ei'ichi—Shakai kigyō-ka no sendansha.* Tokyo: Iwanami shoten, 2011.

Shiseidō Corporate Culture Division. *Bi o tsutaeru hitotachi: Shiseidō byūtī konsarutanto shi.* Tokyo: Kyūryūdō, 2001.

Shiseidō Corporate Museum. *Shiseidō monogatari: Shiseidō kigyō shiryōkan shūzōhin katarogu (1872–1946).* Kakegawa: Shiseidō Corporate Museum, 1995.

Silverberg, Miriam. "Constructing a New Cultural History of Prewar Japan." In "Japan in the World," special issue, *boundary 2* 18, no. 3 (Autumn 1991): 61–89.

——. "Constructing the Japanese Ethnography of Modernity." *Journal of Asian Studies* 51, no. 1 (February 1992): 30–54.

——. *Erotic Grotesque Nonsense: The Mass Culture of Japanese Modern Times.* Berkeley: University of California Press, 2009.

——. "The Modern Girl as Militant." In *Recreating Japanese Women, 1600–1945,* edited by Gail Lee Bernstein, 239–266. Berkeley: University of California Press, 1991.

Sivulka, Juliann. *Soap, Sex, and Cigarettes: A Cultural History of American Advertising.* 2nd ed. Belmont, CA: Wadsworth, 2011.

Skov, Lise. "Fashion Trends, Japonisme and Postmodernism: Or 'What Is So Japanese about Comme des Garçons?'" *Theory, Culture, and Society* 13, no. 3 (1996): 129–151.

Smith, Norman. *Intoxicating Manchuria: Alcohol, Opium, and Culture in China's Northeast.* Vancouver: University of British Columbia Press, 2012.

Soh, Sarah. *The Comfort Women: Sexual Violence and Postcolonial Memory in Korea and Japan.* Chicago: University of Chicago Press, 2008.

Solis, Jesus. "Japan's Black Market: *Yakuza*, SCAP, and the Culture of the *Yami'ichi*." MA thesis, University of Colorado, 2012.

Solt, George Sekine. "Taking Ramen Seriously: Food, Labor, and Everyday Life in Modern Japan." PhD diss., University of California at San Diego, 2009.

Stalker, Nancy. "'Cool Japan' as Cultural Superpower: 1980s–2010s." In *Japan: History and Culture from Classical to Cool,* 362–400. Berkeley: University of California Press, 2018.

Stein, Sally. *The Rhetoric of the Colorful and the Colorless: American Photography and Material Culture between the Wars.* New Haven, CT: Yale University Press, 1991.

Bibliography 375

Stephenson, Shelley. "'Her Traces Are Found Everywhere': Shanghai, Li Xiang-lan, and the 'Greater East Asia Film Sphere.'" In *Cinema and Urban Culture in Shanghai, 1922–1943*, edited by Yingjin Zhang, 222–245. Stanford, CA: Stanford University Press, 1999.

Stirling, Isabel. *The Life and Works of Ruth Fuller Sasaki*. Los Angeles: Counterpoint, 2006.

Sugimori, Hisahide. *Bishu Ichidai: Torii Shinjirō Den. Nihon uisukii monogatari*. Tokyo: Mainichi Shimbunsha, 1966.

Sugimoto, Yoshio. "Making Sense of *Nihonjinron*." *Thesis Eleven* 57, no. 1 (May 1, 1999): 81–96.

Sun Ad Company. *Yatte minaware—Santorii no 70 nen (1)*. Tokyo: Suntory, 1969.

Sunaga, Noritake. "Manshū no kagaku kōjō—jō." *Rikkyō keizaigaku kenkyū* 59, no. 4 (2006): 111–147.

Swader, Christopher S., Olga Strelkova, Alena Sutormina, Victoria Syomina, Volha Vysotskaya, and Irene Fedorova. "Love as a Fictitious Commodity: Gift-for-Sex Barters as Contractual Carriers of Intimacy." *Sexuality and Culture* 17 (2013): 598–616.

Taguchi, Masao. "Ri Kōran ni okuru kotoba." *Eiga no tomo* (June 1941): 98–99.

Takeyama, Akiko. *Staged Seduction: Selling Dreams in a Tokyo Host Club*. Stanford, CA: Stanford University Press, 2016.

Tanaka, Yasuo. *Nantonaku, kurisutaru*. Tokyo: Kawade shobō shinsha, 1981.

———. *Somehow Crystal*. Translated by Christopher Smith. Tokyo: Kurodahan Press, 2019.

Tanizaki, Jun'ichirō. *In Praise of Shadows*. New Haven, CT: Leete's Island Books, 1977.

———. *Naomi*. Translated by Anthony Chambers. London: Vintage Books, 2001.

Thorsten, Marie, and Yoneyuki Sugita. "Joseph Dodge and the Geometry of Power in US-Japan Relations." *Japanese Studies: 1981–2012* 19, no. 3 (1999): 297–314.

Tipton, Elise K. "The Café: Contested Space of Modernity in Interwar Japan." In *Being Modern in Japan: Culture and Society from the 1910s to the 1930s*, edited by Elise K. Tipton and John Clark, 119–136. Honolulu: University of Hawai'i Press, 2000.

———. *Modern Japan: A Social and Political History*. London: Taylor and Francis Routledge, 2002.

———. "Pink Collar Work: The Café Waitress in Early Twentieth Century Japan." *Intersections: Gender, History and Culture in the Asian Context*, no. 7 (March 2002). http://intersections.anu.edu.au/issue7/tipton.html.

Toby, Ronald P. "Reopening the Question of *Sakoku*: Diplomacy in the Legitimation of the Tokugawa Bakufu." *Journal of Japanese Studies* 3, no. 2 (Summer 1977): 323–363.

376 *Bibliography*

Tomii, Reiko. "State v. (Anti-)Art: Model 1,000 Yen Note Incident by Akasegawa Genpei and Company." *Positions: East Asia Cultures Critique* 10, no. 1 (Spring 2002): 141–172.

Toyoda, Takeshi. "Japanese Guilds." *Annals of the Hitotsubashi Academy* 5, no. 1 (October 1954): 72–85.

Tsai, Wan-Hsiu Sunny. "Patriotic Advertising and the Creation of the Citizen-Consumer." *Journal of Media and Communication Studies* 2, no. 3 (March 2010): 76–84.

Uchida, Hoshimi. "The Spread of Timepieces in the Meiji Period." In "The Birth of Tardiness: The Formation of Time Consciousness in Modern Japan," special issue, *Nichibunken Japan Review: Journal of the International Research Center for Japanese Studies* 14 (January 1, 2002): 176–177.

Uchikawa, Yoshimi, and Matsushima Eiichi, eds. *Taishō nyūsu jiten*, vol. 7. Tokyo: Mainichi Komiyunikēshiyon Shuppanbu, 1989.

Uchiyama, Benjamin. *Japan's Carnival War: Mass Culture on the Home Front, 1937–1945*. Cambridge: Cambridge University Press, 2019.

Ueno, Chizuko. "Self-Determination on Sexuality? Commercialization of Sex among Teenage Girls in Japan." *Inter-Asia Cultural Studies* 4, no. 2 (2003): 317–324.

Umemura, Maki, and Rika Fujioka. *Comparative Responses to Globalization Experiences of British and Japanese Enterprises*. London: Palgrave Macmillan, 2013.

United States Strategic Bombing Survey (European War / Pacific War). Maxwell AFB, AL: Air University Press, October 1987. https://web.archive.org/web /20080528051903/http://aupress.au.af.mil/Books/USSBS/USSBS.pdf.

Uozumi, Hirohisa. *Kō kigyō no seiritsu to tenkai: Senjiki. sengō fukkōki no eidan. Kōdan. Kōsha*. Tokyo: Iwanami shoten, 2009.

Usui, Kazuo. *Marketing and Consumption in Modern Japan*. London: Routledge, 2014.

Victoria, Brian Daizen. *Zen at War*. 2nd ed. Lanham, MD: Rowman and Littlefield, 2006.

Vogel, Ezra. *Japan as Number One: Lessons for America*. Cambridge, MA: Harvard University Press, 1979.

———. *Japan's New Middle Class: The Salary Man and His Family in a Tokyo Suburb*. Berkeley: University of California Press, 1963.

Walker, Brett. *Toxic Archipelago: A History of Industrial Disease in Japan*. Seattle: University of Washington Press, 2010.

Walker, Janet A. *The Japanese Novel of the Meiji Period and the Ideal of Individualism*. Princeton, NJ: Princeton University Press, 1979.

Walsh, Anthony. "Economies of Excrement: Public Health and Urban Planning in Meiji Japan." *Historical Perspectives: Santa Clara University Undergraduate Journal of History, Series II* 14, no. 9 (2009): 55–96.

Bibliography 377

Washidani, Hana. "'Idō' to 'henshin'—Ri Kōran, 'Dai TōA kyōei-ken' o." In *Ri Kōran to Higashi Ajia*, edited by Yomota Inuhiko, 40–55. Tokyo: Seikōsha, 2001.

Watts, Alan W. *The Way of Zen*. New York: Pantheon Books, 1957.

Watts, Eric King, and Mark P. Orbe. "The Spectacular Consumption of 'True' African American Culture: 'Whassup' with the Budweiser Guys?" *Critical Studies in Media Communication* 19, no. 1 (March 2002): 1–20.

Weber, Max. *The Protestant Ethic and the Spirit of Capitalism*. New York: Norton Critical Editions, 2009.

Weidman, Rich. *The Beat Generation FAQ: All That's Left to Know about the Angelheaded Hipsters*. Lanham, MD: Rowman and Littlefield, 2015.

Weisenfeld, Gennifer. "'From Baby's First Bath': Kaō Soap and Modern Japanese Commercial Design." *The Art Bulletin* 86, no. 3 (September 2004): 573–598.

———. *MAVO: Japanese Artists and the Avant-Garde, 1905–1931*. Berkeley: University of California Press, 2001.

———. "Publicity and Propaganda in 1930s Japan: Modernism as Method." *Design Issues* (Autumn 2009): 13–28.

Woodcock, George. "The Tyranny of the Clock." *War Commentary—for Anarchism* (Mid-March 1944). http://www.spunk.org/texts/writers/woodcock/sp001734.html.

Wynn, Lesley. "Self-Reflection in the Tub: Japanese Bathing Culture, Identity, and Cultural Nationalism." *Asia-Pacific Perspectives* 12, no. 2 (Spring/Summer 2014): 61–78.

Yabe, Nobuhisa. *Shiseidō hyakunen-shi*. Tokyo: Shiseidō senden-bu, 1972.

Yamada, Shōji. *Kantō daishinsai-ji no Chōsen-jin gyakusatsu to sono ato—gyakusatsu no kokka sekinin to minshū sekinin*. Tokyo: Shōshi-sha, 2011.

Yamaguchi, Yoshiko. *Ri Kōran: Watashi no hansei*. Tokyo: Shinchōsha, 1990.

Yamamura, Kozo. *A Study of Samurai Income and Entrepreneurship: Quantitative Analyses of Economic and Social Aspects of the Samurai in Tokugawa and Meiji Japan*. Cambridge, MA: Harvard University Press, 1974.

Yamashita, Samuel. *Daily Life in Wartime Japan, 1940–1945*. Lawrence: University of Kansas Press, 2015.

———. *Leaves in an Autumn of Emergencies: Selections from the Wartime Diaries of Ordinary Japanese*. Honolulu: University of Hawai'i Press, 2005.

Yanagi, Sōetsu. *The Unknown Craftsman: A Japanese Insight into Beauty*. Translated and adapted by Bernard Leach. Tokyo: Kodansha International, 1972.

———. *Yanagi Sōetsu senshū (dai issen) shinpan: Kōgei no Michi*. Tōkyō: Nihon Mingeikan, 1955.

Yanagihara, Ryōhei. *Yanagihara Ryōhei no shigoto*. Tokyo: Genkō-sha, 2015.

Bibliography

Yano, Christine Reiko. *Pink Globalization: Hello Kitty's Trek across the Pacific.* Durham, NC: Duke University Press, 2013.

Yoneyuki, Sugita. "The Yoshida Doctrine as a Myth." *Japanese Journal of American Studies,* no. 27 (2016): 123–143.

Yoneyuki, Sugita, and Marie Thorsten. *Beyond the Line: Joseph Dodge and the Geometry of Power in US–Japan Relations, 1949–1952.* Tokyo: University Education Press, 1999.

Yoshimi, Yoshiaki. *Grassroots Fascism: The War Experience of the Japanese People.* Translated by Ethan Mark. New York: Columbia University Press, 2015.

———. *Kusa no ne no fashizumu: Nihon minshū no sensō taiken (Atarashii seikaishi).* Tokyo: Tokyo Daigaku shuppankai, 1987.

Young, Louise. *Beyond the Metropolis: Second Cities and Modern Life in Interwar Japan.* Berkeley: University of California Press, 2013.

Yuko, Minowa, and Russell W. Belk. "Gifts and Nationalism in Wartime Japan." *Journal of Macromarketing* 38, no. 3 (May 2018): 298–314.

Index

Note: Page numbers in *italics* indicate illustrations.

advertising: celebrity endorsements, 140,
142, 196, 216–217, 219–222; color
advertising, 114; comparisons to
Western products, 119; consuming
communities and, 2; "Delicious Life,"
196, 219–221; government frugality
campaign, 124; government propaganda and, 222; high class in, 73, 93;
Japanese identity and, 90, 242; Katsumi
Asaba Design Studio, 219; lifestyle
promotion, 61; "new woman," 106;
Nissin Cup Noodles ad, 221; nude
female posters, 81–82; othering of, 48;
political trends in, 123; sustainability,
242; wartime advertising, 127–128,
130, 313n32; women's market, 63;
Yume kaidō (Dream Road) series, 217;
zeitaku wa teki da (luxury is the
enemy), 124, 220
African slavery and slave trade, 31, 293n5
Ai to shihonshugi (Love and Capitalism)
(Nakamura), 16
Akadama Port Wine, 81–82, 152–153,
299n6
Akasegawa, Genpei, 197–198
Allen, Woody, 219–220, 222
Allison, Anne, 164, 169, 188, 239
All Japan Watch and Clock Retail Asso-
ciation, 177
Amakasu, Masahiko, 95
Amano, Yūkichi, 221–222
American Exceptionalism (Lipset), 201
Ametora (American traditional), 236,
246–247, 251
Amino, Yoshihiko, 37
Anderson, Benedict, 2, 285n1
Anderssen, Jörgen, 207
Annie Hall (film), 219

Anno, Hideaki, 16
Anpō Treaty, 166, 196
Anti-Comintern Pact (1937), 125, 127
Aoyama district, 245
Apter, Elaine, 11
Arakawa, Shūsaku, 197–198, 204, 332n7
"Arcades, Magasins de Nouveautés"
(Benjamin), 87
The Arcades Project (Benjamin), 87, 236,
252
Arima, Akie, 274
Arnault, Bernard, 193
art galleries, 44, 204, 209
"The Artisanal Manufacturing Revolu-
tion" (Hendrix), 18
artisan and artisanal production: avant-
garde, 196, 206; clutter and, 12;
Hi-Red Center artists, 198; invented
labor, 19; Kawakubo Paris shows, 206;
Neo-Dadaism Organizers, 197–198;
nostalgia for, 20; performance art, 198;
Shiseidō gift boxes, 138–139; *Yomiuri
Indépendent* exhibition, 197; Zen
influence, 206–207
Art of the In-Between (exhibit), 206–207
Asaba, Katsumi, 217–219, 221–222
Asahi Shimbun (Morning News): beginnings of, 3–4; *imon bukuro* (comfort
bags), 137; Kaō advertisements, 118,
126; Kawakubo interview, 208; Lion
toothpaste advertisement, 128, *129;*
Nanking Victory in advertising, 128;
news and commercialism, 125; Osaka
Asahi Shimbun, 4, 106; Suntory advertisements, 102; wartime advertising, 128, 132–134, 160; wartime
efforts, 135
Asakusa entertainment area, 88, 96, 101

379

380 *Index*

Ashikaga shogunate, 38
Asia-Pacific War: advertising and, 125–130; Allied bombings, 89, 125, 146–147, 153, 156–158, 160–161; celebratory atmosphere of success, 125; commercialism and national news, 128; *Katei biyō* (Household Beauty) column, 127; luxury consumption and, 124–125; military contracts, 124–125; patriotic advertising, 124, 133
ASICS corporation, 241–242, 345n25
Aso, Noriko, 83, 304n77
aspirational luxury, 1, 7, 28, 94, 168, 202
Atwal, Glyn, 227
Au Bonheur des Dames (The Ladies' Paradise) (Zola), 87
Azuma, Hiroki, 255, 257
Azuma area, 157

Bacall, Lauren, 214
Bakumatsu period, 293n7
Balenciaga, 192–193
Balint, Peter, 345n27
Bank of Japan (BOJ), 27
banks and banking, 34, 240
Barber, Sheron, 192–193, 332n155
Bardsley, Jan, 218
Barthes, Roland, 52, 223–225, 298n81, 340n127
Bastien, Vincent, 227, 341n150
Bataille, Georges, 16
bathing and hygiene: indoor plumbing, 68–69; *sentō* (bathhouses), 62, 67–68. *See also* Kaō Corporation
Battle of Nagashino, 217
Battle of Sekigahara, 32
Beasley, William G., 36
Beene, Geoffrey, 210
Beezley, William, 306n19
Belk, Russell W., 313n32
Benjamin, Walter, 49–51, 53, 84, 87–88, 125, 236, 252–254, 281
Bestor, Ted, 259
Between Earth and Empire (Clark), 280
Beyond the Metropolis (Young), 96
Birnbach, Lisa, 248
Blanchard, Tamsin, 212
Bloch, Ernst, 97
Bloomingdale's department store, 211
Bolton, Andrew, 207
Bonnett, Alastair, 171

Borovy, Amy, 172
Bosman, Willem, 10
Boucicaut, Aristide-Jacques, 84
Bourdieu, Pierre, 45, 113
brand-name products: consumption of, 49; exchange for companionship, 16; guaranteed quality and, 48; history of, 56; history of craftsmanship and, 19; lifestyle associations, 218; logos, 51, 192; loyalty, 258; Onitsuka Tiger track shoes, 242; self-indulgence and, 219
Brashear-Alejandro, Thomas, 25–26, 279
Brasor, Philip, 222
Brooks, Louise, 110
Broom, Dave, 266
Brubeck, Dave, 247
Bryson, Douglas, 227
Buck, Cyndi, 272
Buck, John Lossing, 315n67
Buddhist Society of America, 182
Budweiser beer, 48
bunka jūtaku (culture houses), 61
bunka seikatsu (culture life), 93, 115
Buñuel, Luís, 281
Burke, Timothy, 61
Burns, Susan, 72
business organizations: *keiretsu* (shareholding companies), 40, 85; zaibatsu (conglomerates), 34, 40, 165
Butler, Lee, 67

Café Raion (Lion), 79, 101
Capital (Marx), 9–10, 13, 35
capitalism: definition of, 30; globalized world, 49; influences, 35–37, 45
Cartier jewelers, Santos-Dumont wristwatch, 78
cartoon characters, 186, 192
Casio: advertising and marketing, 194, 264; Baby G line, 258; Casiotron digital watch, 179–180; collectors (*otaku*), 260; collectors and luxury, 236, 258–259, 275; Ex-word floris XD-R970, 350n102; Gravitymaster, 262–263; G-Shock, 262–264, 269, 272; innovative wares of, 163; J-Cool and, 258; limited-edition products, 253; luxury products of, 263; manufacturing facilities, 263; quellazaire, 165
Casio Computer Company: calculator, 178; origins of, 177–178

Index

Casio Museum, 178
Casual, Reggie, 243–244
Catapano, Josephine, 181
Chamberlain, Basil Hall, 70
Chen, Diexian, 113
Chieinsutoa kenkyū (The Chainstore Research), 109, 135, *136*
Chijin no ai (A Fool's Love) (Tanizaki), 4
Chimoto, Akiko, 154
China: Communist takeover, 165; *guanxi* (connections), 230; Japanese products in, 196; literacy in, 315n67; logo design, 55; New Year holiday, 144, 316n70; Opening and Reforms, 55; skin whitening and, 233–234; Special Economic Zones, 26
China Conflict, 148
Chisso Corporation mercury emissions, 282
Cho, Margaret, 346n36
Christianity and Christian principles, 31, 35, 86
Chūō kōron (Central Review), 78–79, *79*
Chūō ward, 148
Citizen Watch Company, 156, 176
civil rights movement, 248
Clark, John P., 280–281, 355n8
Cold War, 165–167, 179, 181, 195, 279
The Collector (Benjamin), 236, 252, 281
collectors (*otaku*): definition of, 252–253; history of, 254–256; luxury goods and, 259; online communities, 236; traumatic events and, 257; watches, 258–262, 297n71; watches and, 260
The Comfort of Things (Miller), 184
comfort woman system, 130, 146, 317n86
comics and animated films, 256–257
Comme des Garçons boutique, 22, 195, 205–208, 335n40
commodity fetishism, 188; advertising and, 1, 28, 56–57; artisanal production and, 280; capitalism and, 45, 202; celebrity endorsements and, 222; collectors and, 252; commodified relationships, 289n64; commodities and social relations, 9, 11, 185; commodity fetishization, 17, 19; consumer society, 276–277; definition of, 287n20; department stores and, 87; emotional connections and gifts, 15; extreme endpoint of, 17; fashion victim trope,

203; Japaneseness of Kawakubo collection, 206–207; Kondoization and hoarding, 12–13; labor revealed, 18; late industrial capitalism and, 49; luxuriated products, 22, 138, 261, 279; origin of fetish, 9–11; pocket watch and, 100; psychosexual theory, 11; radical art and, 198; Shintō practice and, 13–14; social labor and, 269; social relations and, 184; social status and, 168; unique high quality and, 237
communism: baseline communism, 295n55; left-leaning *Koza-ha* (lecture faction), 35; *Rōnō-ha* (labor-farmer faction), 35
Confucian influence, 23, 31–33, 37, 46
Connery, Sean, 217
consumer behavior, 52–53, 83, 236
consumer capitalism, 13, 15–16, 169, 185–186, 195, 198, 258
Consumption Activity Index, 27, 292n103
"Cool Japan," 179, 240–242, 267, 274
Cool Japan Fund, 240–241
Coppola, Francis Ford, 217, 222
Coppola, Sophia, 216
cosmetics and perfume: medicinal and herbal extracts in, 267–268; *otona no shichi-nan* (seven difficulties for adults), 273–274; purchaser diversity, 269. See also Kaō Corporation; Shiseidō Company
Cosmopolitan (magazine), 7
Council for Quality Inspection of the Japan-Made Watch and Clock, 177
Cowen, Jessie Roberta "Rita," 101
Creighton, Millie, 171
Crohin-Kishigami, Stéphanie, 68
Cromer, Kiara R., 257
Croutzen, Paul, 280
cultural appropriation, 278, 345n27, 346n36
cultural capital, 112–113

Dah Chong Hong Cosmetics company, 234
Dai-ichi Gekijō (First Theater), 127
Dai Nippon Kajū Kabushiki gaisha (Great Japan Juice Company), 103–104, 150, 152–153, 169, 265. See also Nikka whisky Distilling Company
Daini Seikōsha (Second Seikō Company), 155

382 *Index*

Daiwa Kōgyō (Daiwa Industries), 155
Dapper Dan, 251
de Brosses, Charles, 10
Debt (Graeber), 41
de Certeau, Michel, 60, 299n1
Deflem, Mathieu, 255
de Givenchy, Hubert, 210
democratizing luxury, 1, 24–27, 56, 64–66, 147, 212, 262, 276–278, 281, 283
Deng Xiaoping, 26, 55, 218
department stores: colonial expansion, 109; consumption as religion, 86–88; cultural authorities, 304n77; *Ginbura* (Ginza cruising), 41; history of, 83–84; industrial revolution and, 83; luxury goods in, 91, 107; marketing and, 86; modernity and, 61; wartime challenges, 159–160. *See also* Mitsukoshi department store
department stores, foreign: Au Bon Marché, 84, 87; Harrods, 84; Jewish-owned German, 86–87; Liberty of London, 84; Selfridges, 84–85, 304n83; Wanamaker's, 85–86
Derrida, Jacques, 52
de Villiers, Nicholas, 16
Dewar, Tommy, 171
Di Ser brand, 227
Dodge, Joseph, 165
Dodge Plan, 177
Doi, Takeo, 168
Dress Codes (Rubinstein), 202
drugstores, 66, 112, 230, 273
Duchamp, Marcel, 50, 197
Du Culte des dieux fétiches (The Cult of Fetish Gods) (de Brosses), 10
Duffy, Erin, 7
Dutch East India Company, 31

Echigoya, 41–42
Economic Miracle, 22, 89, 163, 167–168, 199, 232, 246, 249, 255
Edano, Yukio, 58
Edo (contemporary Tokyo), 20, 23, 32, 40–41, 69, 241–242
Eiffel, Alexandre-Gustav, 84
Eisenhower, Dwight D., 166
Elan, Priya, 343n2
electronic goods (*denki yōhin*), 168
Enlightenment project, 4
Enomoto, Ken'ichi, 140

environmental destruction, 280–282
environmental stewards, 282–283
Estée Lauder's Youth Dew, 181

Falk, Peter, 217
fancy goods (*fanshii guzzu*), 185–186, 188–189
Fanning the Flames (Kelly), 258
fascism and fascist regimes, 21, 24, 36, 50, 118, 127, 134, 149, 198
fashion and attire: *Ametora* (American traditional), 246–247, 251; Anglo-American punk currents, 203–204; avant-garde, 203, 209, 234; Balenciaga, 192–193; Bathing Ape (BAPE), 236, 244, 249–252; Black and Latinx influence, 249; celebrity purchasers, 211; DR14, 192; hip-hop fashion, 251, 343n2; influences on, 205–206; international appeal, 204–206; pleated design, 214–215; premodern Japanese styles, 195–196; "preppy," 243, 246–248; semiotics of dress, 202–203; sneakers and sport shoes, 242, 345n25; street fashion, 192, 208, 211, 215, 236, 242–245, 249–253, 262, 275, 343n2; Tokyo Olympics and, 247; *Train Fantôme* scarf, 278–280, 279; *wabi-sabi* ideals, 212. *See also* Hello Kitty; Kawakubo, Rei; Miyake, Issey
Fedorova, Irene, 289n64
"Fetishism" (Freud), 11
fetishism of labor, 20–22, 50, 58
Flanagan, Scott, 201
Food Control Law, 163
Forbes, 193
Ford, Henry, 19
Fordism, 36, 50
Foroudi, Pantea, 55
Fortuny y Madrazo, Mariano, 214
Foucault, Michel, 299n1
Fragrantica (blog), 181
Frazer-Caroll, Micha, 343n2
Frederick, Sarah, 144
Freud, Sigmund, 11
Frost, Randy, 12
Frühstück, Sabine, 82
Fūgetsudō cookies, 62
Fujin Gahō (Women's Pictorial), 5
Fujin kōron (Women's Review), 7
Fujin no tomo (Women's Companion), 5

Index

Fujioka, Rika, 159–160
Fujiwara, Hiroshi, 244, 249–250, 345n30
Fukasawa, Naoto, 44
Fukuhara, Arinobu, 65–66, 77
Fukuhara, Shinzō, 54, 66–67
Fukuzawa Yukichi, 4, 75
Funatsu, Tsuruyo, 167
Fury, Alexander, 206
Fuzai jinushi (Absentee Landlords), 35

Gallagher, William, 67
Garon, Sheldon, 37, 220
Garrett, Kent, 248
Gehry, Frank, 205
geisha and geisha houses, 21, 23, 46, 66, 121
Genroku "golden age," 20, 23
The Gift (Mauss), 15, 184
gift-for-sex (GFS), 289n64
Gijae, Seo, 132
Ginn, Greg, 204
Gins, Madeline, 204, 333n7
Ginza shopping district, 41; cafés and bars in, 80, 101; *Ginbura* (Ginza cruising), 41; Hattori Clock Tower, 96–97; high-end boutiques, 96, 246; logos of, 54; Matsuya store, 53–54; Mitsukoshi department store, 85; Mitsukoshi in, 80; Seikō watch and clock repair shop, 76; Shinzō pharmacy, 66; Tokyo Olympics and, 198
Glamour (magazine), 7
Glaser, Gabrielle, 267
Godzilla films, 238–239
Goldman, Jeremy, 26
Gotanda area, 186
Goto, Yutaka, 223, 225, 339n123
Graeber, David, 41, 43, 45, 185, 295n55
Grandin, Greg, 293n5
Granot, Elad, 25–26, 279
Grant, Melissa Gira, 16
Great Britain, 33, 83–84, 89, 138–139, 150–151, 153, 171, 187, 190, 266
Greater East Asia Co-Prosperity Sphere, 110
Great Kantō Earthquake: cultural impact of, 95; destruction and rebuilding, 93, 95; Ginza café culture, 101; media changes after, 106; Mitsukoshi destruction and, 85; modernity after, 122; rebuilding after, 100, 104, 157,

177; Shiseidō chain store system, 114; Shiseidō Parlour and, 66; violence by *jikeidan* and police, 94–95
Grosberg, Kenneth Alan, 38
Gucci, 251
Gupta, Suraksha, 55

H&M, 207–208
Hagiwara, Shigeru, 274
hair washing and hair products, 120–121. *See also* Kaō Corporation
Hanseikai zasshi (Reflection Society Magazine), 78
Hara, Hiromu, 117
Harajuku area, 208, 244, 250, 258, 345n30, 346n36
Harootunian, Harry D., 94, 97
Harris Treaty of Amity and Commerce (1858), 34, 40, 64
Hasegawa, Hajime, 247
Hasegawa, Kazuō, 140
Hashimoto, Ken'ichi, 164
Hatsuda, Kōsei, 163–164
Hattori, Kintarō, 76–78
Hattori, Tamio, 167
Hayasaka, Shinya, 68
Hayashida, Teruyoshi, 247–248
Heian period, 8, 215, 223, 237, 333n20
Heibon Punch, 246
Heisei era, 54
Hell, Richard, 204
Hello Kitty, 182–183, 185–194
Hendrix, Michael, 18
Her Best-Kept Secret (Glaser), 267
High Snobiety, 345n30
Hillary, Edmund, 297n71
Hindrickson, Hildi, 61
hipster capitalism, 18–20, 237–238
Hirai, Hirokazu, 149
Hirakawa, Hiroko, 218
Hiroshima, 238
The History of Modern Japan (Kaempfer), 293n7
Hitler, Adolf, 51
Hoarders (TV show), 12
Hokkaidō, 34, 104, 152–153, 227, 266
Honda, Ishirō, 238
Hoston, Germaine A., 36
House of Representatives Election Law (1925), 118
Housewife's Friend, 104, 110

Index

Housewife's World, 105
Howell, David, 23, 34, 69
Hrushka, Rachel, 21
HTM, 244
Huruse, Noriko, 216

Ibe, Kikue, 262–263
Ichikawa, Kon, 180, 247
Ie no hikari (Light of the Home), 7
Ihara, Saikaku, 45
Iijima, Kazunobu, 240
Ikebukuro ward, 196, 230
Ikeda, Hayato, 163, 166–167, 183
Ikeda, Shinobu, 144
Imagawa-bashi area, 53
Imagined Communities (Anderson), 2
Iman, 211
imon bukuro (comfort bags), 124,
    130–131, 133, 135–137, *136,* 146, 161
imon ehagaki (comfort postcards),
    131–132
imonpin (comfort items), 130, 132, 135
imperial family, 202
Imperial Japan: battle successes, 130;
    birthrate in, 127, 312n13; China and,
    144–145; colonial acquisitions, 93,
    106, 232; colonial marketing, 112;
    commercial and business interests, 137;
    commercial expansion and, 123; eco-
    nomics of, 70; fascism and, 118; first
    gift of whisky, 152, 318n117; luxury
    products of, 90; mass media and, 134;
    modernity and, 111–112, 299n2; patri-
    otic consumption in, 130, 313n21;
    patriotism in, 132, 139; political cul-
    ture in, 63
imperial palace, 298n81
Imperial Rescript on Education, 2
The Independent, 216
industrial capitalism, 75–76, 83–84, 97,
    188
In'ei raisan (In Praise of Shadows) (Tani-
    zaki), 69
Inoue, Mokuda, 82
internationalization, 269, 275, 278
Internet, 222, 236, 261, 275, 277, 345
interwar years. *See* Taishō era
In the Realm of the Hungry Ghosts
    (Maté), 17
Inukai, Tsuyoshi, 92
Iriye, Akira, 243, 274

Isetan department store, 85, 230, 245
Iseya, Yūsuke, 282–283, 355n13
Ishigure, Masakazu, 163
Ishikawa, Satomi, 200
Ishizu, Kensuke, 245–246
Ishizu, Shōsuke, 247
Isono, Hikaru, 63
Issey Miyake-Kyoto, 44, *210*
Itō, Noe, 95
Itoi, Shigesato, 219, 339n107

Jansen, Maurius, 4
"Japan: Wages of Sinlessness," 163–164
Japan as Number One (Vogel), 8, 201
Japan Clock and Watch Association
    (JCWA), 77, 176–177
Japanese capitalism and economy: Anglo-
    American West and, 119; Bernard
    Arnault, 193; blend of Western and
    Confucian values, 33; "Cool Japan,"
    179, 240–242, 267, 274; democracy
    and, 4, 23; economy and, 92; episode of
    economic uncertainty, 200; fascist state
    and, 21; growth of, 29; Japanese
    uniqueness, 199; "Lost Decade," 239;
    mass production and, 57, 261; new
    products and, 104; origins of, 29–31, 40;
    paternalistic benevolence, 90; post-
    war economic miracle, 167; postwar
    economy, 164, 166, 193, 202; print
    media and, 3, 8; proto-history of, 58,
    62; state intervention, 24–25; transwar
    era, 169, 324n31
Japanese culture: *en* (relationships with
    customers), 42–43; *omotenashi* (rela-
    tionships with customers), 19, 24, 43,
    290n76, 296n60
Japanese financial crises: economic reces-
    sion, 229; Great Depression, 102, 114;
    Great Recession and, 24, 313n21
Japanese imperialism: East Asia and,
    232–233; military product endorse-
    ment, 70
Japanese media: anime and manga, 236,
    239, 242, 255–256; Godzilla films,
    238–239; Pokémon, 238; Power
    Rangers, 238
Japanese society, 200–201, 299n1
Japanese Tax Code, 164–165
Japanese women: consumers, 1–2, 63, 107;
    decisionmakers, 6, 70, 292n96; elite

Index

women, 105; frugality of, 27, 184; hairstyles, 120–121; host clubs and, 15–16; housewifery, 121–122; imperial womanhood, 113; kimono cloth, 183; luxury goods and, 27; *moga* (modern girls), 92–93, 105–106, 115, 122; munitions factory volunteers, 147; "new woman," 104, 106, 120; Rice Riots and, 92; *Ryōsai kenbo* ("Good Wife, Wise Mother"), 6; scientific housewifery, 122; skin whitening and, 118, 127, 142, 230; women's magazines, 4–5, 7, 60, 105, 110, 122; women's suffrage, 104; working women, 218

Japan's Carnival War (Uchiyama), 125

Japan's New Middle Class (Vogel), 168, 202

Japan Times, 221

Japan Watch and Clock Inspection Institute, 177

Jeweler's Circular, 77

Jiji shimpō (Current Events News), 4

Jimmu (emperor), 140

Johansson, Scarlett, 215

Josei (Woman) (magazine), 4

Joseph, Nigel, 299n2

Journal of Political Economy, 164

Kabuki-za (Kabuki Theater), 127

Kaempfer, Engelbert, 293n7

Kagemusha (Shadow Warrior) (film), 217

Kagirinaku tōmei ni chikai burū (Almost Transparent Blue), 199

Kairekiben (Exposition on the Changing of the Calendar) (Fukuzawa), 75

Kaitokudō merchant academy, 33

Kamakura period, 37, 53

Kamen no kokuhaku (Confessions of a Mask) (Mishima), 69

Kamiya, Denbei, 101

kamon (family crests), 29, 51–52, 54

Kanamaru, Shigene, 116–117

Kani kōsen (The Factory Ship), 35

Kantō district, 38, 146

Kaō Corporation: advertisements, 48, 117–118, *119,* 119–121; Asience hair-care product line, 267–268; Chinese and Korean market, 109; company archives, 148; early revenues, 115; equality to Western products, 119;

high-quality cleansers and detergents, 119–120; Housework Science Laboratory, 122; international business, 112, 275; international sales, 268; Japanese customers and, 62; Kaō sekken (Kaō Soap), 70–71; luxury consumer products of, 60; Manshū Kaō soap factory, 149; midrange cosmetics, 116; Nanjing factory, 232; new formula soap advertising campaign, 117; Nihachisui (Two Eight Water), 73, *74;* origins of, 3; overseas markets, 196; product endorsements, 70–71; shampoo products, 120–121, *121,* 268–269; soap and, 62, *116;* traditional cleaning products, 69–70; wartime advertising, 127–128; wartime factory destruction, 157; wartime military contracts, 148; wartime production and profitability, 148; wartime soap advertisement, *126.* *See also* hair washing and hair products

Kapferer, Jean-Noël, 227

Kaplan, Louise J., 11

Kapur, Nick, 166

Kashio, Kazuo, 177

Kashio Seisakujo (Casio Manufacturing Company), 177

Kashio Tadao, 177

Kashio Toshio, 177–178

Kashio Yukio, 177

katakana (phonetic Japanese script for foreign words), 103, 121, 152

Kataoka, Toshiro, 81

Katei no tomo (Home Companion), 5

Katsu, Kōkichi, 33

Kaufman, Cynthia, 13–14, 30

Kawabata, Yasunari, 20–21, 57

kawaii (cute) characters, 168, 187–189, 191, 258, 330n133. *See also* Hello Kitty

Kawakubo, Rei, 203–209, 211–212, 336n60

Kawano, Satsuki, 62

Keaton, Diane, 219

Kelly, William, 258–259

Kelts, Roland, 250

Kennan, George, 165

Kennedy, Edward "Ted," 216

Kennedy, John F., 181, 216

Kennedy, Patricia, 216

Kennedy, Robert "Bobby," 216

Kikuchi, Kan, 97
Kingu (King), 7
Kinsella, Sharon, 185
Kirk, Nicole C., 86
Kitagawa, Naoki, 240
Kitagawa, Utamaro, 46
Kita-no-Mandokoro, 181–182
Klein, Naomi, 56, 297n78
Knight, Diana, 223
Kobayashi, Nobuko, 187
Kobayashi, Takiji, 35
Kōchi Prefecture, 177
Kohlbacher, Florian, 274
Kōkoku hihyō (Ad Criticism), 112, 221–222
Kōkokukai (Advertising World), 124
Kokoro (Sincerity) (Natsume), 4
Komori, Naoko, 70
Kon, Wajirō, 41
Kondo, Dorinne, 206
Kondo, Marie, 12, 257, 283
Konoe, Fumimarō, 149
Korea and Koreans, 31, 91, 94, 107, 196
Korean War, 165
Koren, Leonard, 53, 261, 350n112
Kotobukiya Limited: advertising, 171; Allied postwar purchases, 169; founding of, 81, 91; Hawaiian travel contest, 173–174; hospitality and, 62; Imon-yō Santorii Uisukii ("Comfort-Use" Suntory Whisky), 152; Japanese customers and, 62; Japanese whisky, 82, 101; nude female posters, 82; Old Suntory Whisky Kuromaru (Black Ship), 152; origins of, 3, 60; Palm Curry, 102; postcard advertising, 93–94; postwar affordable products, 162–163; Smoker toothpaste, 102; Suntory Royal Whisky, 173; Suntory Shirofuda (Suntory White Label), 102–103, 151, 308n46; Tori's Black Tea, 102; Tori's Sauce, 102; Torys Whisky, 169, 172–173, 193; Torys Wistan, 173; Uncle Torys mascot, 171–173, 193; wartime aviation fuel production, 152; wartime production and profitability, 150; Yamazaki Distillery, 82, 102, 152–153. *See also* Suntory
Kouishi Kotakubo & Co., 77–78
Kretschmer, Angelika, 14
Kumano brushes, 58

Kunikida, Doppo, 5
Kurayoshi Distillery, 319n125
Kurosawa, Akira, 217–218, 222
Kurosu, Toshiyuki, 247
Kushner, Barak, 124
Kuzuhara Kogyō's (Kuzuhara Industries) Modan Shanpū (Modern shampoo) powder, 120

L'Age d'Or (Golden Age) (Buñuel), 281
Lagerfeld, Karl, 205
Laroche, Guy, 209
Lawford, Peter, 48, 216–217
Leach, Bernard, 138
Lean, Eugenia, 113
LeMay, Curtis, 156–157
L'Empire des Signes (Empire of Signs) (Barthes), 223
Lenard, Patti Tamara, 345n27
Lerner, Paul, 86–87
Leroy, Jean-Yves, 226
Li, Xianglan. *See* Yamaguchi, Yoshiko
Liberal Democratic Party (LDP), 163, 166–167
limited-edition products: ASICS and, 241; collector's items, 253, 278; fashion and, 208, 236, 250–252; frugality and, 1, 24; gifts and, 15, 137–138; Hello Kitty, 194; luxury and, 23, 94, 276; mass production and, 48; rarity of, 48, 297n71; Sanrio cute items, 330n134; seasonal items and, 291n88; Seiko store, 96; Seikō watches, 179; Shiseidō trial kits, 231; Suntory label and, 176; watches, 262, 272; whisky, 264
Lingua Franca, 21, 291n84
Lipset, Seymour M., 201
liquor. *See* whisky
literacy: *hiragana* and *rubi*, 2; Imperial Rescript on Education, 2; universal education and, 3
Live and Let Die (film), 179
Locke, John, 10
logos: artisanal guilds *mon*, 52; Chinese, 55; conglomerates, 54, 58; consumerism and, 56; corporate values and, 55; design of, 55; history of, 30, 58; Japanese-themed, 242; *kanban* (carved signs) and, 42, 52; Matsuya, 53; quality standards and, 1; samurai *kamon*, 52; visual reminder, 3; woodblock prints, 29

Lost in Translation (film), 215–216
Louis Vuitton (LV), 192–193, 208, 227, 251, 332n155, 348n73
Love and Pop (Anno), 16
Love. Angel. Music. Baby (Stefani), 346n36
Lucas, George, 217
Lukacs, Georg, 17, 19, 50, 56
Lutens, Serge, 65, 224–228, 278, 280, 341n152
luxury: advertising and marketing, 22; definition of, 22; democratizing, 24; in Japan, 22; limited-edition products, 23–24, 291n88; populence and, 25–26; product qualities, 22. *See also* democratizing luxury
luxury restaurants: Western cuisine, 190; Yakata no Resutoran (Mansion Restaurant), 190–191

MacArthur, Douglas, 165
Machado, Mark, 243
Machida, Saori, 148, 232
Maeda, Mitsugu, 110
Maeshima, Shiho, 5
magazines, history of, 5
Mainichi Shimbun (Daily News), 4
Manchu Empress Wanrong, 110–111
Manchukuo, 92, 110, 139, 144–145, 148. *See also* Yamaguchi, Yoshiko
Manchuria, 21, 107
Manchurian Incident, 103, 106, 117–118, 123, 135
manufactured artisanality: collectors and, 253; consumers and, 19; craftsmanship of, 58, 275; fashion and, 206, 209, 237; global market, 21, 265; Japanese luxury and, 1, 22, 45, 276; labor and, 19; limited editions and, 194; marketing and, 56, 78, 283; mass production and, 49; nostalgia for hand craftmanship, 53; premodernity and, 24, 28; product value, 57; reification antidote, 17–18
manufacturing authenticity, 7
Mao Zedong, 165
Margiela, Martin, 262
Marotti, William, 198
Marounouchi business district, 99
Marshall, Amy Bliss, 7
Marumo, Toshiyuki, 147
Maruyama, Masao, 201, 333n21

Maruyama, Tomoyoshi, 95
Marx, Karl: capital formation, 35; commodity fetishism and, 9–11, 13, 19, 185, 269, 287n20; Europeans and, 280; industrialization and, 14; influences on, 36; monster metaphors, 17; primitive communities and, 29; reification and, 56
Marx, W. David, 230, 245–246
mass media, 1, 7, 93–94, 117–118, 125, 132, 222
mass-produced products: advertising and marketing, 14–15, 30, 283; brand-name products, 48–49; Chinese knits, 21; clutter and, 12–13; collectors and, 260; constructed artisanality, 57; cosmetics and, 138, 271; craftsmanship and, 19, 194, 237; department store sales, 83, 89; fashion and, 206, 212, 214; fetishism of, 45; Japaneseness and, 261; luxury and, 60, 276; Occupy Movement and, 56; politicization of, 50, 53; reproducibility of, 48; spiritually infused animism, 9; watches and, 77
Maté, Gabor, 17, 279
Matsuda, Takeshi, 239, 255
Matsudaira, Sadanobu, 23
Matsukata, Masayoshi, 34
Matsukata Deflation, 34, 75
Matsushima, Emiko, 82
Matsuya Gofukuten (Matsuya Piece Goods Store), 53–54
Matsuzakaya department store, 41, 133–134
Mauss, Marcel, 15, 41, 43, 184, 296n60
Mavo group, 95, 306n9
McDarrah, Fred W., 238
McFadden, Mary, 214–215
McLaren, Malcolm, 204
McLuhan, Marshall, 221
McNally, David, 17
Meidiya, 63, 80, 127
Meiji era: advertising and marketing, 1; calendar reform, 75; commodity fetishism, origin of, 22; company histories, 54; competition to Western companies, 90; constitution (1889), 63; consuming communities and, 2; department stores, 41, 91; frugality of, 70, 81; industrialization in, 29, 34, 72,

Meiji era (*continued*)
77; Japanese identity and, 53; luxury images, 277; mass consumption, 23; Meiji Civil Code, 6; mercantile presence, 65; Misdemeanor Law, 62; nightsoil collection, 69; personal hygiene and grooming, 73; public hygiene, 67–68; *sentō* (bathhouses), 68; serialized novels, 80–81; status categories, abolition of, 35, 40, 43, 63; time control in, 76; tourism in, 301n26; unequal treaties and, 64; women's magazines, 5

Meiji Revolution, 36; *ashigaru* (declassed samurai), 294n15

Melewar, T. C., 55

Men's Club (magazine), 245

merchant class, 23, 32–33, 43, 45, 52, 88

Metacake, 352n140

Metropolitan Museum of Art (New York), 206–207, 211

Mettler, Meghan, 238

middle class: affordable luxury, 121; aspirational luxury items, 168; conformity and material wealth, 200; consumption by, 61; democracy and, 167; democratizing luxury, 1, 6; disposable income and, 276; frugality of, 24, 70–71, 81, 103; home bathrooms, 68; Meiji era and, 1; new markets for, 36; postwar Japan, 167–168; Seibu Department Store, 196; timepieces and, 62, 97–98, 122–123, 154; travel abroad, 54, 173; wartime Japan and, 158–159; women and housewives, 2, 5–6, 105, 114–115, 117. See also *sarariman*

Miller, Daniel, 16, 183–184

Minami, Hiroshi, 118, 201

Ministry of Agriculture, Forestry, and Fisheries, 146

Ministry of Commerce and Industry, 146, 149

Ministry of Education, 321n161

Ministry of Finance, 34

Ministry of Railways, 96

Ministry of Economy, Trade and Industry (METI), 240

Minowa, Yuko, 313n32

Mitaka area, 177, 197, 333n7

Mitsui, Taketoshi, 88

Mitsui and Company, 3–4, 34, 40–41, 54–55, 58, 85, 88–89, 109

Mitsukoshi department store, 230; advertising for, 107; art gallery in, 44; expansion of, 107; high-end products in, 112; history of, 85; Mimeguri Shrine at, 88–89; Nihonbashi location, 85; origins of, 41; *Tennyo magokoro* (Heavenly Maiden of Sincerity), 89–90; wartime losses, 159–160; wartime overseas colonies sales, 160; watch sales, 78–79, 79

Miyake, Issey, 22, 225, 282; avant-garde, 203; childhood radiation-induced injuries, 336n64; collections of, 211; cult status, 204; high-end boutiques, 44, 195; Miyake Design Studio, 210; Pleats Please brand, 205, 211–214, 221; Shiseidō advertisement, 225; style to the masses, 282; Tokugawa-era elegance, 209

Miyake Issey Exhibition, 337nn80–81

Miyamoto, Mike, 103, 265

Miyazaki, Takashi, 124

Miyazaki, Tsutomu, 256–257, 349n90

Miyuki Tribe, 246

Mizoguchi, Kenji, 97–98, 100

Mizuki, Shigeru, 256–257

modernity, 61, 63, 122

modernization theory, 6, 61, 75, 306n19, 334n29

Moholy-Nagy, Lazlo, 117

monetary system, 39, 41, 87

Moody, Dwight, 86

Moore, Jason, 280

Morinaga caramel, 132–133, *133*

Morphology of Revenge (Akasegawa), 198

Morris, William, 139

Morse, Terry O., 238

Motohashi, Kazuyuki, 182, 222, 228–229

Moto'ori Norinaga, 333n20

Murakami, Ryū, 199, 262, 348n73

Murakami, Shihori, 163

Murakami, Takashi, 251

Murasaki, Shikibu, 8, 215, 237

Muromachi period, 29, 38, 41–42, 53, 68, 300n22

Murphey, Dennis L., 257

Murray, Bill, 215

Index

389

Musashino Department Store, 196
Mutsuhito (emperor), 34, 75
mythical founding of Japan, 139, 142

Nagano Prefecture, 115, 155–156, 176, 221
Nagasaki, 31, 238
Nagase, Shinobu, 268
Nagase, Tomirō, 69
Nagata, Mary Louise, 38–40
Nagrin, Henriette, 214
Nakada, Kinkichi, 300n10
Nakamori, Akio, 255
Nakamura, Masanao, 33
Nakamura, Usagi, 15–17, 24, 33, 255, 258
Nakanishi, Natsuyuki, 197
Namba, Kōji, 220
Nantonaku, kurisutaru (Somehow, Crystal) (Tanaka), 8, 250
Naomi (Tanizaki), 106
National Shōwa Memorial Museum, 158, 321n161
National Socialism, 50–51
Natsume, Sōseki, 4
Necrocene age, 277, 280
NEPENTHES, 245
Nettleson, Taro, 198
A New and Accurate Account of the Coast of Guinea (Bosman), 10
newspapers, 3–5
New York Times, 3, 12, 89, 173, 206
Nickerson, Rebecca, 141
Nigō (Nagao Tomoaki), 244, 249–251
Nihonbashi area, 41, 85, 88–89, 148
Nihonbashi-Kayaba-chō area, 148
Nihonjinron (Japaneseness), 195, 200, 202, 234, 334n31
Nihonjinron no keifu (The Genealogy of a Discourse of Japaneseness) (Maruyama), 201
Nihon Keizai Shimbun (Japan Economics News), 4
Nihon Shoki (Chronicles of Japan), 89
Nike, 243–244
Nikka Whisky Distilling Company, 104, 150, 152, 169, 265–266. *See also* Dai Nippon Kajū Kabushiki gaisha
Nikkei (journal), 4
Nikkei Asia, 187

Nikkei Asian Review, 240, 268
Nishihara, Masashi, 166
Nixon, Richard, 200
No Logo (Klein), 56
Nolte, Sharon, 105
Noma, Caroline, 317n86
Nomonhan Incident, 158
Norgay, Tenzin, 297n71
Norman, E. H., 36
nuclear radiation, 238
Nye, Joseph, 239–240

Occupy Movement, 18, 24, 50, 56, 297n78
Oda, Nobunaga, 39
Okuyama, Gihachirō, 152
omuraisu (omelet-rice), 66
Ōnin War, 39
Onitsuka Tiger, 241–242
Orbe, Mark P., 48
Osaka, 3–4, 23, 33–34, 47, 89, 102, 238, 347n56
Osaka Tokei Manufacturing Company, 76
Ōsugi, Sakae, 95
Ota, Nobuyuki, 240
Otaka, Hiroshi, 145
Otaku Murderer, 256

Parent, Timothy, 55
Parfums Beauté Serge Lutens, 278
"Paris, the Capital of the Nineteenth Century" (Benjamin), 87
Parliamentary Election Law, 4
Patterson, Thomas Stewart, 101
Peace Preservation Law (1925), 93, 118
Peanuts comic strip, 186
People's Rights Movement, 63
Perry, Matthew C., 152
Pew Research Group, 291n89
pharmacies and pharmaceuticals, 64, 70, 72–73, 147. *See also* Shiseidō Company
Pietz, William, 9–11
Pinguet, Maurice, 223, 340n127
Pink Globalization (Yano), 187
Pitelka, Morgan, 47
Planet of the Apes (film), 250
Plazyk, Klaudia, 26
Pleats Please boutique and brand, 205, 211–214

Pogue, William, 260
politics and political parties, 93
post-Kamakura era, 37
postwar Japan: anticommunist role, 165;
    black market (*yami-ichi*), 163–164,
    169; bleak environment of, 163;
    democracy in, 167; Income Doubling
    Plan, 167, 183; legal exports, 164;
    Occupation commodity taxes, 177;
    unemployment during, 163
Prasso, Sheridan, 230
The Preppy Handbook (Birnbach), 248
Prieler, Michael, 274
The Principles of Advertising (Starch), 115
print capitalism, 28
product value, 45
Protestantism, 10, 31, 35, 86
proto-industries, 29–30, 34, 38
punk: appearance and clothing, 206,
    336n60; movement, 197, 199,
    203–205; music, 203
Pu Yi, Aisin Gioro, 110–111

quality standards, 45, 47

rationalization (*gōrika*), 36, 50, 122
Rauschenberg, Robert, 210
Ravo, Nick, 173
Ray, Man, 117
Rebirth Project, 282
reification, 17, 19, 56
Rei Kawakubo / Comme des Garçons
    (exhibit), 206, 297
Renger-Patzsch, Albert, 117
Ri, Kōran. *See* Yamaguchi, Yoshiko
Richie, Donald, 98
Ring of Colour (blog), 345n30
Rolex, 78, 259, 297n71
Roppongi Hills, 212
Rubinstein, Ruth, 202
Russell, Latoya, 26, 279
Russo-Japanese War, 71, 130, 140
Ryang, Sonia, 94

Saikoku risshi hen (Self Help), 33
Saint Laurent, Yves, 206
Saitō, Tadakatsu, 233
Saji, Keizō, 171, 173
Sakai, Naoki, 110
Sakai, Yoshinori, 180
sake, 29, 34, 40, 81, 88, 101, 150–151,
    353n144

sakoku (foreign relations), 293n7
Sakoku Edicts, 39
samurai class, 4, 32–33, 52–53, 63,
    294n15
Sand, Jordan, 6
Sanders, Bernie, 24
Saneyoshi, Yasuzumi, 151
Sankei Shimbun (Industrial and Economic
    News), 4
Sanrio Corporation, 163; cheery optimism
    of, 185; history of, 183; *kawaii* (cute)
    phenomenon, 168; *kyarakutā* (charac-
    ters), 188–189; profits, 192; Sanrio
    Puroland (*Piyūro Rando*), 189–191;
    shopping philosophy, 184. *See also*
    Hello Kitty
Sanrio Greetings Company, Ltd., 186; Gift
    Gate shops, 186
Santiago, Philip, 244, 250
Santos-Dumont, Alberto, 78
Sapporo Beer Company, 172
sarariman (salaryman): in bars and cafés,
    100, 104, 122, 170; personal luxuries,
    2; stress relief for, 176; Uncle Torys
    and, 172–173, 175–176; watches and
    punctuality, 98, 176; whisky, 194, 218
Sasaki, Ruth Fuller, 182
Sasaki, Shigetsu (Sōkei-an), 182
Sato, Barbara, 106
Satō, Gengen, 89
Satō, Namiko, 131
Sawada, Michitaka, 268
Schindler, Oskar, 149
Schmidt, Norman B., 257
Schulz, Charles M., 186
Schwarzenegger, Arnold, 221
Science of Housework Magazine (*Kaji no
    kagaku*), 122
Second Sino-Japanese War (1937–1945),
    125, 128, *129, 133,* 133–134, 135,
    151, 154, 232
Seibu Department Store, 196, 219–221
Seikō Corporation: Astron GPS Solar
    Watch, 179–180; Astron quartz watch,
    178; collectors and luxury, 259–261;
    Empire pocket watch, 77, 306n14;
    Laurel wristwatch, 77–78, 306n14;
    limited-edition products, 236; luxury
    consumer products of, 60; manufactur-
    ing and retail success, 77; milestone
    model, 95–96; origins of, 3; postwar
    benefits, 178; postwar recovery, 176;

Index

punctuality and, 62; Seikō chronograph, 260; technology of, 76–77; Tensoku *tokei* aviators' watch, 320n138; Time Keeper pocket watch, 76; Tokyo Olympics and, 178, 180, 193; wartime military production, 154; wristwatches, 306n14, 320n137

Seikōsha: earthquake destruction and rebuilding, 95; Empire pocket watch, 98; "exquisite manufacture," 78; factory, 76; Hattori Clock Tower, 96–97; Japanese customers and, 64; Ministry of Railways and, 96; Tensoku *tokei* aviators' watch, 155; wartime aviators' watches, 154–155

Seiyō zasshi (Western Magazine), 5

Sek, E., 26

Self Help (Smiles), 33

Selfridge, Henry Gordon, 84–85

Sengoku period, 31, 47, 217

Setouchi, Jakuchō, 211

Shavell, Henry, 164–165

Sheldrake, Christopher, 226, 228

Sherman, Cindy, 205

Shibusawa, Ei'ichi, 34, 63

Shibuya ward, 48, 85, 208, 283

Shimamori, Michiko, 112

Shimbashi district, 66

Shimizu, Keizō, 245

Shimizu, Yuko, 186

Shinagawa ward, 186

Shina no yoru (China Nights), 111, 140–142

Shinjuku area, 16, 186, 191, 230, 239, 274

Shinkō shashin no tsukurikata (The Making of Modern Photography) (Kanamaru), 117

Shinohara, Yasuyuki, 227

Shintō practice, 11–14, 22, 88, 308n47

Shiseidō Company: advertising and marketing, 110–111, 145, 225, 228–229, 233–234, 272, 274; beauty consultants, 112, 272; Blue Bird line, 109–110; Chinese and Korean market, 109–110, 113, 228–230, 234–235; Clé de Peau (Key to Skin), 230; Cold Cream, 67; company magazines and clubs, 93, 114–115; Deluxe perfume, 150; department store profit system, 114; discount stores and products, 229–230; Eudermine, 65–67; face brush, 355n7; Fantasy perfume, 150;

feminine beauty, 62; in France, 224–226, 228, 235, 278; free gifts, 138, 314n43; Fukuhara Sanitary Tooth Powder, 65, 67; Future Solutions LX line, 271–273; *Hanatsubaki* (Camellia), 139; *Hanatsubaki* (Camellia) magazine, 93, 115, 139–140, 147; *Hanatsubaki kurabu* (Camellia Club), 112, 137–138, 147; Hanatsubaki perfume, 67; history of, 56, 65, 67, 277; incentive buying, 137–139; Integrate Gracy, 273; international business, 109, 111, 196, 222–224, 270, 275, 339n123; Japanese customers and, 64; logos of, 54, 58; luxury consumer products of, 60, 223, 272–273, 341n150; Manchurian market, 109–110; mass production and, 57; "Miss Shiseidō" mobile beauty salons (*Biyō idō saron*), 112–113; multiethnic models, 299n98; Nombre Noir (Black Number), 225–226; older consumers and, 273–274; origins of, 3; Parfums Beauté Serge Lutens, 226–227; Prior, 273–274; purchaser diversity, 269–271, 353n153; Rose Cosmetics, 109; sales figures, 231–232, 234; Seoul store, 107, *108;* Seven Colors face powder, 67; Shiseidō Hanatsubaki Hake polishing face brush, 57–58; social media and, 231–232; Synchro Skin foundation line, 270–271; testing headquarters, 270; US subsidiary, 182, 222; wartime lipstick, 147; wartime military work, 149–150; wartime overseas sales, 146; wartime production and profitability, 137, 147, 149; WASO, 231; Yamaguchi Yoshiko and, 141–142, 143–144, *143;* Zen perfume, 181. *See also* Lutens, Serge

Shiseidō geppō (Shiseidō Monthly), 93, 114–115, 122

Shiseidō gurafu (Shiseido Graph), 114–115, 122, 139

Shiseidō Parlour, 66–67, 90

Shizuki, Tadao, 293n7

Shizuoka Prefecture, 138

Shōnen kurabu (Boys Club), 131–132, 134

shopping experience, 41–43, 85

Shoppingu no joō (Shopping Queen), 15

Shōwa: A History of Japan (Mizuki), 257

Shōwa era, 98, 120

392 *Index*

Shufu no tomo (Housewife's Companion), 5
Shufu no tomo and *Fujin kōron* (Women's Review), 7
Shūkan bunshun (Weekly Literary Spring), 15
Silverberg, Miriam, 106
Sino-Japanese War, 71, 150–151
Sivulka, Juliann, 7, 63
Skov, Lise, 203
Smiles, Samuel, 33
Smith, Adam, 10
Smith, Norman, 141
Snyder, Gary, 182
soap wrappers, 71, 72
social capital, 26, 45, 49, 58, 202–203, 233
socialism, views of, 24, 291nn89–91
social media, 232, 236, 277, 345n30
social order. *See* samurai class
social order, merchants, 32–33
Sōgo Kyōryoku Oyobi Anzen Hoshō Jōyaku (Treaty of Mutual Cooperation and Security), 166
Sōin gyokusai seyo! (Let's All "Shatter the Jewels") (Mizuki), 256
Solt, George Sekine, 321n165
spectacular consumption, 41, 47–49, 130, 160
Stalker, Nancy, 240
Starch, Daniel, 115
status categories: abolition of, 63; artisan class, 45; lowest group, 46; merchant class, 45–46; peasant class, 45; samurai class, 45
Stefani, Gwen, 346n36
Steketee, Gail, 12
Strelkova, Olga, 289n64
Stuff (Frost and Steketee), 12
Stussy, Sean, 249
Sugiura, Hisui, 107
Sumida ward, 88, 148
Sumitomo, 34, 40, 300n10
Suntory: advertising, 174–175, 217–218; automatic highball machines, 267; celebrity endorsements, 216–217; clientele of, 81, 104; exports to China, 218; foreign spokespeople, 196; Hibiki, 170, 265–266; highballs, 352n133; history of, 60, 80, 102; Jim Beam company, 266; *koma-inu* (lion dogs) in advertisement, 103, 308n47; mixed drinks and, 266; *mizuwari* (highballs),

170–171; name change, 173–174; single-malt Hibiki whisky, 170; special occasion for, 264; Suntory Scotch, 103; Suntory Whisky Red, 176, 326n62; Suntory Whisky Toki, 266; Torii Shoten (Torii's Store), 80; wartime production and profitability, 150; whisky, 82; whisky advertisements, 48, 102–103, *102;* Whisky Kakubin (Square Bottle), 151–152; whisky production, 80; Yamazaki Distillery, 264; Yamazaki Pure Malt Whisky, 264–265. *See also* Kotobukiya Limited
Suntory Museum of Art, 173
Supreme Commander of the Allied Powers (SCAP), 164–165, 177
Sutormina, Alena, 289n64
Suzuki, Daiki, 245
Swader, Christopher S., 289n64
swastika (*hakenkreuz*), 51–52
Syomina, Victoria, 289n64

Tachibana, Munekazu, 95
Taishō bunka, 1905–1927 (Culture in the Taishō Period) (Minami), 118
Taishō era, 61, 69, 78–79, 90, 92, 106, 117–118
Taiwan, 91, 93, 112–113, 182, 213, 228, 233, 268
Takahashi, Jun, 244
Takamatsu, Jirō, 197
Takanarita, Tōru and Megumi, 170
Takashimaya department store, 96, 107, 109, 112, 160
Take Five (Brubeck), 247
Take Ivy (film and book), 247–248, 347n51
Taketsuru, Masataka, 101–104, 151–152
The Tale of Genji (Murasaki), 8, 215, 237, 333n20
Tanaka, Yasuo, 8, 250
Tang Dynasty, 218
Tanizaki, Jun'ichirō, 4, 69, 106, 286n5
Taylorization, 36, 50, 139
TCJ Animation Center, 172
tea ceremonies, 47
A Theory of Shopping (Miller), 16
Things Japanese (Chamberlain), 70
Thurman, Judith, 205
time and timepieces, 163; calendar reform, 75; clock and watch ownership, 77;

Index

collectors (*otaku*), 262; digital watches, 179; Elgin wristwatch, 78; intellectuals and cultural producers and, 97; Jouvenia wristwatch, 78; Luftwaffe's *Beobachtungsuhr* (observation watch), 155; military watches, 77; Occupation commodity tax, 177; pocket watches, 60, 76–78, 96–100, 155; postwar affordability, 168; railroads and textiles and, 75, 96; standardization of, 74–75, 97, 122; wartime Japan and, 154–156; watch and clock stores, 78; The Watch Site, 261; Watchuseek, 261; wristwatches, 96, 306n19. *See also* Seikō Corporation; Seikōsha
Tipton, Elise K., 82, 101
Tōgo, Heihachirō, 140
Tōhō Studios, 217, 238
Tokugawa, Ieyasu, social order of, 32
Tokugawa period, 43; in advertising, 242; artisanally produced products in, 47; artisanal past, 19–20, 35; artisan class, 30; bathhouses and bathing, 67; capitalism in, 37; company precedents, 3; feudal infantry of, 294n15; Gunboat Diplomacy, 152; home decorating and, 6–7; Japanese uniqueness, 200; Kansei Reforms, 23; Kaō shampoo advertisements, 121; merchant class and, 54, 58, 88; Miyake Issey's work, 209; *mono-uri* (itinerant vendors) in, 42; nightsoil as fertilizer, 69; production in, 34; protocapitalism, 29; quality standards and, 45, 237; *rakugo* art form, 220; shopping experience, 44, 296n64; shopping in, 41; social and economics of, 33; time control in, 74; *tsū* (connoisseurs), 46; *wabi-sabi* ideals, 44; *za* (guilds or brotherhoods) in, 37–39
Tokyo Gekijō (Tokyo Theater), 127
Tōkyō kōshinkyoku (Tokyo March) (film), 97–100
Tokyo Metropolitan Museum of Art, 197
Tokyo Olympics (1964), 174, 178, 180, 193, 197
Tōkyō Orinpikku (Tokyo Olympiad), 180, 247
Tomimoto, Kenkichi, 138–139
Tōno, Yoshiaki, 196
Torii, Shinjirō, 80, 82, 102–103, 151, 173, 303n67

Torys Bars, 169–171
Towards an Anthropological Theory of Value (Graeber), 185
Toxic Archipelago (B. Walker), 282
Toyada, Takeshi, 40
toy industry exports, 164
Toyotomi, Hideyoshi, 181
trade organizations: *ie* (trading houses), 40; *kabu-nakama*, 46; *nakama* (trade associations), 39; *rakuza*, 39; *sōgō shōsha*, 40; *toiya* (trade brokers), 40; *za* (guilds or brotherhoods) in, 37–40, 46, 52, 58
Trader Joe's, 237
trading partners, 31–32
Treaty of Kanagawa (1854), 40
Treaty of San Francisco (1951), 166, 193, 196
Trump, Donald, 24, 263
Tsuji, Shintarō, 183–186, 189, 192
Tsuji, Tomokuni, 189
Tsukiji Fish Market, 170
20.16 Big Ideas for 2016 (Goldman), 26
"The Tyranny of the Clock" (Woodcock), 75, 79

Uchida, Hoshimi, 74, 77
Uchiyama, Benjamin, 125
Ueno district, 134
Uniqlo UT line, 251
United States: focus on Japan, 180; focus on Japanese culture, 237–238; Hawaiian travel, 173; Japanese food products in, 237; Japanese military alliance, 166; modern influence, 255; Occupation government, 164–165, 177, 193; postwar influence, 162, 167, 286n5; postwar Japanese products, 238; "Rent-a-Beatnik" ad, 238; soft power concept, 239–240
US Army and soldiers, 156, 169
Ushiyama, Kazuta, 262
US State Department, 165
Usui, Kazuo, 83

VAN products, 245
Veblen, Thorstein, 25
Victoria, Brian Daizen, 328n89
Vogel, Ezra, 8, 162, 167–168, 201–202
Vogel, Suzanne, 168
von Tobel, Alexa, 26–27

394 *Index*

Vreeland, Diana, 211
Vuitton, Louis, 296n64

wabi-sabi concept, 44, 53, 206–207, 212, 227–228, 261, 298n83, 350n112
Wabi-Sabi for Artists, Designers, Poets, and Philosophers (Koren), 53
Walker, Brett, 282
Walker, Janet A., 80
Wanamaker, John, 86
Warhol, Andy, 211
Warnett, Gary, 249
wartime Japan: air-raid hoods, 158, 321n162; Allied bombings, 162; aviation fuel production, 152; civilian and military morale, 158, 321nn164–165; consumption tax, 146–147; daily-use items, 147; domestic survival, 157–158; effect on civilians, 160; *eidan* (management foundations), 149; food shortages and rationing, 158–159, 321n160; lipstick treatment, 146–147; luxury goods restrictions, 146, 161; Manchukuo POW camp, 148; manufacturing facilities, bombing of, 157; military alcohol incentive policy, 151; military distribution, 150; Mukden Number Two Prison, 148–149; strategic materials, 149–150; Trade Corps (*Kōeki Eidan*), 149–150; whisky consumption, 150
Watson, Burton, 182
Watsuji, Tetsurō, 97
Watts, Alan, 180–181, 223
Watts, Eric King, 48
The Way of Zen (Watts), 180, 223
Weber, Max, 35
Weisenfeld, Gennifer, 117, 144
West African society, 10
Western companies, 95–96
Western society, 61–62, 70
Western-style liquor and cafés: exotic foreign reputation, 79; hostess bars and, 169; ice carving in, 170, 326n56; *jokyū* (female servers), 80; Kamiya Bar, 101; male clientele, 80, 82, 104; pink-collar work, 82, 104; in private homes, 80; whisky in, 101; white-collar workers in, 100. *See also* Akadama Port Wine; Kotobukiya Limited; Suntory

Westwood, Vivienne, 204, 208, 336n60
Whiskey Magazine, 265
whisky: highballs, 170–171; Hokkaidō and, 104; Japanese production of, 266; *mizunari* (*Quercus crispulus,* Japanese oak) barrels, 153, 319n125; postwar affordability, 168; production of, 102; Scotland and, 82, 101, 104, 162, 266; wartime military rations, 150–151; Yamazaki water and, 102
Williams, Pharell, 250
Wolfe, Kenneth Bonner, 156
Women's Review, 104
women's suffrage, 104
Woodcock, George, 75, 79, 97
"The Work of Art in the Age of Its Technological Reproducibility" (Benjamin), 49

Xinhai Revolution, 111

Yajima, Kajiko, 130
yakuza (organized criminal) bands, 169
Yamada, Seizaburō, 21
Yamaguchi, Yoshiko, 111, 140–142, 143–145, *143,* 161
Yamaguchi, Yoshitada, 163–164
Yamamoto, Kansai, 282
Yamana, Ayao, 110
Yamanashi Prefecture, 81
Yamanashi Silk Company, 183, 185–186. *See also* Sanrio Corporation
Yamashita, Samuel, 158
Yanagi, Sōetsu, 139
Yanagihara, Ryōhei, 171–172, 175
Yanase, Masamu, 95, 306n9
Yano, Christine, 187–188, 285n7
Yano, Akiko, 219, 338n104
Yasuhara, Yoshihiro, 219
Yoichi Distillery, 104, 152–153, 265
Yomiuri Shimbun (newspaper), 4, 82, 197
Yonezu, Matsuzō, 63
Yoshida, Shigeru, 166
Yoshida Doctrine, 166
Yoshihito (emperor), 92
Yoshimi, Yoshiaki, 36
Yoshimura, Masunobu, 197
Yōshū tengoku (Liquor Heaven), 171
Young, Louise, 96
Yukiguni (Snow Country) (Kawabata), 20–21

Zen at War (Victoria), 328n89
Zen Buddhism and Buddhist temples:
American craze for, 180, 237; Asakusa
temple, 88; capitalism's ills and, 280;
comparison to France, 223; Daitokuji
(Daitoku Temple), 182; department
stores and, 89; Hungry Ghost Realm, 17;
ideals of, 53; impermanence, 13; Kōdaiji
temple, 181–182; *manji* (swastika), 51;
merchant class and, 88; militarism of,
328n89; Rinzai Zen traditions, 181–182.
See also *wabi-sabi* concept
Zhang, Ziyi, 48
Zola, Émile, 87

About the Author

Annika A. Culver is professor of East Asian history at Florida State University, where she specializes in Japan and Northeast Asia–related topics. She received her doctorate from the University of Chicago and holds an AM degree in Regional Studies East Asia from Harvard University and a history degree from Vassar College. Since 2012, she has served as a scholar in the US-Japan Network for the Future, a group initiated by the late Ezra Vogel that connects academics to foreign policy communities; she is also a member of the editorial board of the *Texas National Security Review*. Her research and publications feature propaganda and advertising, cultural production in Manchuria/Manchukuo and Japan's empire, history of science in Japan, and Japanese consumer capitalism, with funding from the Japan Foundation, the Association for Asian Studies, the D. Kim Foundation for Science and Technology, the Fulbright US Student Program, and other grants. Professor Culver's publications include *Glorify the Empire: Japanese Avant-Garde Propaganda in Manchukuo* (2013), which won the Southeast Conference for the Association for Asian Studies 2015 Book Prize; the co-edited volume *Manchukuo Perspectives: Transnational Approaches to Literary Production* (2019); and *Japan's Empire of Birds: Aristocrats, Anglo-Americans, and Transwar Ornithology* (2022).